The Institute of Chartered Accountants in England and Wales

BUSINESS STRATEGY AND TECHNOLOGY

For exams in 2019

Study Manual

www.icaew.com

Business Strategy and Technology
The Institute of Chartered Accountants in England and Wales

ISBN: 978-1-50972-084-2
Previous ISBN: 978-1-78363-776-8

First edition 2007
Twelfth edition 2018

The content of this publication is intended to prepare students for the ICAEW examinations, and should not be used as professional advice.

British Library Cataloguing-in-Publication Data
A catalogue record for this book is available from the British Library

Originally printed in the United Kingdom on paper obtained from traceable, sustainable sources.

Welcome to ICAEW

As the future of our profession, I'd like to personally welcome you to ICAEW.

In a constantly changing and volatile environment, the role of the accountancy profession has never been more important to create a world of strong economies, together. ICAEW Chartered Accountants make decisions that will define the future of global business by sharing our knowledge, skills and insight.

By choosing our world-leading chartered accountancy qualification, the ACA, you are not only investing in your own future but also gaining the skills and values to meet the challenges of technological change and contribute to future business success.

Joining over 150,000 chartered accountants and over 27,000 fellow students worldwide, you are now part of something special. This unique network of talented and diverse professionals has the knowledge, skills and commitment to help build local and global economies that are sustainable, accountable and fair.

You are all supported by ICAEW as you progress through your studies and career: we will be with you every step of the way to ensure you are ready to face the fast-paced changes of the global economy. Visit page viii to review the key resources available as you study.

It's with our training, guidance and support that our members, and you, will realise career ambitions, develop insights that matter and maintain a competitive edge.

I wish you the best of luck with your studies and look forward to welcoming you to the profession.

Michael Izza
Chief Executive
ICAEW

Contents

The Business Strategy and Technology module provides you with an understanding of how organisations develop and implement strategy, including any ethical implications.

Questions within the Study Manual should be treated as preparation questions, providing you with a firm foundation before you attempt the exam-standard questions. The exam-standard questions are found in the Question Bank.

Permitted texts

At the Professional and Advanced Levels there are specific texts that you are permitted to take into your exams with you. All information for these texts, the editions that are recommended for your examinations and where to order them from, is available on icaew.com/permittedtexts.

Professional Level exams	Permitted text
Audit and Assurance	✓
Financial Accounting and Reporting	✓
Tax Compliance	✓
Business Strategy and Technology	✗
Financial Management	✗
Business Planning	No restrictions

Advanced Level exams	
Corporate Reporting	No restrictions
Strategic Business Management	No restrictions
Case Study	No restrictions

The exams which have no restrictions include the following:

- Business Planning: Banking;
- Business Planning: Insurance;
- Business Planning: Taxation;
- Corporate Reporting;
- Strategic Business Management; and
- Case Study.

This means you can take any hard copy materials into these exams that you wish, subject to practical space restrictions.

Although the examiners use the specific editions listed to set the exam (as listed on our website), you **may** use a different edition of the text at your own risk.

This information, as well as what to expect and what is and is not permitted in each exam is available in the Instructions to Candidates. You will be sent the instructions with your exam admission details. They can also be viewed on our website at icaew.com/exams.

Key resources

We provide a wide range of fantastic resources and services to help you in your studies. Here is some of what we have to offer.

Take a look at the online resources available to you on icaew.com/examresources:

Syllabus, skills development and technical knowledge grids

This gives you the full breakdown of learning outcomes for each module, see how your skills and technical knowledge will grow throughout the qualification.

Study guide

This guides you through your learning process, putting each chapter and topic of the Study Manual into context and showing what learning outcomes are attached to them.

Exam webinars

The pre-recorded webinars focus on how to approach each exam, plus exam and study tips.

Past exams and mark plans

Each exam is available soon after it has been sat, with mark plans available once results have been released. Remember that if you're accessing an exam from 2018, it may not reflect exams for 2019. To access exam-standard questions that reflect the current syllabus, go to the Question Bank.

Errata sheets

These are available on our website if we are made aware of a mistake within a Study Manual or Question Bank once it has been published.

Exam software

You need to become familiar with the exam software before you take your exam. Access a variety of resources, including exam guide, practice software, webinars and sample exams at icaew.com/cbe

Student support team

Our dedicated student support team is here to help and advise you throughout your training, don't hesitate to get in touch. Email studentsupport@icaew.com or call +44 (0)1908 248 250 to speak to an adviser.

Vital and Economia

Vital is our quarterly ACA student magazine. Each issue of Vital is packed with interesting articles to help you with work, study and life. Read the latest copy at icaew.com/vital.

What's more, you'll receive our monthly member magazine, Economia. Read more at icaew.com/economia.

Online student community

The online student community is the place where you can post your questions and share your study tips. Join the conversation at icaew.com/studentcommunity.

Tuition

The ICAEW Partner in Learning scheme recognises tuition providers who comply with our core principles of quality course delivery. If you are not receiving structured tuition and are interested in doing so, take a look at our recognised Partner in Learning tuition providers in your area at icaew.com/dashboard.

CABA

Access free, confidential support to help you take care of your wellbeing, at work and at home. CABA's services are available to you, and your family, face-to-face, over the phone and online. Find out more at caba.org.uk

ICAEW Business and Finance Professional (BFP)

This exciting new designation has been developed as a form of recognition for professionals who have gained the essential knowledge, skills and experience necessary for a successful career in business and finance. Once you have completed the ICAEW CFAB qualification or the Certificate Level of the ACA, you are eligible to apply towards gaining BFP status. Start your application at icaew.com/becomeabfp.

Skills within the ACA

Professional skills are essential to accountancy and your development of them is embedded throughout the ACA qualification.

The following shows the professional skills that you will develop in this particular module. To see the full skills development grids, please go to icaew.com/examresources.

Assimilating and Using Information

Understand the situation and the requirements

- Demonstrate understanding of the business context
- Recognise new and complex ideas within a scenario
- Identify the needs of customers and clients
- Explain different stakeholder perspectives and interests
- Identify risks within a scenario
- Identify elements of uncertainty within a scenario
- Identify ethical issues including public interest and sustainability issues within a scenario

Identify and use relevant information

- Interpret information provided in various formats
- Evaluate the relevance of information provided
- Filter information provided to identify critical facts

Identify and prioritise key issues and stay on task

- Identify business and financial issues from a scenario
- Prioritise key issues
- Work effectively within time constraints
- Operate to a brief in a given scenario

How skills are assessed: students may be required to:

- understand key information from the scenario provided;

- understand the context of the scenario in terms of type of business, industry and wider context;

- recognise key ethical issues for an accountant undertaking work in accounting and reporting; and

- recognise specific issues that may arise in the context of the situation described.

Structuring problems and solutions

Structure data

- Structure information from various sources into suitable formats for analysis

- Identify any information gaps

- Frame questions to clarify information

- Use a range of data types and sources to inform analysis and decision making

- Structure and analyse financial and non-financial data to enhance understanding of business issues and their underlying causes

- Present analysis in accordance with instructions and criteria

Develop solutions

- Identify and apply relevant technical knowledge and skills to analyse a specific problem
- Use structured information to identify evidence-based solutions
- Identify creative and pragmatic solutions in a business environment
- Identify opportunities to add value
- Identify and anticipate problems that may result from a decision
- Identify a range of possible solutions based on analysis
- Identify ethical dimensions of possible solutions
- Select appropriate courses of action using an ethical framework
- Identify the solution which is the best fit with acceptance criteria and objectives
- Define objectives and acceptance criteria for solutions

How skills are assessed: students may be required to:

- identify and use information to define key business issues;

- demonstrate understanding of the business, its strategy, industry and wider context.

- demonstrate the impact of ethics on the objectives and methods of an organisation;

- identify the ethical implications of strategic proposals;

- demonstrate relevant technical knowledge;

- perform appropriate analysis of numerical data and demonstrate an understanding of what is relevant; and

- use data analysis to develop and illustrate an answer.

Applying judgement

Apply professional scepticism and critical thinking

- Recognise bias and varying quality in data and evidence
- Identify assumptions or faults in arguments
- Identify gaps in evidence
- Identify inconsistencies and contradictory information
- Assess interaction of information from different sources
- Exercise ethical judgement

Relate issues to the environment

- Appreciate when more expert help is required
- Identify related issues in scenarios
- Assess different stakeholder perspectives when evaluating options
- Retain an overview of the business issue or scenario
- Appraise the effects of alternative future scenarios
- Appraise ethical, public interest and regulatory issues

How skills are assessed: students may be required to:

- evaluate the impact of a business proposal on an entity;

- assess the reliability, accuracy and limitations of any analysis performed;

- be able to produce arguments integrating numerical and descriptive analysis;

- prioritise the issues facing an entity;

- identify links and relationships between different issues affecting an entity and use these to establish priorities;

- evaluate options for an organisation, taking into account its stakeholders, objectives, priorities, available resources and ethical obligations; and

- provide reasons for the rejection of alternatives.

Concluding, recommending and communicating

Conclusions

- Apply technical knowledge to support reasoning and conclusions
- Apply professional experience and evidence to support reasoning
- Use valid and different technical skills to formulate opinions, advice, plans, solutions, options and reservations.

Recommendations

- Present recommendations in accordance with instructions and defined criteria
- Make recommendations in situations where risks and uncertainty exist
- Formulate opinions, advice, recommendations, plans, solutions, options and reservations based on valid evidence
- Make evidence-based recommendations which can be justified by reference to supporting data and other information
- Develop recommendations which combine different technical skills in a practical situation

Communication

- Present a basic or routine memorandum or briefing note in writing in a clear and concise style
- Present analysis and recommendations in accordance with instructions
- Communicate clearly to a specialist or non-specialist audience in a manner suitable for the recipient
- Prepare the advice, report, or notes required in a clear and concise style

How skills are assessed: students may be required to:

- draw realistic conclusions from an analysis of data and the information provided;
- prepare a report or memorandum structured according to the requirements of the scenario, with appropriate context;
- provide reasoned advice based on an understanding of the business and the relevant scenario, including an assessment of possible alternatives;
- recommend suitable courses of action in a given situation; and
- identify risks and outline reservations about the advice.

CHAPTER 1

Introduction to the Business Strategy and Technology exam

Introduction

Examination context

TOPIC LIST

1   Business Strategy and Technology, and the ACA exams

2   Knowledge

3   Skills

4   Professional experience and common sense

5   Developing business awareness

6   A guide to the marking process

7   Examination technique

Introduction

Learning outcome

Tick off

*   To become familiar with the context of the Business Strategy and Technology exam   ☐

Syllabus links

The purpose of this chapter is as an initial help to approaching the Business Strategy and Technology exam. The knowledge, understanding, skills and business awareness that you will develop in relation to Business Strategy and Technology will be of great benefit when you progress to the Advanced level of the ACA syllabus.

Examination context

Whilst an appreciation of models and theories underlying the exam are important, the focus of your examination is a practical one. You will be required to interpret business scenarios and to provide professional advice to clients and management on what to do. You will not be required to reproduce names and models for the sake of it – knowledge will always need to be applied. It is important not to be deterred by the emphasis on technology in the title of the examination. This will not be a stand-alone aspect of the exam but will be integrated into the scenarios. The emphasis will be upon understanding how technological developments have impacted on modern organisations, the process of setting strategy, and measuring performance. You will not be expected to display a detailed understanding of the internal workings of IT systems, nor will you be required to exhibit knowledge concerning computer algorithms and the internal logic of software applications. You are however required to have a high level understanding of the main technological developments affecting organisations and the business environment. This will include for example a working knowledge and understanding of data analytics and cyber security. It is important to remember that Business Strategy and Technology is a very practical exam, and your ability to apply your knowledge and understanding of a subject to a scenario is crucial.

The models and theories you will cover in this Study Manual are to be used in three ways in the examination:

1   To **analyse and interpret**: applying the appropriate models and perspectives to the situation, data and issues outlined in the scenario will help you to see underlying causes better.

2   To **generate solutions**: many of the models include recommendations or approaches to resolving problems. You may wish to pass this advice on to management.

3   To **substantiate your comments**: the models and their authors are recognised by management who may have studied them too. You would be expected to refer to them as a framework in a real business report. You will not, however, be expected to describe the models in great detail in your answer.

At the beginning of every chapter the examination context comments are there to illustrate how certain topics have been tested in previous sittings. It is important that you take the time to read through this guidance in preparation for your own exam. You may notice that some of the comments made relate to examinations reaching back a number of sittings. Although these questions were set some time ago, they are still very relevant to your studies and have been used within this pack to help you understand how your knowledge may need to be applied. As the examiner highlights, the fundamental concept behind the Business Strategy and Technology examination as a practical, scenario based exam has not changed and therefore students are strongly advised to take notice of the points raised. The reference to previous exam questions is particularly useful and questions set more recently have been included in your Question Bank for you to attempt.

1 Business Strategy and Technology, and the ACA exams

As a chartered accountant you will one day find yourself involved in helping an organisation 'find its way' in the world: taking its resources and capabilities and using them to exploit opportunities in markets and industries to satisfy its stakeholders over time. To 'find its way' the organisation must have an idea of what it wants to achieve and how it is going to achieve it. At its most basic, this is what business strategy means. A key part of business strategy concerns the growing role that technology and data analytics play in the activities of organisations. Such developments around the world are now of strategic significance and are therefore reflected in the ICAEW syllabus. Constant technological change will shape your role as a chartered accountant and could have an impact on the professional advice you will provide.

The purpose of the Business Strategy and Technology examination at the Professional level of the ACA exams is to help you develop and demonstrate your knowledge, understanding and the skills necessary to ensure an organisation with which you are involved can find its way.

All Professional level exams require both factual knowledge and understanding, and analytical skills, plus the ability to apply knowledge in real-life scenarios. It is important to distinguish between what we mean by 'knowledge' and 'skills', and to see how the exam assesses each.

2 Knowledge

The knowledge required to do well in Business Strategy and Technology is primarily built on that acquired at Certificate level in the Business, Technology and Finance, and Management Information exams. Your knowledge and understanding is extended, enhanced and developed at this level but it is assessed very differently. All professional level exams are now computer-based, requiring you to read and interpret exam questions on-screen and to then type up your answers into the designated response area provided by the exam software. This is different to the objective test exams that you have attempted during your earlier Certificate level studies. It is important that you take the time to ensure that you are familiar and fully comfortable with the exam software prior to attempting your Business Strategy and Technology examination. More detail about computer-based exams can be found on the ICAEW website at icaew.com/cbe.

Each question in the exam consists of a 'scenario', often with a data analysis or quantitative element, followed by one or more 'requirements', to which you must prepare answers.

The other major difference between Certificate and Professional level is that knowledge is only assessed in the context of how it is applied to the business scenarios set out in the exam. Knowledge in the Business Strategy and Technology exam requires more than just an ability to display rote learning of the content covered in the Study Manual, it also requires you to display an understanding of that knowledge by applying it to the scenario detail featured in the question.

Thus you would not expect to see a requirement like this:

'Describe the factors incorporated in Porter's Five Forces model'.

But you would expect to see a requirement like this: Q1 from a previous exam, provided a detailed scenario describing the tyre manufacturing industry and a participant in the UK tyre market:

'Using Porter's Five Forces model, identify and evaluate the factors affecting the overall profitability of the UK tyre manufacturing industry.'

While you can assume one or two marks will be available just for the basic knowledge of what each of the five forces is, most of the marks will be going for displaying an understanding of how that knowledge is used to analyse the scenario and explain the pertinent points under each heading.

3 Skills

To be successful in the Business Strategy and Technology exam you have to demonstrate a range of skills in applying knowledge. The table below describes the four categories of skill and gives you an example of how you can expect to have each skill tested in the Business Strategy and Technology exam.

Skill at Professional level	How the Business Strategy and Technology exam might test this skill
Assimilating and using information	
Understand the situation and the requirements	Reading a large amount of material in the scenario including different types of qualitative and quantitative data and distinguishing the parts that are relevant to each requirement
Identify and use relevant information	Taking both narrative and numerical information and combining them to understand and explain a situation more fully
Identify and prioritise key issues and stay on task	Identifying which pieces of data and/or information in the scenario relate to what you already know eg, identifying that information about economies of scale is relevant to the 'threat of new entrants' in Porter's five forces model. You need to be comfortable picking out key pieces of information from the scenario to help you answer the actual requirement set
Structuring problems and solutions	
Structure data	Calculating ratios and using other data relating to performance. Analysis may include identifying trends in both financial and non-financial data in the scenario, or using the headings in a model such as Five Forces, PESTEL or SWOT to break down the information in the scenario
Develop solutions	Drawing together ratios, trends in data, or categorised written information to get a clearer picture of the situation, highlight the key issues and begin to identify possible solutions
Applying judgement	
Apply professional scepticism and critical thinking	Identifying deficiencies in the data and information available and identifying what may be needed to address them. This involves developing a questioning approach when presented with data and information in a scenario
Relate issues to the environment	Using the analysis to date to identify feasible actions that could or must be taken, and their likely consequences

ICAEW 2019

Skill at Professional level	How the Business Strategy and Technology exam might test this skill
Concluding, recommending and communicating	
Conclusions	Applying technical knowledge and expertise to support reasoning and conclusions
Recommendations	Making a choice between possible actions or viewpoints and providing a reasoned explanation of that choice and its potential consequences
Communication	Being professional in producing material for the required purpose and audience

4 Professional experience and common sense

Technical knowledge, understanding, and professional skills are vital to success in Business Strategy and Technology, as we have seen, but the value of your common sense and professional experience should not be underestimated. Your analysis of a situation should always be tempered with your awareness of the 'real world', however this has been obtained. This applies in particular to answers where you make a recommendation: you should think twice for instance about asking for every conceivable piece of additional data or information before reaching a firm conclusion, or recommending a global overseas expansion to a firm with only 10 employees.

There may be occasions where you do not feel you have any technical knowledge to bring to bear on a scenario. In such a situation you may have to adopt a 'common' sense' approach to one or more requirements. While this is never going to earn you full marks it is better than not providing an answer at all.

A key aspect of professional experience that you need to develop is professional scepticism, that is looking at the qualitative and quantitative data and information that you have been given with a questioning eye. Data and information that is provided in-house by the management of a company desperate to raise finance, for instance, should be looked at with some scepticism, on the basis that the management may seek to overplay good news and underplay bad news to secure their objective. Data and information provided by a professional firm such as an independent reviewer of a business on the other hand may be taken with far less scepticism.

5 Developing business awareness

Throughout this Study Manual we will be building up your knowledge and skills, and demonstrating how these apply to exam questions in a large number of topic areas. Each chapter begins with an example of the type of requirement you might expect for that topic area, so you become familiar from the beginning with the context of the exam.

The variety of scenarios and case examples that you will see in this Study Manual will also help you to build up your business awareness. This is a vital element in developing the combination of knowledge, skills, professional experience and common sense that will help you to do well in the Business Strategy and Technology exam, and progress to Advanced level.

You can help yourself further in this respect by taking advantage of resources that are available online in the form of 'real world' case studies. Visiting the business pages of a quality newspaper and news websites is strongly recommended as they often provide useful articles and case studies on topical business and technological issues.

You should look out for case studies covering topics including:

- The external environment
- Technological developments (including automation, intelligent systems, digital assets and cryptocurrencies)
- Big data and data analytics
- Cyber security
- Finance
- Marketing
- Operations
- People (including the concepts of human capital, shared service centres and workforce flexibility)
- Strategy
- Ethics and sustainability (including natural capital)

6 A guide to the marking process

6.1 The distinction between Knowledge and Skills

Business Strategy and Technology (BST) has the highest skills content of all the Professional level examinations and as BST leads on to Advanced level, there may be some relatively open requirements. This is reflected in the marking process where the available marks for each requirement are divided into two pools: Knowledge marks (K) and Skills marks (S), with more marks awarded for skills than knowledge. The knowledge element will usually be approximately 25% to 30% of the marks.

Broadly speaking the K marks are for demonstration of accurate knowledge and understanding from the Learning Materials that is relevant to the requirement ie, the answer is developed using recognised models, tools and frameworks, not just common sense. This demonstration may be explicit or implied. This means that you do not have to set out your knowledge in the abstract before then applying it to the scenario: you can demonstrate your knowledge in the process of applying it to the scenario.

The S marks are for evidence of the skills discussed in the table in Section 3 of this chapter.

6.1.1 Example: K and S marks

Requirement: 'analyse the competitive forces within an industry'.

K marks would be awarded for understanding the right model to select and knowing the key headings, in this case that 'competitive forces' suggests Porter's Five Forces model should be applied under its five headings.

S marks would be gained by:
- Applying the model to the context in the question

  eg, identifying data and information from the scenario under each of the five headings
- Analysing the data and information

  eg, to evaluate the significance of each force
- Reasoning and judgement

  eg, summarising the key forces within the industry and their impact on the business in question

6.2 Marking

For any particular exam there are three marking documents:

- a detailed mark plan for the examination which is a full answer, containing all the likely points that candidates may make; it is not a model answer as it is highly unlikely that any one candidate could produce it in the time allowed;

- a marking grid which breaks the exam down into the K and S mark pools available for each requirement; and

- a separate marking guidance document issued to markers, giving an overview of the typical K and S points for each requirement, to be used in conjunction with the detailed mark plan.

Note that some requirements are marked out of more marks than are actually available, for instance there may be a maximum of 7 skills marks but the total pool is treated as being 9 marks. This headroom increases the chances of a good answer scoring maximum marks.

The marking grid and marking guidance are reproduced below for the September 2017 examination, together with an overview of the key issues and knowledge content.

6.3 September 2017 exam

6.3.1 Overview of key issues and knowledge required:

Q1 – Blakes Blinds Ltd   **(45 marks)**

UK manufacturer and installer of high-quality door and window blinds for the corporate market. The company's customers are UK-based and include restaurant chains, hospitals, educational establishments and owners of commercial buildings. The company acts as sub-contractor to several large building firms installing blinds in new-build developments. The company has recently developed an innovative 'Auto-Close' system, which allows blinds to be operated remotely. The board are considering whether to acquire the company's major Chinese supplier in a bid to boost profitability. The Financial Controller is facing an ethical dilemma following a request from the Managing Director to provide misleading information to the local council in order to obtain a grant.

- Mini case, including data analysis.

- Key issues: sustainable competitive advantage, performance analysis, additional information required, advantages and disadvantages of the proposed acquisition, transfer pricing, ethical issues and actions to address them. .

Q2 – Air Services UK Ltd   **(29 marks)**

A limited company which is responsible for providing airspace management services to all airports and aircraft using UK airspace. The company used to be a non-profit making government body, but has subsequently been established as a limited company, partly owned (49%) by the UK government and partly by private investors (51%). The company has developed an innovative cloud-based system which can be used to manage unmanned aircraft systems (drones). The company's systems were recently hacked which led to severe disruption at airports. Following the incident a new CEO has recently been appointed, and is keen to develop new international revenue streams.

- Key issues: Goals, vision, objectives of stakeholders, Human Resource and Research and Development functional strategies, cyber-security risks and risk management.

Q3 – Purechoc Ltd   **(26 marks)**

Purechoc Ltd is a family-owned business that makes premium, hand-made chocolates and chocolate bars, on a small scale for a niche market. The company operates four UK shops, each of which is managed by a member of the family who own the business. The company only sells chocolates to individuals and does not sell to supermarkets or other retailers. A large American confectionery manufacturer has recently offered to acquire the entire share capital of Purechoc. In response to the acquisition offer some of the directors have proposed opening more shops by pursuing a franchising route.

- Key issues: Evaluate the alternative proposals with reference to control, risks, strategic fit, and providing preliminary advice.

Marks split 25% knowledge, 75% skills

6.3.2   The marking process

The following is one of the requirements in the exam, which will serve as an example of the marking process:

For 7 marks S17 Q1.4 asked candidates to 'discuss the ethical issues arising for BB [Blakes Blinds] and the Financial Controller as a result of the grant application, and recommend appropriate actions.'

The available mark pool was K3, S5 – a total of 8 marks with a maximum possible score of 7.

Knowledge: 3 marks

These were for recognising the difference between 'ethical' and 'legal' implications and dealing with them separately in the answer:

- Ethical issues related to 'doing the right thing'
- Legal issues related to consideration of whether the grant application would constitute fraud.
- Use of ethical language: honesty, transparency and integrity
- Reference to the ICAEW Code of Ethics

Skills: 5 marks

The skills that could be demonstrated here included:

- Identifying the facts – in this case the grant criteria – and showing appropriate professional scepticism: has the Managing Director knowingly made a false statement or misinterpreted the criteria?
- Evaluating the ethical issues by considering the Managing Director's actions, and the implications for the Financial Controller and BB.
- Based on the analysis, provide realistic actions that the Financial Controller in the case should look to take.
- Provide a brief discussion of the likely implications of the actions recommended and made an attempt at some form of conclusion.

6.3.3 Marking grid Business Strategy and Technology September 2017

	Available		Awarded			
	K	S	K	S	Max mark	Total awarded
Q1: Blakes Blinds Ltd						
1.1 Factors creating competitive advantage/sustainability	2	5			7	
1.2 Analysis of performance/areas of concern	1	22			20	
1.3 Advantages/disadvantages of acquisition/transfer pricing	4	8			11	
1.4 Ethical issues	3	5			7	
Total	**10**	**40**			**45**	
Q2: Air Services UK Ltd						
2.1 Consistency of three-year goals	2	9			10	
2.2 Functional strategies (HR and RD)	2	9			10	
2.3 Cyber-security risks/risk management	3	7			9	
Total	**7**	**25**			**29**	
Q3: Purechoc Ltd						
3.1 Control section of report	3	5			8	
3.2 Risks section of report	2	6			7	
3.3 Strategic fit section of report	2	6			7	
3.4 Preliminary advice section of report	1	3			4	
Total	**8**	**20**			**26**	
Overall total	**25**	**85**			**100**	

Q1: Blakes Blinds Ltd	Knowledge	Skills
1.1 Competitive advantage/ sustainability	• Identification of focussed differentiation strategy (Porter) • Explicit or implicit use of Porter's 5 forces or other appropriate model eg, Kay	• Analysis of internal factors creating competitive advantage • Analysis of external industry/ market forces • Conclusion regarding sustainability of competitive advantage
1.2 Analysis of financial performance	• Structured tables of figures	**20X5 compared to 20X6** **Calculations** • GP margin by revenue stream • Sales mix • GP mix • Exchange rate impact • Cost ratios • % changes 20X5 – 20X6 **Discussion** • Acknowledge Board concerns • Fall in operating profit due to reduced GP margin and increased fixed costs • Analysis of different products • Impact of exchange rate movements • Interdependency of product lines **Ability to achieve 20X7 budget** **Calculations** • GP margin • Operating margin • Exchange rate impacts • Margin of safety • Change in sales/overheads • Scale actual figures for 12 months • Variance calculations **Discussion** • Ambitious sales growth • Actions of competitors

Q1: Blakes Blinds Ltd	Knowledge	Skills
		• Seasonality
		• Exchange rate movements
		• Increasing fixed costs
		• Assumptions behind budget
		• Assess likelihood of achieving budget
		Relevant further information
1.3 Acquisition of RX	**Acquisition** • Identification of backwards vertical integration strategy • Acquisition increases operating gearing **Transfer pricing** • Understanding of what transfer price means for each division • Options for setting transfer prices	**Acquisition** • Balanced consideration of advantages and disadvantages related to scenario • Consideration of control, risks, flexibility, overseas risks, new markets **Transfer pricing** • Cost or profit centre • Goal congruence issues • Performance measurement • Behavioural issues • Capacity/external market considerations • Reporting of profit/tax/legal implications **Conclusion** • Viability of acquisition or next steps to allow decision

1.4 Ethical issues	• Demonstration of appropriate ethical language and principles:
	
	   – Honesty/ transparency/integrity
	
	   – Legality/fraud
	
	   – Financial Controller – ICAEW Code of Ethics applies
		• Application of ethical principles to scenario
		
		• Consideration of issues:
		
		   – False statement on grant application
		
		   – Pressure from Managing Director
		
		• Consideration of facts: grant criteria
		
		• Legality if knowingly make false statement
		
		• ICAEW principles/threats for Financial Controller

Q1: Blakes Blinds Ltd	Knowledge	Skills
		• Potential intimidation • Balanced discussion (BB and Financial Controller) • Proposed actions

Q2: Air Services UK Ltd	Knowledge	Skills
2.1 Consistency of three-year goals	• Distinguish difference/links between long-term vision and shorter-term goals and objectives • Conflicting stakeholder objectives	**Consistency of goals and vision** • Areas covered by goals (safety, efficiency, environment) • Areas covered by vision (global, innovation) • Discussion of goals in context of globalisation • Consideration of missing goals eg, relating to innovation **Consistency of goals and stakeholder objectives** • Identification of key stakeholders and likely objectives (shareholders, government, CAA, Airlines, Airports, Passengers, Staff) • Link goals to each stakeholder group • Consider if any stakeholder needs not met/any objectives conflict
2.2 Functional strategies (HR and RD)	Generic understanding of areas covered by: • HR strategy (evaluating people needs/resource requirements and how to meet them) • R&D strategy (product and process improvement)	• Link functional strategies to vision • In context of internationalisation and growth opportunities (tenders) • Recognition of external environment Key issues identified for each of: **Human Resources** • Succession planning • Quantity and quality of people • Short-term/medium-term/long-term issues relating to recruitment and retention

Q2: Air Services UK Ltd	Knowledge	Skills
		• Skills/availability
		• Training/learning
		• Flexibility of workforce
		Research and development
		• Innovation
		• Keep current services going and develop new ones
		• Consideration of technology
		• Risks
		• Investment/funding required
2.3 Cyber-security risks/risk management	**Nature of cyber-security risk** • Use of TARA approach to risk management (transfer/avoid/reduce/accept) • Business continuity plan	**Types of risk** • In context of suspected hacking incident • Identification of specific relevant risks for ASU (hacking, denial of service, sabotage) • Impact of IT failure on ASU – reputational and financial risk, safety (deaths), fines, loss of new contracts • Widespread use of network and cloud-based systems increase risk **Risk management** • Considers appropriate risk management strategies • Board level issue/governance • Need for business continuity plan • Concept of both short-term and long-term continuity

Q3: Purechoc Ltd	Knowledge	Skills
3.1 Control section of report	<ul><li>Report format</li><li>Ownership control</li><li>Operational (day-to-day) control</li></ul>	**Sale of shares**<ul><li>Ownership structure/autonomy</li><li>Bargaining power in relation to Koreto</li><li>Koreto wants to appoint new CEO</li><li>Semi-autonomous subsidiary</li><li>May lose some strategic control but retain operational control</li></ul>**Franchising**<ul><li>Number of partners</li><li>Contractual v operational control</li><li>Control quality</li><li>Bargaining power in relation to franchises</li><li>Control via franchise agreement</li></ul>
3.2 Risks section of report	Recognition of both aspects of risk:<ul><li>Variety/types of downside risk</li><li>Potential for risk reduction/upside risk</li></ul>	**Sale of shares**<ul><li>Key risk is loss of control</li><li>Koreto may not stand by promises</li><li>May require dividends, management fees</li><li>May limit funds available</li><li>May help reduce risks presented by Marine's ill-health</li><li>Sale of shares transfers risk to Koreto</li></ul>**Franchising**<ul><li>Shared risk</li><li>Reduces financial risk but potentially increases reputational risk</li><li>Possible loss of intellectual property</li><li>Purechoc may be unable to provide support to franchisees</li><li>Brand may not attract franchisees</li></ul>

Q3: Purechoc Ltd	Knowledge	Skills
Strategic fit section of report	• Premium product in niche market • Ethics and values	**Sale of shares** • Comparison of Koreto and Purechoc • Resources/funding available • Future operation as single or separate brands • Access to other markets/customers/distribution channels/marketing • Koreto has international knowledge **Franchising** • Individual shops fit Purechoc's ethos/niche market • Obligations on Purechoc to provide resources/support for franchisees • Limited resource/expertise available from individual franchisees • Franchises may provide local knowledge
Preliminary advice	• Demonstrates clear understanding of nature of franchise arrangement v sale of shares	• In context of limited resources for expansion • Comparison of choice of partner: individual franchisees v large American corporate • Views of Marine • Views of other shareholders • Considers other alternatives • Makes a preliminary recommendation

7 Examination technique

The Business Strategy and Technology examiners have the following advice for candidates sitting this examination:

- Take the time to watch the computer-based exam webinars available on the ICAEW website. These short webinars are available for candidates to watch in the lead up to sitting the Business Strategy and Technology exam. They cover a range of issues relating to the Professional level computer-based examinations including overviews of the exam software, tips on attempting computer-based exams, and guidance on practical matters such as how to move and resize the question and answer window when using the software. The webinars are available at icaew.com/cbe. There are also specific exam webinars for each Professional level exam. These are available at icaew.com/examresources.

- Use the practice exam software available via the ICAEW website, to become comfortable with the features and functionality of the software. The 'copy' and 'paste' functionality of the exam software allows for information to be transferred from the question scenario and pasted into the response area. The examiners have commented that candidates need to take care when pasting information in this way as there is a temptation to paste vast amounts of detail from the question with limited attempt made to use it constructively in the creation of answers. Information from the scenario should only really be transferred into the response area if it will help save time in terms of typing it up, and ultimately adds value to the answer the candidate provides.

- When using the exam software candidates need to be mindful that the examiner can only see answers as they appear on the screen. The examiners cannot see the formulae used by candidates in their answers nor can they make the window larger to view narrative answers which extend beyond the view of the screen. As such candidates need to ensure that there is an audit trail for numerate answers, and ensure that all text is clearly visible so that the examiners can fully review the answers provided.

- Read the requirements carefully and select appropriate analytical tools.

- Complete the requirements for each question in the order set out in the question, since very often analysis in the later requirements can be linked back to that in earlier requirements.

- A brief definition of a model is welcomed before going on to apply it in the context of the question.

- Sometimes candidates over-rely on the use of models, as they apply them but do not develop them sufficiently – inclusion of models where not appropriate, and their over-use, can often lead to time-wasting. For example, some candidates will apply a full SWOT analysis to a question which asks them to only identify strengths. This again highlights the importance of reading the requirements carefully. Similarly a long list of points for PESTEL analysis, without considering the implications for the particular business in the scenario or the priority of the points, will score limited marks.

- Avoid the temptation to produce overly detailed answers. This is particularly the case when explaining the key themes around technological developments. Providing lots of detail about how the software behind distributed ledger technology works in the 'real world' but falling to relate it to the scenario will lose you time and earn very few, if any marks. The examiners do not expect you to be technology experts. They do, however, want to see well structured, balanced arguments which answer the questions set.

- Question scenarios will feature different types of organisations operating in a range of different industries and environments and facing a wide range of potential issues . Some questions may feature organisations operating in cutting edge, hi-tech industries. These questions are designed to be accessible to all candidates attempting the exam, not just those candidates working in a hi-tech industry. The range of scenarios illustrates the importance of studying the whole syllabus and also highlights the need to do lots of question practice prior to sitting the exam. The Business Strategy and Technology Question Bank provides a large selection of past exam questions covering a variety of organisations and industries.

- Candidates need to be prepared for question scenarios to include both qualitative data and quantitative data. Regardless of the form the data in a question takes, if data is provided in the question scenario then you are expected to use it. Some requirements explicitly ask for specific data analysis or supporting calculations. Other more open-ended requirements may implicitly require data analysis – eg, where data is presented in the scenario and the requirement asks for a discussion of qualitative and quantitative factors to consider. Ignoring a requirement which explicitly or implicitly requires some data analysis or supporting calculations will make achieving a pass mark significantly more difficult.

- Numerical, quantitative requirements can appear in any of the questions in the exam, and will not solely relate to analysing the performance of the featured entity between two periods in time. Business Strategy and Technology questions often feature requirements which require candidates to undertake some form of calculation and to then comment on the result as part of analysing a proposed business option/decision. As such candidates commonly struggle with break-even and margin of safety calculations. Candidates are advised to spend sufficient time practising business decision calculations such as these.

- Numbers in a scenario help to tell the story, and are backed up by appropriate narrative; candidates should try to adopt a similar approach in their answers. Some candidates spend too much time focusing on numerical analysis in the exam which often limits the amount of time available to expand the narrative aspects of their answer – explaining the significance or implications of the numbers. Candidates are advised to spend some time before attempting numerical requirements to consider the calculations that are likely to be most useful in answering the question. Being selective about the calculations to perform and discuss is central to producing a good answer.

- Responding to the scenario and requirements by addressing the major points will score more highly than a scatter-gun approach. Identifying key points in answers is important, and overall it is the quality of an answer's content, rather than its volume, that is key to gaining marks.

- In the context of the requirement, markers award marks for scripts that are properly presented and they have no objection to appropriate use of bullet points, tables, diagrams, and any technique that helps to present analysed data and information clearly. However, when making points in bullet form, it is important for candidates to write in sentences and to identify causal relationships, elaborating when necessary and applying the information to the scenario.

- Marks are not awarded specifically for the use of headings, but their use will help candidates to structure their answer, leading to a better performance.

7.1 Key tips for exam technique

- Answer all parts of all requirements.

- Identify clearly which requirement is being attempted.

- Demonstrate/apply appropriate knowledge.

- Identify the key data and issues in scenarios.

- Make use of any qualitative and quantitative data provided in the scenario. Spend time deciding which additional calculations are most useful. Always present any supporting numerical analysis in table format with appropriate headings.

- Prioritise issues in answers.

- Use systematic analysis, reasoning and judgement, in particular of cause and effect relationships.

- Balance the arguments not the conclusion.

- Conclude/recommend even when not specifically required to do so.

7.2   Key things to avoid

- Failing to practice questions using the exam software prior to attempting the Business Strategy and Technology exam.

- Ignoring quantitative data that is provided in the question and not including any data analysis in your answers where it is implicitly or explicitly required.

- Simply restating facts from the question without any development, often in the context of models, eg, SWOT, PESTEL, Five Forces.

- Answering requirements in random order.

- Throwing models randomly at a situation, especially as a result of confusing the various ideas of Porter.

- Providing overly theoretical or detailed answers.

- Producing messy, poorly laid out, unprofessional answers.

- Failing to use a report or other specified format for your answer when required to do so.

CHAPTER 2

Strategy and organisations

Introduction

Examination context

TOPIC LIST

Summary and Self-test

Answers to Interactive questions

Answers to Self-test

Introduction

Learning outcome

- Evaluate an organisation's purpose

The specific syllabus reference for this chapter is:1a.

Syllabus links

In the Business, Technology and Finance exam you will have covered the basic objectives and processes of strategic management. This chapter revises these topics and provides a range of alternative perspectives on the role of management in the strategic process.

The following topics, revised and expanded here, were introduced in your Business, Technology and Finance studies:

- General objectives of strategic management.
- The strategic management process.
- Nature and purpose of strategic plans, business plans and operational plans.

The framework of the rational planning model will be employed in subsequent chapters.

Although much of the focus of this chapter (and Study Manual) is upon the strategic management process from a commercial, business perspective it is important to recognise that a number of the key themes explored here will still be relevant to other types of organisations, (for example, not-for-profit organisations). The need for objectives and planning are likely to be common to all organisations.

Examination context

This chapter reviews some of the leading theories of strategy formulation and provides the names of many authorities on strategy. The remaining chapters of this study manual also provide coverage of names and theories.

Q2 in March 2015 (*The Scottish Woodlands Commission*) focused on a government department which was responsible for all state owned forests in Scotland. The Scottish Woodlands Commission (SWC) had been approached by CabinCo Ltd, a private company, which operated up-market, self-catering holiday villages in England and Wales. CabinCo proposed the establishment of a public/private partnership between both organisations which would allow CabinCo to set up rental holiday villages in one of SWC's forests. The intention was that both parties would equally share any profits that the venture generated. Candidates were required to:

'Write a report for SWC's trustees, evaluating the proposed venture.'

(9 marks)

Candidates were expected to structure their answers around four headings, one of which was 'strategic fit'.

Candidates were expected to make use of the detail outlined in the scenario in respect of SWC's and CabinCo's mission statements, objectives and planning horizons when assessing the concept of strategic fit and the proposed new venture. Each of these is a key feature of the formal strategic planning process which is considered in this chapter and the next one.

1 What is strategy?

Section overview

- Strategies are about the long term development and survival of the business.
- Strategy takes place at several levels ranging from the corporate centre down to strategies for functions such as marketing, human resources and finance.

1.1 Approaches to strategy

There are probably as many different definitions of 'strategy' (or 'corporate strategy') as there are textbooks on the subject.

Definitions

'**Strategy** is the direction and scope of an organisation over the long term, which achieves advantage for the organisation through its configuration of resources within a changing environment, to meet the needs of markets and to fulfil stakeholder expectations.' *(Johnson, Scholes and Whittington).*

'**Corporate strategy** is concerned with an organisation's basic direction for the future, its purpose, its ambitions, its resources and how it interacts with the world in which it operates' *(Lynch).*

From these we can say that strategy is therefore concerned with:

- The long-term direction (objectives) of the organisation
- The environment in which it operates
- The resources at its disposal
- Managing relationships with stakeholders

Theories of strategy and of strategic management must be used with caution. They don't apply in all situations and the evidence for them is not always clear cut. Therefore this text draws attention to the limitations of some to help you decide how far you can apply them in the exam.

This chapter reviews two broad approaches to strategy: the **rational planning (traditional) approach** and the **emergent approach**. It also considers whether an organisation can achieve competitive advantage by orientating its strategy around its external environment (**positioning-based approach**) or around its internal competences (**resource-based approach**).

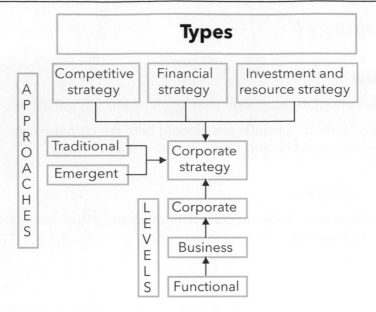

1.2 Levels of strategy

Strategy can exist at several levels in an organisation:

1.2.1 Corporate strategy

Corporate strategy is generally determined at head office/main board level. This covers the business as a whole – its overall mission and objectives, product/market decisions, major investment decisions, financing decisions and relations with external stakeholders.

1.2.2 Business strategy

This normally takes place in strategic business units (SBUs). **Competitive strategy** is normally determined at this level covering such matters as how advantage over competitors can be achieved and marketing issues, such as the marketing mix.

1.2.3 Functional (operational) strategies

This refers to the main functions within each SBU, such as production, purchasing, finance, human resources and marketing, and how they deliver effectively the strategies determined at the corporate and business levels.

2 Overview of strategic planning approaches

Section overview

- There is a contrast between the formal rational approach to strategic planning and the emergent approach to the strategy process.

- The rational planning model, originated by Ansoff, involves strategic analysis, strategic choice, implementation of the chosen strategy, then review and control.

- Mintzberg criticises it as a failure in practice and of dubious validity as an explanation of what does and should happen.

- The emergent approach views strategy as continuously and incrementally evolving.

- Many businesses succeed through the actions of the founder or CEO.

2.1 Contrast between rational planning and emergent approach

Rational approach also called • Top down approach • Formal approach • Traditional approach	• Strategy involves setting goals first and then designing strategies to reach them • Some prediction of the future is possible • Outcomes of strategic choices can be predicted and controlled • Possible to separate the planning and selection of strategies from the implementation of strategies
Emergent approach also called • Bottom up approach	• Builds management team with right strategic skills • Managers of divisions granted significant autonomy • Empowerment of managers to develop and adapt strategies as circumstances change and opportunities and threats arise • Strategic choice and implementation happen concurrently

2.2 Benefits claimed for strategic planning

Strategic planning can achieve several benefits:

- Creates a management process to detect and respond to changes in market and environmental forces and so improve performance.

- Provides a framework for SBUs to produce plans with clear, long term goals thus avoiding short termism.

- Enables derivation of milestones for achievement of goals and monitoring progress by stages.

- Mechanism to ensure harmony of objectives, both between SBUs and over time ('goal congruence'.)

- Improves stakeholder perceptions, for example a clear strategy may improve the share price.

- Investing in the planning process develops future management potential and can aid continuity planning.

2.3 Mintzberg's criticisms of strategic planning

Strategic planning has fallen from popularity and has been criticised. Mintzberg's critique below is amongst the most insightful. Mintzberg argues that planning doesn't work out in practice.

Problem	Comments
Practical failure	Empirical studies have not proved that **formal planning** processes contribute to success.
Routine and regular	Strategic planning often occurs as an **annual cycle**, but a firm cannot allow itself to wait every year for the month of February (for example) to address its problems.
Reduces initiative	Formal planning discourages **strategic thinking**. Once a plan is locked in place, people are unwilling to question it. Obsession with particular performance indicators means that managers focus on fulfilling the plan rather than concentrating on developments in the environment.

Problem	Comments
Internal politics	The assumption of 'objectivity' in evaluation ignores political battles between different managers and departments. The model doesn't describe reality.
Exaggerates power	Managers face limits to the extent to which they can control the behaviour of the organisation. The plans may be ignored by subordinates.
Impractical	The hierarchy of objectives, budgets, strategies and programmes does not reflect the reality of most organisations who prefer simple, more easy to apply programmes such as capital budgeting.

2.4 The role of the leader or entrepreneur in strategy

Many businesses have been successful through the actions of their founders, chief executives or entrepreneurial individuals within the organisation rather than through formal strategic planning.

Interactive question 1: Famous business leaders

1.1 Name some corporations which have been made successful by the business leadership given by a famous individual.

See **Answer** at the end of this chapter.

Entrepreneurs are individuals who build new businesses. An entrepreneur is not just the owner/manager of a small business but is best regarded as a manager who pursues opportunity and drives change to create value.

Entrepreneurship is a style of management, with a particular mix of innovation and risk.

3 A rational (prescriptive) approach to strategy formulation

Section overview

- The rational planning model starts with strategic analysis, which involves internal and external analysis then corporate appraisal. This informs the business's choice of mission, goals and strategic objectives.

- Any resulting gap in where the business wants to be and where it is currently headed is addressed by identifying and evaluating strategic options and selecting the most appropriate.

- Implementing strategies involves planning the appropriate resources and operations, structuring the business effectively and monitoring using appropriate control systems.

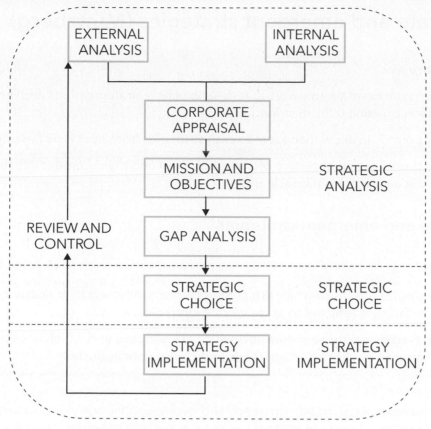

(Diagram: The rational planning model)

The main stages in the rational approach are:

1   **Conduct a corporate appraisal**: This involves assessing both the present business environment and how it may develop over the planning timescale (typically five + years), and the internal position of the business (such as staffing levels, product quality and financial position).

2   **Set mission and objectives**: Management will assess whether the long-term interests of the business are best met in its present industry and competing in its present way or whether the business needs to strike out in a new direction. This is called its mission. Objectives will be set for the coming years. The job of strategy is to attain them.

3   **Gap analysis**: Involves comparing forecast performance with the strategic objectives set by management. If forecast performance is below the objectives set then this exposes a gap which must be filled by new and better strategy.

4   **Strategic choice**: Management generate new business options for the firm, such as new products or markets, and evaluate these to arrive at a set of potentially successful and affordable strategies to help the firm reach the objectives set.

5   **Strategy implementation**: Management carries out the strategy at corporate, business and functional levels by developing organisational structures, policies and programmes to carry it out.

4 Deliberate and emergent strategies (Mintzberg)

Section overview

- Mintzberg provides a framework that describes how strategic plans and incrementalism combine in practice to form strategies.

- The key point is to allow managers to craft strategies from events as time progresses.

- The conclusion is that a mixture of a strategic plan and management initiative will provide control but also organisational learning.

4.1 Deliberate and emergent strategies

Definitions

Intended strategies are those which are conscious plans imposed by management. If they are implemented, they are referred to as deliberate strategies.

Emergent strategies are those behaviours which are adopted and which have a strategic impact. Emergent strategies adapt to human needs and evolve continuously.

Emergent strategies adapt to human needs and evolve continuously. The emergent approach can involve the same degree of strategic analysis as the rational planning approach but the processes of choice and implementation take place together. This is for two reasons:

1. **Identity of decision and action**. The managers that create and choose the strategies are also responsible for carrying them out.

2. **Learning process**. The choice of strategies interacts with implementation. Rather than having a grand scheme for the next five years management tries something out this year, learns lessons from where it succeeds and fails, and develops new initiatives for next year.

In the emergent approach, objectives and strategies are a result of negotiations and discussion, taking into account the human element of the system. A strategy is tried and developed as it is implemented. Alternative strategies will be tried where it fails.

4.2 Five types of strategy

Mintzberg (*The Strategy Process*) identified the following.

- **Intended**: The result of a deliberate planning process

- **Deliberate**: Where the intended plans have been put into action

- **Unrealised**: Not all planned strategies are implemented

- **Emergent**: Strategies are created by force of circumstances

- **Realised**: The final realised strategy results from a balance of forces of the other types of strategies

The interaction of these strategies is illustrated in the following diagram.

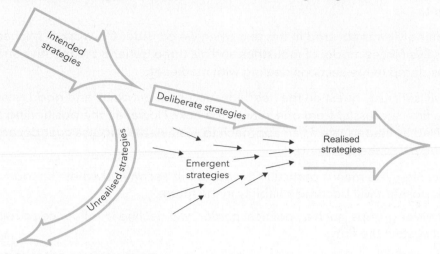

Strategies must still have **purpose** and this will be set by senior management. No actual strategy will be **wholly deliberate** or **wholly emergent**.

The task of **strategic management** is to control and shape these **emergent strategies** as they **develop**.

5 Positioning versus resource-based views of strategic advantage

Section overview

- Early prescriptions for strategy emphasised that success lay in 'fitting' the organisation to its environment better (eg, satisfying shareholders and customers and staying on the right side of the authorities). This is known as the positioning approach.

- Modern resource-based views emphasise that long-term success lies in organisations, 'playing to their strengths' or '**competences**'.

- For competences to be capable of leading to **superior competitive performance** they must **fit** the present environment, **stretch** the firm to innovate and able to admit **leverage** to gain extra value in new lines of business.

5.1 Positioning view of strategic advantage

A firm or industry faced with the imminent obsolescence of one of its core products must decide whether to orientate strategy around external customer needs or rather orientate strategy around its internal resources and competences. Choosing the first is an example of a positioning approach. Choosing the second applies the resource-based approach.

Characteristics of the positioning approach are:

- A **focus on customer needs** and adapting products, and the process of making them, to any changes in these needs.

- The **gaining of a superior position against rivals** through analysis of the industry and marking and adopting strategies to gain relative market share or reduce relative costs.

- The **assessment of relations with stakeholders** such as government, shareholders, suppliers and distributors to use better relationships as a source of advantage.

- **Seeking to gain preferential access to resources** such as materials, low cost labour and scarce skills.

The significant feature is the belief that successful strategy involves the business **adapting to its environment.**

The positioning view is covered in this text when we consider the work of Michael Porter (notably his five forces model of industries and his three generic competitive strategies) and is further considered in the sections dealing with marketing.

No writer will seriously question the need for successful products and good relations in assisting in making a firm successful from one year to the next. However, the positioning approach has been criticised as inadequate as an approach to sustainable success over decades with particular regard to the following:

- Product life-cycle means particular products will become obsolete so today's successful market position will become a liability in the future.

- Stakeholder groups, such as political parties, will decline in influence so relations with them will not sustain the firm.

- Long-term technological changes will eliminate cost advantages or technical superiority of a given product.

Perpetual change of the organisation's skills base and products will be disruptive and eventually leads the firm into fields in which it has little expertise.

5.2 Resource-based view of competitive advantage

Technological changes can destroy industries:

- Downloads damage CD and DVD manufacturers, distributors and retailers

- Electronic methods of communication such as Facebook, instant messaging, email and text messages sent from mobile devices have threatened the traditional postal system

- Genetic modification of organisms can compromise the pesticide and pharmaceutical industries

The **resource-based view** is an **inside-out** view of strategy. Firms do not look for strategies external to them. They develop or acquire resources and **competences**, create new markets and exploit them.

Johnson, Scholes and Whittington say successful strategies require **strategic capability.**

Resources and competences are needed for the successful execution of defined strategies.

Fit	Resources must be available to fit with the current product-market demands and current needs.
Stretch	This means being at the leading/shaping edge of new strategic developments in the industry. This suggests that the organisation's ambitions cannot be met with current resources and competences. Ambition should outpace resources.
Leverage	Existing resources are used in many different ways, so that extra value is extracted from them.

Creation of new markets

A fundamental point made by Prahalad and Hamel (*Competing for the Future*) is that markets are not 'given'. They can be created by corporate action. Companies do not merely 'satisfy' customer needs: they 'create' them.

Interactive question 2: Apple and the chicken and egg question

Apple is often cited as an example of a firm that creates industries through leverage of core competences in technological innovation and design of mobile devices. This has created markets such as:

- Personal audio: Through its portable iPod MP3 player enabling users to download the latest music via Apple iTunes.

- Personal computers: Via the original Apple Macintosh 128K which at the time of its release revolutionised the computing industry by becoming the first mass-market PC. The evolution of Apple's computing division has led to the introduction of tablet computers, eg, iPad.

- Mobile phones: Apple's first iPhone helped to raise the bar in the standard of mobile technologies, heralding the introduction of a new generation of devices. Users are able to synchronise and connect Apple devices to one another due to the products' innovative design.

Requirement

2.1 Was it these technologies that built a whole new industry, or was the industry already there?

See **Answer** at the end of this chapter.

5.3 Comparison of positioning and resource-based views

According to the **resource-based view** of strategy the role of resources is **more than simply to execute** strategies determined by desired positions in product markets. Rather, the focus of the strategist should be on **resources and competences**. These are **assets** for the long term. Such a combination of resources and competences takes years to develop and can be hard to copy.

Some of the implications are explained in the following table.

Factor	Positioning-based view	Resource-based view
Profitability	Industry profitability determined by the five competitive forces. Position of a company in the industry determines its profitability.	Corporate profitability is based on sustainable competitive advantage achieved from the exploitation of unique resources.
Approach	Outside-in, ie, consider outside environment and markets then the company's ability to trade in these conditions.	Inside-out: consider key resources first, then how to exploit competitive advantage in available markets.
Diversity	Maintain diversified portfolio of products (see BCG matrix) to spread risk and generate cash in changing market conditions.	Focus only on products where company has a sustainable competitive advantage.
Key focus	Industry orientation and positioning in the market.	Focus on core competences which competitors do not possess and will find difficult to copy.

6 Planning horizon

Section overview

- Strategic management and strategic planning are often distinguished from operational issues by the length of time concerned: the horizon.

- Most managers have the need to deliver short-term results which can take priority over longer term strategic development of the business.

- The pressure for shorter term results and shorter planning horizons can come from the ownership of the organisation, its capital structure, the industry it is in, its environment and the nature of its management.

6.1 Short, medium and long term planning

There terms are often used but remain ill-defined. A rule of thumb is:

- Short term: Horizon of 1–3 years
- Medium term: Horizon of 3–10 years
- Long term: 10 + years

6.2 Short run/long run trade off

Managers and businesses are frequently evaluated on short term successes such as profits. Strategic thinking requires that managers consider the long term growth and survival of the business.

Therefore management is required to balance short- and long-term considerations.

6.3 Influences on planning horizons

- **Nature of ownership**
  Firms with shareholders are obliged to ensure some financial return each year to their shareholders. Making sufficient profits each year will normally be needed to promote shareholder value. State-owned organisations do not have this obligation (but they will have different ownership issues to contend with, such as the changing nature of political agendas, different governments' attitudes to funding and state control).

- **Capital structure**
  Some investors, such as banks or private equity investors (sometimes called venture capitalists) do not require short term profits. Banks will continue to lend providing assets cover the loans and interest is paid. Private equity investors require profits and share values to grow over a 5–10 year period to give them a substantial capital gain when they sell their holding.

- **Nature of industry**
  Industries such as aircraft development, satellite communications and oil pipelines require large capital investments that take a long time to build and to pay back. Long-term plans are essential to justify these.

- **Nature of business environment**
  In rapidly changing environments it is likely that long-term planning may be futile. For example, industries such as bio-technology, home entertainment and mobile communications, where effects of technology and legislation are hard to predict, will tend to avoid plans and instead adopt a strategic management approach within a series of short-term plans.

- **Nature of management**

  Long-term planning is a skill and it is time consuming. Some entrepreneurial managers will avoid it, for example because they lack the time or skill, or because they are unwilling to become 'tied down by red tape'. Others, for example the management of family firms, are reluctant to consider changing the 'way it has always been done'.

Interactive question 3: Superware products

Superware Products Ltd (hereafter Superware) was formed five years ago, in 20X4, by three colleagues who had left a major software house to work on the development of accounting software for small businesses. Superware currently (20X9) employs 18 staff at the company's head office in Swindon, and a further eight regionally-based salespeople in various parts of the UK.

Company structure

The three directors of Superware are Paul Shaw (Managing), Steven Thomas (Sales) and Mark Greenwood (Development). They each have a small team reporting directly to them and they meet on a daily basis if they are in the office, to discuss the business and to brainstorm a little over coffee. All three directors come from a background of software sales to small and medium-sized organisations. Mark is responsible for six product development staff and two administrators. His staff work full time on developing and upgrading the Superware product, and meet regularly with the sales staff to get feedback from customers and users. In addition to the eight salespeople, Steven has two sales administrators and a secretary working for him. The sales staff meet at head office on a weekly basis and the administrators work closely with the financial accountant. Paul takes responsibility for the remaining staff who perform general administration, reception and clerical tasks. His only specialist staff member is Zandra who, with her assistant, maintains a high level of control over the company's financial reporting and accounts.

Planning and control

Once a year the directors, under the guidance of Paul and with assistance from Zandra, agree a full budget for the next 12 months. The budget is always based on the previous year's performance, with adjustments for known changes such as inflation, costs and forecasts of demand from sales staff feedback. During the discussion of the budget Zandra calculates various ratios to illustrate trends in the company's profitability and liquidity, and the budget is normally adjusted to ensure that trends are as desired. When the budget is agreed, a copy is sent to the bank for its records.

Each month throughout the year, Zandra produces a management report which shows performance against budget for every cost and revenue heading. This report, together with a commentary written by Paul, is sent to each director and they pass copies to their key staff after removing any sensitive information. Four times each year the remaining periods are reforecast and the adjusted end-of-year position (or out-turn) is also compared with the budgeted position. Paul writes an additional commentary in these months which identifies key actions to bring performance back to budget.

The current position

The directors are presently involved in finalising the budget for 20X9 and are concerned that the process of budgeting is becoming increasingly meaningless. The results for 20X8 show a significant shortfall in both revenue and profitability against both the budget and third quarter out-turn for the year, yet Paul is still insisting that the 20X9 budget should be the 20X8 budget uplifted for inflation and known changes. During the 20X9 audit Zandra mentioned the directors' concerns to the audit manager who suggested that you, as a recently qualified member of the audit team with an interest in strategic planning, might be able to advise the company on how to proceed. The directors have agreed that this would be useful, and have arranged a meeting at which you can meet them and discuss the role of planning within Superware.

Requirements

3.1 Prepare briefing notes to present at a meeting with the directors of Superware at which you will be expected to discuss the following:

(a) The current planning process

(b) Weaknesses of the current planning process

(c) Recommendations for improvement of the planning process. Recommendations should be clearly justified

See **Answer** at the end of this chapter.

7 Strategy and ethics

Section overview

- The desire by management to act ethically affects the scope of strategies adopted but also requires that management keep an eye on the ethical consequences of its operations.

7.1 Impact of ethics on strategy

Ethics impacts at several points in the strategy process:

- In the **formulation of strategic objectives**. Some firms will not consider lines of business for ethical reasons.

- External appraisal will need to consider the **ethical climate in which the firm operates**. This will raise expectations of its behaviour.

- **Internal appraisal**: Management should consider whether present operations are 'sustainable', ie, consistent with present and future ethical expectations.

- **Strategy selection**: Management should consider the ethical implication of proposed strategies before selecting and implementing them.

Ethics and corporate responsibility will be covered in more detail in Chapter 16.

Summary and Self-test

Summary

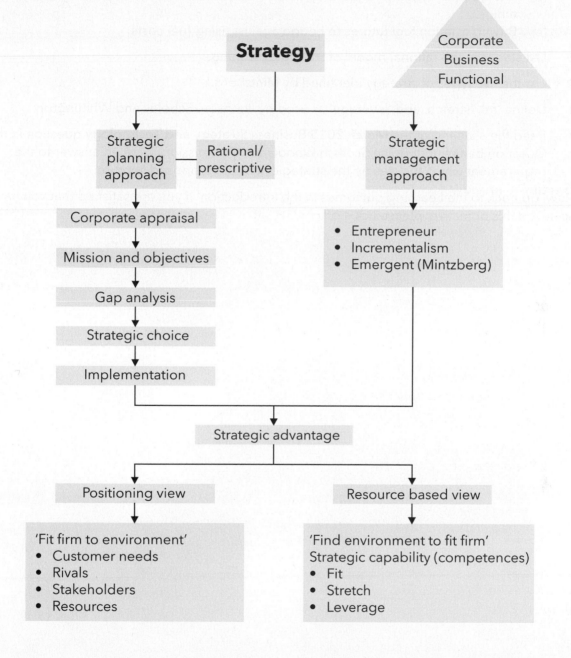

Strategy

Corporate
Business
Functional

Strategic planning approach

Rational/ prescriptive

Strategic management approach

Corporate appraisal

- Entrepreneur
- Incrementalism
- Emergent (Mintzberg)

Mission and objectives

Gap analysis

Strategic choice

Implementation

Strategic advantage

Positioning view

Resource based view

'Fit firm to environment'
- Customer needs
- Rivals
- Stakeholders
- Resources

'Find environment to fit firm'
Strategic capability (competences)
- Fit
- Stretch
- Leverage

CHAPTER 2

Self-test

Answer the following questions.

1   For each of the following issues facing an airline, identify the appropriate level of strategy:

    (a) The decision whether to use permanent or contract staff to work as ground crew.
    (b) The decision whether to develop a no-frills alternative airline to existing full-service airline.
    (c) Buying aviation fuel futures to hedge against rising fuel costs.

2   List stages in the rational model of strategic planning.

3   List the five types of strategy identified by Mintzberg.

4   Define 'fit', 'stretch' and 'leverage' as used by Johnson, Scholes and Whittington.

5   Read the scenario of the **March 2015 Business Strategy and Technology** question in the Question Bank entitled *The Scottish Woodlands Commission*. Draft an answer to the requirement which focuses on the strategic fit of the proposed venture.

Now, go back to the Learning outcomes in the Introduction. If you are satisfied that you have achieved this objective, please tick it off.

Answers to Interactive questions

Answer to Interactive question 1

1.1

Mittal Steel	Lakshmi Mittal
Facebook	Mark Zuckerberg
Berkshire Hathaway	Warren Buffett
Far Eastern Group	Douglas Hsu
Tesco	Sir Terry Leahy
Gazprom	Viktor Zubkov
Ryanair	Michael O'Leary
GE (General Electric)	Jack Welch
TWA	Howard Hughes
Dell	Michael Dell
Tata Group	Ratan N Tata
Hutchison Whampoa	Li Ka-shing
Amazon	Jeff Bezos
Virgin Group	Richard Branson
Apple	Steve Jobs
Microsoft	Bill Gates
Sony	Akio Morita
Bannatyne's Health Clubs	Duncan Bannatyne
Amstrad	Alan Sugar
Ford	Henry Ford

Answer to Interactive question 2

2.1 Like the chicken and egg question this can't be answered.

- Apple provided a new way to make sales by fulfilling some of the same needs that had previously been satisfied by existing mobile phones and portable music players, books and magazines, conventional television programming and personal conversation. So in a sense these needs were already there and were being supplied by different industries.

- The value extracted from the needs through sales of personal computers and portable devices and the creation of a range of associated products, helped the mobile devices industry grow exponentially.

Answer to Interactive question 3

3.1 **Briefing notes**

To	The Directors
From	The Auditor
Date	Today
Subject	The strategic planning process of Superware Products Ltd

(a) **Current planning process**

Currently the planning process in Superware can be illustrated by use of the following model.

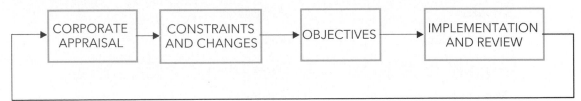

(b) **Weaknesses**

This model is commonly used in smaller organisations, and until 20X8 was perfectly suitable for the purposes of Superware. However, such an 'incremental' model, combined with a 'budget-constrained' management style such as that practised by Paul, does have some weaknesses in a dynamic environment such as the IT industry. These weaknesses, as illustrated by Superware, are as follows.

The use of corporate appraisal at the first stage tends to lead to a blinkered view of strategy, which will necessarily focus on the current products and markets of the company.

The lack of environmental analysis throughout the strategy process, with the exception of known economic changes as a constraint to business, leads to opportunities and threats not being considered until too late.

An incremental approach which led, particularly in 20X8, to an optimistic plan being formalised which was possibly not achievable.

The modification of plans to meet personal objectives of the directors, regardless of the achievability of those objectives.

The short-term nature of the process, concentrating on a 12 month planning horizon, will tend to give a distorted view of the future and lead to a lack of direction and consistency in the goals communicated to managers and staff.

Having said all this, the process does have one significant strength in that the focus on implementation and review is very thorough, particularly in the revision of out-turns and the targeting of performance improvements.

(c) **Recommended modifications**

It is recommended that the company modify the planning process in line with the following model.

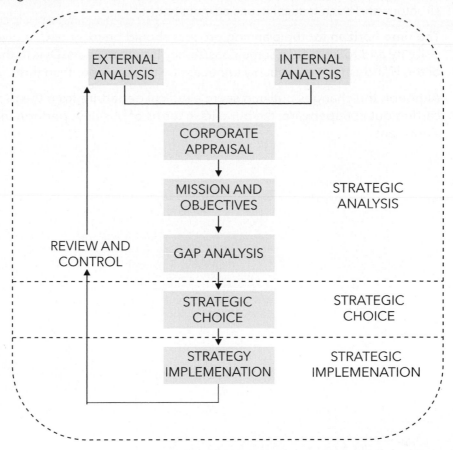

The detailed content and major changes from the current process are explained as follows.

External environmental analysis is a formal analysis of the context in which the company does business. It may well include studies of market size, customer needs, competitor behaviour and changes in technology. Such a study should concentrate on major changes which will affect Superware either as opportunities or threats.

Examples of such changes might include an emerging customer need for a tax module to cope with pay and file, demand for an alternative platform such as UNIX, or an opportunity to launch a totally new product line to meet unsatisfied demand.

Internal analysis of the organisation will identify the current strengths and weaknesses, not merely in terms of the financial performance but also some of the qualitative aspects.

Examples might include the organisation and resources of the company.

Corporate appraisal summarised by SWOT.

Objectives should be agreed, taking into account the requirements of all interested parties, which are perceived as achievable by the managers and staff. Objectives should also take into account the risks and opportunities identified as a result of the environmental analysis.

Strategies can then be formulated, based on all the previous stages, to achieve the company objectives, protect against threats and exploit opportunities.

Examples of such strategies might be product or market development, or even diversification into, for example, management software for doctors or schools.

Implementation and review of strategy should still take place as currently, but as part of the implementation phase it will be necessary to re-evaluate the organisation structure and such tactical issues as investment.

The time horizon for the planning process should be extended to give better strategic visibility and to introduce some consistency between years. Due to the volatile nature of the IT industry, it is probably unnecessary to plan more than three years in advance.

Although the changes outlined seem a radical departure from the process currently carried out in Superware, the benefits in terms of business performance should be significant.

Answers to Self-test

1   (a)   Functional strategy: concerns HRM
     (b)   Corporate strategy: affects shape and scope of business
     (c)   Functional strategy: financial strategy to hedge risk

2   (a)   Corporate appraisal
     (b)   Mission and objectives
     (c)   Gap analysis
     (d)   Strategic choice
     (e)   Strategic implementation

3
- Intended strategy
- Deliberate strategy
- Unrealised strategy
- Emergent strategy
- Realised strategy

4   Fit: Resources able to support current product-market demands and needs

     Stretch: Firm should have resources at cutting edge of the industry or should seek to acquire them

     Leverage: Resources can be used in many ways

5   Refer to the answer to the Scottish Woodlands Commission in the Question Bank.

CHAPTER 3

The purpose of an organisation

Introduction

Examination context

TOPIC LIST

Introduction

Learning outcomes

- Evaluate an organisation's purpose, in terms of its stated mission and objectives ☐
- Consider the different objectives of stakeholders ☐
- Identify the implications for stakeholders, including shareholder value, of choice between strategies ☐

Specific syllabus references for this chapter are: 1a, 2c.

Syllabus links

Some coverage of stakeholders and their interests, and the nature and desirable qualities of business objectives, was given in your Business, Technology and Finance studies.

Examination context

In the exam you may be required to create a mission statement for a given organisation or to identify the inconsistencies and omissions in an existing one. You may also be asked to suggest appropriate goals and objectives. This will involve balancing the needs of different stakeholder groups, identifying possible conflicts of interest and recognising the priorities for the organisation. One of the scenarios in the exam may be a not-for-profit organisation so you must understand the particular issues such organisations face when determining objectives and strategy.

Q2 in the March 2014 exam (*Boom plc*) focused on a company involved in the mining industry. The local government in a South American country is prepared to issue Boom a lease to commence mining operations involving hydraulic fracturing (fracking). Boom's mission statement is 'to maximise the return on investment for our shareholders whilst striving to recognise our corporate responsibility to wider society'. Two of the company's directors have expressed differing opinions on the usefulness of the mission statement. The first part of the question required candidates to:

'Discuss the views of the two directors in relation to Boom's mission statement. In doing so, you should explain the director's duties in respect of corporate governance and corporate responsibility.'

(12 marks)

Corporate governance and corporate responsibility are considered in greater detail in later chapters. As this requirement illustrates, different groups may have different views of an organisation's mission statement. It is important that you realise that questions will require you to apply your knowledge of mission statements using the detail provided in the scenario, in this case comparing the views of the two directors.

Q2 in the September 2017 exam (*Air Services UK Ltd*) focused on a company responsible for providing airspace management systems to all airports and aircraft using UK airspace. The company was partly owned by the UK government and private shareholders, which consisted of several UK-based airlines and Air Services UK staff. Following some recent difficulties the company appointed a new CEO (Joan Louli), who set a new company vision and four key goals to be achieved over the next three years. The first requirement asked candidates to:

'Analyse the extent to which the three-year goals set out by Joan Louli are consistent with both her stated vision for ASU [Air Services UK] and the objectives of ASU's key stakeholders.'

(10 marks)

This requirement nicely illustrates how the topics of vision, goals and stakeholders can be examined in the Business Strategy and Technology exam. As the four new goals focused on different areas of performance, the key stakeholders outlined in the question scenario (government and private shareholders) invariably had different levels of interest in them.

1 The concept of mission

Section overview

- The purpose of an organisation may be communicated in a mission statement. The role and value of such statements has been a matter of debate.

1.1 Mission statements

Definition

Mission: the values and expectations of those who most strongly influence strategy about the scope and posture of the organisation (Johnson, Scholes and Whittington).

Johnson, Scholes and Whittington have suggested that 'the mission of an organisation is the most generalised type of objective and can be thought of as an expression of its *raison d'être*' (reason for existing).

1.2 Elements of mission

The Ashridge College model of mission (Campbell et al, *A Sense of Mission*, 1992) links business strategy to culture and ethics by including four separate elements in an explanation of the **features of a successful mission**.

(a) **Purpose** Why does the organisation exist? Who does it exist for?

- To create wealth for shareholders who take priority over all other stakeholders?
- To satisfy the needs of all stakeholders, including employees, for example?
- To reach some higher goal such as the advancement of society?
- To alleviate the poverty of the needy?

(b) **Strategy:** the competitive position and distinctive competence of the organisation.

(c) **Policies and standards of behaviour:** the policies and behavioural patterns underpinning its work.

(d) **Values:** what the company believes in, which is replicated in employees' personal values.

Worked example: Facebook's mission

Social media platform, Facebook, provides the following detail about its mission statement on the investor relations pages of its website:

'Facebook's mission is to give people the power to build community and bring the world closer together. People use Facebook to stay connected with friends and family, to discover what's going on in the world, and to share and express what matters to them.' (Facebook, 2018).

Source:

Facebook, (2018) *FAQs*. [Online]. Available from: https://investor.fb.com/resources/default.aspx [Accessed 18 April 2018].

1.3 The importance of mission to corporate strategy

The role of mission in strategy is determined by the approach to strategy formulation:

1. **Rational approach**: Mission is the starting-point of strategy formulation. It is the basis on which strategic objectives are set. Any strategy developed must be shown to be consistent with the mission before it is adopted. The culture and values of the organisation must be moulded to serve the strategy.

2. **Emergent approach**: Mission is embedded in the culture of the organisation and used to generate strategic initiatives.

The authors of the Ashridge model claim their model suits either view because, regardless of whether strategy is formulated bottom-up or top-down, all four elements will have to be in place and congruent if the strategy is to be fully successful.

1.4 Mission statements

Mission statements are formal documents that state the organisation's mission. There is no standard format, but the four element Ashridge model of mission is a good basis for writing a mission statement. Mission statements are published within organisations to promote desired behaviour: support for strategy and purpose, adherence to values and adoption of policies and standards of behaviour.

Benefits claimed for mission statements are that they:

- Provide a basis for the control of organisations, ie, managerial and operational goals can be set on the basis of them

- Communicate the nature of the organisation to stakeholders

- Help to instil core values in the organisation

Some commentators are suspicious of mission statements:

- They are often **public relations** exercises rather than an accurate portrayal of the firm's actual values

- They can often be full of **generalisations** from which it is impossible to tie down specific strategic implications or develop meaningful strategic objectives

- They may be ignored by the people responsible for formulating or implementing strategy

2 Organisational goals and objectives

Section overview

- We assume that the primary aim of profit seeking organisations is to increase the wealth of their owners.

- However in practice it seems likely that other factors may force management to offset profitability goals against other objectives.

- Not-for-profit organisations are likely to have multiple aims, reflecting a wider group of stakeholders

2.1 Purpose of the organisation

A basic division of organisational purpose is:

1. **Profit seeking organisations**: the **primary goal** of these is assumed to be to deliver economic value to their owners ie, to increase shareholder wealth. Goals such as satisfying customers, building market share, cutting costs, and demonstrating corporate social responsibility are **secondary goals** which enable economic value to be delivered.

2. **Not-for-profit organisations (NFP)**: the primary goals of these vary enormously and include meeting members' needs, contributing to social well-being and pressing for political and social change. Secondary goals will include the economic goal of not going bankrupt and, in some cases, generating a financial surplus to invest in research or give to the needy. Often the goals of NFP organisations will reflect the need to maximise the benefit derived from limited resources, such as funds. Their objectives may be more heavily influenced by external stakeholders such as the government.

2.2 Shareholder value maximisation

The simple assumption is that profit-seeking organisations seek to maximise shareholder value.

The concept of shareholder wealth maximisation is relied on in several ways:

- As a decision-making criterion: techniques such as NPV and IRR assume this as the goal of the business.

- As a criterion to evaluate divisional managers: using performance measures such as Return on Capital Employed (ROCE) or sometimes Return on Investment (ROI) which should exceed cost of capital and rise from year to year.

- As the basis for financial incentives for managers. Bonuses may be based on improvements in the ROCE, earnings per share (EPS) or share price from year to year.

- As a benchmark against which to evaluate the board. Investment analysts and 'active value' investors use shareholder value measures to evaluate corporate performance and some newspapers publish league tables to name and shame underperforming boards.

2.3 Limitations of shareholder value assumption

Shareholder wealth maximisation may not be an accurate **description** of managerial behaviour and decisions because:

- **Corporate governance is too weak** to give shareholders sufficient information or influence to ensure management maximise shareholder wealth rather than, say, their own emoluments.

- **It ignores the non-financial goals of shareholders**: Family firms, firms with ethical funds holding shares, and firms with substantial shareholdings in the hands of governmental bodies will be also required to satisfy non-economic objectives such as sustainability or employment.

- **It is impossible to verify**: Seen in retrospect a board's decisions may be seen to have failed to maximise shareholder wealth. Yet this is consistent with a board that wished to maximise shareholder wealth but whose decisions were limited by time, information available and their own skills. Also to judge whether wealth was maximised it would be necessary to know the outcomes of all the alternatives the board ignored.

It may not be a suitable **prescription** for management because it:

- **Ignores the nature of the financial return required**: shareholders receive their wealth from dividends and from capital growth. They are assumed to be indifferent between the two, but may not be in practice due to income needs and the different tax treatments of income and capital growth.

- **Overlooks the power of stakeholders** other than shareholders, eg, increasing shareholder wealth at the expense of staff benefits may lead to loss of staff and industrial action.

- **Ignores corporate responsibility (CR)**: many cultures take the view that profits should be balanced against the good of society and the natural environment.

2.4 Setting business objectives

Hierarchically, missions and objectives can be shown as follows.

There should be goal congruence, ie, the mission and objectives set at each level should be consistent with each other and not in conflict.

Quantifying objectives

Objectives must be capable of being quantified, otherwise progress towards them cannot be measured.

For a government agency or charity, for instance, to state its objective as 'to improve the welfare of old age pensioners' is not precise enough. It must state how it is going to measure the achievement – in terms perhaps of the number of places in old people's homes, the number of meals-on-wheels served, the number of patients treated in geriatric wards – so that several targets may make up its overall objective.

In other words, for objectives to be of use in practice, they must be SMART – **S**pecific, **M**easurable, **A**chievable, **R**elevant and **T**imebound – eg, 'increase online revenues by 25% within one year'.

Objectives specified in this way are often referred to as 'closed' objectives.

2.5 Examples of objectives

In practice objectives vary in attributes and in terms of the precision with which they are specified. The following gives some examples:

- **Corporate objective: open**
  Our primary aims are to provide a sound investment for our shareholders by increasing shareholder value and also worthwhile job prospects for our employees. Our objectives are customer satisfaction, real growth in earnings per share and a competitive return on capital employed.

- **Corporate objective: closed**
  The most important objective remains the achievement of a minimum return of 20% on average capital employed, with a target return of 25%.

- **Business unit objective: open**
  One of the main aims for one of the business areas in which the company is involved is to play a leading role in meeting the requirements of the widening and expanding home entertainments industry.

- **Business unit objective: closed**
  In the UK we are budgeting our house building unit to sell 2,500 homes next year – a figure that will put it among the top 10 house builders. Ideally, existing performance statistics should be used to measure objectives; if a new system of data collection or processing has to be instituted to measure progress towards objectives, extra cost will be incurred.

Interactive question 1: Gooseberry Farm Ltd

The current date is May 20X6.

Giles MacDonald and his wife, are the owners of Gooseberry Farm Ltd. Gooseberry Farm operates a 1,200 acre arable site located five miles outside the local country town, Norbridge. As a result of a change in the way government farming subsidies are calculated, Gooseberry Farm Ltd faces a sharp decline in its annual trading profits. The MacDonald's are therefore considering using 200 acres to establish a new exclusive 18-hole golf course, and golf club. In the event that they proceed with the proposal Mr and Mrs MacDonald are keen that the golf club is established as a separate legal entity. Mr and Mrs MacDonald intend to name the business the Millennium Golf Club Ltd.

From some preliminary research conducted into the local golf scene Mr and Mrs MacDonald intend to limit membership to a maximum of 750 players to help create an exclusive environment at the new club. The policy of the club will be to keep the annual subscription fee for members as low as possible while maintaining high quality facilities and helping to preserve the natural wildlife in the surrounding countryside.

A number of local businessmen regard the establishment of the golf course as feasible, since planning permission will readily be forthcoming and membership waiting lists at the two existing clubs in the Norbridge area exceed 350. On the assumption that target membership levels are achieved, annual subscriptions will initially to be set at £500 for each member. This will be £100 less than for full membership at the two rival golf clubs in the area. In addition, no joining fees will be payable in the first year of operation, but thereafter (as with the other two clubs) they will be equal to one year's subscription. On this basis Mr and Mrs MacDonald are certain that they will be able to recruit around 350 members from the existing two clubs, including a good number of influential local businessmen and low handicap players. In addition, the new club expects to recruit most of those currently on the waiting lists at its two local rivals.

Requirements

As an employee of the firm of accountants used by Mr and Mrs MacDonald:

1.1 Draft a mission statement that might be suitable for Millennium Golf Club Ltd and identify possible key objectives.

See **Answer** at the end of this chapter.

3 Stakeholder goals and objectives

Section overview

- Profit, or shareholder wealth, maximisation assumes that management are motivated and free to adopt policies that serve the interests of just one social group: the owners of the business.

- Stakeholder analysis suggests that management may seek to serve, or may be constrained by, a wider group of interested parties.

3.1 Role of stakeholders

Definitions

Stakeholders: Are those groups or persons with an interest in what an organisation does.

Management theory rejects the assumption that firms seek shareholder wealth maximisation as too simplistic. Instead it states that the goals of an organisation will reflect the power and interests of the most powerful stakeholder groups.

There are three broad types of stakeholder in an organisation, as follows:

- **Internal** stakeholders (employees, management)
- **Connected** stakeholders (shareholders, customers, suppliers, financiers)
- **External** stakeholders (the community, government, pressure groups)

Interests of stakeholders

The interests (or expectations) of stakeholders may be in **conflict**. Conflict may arise **between** groups (eg, employee demands for pay rises reduce profits available for shareholders) and **within** groups (eg, institutional shareholders in a recently floated plc may have different objectives from family shareholders).

Which expectations determine the organisation's objectives depends on the relative **power** of the stakeholder groups (see Section 3.6).

3.2 Internal stakeholders: employees and management

Because **employees and management** are so intimately connected with the company, their objectives are likely to have a strong influence on how it is run. They are interested in the following issues:

(a) The **organisation's continuation and growth**. Management and employees have a special interest in the organisation's continued existence.

(b) Managers and employees have **individual interests** and goals which can be harnessed to the goals of the organisation.

Internal stakeholder	Interests to defend	Response risk
Managers and employees	<ul><li>Jobs/careers</li><li>Money</li><li>Promotion</li><li>Benefits</li><li>Satisfaction</li></ul>	<ul><li>Pursuit of 'systems goals' rather than shareholder interests</li><li>Industrial action</li><li>Negative power to impede implementation</li><li>Refusal to relocate</li><li>Resignation</li></ul>

3.3 Connected stakeholders

Connected stakeholders and external stakeholders are both outside the organisation. Their difference lies in the degree of connectedness.

- Connected stakeholders supply resources to the organisation such as capital or sales revenue.

- External stakeholders do not have this direct connection but rather influence the context in which the organisation operates.

Connected stakeholder	Interests to defend	Response risk
Shareholders (corporate strategy)	• Increase in shareholder wealth, measured by profitability, P/E ratios, market capitalisation, dividends and yield • Risk	• Sell shares (eg, to predator) or boot out management
Bankers (cash flows)	• Security of loan • Adherence to loan agreements	• Denial of credit • Higher interest charges • Receivership
Suppliers (purchasing strategy)	• Profitable sales • Payment for goods • Long-term relationship	• Refusal of credit • Court action • Wind down relationships
Customers (product market strategy)	• Goods as promised • Future benefits	• Buy elsewhere • Sue

Worked example: Shareholder activism

A podcast on the *Financial Times* website in April 2016, contained an interview with the newspaper's Corporate Affairs correspondent, David Oakley. The interview explored the growth in shareholder activism. Oakley highlights that the growing disparity between the level of pay between senior management and average workers has increased significantly since the 1990's. Today the most senior officers in large organisations now earn 150 times more than the average worker. As a result this has led to increasing numbers of shareholders challenging the pay packages proposed for company directors. Oakley notes that in 2012, there were a number of such challenges, that resulted in the so-called 'shareholder spring', which led to increased legislation in 2013 around the need for companies to adopt clear pay policies. Although, such measures have eased the pressure on corporate boards, the issue is not likely to disappear anytime soon. In 2016, it was reported that 59% of shareholders in oil company BP voted against the proposed pay package of the company's CEO, Bob Dudley. As Oakley highlighted, although the vote was non-binding on BP it sent a clear signal to the directors that shareholders want a greater say over the corporate matters affecting shareholder wealth.

Source:

Shareholder activism on the rise. (2016) Podcast. [Online]. Available from: www.ft.com [Accessed 6 June 2016].

3.4 External stakeholders

External stakeholder groups – the government, local authorities, pressure groups, the community at large, professional bodies – are likely to have quite diverse objectives.

External stakeholder	Interests to defend	Response risk
Government	• Jobs, training, tax	• Tax increases • Regulation • Legal action

External stakeholder	Interests to defend	Response risk
Interest/pressure groups	• Pollution • Rights • Other	• Publicity • Direct action • Sabotage • Pressure on government

These stakeholders are likely to play a greater role in determining the objectives for NFPs.

3.5 Dependency

A firm might depend on a stakeholder group at any particular time.

(a) A firm with persistent cash flow problems might depend on its bankers to provide it with money to stay in business at all.

(b) In the long term, any firm depends on its customers.

The degree of dependence or reliance can be analysed according to these criteria:

(a) **Disruption**: Can the stakeholder disrupt the organisation's plans (eg, a bank withdrawing overdraft facilities)?

(b) **Replacement**: Can the firm replace the relationship?

(c) **Uncertainty**: Does the stakeholder cause uncertainty in the firm's plans? A firm with healthy positive cash flows and large cash balances need not worry about its bank's attitude to a proposed investment.

The way in which the relationship between company and stakeholders is conducted is a function of the parties' **relative bargaining strength** and the philosophy underlying **each party's objectives**. This can be shown by means of a spectrum:

	Stakeholders' bargaining strength				
	Weak				Strong
Company's conduct of relation-ship	Command/ dictated by company	Consulation and consideration of stakeholders' views	Negotiation	Participation and acceptance of stakeholders' views	Democratic voting by stakeholders	Command/ dictated by stakeholders

3.6 Stakeholder mapping: power and interest

Mendelow suggests that stakeholders may be positioned on a matrix whose axes are power held and the likelihood of showing an interest in the organisation's activities. These factors will help define the type of relationship the organisation should seek with its stakeholders.

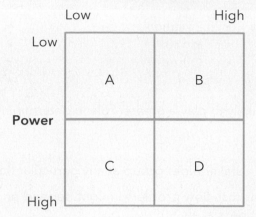

Level of interest

	Low	High
Low	A	B
High	C	D

(with "Power" label on the left axis)

(a) **Key players** are found in segment D: strategy must be **acceptable** to them, at least. An example would be a major customer.

(b) Stakeholders in segment C must be treated with care. While often passive, they are capable of moving to segment D. They should, therefore be **kept satisfied.** Large institutional shareholders might fall into segment C.

(c) Stakeholders in segment B do not have great ability to influence strategy, but their views can be important in influencing more powerful stakeholders, perhaps by lobbying. They should therefore be **kept informed**. Community representatives and charities might fall into segment B.

(d) Minimal effort is expended on segment A.

A single stakeholder map is unlikely to be appropriate for all circumstances. In particular, stakeholders may move from quadrant to quadrant when different potential future strategies are considered.

Stakeholder mapping is used to assess the **significance** of stakeholder groups. This in turn has implications for the organisation.

(a) The framework of **corporate governance** should recognise stakeholders' levels of interest and power.

(b) It may be appropriate to seek to **reposition** certain stakeholders and discourage others from repositioning themselves, depending on their attitudes.

(c) Key **blockers** and **backers** of change must be identified.

Stakeholder mapping can also be used to establish political priorities. A map of the current position can be compared with a map of a desired future state. This will indicate critical shifts that must be pursued.

Interactive question 2: Supavac plc

Supavac plc ('Supavac') is a listed company which manufactures vacuum cleaners. Some 70% of its output is sold to Avold plc ('Avold'), a major UK-based chain of electrical stores. Vacuum cleaners are sold under Avold's own label and are regarded as being in the mid to upmarket range. Manufacturing takes place at Supavac's two factories, both of which are in the UK and are of approximately equal size.

The workforce of Supavac is largely unskilled or semi-skilled and is not unionised.

Avold has been a major customer of Supavac for about 30 years, but a new management team recently took over at Avold. It informed the board of Supavac that a new annual contract is to be arranged which would involve a major reduction in prices offered, and that the volumes purchased next year would be only 60% of previous years. It was also made clear that further price reductions would need to take place in future years if the contract were to be maintained at the new lower volumes.

As employees became aware of the increasingly competitive conditions, the possibility of factory closure emerged.

The board of Supavac identified two strategies:

Strategy 1. Close one factory and attempt to cut costs at the other by a policy of efficiency improvements and redundancies.

Strategy 2. Close both UK factories and open a new factory in Eastern Europe where labour costs are significantly lower than in the UK.

Requirements

2.1 Identify and justify the position of each of the following stakeholder groups in Mendelow's power-interest matrix with respect to the two strategies.

    (a) UK-based employees
    (b) Potential employees in Eastern Europe
    (c) Shareholders in Supavac
    (d) Avold

See **Answer** at the end of this chapter

4 Not-for-profit organisations

Section overview

- The number of not-for-profit organisations potentially outweighs the profit seeking ones if we include voluntary sports clubs, interest groups and associations.

- Understanding how strategy is developed in these is important. It is similar to strategy formulation in businesses but without the comfort of the assumption of a single overriding goal of profit.

4.1 Voluntary and not-for-profit sectors

The term **not-for-profit organisation (NFP)** encompasses many different organisations whose only similarity is that they do not seek to make economic returns for their owners.

NFPs include:

- **Volunteer organisations**: providing services such as neighbourhood improvement, assisting the elderly, providing opportunities for children and youth, visiting the sick.

- **Charitable trusts**: set up around clear objectives to achieve some cultural or social goal eg, education of the young, art and music.

- **Governmental bodies**: these range from departments of central government down to local administrative bodies. Obvious examples include police services, armed forces and education services.

- **Mutually-owned public benefit corporations**: these are effectively companies which do not issue shares to the public but rather whose capital is provided, and debts guaranteed to a certain limit, by others. They are free to raise debt from third parties. Their members are the stakeholder groups they serve and they will have procedures to consult and report to them. In the UK these include rail infrastructure provider Network Rail and Foundation hospitals. A more well-known example are UK Public Schools which are in fact private schools for fee paying pupils but which have the legal status of a public corporation.

The taxation treatment of the incomes of NFPs is likely to be favourable because their surpluses are not treated as profits. For this reason many NFPs have to work hard to defend their status against accusations that they are merely a tax avoidance device. To do this they need to demonstrate a genuine **public interest** motivation.

Business strategy issues are just as relevant to a not-for-profit organisation as they are to a business operating with a profit motive. The tasks of setting objectives, developing strategies and controls for their implementation can all help in improving the performance of charities and NFPs.

4.2 Objectives

Objectives will not be based on profit achievement but rather on achieving a **particular response** from various target stakeholders.

Here are some possible objectives for a NFP:

(a)   Surplus maximisation (equivalent to profit maximisation)

(b)   Revenue maximisation (as for a commercial business)

(c)   Usage maximisation (as in leisure centre swimming pool usage)

(d)   Usage targeting (matching the capacity available, as in the National Health Service (NHS) in the UK)

(e)   Full/partial cost recovery (minimising subsidy)

(f)   Budget maximisation (maximising what is offered)

(g)   Producer satisfaction maximisation (satisfying the wants of staff and volunteers)

(h)   Client satisfaction maximisation (the police generating the support of the public)

There are no buyers in the NFP sector, but rather a number of different **audiences** (or stakeholders):

(a)   A **target public** is a group of individuals who have an interest or concern about the charity.
(b)   Those benefiting from the organisation's activities are known as the **client public**.
(c)   Relationships are also vital with **donors and volunteers** from the general public.
(d)   There may also be a need to lobby **local and national government** and businesses for support.

The objective setting process must **balance** the interests and concerns of these audiences, which may result in a range of objectives, rather than a single over-riding one. To allow for this balance to be achieved:

NFPs will typically feature wide **participation** in the objective setting process. Indeed it may be a legal condition in their constitution and essential to maintaining their legal status.

Stakeholder power and interests are likely to be more obvious in NFPs than in profit-seeking organisations.

Interactive question 3: Foundry Theatre

The Foundry Theatre is a major regional theatre in Westingham and was built 70 years ago. 30 years ago the Arts Council awarded the theatre a grant for the first time 'to allow the theatre to undertake more prestigious productions than their own resources allow'. This grant (of £5,000) was very significant in that it marked the transition from **commercial** to **subsidised** theatre.

A few years after the Arts Council grant was awarded, the theatre was refurbished extensively with money from Westingham City Council at a cost of £884,000. Despite this, the theatre was soon in difficulties and heading for considerable financial losses. In a report published at the time the council's treasurer stated that the theatre should 'slash costs and attract bigger audiences to improve its financial position'. In addition, the theatre was criticised for not staging enough popular shows, for inadequate use of the building and for having a 'top heavy' management structure.

Again the council offered to step in with financial assistance providing the theatre cut its costs and implemented a review of its management structure. The theatre administrator refused the council's terms, indicating that many of the council's proposed savings would severely compromise the theatre's artistic standards.

Changes were eventually made and the theatre survived.

The objectives of the theatre were enshrined in the memorandum of association of the Foundry Theatre Trust as follows.

- To promote, maintain, improve and advance education, particularly by the production of educational plays and the encouragement of the arts of drama, mime, dance, singing and music.

- To receive, educate and train students in drama, dancing, music and other arts and to promote the recognition and encouragement of special merit in students.

The company (and the theatre) has enjoyed varying degrees of success over the last 10 years (attendance figures are given in Appendix I).

The current position

In a recent article in the *Westingham Gazette* the following comment was made.

'The Artistic Director has resigned, attendances are down by 50%, productions planned for the new year are cancelled, the company is heading for a £250,000 deficit – but there is no crisis at the Foundry, said Stephen Appleyard, Chief Executive, Westingham Theatres Committee.'

In carrying out an internal analysis for Westingham Theatres Ltd the following comments have been made.

James Knowles-Cutler (newly-appointed Artistic director)

'The objective of the theatre is clear to me. We should aim to increase our audiences through a programme of challenging plays. Rehashing populist plays is not our role. We should attempt to attract well-known (in theatre terms) classical actors and seek to stimulate debate and interest in theatre through a programme of good classics (for example, *The Caretaker* by Pinter, *Waiting for Godot* by Beckett, etc,) and challenging modern plays. My ultimate objective is to establish ourselves as the leading ''serious'' theatre outside of London.'

Thomas Sutherland (Finance director)

'We are still dependent for a large amount of our funding on central government grants. The percentage of our funding coming from this area looks to be about 50%. This is misleading because the actual amount of this funding has been growing very slowly. The fact that it represents up to 50% is due to a reduced proportion of revenue coming from box office receipts. Therefore, we really have one objective – to boost our sales or receipts from the box office. Our current revenue includes £1,171,856 (20X9) down from a high of £1,596,245. Thus I estimate our ideal objective is to increase our box office receipts by 30% over the next three years. I believe there are a number of ways we can achieve this.

(1) We can reduce the price of our ''Foundry Card''. This is a membership card which allows the holder to attend five peak performances (ie, Friday and Saturday) for the price of four performances. By reducing the price we would encourage demand.

(2) We should also reduce our prices on an individual performance basis. I believe this would increase attendances by such an amount as to increase total revenues overall.

(3) The restaurant/café side could be improved. The theatre occupies a first rate position in the city and has an excellent atrium space in the entrance hall. This is already used at lunchtimes, etc, but could be profitably used in the evenings for pre-theatre dinner.'

Brian Johnson (Westingham City Council, appointed to board of trustees of the Foundry Theatre)

'The trustees for the theatre believe the objective is to broaden the audience. The current composition of our audience is shown in Appendix II. Clearly the greater proportion of the audience comes from A/B income groups. We need to push more into other market segments. By boosting attendances in this manner we can go some way to achieving increased revenue figures. We think focusing on the production of highbrow theatre will only alienate a large group of the very people we are trying to attract.'

Requirements

You are part of a consultancy team appointed by the Westingham Council to investigate the theatre's position.

3.1 In the light of information provided in Appendix II discuss the use of price reductions as a means of achieving the objectives as stated by the finance director.

3.2 Draft a memorandum to the trustees of the theatre explaining the objectives of the theatre as expressed by the artistic director, the finance director and the trustee. You should comment on their compatibility and suggest a possible prioritisation of these objectives.

See **Answer** at the end of this chapter.

Appendix I

Attendances at Westingham Theatre 20X0 to 20X9

Year	Theatre	Studio	Total
20X0	159,700	16,600	176,300
20X1	168,800	12,900	181,700
20X2	167,900	8,000	175,900
20X3	167,700	18,000	185,700
20X4	210,300	21,200	231,500
20X5	206,869	14,902	221,771
20X6	175,064	16,533	191,597
20X7	159,966	13,491	173,457
20X8	175,435	4,903	180,338
20X9	100,807	9,510	110,317

Appendix II

Demographic characteristics of theatre-goers and local population

	Total population in metropolitan county around Westingham	Foundry audiences	Foundry mailing list 20X9	Foundry card holders 20X9
(1) Social class (% A/B/C1)	29%	80%	50%	71%
(2) Education (% completing full-time education, age 19 or over)	3%	50%	N/A	N/A
(3) Age (% under 35)	37%	Main theatre 55% Studio theatre 75%	25%	7%
(4) Sex (% females)	51%	50% apiece in main theatre and studio	66%	64%
(5) Westingham post code	N/A	80% (estimated)	70%	91%

Appendix III

Revenues

Year	Box office £'000	Government grant £'000
20X3	1,144	927
20X4	1,306	1,072
20X5	1,330	1,054
20X6	1,446	1,095
20X7	1,596	1,065
20X8	1,117	1,103
20X9	1,172	1,157

CHAPTER 3

Summary and Self-test

Summary

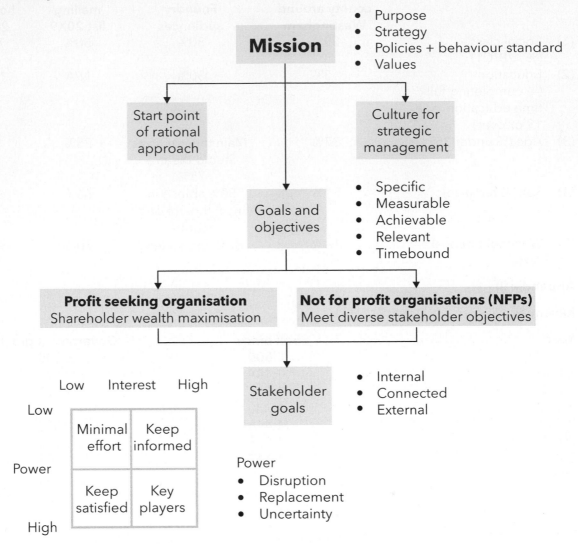

Mission

- Purpose
- Strategy
- Policies + behaviour standard
- Values

Start point of rational approach

Culture for strategic management

Goals and objectives

- Specific
- Measurable
- Achievable
- Relevant
- Timebound

Profit seeking organisation
Shareholder wealth maximisation

Not for profit organisations (NFPs)
Meet diverse stakeholder objectives

Stakeholder goals

- Internal
- Connected
- External

	Low	Interest	High
Low		Minimal effort	Keep informed
Power			
High		Keep satisfied	Key players

Power
- Disruption
- Replacement
- Uncertainty

Self-test

Answer the following questions.

1 What are the four elements in the Ashridge definition of 'mission'?

P ....

S ....

P ....

V ....

2 Mission statements have a standard format.

☐ True

☐ False

3 Fill in the gaps: Most organisations set themselves quantified (a) .... to enact the corporate (b) .... Many objectives are:

(c) S ....
(d) M ....
(e) A ....
(f) R ....
(g) T ....

4 Some objectives are more important than others. These are called .... corporate objectives.

5 (a) 'Increase the number of customers by 15%'
(b) 'Produce reports within three days of month end'
(c) 'Achieve 35% market share'

Are each of the above examples of unit objectives or corporate objectives?

6 There are three broad types of stakeholder. What are these?

(a) ....
(b) ....
(c) ....

7 Define an NFP.

8 Read the scenario of the **September 2012 Business Strategy and Technology** question in the Question Bank entitled *Bigville Council*. Draft an answer for the requirement on the objectives of different stakeholder groups.

9 Read the scenario of the **March 2014 Business Strategy and Technology** question in the Question Bank entitled *Boom plc*. Draft an answer for the requirement concerning the views of the two directors in relation to the company's mission statement.

10 Read the scenario of the **September 2017 Business Strategy and Technology** question in the Question Bank entitled *Air Services UK*. Draft an answer for the requirement on the consistency of the three-year goals and objectives of key stakeholders.

Now, go back to the Learning outcomes in the Introduction. If you are satisfied that you have achieved these objectives, please tick them off.

Answers to Interactive questions

Answer to Interactive question 1

1.1 Mission statement

For Millennium Golf Club Ltd, a suitable mission statement might be:

'Our mission is to become the premier golf club in the Norbridge area by offering excellent value for money. We will achieve this by charging low fees, having high quality facilities and restricting the membership numbers of the club to ensure exclusiveness. At the same time we will protect the environment and help to preserve the local countryside.'

Suitable key objectives might include:

1. To achieve the membership target of 750 members in the first year.

2. To recruit at least 350 members from rival clubs.

3. To ensure 30% of golf club members have a low handicap.

4. To win an award for golf club design and facilities by 20X9.

5. To hold a local golf championship at the club by 20X9.

6. To monitor the wildlife around the golf club and make sure that numbers of breeds of wildlife are maintained.

Answer to Interactive question 2

	Interest	
	Low	**High**
Power **Low**		UK employess Eastern European employess
Power **High**		Shareholders Avoid

2.1 (a) UK-based employees

The power of employees to stop or moderate any closure decision is limited. If the entire UK workforce is united, then significant costs can arise from disruption. However, once the decision is announced the employees at the site that is not to be closed have a much lower negative interest in the decision. Indeed, from the perspective of self-interest their employment might even be more secure as a result of the closure of the other plant; hence they could develop a positive interest.

In general, however, UK employees would favour strategy 1 as there are fewer redundancies.

Perversely, if the redundancy payments are sufficiently high some employees may favour redundancy to continued employment and thus have a positive interest in strategy 2 (eg, if they were going to leave anyway).

(b) **Potential employees in Eastern Europe**

Potential employees have probably not yet been specifically identified but they would have no power to influence the decision in either case.

Clearly, once selected, they would have a strong positive interest in strategy 2, particularly if local unemployment is high and/or Supavac is offering better pay and conditions than local employers.

(c) **Shareholders in Supavac**

The ability to maintain the Avold contract is essential to Supavac shareholders as it counts for 70% of sales. The strategies under consideration appear necessary to reduce costs and thus maintain the Avold contract, even if not at volumes previously attained. The shareholders would favour the strategy that best achieves this, having regard to all other factors (such as quality, certainty of supply, transport costs, labour costs).

The shareholders have the ultimate power to determine the direction of the company. While in the short term the directors are empowered to make the relevant decisions, they can be displaced if these are not in the interests of shareholders.

(d) **Avold**

Given that Avold takes 70% of Supavac's sales, it has considerable power over Supavac and is likely to be in a position to influence the decision of where production should take place. It will undoubtedly need assurances, if vacuum cleaners are to be manufactured overseas, as to quality and delivery schedules. The ability of Supavac to cut costs will have an impact on its ability to deliver price reductions.

Avold is interested in the reorganisation as vacuum cleaner manufacture is a competitive market, with a range of alternative suppliers available if Supavac fails to deliver cost reductions. (Alternatives are possible as there is an element of judgement involved, given the information available.)

Answer to Interactive question 3

3.1 Effectiveness of price reductions

The finance director has a stated objective of increasing sales revenue as far as possible and suggests reducing prices to achieve this.

As a means of enhancing sales the following comments are relevant.

Given the information on the population in Appendix II, 80% of the audience comes from social grouping A/B/C1.

It could be argued that going to the theatre represents a small amount of total expenditure for such groups, and therefore a rise in price may be possible to increase sales revenue.

Alternatively, to attract a wider audience (students, children, unemployed), price reductions may help to raise sales revenues.

The pricing structure needs to be much more precise, ie, it needs to take into account

- Time of week and performance (students, cheap mid-week seats)
- Ability of audience to pay and their income bracket

It also assumes that the demand for theatre seats is driven largely by price. This is a very strong assumption. Non-price factors which would influence the demand would include the programme of plays itself, actors involved, time of year, etc. The implicit assumption made by the finance director is that, *ceteris paribus*, reducing price will increase demand. One badly chosen programme of plays could reduce overall demand in a given season.

3.2 Memorandum

To	Members of the Westingham Council
From	ABC Consultants
Date	Today
Subject	The Foundry Theatre – Objectives and role

The nature of objectives

Objectives differ dramatically between organisations and in the way they are expressed. The most obvious distinction is between open and closed objectives.

Open objectives contain no reference to a quantified target for the objective. For example, a statement such as 'we aim to increase our market share' is open. Thus there is no guidance on by how much to increase the target of the objective nor over what timescale.

Closed objectives contain some quantified target value for the objective in question. The following is an example of a closed objective: 'Our objective is to increase our market share (by volume) by 12% over the next three years.' This contains a criterion by which to assess the target volume. It gives a target (12%) and a timescale (three years).

The final point to be made about objectives is that as far as possible they must be consistent. It is important to have a principal objective in agreement with supporting objectives. It is the duty of senior management to ensure that objectives are consistent and avoid dysfunctional behaviour.

The objectives for the Foundry Theatre

Introduction

Examination of the objectives for the Foundry Theatre are best undertaken from a 'stakeholder' viewpoint.

From the information given it can be seen that two of the objectives are 'open'. It is difficult to see how to assess the theatre against such open-ended objectives.

Clearly, in following the trust's objectives audience surveys could be carried out to determine

- Income bracket
- Residential area
- Frequency of attendance, etc

Thus, given the data in Appendix II on audience composition, this objective will be achieved if, *ceteris paribus*, more C1/C2 males under 35 attend plays and concerts.

The objective can thus be clarified and become closed.

Compatibility of objectives

Clearly the objectives put forward by the artistic director and the trust are mutually incompatible. If either objective is to be pursued to the exclusion of the other, stakeholder conflict is assured. If so, two possible (there may be more) outcomes become apparent.

- The artistic director becomes disgruntled and resigns.

- The trustees become disaffected and attempt to make changes at the theatre (in the absence of more information on the memorandum of association of the trust, it is difficult to say what power they have).

The next issue is to see whether the objective of the finance director is compatible with the other two.

The objective of increasing box office receipts is compatible with either of the other two.

From the viewpoint of the artistic director, increasing audience figures (and therefore receipts) will come from a small percentage of the metropolitan area's population (29% are A/B/C1) and these already provide 80% of the audiences of the Foundry Theatre.

Given the increased ability to pay of the A/B/C1 income groups, increasing the attendance price of tickets and a more challenging series of plays may satisfy both the finance and artistic directors.

From the trust's viewpoint, putting on less 'difficult' plays and increasing the number of popular touring reviews/plays may well boost audiences. Therefore reducing price may well enhance demand in volume terms, thus increasing box office receipts overall.

Prioritisation of objectives

There is an additional important element here and that is the amount of government grant. Appendix III shows the amount of government grant the theatre has received since 20X3.

The percentage of revenue accounted for by government grants is less important than the amount. It can be seen to have grown very little (compound annual growth of just 1.5% between 20X3 and 20X9). In real terms this has almost certainly fallen.

A critical issue facing the theatre therefore is its role as a subsidised theatre.

The current government is not disposed towards subsidies. There appears little hope of the grant increasing as a source of revenue.

The most important objective therefore is for the theatre to increase its box office revenues. Failure to do so (given no growth in subsidy) will eventually diminish the theatre's ability to stage its own productions.

The reduced ability to stage its own productions means that the artistic director's objective cannot be achieved.

Conclusions and recommendations

The main conclusions are as follows.

- Increasing box office revenue is the primary objective for the theatre.

- The finance director's assumptions on how this may be achieved are questionable.

- Audience research should be carried out re frequency/preferences, etc. This will provide information as to programmes and willingness to pay.

- The increased revenue appears likely from three principal sources.

  - Increased prices to current A/B/C1 theatre-goers and a challenging programme.

  - Lower prices to C1/C2/D income groups with a change in programme emphasis to 'popular' plays/musicals.

  - Perhaps a combination of both of these could work with plays/shows at varying prices during the week.

- Using the atrium space to provide a restaurant/café would probably increase non-theatre audience and thus provide an additional source of revenue.

Answers to Self-test

1. Purpose
    Strategy
    Policies and standards of behaviour
    Values

2. False

3. (a) objectives (b) mission (c) specific (d) measurable (e) achievable (f) relevant (g) time bound

4. Primary

5. (a) Unit
    (b) Unit
    (c) Corporate

6. (a) Internal
    (b) Connected
    (c) External

7. An organisation whose attainment of its prime goal is not assessed by economic measures. Their first objective is to be a non-loss operation to cover costs. Profits are made only as a means to an end, such as providing a service.

8. Refer to the answer to Bigville Council in the Question Bank.

9. Refer to the answer to Boom plc in the Question Bank.

10. Refer to the answer to Air Services UK in the Question Bank.

CHAPTER 4

The macro environment

Introduction

Examination context

TOPIC LIST

Summary and Self-test

Answers to Interactive questions

Answers to Self-test

Introduction

Learning outcome

- Analyse for a given situation the external factors which may impact upon an organisation's performance and position, identifying significant issues in areas such as:

    - Sustainability, including natural capital

    - Macroeconomic forces

    - International trade, financial systems and global economic factors

    - Government policies

    - Cultural environment

    - Current technology developments, including those relating to automation and intelligent systems

Specific syllabus reference for this chapter is: 1b.

Syllabus links

Environmental analysis was covered in Business, Technology and Finance. However its coverage was at the level of core knowledge. In the Business Strategy and Technology examination you will be required to apply it.

Examination context

The scenarios in the majority of exam questions will require you to absorb and understand information about the external environment in which an organisation operates based on a scenario. You will also need to assess the implications of the environment and changes in the environment for the strategic positioning and strategic decisions of an organisation. To do this you will need to apply your knowledge using the tools and ideas covered in this chapter.

Q1 in the September 2015 exam (*Kentish Fruit Farms*) focused on an organic fruit farm. The scenario contained information about the farm's external environment. The first requirement asked candidates to:

'Identify and analyse the three key factors from the PESTEL model which are most relevant to the UK organic fruit industry.' **(9 marks)**

While the instruction to use the PESTEL model is very clear, it is particularly important to recognise that in this instance that you only need to analyse three key factors. However, to produce a good answer it was critical that you justify why the factors you have chosen should be considered important. When only part of a model is required it is crucial that you apply those elements most relevant. This will be driven by the scenario detail. In the case of Kentish Fruit Farms, the examiner noted there was plenty of obvious information in the scenario to discuss social, technological, ecological or legal factors. There was less in the scenario to support political or economic considerations.

Although in this question you only needed to analyse three factors, the question requirements in other exams might ask you to apply the PESTEL model as a whole to the scenario, in which case you should aim to analyse all of the factors when attempting the question. It is important to note however, that some requirements may not specify a particular model to use to all, in which case you will need to use your judgement as to whether the use of a model or framework in your answer will add value.

In light of the name of the exam, Business Strategy and Technology, it is important that you appreciate the impact that technology and technological change is having on organisations. Exam questions could easily feature organisations which are dependent on the use of technology in delivering a service or as part of the process for new product development. Clearly, in such cases, technology will be vital to the organisation's ability to operate effectively.

Q1 in the March 2017 exam (*Ignite plc*) focused on a company which manufactures luxury cigarette lighters, and other types of products. It was set up when smoking was fashionable but has subsequently experienced declining sales as smoking has become unpopular and many people who continue to smoke have switched to e-cigarettes. The first requirement asked candidates to:

'Analyse the external factors that have influenced the changing demand for Ignite's cigarette lighters in the UK between 1950 and 2016.'   **(9 marks)**

Although, no specific model was requested in the requirement the level of detail outlined in the scenario regarding changes in social attitudes, government legislation and technological developments provided a strong clue that use of the PESTEL model was highly appropriate.

1 The business environment

Section overview

- Strategy is concerned with matching the organisation to the threats and opportunities in its environment.

- The process of gathering and disseminating the necessary knowledge about a firm's external environment is a specific example of knowledge management.

1.1 Importance of management understanding business environment

The environment contains those factors 'surrounding the organisation'. It includes the general macro-economic environment (the political, economic, social, technological, ecological and legal influences in the countries a business operates in); and factors particular to the firm or industry such as competitors, customers and suppliers.

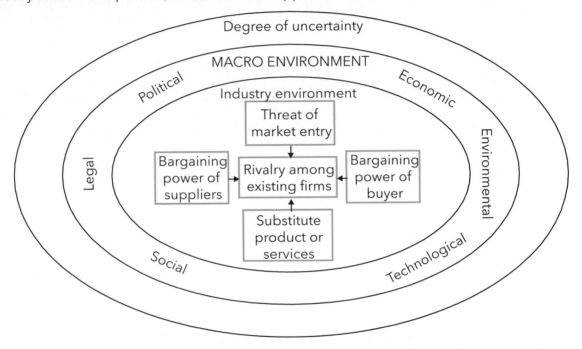

(Diagram: Tiers within the business environment)

To be viable (eg, able to sustain itself through time) the organisation must achieve an appropriate 'fit' with this environment. This includes:

- Results that meet the expectations of its owners (shareholders, government, members etc,)
- Products and services that meet its clients' expectations at least as well as rivals'
- Ability to remain within the legal and ethical codes of the societies it works in
- Attractive as a place to work for its staff
- Satisfying the needs of other powerful or influential stakeholders

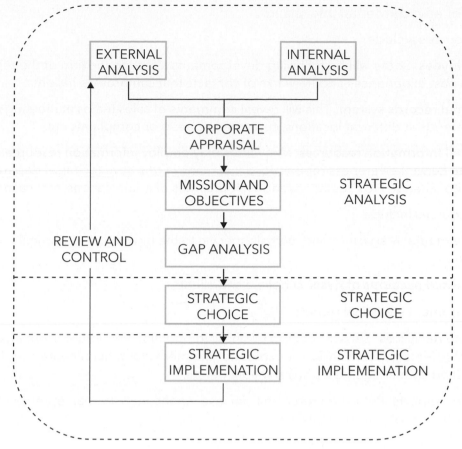

(Diagram: The rational planning model)

Rational planning approach: Environmental appraisal is a **one-off assessment** which establishes the forces acting on the business at present and **forecasts** how these may develop during the years of the plan.

Strategic management approach: The need for **environmental scanning**. This is a continuous awareness by management of environmental issues enabling them to be routinely considered in decision making.

Interactive question 1: Considering the business environment

For a professional accountancy practice, answer the following questions.

1.1 What are the main external factors, in your view?

1.2 How do these main environmental/external factors affect the strategies of the practice?

1.3 In your view, how do managers perceive change in the environment of the organisation?

1.4 How do you think managers incorporate environmental/external issues into decision-making?

See **Answer** at the end of this chapter.

1.2 Gathering and disseminating environmental information

An effective information system:

- Gathers environmental information.
- Validates and corroborates the information.
- Disseminates the information so that people who need it can find it.

1.2.1 Sources of environmental information

Internal sources include:

- **Employees**: Some will be following developments affecting the firm or their field of work, or have past experiences and networks of contacts that can provide insights.

- **Internal records system**: This will reveal comments of sales teams at meetings, revenue and cost trends at different locations, customer requests or complaints etc.

- **Formal information resources**: Many firms may employ information resources specialists to create current awareness reports eg, accountancy firms have technical departments that monitor changes to regulations and the outcomes of adjudications, test cases and appeals.

External sources include:

- **Trade media**: Magazines and journals specific to the industry or to particular business functions.

- **Published accounts of rivals**, suppliers and clients.

- **Government statistical reports.**

- **Online resources**: Subscriptions to business information vendors, current awareness services (emails from vendors who monitor the media for articles containing keywords specified by management). Social media trends.

- **Market reports**: Published research from investment analysts, market researchers, trade departments of governments etc.

1.2.2 Validating environmental information

Professional scepticism should be applied when considering environmental information. Is it valid and fit for the purpose of analysis? Issues to consider in validating environmental information include:

- Integrity of the source: internet gossip and market rumours lack integrity on their own.

- Forecasting and predictive record in the past.

- Degree of substantiation: is there more than one report or instance of this from independent sources?

- Age of the information: how up to date is it?

- Motivation of provider: does the provider have something to gain from convincing the firm of this information?

1.2.3 Disseminating environmental information

Dissemination can be assisted by:

- A well designed intranet with clear files and a search facility. This can be supplemented by regular vlogs and webinars prepared and delivered by management.

- Periodic briefing reports with a digest of the most significant information.

- Periodic seminars to brief management.

- Annual management development sessions at an internal or external business school to introduce and discuss new environmental issues.

2 Environmental dynamics

2.1 Environmental uncertainty

Strategic planning takes place in the context of an uncertain future environment as competitors enter and leave the market, governments and their policies change, technology develops.

Changes in the external environment which have a long-term impact may be dealt with by strategic planning, but dealing with changes that have an immediate short term impact may involve crisis management.

The intensity of environmental issues varies from sector to sector and company to company.

Some businesses exist in relatively **static** environments, where the environment is simple (few competitors, limited products, slow rate of change) but many face environments which are **dynamic** – complex and characterised by rapid change.

In static environments, the business's historic and current environment will be a useful predictor of the future. In dynamic environments this will be of little benefit.

The degree of uncertainty and pace of change will affect the amount of resources devoted to environmental assessment. For example, investment banks employ substantial research departments and each day begins with dissemination of relevant environmental information to traders and managers. Airlines also have research departments which 'red flag' issues on a regular basis and also provide reports and forecasts as inputs into their strategic planning process.

2.2 Scenario planning

Definition

Scenario planning: Concerns the development of pictures of potential futures for the purposes of managerial learning and the development of strategic responses.

2.2.1 When is scenario planning useful?

Scenario planning is useful where a long-term view of strategy is needed and where there are a few key factors influencing the success of the strategy, eg, in the oil industry there may be a need to form a view of the business environment up to 25 years ahead, and issues such as crude oil availability, price and economic conditions are critical. For example, Shell was the only major oil company to have prepared its management for dealing with the shock of the 1970s oil crisis through scenario planning and was able to respond faster than its competitors.

It is important to understand how scenario planning differs in nature from the normal strategic planning exercise. Scenario planning is a wider exercise than simply viewing the entity's operations at a company level and considering a range of external variables likely to impact on the ability of the entity to achieve its objectives. It tries to take a longer term view of the different ways in which an industry may develop. Ultimately, strategic planning results in an organisation developing a strategy, whereas scenario planning is focused on identifying a range of plausible alternatives which give an indication as to the future state of an industry.

Factors such as technology may cause major uncertainty regarding the future shape of an industry (consider for example the impact that email has had on the delivery of letters and that e-readers have had on the book industry.) So in scenario planning a key question might be to consider where the industry will be in 10 years' time. An organisation that wishes to have a sustainable business needs to ask ''what if'' questions and come up with contingency plans.

The nature of scenario planning means that precision is not possible, but it is important to develop a view of the future against which to evaluate and evolve strategies.

Scenario building attempts to create possible future situations using the key factors. The aim is to produce a limited number of scenarios so that strategies can be examined against them in terms of 'what if ...?' and 'what is the effect of ...?'.

A UK-based car manufacturer could assess the impact of 'political changes' or 'opposing moves by competitors' such as the introduction of driver-less cars on its business. Financial models of the firm are often used in conjunction with this approach to assess impact on profit. Although these provide a useful approach, it is important not to become too committed to one scenario; after all, they are only forecasts which might not in the event be valid.

2.2.2 Steps

- Identify key forces which might affect an industry or market, using techniques such as PESTEL analysis (see section 3).

- Understand the historic trend in respect of the key forces.

- Build future scenarios, eg, optimistic, pessimistic and most likely.

The scenarios generated are then 'plots' to be played out making managers consider future possibilities and encouraging them to think about strategy more flexibly. In Chapter 10 we shall explore the role of scenario building and its use in risk management.

3 PESTEL analysis

Section overview

- In your Business, Technology and Finance studies, you will have encountered PESTEL factors in your studies of the environment of business.

- This section provides a recap of the key PESTEL factors and identifies how each may impact on the strategy of the organisation.

- Later sections extend analysis to the global business environment.

3.1 Recap of PESTEL analysis

PESTEL was introduced in Business, Technology and Finance, but we will recap its key themes here. PESTEL is a handy checklist for identifying environmental factors:

- **P**olitical
- **E**conomic
- **S**ocial/cultural
- **T**echnological
- **E**cological/environmental
- **L**egal

PESTEL identifies the macro factors in the external environment which may affect a particular industry. Depending on the industry, some factors will be more significant, eg, legal and ecological issues may have a major influence in the airline industry, whereas political issues will play a major part in the healthcare industry.

The organisation must focus on the key influences currently affecting its industry and those that might become significant in the future ie, the key threats and opportunities that arise for the organisation as a result of the PESTEL analysis.

3.2 Political factors

Political factors relate to the distribution of power locally, nationally and internationally.

Political risk is the possibility that political factors will have an impact on the business's environment or prospects. The impact could be positive or negative; the issue is the uncertainty created.

Types of risk include the following.

- **Ownership risk**: A company or its assets might be expropriated (or nationalised) by the state, normally with compensation. Confiscation is, effectively, expropriation without compensation.

- **Operating risk: Indigenisation/domestication**. The firm may be required to take local partners. There may be a guaranteed minimum shareholding for local investors.

- **Transfer risk** may affect the company's ability to transfer funds or repatriate profits.

- **Political risk**: The government of the host country may change taxes or seek a stake in the business to increase its power or to satisfy local public opinion.

Managing political risk

Companies, especially transnational corporations, might take measures to reduce political risk. These include:

- Detailed risks assessments prior to investing in the country.

- Partnering with a local business to increase acceptance of the project and to lobby for political support.

- Avoid total reliance on one country, eg, oil companies extract oil from many countries to offset risks of interrupted supplies or spiralling costs.

3.3 Economic factors

The economic structure of a country should be considered in strategic decision-making. Countries typically progress from reliance on primary industries (eg, agriculture, minerals, forestry) through manufacturing to tertiary services (eg, financial and commercial sectors).

A country's economy will affect overall wealth, financial stability and patterns of demand.

In setting strategy an organisation needs to consider where the economy is currently and where it is heading.

- Long-term exchange rates' behaviour affect the relative competitiveness of imported and domestically produced products and exports. A falling domestic exchange rate makes firm's exports more competitive and imported inputs more expensive. This may be determined by the value of key exports such as oil, minerals, crops, manufactured goods etc.

- Interest rates (long-term and short-term) affect cost of finance and also levels of demand in the economy.

- The economic infrastructure, for example access to payments systems, consumer and trade credit, access to venture and other capital, the quality of the stock exchanges.

3.4 Social/cultural factors

Social factors include

- **Make-up of population**: eg, growth rate, proportion of old and young people.

- **Family structure** and size; the importance (or lack of it) of the extended family and relationships with non family members; the extended family provides contacts and work.

- **Attitudes to diversity**: eg, the existence of gender and other stereotypes. In some cultures, gender stereotypes are more sharply drawn.

- Extent of **social mobility**: the degree of social stratification and difference within each society and whether people can move between them, the changes in size, wealth and/or status of different groups within the population and the geographical distribution of the population between regions and urban, suburban and rural areas.

Cultural factors affect strategy in several ways:

- The **market for products**, eg, religious prescriptions on food, financial services

- **Promotional strategies**, eg, language of adverts, considerations of imagery and decency

- **Methods of conducting business** in countries, eg, conventions of negotiation, giving and receiving gifts, ensuring 'face' for contacts (ie, maintaining self-respect and status)

- **Methods of managing staff**, eg, language differences, attitudes to managerial authority

- Expectations of **business conduct**, eg, extent of engagement with corporate responsibility (CR), time horizon of investment, engagement in political matters

3.5 Technology

The strategic significance of the technological environment includes:

- Technological base, and therefore customer and staff familiarity with it, varies across countries. Operations will have to take this into account.

- Technological change challenges existing industry structure and competitive advantages and so strategies to harness or evade it are necessary.

- Technological change can render existing products obsolete but can also provide opportunities to develop new products and ways of doing business. Therefore continuous R&D and learning is necessary to remain competitive. The growing role of technology is explored in greater detail later in the Study Manual.

- Technological change creates uncertainty which may influence the approach to strategy formulation that is adopted.

- Advances in technology may also provide new channels to get products and services to market.

- Technological change in the form of automation and intelligent systems (Artificial Intelligence and Machine Learning) are rapidly changing how organisations structure the activities they undertake, as computers, robots and machines increasingly perform tasks traditionally carried out by people. In Chapter 6 we discuss the topics of automation and intelligent systems in greater detail, when we consider the important area of strategic capability.

3.6 Ecological environment factors

There is an increasing focus on maintaining the world's resources rather than depleting or destroying them, in order to ensure that they support human activity now and in the future.

This desire for 'sustainability' encompasses environmental issues such as:

- **Climate change and pollution**. Global warming is forecast to cause polar ice caps to melt, leading to a chain of events including rises in sea levels and climate change.

- **Energy gap** as fossil fuels diminish while, for example, countries such as Brazil, Russia, India, China and South Africa (the BRICS economies) are growing rapidly and demand more energy.

- **Waste recycling** issues as developed countries recognise the forecast use of landfill and also realise that much landfill is hazardous waste (eg, batteries, electronic circuitry, oil and solvents in car engines).

- **Bio-diversity** issues as growing of cash crops and destruction of forests for grazing or building land also destroys species of plant, insects and animals.

- Introduction of **genetically modified organisms** into the food chain leading to loss of species and potentially hazardous future effects.

Main government policies are:

- Reduce carbon emissions through targets set in cross governmental accords such as the 1992 Kyoto and 2015 Paris agreements.

- Penalisation of carbon creating industries through taxes levied on emissions or on fossil fuels used.

- Investment in non-carbon creating technologies such as nuclear energy, wind and wave power and electric or hybrid cars.

- Making foreign aid dependent on acceptance of environmental policies by recipient countries.

- Regulations covering hazardous waste.

Implications for business strategy

- Need to accept 'polluter pays' costs – taxes on emissions and requirements that firms buy certificates from refuse firms confirming recovery or destruction of materials the firm introduces into the supply chain.

- Increased emphasis on businesses acceptance of corporate responsibility (CR) and principles of sustainable development.

- Potential for economic gain from cleaning-up operations and selling surplus 'permits to pollute' to firms that have not cleaned up.

- Potential competitive advantage from development of products that ecologically conscious buyers will favour.

- Need to monitor ecology-related geo-political and legislative developments closely.

3.6.1   Natural capital

Linked to the concept of ecology and sustainability is that of natural capital.

Definition

Natural capital: The 'natural assets (eg, air, water, land, habitats) that provide everyday resources including timber, agricultural land, fisheries and clean water as well as services such as air and water filtration, flood protection and pollination for crops (otherwise known as 'ecosystem services') (Dunscombe and Glover, 2016:p.2, *ICAEW Natural capital in practice*).

The focus on natural capital has increased dramatically in recent years as organisations begin to better understand how their activities affect the natural world. The Natural Capital Forum (2018) compares the concept of natural capital to that of an organisation spending more than it earns, in as much that it will eventually run up a debt. When organisations take more out of the natural environment than they give back, they have run up a debt which needs to be paid back. This can be achieved, for example, through repairing the damage caused by polluting activities, or replanting forests where trees have been felled to provide timber for production. Organisations that 'keep drawing down stocks of natural capital without allowing or encouraging nature to recover, run the risk of local, regional or even global ecosystem collapse. Poorly managed natural capital therefore becomes not only an ecological liability, but a social and economic liability too'. (Natural Capital Forum, 2018).

The increasing focus on natural capital is starting to change the way in which organisations report on their activities, with many now attempting to place financial values on the natural assets they use, to enable them to make more informed business decisions.

We will look at the increasing focus on sustainable business practices and sustainability reporting in more detail in Chapter 16.

3.7 Legal factors

Legal factors relate to the role of law in society and its role in business relationships. This can be assessed in terms of:

- **Systemic factors**: How effective is the legal system at enforcing contracts? To what extent are legal decisions likely to be interfered with by politicians ie, are the courts independent of government? How easy is it to get hold of legal advice? How speedy are the courts? To what extent is regulation delegated? Are rights of private property genuinely enforceable?

- **Cultural factors**: To what extent are business relationships conducted formally or informally? The USA is regarded as a litigious society; in Japan (partly because of the small size of the legal profession), business is widely believed to be based more on long-term relationships.

- **Context and regulatory factors**: Cover civil and criminal law, laws relating to consumer protection and advertising, employment, health and safety and so forth. Furthermore, to what extent is competition promoted, regulated and enforced? Intellectual property rights are examples of specific issues which need to be considered.

Interactive question 2: Estate agent industry

The following interactive question provides an opportunity for you to apply the PESTEL framework to the UK estate agent industry.

Estate agents are residential property agencies which act on behalf of individual vendors to assist in the sale of their home. Revenues are derived from financial services, lettings, valuations and surveys. However, the main source of revenue is commissions on the sale of residential property.

Agencies are regulated in the UK by the Estate Agents Act 1979, which aims to ensure that agents act in the best interests of sellers, and that both buyers and sellers are treated honestly and fairly. Agencies must also comply with money laundering legislation. Agency employees are not currently required by UK law to be either licensed or formally qualified. However, many employees belong to a professional body and must comply with that body's code of professional ethics.

In recent times traditional estate agents operating physical branches have struggled. The traditional estate agency business model has suffered as a direct consequence of the continuing rise of technology start-up companies which are now challenging existing ways to sell property.

The rise of so-called 'proptech' firms has seen increasing numbers of house sellers turn to online estate agencies like Purplebricks..

Unlike traditional estate agents, which operate from physical branches often located on busy UK high streets employing teams of estate agents, companies like Purplebricks operate a hybrid strategy. This strategy does not require the use of high street branches as the company operates from an online platform where sellers are assisted through the selling process by a dedicated property expert contracted on a freelance basis by Purplebricks. Websites charge private sellers commission fees which are a fraction of those being charged by traditional estate agents. One newspaper article (Fraser, 2016) reported that Purplebricks controlled 65% of the online estate agency market. The article also noted that in recent times a number of established estate agencies have invested in similar online 'proptech' companies in recognition of the changes this is creating in the industry. It is estimated that online agencies represented sellers in 15% of UK property sales in 2018.

In early 2017, the UK government announced plans to help first-time buyers to get onto the property ladder by allowing councils to build houses on hundreds of brownfield sites, being land which was previously deemed unusable. A second newspaper article (McCann, 2017) highlighted that the government's financial support for the scheme would see housing developers sell the properties at a discount of 20%, to help first-time buyers. In November 2017, changes were made to the stamp duty thresholds in the UK with the aim of making it cheaper for first-time buyers to purchase property. (In the UK when a buyer purchases a home they pay a tax known as stamp duty, and the amount of tax paid depends on the value of the property.) The changes meant that first-time buyers purchasing a property with a value up to £300,000 would not have to pay stamp duty, and thereby able to save thousands of pounds in tax. However, some observers have suggested that the stamp duty changes have in fact slowed the first-time buyer property market, as buyers were instead choosing to wait longer, save more, and then purchase a larger property from which they could eventually start a family, instead of purchasing a smaller home first (Morley, 2018).

A common feature of the UK housing market for a number of years has been rising property prices. According to the Royal Institution of Chartered Surveyors, the growth in house prices in the UK had been caused by a shortage in the number of properties coming onto the market coupled with increases in the number of buyers (Osborne, 2016). The population in the UK is expected to reach 73 million people by 2037, with an increase in the requirement for single occupant households as the demographics in the UK change. This is predicted to increase the demand for houses in the long term.

Requirements

2.1 Discuss the environmental factors that affect the estate agent industry, using the following headings.

    (a) Political
    (b) Economic
    (c) Social
    (d) Technological
    (e) Ecological
    (f) Legal

See **Answer** at the end of this chapter.

Sources:

Fraser, I. (25 December 2016) The rise of 'proptech': how the fall of the traditional estate agent has opened the door to upstarts. *The Telegraph*. [Online] Available from: www.telegraph.co.uk [Accessed 25 April 2017].

Osborne, H. (26 December 2016) UK housing market: what to expect in 2017. *The Guardian*. [Online] Available from: www.theguardian.com [Accessed 25 April 2017].

McCann, K. (3 January 2017) Theresa May promises thousands of new homes for young first-time buyers. *The Telegraph*. [Online] Available from: www.telegraph.co.uk [Accessed 25 April 2017].

Morely, K. (27 February 2018) Stamp duty changes slowing first-time buyer market as they shun flats for family homes. *The Telegraph*. [Online]. Available from: www.telegraph.co.uk [Accessed 19 April 2018].

4 The international business context

Section overview

- Few if any businesses are unaffected by global influences from competition, new markets or, at the very least, cheaper sources of supply.

- The view that certain nations have built-in advantages from low costs or harder-working staff has given way to a more sophisticated view that home factors may configure to give advantages to a handful of specific industries.

- This is illustrated using – Porter's Diamond model.

4.1 The importance of the global business environment

Rapid industrialisation from the 18th century was a consequence of early involvement of merchants and businesses in trade. In the 21st century improved transportation and communications and cross-border business ownership have created, for most industries, a global business environment.

Global competition affects firms in several ways. It:

- Provides the opportunities of new markets to exploit.

- Presents the threat of new sources of competition in the home economy from foreign firms.

- Offers an opportunity of relocating parts of business activity (or **supply chain**) to countries able to perform them better or more cheaply.

- May drive cross border acquisitions and alliances.

This leads management to make significant strategic investment decisions that rely on assessments of the stability and trends of the global business environment:

- Development of products for international markets.

- Advancing credit to clients in international markets or investing in businesses and assets in host countries.

- Reliance of international sources for supplies of crucial inputs.

4.2 The global corporation

Definition

Globalisation: The production and distribution of products and services of a homogenous type and quality on a worldwide basis.

Levitt (*The Globalisation of Markets,* 1983) described the development of a 'global village' in which consumers around the world would have the same needs and attitudes and use the same products. A global corporation would be one that operated as if the entire world was one entity, to be sold the same things everywhere.

Levitt's focus was on the marketing aspects of globalisation. The global business corporation will also be characterised by

- **Extended supply chains**: Instead of making the product at home and exporting it, or setting up a factory in the host country to make it, the global corporation may factor out production so that different parts of the product (or service) originate in different countries. Womack et al (*The Machine That Changed The World*) suggest that the globalisation of the automobile industry led the way for this model.

- **Global human resource management**: This involves pan-national recruitment and development of human resources.

Interactive question 3: A global corporation?

Some would say that such purely global organisations are rare. Industry structures change and foreign markets are culturally diverse. Even within the USA, there is an enormous variety of cultural differences.

Requirement

3.1 Can you think of a global corporation that fulfils the requirements of the definition given above?

See **Answer** at the end of this chapter.

4.3 Ohmae's five Cs: factors encouraging development of global business

Ohmae (*The Borderless World*) has identified a number of reasons which might encourage a firm to act globally arranged into a 'five C's' framework.

The customer	Are consumer tastes across the world converging upon similar product characteristics?
The company itself	Selling in a number of markets enables fixed costs to be spread over a larger sales volume.
Competition	The presence of global competitors, who are enjoying the benefits of global commitment, could encourage a previously local or regional operator to expand its activities.
Currency volatility	Setting up assembly overseas is a way of reducing the exchange rate risks inherent in exporting and may also help to get around government imposed trade barriers.
Country	Locating business activities overseas may provide cheaper access to labour, materials and finance, along with the goodwill of host governments.

The continuing political acceptance of free-trade by international economies is essential to the success of these strategic investments.

4.4 Porter's Diamond: *The Competitive Advantage of Nations*

Management developing strategy in a global environment needs to understand the competitive advantages they have over firms from other countries.

Porter (*The Competitive Advantage of Nations*) seeks to 'isolate the national attributes that foster competitive advantage in an industry'.

Porter identifies determinants of national competitive advantage which are outlined in the following diagram. Porter refers to this as the Diamond.

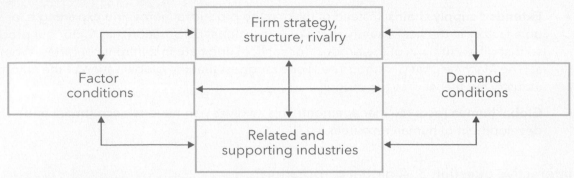

Role of factor conditions	Basic factors	Advanced factors
Human resources skills, (price, motivation, industrial relations) Physical resources (land, minerals, climate, location relative to other nations) Knowledge (scientific and technical know-how, educational institutions) Capital (ie, amounts available for investment, how it is deployed?) Infrastructure (transport, communications, housing)	Basic factors include: natural resources, climate, semi-skilled and unskilled labour. Basic factors are inherited, or at best their creation involves little investment.	Advanced factors include modern digital communications, highly educated personnel, research laboratories and so forth. They are necessary to achieve high order competitive advantages such as differentiated products and proprietary production technology.

Role of demand conditions	Comment
The home market determines how firms perceive, interpret and respond to buyer needs. This information puts pressure on firms to innovate and provides a launch pad for global ambitions.	• There are few cultural impediments to communication in the home market. • The segmentation of the home market shapes a firm's priorities: companies will generally be successful globally in segments which are similar to the home market. • Sophisticated and demanding buyers set standards. • Anticipatory buyer needs: if consumer needs are expressed in the home market earlier than in the world market, the firm benefits from experience. • The rate of growth: slow growing home markets do not encourage the adoption of state of the art technology. • Early saturation of the home market will encourage a firm to export.

Role of related and supporting industries	Comment
Competitive success in one industry is often linked to success in related industries. Domestic suppliers are preferable to foreign suppliers, as 'proximity of managerial and technical personnel, along with cultural similarity, tends to facilitate free and open information flow' at an early stage.	This facilitates the generation of clusters. These are concentrations of many companies in the same industry in one area, together with industries to support them. For example, London in the UK is a global financial services centre, with a concentration of banks, legal services, accounting services and a depth of specialist expertise. Silicon Valley is a further example.

Role of strategy, structure and rivalry	Comment
Structure	National cultural factors create certain tendencies to orientate business people to certain industries. German firms have a strong presence in industries with a high technical content.
Strategy	Industries in different countries have different time horizons, funding needs and so forth. • National capital markets set different goals for performance. In some countries, banks are the main source of capital, not equity shareholders. • When an industry faces difficult times, it can either innovate within the industry, to sustain competitive position or shift resources from one industry to another (eg, diversification).
Domestic rivalry	• With little domestic rivalry, firms are happy to rely on the home market. • Tough domestic rivals teach a firm about competitive success. • Each rival can try a different strategic approach.

Two other variables, **chance events** and the **role of government**, also play their part in determining the competitive environment.

4.4.1 Interactions between the determinants

The factors in the 'Diamond' are interrelated. Competitive advantage in an industry rarely rests on a single determinant.

- Related industries affect demand conditions for an industry. For example 'piggy-back' exporting is when an exporting company also exports some of the products of related industries.

- Domestic rivalry can encourage the creation of more specialised supplier industries.

4.4.2 Clusters

Related business and industries are geographically clustered. A cluster is a linking of industries through relationships which are either vertical (buyer-supplier) or horizontal (common customers, technology, skills). Clusters are supposedly a key factor in the competitive advantage of nations.

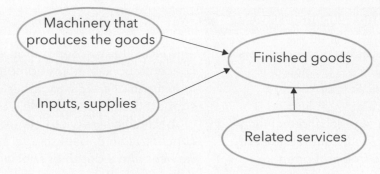

Within a country, the industry may be clustered in a particular area.

- The Indian software industry is based in Bangalore.
- The UK investment banking industry is largely based in London.

Interactive question 4: Why do banks cluster?

4.1 It is easy to see why mining companies should congregate in a cluster around coal seams, or shipping services would congregate around ports, but why should banks and software companies be clustered in the same way, given plentiful IT and broad bandwidth communications?

See **Answer** at the end of this chapter.

4.4.3 Using Porter's Diamond to develop business strategies

Porter claims that firms gain competitive advantage from either of two sources.

- Lower costs of supply to customers which result in higher profitability (cost leadership).

- Differentiated service or reputation resulting in higher prices and sales revenues (differentiation).

Porter advises management to consider the diamond factors in their home country and to compare them with the diamond factors available to rivals from other countries.

He offers the following prescription.

- If the home diamond factors give a comparative cost advantage over those of foreign rivals then management should adopt strategies based on **overall cost leadership**. This may explain the strategies of South Korean car manufacturers like Hyundai/Kia, Daewoo and SsangYong (the latter two being respectively offshoots of General Motors and Daimler Chrysler).

- If the home diamond factors give a differentiation advantage over foreign rivals management should adopt strategies based on **differentiation**. This may explain why car manufacturers Mercedes, BMW and Audi tend to develop and initially produce their limousines in Germany but build vans and utility cars in Spain, South Africa and Brazil.

- If the diamond does not confer advantage over rivals then management must **focus** on sub-sections of the industry which large players may have overlooked or not be able to exploit commercially. This may explain the large number of private banks in Switzerland or the boutique sports car makers in Italy (Ferrari, Lamborghini, Maserati etc).

Interactive question 5: Chinese car industry

At the end of the 20th century, China's car production did not match any single large auto company in the developed world. In 2018 the International Organization of Motor Vehicle Manufacturers (2018) reported China was the world's largest car producer. But it is not just volumes. China's car makers now produce not just low-cost runabouts, but also luxury and sports models, 'concept cars' and even a few hybrid and electric vehicles. Local car makers in the fastest-growing car market would appear to have come of age.

Until recently many Chinese car makers built thinly-disguised copies of vehicles made by Volkswagen, GM and Toyota. In the past few years things have changed. In preparation for a push overseas local firms such as Chery, Great Wall and Geely have proved they can develop their own vehicles too. Buying designs from international specialists and installing robotic production lines have led to an increase in the types of cars produced. Chery was reported to be working on developing more than 100 new models, however this figure was subsequently revised downwards.

For a number of years foreign car makers had been worried by the Chinese firms' ultra low prices, however this has been changing in recent times. The rise of China's affluent middle class has led increasing numbers of Chinese consumers to switch to more expensive Western brands renowned for safety and flair. Chinese domestic car brands have also been damaged by poor safety crash results. Chinese cars exported today mostly go to Africa, south-east Asia and the Middle East, where expectations are lower and price matters more.

The development of China's car manufacturing business has been helped by a number of factors. A lot of early technology was borrowed. The government also offered support to fledgling firms via direct investments, guaranteed loans and a programme aimed at supporting Chinese production of electric cars. Universities provided technical help, especially in the development of expensive engines. Future legislation is likely to force foreign firms to do more research and development in conjunction with Chinese partners to ensure continued access to cutting-edge engineering skills.

Requirement

5.1 Identify, using Porter's Diamond, the sources and nature of any competitive advantage enjoyed by Chinese car manufacturers.

See **Answer** at the end of this chapter.

Source:

International Organization of Motor Vehicle Manufacturers. (2018) *2017 Production Statistics*. [Online]. Available from: http://www.oica.net/category/production-statistics/2017-statistics/ [Accessed 19 April 2018].

5 Limits to globalisation of business

Section overview

- Despite the forecasts there are many impediments to the development of global businesses such as protectionism. These are reviewed here.

- Pursuing a global strategy is a source of risk to a business, either because the forecast opportunity doesn't come about or because host governments change their policies towards 'foreign' investment and render it no-longer valuable.

5.1 Political risks in international business

The development of plans for international business will depend on the following factors:

1. The stability of the government. Rapid changes or political unrest make it difficult to estimate reactions to an importer or a foreign business.

2. International relations. The government's attitude to the firm's home government or country may affect trading relations.

3. The ideology of the government and its role in the economy will affect the way in which the company may be allowed to trade, and this might be embodied in legislation.

4. Informal relations between government officials and businesses are important in some countries. Cultivation of the right political contacts may be essential for decisions to be made in your favour.

Political risk is still relevant with regard to overseas investment, especially in large infrastructure projects overseas. History contains dismal tales of investment projects that went wrong, and were expropriated (nationalised) by the local government.

*   Suspicion of foreign ownership is still rife, especially when prices are raised.

*   Opposition politicians can appeal to nationalism by claiming the government sold out to foreigners.

*   Governments might want to re-negotiate a deal to get a better bargain, at a later date, thereby affecting return on investment.

In addition to expropriation, there are other dangers:

*   Restrictions on profit repatriation (for example, for currency reasons).
*   'Cronyism' and corruption leading to unfair favouring of some companies over others.
*   Arbitrary changes in taxation.
*   Pressure group activity.

Worked example: Brexit

A good example of political risk and uncertainty in international business concerns Britain's decision to leave the European Union, following a referendum in June 2016. In March 2017 Sir Tim Barrow, the UK's ambassador to the EU, submitted a letter to EU Council President Donald Tusk formally triggering the 2 year process of the UK's withdrawal from the EU. Since this time many business leaders have expressed concern over the uncertainty surrounding the eventual trading relationship that Britain will have with its European neighbours when the country leaves the EU. In response, many large multinational businesses in a range of sectors have turned to various forms of scenario planning to better understand the potential impact that the failure of Britain and the EU to reach a tariff-free trade deal could have on their respective industries.

5.2 Protectionism in international trade

Protectionism is the discouraging of imports by, for example, raising tariff barriers and imposing quotas in order to favour local producers. It is rife in agriculture.

Protectionist measures include:

Tariffs or customs duties: A tax on imports where the importer is required to pay either a percentage of the value of the imported good (an *ad valorem* duty), or per unit of the good imported (a specific duty).

Non-tariff barriers: Restrictions on the quantity of product allowed to be imported into a country. The restrictions can be imposed by import licences (in which case the government gets additional revenue) or simply by granting the right to import only to certain producers.

Minimum local content rules: A specified minimum local content of products should be made in the country or region in which they are sold to qualify as being 'home made' and so avoid other restrictions on imports. This leads manufacturers to set up factories in the country.

Minimum prices and anti-dumping action: To stop the sale of a product in an overseas market at a price lower than charged in the domestic market, anti-dumping measures including establishing quotas, minimum prices or extra excise duties are used

Embargoes: A total ban or zero quota.

Subsidies for domestic producers: Financial help and assistance from government departments that give the domestic producer a cost advantage over foreign producers in export as well as domestic markets.

Exchange controls and exchange rate policy: Regulations designed to make it difficult for importers to obtain the currency they need to buy foreign goods.

Unofficial non-tariff barriers: Administrative controls such as slow inspection procedures or changing product standards which are hard for foreign suppliers to anticipate and respond to.

5.3 Trade blocs and triads

Trading blocs

Currently, a number of regional trading arrangements (or 'blocs') exist, as well as global trading arrangements. These regional trading groups take three forms.

1. Free trade areas – members in these arrangements agree to lower barriers to trade amongst themselves, eg, NAFTA (USA, Canada, Mexico).

2. Customs unions – these agree a common policy on barriers to external countries. Tariffs, taxes and duties are harmonised amongst members.

3. Common markets – in effect, the members become one trading area. There is free movement of all factors of production. The European Union (EU) features a common political decision making process and a single currency and has economic union as an aim.

In addition to NAFTA and the EU, other major regional trade organisations include:

*   Mercosur – Brazil, Argentina, Paraguay, Uruguay and Venezuela

*   The Economic Community of West African States (ECOWAS)

*   The Association of Southeast Asian Nations (ASEAN) – Indonesia, Malaysia, Philippines, Singapore, Thailand, Brunei, Cambodia, Laos, Myanmar , and Vietnam.

Triad theory describes the international business environment as a limited number of 'superblocs'.

The Triad

Ohmae developed the concept of a global economic triad in 1985, consisting of three main economic blocs: the USA, the EU and Japan, which controlled 75% of world trade at the time.

Triad theory rejects the idea that homogenous products can be developed and sold throughout the world. Multinationals have to develop their products for the circumstances of each triad.

The Triad theory which applied in the latter part of the 20th century may be out of date now. The emerging markets, particularly those of China and India, but also Eastern Europe may give rise to additional trading blocs or a shifting economic triad for the 21st century of China, India and the US.

Summary and Self-test

Summary

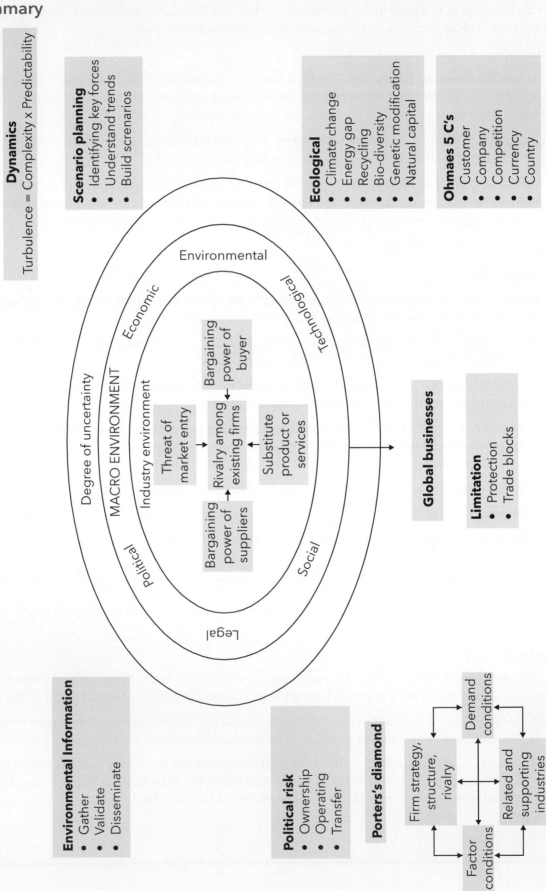

Dynamics
Turbulence = Complexity x Predictability

Scenario planning
- Identifying key forces
- Understand trends
- Build scenarios

Ecological
- Climate change
- Energy gap
- Recycling
- Bio-diversity
- Genetic modification
- Natural capital

Ohmaes 5 C's
- Customer
- Company
- Competition
- Currency
- Country

Environmental

Economic

Technological

Degree of uncertainty

MACRO ENVIRONMENT

Industry environment

Political

Legal

Social

Threat of market entry

Bargaining power of buyer

Rivalry among existing firms

Substitute product or services

Bargaining power of suppliers

Global businesses

Limitation
- Protection
- Trade blocks

Environmental Information
- Gather
- Validate
- Disseminate

Political risk
- Ownership
- Operating
- Transfer

Porters's diamond

Firm strategy, structure, rivalry

Demand conditions

Related and supporting industries

Factor conditions

Self-test

Answer the following questions.

1   PDB Motors plc is a major UK car manufacturer with plants in the UK and Europe. It is seeking to exploit both the buoyant North American and Brazilian markets for car sales.

Suggest two reasons why it would be a logical strategy for PDB Motors plc to build an assembly plant in Mexico.

2   Social and technological factors always need to be assessed when analysing the environment within which a business operates.

Give two examples of each of these factors which would be relevant to Busline plc, a UK operator of coach tours to Scarborough and Whitby (seaside towns in the North of England).

Suggest how each of your factors may impact future demand.

3   Read the scenario of the **September 2015 Business Strategy and Technology** question in the Question Bank entitled *Kentish Fruit Farms*. Draft an answer to the question which requires the completion of partial PESTEL analysis.

4   Read the scenario of the **March 2017 Business Strategy and Technology** question in the Question Bank entitled *Ignite plc*. Draft an answer to the question which requires the analysis of the external factors that have influenced the changing demand for Ignite's cigarette lighters.

Now, go back to the Learning outcomes in the Introduction. If you are satisfied that you have achieved the objective, please tick it off.

Answers to Interactive questions

Answer to Interactive question 1

1.1 External factors would include:

- Rival accounting firms seeking to take clients themselves.
- Other professional practices which may direct work toward us.
- Regulations such as tax laws, accounting standards and audit standards.
- The labour market for post-qualified and qualified accountants.
- The general state of the economy and its effect on business.

1.2 These factors create opportunities and threats. New regulations create a need for professional advisers to provide guidance to clients. Competitors or a thriving labour market with higher pay create threats (incidentally notice how you changed your perspective on the last point because you would like to have the higher pay but you are calling it a threat for your firm). This illustrates how flawed the distinction between 'internal' and 'external' is when we discuss environmental analysis.

1.3 This will depend on the managers' psychological make-up. Some will see it as a tiresome bind that makes them have to keep changing things and also which makes it hard to plan or feel certain. Others will see it as invigorating.

A very interesting test of management is the extent to which they see themselves as powerless in the faces of environmental changes or whether they believe they can shape and respond to them.

1.4 Again, this varies. Some will avoid making decisions which could be affected by environmental uncertainty, and will wait till it settles down (hence incrementalism). Some will simply ignore environmental issues that cannot be proven. Perhaps a more balanced approach is to adopt strategies that would still deliver benefit under a number of environmental developments or perhaps have several courses of action running at the same time, with each one designed to take advantage of different environments. In another context, energy companies invest in several different technologies because they do not know how oil prices and environmental regulations will develop.

Answer to Interactive question 2

2.1 **PESTEL analysis**

The factors affecting the estate agent industry are very closely linked to prosperity and activity in the residential housing market. The PESTEL analysis therefore needs to consider the wider housing market as well as factors directly affecting the estate agent industry

(a) **Political**

Political influences relate to the extent to which it is government policy to support and promote the housing market. The UK government's plans to help first-time buyers get onto the property ladder by allowing the development of brownfield sites is aimed at increasing the national housing stock. The planned subsidisation in the form of the 20% discount for first-time buyers removes a barrier to buying a house. The government's scheme is likely to be positive for the UK estate agency industry if the new homes are sold through those estate agents in close proximity to the brownfield sites.

The proposal to remove stamp duty for first-time buyers purchasing houses for less than £300,000 was also designed stimulate demand. However, this initiative may not be as positive for estate agents as might have first been expected, because some buyers are choosing to delay purchasing a home in order to allow them to purchase a larger property in the future.

(b) **Economic**

Political considerations are closely linked to economic factors. The dependence of the housing market on the prosperity of individuals is heavily influenced by the success of the government's economic policy. Despite the growth in house prices, traditional estate agents have struggled to capitalise. The buoyancy of the economy generally and the housing market in particular appears to have helped new start-up firms to enter the industry to compete with established players.

(c) **Social**

The increasing population and the change in demographics have expanded the long run potential growth of the housing market. In particular the increased proportion of single occupancy dwelling increases the volume, but changes the mix, of desired housing. Whilst this may appear to be positive for estate agents in general, social changes in how people buy and sell property are undermining the ability of traditional estate agents to benefit from the demographic changes. The rise of online estate agents, which provide services at lower fees than those charged by traditional agents, suggests that sellers do not regard the service offering of existing players to be worth paying for. The rise of companies such as Purplebricks is considered in the following section on technological factors.

(d) **Technological**

Increased usage of the internet, and other electronic means of communication, is a threat to estate agents as a substitute sales channel for direct transactions between buyer and seller. The significance of this threat is evident as Purplebricks alone controls 65% of the UK online estate agency market. The ability of such a relatively new player to become established in the online estate agency market is likely to increase the difficulty in the long-term for traditional players to compete. Furthermore, as a number of established estate agents have invested in 'proptech' companies this indicates that they perceive an increasingly greater role for online estate agents in the future. Despite these changes in 2018 online agents were estimated to have been involved in just 15% of all property sales made in the UK, all of which reduces the short-term significance of the threat posed to traditional estate agents.

(e) **Ecological/environmental**

The UK governments proposal to allow councils and developers use brownfield sites indicates a willingness to make better use of land previously deemed unacceptable for development. This will reduce the price of new houses for eligible first-time buyers, and may result in increased business for estate agents in the event the house builders choose to sell via an agent.

(f) **Legal**

Legal issues can be both a benefit and a cost to the industry. Legislation may directly affect the practices of estate agents, but could also have an impact upon the housing market (as we have already noted in relation to stamp duty). In the UK, estate agents are required to comply with two key pieces of legislation: the Estate Agents Act 1979, and Money Laundering regulations. The need to comply with the provisions of such legislation will attract its own costs, in terms of providing staff with relevant training and paying penalties for any breaches.

Answer to Interactive question 3

3.1 Levitt cited examples such as Coca-Cola in his article. More recently, examples such as Starbucks, Mercedes Benz, Facebook, Google, Microsoft and Disney have been called global businesses.

In practice, these corporations offer subtly different products in different markets and their appeal is not global. For example, Coca-Cola has suffered badly from an anti-American sentiment.

Answer to Interactive question 4

4.1 The reasons cited for geographical clustering of financial and IT businesses are:

- Proximity to educational and research centres. For example, in USA the IT industry clusters around its universities.

- Networking and mutual exchanging of staff.

Answer to Interactive question 5

5.1 The scenario suggests the following sources of the cost leadership advantages enjoyed by the Chinese car industry:

Demand conditions: China is a very large market and fast growing. This enables firms to gain significant economies of scale and also to justify investment in the new models and production equipment. Although demand is still high for domestic brands this appears to be changing as the number of affluent Chinese middle-class buyers continues to grow. Buyers from this group are now preferring to purchase foreign models. Historically, demand in China was driven for low price cars and which had forced car makers to concentrate on reducing costs.

Related industries: The only cited example is the assistance from universities in R&D. This provides significant cost advantages compared with in-house development. The low price of the Chinese vehicles suggests that steel and other components are being sourced cheaply too.

Factor conditions: China clearly has a good technical education system. It is also known for having abundant cheap labour and land available for building car plants. It has good sea links and freight handling for the purposes of exporting.

Firm strategy, structure and rivalry: The Chinese government is keen for the market to achieve future growth among Chinese brands and has put in place measures to support local car makers. This will give each significant economies of scale and an incentive to invest in product and process improvement. That foreign-made cars are allowed into China gives a stimulus to product development and the search for competitive advantage.

Answers to Self-test

1   Two reasons from the following:

    - This would allow PDB to take advantage of low labour costs in Mexico.

    - The location would be close to potential major markets, cutting transport costs and reducing lead time.

    - The North American Free Trade Agreement (NAFTA) will avoid sales to the USA and Canada being subject to import restrictions.

    - It delivers sales growth prospects to a company facing a saturated European market.

2   **Social factors**

    Two examples form the following:

    - Increasing car ownership (lower demand)
    - Higher proportion of older people in society (higher demand)
    - Cheap overseas packages available (lower demand)

    Technological factors

    Two examples from the following:

    - Development of faster trains (lower demand).

    - More comfortable coaches being developed (higher demand).

    - Greater internet accessibility, creating more awareness of other travel options (lower demand). However, the ability to book coach tour tickets online coupled to a dynamic pricing approach may actually increase demand (higher demand). Furthermore, customers may demand improved functionality when using coaches, for example, free Wi-Fi.

3   Refer to the answer to Kentish Fruit Farms in the Question Bank.

4   Refer to the answer to Ignite in the Question Bank.

CHAPTER 5

The industry and market environment

Introduction

Examination context

TOPIC LIST

Introduction

Learning outcomes

- Analyse for a given situation the external factors which may impact upon an organisation's performance and position, identifying significant issues in areas such as:

    - Its industry and markets, including competition

- Analyse an organisation's current markets and competitive strategy in sufficient detail for decisions to be made, drawing conclusions consistent with the qualitative and quantitative data available and highlighting relevant issues in terms of their likely impact on the strategy of the organisation

- Explain, in a given scenario, how products and services must evolve in the face of changing technologies, consumer demand and industry competition

The specific syllabus reference for this chapter are: 1b, 1c, 2h.

Syllabus links

This chapter covers some of the same objectives as Chapter 4 through the use of additional models. Some of the models covered here will be familiar to you from the Business, Technology and Finance syllabus.

Examination context

This chapter looks at models such as Porter's Five Forces and life cycle analysis. Applying the appropriate models to the scenario in the exam will help you understand and analyse the wider context in which the organisation is operating and the factors that are likely to impact on business performance.

The examiners have highlighted that candidates need to be prepared for exam questions to ask for the use of models in a number of different ways. Questions may ask you to apply specific elements of a model to a scenario for which roughly equal marks will be awarded. You may be asked to apply a whole model where the marks are allocated unevenly in a question, this is due to the fact that certain parts of the model provide more scope for application to the scenario than other aspects.

In Q2 March 2016 (*Dreamy Potato Products Ltd*) the scenario focused on a food processing company based in the west of England. The company bought potatoes from local farmers, peeled, washed and processed them before selling them to various food manufacturers. The first part of the question focused on Porter's Five Forces Model:'

'In relation to the potato processing industry, prepare an analysis of the following elements of the Porter's Five Forces model:

- Barriers to entry
- Power of suppliers
- Power of customers

You should explain the relevance of each force for DPP.   **(9 marks)**

As the requirement was worth 9 marks and candidates were expected to discuss three of Porter's five forces this should have been a clue that there were 3 marks on offer for discussing each of the forces specified. As this question only asked candidates to consider three of Porter's Five Forces, providing detail on the two other forces would have cost time when attempting the other elements of the question, and gained no marks.

1 Porter's Five Forces approach

Section overview

- Strategic analysis requires management to consider the competitive forces in the organisation's industry, and Porter's Five Forces is one of the most influential models used. Porter's Five Forces was introduced in your Business, Technology and Finance studies.

- Long term profitability determined by the extent of competitive rivalry and pressure on an industry.

- By considering the strength of each force and the implications for the organisation, management can develop strategies to cope.

- Like all models of analysis it has limitations particularly in industries that are rapidly changing.

1.1 The Five Forces model

The Five Forces model was introduced in your Business, Technology and Finance studies, so we will only highlight its key themes here, rather than looking at it again in detail.

According to Porter, five competitive forces influence the state of competition in an industry. These collectively determine the profit (ie, long-run return on capital) potential of the industry as a whole.

(Adapted from Porter M, *Competitive Strategy* (1980) New York: Free Press)

Porter claims that the intensity of the fifth force, that is the rivalry amongst industry competitors, is driven by the intensity of the other four forces. If these other forces are driving profitability down, the firms in the industry will compete more intensely to restore their own profits.

1.2 The threat of new entrants

A new entrant into an industry will bring extra capacity and more competition. The strength of this threat is likely to vary from industry to industry, depending on the strength of the barriers to entry. Barriers to entry discourage new entrants and influence the likely response of existing competitors to the new entrant. These will include:

- economies of scale and scope
- product differentiation
- capital requirements

- switching costs
- access to distribution channels
- cost advantages of existing producers, independent of economies of scale
- response of incumbents

Entry barriers might be lowered by:

- changes in the environment
- technological changes
- new distribution channels for products or services

Generally an industry with low barriers to entry will be characterised by a large number of small firms.

The impact of e-commerce on traditional business models over the last 20 years has been significant, and has helped to break down traditional barriers to entry in certain industries. A number of well-known retailers around the world have gone out of business after failing to recognise (and respond) to the fact that traditional barriers to entry, such the associated costs of establishing physical stores, can now easily be overcome by competitors selling the same goods online directly to customers.

1.3 The threat from substitute products

A substitute product is a product/service produced by another industry which satisfies the same customer needs.

Substitutes affect profitability of an industry through:

- Putting a ceiling on prices eg, air fares will determine the maximum level of train fares over similar routes
- Affecting volumes of demand
- Forcing expensive investments and service improvements eg, DVDs supplied with booklets, posters and other offers to make them more attractive as artefacts compared to virtual downloads

Threat from substitutes is determined by:

- Relative price/performance eg, speed of plane travel against the speed of train travel may be higher but does it justify the higher price?
- Switching costs from one to another eg, downloads may be cheap but necessitate buying a smart phone or computer.

Interactive question 1: Blockbuster

Launched in 1985, American company Blockbuster became the largest film rental company in the world. It offered customers the ability to rent video games and movies (initially on video cassettes and later DVDs) for a short period, from its owned and franchised stores. By the mid-1990s, it employed 60,000 staff and operated 9,000 stores worldwide.

However, although it had once been a leading provider of home entertainment, the company finally closed down its operations in late 2013.

Requirements

1.1 Identify the factors that enabled substitutes to cause the financial decline of Blockbuster.

See **Answer** at the end of this chapter.

1.4 The bargaining power of buyers (customers)

Buyers (customers) may include:

- Industrial customers and distributors seeking to obtain lower costs to boost their own margins, or better inputs and smoother transactions with suppliers.

- Governmental or other not-for-profit organisations seeking to gain more benefit for their clients.

- Consumers wanting better quality or technologically advanced products and services at lower prices.

Worked example: Toys R Us

In early 2018 it was announced that toy retailer, Toys R Us, would close all of its UK stores in April. The BBC (2018) highlighted that the company's demise was in part due to failing to recognise the impact that changes in technology were having on demand for its products. Kate Hardcastle a retail analyst from Insight With Passion, explained that 'kids are changing, an eight year-old now […] can download an app in 30 seconds to distort their face and make them look like Spiderman. Retail almost can't keep up'. (BBC, 2018). The article highlighted that children's birthday presents are becoming increasingly more technologically advanced, with VR (virtual reality) headsets, drones and go-pro cameras becoming ever more common. These changes effectively broadened the range of competitors that Toys R Us was competing against to include hi-tech retailers. As Hardcastle noted, selling hi-tech products was not something which 'Toys R Us was able to get into very successfully'. (BBC, 2018).

Source: BBC (2018) *Five Reasons Toys R Us failed*. [Online]. Available from: www.bbc.co.uk [Accessed 19 April 2018].

Buyer power may depend on the number of alternative suppliers in the industry. Buyer power is increased by:

- The customer buying a large proportion of total industry output.

- The product not being critical to the customer's own business and a lack of proprietary product differences which would otherwise make them favour or be locked into one supplier.

- Low switching costs (ie, the cost of switching suppliers).

- The size of the purchase relative to the size of the supplier.

- High degrees of price transparency and supplier information available in the market.

1.5 The bargaining power of suppliers

Industry profitability can be affected by powerful suppliers. Suppliers can exert pressure for higher prices but this depends on a number of factors.

- The number and size of suppliers – are there just one or two dominant suppliers to the industry, able to charge monopoly or oligopoly prices?

- The threat of new entrants or substitute products to the supplier's industry.

- Whether the suppliers have other customers outside the industry, and do not rely on the industry for the majority of their sales. If the industry supplied is not an important customer, suppliers may be unwilling to negotiate or discount.

- The importance of the supplier's product to the customer's business.

- The extent to which the supplier has a differentiated product.

- The level of switching costs for their customers. The internet tends to lessen supplier power, reducing barriers to different supplier migration.

1.6 Competitive rivalry

If rivalry is fierce, firms compete aggressively which reduces the profit potential for all players in the industry.

The intensity of competition will depend on the following factors:

- Rate of market growth: The level of rivalry in an industry is intensified when market growth is slowing or stagnant.

- Level of fixed costs: High fixed costs make it more likely that competitors will compete on price in the short-term in order to earn a contribution from sales to help cover costs.

- Ease and cost of switching for buyers: Suppliers will compete aggressively if buyers can, and do, switch easily.

- Importance of capacity utilisation/economies of scale: A supplier might aim to achieve a significant increase in output, in order to obtain reductions in unit costs.

- Degree of uncertainty regarding the actions of rival firms: a key characteristic of an oligopoly is that the actions of one firm produce a response from rivals. When a firm is uncertain about the behaviour of a competing firm, there is a tendency to respond by formulating a more aggressive strategy.

- Strategic importance: Where success in a particular market is a prime strategic objective, firms are more likely to act increasingly competitively to meet their targets.

- Exit barriers: High exit barriers (non-current assets with a low break-up value; redundancy payments, effect of withdrawal on the other operations within the group) increase the cost of ceasing operations and cause firms to try and earn profits by any means available.

1.7 Using the Five Forces framework

The Five Forces framework should be used to identify the key forces affecting an organisation and hence the opportunities available and threats to be considered. The key forces will tend to differ by industry so, for example, in the UK for producers of own branded food products, the power of the large UK retail buyers (eg, Sainsbury's, Tesco, Asda, Marks & Spencer, etc,) will be very important.

Consideration should be given to whether the forces will change over time and if so, how. Strategies will need to be developed to adapt to these changes.

It is essential for an organisation to determine not only how it stands in relation to the forces but also how its competitors stand.

Competitive strategy will be concerned with how an organisation can influence the competitive forces, eg, can competitive rivalry be diminished? Can barriers to entry be created?

The ideal market, in which profits are easiest to make, is one where there is:

- Low supplier power
- Low customer power
- Little prospect of substitutes emerging
- High barriers to entry
- Weak inter-firm competition

1.8 Limitations of the Five Forces model

- **Ignores the role of the state**: In many countries, the state is a factor in the industry and influences the forces via ownership, subsidy, or presentation or regulation of competition. The Five Forces model seems to present government as just a rule setter.

- **Not helpful for not-for-profit organisations**: The Five Forces are those which determine industry profitability. If profitability is not a key objective for managers, they might not consider five forces analysis to be helpful.

- **Positioning view and not resource-based**: It assumes profitability will be determined by dealing better with the five forces ie, outside-in. Individual business', strategic decision-makers should focus on product-market strategy. This ignores competence building for innovation to enter new industries.

- **Assumes management are required to maximise shareholders' wealth**: In some countries, companies pursue market share objectives instead, as has been the case in Japan, traditionally, and South Korea, where large groups, with easy access to credit (and low cost of capital) did not overtly pursue profit objectives.

- **Dynamic industries**: The model is less useful in industries that are rapidly changing as it is difficult to predict how the forces may change. Dynamic industries may require a greater focus on risk management.

- **Ignores potential for collaboration to raise profitability**: The model underplays the potential for collaboration (eg, supply chain collaboration) to build long-term relationships with suppliers, customers or distributors, joint ventures, to avoid substitutes, and so on.

- **Some industries may include additional forces**: Porter's Five Forces model can be extended to include a sixth force, referred to as 'complementors'. Complementors are those entities that enhance the attractiveness of an organisation to its customers or suppliers. For example, app developers complement the offering of smartphone and tablet computer makers. As this illustrates some industries will be affected by a wider range of factors than those in the traditional Five Forces model.

2 Industries, companies, markets and technologies

Section overview

- The industry life cycle model describes the stages of development from introduction, through growth, shakeout and maturity, into decline.

- The phase that an industry is at will affect the behaviour of the competitive firms within the industry and have implications for choice of strategy.

2.1 Industry life cycles

Definition

Industry: A group of organisations supplying a market offering similar products using similar technologies to provide customer benefits.

The concept of life cycle analysis is popular in strategic management and can be used to describe the phases of development that an industry , or market segment within an industry, goes through.

The key stages of the industry life cycle are:

- **Introduction** – newly invented product or service is made available for purchase and organisations attempt to develop buyer interest. There may be significant competitive advantage to those firms who are first in the industry.

- **Growth** – a period of rapid expansion of demand or activity as the industry finds a market and competitors are attracted by its potential.

- **Shakeout** – a period in which market growth begins to slow. Weaker players are forced to leave the industry.

- **Maturity** – a relatively stable period of time where there is little change in sales volumes year to year but competition between remaining firms intensifies as growth continues to slow down.

- **Decline** – a falling off in activity levels as firms leave the industry and the industry ceases to exist or is absorbed into some other industry.

Each phase has different implications for competitive behaviour and corporate strategy eg, if an industry is growing, the organisations operating in that industry can grow as the market develops; in a mature industry, growth can only be achieved by stealing market share from other competitors and typically the market becomes more fragmented.

Some industry life cycles are identical in pattern and timing to that of their product (eg, in the hat industry, or steel industry). Others have longer life cycles than the particular products, eg, the music industry which has endured from sheet music till MP3 and downloads, merely releasing (and re-releasing) its music as new products as the format changes.

Many businesses will not wish to risk having only a single product or all their products at the same stage of development as they may all decline together. This leads to the concept of a balanced product portfolio which is discussed further in Chapter 6.

The financial returns to firms in an industry vary according to the stage:

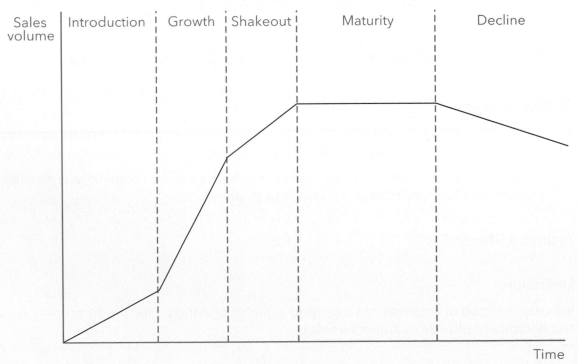

2.2 Characteristics of the industry at different phases

	Introduction	Growth	Shakeout	Maturity	Decline
Customers	Experimenters, innovators	Early adopters	Growing selectivity of purchase	Mass market, brand switching is common	Price competition Commodity product
R&D	High	Extend product before competition	Seek lower cost ways to supply to access new markets	Low	
Company	Early mover Production focused	React to more competitors with increased marketing	Potential consolidation through buying rivals	Battles over market share Seek cost reduction	Cost control or exit
Competitors	A few	More entrants to the market	Many competitors, price cutting but winnowing out of weaker players	Depending on industry, a few large competitors	Price-based competition, fewer competitors
Profitability	Low, as an investment	Growing	Levelling off	Stable, high or under pressure	Falling, unless cost control

2.3 Strategic implications of life cycles

Both industries and products have life cycles and management must pursue different strategies at each stage:

Introduction stage

- Attract trend-setting buyer groups by promotion of technical novelty or fashion.
- Price high (skim) to cash in on novelty or price low (penetration) to gain adoption and high initial share.
- Support product despite poor current financial results.
- Review investment programme periodically in light of success of launch (eg, delay or bring forward capacity increases).
- Build channels of distribution.
- Monitor success of rival technologies and competitor products.

Growth stage

- Ensure capacity expands sufficiently to meet firm's target market share objectives.
- Penetrate market, possibly by reducing price.
- Maintain barriers to entry (eg, fight patent infringements, keep price competitive).
- High promotion of benefits to attract early majority of potential buyers.
- Build brand awareness to resist impact from new entrants.

- Ensure investors are aware of potential of new products to ensure support for financial strategy.

- Search for additional markets and product refinements.

- Consider methods of expanding and reducing costs of production (eg, contract manufacturing overseas, building own factory in a low cost location).

Shakeout phase

- Monitor industry for potential mergers and rationalisation behaviour.
- Seek potential merger candidates.
- Periodic review of production and financial forecasts in light of sales growth rates.
- Shift business model from customer acquisition to extracting revenue from existing customers.
- Seek to extend growth by finding new markets or technologies.

Maturity phase

- Maximise current financial returns from product.

- Defend market position by matching pricing and promotion of rivals.

- Modify markets by positioning product to gain acceptance from non-buyers (eg, new outlets or suggested new uses).

- Modify the product to make it cheaper or of greater benefit.

- Intensify distribution.

- Leverage the existing customer database to gain additional incomes (eg, mobile phone operators seeking to earn from content management).

- Engage in integration activities with rivals (eg, mergers, mutual agreements on competition).

- Ensure successor industries are ready for launch to pick up market.

Decline phase

- Harvest cash flows by minimising spending on promotion or product refinement.

- Simplify range by weeding out variations.

- Narrow distribution to target loyal customers to reduce stocking costs.

- Evaluate exit barriers and identify the optimum time to leave the industry (eg, leases ending, need for renewal investment).

- Seek potential exit strategy (eg, buyer for business, firms willing to buy licences etc).

- The response of competitors is particularly important – there may be threats as they attempt to defend their position, or opportunities, eg, when a competitor leaves the market.

Worked example: Apple's iPhone

A company's policy on innovation will be linked to its assessment of how the product lifecycle concept applies to its portfolio. Apple has tended to launch a new version of its iPhone device every 12 months. Each new version offers users more advanced features than previous models. Once older models of the iPhone have reached a certain age Apple has tended to withdraw certain elements of user support. In October 2016, Apple began warning users that support for 32-bit applications using the Apple operating system (iOS) would come to an end. The announcement came amid Apple's plans to move all of its future iPhone devices onto a 64-bit operating system architecture. In late 2017, Apple launched the iPhone X. In addition to the near bezel-less frame and wireless charging capability, Apple removed the iconic home button which had become a staple feature of the devices' previous incarnations, to improve the users' visibility of the screen.

Interactive question 2: Profitability of airlines

The airline industry as a whole is loss making (ie, adding profits of successful airlines to losses of unsuccessful ones). Even successful airlines struggle to get an operating margin above 10%.

Requirements

2.1 Using the following models identify contributory factors to the low rates of profits in airlines.

    (a) Industry life cycle
    (b) Porter's Five Forces

2.2 Identify potential strategies to restore profitability in the light of your analysis.

See **Answer** at the end of this chapter.

3 Product life cycles and international activities

Section overview

- Global firms recognise that markets develop at different rates.

- These differences in stage of development mean that products can be managed differently across the world.

3.1 Extending product life cycles through operating abroad

When domestic performance declines, some firms try to close the gap by exporting.

This is possible only if there are **different product life cycle patterns** in different countries as shown in the diagrams below.

Product life cycles in different countries

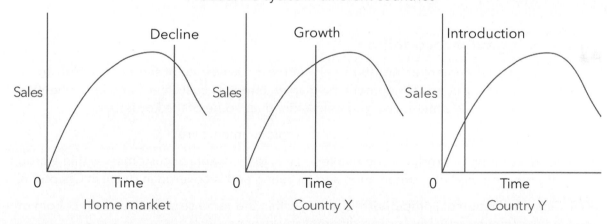

International business must consider many markets simultaneously, with a view to implementing a global introduction and manufacture. The financial returns to an investment may depend on the roll-out of this strategy.

3.2 International Trade Life Cycle

The International Trade Life Cycle is used in developing long-term product strategy. It postulates that many products pass through a cycle during which high income, mass-consumption countries are initially exporters but subsequently lose their export markets and ultimately become importers of the product from lower-cost economies.

From the perspective of the initiator high income country, the pattern of development is as follows.

- **Phase 1. The product is developed in the high income country** (eg, the USA). There are two main reason for this.

    - High income countries provide the greatest demand potential

    - It is expedient to locate production close to the market during the early period so that the firm can react quickly in modifying the product according to customer preferences

- **Phase 2. Overseas production starts**. Firms in the innovator's export markets (such as the UK) start to produce the product domestically. Thus, for example, the UK market is then shared by the innovative US firm and the UK firms.

- **Phase 3. Overseas producers compete in export markets**. The costs of the UK producers begin to fall as they gain economies of scale and experience. They may also enjoy lower costs of labour, materials etc, than the US firms. The UK firms now start to compete with the US producers in third-party export markets such as, say, India or Brazil.

- **Phase 4. Overseas producers compete in the firm's domestic market**. The UK firms become so competitive, due to their lower production costs that they start to compete with the US firms in the US domestic market. The cycle is now complete.

4 Industry segments and strategic groups

Section overview

- Returning to concepts of an industry it is possible to see segments or strategic groups within the same industry.

- Competitive strategy should be based on choosing the right segments for the organisation to operate in, and achieving success in each chosen segment by defending the firm's position there.

4.1 Industry segment recognition

Assessing the environment at industry level ignores the existence of segments within an industry. A company needs to segment the market, target its customers, and implement a marketing mix to satisfy them. The grid below identifies some of the key issues.

Benefits to management from recognising strategic segments are:

- Better tailoring of products and marketing mix to the wants of customers within a group (this is called market segmentation and targeting and is covered in detail in Chapter 8).

- Closer definition of competitors (ie, those within the same segment) as distinct from others in the same industry but serving different sub-groups.

- Identification of mobility barriers, ie, factors preventing potential rivals entering the segment or preventing management from taking firm into new segments.

4.2 Key considerations

The grid below identifies some of the key considerations in identifying strategic segments:

The product	What category of product is it?
	Eg, consumer product, consumer service, specialist business product, business service, component, raw material etc
The customer	Who is the primary customer? eg, consumer, business, organisation, government
	What is the location of the customer? eg, local, national, regional or global basis
	Is the buying decision made centrally or locally?
	Cultural differences might affect buying behaviour, especially in negotiation and necessitate a difference in approach eg, the appointment of go-betweens.
Segmentation	Are there different groups of customers with different buying characteristics?
	Is industry divided naturally by country or region? Do trade barriers or tariffs enforce segmentation?
	Does the industry effectively straddle several borders? In a global industry there may be no point in segmenting by country.
	If there are many competitors, a potential supplier might prefer to stay close to one particular market.
	A supplier may, because of its size or because of transportation differences, be unable to serve the entire industry.
Competitors	Where is rivalry strongest?
	Are there any niches with less competition? The identification of industry segments can enable firms to defend niche segments against larger, less focused, rivals.

4.3 Identifying country clusters

In choosing which groups of **countries** to enter, a firm might focus on particular countries or regions or groups of countries with similar characteristics using the following bases.

Basic data	Issues
Level of economic development, infrastructure and so on.	For example, the lack of a fixed line telecommunications network in Africa may encourage take-up of mobile telecommunications.
Cultural similarities (eg, for intellectual property, common language).	It is easy to overestimate the similarities between two countries that might be assumed because they speak the same language. For example, despite the common use of English, there are distinct cultural differences between the US and the UK.
Member of economic groupings (eg, a strategy for the EU).	Economic groupings such as the EU have tariff barriers for some external goods. They may have common product standards which must be adhered to.

Basic data	Issues
Similar market or regulatory structures.	This suggests similar marketing mixes may be appropriate to more than one market. American credit card companies have expanded in the UK because UK consumers use credit cards. German consumers tend not to use credit cards as frequently.
Inter-market timing differences: life cycles.	Certain markets have similar demand patterns for similar goods but that one leads and the other lags. For example, it is assumed that internet penetration will rise in the developed world, but that the US will lead, and other countries will follow as innovations spread.

If countries are deemed to be similar, then it may be possible to use one country to 'predict' the behaviour of another.

4.4 Mobility barriers

These are factors that make it hard for a firm in one strategic group to develop or migrate to another. They function as barriers to entry and, as such, can enable superior rates of profit to be enjoyed by firms within a strategic group.

They relate to the following.

- **Characteristics**, such as branding, user technologies and so on, specific to markets overseas or to geographical regions within a country.

- **Industry characteristics**: to move into a mass volume end of the market might require economies of scale and large production facilities. To move to the **quality end** might require greater investment in research and development.

- The organisation may lack the **distinctive skills** and competences in the new market area.

- **Legal barriers**.

4.5 Buyers in the public sector

Developing business in industrial segments where governmental institutions are significant buyers raises special considerations:

- **Public accountability**: Governmental use of public money is often subject to controls and scrutiny that would be unthinkable in private corporations. This will vary from country to country according to the extent to which public accountability for expenditure is deemed to be important to the political system.

- **Governments are rarely monolithic**: Different government departments may have different cultures, agendas and resources. Regional political variations mean that local government purchasing units may have different processes.

- **Political considerations**: Public procurement will look at the whole social benefit and not merely costs. Therefore employment effects, and factors such as pollution will be considered. Government bodies may also require that its suppliers can show they conform to its own policies in matters of non-discrimination, sustainability etc.

- **Purchasing by tender**: Usual forms of buying procedure are the open tender and the selective tender. For a selective tender process, the firm needs to be accepted on the appropriate list. In some countries, it takes considerable persistence to get to that stage, since it may take several visits to appropriate government officials to establish a good working relationship.

Summary and Self-test

Summary

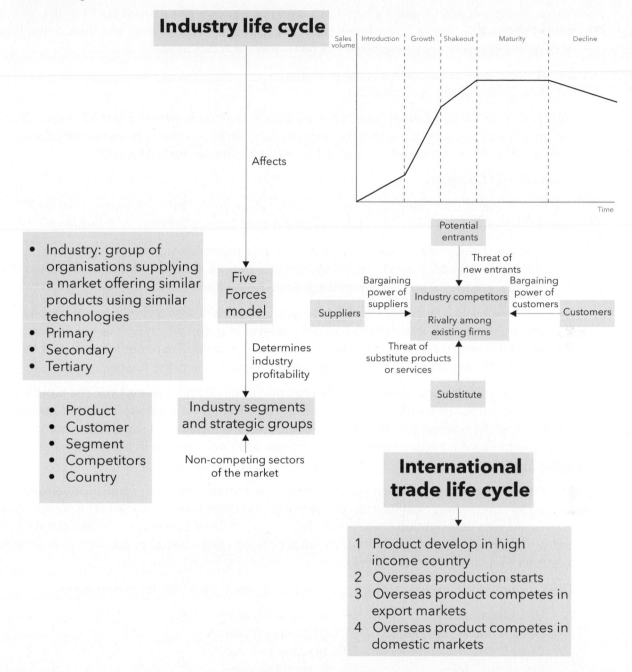

Industry life cycle

Sales volume | Introduction | Growth | Shakeout | Maturity | Decline
Time

Affects

- Industry: group of organisations supplying a market offering similar products using similar technologies
- Primary
- Secondary
- Tertiary

- Product
- Customer
- Segment
- Competitors
- Country

Five Forces model

Determines industry profitability

Industry segments and strategic groups

Non-competing sectors of the market

Potential entrants

Threat of new entrants

Bargaining power of suppliers

Suppliers

Industry competitors

Rivalry among existing firms

Bargaining power of customers

Customers

Threat of substitute products or services

Substitute

International trade life cycle

1. Product develop in high income country
2. Overseas production starts
3. Overseas product competes in export markets
4. Overseas product competes in domestic markets

C H A P T E R 5

Self-test

Answer the following questions.

1 Mr Mavers runs a small newspaper and sweet shop in the centre of a large city. Will his customers exert a high or low bargaining power over him? Justify your answer.

2 "Large companies often exert a high bargaining power over their suppliers." For the following two businesses, identify the types of suppliers they will have, and discuss the level of bargaining power these suppliers will have over each business.

    (a) A large, mid-price chain of clothes shops
    (b) A large top division football club

3 "Audit fees for UK companies have fallen by 20% in real terms over the last 10 years." Given the intensity of competition within the industry, why do accountancy firms not withdraw from audit and focus their efforts instead on more profitable areas of work?

4 **Gizmo Petrol Company**

The Gizmo Petrol Company is a large company selling petrol through approximately 200 petrol stations, half of which are concentrated in the North-West region of England.

It has always maintained a strong presence in residential locations, as the Managing Director of the firm, Mr Macari, has always felt that people are more likely to purchase petrol as they leave for work or when they return home from work.

Gizmo operates its petrol stations via a five-year agreement with a single petrol supplier. The agreement is such that there is a minimum level of petrol which Gizmo has to purchase; at present the amount purchased is twice the minimum level. There are a number of other suppliers in the market should Gizmo require a new supplier in the future.

The company has been able to fund its expansion policy by borrowing from the bank and at present the company's gearing ratio stands at 32%. The company benefits from a strong positive cash flow which has allowed it easily to meet its repayment requirements and earn a reasonable profit margin. However, this margin has been eroded in recent years as a result of a recession which has left consumers more price-conscious.

The market as a whole has seen consolidation over recent years with small independent petrol stations finding it difficult to compete with the large multi-nationals. The company is now faced with competition from two slightly larger national companies, local independent petrol stations and supermarkets which are supplying cheap petrol to customers in an effort to attract them into their stores.

The product range offered by Gizmo at present is made up of the following items.

Unleaded petrol	44% of company sales
Lead replacement petrol	31% of company sales
Diesel	23% of company sales
Non-petrol sales	2% of company sales

The move towards environmentally-friendly products within society and the taxation system benefiting unleaded petrol have allowed Gizmo to expand its sales of this product at the expense of lead replacement petrol.

The transport system within Britain is still largely dominated by cars, as individuals enjoy the freedom and flexibility of the motor vehicle and the government has maintained its road building policy. Despite this, train travel throughout the country has increased in recent times due in part to significant improvements to the railway network infrastructure. Competitors have also taken the lead in the development of improved petrol stations offering more services than selling petrol only. One such development has been the introduction of electric charging stations to accommodate the growing number of drivers owning electric cars. Gizmo has never been at the leading edge of developments within the industry and still largely sees the purpose of a petrol station as merely providing petrol. Gizmo's non-petrol sales are mainly made up of confectionery and cold snacks.

Requirements

Prepare briefing notes for Mr Macari containing an analysis of the external position of Gizmo within the marketplace.

6   Read the scenario of **the March 2013 Business Strategy and Technology** question in the Question Bank entitled *Mayhews Ltd (amended).* Draft an answer to the requirement on Porter's Five Forces Model.

7   Read the scenario of the **March 2016 Business Strategy and Technology** question in the Question Bank entitled *Dreamy Potato Products Ltd.* Draft an answer to the requirement which asks for the completion of a partial Five Forces analysis.

Now, go back to the Learning outcomes in the Introduction. If you are satisfied that you have achieved these objectives, please tick them off.

Answers to Interactive questions

Answer to Interactive question 1

1.1 Substitutes include:

- Supermarkets sell many of the most popular film titles at low prices.

- Online shops such as Amazon provide DVDs (in addition to its own streaming service, Amazon Prime).

- Downloads from Netflix and Apple.

- Piracy of movies by unregulated download sites and file sharing.

These substitutes predominantly reduced the willingness of customers to visit Blockbuster stores with the consequence that the company's sales revenue fell.

The principal reason is the improvement in price/performance of these substitutes.

Supermarkets may be cheaper but are, importantly, convenient because households shop there each week and so simply add the latest film release to their trolley. Furthermore, purchasing the latest films removes the need for customers to return to a Blockbuster store once the rental period has finished. Where the households are not minded to follow film releases they were unlikely to visit Blockbuster.

Film downloads may be free or cheaper. They are also more convenient because again no special visit to a store is needed, the film trailer can be sampled and be immediately available for watching on various computer platforms.

Amazon may be cheaper but also provides customer film reviews which enable buyers to have more information before buying than could be gained by a visit to a Blockbuster store.

The introduction of new technologies indicates that traditional Blockbuster customers had little loyalty to the company as they were able to easily switch to different substitute providers of film entertainment products.

Answer to Interactive question 2

2.1 (a) **Industry life cycle**

The industry seems to be at the shakeout phase with overcapacity due to many operators and liberalisation of competition (so-called 'open skies') leading to greater competition on profitable routes.

Consolidations (eg, Air France with KLM) and failures (eg, Swiss Air) have occurred.

(b) **Porter's Five Forces**

Buyer power	• Increased availability has led to more choice in the market.
	• The growth of electronic booking services (eg, e-bookers, expedia.com, lastminute.com) has restricted ability of airlines to charge full price.
	• The change in the nature of the buyer towards short-haul leisure where price is more important than it was to business travellers.

Supplier power	• Aviation fuel accounts for 30 – 35% of costs and is determined by oil producer cartels and large oil companies.
	• Airframes are provided by two firms (Boeing and Airbus) and engines by three firms (GE, Pratt and Whitney, Rolls Royce).
	• Airport landing plots and services are provided by national monopolies.
Substitutes	• Faster trains with better facilities which travel to centre of cities.
	• Alternative leisure eg, cruises.
	• Technologies such as video-conferencing, Facetime and Skype.
Entrants	• Low cost point-to-point providers attack by short-haul router.
	• Opening up of competition by bi-lateral agreement (eg, USA and EU) or under pressure from World Trade Organisations.
Competitive rivalry	• Very high fixed cost industry makes competition for volume force prices down towards marginal cost.
	• Limited opportunities for differentiator given similarity of aircraft and destinations.
	• Volatile demand due to seasons and economic/political factors.

2.2 Restoring profitability

Consolidation of airline industry to reduce capacity.

Operate alliances to rationalise competition and benefit from economies of scale (ground handling, fuel purchase etc).

Oppose increasing take off and landing slots or greater competition.

Reduce fixed costs, eg, by outsourcing, better capacity planning.

Differentiate service to gain higher yield per passenger.

Answers to Self-test

1   High bargaining power.

    Presumably there are many other similar shops nearby, so customers will go elsewhere if he does not stock the products they want.

2   (a)   Chain store

    - Suppliers will be small independent manufacturers of clothes.

    - Many suppliers will exist.

    - All suppliers will have very similar products.

    - High bargaining power over suppliers is likely, given that if the chain store is dissatisfied with one supplier, there is unlikely to be a problem finding an alternative.

    (b)   Football club

    - Main suppliers are players.

    - Players are highly skilled individuals.

    - Each player's specific attributes will differ.

    - Low bargaining power is therefore likely, given that some players will not be easily replaceable.

    - This contradicts the quotation, but the situation arises because the suppliers, although small, do not offer a standard service.

3   Accountancy firms have a strategic need to offer audit in the sense that clients will expect a range of services. The audit is often the loss leader that introduces the client to the firm. Other more profitable services can then be offered.

    All large companies are obliged by law to have an audit, so accountancy firms will always have a market.

4   **Gizmo Petrol Company**

    Briefing notes

To	Mr Macari
From	Mr Smith
Date	Today
Subject	Analysis of the external position of the Gizmo Petrol Company within the market place

    Gizmo's external position

    Gizmo's position within the market place can be analysed according to the opportunities and threats that it faces.

    (a)   **Opportunities**

    Product range

    The company should follow the lead of competitors and take advantage of the move by consumers towards convenience shopping. The provision of essential everyday household items, such as light bulbs, should be seriously considered, given the company's location in residential areas. Gizmo should also look to exploit the opportunities to attract customers with electric cars. This could be achieved by introducing electric charging stations at its sites.

Expansion

Gizmo's operations are largely concentrated in the North-West of Britain. Given the company's experience, consideration should be given to moving towards other areas.

Political

The government's road building policy should provide motorists with improved transport facilities and hence ensure that petrol is still a highly desired product.

Independent retailers

The increased competition within the market place has already seen many small independent petrol firms ceasing to trade. This situation is likely to continue in the future and therefore Gizmo should use this as an opportunity to purchase petrol stations at a reasonable price to aid its nationwide expansion.

Location

Given that Gizmo has the opportunity to expand, it should look towards locating in areas other than residential, eg, sites near towns would provide consumers with convenient places to fill up with petrol.

(b) **Threats**

Demand for Gizmo's products is derived from vehicle ownership and usage. A number of the points outlined below highlight that changes to vehicle ownership and usage will have a direct impact on Gizmo's future performance due to reduced demand for petrol.

Substitutes

Increasing train travel throughout the country is a threat to traditional car usage as it presents motorists with an alternative to driving. As such this may lead some motorists to abandon their cars.

Political

The government may influence the price of petrol by tax rises, which again may deter motorists from using their cars.

Competitors

Supermarkets may further drive down the price of petrol or offer cheaper petrol to attract customers to improve their sales. As customers are also becoming more price-conscious prices may also generally fall, putting pressure on margins and cash flows.

Technology

Gizmo's lack of technological development may leave it open to attacks from competitors who have developed improved service stations, and offer electric car charging facilities.

Supplier

The fact that Gizmo is supplied by only one company may cause future problems with quality and price flexibility if the market price fluctuates.

Social attitudes

Consumers may turn towards public transport as being more environmentally-friendly. Consumers may also change the types of vehicle that they own, switching from petrol engine cars to hybrid and electric cars.

6   Refer to the answer to Mayhews Ltd in the Question Bank.

7   Refer to the answer to Dreamy Potato Products Ltd in the Question Bank.

CHAPTER 6

Strategic capability

Introduction

Examination context

TOPIC LIST

Summary and Self-test

Answers to Interactive questions

Answers to Self-test

Introduction

Learning outcomes

In the context of a business scenario:

- Evaluate an organisation's critical success factors ☐

- Analyse for a given situation the external factors which may impact upon an organisation's performance and position, identifying significant issues in areas such as: ☐

  - Markets for finance, labour and other resources

  - Supply chain factors

  - Current technology developments, including those relating to automation and intelligent systems

- Identify the significance and effect of the internal factors in a given situation which affect or may influence an organisation's ability to achieve its chosen strategy including its current resources, product/service portfolio, value chain, organisational and operational capabilities, (including core competencies, existing business processes, human capital and workforce flexibility), use of developing technology (including digital assets, cryptocurrencies, big data, internet of things, automation and intelligent systems) ☐

- Explain in a given scenario, how products and services must evolve in the face of changing technologies, consumer demand and industry competition ☐

- Evaluate how strategies for technology and innovation, including digital assets, automation, intelligent systems, workforce flexibility and shared service centres, can support the organisation's achievement of its overall strategy

- Identify and evaluate methods of further developing a specific organisation which adjust existing strategies or implement new strategies to take account of changing position and risk ☐

The specific syllabus references for this chapter are 1a, 1b, 1d, 2h, 3b, 3e.

Syllabus links

You will have been briefly introduced to most of the concepts in this chapter in your Business, Technology and Finance syllabus.

Examination context

This chapter includes key principles of strategic capability, core competences and resource based strategy. Questions are likely to focus on the linkages between elements and the manner in which, when used together, they can facilitate strategy and leverage competitive advantage. In this chapter we also explore the increasingly important role that technological capabilities now play in modern organisations. Terms including big data, data analytics, artificial intelligence, automation, cloud computing and crowdfunding are increasingly mentioned in the media as they become part of everyday business language. Having a good understanding of this content is important as you prepare for your Business Strategy and Technology exam. However, as mentioned in Chapter 1, the inclusion of these topics in the learning materials does not mean that you will be required to display a detailed understanding of the internal workings of IT systems, nor will you be required to exhibit knowledge concerning computer algorithms and the internal logic of software applications.

You will, however, be required to have a high level understanding of the main technological developments affecting organisations, and how technology can affect their strategies, or their ability to implement those strategies successfully. Remember that the Business Strategy and Technology exam is a very practical exam, and your ability to apply your knowledge is crucial.

In Q3 of the March 2017 exam (*Gighay Ltd*) the scenario focused on a company called Gighay, which provided IT services. Information was provided about two potential new clients. The first client Oxna, a publishing business, had limited in-house IT expertise and, following recent cyber-security issues, was considering whether to outsource management of all its IT needs to Gighay. The first requirement asked:

'Explain the benefits and problems for Oxna of outsourcing all of its IT needs to Gighay and suggest some KPIs that could be included in the service contract between the companies.'

(11 marks)

This requirement nicely illustrates how traditional business topics can be combined in a scenario with a technological angle to test a candidates understanding of key topics such as outsourcing and performance measurement in a very practical, applied way.

In Question 1 of the March 2014 exam (*Emelius Ltd*) the scenario focused on a company which offered paper document storage and management services. The company had recently developed a new digital data capture service whereby paper documents could be scanned in and then made available on an electronic platform. The second requirement asked:

'Explain four key drivers in the value chain for Emelius' new digital data capture service.'

(12 marks)

As the examiner noted 'Better candidates discussed their answer in the context of Emelius' generic strategy using value chain terminology; identified and explained a range of both cost and value drivers; and brought out the importance of linkages in the value chain'.

The examiner's comments again highlight the importance of being able to apply your knowledge to the scenario. This requirement considers how IT can be used to develop an organisation's competitive advantage and the implications that reliance on IT may have for other activities in the value chain. In this case Emelius' competitive advantage centres on the speed, security and reliability of access to digital information, once captured. Analysis of the value chain showed that, as might be expected with digital data, Emelius makes heavy use of technology throughout the chain to address these critical success factors.

1 Analysing an organisation's strategic capability

Section overview

- Having analysed its external environment, an organisation must assess its strategic capability as the next step in strategic analysis.

To develop a strategic plan, an organisation must be aware of its current position. In the rational approach to strategic planning, having completed an analysis of the external environment, management needs to undertake internal analysis. This involves consideration of:

- Critical success factors and competences
- Resources
- Value chain
- Supply chain
- Product/service portfolio

2 Critical success factors and core competences

Section overview

- Critical Success Factors (CSFs) are the areas at which an organisation must excel if it is to achieve sustainable competitive advantage (SCA).

- Threshold resources and competences are the basic resources and activities required by all firms in the market and which are necessary to stay in business.

- Only by having unique resources and core competences can a firm generate SCA.

- Kay identified three distinct capabilities or sources of core competence: competitive architecture, reputation and innovative ability.

2.1 Critical success factors

Definition

Critical success factors (CSFs) are a small number of key goals vital to the success of an organisation ie, 'things that must go right'.

An alternative definition is provided by Johnson, Scholes and Whittington.

Critical success factors 'Those product features that are particularly valued by a group of customers, and, therefore, where the organisation must excel to outperform the competition.'

This second definition is more restricted because it deals merely with product features rather than considering additional factors which are vital to commercial success such as product availability, competitive knowledge or cost and performance control.

2.2 Identifying CSFs

The concept of CSFs was originally developed by Daniel in 1962 and refined by the Massachusetts Institute of Technology (MIT) as a device for aligning the information provided by a firm's information systems to the firm's business needs to ensure it is relevant and complete (this aspect is discussed further in Chapter 14).

MIT proposed five areas in which CSFs should be identified.

1. **The structure of the particular industry**: These are the factors shaping the success of the industry as a whole and the factors that will determine the number and profitability of the players within it eg, consumer adoption of genetically modified foods is a CSF for any firm involved in developing or growing GM crops.

2. **Competitive strategy and position**: The key elements of the business strategy that must be delivered. For example growth in market share or percentage coverage of target market.

3. **Environmental factors**: Although not directly under the influence of management these must be monitored and action taken if they deviate from the firm's plan. For example a house building firm would regard the state of the economy and lending rates as CSFs and if they were to become adverse would cut back on its new-starts.

4. **Temporary factors**: These could be internal changes that are being made to organisational structure, or cost reductions. The success of these short-term projects is critical to the overall success of the business.

5. **Functional managerial position**: Each managerial role will have CSFs associated with it related to the manager's performance of their role.

Worked example: CSFs for M-Payment firms

M-Payment refers to the use of mobile phone (cell-phone) credits to pay for goods and services. The owner waves their mobile phone handset over the shop's sensor and the transaction fee is charged to the mobile phone operator and billed to their customer in due course. Where goods are purchased using the mobile phone, such as tickets where the handset is used to navigate through an automated switchboard or web-enabled mobile phones accessing websites, the funds can be transferred at the time of purchase.

The benefits are:

- Individuals will not have to carry separate credit cards, cash etc.

- Security will improve because there will be no opportunity to try to capture Personal Identification Numbers (PIN numbers) from terminals.

- Individuals denied credit cards will be able to use virtual payments systems.

- Provides methods of payment in countries that lack the infrastructure of banks etc, providing the country has a retail network for 'pay as you go top-up' cards.

Research carried out by Booz Allen and Hamilton indicate that the following industry CSFs will determine the uptake of M-Payment around the world.

- Banks and credit card companies must evaluate ways to let mobile telecoms participate in collaborative ventures rather than setting up rival payment systems.

- Mobile operators must consider new mobile payment systems in the context of new ways to open up revenue streams, especially from monthly m-payment subscription charges or per transaction fees. Operators must also take full advantage of the positive side effect of embedding the mobile phone even deeper into the life of the subscribers – a significant motivator in the Japanese model.

- Handset suppliers must embrace new approaches and start to consider active integration of mobile payment capabilities into product road maps and line-ups. Mobile payment capabilities are seen by some as the next big thing to drive handset replacement, making standardisation and compatibility across operators and platforms critical to preserve user attractiveness and scale benefits.

- Merchants must use their vast experience with cashless payments to drive further cost decreases that accrue from giving up cash, and to offset point of sale (POS) technology upgrade costs.

- Finally, it needs to be demonstrated to mobile phone users that mobile payment is much more attractive than other more familiar payment schemes. The bundle of convenience aspects (safe, secure, available, fast, transparent, etc,) needs to be packaged and sold to target groups individually.

2.3 CSFs and competitive advantage

CSFs differ from one market segment to another, eg, in some price may be key, in others quality, in others delivery, etc.

CSFs concern not only the resources of the business but also the competitive environment in which it operates, discussed in Chapters 4 and 5, ie, how will the business achieve a **sustainable competitive advantage (SCA)** over its competitors?

The following diagram shows the relationship between the different **resources** of an entity and the activities and processes which transform those resources into outputs to create added value (**competences**). It also shows the way in which entities can generate a SCA over their competitors by their unique control/ownership of particular core competences in these processes and activities.

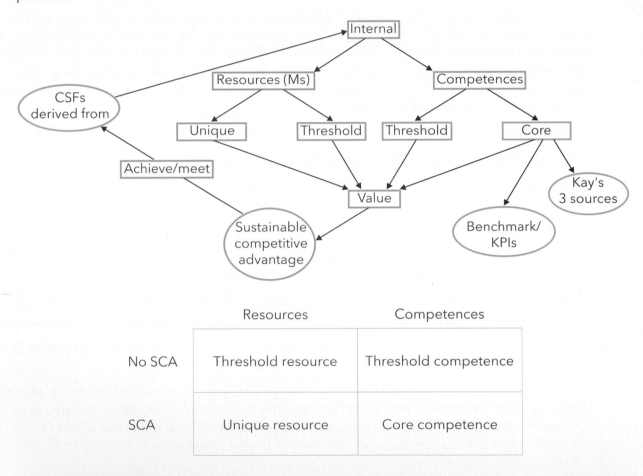

	Resources	Competences
No SCA	Threshold resource	Threshold competence
SCA	Unique resource	Core competence

Threshold resources	The **basic** resources needed by **all** firms in the market.
Unique resources	Those resources which give the firm a sustainable competitive advantage over its competitors, enabling it to meet the CSFs. They are resources which are **better** than those of the competition and **difficult to replicate**.

Threshold competences	The activities and processes involved in using and linking the firm's resources **necessary to stay in business**.
Core competences	The critical activities and processes which enable the firm to meet the CSFs and therefore achieve a sustainable competitive advantage. The core competences must be **better** than those of competitors and **difficult to replicate**.

2.4 Core competences – Kay's three sources

Kay (1993) argues that there are three distinct capabilities a company can develop that add value. These capabilities or core competences can originate from three sources.

Competitive architecture

This is the network of relationships within and around a business. There are three divisions as described below.

- Internal architecture – relationships with employees.
- External architecture – relationships with suppliers, intermediaries and customers.
- Network architecture – relationships between collaborating businesses.

The knowledge, routines and information exchanges created by these relationships (particularly those which are long term) can produce core competences which other businesses cannot replicate.

Reputation

This is the reason why customers come back, investors invest, potential employees apply for jobs and suppliers supply. Reputations (at least good ones) are not developed overnight – they can take years. Once a business has a good reputation it provides a core competence that rivals cannot match. Examples (may) include BMW and Virgin Atlantic (reputation for quality and service).

Innovative ability

This is the ability to develop new products and services and maintain a competitive advantage. Organisation structure, culture, routines, etc, and collaboration between employees, customers and suppliers (ie, the architectures discussed above) influence the ability of a business to innovate. Apple, for example, has consistently been innovative.

3 The resource audit

Section overview

- A resource audit catalogues the assets by considering physical resources, intangibles, human resources, technological resources and financial resources.

- An alternative and handy checklist is the 9Ms.

- Firms own many assets. Some of these assets will be sources of superior earnings in the future for the business and are called strategic assets.

- Therefore it is not sufficient to simply identify the resources. A business must understand whether they are strategic assets ie, unique resources that underlie the firm's SCA.

The **resource-based** approach views the resources of the organisation not just as facilitators to gain competitive advantage from product-market strategies but as sources of strategic advantage in themselves.

In reviewing strategic capability, a first step is to conduct a **resource audit**. This covers physical resources, intangibles, human resources, technological resources and financial resources.

The audit should be comprehensive, but it is useful to identify the unique resources which underlie the firm's sustainable competitive advantage (ie, what sets it apart from other organisations) as opposed to those that are necessary (ie, threshold) but do not form the basis of SCA.

3.1 Physical resources

These include resources owned by the firm and resources to which the firm has access, for example in a supply chain or network.

- Physical assets should be audited reviewing how cost-effectively they are used. A measure of **capital productivity** is profit per unit of capital.

- **Inventories** and working capital are also resources, but they have to be financed. The focus of just-in-time approaches to inventory management and production (JIT) has been to reduce the need to finance working capital.

- Raw materials. Is the firm vulnerable to sudden changes in prices – are there long-term supply contracts or hedging instruments which can overcome this?

- Finally, are physical resources constraints on strategic activity (ie, **limiting factors**)?

3.2 Intangibles and other resources

Brands and other reputational assets are resources created by a firm through the process of transforming inputs into outputs. Patents and other aspects of intellectual property are also intangibles.

These also include customer relationships and relationships with other key stakeholders such as media, and governments.

3.3 Human resources and labour markets

Human resources comprise the productive services people offer to the organisation. An audit of human resources can include more generally the following:

- **Headcount**: Does the firm have enough people to do the task or can the work be done more productively with fewer?

- **Skills base** available to the firm: measured though qualification and training, and the social and psychological aptitudes linking the technical skills to performance.

- **Culture**: The emotional and motivational climate of an organisation is critical to its success particularly in industries where personal service is essential to the 'experience' the company is offering.

- **Workforce structure** and organisation structure

- **The right mix of labour and capital**

  There is a trade-off, in some respects, between using people and using equipment to save money or to increase efficiency. For example, reducing the costs of a call centre can be achieved by:

  - Voice activated software and voice recognition software to process simple transactions
  - Outsourcing it off-shore to a country where labour costs are lower

  The choice will depend on the potential cost savings and benefits and perhaps customer resistance and the firm's attitudes to reputational risk if it cannot achieve its level of service. In addition to achieving the right balance of labour and capital many larger organisations have become increasingly focused on achieving the right mix of labour. Issues relating to workforce inclusion and diversity are highly topical.

- **Service levels**

  Whilst some services can be automated, others cannot – customer service staff are often those who encounter the most moments of truth with the customer. In a service-led economy, the quality of human interaction is an important element of customer satisfaction. To provide good service, those at the customer interface must be supported by a management infrastructure of robust information systems and good training and supervision.

- **Intellectual property and knowledge**

  Knowledge based industries require the creation of and use of intellectual property. The skills and mindset necessary for this may often rely on the education and culture of the country of operation.

3.3.1 Human capital and workforce flexibility

Two important issues to consider when undertaking an audit of an organisation's human resource capabilities are: **human capital** and **workforce flexibility**.

Definition

Human capital: Is concerned with the collective attributes of an organisation's human resources. It includes the capabilities, creativity, skills and knowledge of an organisation's staff which combine to enable the organisation to create economic value.

Over the last 50 years, especially in many of the world's most advanced economies, there has been a gradual shift in the types of jobs being undertaken by the general population, with fewer people now working in traditional production and manufacturing roles. Growing numbers of workers are now involved in increasingly innovative, creative processes, often in hi-tech environments. As such, organisations need to think carefully about how they can get the best out of these workers to realise their strategies and to generate acceptable returns for their shareholders.

To increase the value of the human capital at their disposal many organisations have developed their own programmes specifically designed to get the most from their staff.

Practical ways in which human capital can be enhanced include:

- **Education and training:** Providing employees with the opportunity to learn more about a subject or skill, which they can then apply to their roles in the workplace, may help to boost productivity. Providing opportunities for education and training is likely to be critical to organisations operating in hi-tech, fast-paced industries as the need to keep products and services relevant to the needs of customers is likely to be an ongoing challenge.

- **Allowing creativity:** Organisations should encourage workers to be creative and to try out new ideas, and to challenge existing ways of doing things. This requires management to adopt a more open mind-set and to accept that the outcomes of some employee-directed schemes may not result in a commercially viable solution.

- **Infrastructure:** To get the best from employees, organisations need to ensure that workers have access to the necessary equipment and resources to perform their jobs effectively. Infrastructure in the form of internet and communications technologies are critical to most workers nowadays. Infrastructure in the form of knowledge management systems can also play an important role in sharing information among co-workers. Knowledge management is considered in more detail in Chapter 14.

- **Recognising the intellectual property within the workforce:** Organisations need to recognise the value of their workers in terms of the intellectual property (IP) that they can create. The ability to capture and share the ideas of workers which can be turned into IP may be achieved in part by the use of knowledge management systems mentioned above.

- **Motivation:** Organisations need to devise ways of keeping workers motivated. As such management need to recognise the talents and efforts made by employees, this may be achieved through offering appropriate financial and non-financial incentives. Today many organisations operate their own talent management programmes which are aimed at identifying and retaining individuals considered to be important to the future of the organisation.

- **Competition:** Organisations may attempt to harness the creative abilities of the workforce through establishing competitive working environments. Organisations can achieve this by framing work in the context of a 'problem' to be solved. Such an approach may be appropriate when developing highly innovative products as workers are encouraged to be creative and to draw on their expert knowledge to find a solution.

- **Participation in activities:** Allowing workers greater participation in decisions affecting their work may help to bring a fresh perspective to achieving work-related tasks.

The value generated by organisational activities aimed at improving human capital should form part of the human resource audit. Consideration needs to be given to whether the associated cost and effort of developing human capital programmes provides the intended benefit to the organisation.

Workforce flexibility

Flexibility has become a key feature of the relationships that exist between workers and employers. Organisations wishing to maximise the benefits from these relationships need to consider a number of developments as they have implications for the organisation's audit of its human resources. Recent developments here include:

Flexible workplace arrangements

Many organisations now provide their workers with greater autonomy in terms of when and where they work. This approach has been driven, in part, by the recognition that people are unique, and that instigating mandatory hours of work eg, 9am to 5pm, represents a failure to take account of the fact that some workers are more productive at different points in the working day (eg, late at night or earlier in the morning). In addition, many organisations now offer flexible workplace arrangements having recognised that workers increasingly have varied lifestyles and commitments outside of the work environment, for example, some workers may act as carers for relatives in addition to working. This change in approach represents a desire among organisations to actively encourage a better work-life balance for employees. The introduction of flexible workplace arrangements is particularly pertinent to the concept of human capital as it can help organisations not only to retain the best talent in its workforce but also to attract potential recruits.

Home working

The widespread use of internet enabled technologies have fundamentally changed the way in which many people now work, with growing numbers now working from home. This brings benefits to the worker and employer. For many employees, home working offers a better work-life balance, and reduces the associated cost of commuting to work, while from the organisations perspective, some studies suggest that home working improves engagement and worker productivity. Home working does however present some challenges for employers and employees alike. Home working weakens the traditional mechanisms of control that many organisations have grown accustomed to in relation to monitoring their employees. This in turn heightens the risk that managers lose contact with their staff and colleagues. From the employees perspective home working may result in feelings of isolation and cause stress.

Responding to changing needs

Organisations in many industries now employ workers under different types of employment contract. In a bid to maintain flexibility in response to changing business needs some organisations have started to restrict the number of workers employed on full or part time contracts, with many workers increasingly being hired on a temporary, freelance basis. This change is associated with the continuing trend towards the creation of the gig economy, which is discussed in a later chapter. Such flexibility presents benefits for organisations and workers alike. For organisations, particularly those involved in project work, the use of short-term contracts enables particular skills to be brought in as and when required on an ad-hoc basis, thereby avoiding the need to pay salaries and to make pension contributions. Workers hired in this way are able to be selective about the work they undertake based on those projects that they are most interested in. Arrangements such as these are associated with Handy's shamrock (flexible firm) theory, which is discussed in Chapter 9.

Changing make-up of the workforce

The ageing population in many of the world's most advanced economies is predicted to lead to an increase in the pensionable age for most workers. A consequence of this is that governments are increasingly putting pressure on organisations to employ greater numbers of older workers. PwC's 'Golden Age Index' for 2017 highlighted that the UK economy would gain up to £80 billion if more organisations employed a greater number of workers aged over 55 years old (PwC, 2017). For many organisations, retaining and employing a greater number of older workers will require a change in the mind-set of management, as they need to able to recognise the value of the work experience that older workers bring. PwC (2017) highlight that this will require organisations to change their human resource practices by offering 'flexible working, partial retirement options and role redesign'. Issues around diversity and inclusion have also become increasingly important in recent times. Many organisations today aim to pro-actively manage issues relating to diversity having recognised that diversity extends beyond issues related to race, ethnicity, age and gender. Diversity is also concerned with the fact that as individuals people have different personalities, preferred working styles and individual needs.

Technology and workforce flexibility

Closely connected to the issue of workforce flexibility is the important role that technology has played in facilitating this. As such, it is important that the technological resources associated with workforce flexibility are included as part of the organisation's resource audit. As mentioned above, the ability for workers to perform their jobs not only from home, but from other parts of the world has only been possible due to the growing use of internet technologies. For organisations to get the maximum benefit that such flexibility offers it is important that careful consideration is given to the creation of appropriate strategies for technology. Devising effective strategies will require management to consider the following:

- Flexible workers based from home or other parts of the world need to be provided with the hardware and software necessary to undertake the work required. Such equipment needs to have internet connectivity, especially if files and work resources are only available via cloud based servers.

- Management need to consider the work environments of those flexible workers based offsite, especially as the employing organisation may owe a duty of care to protect such workers under health and safety regulations. Where flexible workers are expected to deal with customers, for example via video conferencing technologies such as Skype, management need to consider whether such arrangements are likely to be appropriate in terms of promoting a consistent image.

- Management need to ensure that sufficiently robust security measures are in place to protect organisational data used away from the office. This is particularly important given the risks of confidential data getting lost, hacked or corrupted.

- In the case of IT related problems occurring, flexible workers need to have access to IT support from a helpdesk.

3.4 Financial resources

An organisation will need finance for any expansion. One aspect of a resource audit would be to simply look at the different sources of finance available to the organisation – internal generation, loans, equity, credit etc. However, it should be noted that there will be implications arising from obtaining finance from external sources, such as ceding control to other stakeholders, unavoidable interest payments in the future, the need to keep the investment markets informed. Management may prefer to invest from retained profits as there is not the management time (or scrutiny) involved in getting outside parties to invest more. In recent times crowdsourcing, and more specifically crowdfunding has become an increasingly effective way for smaller organisations to access funding from external parties.

Definition

Crowdsourcing: The process of getting work or funding, usually online, from a network of people. *(Oxford Dictionary)*.

Crowdfunding: Is a way of raising finance by asking a large number of people for a small amount of money. *(The UK Crowdfunding Association)*.

Advances in internet technologies have changed the way in which organisations can raise finance. Historically, organisations would need to approach a handful of finance providers (for example, banks) to raise funds, but nowadays it is possible for organisations to access thousands and even millions of individuals willing to fund a business expansion or project. Crowdfunding involves an individual and/or organisation posting details of its project on a website through which individuals can choose to provide funding to support the project.

Worked example: Crowdfunding

The UK Crowdfunding Association identifies the following as the most common types of crowdfunding:

Donation/reward crowdfunding attracts people who invest in a project as they believe in the cause, ie, supporting a charitable cause in order to make a positive difference. In some cases rewards might be offered in exchange for providing funds, for example in the case of a band wishing to attract funding to play a concert, contributors may receive 'acknowledgments on an album cover, tickets to an event, regular news updates'.

Debt crowdfunding attracts investors which receive their original funds back with interest. This is also known as peer-to-peer lending (P2P). This approach is similar to traditional bank lending, whilst the returns are financial (interest on the loan), investors benefit from supporting a project that they believe in.

Equity crowdfunding attracts those investors which provide funding in exchange for equity, for example, shares or a stake in a project. As with traditional business shares, the investor takes a risk that the value of their investment may go down as well as up.

Source:

UK Crowdfunding Association, (2017) *What is Crowdfunding?* [Online]. Available from: https://www.ukcfa.org.uk/what-is-crowdfunding/ [Accessed 3 May 2017].

3.5 Technological resources

Technology is a resource in many different ways. Here we focus on two aspects.

- The organisation's capability to manage technology projects, especially IT projects. The costs and complexities of such projects means there is potential for failure (and success) on a huge scale.

  Implementing a successful technology solution enabled low cost carriers such as easyJet and Ryanair to reduce their cost structures and to open low cost air travel to many people. Alternatively, failed technology implementations can drive away customers.

- The impacts of the technology itself:

  - Enable the development of a new product or service generated by technology.

  - Have a disruptive impact on an industry (eg, digital music downloads threaten to overturn the traditional music industry business model).

  - Enable increase in productivity.

  - Engender additional risks.

3.6 Big Data and data analytics

Advances in technology have helped to make data an increasingly important resource in business. Making use of the insights that can be gained from data analysis has made data management a strategic issue for many organisations. As a result, assessing how an organisation manages the data it holds should form an important part of a strategic capability review. The increased emphasis on the importance of data has given rise to the now widely used terms of big data and data analytics. In this section we introduce the concept of the big data and data analytics, in Chapter 14 we consider how the use of big data can help organisations achieve a competitive advantage.

Definitions

Big data: Is a term that describes those 'datasets whose size is beyond the ability of typical database software to capture, store, manage and analyse.' (*McKinsey Global Institute, Big data: The next frontier for innovation, competition and productivity*)

An alternative definition is provided by Gartner.

Big data concerns 'high-volume, high velocity and high-variety information assets that demand cost-effective, innovative forms of information processes for enhanced insight and decision making.' (*Gartner*)

Data analytics: The process of collecting, organising and analysing large sets of data to discover patterns and other information which an organisation can use for its future business decisions.

Closely, linked to the term data analytics is data mining.

Data mining: The process of sorting through data to identify patterns and relationships between different items. Data mining software, using statistical algorithms to discover correlations and patterns, is frequently used on large databases. In essence, it is the process of turning raw data into useful information.

Cloud computing: 'Is a model for enabling ubiquitous, convenient, on-demand network access to a shared pool of configurable computing resources (eg, networks, servers, storage, applications, and services) that can be rapidly provisioned and released with minimal management effort or service provider interaction'. (*US Department of Commerce, National Institute of Standards and Technology*)

Internet of things: A system of interrelated computing devices, mechanical and digital machines, or objects that are provided with unique identifiers and the ability to transfer data over a network without requiring human-to-human or human-to-computer interaction.

3.6.1 Growth in the amount of data in business

Today, organisations have access to greater quantities of data than in the past, with vast amounts of transactional data available from a number of internal and external sources, such as suppliers and customers.

The growth in the amount of data now available has been largely fuelled by increasing internet usage and by developments in communication methods such as wireless networks, social media sites and smartphones. An increasing number of organisations have embraced the so-called 'internet of things' by embedding sensor technologies, such as RFID tags (Radio Frequency Identification) and tracking devices, into their operations to gather data from a diverse range of activities. Companies including British Gas, an energy supplier in the UK, have introduced so-called smart meters as a way of measuring the amount of electricity consumers are using on a daily basis. Such meters also allow home owners to better manage their household energy costs as the meter records and wirelessly transmits the level of energy consumption back to the energy provider.

Leading data analytics software firm, SAS, offers the following explanation of big data and its importance for businesses.

'Big data is a term that describes the large volume of data – both structured and unstructured – that inundates a business on a day-to-day basis. But it's not the amount of data that's important. It's what organisations do with the data that matters. Big data can be analysed for insights that lead to better decisions and strategic business moves.'

(SAS, *big data – What it is and why it matters*. [Online] SAS. www.sas.com)

Data analytics concerns the ability to analyse large sets of data to reveal meaningful insights. As the definition outlined at the beginning of this section highlights, data analytics involves the discovery of patterns and trends which can be used by organisations when making decisions. Data analytics often involves the use of software and IT/IS infrastructures. Traditionally, the ability for most organisations to analyse such vast quantities of data was too prohibitive due to the cost and difficulties involved. This however is gradually changing as the use of increasingly cost-effective technologies such as cloud computing architectures and open source software become more readily available.

Nonetheless the possession of data analytics tools can be regarded as an important part of an organisation's strategic capability. As we shall explore here and also in Chapter 14, big data in a commercial setting is increasingly being used to identify trends that may exist in vast quantities of data in the pursuit of building a competitive advantage and value creation.

3.6.2 The Vs of big data

Doug Laney, an analyst with technology research firm Gartner, suggests that big data can be defined with reference to the three V's of volume, velocity and variety.

Volume

The vast quantities of data generated are a key feature of big data. Advances in technology and data analytics software have enabled very large data sets to be processed. This is helping organisations to gain a deeper understanding of customer requirements. For example, organisations can collect large amounts of external data about their customers from customers' use of the internet and social media. This data can now be combined with internally generated data for example, from customer loyalty cards or transactions recorded at shop tills, to build up a more detailed profile of the customer.

The volume aspect of big data has challenged the strategic capabilities of many organisations wishing to exploit its potential. Most notably, these have involved enhancing existing IT infrastructures through the use of cloud computing architectures so that they are capable of holding greater amounts of data.

Velocity

Velocity refers to the speed at which 'real time' data flows into the organisation and the speed at which the data is processed by the organisation's systems to produce a meaningful output. Many online retailers have developed capabilities which enable them to record the movements and 'clicks' made by a customer when using the organisation's website. As such, online retailers are now able to build up a better picture of those products and services the customer found most interesting as opposed to only recording the final sale transaction with the customer. Analysing the customers' clicks while still visiting the website has enabled online retailers to recommend relevant additional items for purchase based on those items already viewed. Online websites including Amazon and eBay use this tactic to encourage customers to make extra purchases.

Variety

Variety is concerned with the diverse range of forms that big data can take. An increasing amount of data generated comes in an unstructured form, ie, data which is not easy to hold in a database. Unstructured data may take the form of words used by people on social media sites such as Facebook and Twitter, along with shared content such as photographs or video recordings.

Capturing, processing and storing unstructured data presents further challenges to organisations which may need to develop their existing IT/IS capabilities to be able to firstly store such data and secondly extract meaning from the data they hold. Data which is too large, moves too fast or fails to fit neatly with existing IT infrastructures reduces the value which can be derived from it.

The three V's of big data can also be extended to include an additional characteristic: veracity.

Veracity

Veracity (value) is concerned with the truthfulness of the data collected. For data to have any value when being used for decision-making in an organisation, it needs to be truthful, ie, it must not present a bias or contain inconsistencies. The use of poor quality data may have expensive and far reaching consequences for those organisations which rely on it for making strategically important decisions. For example, an organisation may decide to introduce a type of product in the belief that there is sufficient customer demand for it, when in reality this may not be the case.

Worked example: Data and cloud computing

The growth in the amount of data generated today presents organisations with a choice: to set up their own data storage facilities on site or to adopt a cloud-based approach where data storage is handled remotely by a service provider.

An article written by Jessica Bown in 2016 highlights some of the benefits of cloud computing. Bown notes research by Temenos, a Swiss software company, which suggests that nearly 9 in 10 financial institutions run at least some business applications in the 'cloud'. The services being offered by cloud computing service providers, such as Amazon Web Services (AWS) and Google Cloud, are enabling new financial technology companies to create new businesses. Bown (2016) notes the rise of Norwegian technology company, Auka, which created 'the first mobile payments platform run entirely on Google Cloud. Meanwhile, customer relationship management specialist Salesforce now allows banks to offer personalised financial advice on any device'.

The drive towards the adoption of cloud computing in recent years is due in no small part to the flexibility and significant cost savings it offers. Setting up the required software to access the services provided by cloud service providers can take anywhere from a few days to a matter of minutes. This is considerably quicker than the time needed to establish an in-house IT facility.

It's not just the speed of establishing access to such services which is tempting users, it is also the ability for organisations to access their own real time data from pretty much anywhere in the world.

Furthermore, the creation of in-house IT infrastructures and data storage centres is highly expensive. Bown's article highlights comments made by Allan Brearley, Head of Transformation at Tesco Bank, 'when we evaluated the solutions for a new [web] page using our traditional on-premises delivery model, it was going to cost about £3,500 and take around three months to deliver. However, we evaluated the AWS option using exactly the same design solution and it cost £66 a month and took less than a week. We later realised we could just host these things as a static page costing 13p a month'.

Interestingly, it is not just financial institutions which are turning to the use of cloud-based services. An article by Suzanne Bearne in 2016, highlighted that a number of small businesses have also started to outsource business functions to cloud-based service providers. Bearne highlights the case of London-based wine retailer, Baacco, which has managed to attract customers in a number of European countries with the use of cloud-based tools.

Tai Alegbe co-founder of Baaco notes that 'analytical tools from companies like Mixpanel, Crazy Egg and Google Analytics combined with cloud-based infrastructures have been instrumental in helping Baacco grow overseas. They allow us to build, measure and learn about our customers far quicker than any other method.' Bearne (2016) notes that Baacco 'realised they had higher-than-usual drop-offs at the checkout from its French and Spanish consumers, they analysed the data provided by cloud-based tool Crazy Egg and learnt that they were being put off by the unfamiliar payment logos'.

Sources:

Bown, J. (2016) *Fast cash: The high-speed world of cloud-based finance*. [Online]. Available from: www.bbc.co.uk [Accessed 2 May 2017].

Bearne, S. (2016) *From wetsuits to wine: Small firms embrace the cloud*. [Online]. Available from: www.bbc.co.uk [Accessed 2 May 2017].

3.6.3 Practical considerations with big data

Before organisations introduce a big data programme there are a number of practical issues which should be considered. These include:

Will a big data programme give the organisation a competitive advantage? Does the organisation have the requisite capabilities to get the most from introducing a big data programme? Factors here might include:

(a) Are there workers within the organisation or in the job market with the required skills capable of analysing large data sets?

(b) Storing vast quantities of data places a greater emphasis on organisations having robust data security measures in place. Are these security measures in place or do they need to be developed? (The concept of cyber security is considered later in the Study Manual.)

(c) Does the organisation have the financial resources and time available to invest in or upgrade IT/IS?

(d) Furthermore, the issue of data ownership is likely to present challenges for organisations, ultimately who owns the data held? Does it belong to the organisation or customer?

In Chapter 14 we return to the topic of big data when we consider how it can help organisations to implement and monitor a strategy and assist in the creation of a competitive advantage.

Worked example: Big data, big considerations

An article by Matthew Wall entitled 'Big Data: Are you ready for blast-off?' published on the *BBC* website highlighted some interesting considerations in relation to the adoption of big data.

The article highlights that one of the biggest challenges when introducing big data concerns finding workers with the capabilities to get the most from the data an organisation may capture, Wall notes that 'big data needs new skills, but the business and academic worlds are playing catch up'.

Duncan Ross, director of data science at Teradata highlights that 'the job of the data scientist didn't exist five or 10 years ago'. As a result this has created a shortage of skills in the job market. Wall notes that 'many businesses are only just waking up to the realisation that data is a valuable asset that they need to protect and exploit.' This sentiment is supported Ralf Dreischmeier, head of the Boston Consulting Group's information technology practice, who noted 'banks only use a third of their available data because it often sits in databases that are hard to access. We need to find ways to make this data more easily accessible'.

However, as Dreischmeier notes this desire to access data presents further complications as both private and public sector organisations battle to 'keep sensitive data safe from hackers, spies and natural disasters – an increasingly tall order in this mobile, networked world'.

Questions have also been raised over who ultimately owns the data that organisations hold and who is responsible for keeping such data safe from hackers. Does it belong to the individual or customer, the company, the service provider hosting the data or the national jurisdiction where the data is held? Such questions are unlikely to go away in the short term, and, as Laurie Miles, head of analytics for SAS, highlights, it is a 'legal minefield'.

Source:

Wall, M. (2014) *Big Data: Are you ready for blast-off?*. [Online] . Available from: www.bbc.co.uk [Accessed 6 June 2016].

3.7 Developments in technology

It is important to recognise that big data and data analytics are just one of a number of technological developments which could have a significant impact on the strategic capabilities of organisations, and ultimately the ability of these organisations to realise their strategies. Ensuring that management considers an organisation's use of developing technologies will form an important element of the technology resource audit.

This section focuses on the following technological developments:

- Automation
- Intelligent systems
- Digital assets
- Cryptocurrency

3.7.1 Automation

Definition

Automation: 'the creation and application of technology to monitor and control the production and delivery of products and services'. (The International Society of Automation, 2018).

Technological advances have rapidly increased the ability for organisations of all sizes to automate activities which had historically been carried out by human workers. The concept of automation in business is not new, as many examples exist of machines having taken over the work traditionally carried out by human beings. The use of robots to complete a variety of pre-programmed production activities is today standard practice in many of the world's manufacturing industries. However, as the definition provided above highlights, the automation of business processes is not solely restricted to traditional manufacturing type businesses, and is now in widespread use in many service industries. In recent times, automation has become increasingly associated with the concept of intelligent systems, which enable computer systems to undertake evermore complex tasks.

3.7.2 Intelligent systems

Definition

Intelligent system: 'a computer-based system that can represent, reason about, and interpret data. In doing so it can learn about the structure of the data, analyse the data to extract patterns and meaning, derive new information, and identify strategies and behaviours to act on the results of its analysis'. (University College London, 2018).

An alternative definition is:

Definition

Intelligent systems: 'are technologically advanced machines that perceive and respond to the world around them.' (University of Nevada, 2018).

As both definitions above illustrate, intelligent systems in their broadest sense have the functionality to interpret some form of stimulus, and are then capable of responding in some fashion. Intelligent systems are closely associated with the concepts of Artificial Intelligence (AI) and Machine Learning. Although often used interchangeably, it is important to recognise that the terms AI and Machine Learning are in fact subtly different. Artificial Intelligence (AI) is concerned with creating advanced computer systems which have the ability to think for themselves, in much the same way that humans use their intelligence to weigh up information as the basis for determining appropriate actions. Machine Learning is focused on the science associated with getting computer systems to learn how to act without being specifically programmed to do so.

Automation, intelligent systems and strategy

It is important to recognise that a number of different automated and intelligent systems exist in different organisations and industries. In this section, some consideration is given to the types of systems commonly used, and the different ways they can help support organisations to achieve their strategies.

- Intelligent systems can operate robotic machinery at a far higher level of precision and accuracy than human beings, thereby reducing the rates of error in a production environment to almost zero. This allows organisations to reduce the costs of wasted, damaged materials in production, and to reduce the number of physical staff employed in production roles. Unlike human beings, automated intelligent systems can be used 24-hours a day, 7 days a week, thereby providing organisations with far greater flexibility than that offered by human workers, who are protected by health and safety and employment rights in many parts of the world.

- Companies including Apple and Amazon have made the use of intelligent system technologies a key part of their product development strategies. Apple's development of its personal assistant Siri, and Amazon's creation of its home hub, Alexa, use voice activated and internet technologies to undertake different user commands. Such technologies enable users to request information from the internet, schedule appointments, and send emails. Apple has integrated its Siri technology into a number of its hardware devices (including iPhones and iPads) as a means of keeping its product offering attractive to customers.

- Intelligent systems such as virtual assistants, sometimes referred to as 'chatbots' use Artificial Intelligence (AI) to undertake repetitive tasks, such as replying to frequently asked questions raised by an organisation's customers. A number of websites offer customers the opportunity to enter into conversational dialogue with a virtual assistant in real time, and the virtual assistant is capable of answering simple questions such as providing details about the company's products while the customer is shopping on the company's website. The use of virtual assistants in this way can help enhance the customer experience, as the need for customers to call a company's customer service centre is reduced, thereby increasing the likelihood that customers will make a purchase while online instead of switching to a competitor.

- Although, online shopping is not new, Amazon has automated this process further having introduced its 'dash button' technology, which aims to empower customers to make shopping easier. Amazon's dash button is a physical button which shoppers can use to order everyday items directly from their home without the need to visit the Amazon website. Each dash button is linked via the customer's home Wi-Fi connection to Amazon's ordering system for a particular product – when the button is pressed, an order for that product is automatically generated and issued to the customer's home address. The dash button is connected to the customer's Amazon account, which allows the user to specify the order quantity and type of product to be delivered. The system is designed to save the customer's time and reduces the scope for running out of regularly purchased items, provided the dash button is used prior to this point.

- A number of high profile business projects aimed at developing automated and intelligent systems technology are currently being undertaken. Online retailer Amazon undertook a trial project to assess the viability of using drone technology to deliver goods to customers' homes. This was part of the company's bid to enhance its supply chain strategy by reducing delivery costs and getting orders to customers more quickly. Another development, which could revolutionise the automobile industry, is the strategy being pursued by a number of technology firms to develop self-driving cars. Waymo which is owned by Alphabet, the owner of Google, is one of many companies (including Uber and Tesla) undertaking a project to develop a safe driver-less car which incorporates automated intelligent system technology. The advent of driver-less car technology is predicted to enable companies such as Waymo, to develop and deliver its own self-driven 'ride-hailing' strategy, to compete with traditional taxi firms.

Key considerations

To be able to make effective use of developing technologies such as automation and intelligent systems, organisations need to give careful consideration to a number of factors which may affect their ability to leverage the benefits offered:

- **Impact on human resources** – Often the rationale for using developing technologies is that it enables organisations to save the cost of employing staff to undertake lower-level, routine, repetitive tasks. Organisations need to carefully factor in the associated redundancy costs of replacing staff with automated intelligent systems. Replacing workers with new technologies also raises ethical considerations as to whether such strategies are fair. Negative perceptions of this among customers may cause reputation damage. A counter argument to these negative aspects is that the use of developing technologies will remove the need for human beings to undertake routine tasks, and should instead allow organisations to retain, and use these workers to perform more value-adding tasks, such as using their creativity to help improve organisational processes, products and services. This approach may require organisations to invest in human capital programmes to be able to more effectively utilise the workers at their disposal.

Worked example: Automation and Intelligent Systems

As the use of automated and intelligent systems gathers pace many workers are facing increasingly uncertain futures. Wall (2018) notes that 'software automation, informed by machine learning and artificial intelligence (AI), will have a profound effect on [...] workplaces and the jobs people currently do. Those workers under the greatest threat from the increasing use of intelligent systems are those in low-skilled, lower paid jobs, such as call centre workers. The need for call centre workers is diminishing as a greater number of the interactions that take place between an organisation and its customers are being performed by 'virtual assistants' known as 'chatbots'. Wall (2018) notes the words of Bernard Louvat, the general manager of digital customer engagement solutions at tech firm, Nuance, 'a virtual assistant can handle 60%-80% of all customer conversations now without any need for a human agent to intervene – five years ago it would have been 25%-30%. Chatbots are certainly eliminating jobs – we need fewer and fewer human agents each year. The ones that are left will be highly skilled super-agents looking after the most complicated cases'. Hudson (2017) highlights research from accountancy firm, PwC, which suggests that as many as 40% of jobs in the US, and 30% of jobs in the UK will be lost as a result of the widespread use of intelligent systems by 2030.

Whether this change materialises is open to much debate.

Sources:

Hudson, A. (10 May 2017) '40% of jobs' taken by robots by 2030 but AI companies say they're here to help. *Metro*. [Online]. Available from: http://metro.co.uk [Accessed 20 April 2018].

Wall, M. (2018) *Adapt or die: How to cope when the bots take your job*. [Online]. Available from: www.bbc.co.uk [Accessed 20 April 2018].

- **Costs** – The introduction of developing technologies will present organisations with a number of significant costs. Costs here will most likely include the associated costs of purchasing the physical hardware and software to be used, and the infrastructure needed to support the technology. In the case of smaller organisations, the costs of introducing developing technologies may in fact prove prohibitive. Careful consideration needs to be given to the associated costs of hiring in workers (either on a permanent or contract basis) to help the organisation develop the necessary infrastructure. The associated costs of training staff to use developing technologies, especially where automated robotic systems are integrated into human workspaces also need to be factored in.

- **Speed of change and competitive advantage** – Organisations need to carefully consider the rapid speed with which developing technologies evolve. Constant change increases the likelihood of technological obsolescence in relatively short time frames. As such, management need to consider the impact that updating developing technologies will have on an organisation's financial resources not only at the point of introduction but also into the longer term as system updates and upgrades are required. Consideration should also be given to the potential competitive advantage that organisations are likely to gain when introducing new technologies. The fact that the use of automated and intelligent systems is so widespread in certain industries raises doubts as to whether organisations adopting their use will be able to create a sustainable competitive advantage. Consideration also needs to be given to extent that organisations may suffer a competitive disadvantage by failing to introduce new technologies, as in time they may come to represent a threshold resource.

- **Impact on customers** – Organisations also need to consider the impact that the introduction of developing technologies will have on customers. For example, it is unlikely that all of a company's customers would want to engage with a 'chatbot' when visiting a website, with some still preferring to deal with a human being.

3.7.3 Digital assets

Definition

Digital assets: Assets which are held in digital form, that is to say assets which are not available in physical form. Common examples of digital assets include: PDF files, images, audio and video files.

The widespread use of computer systems around the world means that most organisations now hold at least some of their assets in digital form. Digital assets represent strategically important resources for most organisations as they are ultimately linked to an organisation's ability to deliver its selected strategy. As such, many organisations have moved to enhance their strategic capabilities in terms of how they manage their digital assets by implementing digital asset management (DAM) systems.

Most **digital asset management systems** are effectively a centralised, easy to use, repository in which different types of digital asset can be stored. Demand for digital asset management systems, especially among larger organisations, has been driven by the sheer volume of digital assets in existence which are held by different individuals, in different locations, across organisational networks. Common problems associated with this approach include: difficulties in finding digital assets (files, photos etc) on the network especially when required for use by more than one individual or department; digital assets getting lost; and issues around version control of digital assets saved on the network. Such occurrences hinder workforce productivity and ultimately the ability of organisations to utilise their digital assets in the realisation of their overall strategy.

Features of digital asset management systems

Digital asset management systems can support organisational strategies by ensuring that digital assets are easily accessible and available to use as required.

Common features of digital asset management systems:

- Digital assets are saved centrally to avoid the need for multiple network locations;

- Access rights can be set so that only individuals with appropriate authorisation can access and amend digital content;

- Digital assets can be saved according to their file type which is designed to support ease of use;

- A search function which allows users to search for digital assets in the event that the asset name cannot be recalled (ie the file name). Search functions allow the user to search for content using everyday language ie December's budget file 20X8;

- Many digital asset management systems are integrated with cloud-based technologies so that the organisation's digital assets can be securely stored and can be accessed around the world.

Worked example: Digital asset management in action

This example focuses on the key points included in an article written by ResourceSpace (2017), a provider of digital asset management systems.

ResourceSpace (2017) highlighted the benefits that digital asset management systems can bring international charities when designing marketing campaigns to support strategic objectives. The use of digital asset management systems:

- Helps charities with internationally dispersed operations to ensure consistency in the brand message they promote, as the same digital assets are available to all branches of the charity.

- Allows charity workers, wherever they are based in the world, to access key digital assets, for example, a powerful image captured for use in a marketing campaign.

- Provides users with instant access to digital assets. This functionality is likely to be critical when designing marketing content in response to major incidents. For example, to maximise support among donors during an unfolding humanitarian disaster.

- Means that less time and effort is needed when designing marketing campaigns as all digital assets are held centrally. This enables charity workers to spend more time on value-adding activities, such as supporting those in need.

Source: ResourceSpace (2017), *How can better Digital Asset Management help charities?* [Online]. Available from: www.resourcespace.com/blog/dam_for_charities [Accessed 23 April 2018].

Implementing a digital asset management strategy

The successful implementation of a digital asset management strategy requires the consideration of a number of practical issues, many of which are pertinent to an organisation's technology resource audit:

- **Infrastructure capabilities and storage needs** – management need to assess the organisation's current approach to the storage of digital assets in order to determine how best to configure and structure their digital asset management system. This is important in ensuring that it meets their needs.

- **Management support** – the introduction of a digital asset management system for most organisations will require senior management support, especially as the upheaval to existing work patterns is likely to be extensive during the implementation stage.

- **Selection of supplier** – organisations which have not previously used a digital asset management system need to take care to ensure that the supplier of the system is appropriate to the organisation's needs.

- **Project team** – given the strategic importance of many digital assets, the implementation of a digital asset management system should be overseen by a dedicated project team to ensure that any disruption caused by the implementation of the system is minimised.

3.7.4 Cryptocurrency

Definition

Cryptocurrency: A form of decentralised, digital currency, designed to facilitate the virtual exchange of transactions. Cryptocurrency is encrypted through the use of cryptography.

Cryptography is concerned with the creation of codes which are difficult to break. It is commonly used in computer science as a way of securing communications and information. In recent years cryptography has become associated with a form of digital money known as cryptocurrency.

Cryptocurrencies allow users to pay for items purchased online, and to receive payments in anonymity. Unlike traditional currencies, cryptocurrencies are not controlled by a central banking mechanism, and as such the value of cryptocurrencies has been known to fluctuate dramatically. This is due to market forces leading to changes in supply and demand for currency. Transactions using cryptocurrencies are recorded through a network of computers which collectively act to maintain a distributed ledger, known as a blockchain. Blockchain is effectively a public form of bookkeeping in which all transactions between participants in the network are logged and verified. (Blockchain is discussed in greater detail in Chapter 14.)

Units of cryptocurrency are generated through a process known as 'mining'. Cryptocurrency mining involves the use of computer mining software to add records of new transactions to the blockchain. 'Miners', being those individuals operating the software, are then rewarded with cryptocurrency in exchange for their efforts. It is important to note however, that cryptocurrencies can also be purchased from online brokers. A number of different types of cryptocurrency exist, however the best known cryptocurrency, is Bitcoin.

Worked example: Bitcoin

In April 2018 the Bitcoin website presented a short video titled '*What is Bitcoin?*'

Bitcoin allows users to enter into peer-to-peer transactions with one another without the need for an intermediary like a bank. This enables users of Bitcoin to enter into transactions with other parties potentially located in different parts of the world. Unlike traditional banking arrangements, users cannot have their bank accounts frozen. Bitcoins are stored in a 'digital wallet' which can be accessed via the user's computer or mobile device. (Bitcoin, 2018).

According to Bitcoin (2018) users can purchase anything using their Bitcoins.

Source: Bitcoin (2018), *What is Bitcoin?* [Online]. Available from: https://bitcoin.org/en/ [Accessed 23 April 2018].

In recent times a number of larger organisations have started to accept Bitcoin transactions as a form of payment. One of the most well-known, is the online travel agency, Expedia, which allows users to pay for hotel bookings using Bitcoin.

Factors for consideration

The widespread use of internet technologies around the world is likely increase the demand for cryptocurrencies, especially in those parts of the world where the majority of the population do not have access to conventional banking services. However, organisations interested in accepting cryptocurrencies, such as Bitcoin, as a form of payment for goods supplied need to give careful consideration to the following factors:

- **Impact on reputation** – the ability of users to anonymously send and receive cryptocurrencies around the world has caused concern in some quarters over the suitably of their use in business. Concerns have been raised that criminals have started to use Bitcoin and other cryptocurrencies as a means of transferring the proceeds of crime. Organisations considering accepting cryptocurrency payments therefore need to weigh up the negative connotations that this may bring and the potential for reputation damage.

- **Capabilities required** – an organisation's ability to accept cryptocurrencies will be dependent on having the appropriate infrastructure capabilities in place. The volatility in the value of many cryptocurrencies has led many organisations which accept cryptocurrency payments, to do so through the use of online intermediaries. Intermediaries such as BitPay enable an organisation's customers to pay for goods in Bitcoin, at a 'locked-in' exchange rate and then instantly convert the value of the Bitcoin into the organisation's preferred stable currency (for example, Euro, British Pound, or American Dollar), and deposit the funds into the organisation's bank account. As such intermediaries bear all of the risks in this relationship, organisations using their services are required to pay a settlement charge.

3.8 The need for integration

Resources considered on their own are inert. **Resources are of no value unless they are organised into systems**, and so a resource audit should go on to consider how well or how badly resources have been utilised, and whether the organisation's systems are **effective** and **efficient**.

Resource	Utilisation
Technical resources	For example, processes for new product development, ability to serve customers efficiently.
Managerial skills	An effective management is a key organisation resource in planning activities, controlling the organisation and motivating staff.

Resource	Utilisation
Organisation	Organisation structure is critical. For example product or brand divisionalisation or brand management should facilitate communication and decision-making, at the level of the brand.
Information and knowledge systems	These have a strategic role.

The organisation and transformation of resources to create value is covered in more detail in section 5, which looks at value chain analysis.

3.9 The 9Ms checklist of resources

The **9Ms model**, was introduced in your Business, Technology and Finance studies, it provides another way of summarising the resources and sources of competences to be evaluated:

- **Machinery**
- **Make-up**
- **Management**
- **Management information**
- **Markets**
- **Material**
- **Men and women**
- **Methods**
- **Money**

3.10 Limiting factors

Definition

Limiting factor: A factor which at any time, or over a period, may limit the activity of an entity, often occurring where there is shortage or difficulty of availability.

In the short term a business must make the best use of the resources available to it.

In the long-term, the company may wish to:

- Reduce the shortfall by obtaining more of the resource
- Economise on use by reconsidering the activities consuming the resource, eg, redesign a product to use less machine time

Worked example: Easing limiting factors in banks

Banks have shifted their business from reliance on providing accounts for money transmission and loans to a wider portfolio of products including pensions, home loans, credit cards, and insurances. This presented problems because the floor space of banks is limited, as are staff numbers and staff accommodation. The banks responded to these limiting factors by:

- Increasing the number of Automated Teller Machines (ATMs) both in branch and available for customers to access outside of branch opening hours, which dispense cash and account balances but also can be used to make deposits and pay bills.

- The provision of telephone and online banking services to reduce the volume of transactions taking place in the bank branches.

- Reducing the number of cashier places to make room for front-office cubicles housing financial advisers. The resulting queues encouraged customers to use the ATMs and online services.

- Recruitment of staff predominantly to sell financial service products.

4 Benchmarking competences

Section overview

- Benchmarking compares the use of assets across the firm or across the industry and indicates where they might be used better or where they are already a source of superior performance.

Once a business has identified its CSFs and core competences, it must identify performance standards which need to be achieved to outperform rivals and achieve SCA. These standards are sometimes called key performance indicators (KPIs).

One way of setting KPIs is to use benchmarking. Benchmarking is defined by the Chartered Institute of Management Accountants (CIMA) as: 'The establishment, through data gathering, of targets and comparators, through whose use relative levels of performance (and particularly areas of underperformance) can be identified. By the adoption of identified best practices it is hoped that performance will improve.'

To ensure a balanced and comprehensive range of performance measures are set, the Balanced Scorecard can be used.

4.1 Purposes of benchmarking

Benchmarking encourages improvement and change to achieve strategic competitive advantage over competitors, or at least to reduce costs and streamline operations.

4.2 Bases for benchmarking

Ensuring that you have an understanding of the different types of benchmarking covered in this section is very important. Benchmarking could easily appear in any of the three questions in the Business Strategy and Technology exam. Commenting on candidate performance in previous sittings, the examiner noted that many candidates struggle to gain the marks on offer when attempting requirements which required an understanding of the four bases of benchmarking outlined below.

Internal benchmarking

- Historical comparison looks at performance over time to ascertain trends/significant changes, etc, but the danger is that performance against competitors is ignored.

- Branch comparisons within the same organisation may help to identify best practice which can be implemented in all branches. Again, the danger is ignoring competitors.

Competitive benchmarking

This involves comparing performance with other firms in the same industry or sector. This may involve the use of league tables (eg, schools, hospitals, universities). The problem with industry norm comparisons is that the whole domestic industry may be performing badly (so international comparisons are better) or the whole international industry is losing out to other industries (so a wider perspective is needed – see below).

Activity (or best in class) benchmarking

Comparisons are made with best practice in whatever industry can be found. British Airways improved its aircraft maintenance, refuelling, turnaround, etc, by studying Formula One motor-racing pit teams.

Generic benchmarking

Benchmarking against a conceptually similar process. Again, Formula One was used by car manufacturers to help reduce changeover times on production lines.

Interactive question 1: Car seats

Yaz plc manufactures car seats for children. Yaz's home country, Z land, has extensive legislation on car safety for many years and child seats are compulsory. The company was formed 10 years ago by an entrepreneur who had previously worked as a technical consultant for an industrial foam company. Despite strong competition, Yaz plc has succeeded largely by careful marketing.

The car seats come in a range of sizes and there are a variety of options from fully integrated seats for very young babies to booster seats for older children. The company's main customer is an accessory manufacturer with a major presence in Yaz plc's home market. It buys the car seats from Yaz plc and sells them under its own brand as 'safety approved'. It advertises the car seats in accessory brochures and on its website. The company's second major customer is a large superstore in the home country which specialises in children's clothing and accessories such as prams and pushchairs. The remaining sales are to a varied mix of large and small mainly independent car accessory retailers.

The car seats have historically all been produced on a single site in the north of the home country. The Managing Director uses his connections to source the foam padding from several suppliers with a commitment to achieving the lowest price but complying with safety standards and expectations. Z land has sophisticated economy with efficient capital markets; JIT logistics are common in all forms of manufacturing.

The company is considering possible methods of expansion and is currently considering exports to neighbouring countries.

Requirements

1.1 Explain how conditions in Z land could give Yaz plc a competitive advantage when it starts its export operations.

1.2 The Managing Director of Yaz plc is constantly trying to improve the productivity and quality of his manufacturing operations and is considering a programme of benchmarking. Explain why a benchmarking programme would help Yaz plc and suggest how it might be carried out.

See **Answer** at the end of this chapter.

5 Transforming resources: the value chain

Section overview

- Porter's value chain encourages management to perceive of the business as a sequence of activities that add value to inputs so that the final good or service shall command a profitable price on the market. This model was introduced in Business, Technology and Finance, and, is recapped here.

- The crucial activities that sustain competitive advantage are called cost drivers and value drivers.

- Competitive advantage can be created and sustained by linkages in the value chain which help to co-ordinate and optimise activities.

- Extending the value chain to an underlying value system of suppliers, distributors and customers makes it hard for competitors to replicate.

5.1 Recap of Porter's value chain model

Definition

Value chain: the sequence of business activities by which value is added to the products or services produced by an entity.

In overview, value chain analysis sees the firm as an input/output device.

The value chain consists of the organisation's resources, activities and processes that link the business together, and the profit margin. Together these create the total value of output produced by the business, quantified by the price paid by the customer.

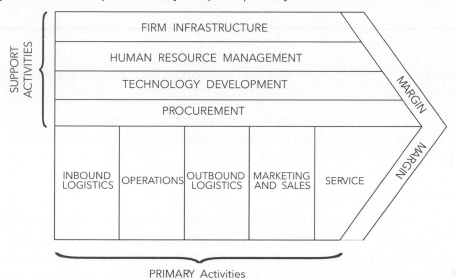

Porter's Value Chain model, (source: Porter, *Competitive Advantage*)

The **margin** is the excess the customer is prepared to **pay** over the **cost** to the firm of obtaining the necessary resource inputs and of performing value-creating activities upon them before selling them to the customer.

5.2 Value chain activities

Primary activities relate to production, sales, marketing, delivery and service, in other words anything directly relating to the process of converting resource inputs into outputs.

Activity	Comment
Inbound logistics	Receiving, handling and storing inputs to the production system (ie, warehousing, transport, stock control etc).
Operations	Convert resource inputs into a final product or service. Resource inputs are not only materials. 'People' are a 'resource', especially in service industries.
Outbound logistics	Storing the product and its distribution to customers: packaging, warehousing etc.

Activity	Comment
Marketing and sales	Informing customers about the product, persuading them to buy it, and enabling them to do so: advertising, promotion etc.
After sales service	Installing products, repairing them, upgrading them, providing spare parts, advice (eg, helplines for software support).

Support activities provide purchased inputs, human resources, technology and infrastructural functions to support the primary activities. Each provides support to all stages in the primary activities. For instance procurement where at each stage items are acquired to aid the primary functions. At the inbound logistics stage it may well be raw materials, but at the production stage capital equipment will be acquired, and so on.

Activity	Comment
Procurement	Acquire the resource inputs to the primary activities (eg, purchase of materials, subcomponents, equipment).
Technology development	Product design, improving processes and/or resource utilisation.
Human resource management	Recruiting, training, developing and rewarding people.
Management planning and firm infrastructure	Planning, finance, and quality control: these are crucially important to an organisation's strategic capability in all primary activities.

Worked example: Maple plc

Maple plc is a manufacturer and online retailer of bespoke furniture designed entirely to the consumer's specification. The furniture is made using high quality materials and skilled craftsmen to produce exquisite one-off items of furniture. Their furniture is considered a high added-value product that sells at a high price. Significant advertising supports the brand image of the product. Every element of the supply to the customer is controlled by Maple as the company manufactures, sells and delivers the furniture directly to the consumer.

An outstanding level of after-sales service is also provided as each piece of furniture is sold with a 10-year guarantee, two years interest free credit, optional treatments to prevent stains or damage and optional furniture cleaning services. Customer satisfaction is a key value of the company and a strict approach is taken to discipline in relation to customer complaints.

The staff are all either skilled or semi-skilled and the company runs a highly respected training programme to ensure they continue to develop their skills. The production machinery has recently been upgraded to the highest standard following a tendering exercise from equipment suppliers.

Inventory is well controlled and the strong links with the suppliers via integrated systems allows the correct materials to be automatically ordered when an order from a customer is confirmed. Strong IT systems also support the finance and marketing functions of Maple.

The company operates online, with no physical presence, which allows it to offer a wide range of choice to the customer allowing them to select different elements and 'build' their furniture to their own specifications. Once complete, delivery is made using their own vans and the furniture is carefully installed by experienced staff.

Requirement

Draw the value chain for Maple plc

Solution

Firm Infrastructure	Profit-orientated culture, tight financial control				
Technology Development	IT ordering systems, inventory control, payables management		Delivery IT systems		IT credit arrangement systems
Human Resource Management	Training HO supply staff generally and in IT system	Manufacturing skills training, working practices	Delivery IT systems training	Discipline relating to customer issues	Training of delivery/ Installation staff
Procurement	Managing supplier relationships, payables management	Tendering system for new equipment, significant financing support		Marketing department	Financing and administration of customer credit facilities
Primary activities	Optimal delivery, sourcing high quality materials	Latest equipment, prime site factory, skilled labour	Prime sites for shops, delivery to customers	Installation for customers, advertising	Optional cleaning service, 10-year guarantee
	Inbound Logistics	Operations	Outbound Logistics	Marketing and Sales	Service

MARGIN

MARGIN

In the Business Strategy and Technology exam, you will not be required to draw diagrams consisting of specific shapes such as the one shown above which is in an arrow like form. You may however be required to present your value chain answer in a tabular or columnar format using the exam software provided.

5.3   Cost and value drivers

Cost drivers

Using the value chain as a basic analysis tool, it is possible to look at each of the value activities and identify the major influences on the costs incurred. These structural factors which influence cost are the cost drivers. For example supermarkets regard the diversity of products (food, clothes, spirits, audio, etc,) stocked as cost drivers because for each additional product line stocked the supermarket incurs the costs of logistics, stocking, stacking, programming electronic point of sale systems (EPOS), product training and promotion costs.

The factors which influence the cost of a given activity may vary, even between competitors in the same industry. An understanding of cost behaviour will allow a firm to assess the possibilities of adopting a least cost competitive stance.

Value drivers

Unlike cost drivers, the potential sources of value are likely to be many and varied. An understanding of the value drivers for a particular key value activity is essential for a firm trying to differentiate itself from its competitors.

For example, if competitive advantage centres on the durability of a product, then this can be supported by the sourcing of components, product design and maintenance services offered (the key value activities). In turn the value drivers for these support activities might be supplier vetting and approval procedures, the use of freelance designers and in-house after-sales service teams.

5.4 Linkages

One of the key aspects of VCA is that it recognises that the firm's resources are not a random collection but are organised in such a way that the firm's products or services are valued by its customers.

Activities in the value chain affect one another. **Linkages** connect the activities in the value chain. They have two roles.

- They **optimise activities** by enabling trade-offs. For example, more costly product design or better quality production might reduce the need for after sales service.

- Linkages reflect the need to **co-ordinate** activities. For example, Just In Time (JIT) requires smooth functioning of operations, outbound logistics and service activities such as installation.

These linkages are often unrecognised, especially if there is a rigid functional structure. A value chain analysis can help draw them to management's attention and so improve business performance. Increasingly linkages between activities are achieved through the use of IT/IS system applications. For example, in respect of procurement activities organisations now use EDI (electronic data interchange) as a way of placing orders with suppliers. Internet technologies can reduce production times and costs by improving information flows as a way of integrating value chain activities, eg, by making procurement more efficient or sharing demand information with suppliers.

In respect of human resource management linkages between staff in different departments is increasingly being achieved through the use of self-service portals for employees to book holiday or make training requests. In terms of primary activities, the use of robots and 3D printing are creating stronger ties between product design activities and production activities. Furthermore, linkages between operational activities and outbound logistics are now increasingly supported through the use of RFID technology, which can track the progress of goods from pick-up at the warehouse to delivery to the end customer, all of which should help improve organisational performance.

5.5 The value system

A firm's value chain is connected to what Porter calls a **value system**, ie, activities that add value that extend beyond the organisation's **boundaries**.

For example, when a restaurant serves a meal, the quality of the ingredients – although the cook chooses them – is partly determined by the grower. The grower has added value, and the grower's success in growing produce of good quality is as important to the customer's ultimate satisfaction as the skills of the chef.

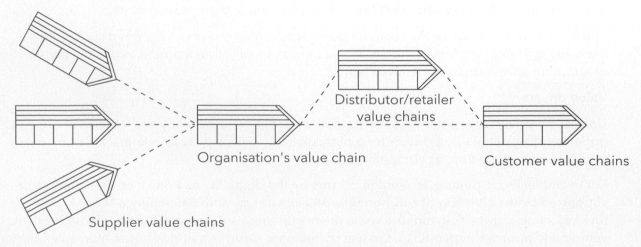

Supplier value chains

Organisation's value chain

Distributor/retailer value chains

Customer value chains

5.6 The value chain and competitive advantage

Competitive advantage can be **sustained by linkages** in the value chain and also in the wider **value system** of suppliers, distributors and customers. The planning of these linkages can provide the basis for cost advantages or become the basis on which the firm's products are differentiated from those of competitors. **Competitors can often replicate parts of a value chain but it is more difficult to copy linkages**. As businesses outsource more and more activities, the links in the value system become more important. Electronic communications enhance the ability of businesses to outsource.

5.7 Use in strategic planning

The principal use of the value chain is to assist in understanding the business and its strengths and weaknesses, as a form of position analysis. However, the value chain can be used specifically to:

- Identify strategically significant activities (the value activities) as an aid to targeting capital investment.

- Compare with the value chains of competitors, to identify sources of differentiation.

- Identify opportunities for synergy between the firm and a potential acquisition, for example opportunities to transfer skills or share activities.

The value system highlights the relationship between a firm and its customers and suppliers.

- This will assist managers in identifying competitive forces in the system, and targeting potential vertical integration prospects.

- Management of these wider linkages can make it more difficult for competitors to replicate the organisation's value chain and hence contributes to sustainable competitive advantage.

Interactive question 2: Hairdressers

Xena Ltd is a chain of hairdressers with 14 sites operating in the business districts of the capital and three other major cities. It has a very simple philosophy – quality haircuts for women who are short of time. It operates a no appointment, drop-in system. Customers take a ticket on arrival and wait in a large comfortable seating area until their numbers are called. All staff are multi-skilled and there are no specialists. The company aims to keep waiting times below 15 minutes.

The salons offer a wide range of services from very simple cuts to more complex styles and treatments. In 50% of their stores Xena Ltd also offers beauty treatments, such as facials, in a separate salon on site. The company's main publicity comes from personal recommendation by satisfied customers, but they also occasionally advertise in high quality women's magazines.

After a recent period of expansion, the management team of Xena Ltd feel that their business model is not being applied consistently throughout the organisation and they have decided improvements and adjustments need to be made. However, none of the management team knows how to relate their philosophy to their operations to the best effect.

Requirements

2.1 Using the concept of the value chain, explain how Xena Ltd can adopt the quality and speed approach throughout its activities.

2.2 What are the benefits and problems of value chain analysis for a company such as Xena Ltd?

See **Answer** at the end of this chapter.

6 Outsourcing and shared service centres

Section overview

- Outsourcing is the use of an external supplier as a source of components, products or services previously provided in-house.

- The practice of **outsourcing** may be used to strengthen an organisation's value chain.

- **Shared service centres** provide an alternative to outsourcing.

6.1 Outsourcing

Definition

Outsourcing: The strategic use of outside resources to perform activities traditionally handled by internal staff and resources. (*thebalance.com*).

With the help of technology and telecommunications it is now possible for **one service provider** to devise a common process to deal with those activities common to **many different organisations in a single location**.

In addition to cost considerations, management may take the view that a chain is only as strong as its weakest link and therefore supply chains can be strengthened by outsourcing weak links to more competent providers.

Interactive question 3: Outsourcing and core competences

3.1 Should a core competence ever be outsourced?

See **Answer** at the end of this chapter.

The issues to be considered in deciding **whether to outsource** include:

- The firm's **competence** in carrying out the activity itself. Low competence implies high cost and risk of poor performance.

- Whether **risk** can be managed better by outsourcing, eg, shift legal liability to the provider and possibly also levy charges for breakdowns in performance that will mitigate losses.

- Whether the activity can be **assured and controlled** by the framework of a contract and performance measures, eg, outsourcing payroll can normally be done relatively easily but systems development is more open-ended.

- Whether **organisational learning and intellectual property** is being transferred. The in-house operation may be a source of significant learning leading to product and process improvement. This is one reason that in the early stages of the international production life cycle (Chapter 4) firms keep manufacturing in-house rather than outsource to cheaper contract manufacturers.

The issues to consider in deciding **whom to outsource to** include:

- The **track record** of the provider and its experience of similar partnerships.

- The **quality of relationship** on offer, eg, will they place staff at your premises, hold regular meetings, provide open-book accounts?

- The **strategic goals** of the provider, eg, is this their core business, will they operate globally alongside the firm?

- The **economic cost** of using them (including whether they will take staff over and pay for transferred assets).

- Their **financial stability.**

Worked example: Airlines and outsourcing

The following case explores how major airlines have embraced outsourcing.

'No frills' airlines have focused for a number of years on keeping costs low. Warwick Brady, the then Chief Operations Officer at easyJet, noted 'we outsource everything that we can outsource…as long as we can manage it and control it, it gets outsourced'. Wild notes an estimate by KPMG which suggests the value of outsourced services provided to airlines (excluding back-office functions) is €200bn globally. At easyJet only staff working in core functions (such as the crew and pilots) are employed by the airline, 'with services such as passenger helplines and crew rosters outsourced to specialists in Montreal and Krakow respectively'.

Other established airlines have also taken to outsourcing operations. German carrier Lufthansa has outsourced the maintenance and support of its ticketing and booking system, while US airline Delta Air Lines signed a deal in January 2014 with Gate Gourmet to increase the range of services the catering firm provides.

Source:

Wild, J. (21 April 2014) Airlines turn to outsourcing to keep lid on costs. *Financial Times*. [Online] Available from: www.ft.com [Accessed 6 June 2016].

Interactive question 4: Outsourcing R&D

4.1 Give two advantages and two disadvantages of a computer software company outsourcing its research and development.

See **Answer** at the end of this chapter.

6.2 Shared service centres

Definition

Shared service centre: a number of internal transaction processing activities which had previously been conducted in a number of different departments, or business units, are brought together into one site within an organisation.

Shared service centres provide large organisations with an alternative to outsourcing activities. Any organisational activity can be consolidated into a shared service centre. However, activities commonly performed through shared service centres include: purchasing, human resource management, payroll and finance. Organisations that have established shared service centres have tended to do so to in order to realise their overall strategy, which in the case of most commercial entities is often driven by the objective of reducing costs in order to generate improved profits. The use of standardised technologies and service level agreements have been key enablers of shared servicing.

Worked example: NHS Shared Business Services

NHS Shared Business Services (NHS SBS) is a joint venture established between private consulting firm, Sopra Steria and the Department of Health. The arrangement was established in 2005 with the aim of reducing business service costs incurred by the NHS. The NHS SBS offers a number of finance and accounting support services including payroll, general ledger processing and compliance reporting. Over 35% of NHS organisations use the services provided. The NHS SBS website claims to have delivered audited savings of £400 million to date. (NHS Shared Business Services, 2018).

Source:

NHS Shared Business Services (2018) *About Us*. [Online]. Available from: https://www.sbs.nhs.uk/nhs-sbs-about-us [Accessed 3 July 2018].

Shared service centres present organisations with a number of advantages and disadvantages.

Advantages

- **Cost savings** from reduced headcount and the realisation of the associated economies of scale resulting from operating from a single location.

- **Knowledge** between those based in the shared service centre can be more easily shared than when activities were embedded in different parts of the organisation. For example, a company has just created a new shared service centre to provide payroll services to the entire organisation. The new centre has brought together six payroll teams each of which had previously been responsible for providing payroll services to one of the organisation's departments. By consolidating the payroll teams in this way members of the new shared service centre can more easily share their knowledge of best practice in payroll processing.

- The use of **standard processes** by shared service centres ensures that all departments or business units in receipt of these services are treated consistently.

Disadvantages

- Department or business **specific knowledge may be lost**. For example, the creation of a shared service centre to manage all of an organisation's finance matters may not be able to provide financial information to an individual department with the same degree of insight than would be the case if the finance team were integrated within that department.

- Closely connected to the previous point is that staff based in shared service centres are often **removed from the day-to-day realities** facing the departments or business units that they serve. This diminishes the value that they might be able to add to the departments.

- The physical distance between the shared service centre and the business areas that it serves may **weaken the relationships** that exist between the two.

7 Supply chain management

Section overview

- Supply chain management (SCM) is the management process, often assisted at the operational level by high power IT applications, of synchronising the networks in the service of the final customer.

7.1 What is supply chain management?

Definition

Supply chain management (SCM): The management of all supply activities from the suppliers to a business through to delivery to customers.

This may also be called **demand chain management** (reflecting the idea that the customers' requirements and downstream orders should drive activity) or **end-to-end business** (e2e). In essence it refers to managing the value system.

The main themes in SCM are:

- **Responsiveness** – the ability to supply customers quickly. This has led to the development of Just In Time (JIT) systems to keep raw materials acquisition, production and distribution as flexible as possible.

- **Reliability** – the ability to supply customers reliably.

- **Relationships** – the use of single sourcing and long-term contracts better to integrate the buyer and supplier.

7.2 Technology and SCM

Technology is vital to SCM, given the vast flow of information between suppliers, customer and intermediaries.

Technology applications which have facilitated SCM include:

- Email

- Web-based ordering and tracking. This involves outsiders seeing some management information on an extranet.

- Electronic data interchange (EDI) of invoices and payments, ordering and sharing of inventory information.

- Satellite systems able to track positions of trucks.

- Radio data tags fixed to pallets or boxes of valuable items to enable them to be located in the supply chain (including within a warehouse).

This has led to:

- Reductions in costs

- Better outsourcing opportunities

- Increased product and service innovation

- Mass-customisation of products: ie, customised products made by mass production methods, eg, Dell computers, superior car marques.

7.3 Supply chain networks

Supply chain management involves optimising the activities of companies working together to produce goods and services. It can involve the following:

- Closer **partnership** relationships with a **reduced number of suppliers.**

- **Reduction in customers served**: For the sake of focus, companies might concentrate resources on customers of high potential value.

- **Price and stock co-ordination**: Firms co-ordinate their price and stock policies to avoid problems and bottlenecks caused by short-term surges in demand, such as promotions.

- **Linked computer systems**: Electronic data interchange and use of intranets saves on paperwork and warehousing expense.

- **Early supplier involvement** in product development and component design.

- **Logistics design**: A major technology firm restructured its distribution system by enabling certain product components to be added at the distribution warehouse rather than at the central factory, for example user-manuals which are specific to the market (ie, user manuals in French would be added at the French distribution centre).

- **Joint problem solving** among supply chain partners.

- **Supplier representative on site**.

The aim is to co-ordinate the whole chain, from raw material suppliers to end customers. The chain should be considered as a **network** rather than a **pipeline** – a network of vendors support a network of customers, with third parties such as transport firms helping to link the companies.

Worked example: KFC's supply chain problems

In late February 2018, fast-food chain, KFC, made news headlines for the wrong reasons when a number of its outlets ran out of fresh chicken. Problems with the company's supply chain forced the majority of its UK outlets to close for a number of days. The closures were all the more embarrassing for KFC, as the company had only days before changed to a new logistics supplier, responsible for handling its nationwide chicken deliveries. The BBC (2018) reported that 'until 13 February, all of KFC's chicken was delivered by Bidvest. But after the contract switched to DHL […] many of the food giant's outlets began running out of chicken products'. (BBC, 2018).

According to Weaver (2018), DHL blamed the disruption caused on its use of a cold storage warehouse, located in Rugby, which had not been registered with the local council to be used as a fresh food store. The registration required to operate the warehouse was subsequently granted by Rugby Borough Council within days of the disruption starting. Speaking at the time a KFC spokesperson explained that some of the poultry at the depot would have be destroyed, amid food safety concerns (Weaver, 2018).

In early March 2018 it was reported that KFC had entered into a contract to return some of its chicken delivery operations to its previous supplier, Bidvest. The highly publicised move resulted in Bidvest signing 'a new agreement with KFC UK & Ireland to supply up to 350 of its 900 restaurants' (BBC, 2018).

Sources:

BBC (2018) *KFC in partial return to ex-distributor Bidvest*. [Online]. Available from: www.bbc.co.uk [Accessed 25 April 2018].

Weaver, M. (21 February 2018) Hundreds of KFC shops closed as storage depot awaits registration. *The Guardian*. [Online]. Available from: www.theguardian.com [Accessed 25 April 2018].

7.4 Supply chain management and cyber security

In Chapter 14 we explore the increasing need for organisations to have in place robust measures to reduce the threats facing IT/IS infrastructures.

7.4.1 Importance of cyber security in supply chain management

The desire to protect systems from external third parties, such as hackers, intent on stealing corporate data is well documented, however, the increasing use of IT systems in linking together the organisation's information systems with those systems of its suppliers is now presenting new challenges. As a result, the issue of cyber security in the supply chain has risen up the agenda in recent years. Linking the organisation's supply chain systems with those of its suppliers represents the opening up of another point of entry for undesirable third parties.

7.4.2 Consequences of poor IT security

The case of US retailer Target which had its IT infrastructure compromised by hackers in 2013 was believed to have been caused in part by the failings in the IT systems of one its air-conditioning suppliers. Hackers were able to gain access to Target's billing system by infiltrating the supplier's IT infrastructure which was linked to Target's own IT systems.

7.4.3 ICAEW's 2015 Audit insights: cyber security report

ICAEW's 2015 *Audit insights: cyber security* report highlights that organisations need to change their focus in respect of how they manage the supply chain. Organisations need to prioritise and target supply chain assurance activities around those areas which represent the greatest risk. The report highlights that the growing threat posed by cyber risks represents a significant opportunity to make positive changes to the way in which the supply chain is managed. The following extract from the report raises some interesting considerations:

> Traditional approaches to supply chain risk, for example, prioritise the suppliers associated with the highest value spend. While this may be appropriate for many types of risk management, it is unsuitable for cyber risk management. Instead the key selection criteria should relate to access to critical data or systems. A company dealing with records management, for example, might have a relatively small spend associated with it, but expose the business to high levels of cyber risk.

> Efforts also typically focus on procurement processes, for example requiring compliance with specific standards to tender for work or requiring bidders to complete questionnaires about their practices as part of the bidding process. Less attention is paid to ongoing assurance processes. However, it is crucial for businesses to gain assurance through the life cycle of contacts. Otherwise there will be no way to check that suppliers are doing as they promised through the bidding process or to review the risks if the environment changes.

The report also highlights that as the approach adopted by businesses in managing their supply chains continues to evolve, organisations should be increasingly prepared to answer questions about the cyber security measures that they have in place. These questions are likely to come from potential customers or clients wishing to gain some assurance over how their own systems and data will be protected.

In Chapter 14 further consideration is given to the practical measures that organisations can take to reduce the cyber risks they may encounter. Chapter 9 considers the role of the board of directors in managing cyber risks.

8 Networks, relationships and architecture

Section overview

- Network analysis recognises that businesses are frequently webs of networks between internal departments and also with outside contractors, customers, and suppliers.

- This gives rise to the importance of understanding the relationships between the partners and the value of **relational contracts** based on trust and commitment to replace **transactional contracts** in which each side tries to get the greatest gain for itself.

- The virtual firm is introduced and a modern organisational structure which replaces vertically integrated businesses with a high reliance on networks.

8.1 What do we mean by architecture?

The concept of the **value system** suggests a variety of interrelationships between different businesses. We shall now explore the nature of some of these relationships.

Definition

Network architecture: the network of relational **contracts**, within or around, the firm.

A **relational contract** contains parties doing business with each other in a long term relationship. Its provisions are only partly specified but it is enforced not by legal process but by the needs the parties have to go on doing business with each other (as opposed to a **spot contract** which is a one-off transaction).

These **relational contracts** may have a **legal basis**, but also include a **pattern of expectations** that the parties have of each other.

Firms may establish these relationships in two ways, internally and externally.

Internal networks ...with and among their employees (internal architecture)	Organisation structure and culture; job descriptions and work patterns to encourage development; employment contracts (eg, employer commitment vs 'short term hire'); remuneration structure to encourage 'loyalty', 'creativity' and a willingness to satisfy individual preferences for the collective's benefit.
External networks ...with their suppliers or customers (external architecture) among firms engaged in related activities (Kay, 1993)	Relationships with suppliers – eg, long-term supply contracts, detailed design specifications – firms share knowledge and establish fast response times on the basis of relational contracts. Networks are **groups** of firms making relational contracts with each other, who need to do business together in the long term, and who arguably depend on a common skills base.

The type of network relationship can range from the **collaborative** (founded **on commitment and trust**) to mainly **transactional** (just a buy-sell relationship). A **collaborative** network involves a great deal of co-operation, which may be enshrined in joint venture agreements. In a **transactional relationship**, there is no commitment to the long term.

Drivers of collaboration strategies that result in network arrangements can be characterised as follows:

- **Blurring of market boundaries**: Eg, convergence of telecommunications and computing. This increases the complexity of technologies.

- **Escalating customer diversity**: Customers are becoming more demanding. In global markets, customers are more diverse almost by definition.

- **Skills and resource gaps**: Firms need to collaborate in technologically demanding markets.

Definition

Asset specificity: Where investments are made to support the relationship which have the effect of locking parties into a relationship to some degree.

An example is the investment by the Anglo-French company Eurotunnel in an undersea rail link that locks Eurotunnel into partnerships with the rail operators using it from either end, (ie, Eurostar and SNCF). Both sides required long-term contracts before they would make the commitments necessary.

If a firm makes a **relationship-specific investment,** this implies that it would not make sense to make the investment **outside** the business relationship (eg, if the component was so specialised no-one else would buy it).

8.2 Types of external network

The **relationship** between firms in a network can be close or distant, and we can model them as follows.

Distant   Outsourcing – purchase of goods/services

Partnership – co-ordinated/integrated activities

Alliance – joint ventures: shared ownership

Close   Ownership – for example, vertical integration

Definitions

Alliance: An agreement between firms to share a commercial opportunity characterised by each member of the alliance retaining autonomy and pursuing its own commercial interests.

Partnership: Joint participation between two or more organisations in the serving of a market or project, characterised by the close interrelationship of operations, exchange of staff and mutual trust and commitment to working with the other(s).

In many industries, collaborative ventures and strategic alliances are becoming increasingly common. They can be very complex.

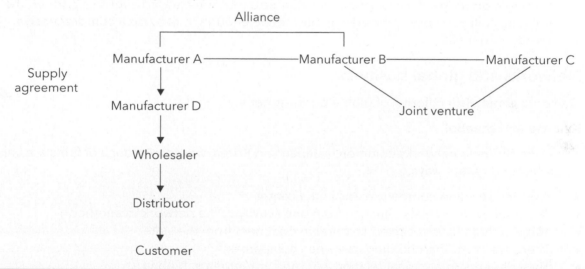

Networks display **horizontal** (eg, joint ventures) and **vertical** (supply chain) linkages.

8.3 Choosing alliance partners

Firms enter long-term **strategic alliances** with others for a variety of reasons.

* They share development costs of a particular technology.
* The regulatory environment prohibits take-overs eg, most major airlines are in strategic alliances because in most countries there are limits to the level of control an 'outsider' can have over an airline.
* Complementary markets or technology.

Strategic alliances only go so far, as there may be disputes over control of strategic assets.

Choosing alliance partners

The following factors should be considered in choosing alliance partners.

Drivers	What benefits are offered by collaboration?
Partners	Which partners should be chosen?
Facilitators	Does the external environment favour a partnership? Relevant factors here would include the availability of suitable providers, legal environment that does not outlaw collaboration as anti-competitive, and high investment costs involved in establishing provision that could not be borne by a single user of the service.
Components	Activities and processes required by the network. What will the alliance partner contribute?
Effectiveness	Does the previous history of alliances generate good results? Is the alliance just a temporary blip? For example, in the airline industry, there are many strategic alliances, but these arise, in part, because there are legal barriers to cross-border ownership.
Market-orientation	Alliance partners are harder to control and may not have the same commitment to the end-user.

Alliances have limitations

1. **Core competence**: Each organisation should be able to focus on its core competence. Alliances do not enable it to create new competences.

2. **Strategic priorities**: If a key aspect of strategic delivery is handed over to a partner, the firm loses flexibility. A core competence may not be enough to provide a comprehensive customer benefit.

8.4 Networks and global business

There are some distinct forms of global business network.

Keiretsu and chaebol

These are business networks common in Japan and Korea, whereby groups of firms are linked in a number of different ways.

- A general trading company exists at the centre
- A central bank circulates finance from one activity of the network to another
- Many of them have received favourable treatment from the state
- There are cross shareholdings between companies
- They depend on personal relationships and agreements: high trust

In both countries, such firms have made high investments and typically result in conglomerate diversification. This business model has come under attack, as a number of chaebol have collapsed recently.

Family networks

Networks based on family structures are common in businesses run by overseas Chinese according to Dicken (*Global Shift*). The family – a relatively small group of insiders – is key to decision making, and operates on the following principles.

- The purposes of the firm is 'the long-term interest on family prosperity'
- Risks must be hedged to protect family assets.
- Key decision makers exist in an inner circle.
- Such firms do not trust non-family members.
- Personal obligations cement and reinforce non-contractual business relationships.

The network is exclusive, but family loyalties mean effective business co-ordination in many countries.

Networks and globalisation

Networks and relationships on any number of levels may be suitable for global businesses. When these are linked to the type of geographic cluster identified in Chapter 4 there is the potential for considerable complexity.

8.5 The virtual firm

An extreme example of networking is the so-called **virtual firm**. It is created out of **a network of alliances and subcontracting arrangements**. It is as if most of the activities in a particular **value chain** are conducted by different firms, even though the process is loosely co-ordinated.

9 The product-service portfolio

Section overview

- Firms with multiple products (eg, consumer goods firms like Heinz) or multiple business units (eg, GE) are said to be managing a portfolio of businesses in the same way as a fund manager might manage a portfolio of stocks and shares.

- The Boston Consulting Group matrix (BCG matrix) is a technique to assist management to visualise their portfolio and to manage it to improve the financial performance of the corporation as a whole. The BCG matrix was introduced in Business, Technology and Finance, and is recapped in this section.

- Treating businesses as investment portfolios was popular in USA and Europe in the 1960s and 1970s but has declined in favour since, with the search for core competences and core businesses. This has led to a re-evaluation of the concept of portfolio analysis.

9.1 The need for a mix of products and services

Many businesses sell more than one type of product or service. For example:

- Accounting firms sell audit services, tax advisory services, accounting services and so on.

- Consumer goods companies such as Procter and Gamble sell a mix of products such as soap powder, children's nappies, cosmetics, drinks, dental hygiene products and shaving products (amongst many others).

These are sold in different markets because of technological and social change, the influence of competition, the demands of shareholders that their investments grow and so on.

The product life cycle and BCG models (to be discussed shortly) can help assess the balance of a product portfolio.

Worked example: Apple and portfolio management

American technology giant Apple, maker of the iPhone, iWatch, and iPad actively manages its product portfolio to keep ahead of the competition. Dou (2014) reported that the company had taken to hiring engineers from competing technology companies, including HTC. Apple's recruitment drive has been largely driven by the need to produce new products faster in response to demand for the latest devices. In recent years the lifecycle of many of Apple's products has reduced as competitors including Samsung have been increasing the speed at which they develop their own range of mobile devices (Dou, 2014). To date, Apple has taken to releasing a new iPhone mobile phone nearly every year to replace older models which are nearing the end of their lifecycle.

Apple has also stepped up its recruitment efforts to attract workers with knowledge of developing technologies, as the company has started to post job adverts for specialists with Artificial Intelligence (AI) expertise. Love (2015) reported that Apple's on-going recruitment drive is part of the company's push to challenge Google in the field of internet searches. Apple is keen to develop smartphone features capable of giving users what they want before they ask.

In an interesting development in early 2018 it was widely reported that Apple had poached the head of Google's Artificial Intelligence (AI) unit to run its own Machine Learning and AI operations. Hern (2018) noted that John Giannandrea's appointment represented part of Apple's push to become the market leader in Artificial Intelligence (AI). 'Under his [John Giannandrea's] command, Google Brain, the company's main AI research team, has rebuilt the technology that underpins some of Google's landmark products, including search, translation and voice recognition' (Hern, 2018).

Sources: Dou, E. (3 March 2014) Apple Goes on Hiring Binge in Asia to Speed Product Releases. *The Wall Street Journal*. [Online]. Available from: http://www.wsj.com [Accessed 8 June 2016].

Love, J. (2015) *Apple ups hiring, but faces obstacles to making phones smarter*. [Online]. Available at: www.reuters.com [Accessed 8 June 2016].

Hern. A. (4 April 2018) Apple poaches Google's AI chief in push to save Siri. *The Guardian*. [Online]. Available from: www.theguardian.com [Accessed 26 April 2018].

9.2 Product life cycle (PLC) revisited

The concept of a life cycle for an industry or product was explored in Chapter 5, along with the strategic implications for each stage of the cycle.

Many businesses will not wish to risk having only a single product (or group of closely related products) or all their products at the same stage of development as they may all decline together.

The business should seek to maintain a balanced portfolio of products with variety to protect against downturns in the fortunes of individual products and to have products at different stages of development. Thus a business needs:

- A mix of yesterday's products, today's products and the products of tomorrow.
- A range of products with different length cycles.
- Lots of products in development/introductory stage.
- Lots of products in maturity to support others.

In the strategic analysis process, a firm should assess:

- The stage of life cycle that any particular product has reached.

- Each product's remaining life (how long it will continue to contribute to the portfolio).

- How urgent is the need to develop and innovate new and improved products.

- Whether the life can be extended or the balance of the portfolio improved by targeting other markets. Different markets may be at different stages in the life cycle, so a company can increase the balance of its portfolio by developing overseas markets. Eg, the market for luxury cars is mature in the USA and Europe but growing in India and China.

9.3 Recap of the Boston Consulting Group matrix

9.3.1 The basics

This matrix was developed by the Boston Consulting Group (BCG) in 1968.

BCG analysis can be applied to:

- **Individual products**
- **Whole strategic business units (SBUs)** and business streams

A company analyses its products or SBUs along two dimensions:

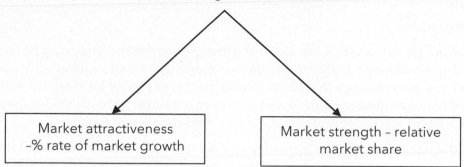

This gives the following matrix:

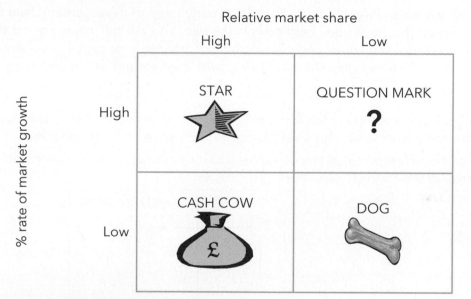

The BCG matrix differs from the product life cycle in that it takes account of external market factors, such as growth rate and share.

- Just as a firm might have a portfolio of products at different stages of the life cycle, it can have a portfolio of different products on the matrix.

- The objective (again) is for the company to have a balanced portfolio.

9.3.2 Boston classification of quadrants

- **Stars**

    Stars are products with a high share of a high growth market. In the short term, these require capital expenditure in excess of the cash they generate to maintain their market position, but promise high returns in the future. High growth rates will however attract newcomers/ competition.

- **Cash cows**

    In due course, stars will become cash cows, with a high share of a low-growth market. Cash cows need very little capital expenditure and generate high levels of cash income. Cash cows generate high cash returns, which can be used to finance the stars. Low growth make attacks by new firms wishing to enter the market unlikely.

- **Question marks (also known as a 'problem child')**

  Question marks are products in a high-growth market, but where they have a low market share. Do the products justify considerable capital expenditure in the hope of increasing their market share, or should they be allowed to die quietly as they are squeezed out of the expanding market by rival products? Because considerable expenditure would be needed to turn a question mark into a star by building up market share, question marks will usually be poor cash generators and show a negative cash flow.

- **Dog products**

  Dogs are products with a low share of a low growth market. They may be ex-cash cows that have now fallen on hard times or question marks that never succeeded in gaining critical mass in a market. Dogs should be allowed to die, or should be killed off. Although they will show only a modest net cash outflow, or even a modest net cash inflow, they are 'cash traps' which tie up resources and provide a poor return on investment.

  Although the best strategy is often to exit the market, this is not the case for all dogs. They can be a valid part of a product portfolio, for example to complete a range, or to fill a niche market.

  There are also **infants** (ie, products in an early stage of development), **war horses** (ie, products that have been cash cows in the past, and are still making good sales and earning good profits even now) and even cash dogs, which are dogs still generating cash, and dodos, which have low shares of low growth markets and which are losing cash.

Notes

1   Clearly if the company has four cash cows – good. However, if they are a small proportion of the company's total sales then it is not as impressive as it first appears.

2   For individual products the objective is to move the product in an anticlockwise direction around the matrix to become a cash cow, ie:

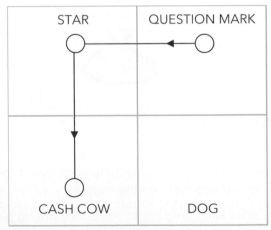

9.3.3   Plotting a BCG matrix

How are products plotted onto the matrix? For each of the company's products, calculate the following:

- Relative market share. A typical method is to use: $\dfrac{\text{Your sales}}{\text{Largest competitor sales}}$

- Percentage growth rate of the market. In excess of 10% growth is often regarded as high, but it will depend upon the type of market.

- Express the sales of each product as a percentage of the company's total sales. Each product is then represented by a circle – the area of which is proportional to the sales of that product.

Worked example: Plotting a BCG matrix

An industrial equipment company has five products with the following sales and market characteristics.

Company's product	Sales £m	£m sales Top 3 firms			Market growth rate %	Relative share
A	0.5	0.7	0.7	0.5*	15%	0.71
B	1.6	1.6	1.6*	1.0	18%	1.0
C	1.8	1.8*	1.2	1.0	7%	1.5
D	3.2	3.2*	0.8	0.7	4%	4.0
E	0.5	2.5	1.8	1.7	4%	0.2

* Company sales within the market

Relative share calculated as Company sales/Top firm sales or Company sales/Sales of next nearest competitor.

This information can then be plotted on to a matrix.

- The size of the circles indicate the contribution the product makes to overall turnover.
- The centre of circles indicates their position on the matrix:

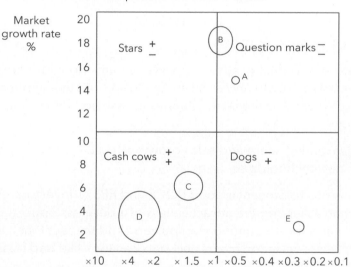

Market share (relative to major competitor)

The evaluation and resulting strategic considerations for the company in the matrix above are:

- There are two cash cows, thus the company should be in a cash-positive state.

- New products will be required to follow on from A.

- A is doing well but needs to gain market share to move from position 3 in the market – continued funding is essential. Similar for B.

- C is a market leader in a maturing market – strategy of consolidation is required.

- D is the major product which dominates its market; cash funds should be generated from this product.

- E is very small. Is it profitable? Funding to maintain the position or selling off are appropriate strategies.

The **product life cycle** concept can be added to a market share/market growth classification of products, as follows.

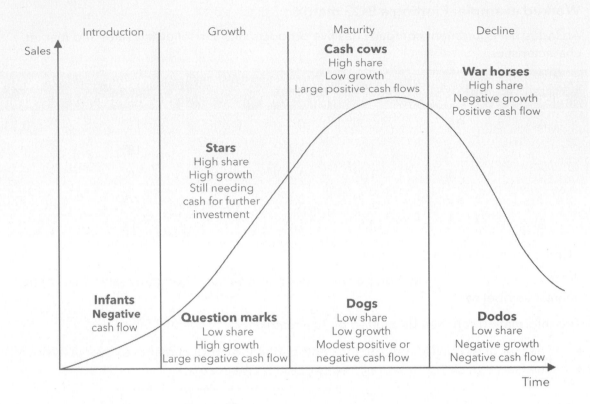

9.4   Shortcomings of the BCG matrix

BCG portfolio analysis is useful because it provides a framework for planners to consider and forecast potential market growth and to evaluate the competitive dimension through an evaluation of market share and the likely changes in cash flow. However, it should not be used uncritically, as follows.

- Factors besides market share and sales growth affect cash flow, eg, amount of R&D and investment in new technologies.

- Many firms, anxious to present a good ROCE and EPS to investors, still use return on investment when assessing the attractiveness of a business opportunity, despite the opportunity it gives for accounting manipulation and the fact that it ignores the time value of money. Therefore question marks and stars can look like bad businesses.

- The model provides no real insight into how to compare one opportunity with another when considering which opportunity should be allocated investment resources, eg, how does a star compare with a question mark?

- Rates of profit of some small businesses can be very high. Therefore in the right conditions a firm can profit from a low share of a low-growth market. (This point is made by Porter in his criticism of the BCG and he uses it to justify focus strategies to gain competitive advantage. See Chapter 7.)

- The model does not take risk into account, which is a crucial difference from the investment portfolio approach from which it takes its inspiration.

- The matrix focuses on known markets and known products. As a generation tool, it sits firmly in the rational planning model and also within the positioning approach to strategy.

- The model assumes industry and market can be defined for purposes of calculating share and growth. Ignoring substitute products can lead management to overestimate the attractiveness of a business unit for investment purposes.

- The model suffers from difficulties in forecasting growth.

9.5 General criticisms of portfolio analysis

Portfolio analysis invites management to view their businesses as a collection of income generating assets which, combined, create a corporation with a financial performance that mixes risk and returns in a way that will appeal to shareholders. In recent times there has been a greater focus among organisations to concentrate on their 'core businesses' and 'core competences' with less focus on creating a balanced portfolio.

Drawbacks of portfolio planning approaches:

- Portfolio models are simple; they do not reflect the uncertainties of decision-making.

- BCG analysis, in particular, does not really take risk into account.

- They ignore opportunities for creative segmentation or identifying new niches.

- They assume a market is given rather than something that can be created and nurtured. After all, industries may be unattractive because customer needs have not been analysed sufficiently.

- They rely on identifiable products rather than services, or more nebulous relationships.

- They ignore the profit-generating capability of business relationships.

- Creating a corporation with the financial characteristics of a well-balanced portfolio does not increase the share price. This is because investors can diversify risk in how they construct their own portfolio.

- Recycling cash flows from cash cows to question marks ignores the alternative of paying out dividend and letting shareholders decide where to invest the money.

- Creation of portfolios may cause the business to move beyond its core competences and so lead to diminishing returns on investment through time.

Summary and Self-test

Summary

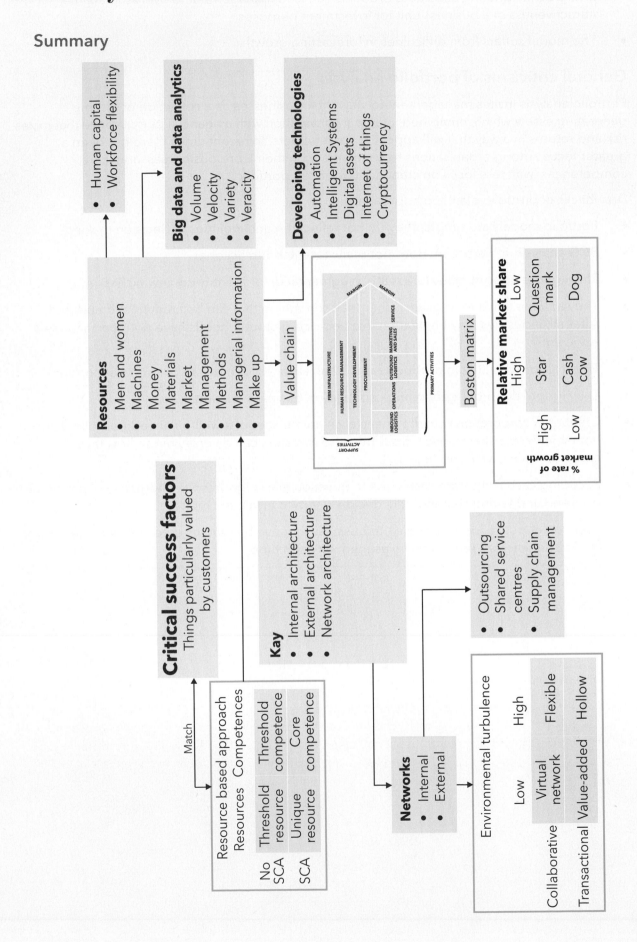

Self-test

Answer the following questions.

1   A major UK chain of betting shops has decided to establish an offshore operation based on the Channel Island of Alderney. This is because such locations do not need to charge punters a tax levy. Bets would be placed by telephone, email or over the internet.

   Describe three key resources that would be required to offer such a service.

2   What is internal benchmarking? Suggest two ways a chain of pubs could use internal benchmarking to improve performance.

3   Rapid Fit UK (RFUK) is a highly profitable listed company specialising in fitting new tyres, brake pads, exhausts etc, to cars and vans. It is now seeking to diversify and has decided to offer fixed price servicing on a while-you-wait basis. This would be pre-booked by motorists over the internet. RFUK's managers believe that they can undercut franchised dealers by offering a quick, no frills service for routine servicing, but are worried about their fitters' ability to tackle complex repair jobs on a wide range of vehicles.

   Evaluate the effect of the following four factors on RFUK's ability to deliver this strategy: financial resources, human resources, current services offered, and information systems.

4   Explain what is meant by benchmarking and suggest why organisations might use it.

5   What is a 'cash cow' in the Boston Consulting Group (BCG) matrix? Suggest two examples.

6   Gaddes Ltd is the UK's largest manufacturer of digital radios. Sales for the year ended 31 January 20X4 were £42 million, with an estimate of £48 million for the following year in a market that is expanding by 12% a year. Gaddes Ltd's major competitor had sales of £36 million in the year ended 31 January 20X4.

   Explain how Gaddes Ltd's radios would be characterised when applying the Boston Consulting Group (BCG) matrix. Describe how existing competitors are likely to react in this market.

7   **APCS plc**

   APCS plc is a large international manufacturer of personal computers. Within Europe it sells four main types of PC – those aimed at the home market, those aimed at the commercial market, laptops and PC servers for networks.

   After-sales service for the whole of Europe is provided by a call centre in Scotland. For example, a customer in Germany rings a number in Germany and the call is then automatically routed to a German speaker at the Scottish call centre. The customer pays for a local call and will be totally unaware that the call is being dealt with in another country. APCS plc pays the cost of the international call.

   The organisation of the call centre is critical, with telephone operators speaking 11 languages. The technology must ensure that the call is routed to the appropriate operator. In addition there are three levels of call taken at the centre. The first level operators deal with routine questions. Second and third levels of operators exist to deal with questions that cannot be answered at a lower level.

   The main costs of the call centre are telephone bills and salaries. An important financial measure is the cost per call, which varies from country to country. Non-financial measures are the following:

   •   Call drop-out rate, ie, the percentage of customers who are put in a queue but hang up before reaching an operator

   •   Average duration of each call

The current focus is on improving these measures from month to month, rather than comparing with other call centres.

The management team is currently reviewing the performance appraisal system and have asked for your advice. In particular they would like some thoughts on benchmarking the call centres.

Requirements

As a member of the accounts department, draft a memorandum to the management team dealing with the following matters.

7.1 An appraisal in terms of strengths and weaknesses of the current performance measures used.

7.2 What benchmarking is and how it is done.

7.3 Whether benchmarking would be suitable for APCS plc.

8   **Gizmo Computer Games Ltd**

Geoff Carter is the Managing Director of Gizmo Computer Games Ltd ('Gizmo'), a growing software house that specialises in writing computer games.

Recently the firm was visited by Peter Ng, a student on placement as part of his MBA course. An extract from his report is given below.

'I feel that Gizmo's main critical success factors (CSFs) are innovation, command of technology, bug rate and graphics skills and you should look to measure and control key performance indicators (KPIs) in these areas.'

Geoff is completely confused by the jargon in the report and has asked you to prepare a brief memorandum to explain what Peter is talking about before he talks to him on the telephone tomorrow.

Requirement

Write a memorandum to Geoff, giving reasons why the CSFs highlighted might be important to Gizmo, and suggestions for a suitable KPI to measure each CSF.

9   Read the scenario of the **December 2014 Business Strategy and Technology** question in the Question Bank entitled *Radar Traditional Radios Ltd*. Draft an answer to the requirement which asks for a discussion of the factors to be considered in abandoning the production of analogue radios.

10   Read the scenario of the **March 2014 Business Strategy and Technology** question in the Question Bank entitled *Emelius Ltd*. Draft an answer to the requirement on the value chain.

11   Read the scenario of the **March 2017 Business Strategy and Technology** question in the Question Bank entitled *Gighay Ltd*. Draft an answer to the requirement on the benefits and problems of outsourcing.

Now, go back to the Learning outcomes in the Introduction. If you are satisfied that you have achieved these objectives, please tick them off.

Answers to Interactive questions

Answer to Interactive question 1

1.1 Porter identifies four elements of national competitive advantage that support the export efforts of successful firms.

These elements and how they can be applied to Yaz plc are explained below.

Factor conditions are a country's endowment of the inputs to production, such as human resources, physical resources, knowledge, capital and infrastructure. Porter distinguishes between basic and advanced factors. The latter are more important for sustained success, and include modern communication and investment in facilities and highly educated personnel. Z land appears well-endowed with these advanced factors, having sophisticated financial markets and industries using modern systems such as JIT.

Demand conditions in the home market have determined how Yaz has responded to customer needs. Careful marketing has made this response successful and Yaz has an enviable reputation at home for quality, innovation, reliability and customer focus that should transfer well to the world market. The success that has been achieved to date has meant that Yaz has the necessary economies of scale to be able to compete globally.

As the home market has shaped Yaz's priorities, the company would be well advised to use this experience and seek abroad those segments that have been successfully targeted in the domestic market. This will require an investment in market research, as the company must determine how well the products will be received abroad. This is vital, as there is little point in launching products if the customers do not want them or can see little difference from existing offerings towards which they may already feel very loyal.

The impact on the home market of more international activity must also be considered. Does Yaz plc have the resources to be able to support both markets, and continue to maintain its accustomed high standards?

The presence of **related and supporting industries** at home, which have to date supplied Yaz with the components it has needed for its successful products, will be important in launching those products internationally. The continued support of these suppliers will be vital, at least in the initial stages of international development. Yaz must assure itself that these suppliers have the resources to provide a higher level of support. Otherwise, international suppliers may need to be sought and this will demand closer and more complex supply chain management.

National firm strategy, structure and rivalry issues create distinctive business environments in different countries. For example, domestic rivalry is important because tough domestic rivals teach a firm about competitive success, and rivals for the home market have to try different strategic approaches.

Yaz has been successful against strong competition in the domestic market and this has provided good training for the international market, which may feature more, and larger, competitors than Yaz has been used to facing at home. However Yaz must ask itself whether its reputation for supplying reliable and good quality products will be enough to guarantee its success in a wider competitive market. It could be that the wider market does not value reliability and quality as highly as Yaz's domestic customers. This would wipe out its main differentiating factor.

1.2 Benchmarking can be very useful for business, both in relation to internal processes and to wider management concerns.

Internally, the adoption of best practice should improve productivity; reduce waste and costs associated with quality failures; and contribute to increased customer satisfaction.

At the **operational** management level, benchmarking is useful if there is any tendency to complacency and it can improve awareness of the processes by which value is currently created and how they could be improved in the future.

At the **strategic** level, benchmarking can be an important contributor to awareness of competition in the changing task environment and how the company is responding to it, both practically and strategically.

There are **disadvantages** to benchmarking. A full programme can overload managers with demands for information, restrict their attention to the factors that are to be benchmarked and affect their motivation by seeming to reduce their role to copying others. It can also undermine competitive advantage by revealing trade secrets. Strategically, it can divert attention away from innovation and the future by focussing it on the **efficiency of current operations**. This is a particularly important point for Yaz , with its current move towards exporting: this will require a great deal of attention by managers at all levels.

If Yaz were to undertake a programme of benchmarking, firm commitment by the Managing Director would be essential to drive it along. It would then be necessary to identify the areas in which improvement was sought and to decide how such an improvement would be identified and measured. Since benchmarking is about **processes rather than results**, measures would have to be rather more detailed than the usual summary measures used in normal management reports.

It would then be necessary to **identify suitable benchmarking partners**. Some industries, such as printing in the UK, run sophisticated benchmarking programmes; Yaz may be able to join such a scheme. Alternatively, trade associations or chambers of commerce may be able to help. Yaz need, not, of course, benchmark against competitors, or even against other motor accessory manufacturers. Its distribution operation, for instance, might be compared with a similar operation in a completely different industry.

Once a scheme of measurement and comparison is in place, it is necessary to determine what **improvements** are possible and to implement them. It will be tempting for the Managing Director of Yaz to delegate this role to a single manager, but better results will be obtained if the responsibility for making and monitoring the necessary changes is embedded in the normal management structure. Success and failure in making and continuing the agreed improvements can then be monitored as part of the **normal performance review process**.

Answer to Interactive question 2

2.1 The value chain is a model of how firms create value for their customers. The value chain describes a number of activities carried out in the firm.

Primary activities are directly related to the processes of production and sales.

Inbound logistics are those activities involved with receiving, handling and storing inputs to the production system.

Operations convert the resource input into the end product.

Outbound logistics relate to storage and distribution.

Marketing and sales inform customers about the product, and include advertising and promotion

After sales service

Support activities obtain purchased inputs, human resources, technology and infrastructure to support the primary activities

Competitive advantage is obtained by configuring the value chain in certain ways. Xena Ltd can use the value chain to ensure that their philosophy of quick, quality haircuts can be adopted and maintained throughout the business. The main areas that Xena Ltd needs to concentrate on are Human Resource Management, Procurement, Technology Development, Operations, Marketing and Sales.

Human Resource Management

An important way Xena Ltd generates value for its customers is by operating without appointments and with multi-skilled staff. This means that whatever a customer needs, she can expect to be attended to quickly and efficiently without having to plan ahead for an appointment.

The company therefore must ensure their staff have the capabilities to meet the objectives of quality and speed. It is clear that they need to be highly trained as they need to be able to work quickly and avoid making mistakes. They need to be multi-skilled so that each member of staff can achieve maximum utilisation and be in a position to deal with any customer and her needs. The company also needs to ensure that they have an adequate workforce of trained juniors to deal with washing hair, cleaning of the salon and general fetching and carrying. This will ensure that the stylists themselves are not wasting time when they could be generating income for the salon.

Technology development

There are many areas in this kind of business where technology can help to achieve the organisation's stated aims. The simple ticket waiting system might be developed to provide an indication of waiting time and an option to prefer a particular stylist, for example. The salons could also use modern technology to make the salon experience more appropriate for their target clientele. This could include free Wi-Fi or tablet computers in the waiting area for busy clients to use while they wait.

Operations

Xena Ltd should consider making the beauty salon business entirely separate from the hairdressing salon as the two businesses seem to offer a mixed message to clients – one of speed but also relaxation. Furthermore the company needs to analyse its current and potential market and determine whether they will require more complex services such as colouring as this kind of procedure would add to the time the stylist needs to spend with each client. They could consider offering a separate area for such services and having dedicated staff working in this area.

There is potentially a new market for Xena Ltd to explore by considering the people who are just too busy to leave the office for a haircut. They could target large office complexes and offer in-house hairdressing services at convenient times.

Marketing and sales

Xena Ltd has been fortunate in that its name has become well-known through personal recommendation. However, it would be unwise to reply on this simple recipe. A sophisticated business needs an appropriate marketing communications strategy. In the case of Xena this may also include the use of social media marketing. This may require the assistance of consultants to develop properly, but Xena Ltd should certainly consider some kind of targeted campaign, even if only run at a low level of intensity to ensure its services are known to potential customers. Careful advertising in local and even national newspapers might be appropriate, though it would be expensive. A high quality direct mail campaign to business addresses might be more appropriate.

2.2 By performing a value chain analysis a company such as Xena Ltd is forced to look in detail at its activities and identify areas for improvement. This may never be achieved if the company is simply concentrating on external analysis as a source of new opportunities

Businesses need to focus on trying to achieve sustainable competitive advantage; by considering each activity of the business as a potential source of strength or a possible weakness, the company can ensure that it maximises the value that it offers. This analysis can also help to identify core competences, which are particularly appropriate source of competitive advantage in the long term.

All companies should concentrate on achieving consistency throughout their operations. That is, if a particular target is set, such as quality or speed or value, then this should be applied to all the activities of the business to ensure that achievement in one area is not negated by failure in another. Examining the business in the light of the value chain is a method of ensuring that value created in one area is not destroyed in another. In the case of Xena Ltd there is, for example, an element of contradiction between the aim of targeting women who are short of time and the use of a queuing system rather than appointments.

A further aspect of the value chain that needs to be considered is the application of this concept to the entire value system and the linkages between that system. By considering these linkages, a company can achieve better relationships with its customers and suppliers and ensure partners are sought who hold similar values and conduct business in a similar manner ie, are compatible.

The value chain also has some limitations in its application. Fairly obviously, it was based on a manufacturing model and it may be difficult to apply to businesses in the service sector such as Xena Ltd. Companies in this situation need to ensure they are comfortable with general principles of the exercise and not get too caught up in trying to make their business fit within a certain framework. Companies also need to ensure they don't focus on value chain analysis to the detriment of environmental analysis and a consideration of competitive forces.

Answer to Interactive question 3

3.1 (a) The firm may effectively be surrendering its source of competitive advantage.

   (b) If all the knowledge needed to run a business is held 'outside' it, short-term profit improvements may be made at the (long-term) expense of the ability to innovate.

   (c) A current competence may be less relevant in future, in which case outsourcing may be part of an exit strategy.

   (d) Managers may disagree as to the business and processes they consider to be core.

Answer to Interactive question 4

4.1 **Advantages of outsourcing R&D**

   (a) Potentially less expensive if R&D is used on an *ad hoc* basis
   (b) Gain from outside expertise and competence
   (c) Flexibility to cope with larger projects or to render cost base more variable
   (d) Frees management up to focus on more important or strategic issues

Disadvantages of outsourcing R&D

   (a) May be cheaper in-house if R&D is a perpetual and continuing activity

   (b) Exposes firm to risk from poor quality or unreliable/unstable provider

   (c) Loss of organisational learning

   (d) Loss of control over intellectual property (IP). For example, who owns the developments?

Answers to Self-test

1. • Staffing will be a major issue, since a small island will not have a large number of available and suitable staff, and relocation from the UK would be costly.

   • Technology will also be important, given the variety of ways of placing bets. The company will have to invest heavily to ensure the systems work.

   • Finance to acquire and equip suitable premises will be significant.

   • Gambling licence is an example of a threshold resource as without it the company would be unable to operate.

2. • Internal benchmarking is the comparison of current results with other results recorded by the same organisation.

   • A chain of pubs could compare the performance of individual pubs in the chain to identify best practice. Overall results could be compared year on year to monitor improvements.

3. • Financial resources: as a profitable listed company RFUK should easily be able to afford what is really only an extension of its current service.

   • Human resources: this is a key constraint because the current staff may lack the skills needed. A programme of recruitment and training will probably be required.

   • Current services offered: this strategy seems like a sensible addition to the current service and is a logical fit – it is product development.

   • Information systems: the service will be unpopular unless RFUK can rely on the internet booking idea working properly. Again, a key issue.

4. Benchmarking is the establishment through data gathering of targets and comparators, by the use of which can be identified relative levels of performance (and particularly areas of underperformance).

   Four sources of comparative data are: internal, competitive, activity (or process) and generic.

   By adoption of identified best practices, it is hoped that performance will improve.

5. The BCG matrix is a way of analysing a portfolio of products by considering their market share and market growth.

   On this matrix a 'cash cow' is a product with a high market share and low market growth.

   A high market share implies that the product is well established. Low market growth implies that it is probably nearing the end of the product life cycle. The product therefore has few serious competitors, and this is unlikely to change in the future.

   In the short term this product is a money spinner, but in the longer term sales may well die away.

   Examples may include Bic biros and Casio electronic calculators.

6. **Gaddes Ltd**

   Company sales are forecast to grow at 14%, whilst the market generally is growing at 12% – according to the BCG model the growth rate is likely to be considered high.

   As market leader, Gaddes Ltd's sales are almost 17% higher than their major competitor. Thus they also have a high relative market share.

   As a result the radios are likely to be categorised as a star product.

   Competitors are likely to be attracted to the market by the high growth rate and the prospect of generating good returns. These factors may give rise to moderate cash investment by competitors.

7   **APCS plc**

Memorandum – draft

To	The management team
From	An accountant
Date	Today
Re	The current system of performance measurement

Introduction

This memorandum looks at the current system of performance measurement and at how benchmarking could improve matters.

7.1 **An appraisal of current measures**

Strengths	Weaknesses
• The current system looks at three measures and is good in so far as non-financial aspects are included along with financial aspects.	• Difficulties in comparing costs between countries and from month to month as tariffs and exchange rates change.
• Cost per call is vital as the cost of telephone calls is the major cost of the call centre and must be monitored to control it.	• The cost per call measure could encourage operators to give customers a shorter (but probably inferior) answer. This is also a problem even with the non-financial measures used.
• Call drop-out rate is a very useful indicator as customer goodwill will be lost if people find themselves queuing for a long period of time. This could also indicate if more operators are needed.	• The main weakness of the approach is that no indication is given as to whether customers actually get a satisfactory response. Some form of customer survey is necessary – perhaps a sample of customers could be called back and views sought.
• Average call duration is probably more useful than cost as if affords better comparability.	• The measures do not seem to be broken down by operator level – one would expect level three queries to take much longer to solve than level one.
	• The lack of some form of comparison with other call centres. It may be that the call centre is very efficient but keeps being asked to improve.
	• The use of last month's figures as this month's target. This could encourage staff to work at less than maximum efficiency to avoid setting a more difficult target for next month.

7.2 **What is benchmarking and how is it achieved?**

Benchmarking involves setting targets by looking at comparable organisations – preferably at 'the best of the rest'. Such organisations could be drawn from any of the following.

- Internal benchmarking: look at other call centres within APCS plc

- Competitive benchmarking: look at competitor companies, such as IBM

- Activity benchmarking: look at any companies with call centres

- Generic benchmarking: look at conceptually similar processes, such as order processing at a large mail order company

The following steps are required to implement and run a system of benchmarking.

1 Gain senior management commitment
2 Decide which processes and activities need to be benchmarked
3 Understand the processes and develop appropriate measures
4 Monitor the process measuring system
5 Choose appropriate organisation against which to benchmark
6 Obtain and analyse data
7 Discuss results with process management and staff
8 Develop and implement improvement programmes
9 Monitor results

7.3 Suitability for APCS plc

(1) Management commitment should be forthcoming due to the team leadership style. Once the team has decided on benchmarking, all members will support it.

(2) The main process to be benchmarked relates to the answering of customer queries, so this step is fairly easy. However, it must be decided, for example, whether to split the processes into different levels.

(3) Developing appropriate measures – as mentioned above, we need measures more focused on whether operators are giving customers satisfactory answers.

(4) Monitoring should be straightforward, though calling back customers will involve more cost. There is also the problem that questions which need to be asked are not too vague or subjective.

(5) Choosing appropriate organisations for comparison – APCS plc does have other call centres, so non-financial measures can be compared between them. The problem of changing exchange rates could make costs difficult to compare.

(6) With competitive benchmarking the main issue will be obtaining data – perhaps they could be called to determine average response times, etc. However, it would not be possible to find drop-out rates.

(7) A forum for discussion will need to be set up – a minor problem.

(8) It is vital that results will be acted upon for the system to have credibility. A settling-in period would also help.

(9) Perhaps a team member should be assigned to take control of the whole process.

In summary, APCS plc is already well on the way towards benchmarking, and the introduction of the approach should not involve much painful change and cost. Internal benchmarking will be much easier but competitive benchmarking will give a much better idea as to whether or not APCS plc has a competitive advantage in this area.

8   **Gizmo Computer Games Ltd**

Memorandum

To	Geoff Carter
From	An Assistant
Date	Today
Subject	Strategic planning

A competence-based approach to strategic planning involves looking at what we are good at – our core competences. Ideally these are areas that we have to be good at to succeed ('critical success factors' or 'CSFs') and are also difficult for competitors to copy.

Once CSFs have been identified, they need to be measured and controlled. This is done by setting targets for related areas. Each CSF could involve looking at many key performance indicators ('KPIs').

Critical success factors of Gizmo and suggested KPIs

Peter has suggested four areas to consider. My thoughts on these are as follows.

- **Innovation**. Given the rate of change in the industry, it is vital that Gizmo's games are seen to be up to date, even 'cutting-edge'. One way of measuring this is to look at the number of extra features or gimmicks in each new game compared with its predecessor.

- **Command of technology**. With technology changing so rapidly it is vital that programmers are totally aware of what the hardware is capable of doing. It will be difficult to find suitable KPIs for this as it is very difficult to quantify. One way could be to send staff on external specialist update courses that include tests or exams at the end. Scores on these tests could be monitored.

- **Bug rate**. Nothing will alienate customers more quickly than bugs in games that prevent them being played correctly. It is thus vital that games are bug-free. This can be measured easily by looking at the number of bugs found once a game is sold, within say six months. Ideally this would also involve assessing whether or not bugs are serious.

- **Graphics**. Many players are impressed more by the graphics than they are by the complexities of a game, so again Peter has identified a key area. Assessing graphics performance will be difficult – possibly the best way is to look at consumer reviews in magazines which will grade games. We want at least a 4 star score.

In summary, Peter has suggested some important areas that Gizmo needs to consider. However, these should be reviewed along with more conventional measures, such as cost control.

9   Refer to the answer to Radar Traditional Radios Ltd in the Question Bank.

10   Refer to the answer to Emelius Ltd in the Question Bank.

11   Refer to the answer to Gighay Ltd in the Question Bank.

CHAPTER 7

Strategic options

Introduction

Examination context

TOPIC LIST

Summary and Self-test

Answers to Interactive questions

Answers to Self-test

Introduction

Learning outcomes

Tick off

- Evaluate an organisation's purpose, highlighting omissions, inconsistencies and weaknesses.

- Analyse an organisation's current markets and competitive strategy in sufficient detail for decisions to be made, drawing conclusions consistent with the qualitative and quantitative data available and highlighting relevant issues in terms of their likely impact on the strategy of the organisation

- Identify, describe and evaluate in a given scenario the alternative strategies available to an organisation

- Explain how to position particular products and services in the market place to maximise competitive advantage by extracting and analysing relevant data

Specific syllabus references for this chapter are: 1a, 1c, 2a, 2i.

Syllabus links

The basic concepts of competitive strategy and strategic growth were covered in your Business, Technology and Finance studies. The topics are summarised again here as the concepts covered in this chapter form a core area of Business Strategy and Technology. As well as developing the ideas further they are also applied to scenario problems of the sort you may face in your examination.

Examination context

This chapter looks at various models which can assist an organisation in developing its products and markets and in choosing strategies for competitive advantage. In the exam these models can be used to assess the strategies already identified in the question or as a way of generating strategic options for the business. Either way, the concepts of SWOT analysis, Porter's generic strategy model and Ansoff's growth matrix are fundamental knowledge for the Business Strategy and Technology exam.

The scenario for Question 2 in the June 2017 exam (*Jason Smyth Textiles (JST) Ltd*) focused on a UK-based manufacturer of soft furnishings. The company's business model had historically been based on pursuing a competitive strategy of cost leadership. However, this model was starting to become difficult to sustain, so a new business model had therefore been proposed. This involved a move upmarket by producing better quality soft furnishings in a new range of higher priced fabrics. The second part of the first requirement asked candidates to:

'Explain how the elements of JST's value chain support its current low cost strategy.'

This requirement nicely illustrates how questions in the Business Strategy and Technology exam can test more than one piece of theory in the same requirement. In this case candidates had to display a clear understanding of Porter's value chain (which was considered in Chapter 6), and also draw upon their knowledge of competitive strategies (which are the focus of this Chapter). Remembering that the company was pursuing a cost leadership strategy was important here, and good answers linked the company's strategy to the value chain activities as part of their discussion of value and cost drivers. This again illustrates the importance of being able to apply your knowledge to the question scenario detail.

The next requirement in the exam asked candidates to do the following:

'With respect to JST's proposed new business model:

Describe its benefits and problems, and make a reasoned recommendation as to whether JST should implement the new business model.'

This requirement effectively built upon the earlier consideration of the company's cost leadership strategy, as candidates were expected to identify the fact that a move 'upmarket' would require a change in generic strategy. The question scenario made it clear that a move towards a strategy of differentiation in this case would not be appropriate. Candidates who produced the best answers structured their work around the headings of benefits and problems of the new business model, and clearly stated their recommendations. As this example shows, structuring your answer in an easy to follow manner will improve your chances of earning the marks on offer.

1 Rational planning model revisited

Section overview

- The development of strategic options involves the final three steps of the rational model.

- Choices involve understanding the present situation, identifying gaps, and developing potential ways to deal with this.

1.1 The rational model

Chapter 2 introduced the rational model.

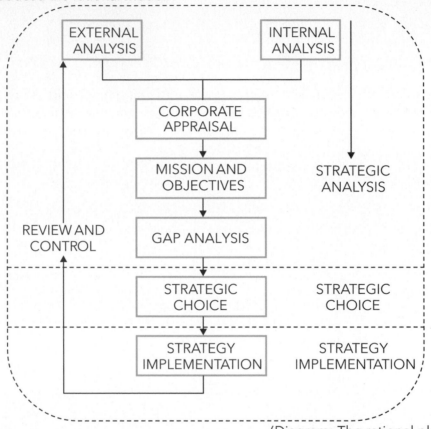

(Diagram: The rational planning model)

The present chapter considers three of the stages:

- **Corporate appraisal**: Combining assessment of environment (Chapters 4 and 5) with assessment of resources, competences and capabilities (Chapter 6) to help management identify the strategic position of the business and its forecast performance.

- **Gap analysis**: Management compare forecast performance with the strategic objectives of the business to identify where strategic adjustments are needed to deliver planned performance.

- **Strategic option development (Strategic choice)**: Management generate and evaluate strategic options to close the planning gap identified.

1.2 Three strategic choices: overview

Johnson, Scholes and Whittington (in *Exploring Corporate Strategy*) identify three distinct groups of strategic options. Strategic choice requires that management makes choices under each of the following:

- **Competitive strategy**: The way that the firm will seek to win customers and secure profitability against rivals. This is covered in the present chapter and continued in Chapter 8 where marketing strategy is discussed.

- **Product/market strategy**: The decision on what products to offer over the coming years and the markets to be served. This is covered in section 5 of this chapter and again continued in Chapter 8.

- **Development strategy**: The decision on how to gain access to the chosen products and markets. Discussion of this choice is reserved until Chapter 11.

Worked example: Virgin group

The following extracts have been adapted from the Virgin website (2016) and illustrate the way this international consumer goods and services corporation applies the 'three strategic choices' approach.

Competitive strategy

Virgin is a leading international investment group and one of the world's most recognised and respected brands. Conceived in 1970 by Sir Richard Branson, the Virgin group has gone on to grow successful businesses in sectors ranging from mobile telephony, travel, financial services, leisure, music, holidays and health & wellness. Virgin employs more than 70,000 people around the world, operating in 35 countries. According to Virgin website in 2016 the group had annual global brand revenues of $24 billion.

All the markets in which Virgin operates tend to have features in common: they are typically markets where the customer has been under-served, where there is confusion and/or where the competition is complacent.

In these markets, Virgin is able to break into the market and shake it up. Virgin's role is to be the consumer champion, and we do this by delivering to our brand values, which are:

Value for money

eg, Virgin Australia – low cost airlines with transparent pricing.

Good quality

High standards, attention to detail, being honest and delivering on promises.

eg, Virgin Atlantic Upper Class Suite – on-board bar, large flat bed on board, touchscreen monitor, mood lighting etc.

Innovation

Challenging convention with big and little product/service ideas; innovative, modern and stylish design.

eg, Virgin Galactic – space travel experiences.

Brilliant customer service

Friendly, human and relaxed; professional but uncorporate.

eg, Virgin Mobile Australia has won awards for its customer service as the company treats its customers as individuals.

Competitively challenging

Sticking two fingers up to the establishment and fighting the big boys – usually with a bit of humour.

eg, in 2012, Richard Branson and Virgin Trains successfully forced the UK government to back track on its announcement that the franchise to run the West Coast Main Line had been awarded to FirstGroup, a rival train line operator. Virgin appealed the government's decision after it came to light that the process for awarding the route was based on flawed information and passenger projections.

Fun

Every company in the world takes itself seriously so we think it's important that we provide the public and our customers with a bit of entertainment.

Product/market strategy

Travel	Entertainment	People and planet
• Virgin Atlantic	• Virgin Games	• Virgin Racing
• Virgin Holidays	• Virgin Casino	• Virgin Start-up
• Virgin Trains	• Virgin Radio	• Virgin Earth Challenge
• Virgin Galactic		

Leisure	Telecom and tech	Money
• Virgin Wines	• Virgin Mobile	• Virgin Money
• Virgin Balloon Flights	• Virgin Media	• Virgin Money Giving

Development strategy

We draw on talented people from throughout the group. New ventures are often steered by people seconded from other parts of Virgin, who bring with them the trademark management style, skills and experience. We frequently create partnerships with others to combine skills, knowledge, market presence and so on.

Once a Virgin company is up and running, several factors contribute to making it a success. The power of the Virgin name; Richard Branson's personal reputation; our unrivalled network of friends, contacts and partners; the Virgin management style; the way talent is empowered to flourish within the group. To some traditionalists, these may not seem hard headed enough. To them, the fact that Virgin has minimal management layers, no bureaucracy, a tiny board and no massive global HQ is an anathema.

Our companies are part of a family rather than a hierarchy. They are empowered to run their own affairs, yet other companies help one another, and solutions to problems come from all kinds of sources. In a sense we are a community, with shared ideas, values, interests and goals. The proof of our success is real and tangible.

Exploring the activities of our companies through this website demonstrates that success, and that it is not about having a strong business promise, it is about keeping it!

Although the Virgin group is a family of businesses with a shared brand, all of the companies run independently. Often the companies are set up as joint ventures with other partners, so they all have different shareholders and boards.'

Source:

Virgin Group (2016) *About us*.[Online]. Available from: https://www.virgin.com/virgingroup/content/about-us [Accessed 8 June 2016].

2 Corporate appraisal (SWOT analysis)

Section overview

- Before dreaming up options, management needs to take stock of the present position of the business.

- A SWOT analysis is an important technique for visualising the situation and is drawn from the environmental assessment and internal appraisal already conducted. SWOT analysis was introduced in your Business, Technology and Finance studies; as a result the material covered here should serve as a recap of your earlier studies.

2.1 Role of corporate appraisal

A complete awareness of the organisation's environment and its internal capacities is **necessary** for a rational consideration of future strategy, but it is not **sufficient**. The threads must be drawn together so that potential strategies may be developed and assessed. The most common way of doing this is to analyse the factors into **strengths**, **weaknesses**, **opportunities** and **threats**. Strengths and weaknesses are diagnosed by the internal analysis, opportunities and threats by the environmental analysis.

SWOT analysis is covered in detail in the Business, Technology and Finance text.

2.2 Bringing them together – the cruciform chart

A cruciform chart (literally 'cross form') can be drafted on a flip-chart by the person facilitating the strategy discussions. Its benefits are:

- Limitations on space restricts management to focusing on the big points.
- Allows mapping of connections between points (see below).

However, effective SWOT analysis does not simply require a categorisation of information; it also requires some **evaluation of the relative importance** of the various factors under consideration. In the exam it is vital that you indicate the relative importance of points that you identify and r provide a summary of the key issues to go with your cruciform.

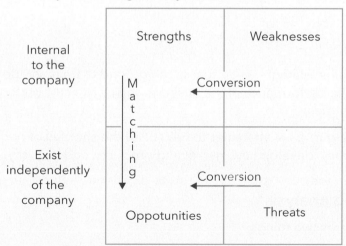

- **Match strengths with market opportunities**
  Strengths which do not match any available opportunity are of limited use while opportunities which do not have any matching strengths are of little immediate value.

- **Conversion**
  This requires the development of strategies which will convert weaknesses into strengths to take advantage of some particular opportunity, or converting threats into opportunities which can then be matched by existing strengths.

2.3 Weihrich's TOWS matrix

Weihrich, one of the earliest writers on corporate appraisal, originally spoke in terms of a TOWS matrix to emphasise the importance of threats and opportunities. It has several benefits:

- It provides a clear set of steps to move from SWOT to the formulation of strategic options.

- It makes management aware of the need for **defensive** strategies (WT) in addition to strategies to grasp opportunities.

	Strengths	Weaknesses
Opportunities	SO Strategies	WO Strategies
Threats	ST Strategies	WT Strategies

Note that this is therefore an inherently **positioning** approach to strategy. A further important element of Weihrich's discussion was his categorisation of strategic options:

- SO strategies employ strengths to seize opportunities.
- ST strategies employ strengths to counter or avoid threats.
- WO strategies address weaknesses so as to be able to exploit opportunities.
- WT strategies are defensive, aiming to avoid threats and the impact of weaknesses.

One useful impact of this analysis is that **the four groups of strategies tend to relate well to different time horizons**. SO strategies may be expected to produce good short-term results, while WO strategies are likely to take much longer to show results. ST and WT strategies are more probably relevant to the medium term.

3 Gap analysis

Section overview

- Gap analysis helps management visualise the ground to be made up between their intentions for the performance of the business and its forecast performance without new initiatives (strategies).

- There are three groups of strategies to help close the shortfall of performance (gap): improve efficiency, develop new market and products, and diversify.

3.1 Overview of gap analysis

Gap analysis compares two things:

- The organisation's **targets** for achievement over the planning period.

- What the organisation would be **expected to achieve** if it carried on in the current way with the same products and selling to the same markets, with no major changes to operations. This is called an F_0 **forecast**, by Argenti.

Definition

Gap analysis: The comparison between an entity's ultimate objective and the expected performance from projects both planned and under way, identifying means by which any identified difference, or gap, might be filled.

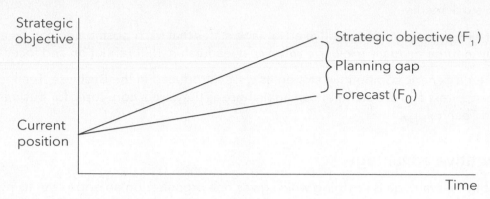

3.2 Strategies to fill the gap

The planning gap may originate from a number of causes:

- Ambitious objectives being set by management (or imposed on management by investors).
- Underperformance of existing product portfolio (eg, maturity stage approaching).
- Difficult environment (eg, industry or economic slow-down).

The gap could be filled by new product-market growth strategies. For example a management team wishing to increase profitability might consider:

- **Efficiency strategies**: reduce the costs of present products and economise on the assets used.
- **Expansion strategies**: develop new products and/or new markets.
- **Diversification strategies**: enter new industries which have better profit and growth prospects.

These are illustrated below.

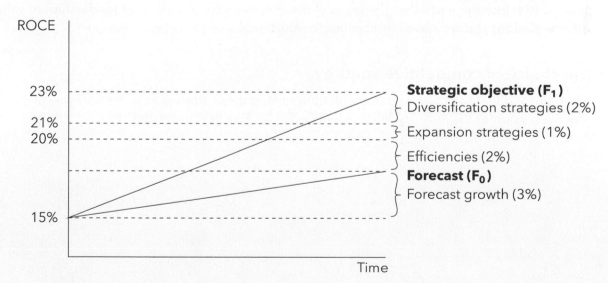

Gaps can also be closed by the simple expedient of setting the objectives lower. Most writers on strategy regard this remedy as an unacceptable admission of defeat by management.

4 Generic competitive strategies: how to compete

Section overview

- Firms must position themselves well in two markets: the market for their products; and in the stock market.

- Porter's concept of competitive advantage states that such positioning can be achieved only in three mutually exclusive ways: cost leadership, differentiation and focus.

- Porter's generic competitive strategies were introduced in the Business, Technology and Finance text and are summarised again here as they are a core topic for Business Strategy and Technology.

4.1 Competitive advantage

Competitive advantage is anything which gives one organisation an edge over its rivals.

In the 1960s and 1970s this tended to be interpreted solely in terms of the marketing concept of providing the customer with superior benefits and so winning sales.

Porter widened the concept of competitive advantage in 1980 by stating that competitive advantage is the consequence of a successful competitive strategy.

Competitive strategy means 'taking offensive or defensive actions to create a defendable position in an industry, to cope successfully with competitive forces and thereby yield a superior return on investment for the firm. Firms have discovered many different approaches to this end, and the best strategy for a given firm is ultimately a unique construction reflecting its particular circumstances.' (Porter)

Note that Porter defines competitive advantage in terms of 'superior return on investment' rather than simply superior sales or higher sales revenue.

In Chapter 6 we examined the concept of the value chain and discussed how a business can create and sustain competitive advantage using cost or value drivers. The choice of competitive strategy will determine whether the focus of the chain should be cost (**cost leadership**) or value (**differentiation**) and will have implications for functional strategies (see Chapter 13).

4.2 The choice of competitive strategy

Porter argued that selecting and implementing one of these strategies is the only way to effectively counter the industry forces identified in his Five Forces model.

The diagram below summarises his argument.

Cost leader	Stuck in the middle	Differentiator
High profit	Low profit	High profit
Lower costs	Higher costs	Higher costs
✓	✗	✓

Competitive pressures will increase as a market ages so that once the mature stage of the industry is reached only two competitive strategies will deliver competitive advantage (ie, superior ROI).

- **Low cost**: A firm following this strategy will withstand the shrinking margins better and so, as rivals fall away, may be left as a major player with enhanced power against the power of suppliers and buyers.

- **Differentiation**: A firm presenting itself as a superior provider may escape price pressure by avoiding straight-forward price comparisons with rivals.

A **stuck in the middle** strategy is one where the firm has sought to attract many segments at different price points and so is seen as not being as differentiated as the market leader but, perhaps because of the costs of serving the differentiated segment, not able to make good profits at the cost leader's prices.

4.3 Porter's generic strategies

Porter's generic strategies are illustrated in the diagram below:

4.3.1

Competitive basis

	Low cost	Differentiation
Broad	Cost leadership	Differentiation
Narrow	Cost focus	Differentiation focus

Competitive scope

4.3.2 Cost leadership

A cost leadership strategy seeks to achieve the position of lowest-cost producer in the industry as a whole. By producing at the lowest cost, the manufacturer can compete on price with every other producer in the industry, and earn the higher unit profits, if the manufacturer so chooses. A cost leadership strategy can be achieved in a number of ways including: supply chain management, establishing production facilities to obtain economies of scale, using the latest technologies to reduce costs, benefiting from the learning curve effect, and reducing overhead costs.

Classic examples of companies pursuing cost leadership are Ryanair and Lidl. Large out-of-town stores specialising in one particular category of product are able to secure cost leadership by economies of scale over other retailers.

4.3.3 Differentiation

A differentiation strategy assumes that competitive advantage can be gained through **particular characteristics** of a firm's products.

How to differentiate

(a) **Build up a brand image** (eg, Pepsi's blue cans are supposed to offer different 'psychic benefits' to Coke's red ones).

(b) **Give the product special features** to make it stand out (eg, Mercedes finger print recognition security system).

(c) **Exploit other activities of the value chain** (see Chapter 6) eg, marketing and service.

(d) Use **IT** to create **new services** or **product features**.

4.3.4 Generic strategies and the Five Forces

Competitive force	Advantages		Disadvantages	
	Cost leadership	Differentiation	Cost leadership	Differentiation
New entrants	Economies of scale raise entry barriers	Brand loyalty and perceived uniqueness are entry barriers		
Substitutes	Firm is not so vulnerable to less cost-effective alternatives	Customer loyalty is a weapon against substitutes		
Customers	Customers cannot drive down prices further than the next most efficient competitor	Customers have no comparable alternative Brand loyalty should lower price sensitivity		Customers may no longer need the differentiating factor Sooner or later customers become price sensitive

Competitive force	Advantages		Disadvantages	
	Cost leadership	Differentiation	Cost leadership	Differentiation
Suppliers	Flexibility to deal with cost increases	Higher margins can offset vulnerability to supplier price rises	Increase in input costs can reduce price advantages	
Industry rivalry	Firm remains profitable when rivals go under through excessive price competition	Unique features reduce direct competition	Technological change will require capital investment, or make production cheaper for competitors Competitors learn via imitation Cost concerns ignore product design or marketing issues	Imitation narrows differentiation

4.3.5 Focus (or niche) strategy

In a focus strategy, a firm concentrates its attention on one or more particular segments or niches of the market, and does not try to serve the entire market with a single product. Within the niche, the firm can either aim to be a cost leader or pursue differentiation

Porter suggests that a focus strategy can achieve competitive advantage when 'broad-scope' businesses fall into one of two errors:

- Under-performance occurs when a product does not fully meet the needs of a segment and offers the opportunity for a differentiation focus player.

- Over-performance gives a segment more than it really wants and provides an opportunity for a cost focus player.

Advantages

- A niche is more secure and a firm can insulate itself from competition.

- The firm does not spread itself too thinly.

- Both cost leadership and differentiation require superior performance – life is easier in a niche, where there may be little or no competition.

Drawbacks of a focus strategy

- The firm sacrifices economies of scale which would be gained by serving a wider market.

- Competitors can move into the segment, with increased resources (eg, Lexus moved into the US luxury car market, to compete with Mercedes and BMW).

- The segment's needs may eventually become less distinct from the main market.

4.4 Conceptual difficulties with generic strategy

In practice, it is rarely simple to draw hard and fast distinctions between the generic strategies as there are conceptual problems underlying them.

- **Cost leadership**

    - **Internal focus**: Cost refers to internal measures, rather than the market demand. It can be used to gain market share: but it is the **market share which is important,** not cost leadership as such.

    - **Only one firm**: If cost leadership applies cross the whole industry, only one firm will pursue this strategy successfully. However, the position is not clear-cut.

        - More than one firm might **aspire** to cost leadership, especially in dynamic markets where new technologies are frequently introduced.

        - The boundary between cost leadership and cost focus might be blurred.

        - Firms competing market-wide might have different competences or advantages that confer cost leadership in different segments.

    - **Higher margins can be used for differentiation**: Having low costs does **not** mean you have to charge lower prices or compete on price. A cost leader can choose to 'invest higher margins in R&D or marketing'. Being a cost leader arguably gives producers more freedom to choose **other** competitive strategies.

- **Differentiation**: Porter assumes that a differentiated product will always be sold at a **higher** price.

    - However, a **differentiated product** may be sold at the same price as competing products to **increase market share**.

    - **Choice of competitor**. Differentiation from whom? Who are the competitors? Do they serve other market segments? Do they compete on the same basis?

    - **Source of differentiation**. This can include **all** aspects of the firm's offer, not only the product. Restaurants aim to create an atmosphere or 'ambience', as well as serving food of good quality.

Focus probably has fewer conceptual difficulties, as it ties in very neatly with ideas of market segmentation. In practice most companies pursue this strategy to some extent, by designing products/services to meet the needs of particular target markets.

4.5 Bowman's strategic clock

Porter's basic concept of generic strategies has been the subject of further discussion. Bowman's clock model was developed from surveys of practising managers attending MBA programmes who were asked to describe the competitive strategies being followed by their own firms, which represent possible combinations of price and quality across a whole spectrum.

The strategy clock

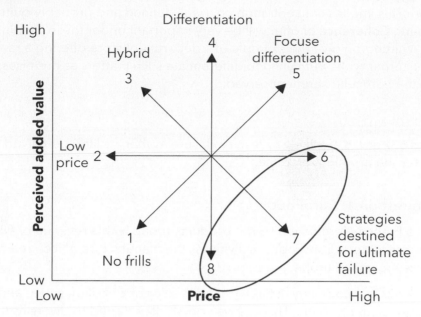

4.5.1 Price-based strategies

Strategies 1 and 2 are price-based strategies.

- A **no frills** strategy (1) is aimed at the most price-conscious and can only succeed if this segment of the market is sufficiently large. This strategy may be used for market entry, to gain experience and build volume. This was done by Japanese car manufacturers in the 1960s.

- A **low price** strategy (2) offers better value than competitors. This can lead to price war and reduced margins for all. Porter's generic strategy of **cost leadership** is appropriate to a firm adopting this strategy.

4.5.2 Differentiation strategies

Strategies 3, 4 and 5 are all differentiation strategies. Each one represents a different trade-off between market share (with its cost advantages) and margin (with its direct impact on profit). Differentiation can be created in three ways:

- product features
- marketing, including powerful brand promotion
- core competences

The pursuit of any differentiation strategy requires detailed and accurate **market intelligence**. The customers and their preferences must be clearly identified, as must the competition and their likely responses. The chosen basis for differentiation should be inherently difficult to imitate, and will probably need to be developed over time.

The **hybrid** strategy (3) seeks both differentiation and a lower price than competitors. The cost base must be low enough to permit reduced prices and reinvestment to maintain differentiation. This strategy may be more advantageous than differentiation alone under certain circumstances.

- If it leads to growth in market share.
- If differentiation rests on core competences and costs can be reduced elsewhere.
- If a low price approach is suited to a particular market segment.
- Where it is used as a market entry strategy.

The basic **differentiation** strategy (4) comes in two variants, depending on whether a price premium is charged or a competitive price is accepted to build market share.

A strategy of **focused differentiation** seeks a high price premium in return for a high degree of differentiation. This implies concentration on a well defined and probably quite restricted market segment. **Coherence** of offer will be very important under these circumstances. Johnson, Scholes and Whittington give the example of a department store offering a range of products to a variety of customer types but failing to differentiate such matters as premises, décor and staff according to the particular segment served.

4.5.3 Failure strategies

Combinations 6, 7 and 8 are likely to result in failure as there is little perceived added value to compensate for the premium on price.

Interactive question 1: EuroFoods

EuroFoods is a French-German consumer products group with a revenue of €8 billion a year at 20X2 retail prices. One of EuroFoods' activities is the manufacture of ice-cream. It is the largest producer of ice cream in Europe.

Medley is an American company. It has worldwide sales of €5 billion a year and these come mainly from chocolate products. Three years ago Medley started to diversify. It did this by selling a new product, ice-cream, in one of its existing markets, Europe. Although Medley had no prior experience of ice-cream, it believed that it could exploit its existing expertise in food products, marketing and distribution in this new area. Medley's products are renowned for their quality, and all of its ice cream products are sold at higher prices than those of competitors to help reinforce the company's image of being a premium brand.

The European ice-cream industry revenue is €6 billion at 20X2 retail prices.

Market share	%
EuroFoods	60
Medley	10
Local producers*	30
	100

* These are defined as manufacturers who sell within only one European country.

Distribution has always been a very important aspect of the food industry. However, it is particularly so in the ice-cream business. This is because the product must be kept refrigerated from factory to shop, and also whilst it is stored in the shop.

Many of the shops which sell EuroFoods' ice-cream are small businesses and the freezer which is required for storage is a costly item for them to buy. EuroFoods has therefore developed a scheme whereby it will install and maintain such a freezer in these shops. The shop owner does not have to pay for the freezer. The only condition which EuroFoods imposes is that the freezer must be used exclusively for the sales of its products.

EuroFoods believes that this arrangement has worked well for everybody in the past. EuroFoods' expenditures on the freezers have ensured that its products have reached the consumer in good condition and also enabled it to simplify inventory control. It has also played a part in building its market dominance by enabling shops which otherwise would not be able to do so, to sell its products.

The European ice-cream business

The peak time of year for sales of ice-cream in Europe is from mid-June to mid-August. These summer sales are deemed 'impulse' sales by the trade and are traditionally made from small retail outlets where EuroFoods tends to have its exclusive arrangements. The other sort of sale is the 'take-home', which are purchases made in larger quantities at supermarkets. These outlets do not have exclusive agreements with EuroFoods.

Analysis of European ice-cream sales in 20X2 is as follows.

	Volume %	Value € bn	Return on sales – Profit before tax € bn
Impulse sales	40	4	0.48
Take-home sales	60	2	0.12
Total	100	6	

Medley

Medley would like to obtain its future growth from the impulse sector of the market. It owns 14,000 non-exclusive freezer cabinets, mainly in Ireland. However, it is costly to maintain these to sell the eight products which constitute its product range. Another problem is that in many cases small shops have room for only one freezer and this has often already been supplied by EuroFoods. As Medley's Ireland Managing Director said:'It means only big competitors with a full range of products can enter the market'.

Medley would like to be able to place its products in the freezers provided by EuroFoods. However, when it tried to do this two years ago in Spain, EuroFoods was successful in a legal action to prevent this.

Medley has now complained to the European Union that EuroFoods' exclusive freezer arrangements restrict competition and are unfair.

You are presently working for Thunderclap Newman, a merchant bank, as a business analyst in its Confectionery Division.

Requirements

Write a report to the head of the Confectionery Division of your bank, which

1.1 Identifies strategies which lead to competitive advantage.

1.2 Makes recommendations to **both** companies on their possible future strategy options if the EU decides that exclusive freezer arrangements are:

- Anti-competitive and, in future, freezers should be available to any manufacturer
- Not anti-competitive and EuroFoods can continue to protect the use of its freezers

Note: A billion equals one thousand million.

See **Answer** at the end of this chapter.

5 Product-market strategy: direction of growth

Section overview

- The second strategic choice, outlined in section 1 above, is which products and markets to serve.

- Ansoff classifies the choices on a matrix into market penetration, product development, market development and diversification. Ansoff's growth vector matrix was introduced in your Business, Technology and Finance studies, and is recapped in this section.

- Each strategy has its particular benefits and drawbacks.

5.1 The product-market growth matrix

Ansoff drew up a **growth vector matrix**, describing how a combination of a firm's activities in current and new markets, with existing and new products can lead to **growth**. The four available growth strategies are: market penetration, product development, market development and diversification.

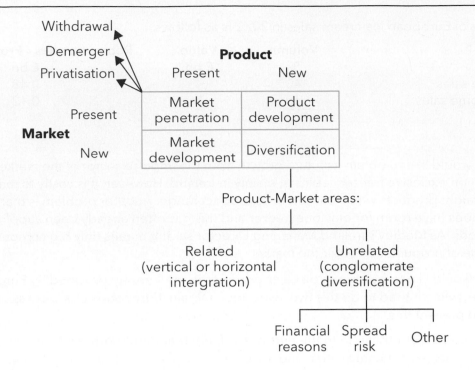

5.2 Growth vectors

Ansoff identifies four directions (or vectors) of growth available to the business which were introduced in the Business, Technology and Finance text. Unlike Porter's generic strategies, where only one should be followed, management can pursue all four of Ansoff's vectors if it wishes to, although some eg, diversification, are more risky than others. In the Business Strategy and Technology exam you may be required to use the Ansoff matrix to analyse the ways in which a business has grown.

5.2.1 Market penetration

The firm seeks to do four things:

- **Maintain or to increase its share** of current markets with current products, eg, through competitive pricing, advertising, sales promotion.

- **Secure dominance** of growth markets.

- **Restructure** a mature market by driving out competitors.

- **Increase usage** by existing customers (eg, airmiles, loyalty cards).

5.2.2 Market development: present products and new markets

There are many possible approaches. Here are some examples.

- **New geographical areas** and export markets (eg, a radio station building a new transmitter to reach a new audience).

- **Different package sizes** for food and other domestic items so that both those who buy in bulk and those who buy in small quantities are catered for.

- **New distribution channels** to attract new customers (eg, organic food sold in supermarkets not just specialist shops, internet sales).

- **Differential pricing policies** to attract different types of customer and create **new market segments**. For example, travel companies have developed a market for cheap long-stay winter breaks in warmer countries for retired couples.

5.2.3 Product development: new products and present markets

This has several advantages.

- The company can exploit its existing marketing arrangements such as promotional methods and distribution channels at low cost.
- The company should already have good knowledge of its customers and their wants and habits.
- Competitors will be forced to respond.
- The cost of entry to the market will go up and newcomers may be discouraged.

5.2.4 Diversification: new products and new markets

Diversification occurs when a company decides to make **new products for new markets**. It should have a clear idea about what it expects to gain from diversification. Diversification is the most risky of the four strategies.

- **Growth**: New products and new markets should be selected which offer prospects for growth which the existing product-market mix does not.
- **Investing surplus** funds not required for other expansion needs, bearing in mind that the funds could be returned to shareholders. Diversification is a high risk strategy, having many of the characteristics of a new business start-up. It is likely to require the deployment of **new competences**.

5.3 Types of diversification

Ansoff identifies **two classes** of diversification:

1. **Related diversification**: Integrating activities in the supply chain or leveraging technologies or competences. This involves either horizontal or vertical integration.

2. **Conglomerate diversification**: The development of a portfolio of businesses with no commercial similarity or links between them.

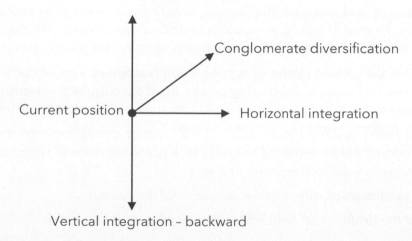

5.3.1 Horizontal integration (related diversification)

Horizontal integration is development into activities which are competitive with or directly **complementary** to a company's present activities. There are three cases:

- **Competitive products**: Taking over a competitor can have obvious benefits, leading eventually towards achieving a monopoly. Apart from active competition, a competitor may offer advantages such as completing geographical coverage.

- **Complementary products**: For example, a manufacturer of household vacuum cleaners moving into commercial cleaners. A full product range can be presented to the market and there may well be benefits from having many of the components common between the different ranges.

- **By-products**: For example, a butter manufacturer discovering increased demand for skimmed milk. Generally, income from by-products is a windfall to be counted, at least initially, as a bonus.

5.3.2 Vertical Integration (related diversification)

Vertical integration occurs when a company becomes its own supplier (backward) or distributor forward).

- **Backward integration**: taking over responsibility for **upstream processes** eg, a clothing retailer producing or designing its own clothes.

- **Forward integration**: taking over responsibility for **downstream processes** eg, an electrical goods retailer setting up its own installation, servicing and repairs service.

Advantages of vertical integration

- **Economies of combined operations**, eg, proximity, reduced handling.

- **Economies of internal control and co-ordination**, eg, scheduling and coordinating operations should be better. Information about the market can be fed back to the production companies.

- **Economies of avoiding the market**. Negotiation, packing, advertising costs are avoided.

- **Tap into technology**. Close knowledge of the upstream or downstream operations can give a company valuable strategic advantages. For example, computer manufacturers have instituted backwards integration into semi-conductor design and manufacturing to gain a better understanding of the technology and its potential.

- **Safeguarding proprietary knowledge**. If a firm makes components itself, it does not have to supply specifications to its suppliers; this information therefore stays confidential.

- **Assured supply and demand**. The firm will have first call on supplies in scarce periods and the greatest chance of having an outlet in periods of low demand. Fluctuations in supply and demand are not eliminated but can, perhaps, be better planned for.

- **Reduction in bargaining power of suppliers and customers**. Two of Porter's forces on a firm are customer and supplier bargaining power. So, if our suppliers are giving us a rough time, we take them over or set up our own supply company. Similarly with distribution channels.

- **Enhanced ability to differentiate**. More of the product comes under control so we have a greater ability to differentiate it. For example, a specialist chain of shops could be established with a distinctive brand image.

- **Stronger relationships** with the final consumer of the product.

- A share of the **profits** at all stages of the value chain.

- Creation of **barriers to entry.**

Disadvantages of vertical integration

- **Vertical integration increases the proportion of the firm's costs which are fixed**. For example, if the firm purchases from an outside source, all those costs will be variable. If the input is produced internally, the firm has to bear all the fixed costs of production. Vertical integration increases business risk from this source.

- **Reduced flexibility to change partners**. If the in-house supplier or customer does not perform well, it is not easy to switch to outsiders. You will probably have to get rid of the in-house company first.

- **Capital investment needs**. Vertical integration will consume capital resources. For integration to be a good choice it must yield a return greater than, or equal to, the firm's opportunity cost of capital, adjusting for strategic considerations.

- **Cut off from suppliers and customers**. By integrating a firm may cut itself off from the flow of technology from its suppliers or market research information from its customers. For example, a firm will have to take responsibility for developing its own technology. Other potential suppliers may be reluctant to share their technology as they would be supplying it not just to a customer, but a customer who is also a competitor.

- **Dulled incentives**. The captive relationship between buyer and seller can quickly lead to inefficiencies. These can quickly spread through the group as products produced at too high a cost are passed through.

- **Differing managerial requirements**. Different businesses need different management skills. Because a company is a successful manufacturer, this does not mean that it can turn its hand to retailing with a reasonable chance of success.

- Avoid transaction costs arising from external relationships. Costs arise over contract negotiation, compliance monitoring, redress actions etc.

- **Overconcentration**: A company places 'more eggs in the same end-market basket' (Ansoff). Such a policy is fairly inflexible, more sensitive to instabilities and increases the firm's dependence on a particular aspect of economic demand.

- The firm **fails to benefit from any economies of scale** in the industry into which it has diversified. This is why, in the publishing industry, most printing is subcontracted to specialist printing firms, who can work machinery to capacity by doing work for many firms.

5.3.3 Conglomerate diversification

Conglomerate diversification has not been very fashionable in the USA and Europe where its financial returns have been disappointing. However, it has been a key strategy for companies in Asia, particularly South Korea. In the previous chapter we explored the role of chaebol (conglomerates) in Japan and South Korea.

Conglomerates

- The characteristic of conglomerate (or unrelated) diversification is that there is no common thread, and the only synergy lies with the management skills. Outstanding management seems to be the key to success as a conglomerate, and in the case of large conglomerates they are indeed able, because of their size and diversity, to attract high-calibre managers with wide experience.

- Two major types of conglomerate can be identified. The **financial conglomerate** provides a flow of funds to each segment of its operation, exercises control and is the ultimate risk taker. In theory it undertakes strategic planning but does not participate in operating decisions. The **managerial conglomerate** extends this approach by providing managerial counsel and interaction on operating decisions, on the assumption that general management skills can be transferred to almost any environment.

Advantages of conglomerate diversification

- **Risk-spreading**: entering new products into new markets offers protection against the failure of current products and markets.

- **High profit opportunities**: an improvement of the **overall profitability and flexibility** of the firm through acquisition in industries which have better economic characteristics than those of the acquiring firms.

- **Ability to grow** quickly by making acquisitions in diverse fields.

- **Escape** from the present business.

- **Better access to capital** markets on mergers and acquisitions.
- **No other way to grow.**
- **Use surplus cash.**
- **Exploit under-utilised resources.**
- **Obtain cash**, or other financial advantages (such as accumulated tax losses).
- **Use a company's image and reputation** in one market to develop into another where corporate image and reputation could be vital ingredients for success.
- Avoidance of the disadvantages of other types of diversification, eg, anti-monopoly legislation.

Virgin Group, which we looked at earlier in the chapter, could be seen as an example of conglomerate diversification.

Disadvantages of conglomerate diversification

- The **dilution of shareholders' earnings** if diversification is into growth industries with high P/E ratios.
- **Lack of a common identity and purpose** in a conglomerate organisation. A conglomerate will only be successful if it has a high quality of management and financial ability at central headquarters, where the diverse operations are brought together.
- **Failure in one of the businesses will drag down the rest**, as it will eat up resources.
- **Lack of management experience**: Japanese steel companies have diversified into areas completely unrelated to steel such as personal computers, with limited success.
- **Poor for shareholders**: conglomerate acquisitions give no additional benefit to the shareholders – since there is no synergy, the individual investor will do no better investing in a subsidiary company through a holding company than he would have done if he had invested in the subsidiary directly. Shareholders can spread risk quite easily, simply by buying a diverse portfolio of shares. They do not need management to do it for them.
- Since there is **no synergy** there is no operating advantage over several smaller firms.
- Earnings of conglomerates and the price-earnings ratios of their shares seem to be particularly **badly affected by economic recession** (and this may mean that during a recession they are unable to continue with acquisitions).

The methods by which Ansoff's growth strategies can be implemented (eg, organic growth, acquisition etc,) will be considered in Chapter 11.

Interactive question 2: Blue Jeans Group

Note: Assume that the current date is March 20X9. The currency in Blue Jeans' country is the dollar.

The Blue Jeans Group was floated in March 20X4 on a major European stock market with a capitalisation of over $22 million. The company was founded 11 years earlier by three Kenyan Asian brothers who began their venture with a market stall based in the capital city of a developed European country which is outside of the Eurozone.

Eight years prior to flotation, the business had been built up to such an extent that the brothers were forced to choose between the wholesaling and retailing arms of their operation. In the event, they decided to focus their effort on the faster-growing wholesaling activities. The capital released by the sale of the retail outlets was then used to purchase a warehouse near to the capital city to stock the garments. It was at this time that the decision was taken to develop Blue

Jeans as the brand name for the range of jeans and fully co-ordinated casual wear in which they were trading.

When the brothers began their wholesaling operations, the rapid growth in the market for jeans meant that their largest competitors had full order books and were not in a position to satisfy market demand. Therefore there was plenty of 'market room' for a company like Blue Jeans. The brothers decided to concentrate their effort initially on smaller retailers, since many of these were not being adequately supplied by the larger (mainly US) manufacturers.

Eventually contracts were obtained with some major European retailers. The small retailer was not ignored but, as Blue Jeans grew, it was forced to direct its efforts towards the more established shops rather than market traders.

Manufacturing – sourcing policy

In the first instance Blue Jeans turned to Hong Kong to obtain the larger quantities which it required for its expanding business. It generally takes seven or eight months for a new manufacturing unit to attain the standards which are demanded by Blue Jeans. Around 90% of the company's orders are now produced in Hong Kong. Blue Jeans considers that its policy of contracting out the manufacture of its garments has generally been successful. However, recent delays in producing new styles of jeans from new patterns have caused problems.

Currently Blue Jeans is radically restyling part of its Big Stuff Company brand (BSCO) brand and hopes to take the market by surprise. A contract to produce the first batch of 5,000 pairs of the new design is about to be awarded. Two competing tenders are being considered.

Supplier A An existing Hong Kong based supplier, offering to deliver the garments in three to six months' time at a cost of $10 per pair payable on delivery.

Supplier B A new supplier to Blue Jeans, which in the past has worked almost entirely for one of its smaller competitors. Supplier B is offering to produce the jeans at $9 per pair payable in advance. It will deliver in nine months and will pay a penalty fee of $0.50 per garment per month for any late deliveries.

On only one occasion has Blue Jeans become involved in the manufacture of its own garments. The outcome of which was near disastrous. The experience led the brothers to make two important policy decisions.

First, they decided not to go into manufacturing themselves but to concentrate on buying and selling. Secondly, they decided to stick with experienced manufacturers and not to attempt to obtain too great a degree of manufacturing process innovation. Recent changes in textile industry technology, eg, flexible manufacturing, JIT, etc, have led one of the brothers to question this approach.

Product market strategy

During the past decade considerable changes have taken place in the jeans market. Therefore flexibility and ability to respond to fairly rapid changes in fashion are an essential component of the ability of a company, such as Blue Jeans, to survive in the jeans business.

The current jeans product strategy of Blue Jeans is based upon a portfolio of four brand names, each of which has its distinctive appeal and identity. First, there is the Blue Jeans brand itself. This is the original brand and is the leader in the group's international activities. The Blue Jeans brand, which is targeted at fashion-conscious men and women in the 15–25 age bracket, consists of two main elements. There are basic denim jeans which are offered on an all the year round basis and there is a casual collection offered on a seasonal basis. The jeans brand is from time to time strengthened by the addition of jeans-related products. These have included footwear, marketed under licence, leather jackets and a range of accessories such as belts and watches. It is envisaged that bags, holdalls and grips will also be introduced.

The Big Stuff Company brand (BSCO) is more 'classical' leisurewear with more contemporary fashions. The BSCO brand is aimed at both men and women in the 16–25 age group. The

Buffalo brand, which was designed in Bordeaux initially for the French market, has its own distinctive French flavour. Moreover, its sales are biased heavily towards women, although it caters for both sexes in the 16-24 age group. By contrast, Hardcore is tough and masculine, based upon a traditional 'macho' image. Since it was introduced it has developed its own clearly defined niche within the men's jeans market – namely the 16-35 age group.

Company financing

The development of Blue Jeans during its early years was reflected in a steady expansion in its revenue and profitability. However, five years on, losses were incurred due to a number of unfortunate events. By the 20X2/X3 financial year profitability had recovered and had reached a total of almost $1 million. To maintain growth in March 20X4 five and a half million shares, representing almost one quarter of the group's equity, were sold at 100 cents on a major European stock market. This sale raised over $5 million for investment purposes.

Since the floatation of the Blue Jeans Group in March 20X4, the company has gone from strength to strength, with average sales growth being roughly 50% per annum. (The Appendix contains Blue Jeans' financial details). Turnover in the year ending 31 March 20X9 is expected to be over $100 million with profits of over $10 million. The brothers are keen to maintain this record of sales growth, while at the same time providing the highest possible returns to their shareholders.

The jeans market

During 20X4 a revival in the jeans market occurred, stimulated by Levi's successful reintroduction of its five pocket, fly button 501 jeans. This development, backed by a heavy advertising campaign, may be seen in terms of a more general appeal to nostalgia in society which was prevalent at that time. A craze for stone-washed jeans also helped to boost sales temporarily. However, this fad had fizzled out by 20X7, by which time overall sales were again static.

A more important trend during the mid to late 20X0s was for the jeans market to become increasingly fashion conscious. Traditionally the style of jeans has changed relatively slowly and manufacturers have relied on making standardised products at high volume. This has tended to accentuate the importance of production economies of scale.

Jeans market 20X6

United States (490m pairs)
Levi Strauss 24%
Diesel 14%
Lee 10%
Wrangler 10%
Guess 3%
Others 39%

Europe (180m pairs)
Levi Strauss 11%
Diesel 4%
Wrangler 3%
Lee 2%
Lee Cooper 2%
Blue Jeans 2%
Others 76%

More recently, rapid changes in style have required companies to exhibit greater flexibility. Designer jean companies, such as Blue Jeans, have generally done well. Of the major manufacturers, Levi and Diesel have prospered. By contrast, Wrangler and Lee Cooper have suffered from their 'cowboy' and 'old fashioned' images respectively.

In an attempt to reverse the adverse trend, Wrangler initiated a major TV advertising campaign. This followed an expansion of such activity by Levi and Blue Jeans. Each of the campaigns had one factor in common – targeting of adolescents, the chief consumer of jeans.

A common feature of the strategic response of the major manufacturers to their business environment has been a decision to withdraw from manufacturing and source their output from contract manufacturers in the Far East. The unquestioned European leader in this respect has been Blue Jeans.

Blue Jeans plc financial details

Blue Jeans: Five year trading summary

	20X8 $'000	20X7 $'000	20X6 $'000	20X5 $'000	20X4 $'000
Revenue	97,461	72,241	50,242	31,113	19,906
Profit on ordinary activities before taxation	12,756	8,399	5,905	4,208	2,633
Taxation	5,019	2,867	2,010	1,718	1,177
Profit on ordinary activities after taxation	7,737	5,532	3,895	2,490	1,456
Minority interests	240	180	160	47	36
	7,497	5,352	3,735	2,443	1,420
Earnings per share	31.9c	22.8c	15.9c	10.4c	7.8c

Requirements

2.1 Outline the factors Blue Jeans should consider in awarding the contract to produce the first batch of the new style BSCO jeans.

2.2 As a management consultant, prepare a memorandum to the Managing Director which

(a) Performs a corporate appraisal of Blue Jeans at March 20X9.

(b) Uses Ansoff to analyse its future strategy options.

See **Answer** at the end of this chapter.

6 Other strategies

Section overview

- The growth strategies identified by Ansoff involve essentially successful business divisions.
- Where divisions are less successful there are strategic choices involving letting them go.

6.1 Withdrawal

Withdrawal may be an appropriate strategy under certain circumstances.

- Products may simply disappear when they reach the end of their life cycles.

- Underperforming products may be weeded out.

- Sale of subsidiary businesses for reasons of corporate strategy, such as finance, change of objectives, lack of strategic fit.

- Sale of assets to raise funds and release other resources.

Exit barriers may make this difficult and/or costly.

- Cost barriers include redundancy costs, termination penalties on leases and other contracts, and the difficulty of selling assets.

- Managers might fail to grasp the idea of decision-relevant costs ('we've spent all this money, so we must go on').

- Political barriers include government attitudes. Defence is an example.

- Marketing considerations may delay withdrawal. A product might be a loss-leader for others, or might contribute to the company's reputation for its breadth of coverage.

- Psychology. Managers hate to admit failure, and there might be a desire to avoid embarrassment.

- People might wrongly assume that carrying on is a low risk strategy.

6.2 Divestment and demerger

Divestment and demerger have become more common as companies seek to reverse the diversification strategies they once pursued. There are several reasons for this.

- To rationalise a business as a result of a strategic appraisal, perhaps as a result of portfolio analysis, where a lack of fit has been identified. Another reason might be to free up management time to concentrate on core competences and synergies.

- To sell off subsidiary companies at a profit, perhaps as an exit route after managing a turn-round or as a management defence strategy to avoid a potential take-over of the whole company.

- To allow market valuation to reflect growth and income prospects. Where a low growth, steady income operation exists alongside a potentially high growth new venture, the joint P/E is likely to be too high for the cash cow and too low for the star. The danger is that a predator will take over the whole operation and split the business in two, allowing each part to settle at its own level.

- Satisfy investors: diversified conglomerates are unfashionable. Modern investment thinking is that investors prefer to provide their own portfolio diversification.

- To raise funds to invest elsewhere or to reduce debt.

Demerger can realise underlying asset values in terms of share valuation. ICI's demerger of its attractive pharmaceuticals business led to the shares in the two demerged companies trading at a higher combined valuation than those of the original single firm.

Summary and Self-test

Summary

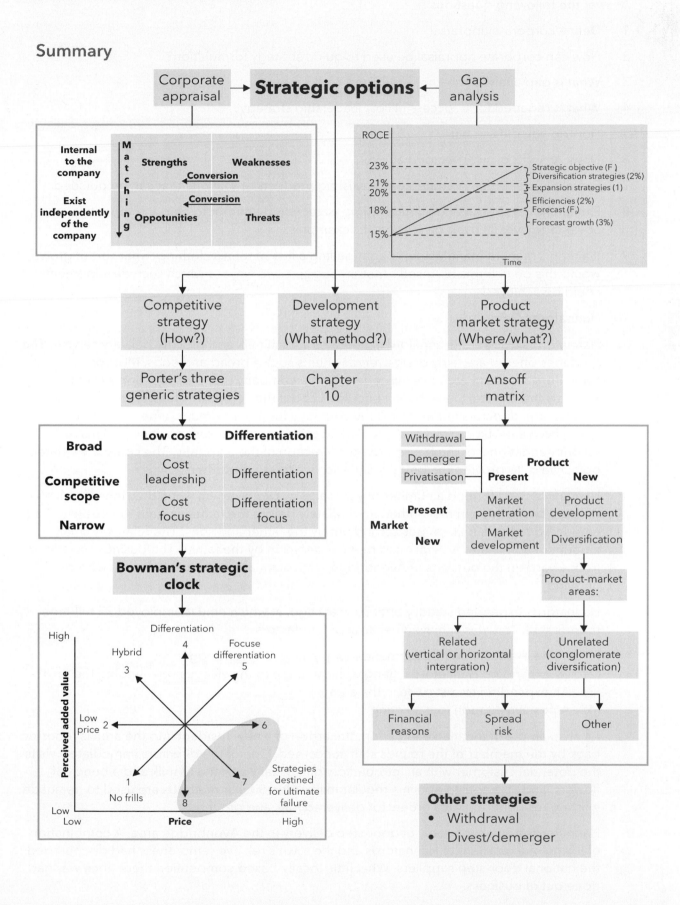

Self-test

Answer the following questions.

1 Define corporate appraisal.

2 How can corporate appraisal be used to guide strategy formulation?

3 What is gap analysis?

4 What is required for a successful cost leadership strategy?

5 How do you differentiate?

6 Draw Ansoff's growth vector diagram.

7 Explain two alternative strategies for existing products or markets that can be pursued.

8 Explain how a producer of natural spring water could attempt to gain a competitive advantage over its rivals giving specific examples.

9 If a tennis racquet manufacturer began selling a line of tennis clothing, what sort of growth would this be in terms of Ansoff's matrix? Suggest two ways in which such development could be achieved.

10 **Hannafords Dairy Ltd**

Hannaford's Dairy Ltd (Hannafords), operates a fresh milk and grocery delivery service. The groceries offered are fairly basic everyday items such a bread and eggs. Most of Hannaford's sales relate to its milk offering. The company is one of your firm's clients. Recently the directors have been concerned about the company's future. This is partly because the directors intend to sell the company for the maximum value, and retire, in about five years' time. You have been asked to assess the current position and make recommendations for the future strategic direction of the company. The company's stated objective is 'to provide the best possible service to our customers.'

Hannafords was formed a number of years ago by two brothers when they inherited a milk delivery business from their father. Immediately before the father's death the business had amounted to three milk rounds carried out by the father and sons. The relatively small amount of administrative work had been undertaken by the father. The business operated from a yard on the outskirts of Avonbridge, a substantial town in the far south west of England.

Hannafords expanded steadily until 30 years ago, at which time it employed 25 full-time rounds staff. This was achieved because of four factors.

(1) Some expansion of the permanent population of Avonbridge
(2) By expanding Hannafords' geographical range to the villages surrounding the town
(3) An expanding tourist trade in the area
(4) A positive attitude to marketing

As an example of the marketing effort, the arrival of a new resident into the area is reported back by the member of the rounds staff concerned. One of the directors immediately visits the potential customer with an introductory gift, usually a bottle of milk and a bunch of flowers, and attempts to obtain a regular milk order. Similar methods are used to persuade existing residents to place orders for delivered milk and groceries.

Hannafords had a monopoly of door-step delivery in the Avonbridge area. A combination of losing market share to Hannafords and the town's relative remoteness had discouraged the national door-step suppliers. What little locally-based competition there once was had gone out of business.

Supplies of milk come from a bottling plant, owned by one of the national dairy companies, which is located 50 miles from Avonbridge. The bottlers deliver nightly, except Saturday nights, to Hannafords' depot. Hannafords deliver daily, except on Sundays.

Hannafords bought and developed a site, for use as a depot, on the then recently established Avonbridge Trading Estate. This was financed by a secured loan which the company subsequently paid off. The depot comprises a cold store, a parking area for the delivery vans, a delivery van maintenance shop and an office.

Profits after adjusting for inflation, have fallen over the last 30 years. Volumes have slipped by about a third, compared with a decline of about 50% for door-step deliveries nationally over the same period. New customers are increasingly difficult to find, despite a continuing policy of encouraging them. Many existing customers tend to have less milk delivered. A sufficient profit has been made to enable the directors to enjoy a reasonable income compared with their needs, but only by raising prices. Currently Hannafords charges 40 pence for a standard pint, delivered. This is fairly typical of door-step delivery charges around the UK. The Avonbridge supermarket, which is located in the centre of town, charges 26 pence a pint and other local stores charge between 35 pence and 40 pence.

Currently, Hannafords employs 15 full-time rounds staff, a van maintenance mechanic, a secretary/bookkeeper and the two directors. Hannafords is regarded locally as a good employer. The company pays good salaries and the directors have always taken a paternalistic approach to the employees. Regular employment opportunities in the area are few. Rounds staff are expected to, and generally do, give customers a friendly, cheerful and helpful service.

The two brothers continue to be the only shareholders and directors, and comprise the only level of management. One of the directors devotes most of his time to dealing with the supplier and with issues connected with the rounds. The other director looks after administrative matters, such as the accounts and personnel issues. Both directors undertake rounds to cover for sickness and holidays.

Requirements

10.1   Comment on the company's stated objective ('to provide the best possible service to our customers') as a basis for establishing a corporate strategy.

10.2   As far as the information given in the question will allow, undertake an analysis of the strengths, weaknesses, opportunities and threats (SWOT analysis) of the company.

      You should explain each point you make and provide some indication of the importance which you attach to each.

      Indicate what additional information you would need to obtain and why you need it, to enable you to complete your SWOT analysis.

10.3   Indicate how the resources of the company could form the basis of its future strategy.

11   Read the scenario of the **March 2015 Business Strategy and Technology** question in the Question Bank entitled *WeDive Ltd*. Draft an answer to the requirement which asks for an evaluation of the two strategic options being considered by the directors.

12   Read the scenario of the **June 2017 Business Strategy and Technology** question in the Question Bank entitled *Jason Smyth Textiles Ltd*. Draft an answer to the requirement which asks for an explanation of how elements of the company's value chain support its low-cost strategy. You should also take the time to attempt the requirement which asks for the benefits and problems of implementing the new business model.

Now, go back to the Learning outcomes in the Introduction. If you are satisfied that you have achieved these objectives, please tick them off.

Answers to Interactive questions

Answer to Interactive question 1

Report

To   Head of Confectionery
From   Business Analyst
Date   Today
Subject EuroFoods and Medley – the international ice-cream market

1.1 Terms of reference

This report outlines the strategy options for EuroFoods and Medley under the alternative scenarios resulting from the pending EU decision on exclusive freezer arrangements.

Competitive advantage

There are a number of different generic strategies which lead to competitive advantage for a firm's products, and these were identified by Michael Porter of the Harvard Business School.

- **High volume/low cost (overall cost leadership)**
  The cost of manufacture of the product is reduced to the lowest level in the market, thus leading to increased margins. The firm is also able to engage in price wars more effectively than its competitors.

- **Differentiation**
  Significant differences are developed in the quality, features and marketing of the product. Customers are therefore willing to pay a higher price, or the market might fragment altogether, leading to total domination of a niche.

- **Focus**
  Either of the above strategies can be combined with a greater or lesser degree of concentration on a smaller number of potential customers. Use of a focus strategy may defeat competitors using either of the two strategies above, but targeting a wide market.

It will also be important in devising strategies for EuroFoods and Medley to consider the effects of the competitive forces in the marketplace.

1.2 Scenario 1 – EU decision outlaws exclusive freezer arrangements

This decision will have a profound impact on the ice-cream market throughout Europe, as it will directly threaten the strong supplier status of EuroFoods in the impulse market. An indication of how significant this might be can be gained from some analysis of the market data.

Current position

% of European market	Volume	Revenue	Profit
Impulse sales	40	67	80
Take-home sales	60	33	20
	100	100	100

It is not clear from the data given exactly what share EuroFoods has of the impulse sales market, but it is unlikely to be less than its 60% overall share of the market, due to the competitive advantage gained from its exclusive freezer arrangements. Indeed, the commentary suggests EuroFoods to be dominant in this lucrative market segment. The outcome of an EU judgement in favour of Medley would therefore be to remove a significant entry barrier – the control of distribution.

EuroFoods' strategic options

The threat of new entrants to the market must be considered by EuroFoods as significant when forming a competitive strategy to take account of this scenario. Ideally, the entry barrier to the impulse sector formerly provided by the exclusive freezer arrangement must be replaced by another of equal effectiveness.

It would appear that the greatest current advantage that EuroFoods possesses in the EU impulse sales market, with the exception of the exclusive freezer arrangement, is its scale of production and established position as market leader.

This suggests that barriers to entry are available in the areas of economies of scale and the experience effect, both of which should lower the cost of production. It seems clear that an 'overall cost leadership' strategy may well be open to EuroFoods, which would enable super-profit to be taken.

It is therefore appropriate to recommend that EuroFoods invest heavily in product development and marketing to produce, brand and place newer, cheaper products, as such an approach is likely to be more effective when competing with Medley.

Medley's strategic options

The removal of exclusive freezer arrangements by the EU will present Medley with a major opportunity for growth. Although there will be a cost impact, as Medley may have to negotiate a fee for the use of the EuroFoods freezers, this will be far less significant than the removal of a major entry barrier.

The EU is likely to view a punitive fee strategy by EuroFoods as being similarly anti-competitive. In order to capitalise on the EU's decision, Medley will need to ensure that the products it develops in the future are sufficiently appealing to customers as they will be able to directly compare, and choose between EuroFoods' offering and Medley's when they are stored in the same freezer.

Medley's strength seems to lie in its ability to demand higher prices as it offers a differentiated product. Therefore any strategy that it pursues must not damage this approach. Profits earned by Medley should be reinvested in widening the distribution network into outlets previously dominated by EuroFoods, and upon reinforcing the brand image of its ice cream products.

For Medley maintaining the focus on the impulse sales segment seems preferable to attempting to compete in the take-home market which yields far lower margins.

Scenario 2 – Exclusive freezer arrangements remain

This represents a continuation of the current market conditions, which suggests that EuroFoods will find it easier to maintain its dominance of the market. However, Medley has already achieved a 10% market share with a new product and further penetration is likely.

EuroFoods' strategic options

EuroFoods must continue to exploit its competitive advantage in the impulse segment by entering into more exclusive freezer arrangements in areas of Europe not significantly penetrated.

In the take-home sector, however, EuroFoods is very vulnerable to attack even though margins are lower and branding is probably less significant.

EuroFoods may like to consider supplying major supermarket chains with a low-price product, possibly under an own brand.

Any cost advantages enjoyed by EuroFoods will ensure that Medley cannot compete without a significant subsidy from the other (non ice-cream) areas of the business.

Medley's strategic options

If the exclusive freezer arrangements are to continue, Medley might try to develop more of a differentiation-focus strategy by supporting the brand in the impulse segment.

Significant capital expenditure will be required to supply and maintain freezers in competition with EuroFoods, and many small retailers will be unable to provide space for both.

Medley will have to examine opportunities for alternative retail methods which are less expensive and more attractive to the retailers.

It may be possible, for example, to invest in the development of smaller freezers which could be placed on the counter. This may require Medley to limit the number of lines on offer to make the best use of the limited display space and avoid stock-outs or heavier distribution costs due to more frequent deliveries.

In the take-home segment, the exclusive freezer arrangements do not apply, and Medley has an opportunity to penetrate the market with multi-buy packs of the same branded product.

However, the brand will have to be heavily supported by advertising to guard against countermoves by EuroFoods. It may be possible to widen the range of lines using other Medley brand names, if the impulse sale segment seems out of reach.

Medley cannot rely on retailers breaking the exclusive freezer arrangement with EuroFoods, but can make it known that it will supply non-exclusive freezers if retailers have problems with EuroFoods. This strategy may backfire if EuroFoods refuses to supply retailers which break the agreement.

Conclusions

It can be seen that the decision in the EU is fundamental to the strategy formulation of both companies.

Answer to Interactive question 2

The Blue Jeans Group

2.1 Choice of supplier

Many factors should be taken into account in selecting a supplier. The main considerations are the following.

- **Cost**

  Supplier A is more expensive but is paid on delivery. Once penalty payments are incurred B becomes even cheaper.

- **Delivery**

  The importance of prompt delivery needs to be considered. Delivery by B is very late whilst A's is earlier but uncertain. Late delivery by B may save cost but it could lead to a loss in profits. Delivery dates quoted on both tenders could be considered to be unacceptably long.

- **Quality**

  Supplier B is new to Blue Jeans and may fail to meet the required quality standard.

- **Reliability**

  Supplier B is new to Blue Jeans and two significant risks are involved.

  Credit risk – payment is in advance and Blue Jeans are therefore carrying the credit risk.

Security – there is some danger that the design of the new jeans may be 'leaked' to Supplier B's existing customers.

In conclusion, Supplier A appears the safer option but delivery dates need to be renegotiated. It would probably be better to test Supplier B on a less important order before allowing it to work on new designs.

2.2 Memorandum

To   Board of Directors, Blue Jeans Group
From   A Consultant
Date   March 20X9
Subject Strategic position of Blue Jeans Group and future strategy options

(a) **Current strategic position**

- The current financial position of the firm is strong in terms of profit and sales growth. EPS has shown a dramatic increase. Its past profit problems now appear to be resolved. No information is available on liquidity and financial structure and it is necessary to examine these areas before making a final recommendation.

- It has a range of products aimed at particular market segments and a 'designer image which is important in the current market for jeans. It has a clearly focused strategy based on product differentiation.

- Its share of the European market is low (20X6) and it appears to have no stake in the large US market. However, in Europe it is of similar size to most other companies, apart from Levi Strauss. The jeans market is currently static and intense competition can be expected. Competition from other leisurewear manufacturers (eg, track suits, etc,) is also possible.

- It is currently supplied almost exclusively from Hong Kong. This could well have cost advantages, but several problems are apparent.

  (1) If the political situation in Hong Kong becomes unstable then this could eventually threaten supplies.

  (2) Exchange rate changes could lead to uncertainty over costs of products to be sold in the European market.

  (3) A danger of forward integration by existing suppliers also exists.

  (4) Long lines of supply and a long lead time in bringing new suppliers up to the required quality standard may hamper Blue Jeans' ability to exhibit the greater flexibility needed to cope with rapid changes of style. Changes in production technology may now be increasing the attractiveness of in-house manufacturing.

- Little information is available as to Blue Jeans' existing customer base and detailed information will be required before a final recommendation can be made.

(b) **Future strategy options**

Introduction

The objectives of the firm are expressed in terms of sales and profits. To a certain extent these two factors are in conflict as sales can often be increased at the expense of profit although this has not appeared to be a problem in the past. Maintaining past growth in both these areas is a considerable task in the face of a static market for jeans, and unless Blue Jeans can make advances in market share, a gap between objectives and actual performance is likely to develop if it simply continues with its existing strategy.

Options

The options for future strategy can be thought of under four headings.

Diversification – moving into new areas

Product development – selling new products to existing customers

Market development – selling existing products in new markets

Market penetration/internal efficiency – growth in sales and profits by increasing share of existing market, and/or reducing cost.

Diversification

- Blue Jeans has no experience of diversification into totally different product markets so this possibility is discounted.

- Horizontal diversification is a possibility, involving the takeover of an existing competitor. Two existing competitors (Lee and Wrangler) are currently experiencing difficulties due to their old fashioned image and could be potential targets. They would both provide footholds in the US market and possibly allow Blue Jeans to generate economies of scale. However, on the evidence available both of these companies are considerably larger than Blue Jeans (see US market share) which could make any takeover difficult (but not impossible).

- Vertical integration. Two possibilities exist here.

    - Forward integration into retail. Given the nature of jeans retailing this seems unlikely, however, more detail on existing customers is required before this can be ruled out.

    - Backward integration into manufacture. Although previous attempts have been unsuccessful, this does not mean that the strategy should be dismissed out of hand. It is investigated in detail in the next section.

Establishment of a manufacturing facility

Advantages

- Savings in transportation costs, search costs, etc.

- Improved quality.

- Greater flexibility in design and manufacture if features such as flexible manufacturing, JIT, etc are introduced.

- More rapid response to changes in styles.

- 'Secrecy' of new designs is also maintained.

- Avoidance of exchange risk if manufactured in the home country. (Exchange risk on exports would still exist.)

Disadvantages

- Blue Jeans will carry the 'volume risk' of manufacture. If demand falls it will still have to cover its fixed manufacturing costs.

- Subcontracted suppliers, due to their experience or location, may offer cost advantages.

Product development

- Some attempts have already been made to broaden Blue Jeans' product range by the addition of jeans-related products.

- This trend could be continued by the introduction of other products such as sportswear or similarly related products, which could be sold through existing distributors. Careful analysis of the demand for these new products would be required. Significant marketing expenditure could be required to promote these products.

- The possibility of online sales should be investigated. This would avoid the need to find new distributors.

Market development

- Blue Jeans' coverage of the European market should be reviewed. As only limited information about existing coverage is available investigating other countries in which Blue Jeans' could sell to should be undertaken.

- Blue Jeans has no stake in the US market which in 20X6 was almost three times larger than the European market.

- Licensing of the Blue Jeans name to manufacturers in other countries could be considered, although this could detract from quality and hamper any export drive at a later date.

- Online sales could enable Blue Jeans to enter new markets/market segments without the necessity of a physical presence. This could be a first step before any overseas expansion is considered.

Market penetration

- The situation in the jeans market appears to be changing from one requiring high volume at low cost to one of product differentiation.

- Blue Jeans should therefore continue to differentiate its product through advertising and aiming at particular market segments. New brands for new segments could be introduced. Online sales/website may encourage loyalty and repeat purchases.

- Cost reduction is of course important but this should not be at the expense of the policy of differentiation. This will be a major consideration in the decision to establish manufacturing facilities. The increased flexibility of own manufacture and the ability to introduce new products rapidly may outweigh the benefits of reduced cost and risk from out-sourcing. Alternatively the internet could be used to seek new supplies and reduce costs.

Conclusions

- The recent financial performance of Blue Jeans has been strong but in a static jeans market existing growth rates will be difficult to maintain.

- Changes in the competitive nature of the jeans markets may lead to a greater emphasis on flexibility, rather than cost. A detailed financial appraisal of in-house manufacturing is now required. This could either be by a green field start-up or an acquisition.

- Blue Jeans' existing policy of differentiation should be continued.

Answers to Self-test

1   A critical appraisal of strengths, weaknesses, opportunities and threats.

2   Match strengths with market opportunities; convert weaknesses into strengths and threats into opportunities.

3   Comparison of the objective with the outcomes of already-planned activities.

4   Economies of scale; latest technology; learning curve effect; improved productivity; minimised overhead costs; favourable access to sources of supply.

5   Build brand image; create special features in the product; exploit the value chain.

6

		Product	
		Present	New
Market	Present	Market penetration	Product development
	New	Market development	Diversification

7   Using the BCG matrix, one of four strategies can be pursued for each product.

Building market share: This is an appropriate strategy if

- Market growth rate is high
- The product is in its growth stage (of the product life cycle)

Such a strategy is appropriate for stars and some (if not all) problem children but requires considerable cash to fund high marketing expenditure.

This strategy involves heavy advertising, discounted pricing and intensive use of promotional techniques.

Holding market share: This is appropriate where both the product and market are mature, as in the case of cash cows, but could be applied to some stars.

Holding is achieved by ensuring that advertising expenditure and prices are comparable to those of competitors.

Harvesting: This strategy allows market share to decline, thus allowing the company to maximise its short-term earnings.

It could be applied to the problem children which the firm does not wish to or does not have the resources to turn into stars.

Harvesting is typically achieved by cutting marketing expenditure and/or raising prices.

Withdrawal: This is an appropriate strategy where the product has a lower than viable market share with no realistic hope of an improvement – typically applicable to dogs.

The product is in an unattractive market, and there is thus little purpose in improving market.

8   Product differentiation:

- Advertising campaign to stress health giving properties
- Package in fancy glass bottles
- Label the bottle using more stylish design

Cost leadership:

- Use plastic bottles
- Bring prices per litre down below competitors
- Sell in multi-packs to increase volume

9 Product development – sales of a new and different product are made but to the same (original) market or customer base.

This could be achieved by:

- Buying in tennis clothing made by another manufacturer and rebadging it
- Developing their own range of clothes from scratch
- Entering into a strategic alliance with a clothes manufacturer to develop the range together

10 Hannafords Dairy Ltd

10.1 Objective

Objectives need to provide a practical basis for the establishment of a strategy.

Hannafords' objective – 'to provide the best possible service to our customers' – lacks most of the elements in 'SMART', an often-used technique for evaluating objectives.

Specific. 'Best possible service' is rather vague and needs expansion into more specific areas, eg, all deliveries by 8 am.

Measurable. There is no readily available scale on which to measure whether 'the best service' has been given.

Achievable. It is hard to say whether the objective is achievable given the comments on specific/measurable above.

Relevant. The objective is very relevant if the business is to survive in the face of increased competition from supermarkets.

Timescale. No timescale is mentioned but is not perhaps necessary. Given the way the objective is expressed and the current position of Hannafords (see (10.2) below), it is probably a day-to-day objective!

10.2 SWOT analysis

This analysis looks at the immediate strengths and weaknesses of the company itself and the opportunities and threats presented by the environment in which it operates.

Strengths of Hannafords

(1) The main strength of the company is its monopoly of milk delivery in a fairly isolated area.

(2) It has a good reputation locally so that even with a price more than 50% above that of the supermarket, it is losing business more slowly than the industry average.

Other, less significant strengths include the following.

(3) It has no loans outstanding and owns its premises.

(4) It has a reputation for being a good employer with good wages, and the staff respond to this.

(5) The directors have shown some skill in marketing as all new residents in Avonbridge are targeted with an introductory gift as an incentive to have a daily milk delivery.

Weaknesses of Hannafords

(1) A significant weakness is the reliance on one source, owned by a national dairy. Although it would seem unlikely the dairy would withdraw supplies, it may be able to force price increases on Hannafords.

Threats

(1) A significant threat is in relying on a limited range of products ie, doorstep deliveries of milk and everyday groceries with reducing sales in a declining market. If it continues to decline this will not be a sustainable position.

(2) Another main threat is that posed by the supermarket and town shops which undercut on price by up to 35%.

(3) A less immediate threat is that the cultural acceptance of the milkman is being gradually eroded, so that for many people all their grocery shopping, including milk, is done at the supermarket. The milkman is therefore not considered.

Opportunities

(1) The most important opportunity presented is to take advantage of the company's position as the only doorstep delivery operation by diversifying and offering a broader range of products.

(2) A further significant opportunity is to cut the cost base by only delivering every other day. This would require careful handling to ensure it had customer support but would allow for a halving of the delivery fleet. Given the company's employment reputation this may have to be achieved through normal turnover of staff, unless other opportunities for the workforce can be found.

Other, less significant, opportunities include the following.

(3) Free or cheap 'cool boxes' for keeping the milk and groceries fresh when people are at work all day.

(4) Carrying advertisements on the milk floats or on the milk bottles.

(5) Considering diversifying into cheese production, which could be marketed to tourists both through local shops and on the milk rounds.

(6) Explore selling milk to the local supermarket as part of a 'buy British' campaign. This is quite topical as a number of supermarket chains now actively purchase goods for resale from local communities.

(7) There may be scope for the brothers to sell the company to the local milk supplier when the time for them to retire comes.

Summary

Overall, Hannaford's Dairy Ltd is performing well. The brothers' experience of the milk delivery market in Avonbridge has been invaluable in helping them exploit the company's position over local rivals, who have gone out of business. The company's position has been supported in part by its remote location which has helped to deter potential competitors.

The continued success of Hannaford's Dairy is likely to depend on the brothers' ability to make its operations more cost efficient in the long term without damaging the company's local image as a good employer and supplier.

Additional information

To complete the SWOT analysis it would be useful to have the following information.

- The financial statements of the last three years and budgets for the next year, to assess its financial strength and cash reserves. This will give an idea of the timeframe within which any changes have to be made.

- How close is the nearest rival to assess the likelihood of the monopoly position being threatened.

- An analysis of past prices from the dairy to see whether it tries to impose price increases regularly.

- The relative remoteness of the outlying villages and the public transport facilities. This would be to assess the usefulness to those without cars of Hannafords offering other products on their deliveries.

- A market survey of the likely customer reaction to deliveries on alternate days.

- The demand for local advertising.

- The location of any other cheese makers and their proximity.

10.3 Resources and strategy

It is important for the company to identify its core competencies from which it can develop its strategies. These appear to be as follows.

Competitive architecture

- Internal: Good (paternalistic) relationships with staff.

- External: Losing customers at a slower rate than national experience so there appears to be some degree of customer loyalty.

Reputation

- Good in terms of home deliveries as it has established a monopoly position. Service regarded as friendly, cheerful and helpful.

Innovative ability

- Marketing innovation, eg, flowers for new customers.

Ownership of strategic assets

- Monopoly on doorstep deliveries.

Based on these core competencies possible strategies to improve profits are to use the delivery network to expand the product range, eg, fruit drinks, milk drinks, fruit, vegetables, and fresh/frozen meats. Alternatively or in addition the network could be used for deliveries of a different nature, eg, mail, parcels, prescriptions (particularly for the elderly), dry cleaning, etc.

11   Refer to the answer to WeDive Ltd in the Question Bank.

12   Refer to the answer to Jason Smyth Textiles Ltd in the Question Bank.

CHAPTER 8

Strategies for products and markets

Introduction

Examination context

TOPIC LIST

Summary and Self-test

Answers to Interactive questions

Answers to Self-test

Introduction

Learning outcomes

Tick off

- Explain and demonstrate how an organisation can capture and analyse qualitative and quantitative data, presented in different formats, to provide relevant information for decision making at an appropriate level within the organisation ☐

- Explain, in a given scenario, how products and services must evolve in the face of changing, technologies, consumer demand and industry competition ☐

- Explain how to position particular products and services in the market place to maximise competitive advantage and develop a marketing strategy by extracting and analysing relevant data ☐

Specific syllabus references for this chapter are: 2b, 2h, 2i.

Syllabus links

In your Business, Technology and Finance studies you will have covered the basic objectives and processes of marketing management. You will also have considered how the marketing function assists in the achievement of business objectives.

This chapter revises these topics and explains how marketing is an essential part of management both in understanding the environment within which the organisation operates and as a means of promoting growth and developing other strategic objectives.

Examination context

This chapter is important for the exam. Questions may test your understanding of marketing concepts in a variety of different scenarios. An understanding of product and marketing strategies may also involve a particular issue, such as pricing. When faced with a requirement on marketing, it is important that you give consideration to the wider business strategy of the organisation featured, as any marketing activities undertaken need to be consistent with this.

In Question 1 of the March 2016 exam (*Outil plc*) the scenario focused on a large listed home improvement retailer that operated three divisions: Homestyle and Fixings in the UK, and the Targi division based in Eastern Europe. It was proposed that the Homestyle division be sold off in order to fund the opening of four trial stores (Fixing stores) in Germany. The final requirement asked candidates to:

'In relation to the Fixings division, discuss:

- the merits of undertaking test marketing before a full international expansion, and
- the strategy of opening four stores in Germany, on a trial basis.' **(8 marks)**

The examiner noted that 'this was the lowest scoring requirement in question 1, but was still reasonably well answered. In general, candidates coped well with identifying the benefits of test-marketing prior to international expansion, although only the better candidates identified this as a risk management strategy. Stronger candidates then went on to consider the merits of the specific proposal to open up four trial stores in Germany. Weaker candidates tended to mix up both elements of the requirement in one discussion, often focussing on one part to the detriment of the other.'

As the examiner's comments highlight, is important that you have a good grasp of the concept of marketing research and marketing, as this could very easily form the basis of an exam question. You need to be confident in developing your answer by applying it to the scenario.

1 Revision of product market strategies

Section overview

- Marketing is one of the functional strategies responsible for implementing the strategic choices of management.

- Marketing can help create Porter's generic strategies of cost leadership, differentiation or focus through how it targets and positions products.

- Marketing strategy identifies and helps develop new products and markets in the Ansoff matrix.

1.1 Marketing terminology

Definitions

Marketing: Can be defined as the set of human activities directed at facilitating and consummating exchanges. From this it can clearly be seen that it covers the whole range of a firm's activities.

Marketing: Alternatively marketing can be defined as 'the management process which identifies, anticipates and supplies customer requirements efficiently and profitably'. *(Chartered Institute of Marketing).*

Customer, consumer and targeting

A distinction can be made between:

- The customer, who purchases and pays for a good or service.
- The consumer, who is the ultimate user of the good or service.

Thus if a company makes corn flakes, its customers are supermarkets etc, but the consumer is the individual who eats the corn flakes. Both customer and consumer need to be targeted.

To obtain greater precision a firm may segment its market, ie, divide it into smaller parts where the parts can be treated differently for marketing purposes. The firm can then target particular segments. Segmentation is covered in section 2 below.

Marketing orientation

A firm which has a marketing orientation will see the needs of consumers/customers as vital. If it develops and markets products to meet these demands (ie, to meet the critical success factors), certain structural characteristics will be apparent within the company, ie:

Function	Activity/department in the company
Identifying customer/consumer needs	Marketing research
Developing products to meet consumer/customer wants/needs	R&D/production
Determining the value of the product to the customers	Pricing
Making the product available to the customer	Distribution
Informing the customer/consumer of the product's existence and persuading them to buy it	Promotion

1.2 Product-market strategy: direction of growth

In Chapter 7, we noted that when deciding their strategies, organisations have to make three key choices:

How to compete: Competitive strategies include cost leadership, differentiation or focus.

Direction of growth: Product/market strategy refers to the mix of product and markets (new or existing) and what the firm should do.

Method of growth (acquisition or organic growth): This will be covered in Chapter 11.

Marketing strategy deals with the first two of these because it enables an organisation to concentrate its limited resources on the greatest opportunities, defining how the organisation will engage customers, prospects and the competition in the market arena, to increase sales and profits and so achieve a sustainable competitive advantage.

1.3 Marketing strategy and Porter

Porter's **three generic strategies** are recipes to create superior long-term profitability.

Overall cost leadership – achieve lowest delivered cost to customer to boost margins and survive market entry and price wars better than competitors.

Differentiation – acquire status of premium perceived value in the market to enable higher prices to be charged and to resist competition from cheaper 'follower' products.

Focus – monopolise a niche segment by provided either a specifically tailored product of very high perceived value or by cutting extraneous costs to gain access to the lowest price segments.

Marketing strategy positions products in the market place according to these generic strategies. This will involve correct tailoring of the main elements of marketing, the **marketing mix**:

- **Product** – the offering the customer consumes.
- **Price** – the pricing point and actual cost in use to the customer.
- **Promotion** – how a product or service is advertised and sold.
- **Place** – where it is available, can be accessed or bought from.
- **People** – the personnel the customer meets.
- **Physical evidence** – the look and feel of the business premises, publicity etc.
- **Process** – the way the customer makes a purchase or the way the customer is dealt with.

The final three Ps are particularly important for service companies' marketing.

1.4 Marketing strategy and Ansoff

Product-market strategy is the mix of products and markets. **Market segmentation** is a tool of marketing strategy that helps management to identify new markets, and to use a **marketing mix** to arrive at a desirable market position. The Ansoff matrix identifies various options (see details in previous chapter).

	Product	
	Present	New
Market Present	Market penetration	Product development
Market New	Market development	Diversification

Market penetration: Maintain or to increase its share of current markets with current products, eg, through competitive pricing, advertising, sales promotion and to increase usage by existing customers.

Market development: Expand into new market segments or geographical areas.

Product development: Launch of new products to existing customers or similar markets.

Diversification: Develop into new industries.

1.5 Danger in assuming 'one size fits all'

Market segmentation refers to the practice of looking for sub-groups in a market.

Focus players obviously depend on this, but it is also practised by broader market players too:

- Differentiated breakfast cereal manufacturer Kellogg's segments the market into children's cereals (Rice Krispies, Frosties etc), adult cereals (Corn Flakes), commuters (cereal brands in a bar).

- US-based cost leader supermarket chain Wal-Mart segments the market into geographical locations where its price-conscious positioning will appeal.

The argument for **mass marketing** is that it creates the largest potential market, which leads to the lowest costs, which in turn can lead to lower prices or higher margins.

Critics point to the increasing splintering of the market, which makes mass marketing more difficult and denies the firms that use mass marketing the opportunities of niche markets.

A proliferation of media (internet, cable TV, mobile phones) and distribution channels (download, social media, direct selling from websites) is allowing more personalised shopping and more personalised marketing messages. It is difficult to practice 'one size fits all' marketing and some observers even claim that mass marketing is dying. It is being replaced by **target marketing** and **personalised marketing**.

2 Segmentation, targeting and positioning

Section overview

- Market segmentation divides markets into sub-units to help target the marketing effort.

- Segmentation bases are the methods used to divide consumer and industrial markets.

- Positioning a product involves putting in the market at a point that will attract the interest of its target segments and able to satisfy their requirements.

2.1 Market segmentation

Definition

Market segmentation: The division of the market into homogeneous groups of potential customers who may be treated similarly for marketing purposes.

Segmentation allows the organisation to vary its marketing mix to each segment it chooses to enter.

Alternatives are:

- Mass (undifferentiated) marketing – no segmentation eg, sugar.

- Niche (concentrated) marketing – concentrate on one or two market segments eg, Morgan cars.

- Micro marketing – complete segmentation, tailoring products and services to individual needs eg, greetings card manufacturer, Moonpig, allows customers to design and customise their own cards.

2.2 Benefits of market segmentation

- The organisation may be able to identify new marketing opportunities, because it will have a better understanding of customer needs in each segment, with the possibility of spotting further sub groups.

- Specialists can be used for each of the organisation's major segments. For example, small business counsellors can be employed by banks to deal effectively with small firms.

- The total marketing budget can be allocated proportionately to each segment and the likely return from each segment. This optimises return on investment.

- The organisation can make adjustments to the product, price and other elements of the marketing mix to improve returns.

- The organisation can try to dominate particular segments, gaining the competitive advantage from a Focus strategy.

2.3 The bases for segmentation

The methods used to split the market up into segments are called **segmentation bases.** They will seek to segment markets according to factors such as:

- Type of customer, eg, business, personal, own use, presents etc.

- Different needs and tastes of the customer.

- Location of the customer.

- Spending potential of customer.

- Circumstances of the customer, eg, loans targeted at new businesses or those with poor credit ratings.

Segmentation can be divided into industrial segmentation and consumer segmentation.

Industrial segmentation includes:

- Geographic: eg, as basis for sales force, distribution or because industries cluster.

- Purchasing characteristics: eg, order size, frequency of order.

- Benefit, eg, reliability, economy, durability, versatility, safety, value for money.

- Company type: eg, type of business, sole trader, partnership, limited company.

- Company size: eg, number of employees, profits, revenue.

- Technological eg, capable of/willing to buy online and to make use of developing technologies.

Consumer segmentation includes:

- Geographic: eg, as by country, region, city etc.

- Psychological: groups sharing common psychological characteristics, eg, old people may be security-oriented.

- Purchasing characteristics: eg, heavy user, medium user, low user.

- Benefit: eg, soap powders – smell, whiteness, economy, stain removal.

- Demographic: divides the market into groups based on such things as age, gender, family size, income, occupation, race etc. One method – socio-economic grouping – is explored further below.

- Technological: eg, whether the customer uses technology, eg, social media, mobile devices etc

2.3.1　Socio-economic grouping

Socio-economic	Social status	Job description
A	Upper middle class	Higher managerial, administrative and professional eg, chief executive, surgeon
B	Middle class	Middle management, administrative and professional eg, teacher, bank manager
C1	Lower middle class	Supervisory, clerical, junior management, administrative, non-manual eg, bank clerk, sales person
C2	Skilled working class	Skilled manual workers eg, electrician, carpenter
D	Working class	Semi and unskilled manual jobs eg, assembly line worker, refuse collector
E	Subsistence	Pensioners, widow(er)s, lowest grade workers, unemployed eg, casual workers

Modern information and communications technology, especially social media, make it possible to create 'segments of one' for personalised marketing.

- Personalised versions of home pages for online stores (eg, Amazon 'page you made').

- Loyalty cards allowing personalised offers to be given at the check-in (eg, screens on shopping carts in supermarkets), check-out or in personalised mailings.

- Interactive TV with specifically tailored advertisements in the commercial breaks.

- Personalised email, social media promotions, text messages and alerts.

2.3.2　Buyer and customer behaviour

A crucial element in the marketing process is understanding **why** a buyer does or does not purchase an organisation's goods or services. If the organisation does not understand the process, it will not be able to respond to the customer's needs and wishes.

Due to the differences that often exist between 'consumer buyers' (those who purchase items for personal consumption), and 'industrial buyers' (those who purchase items on behalf of their organisation and where there are far fewer but larger buyers), it is traditional to split buyers into these two broad groups for analysis.

Consumer adoption model

The people who first buy one type of consumer goods are frequently the same people who first try others. Customers can be divided into groups according to the speed with which they adopt new products.

The **innovators** are relatively young, technology savvy, lively, intelligent, socially and geographically mobile and of a high socio-economic group (largely AB).

Conversely, the **laggards**, who are slow to accept new products, are older, less intelligent, fixed in their job and residence, less well off, and lower on the socio-economic scale. It can be seen that when a company launches a new product, its early customers are likely to be significantly different from its later ones. The consumer adoption model is also consistent with the product life cycle.

This concept can be very useful for marketers trying to assess for example, future demand for technological products such as virtual personal assistant devices.

2.4 Targeting

Definition

Targeting: Involves selecting the most attractive market segments.

The attractiveness of a market segment depends on it being:

- **Measurable**: the ability to forecast the sales or market potential of the segment. Knowing this will be essential for production and distribution planning and also for financial forecasting.

- **Accessible**: the ability of the firm to make and distribute a product to and the availability of suitable promotional media.

- **Stable**: the likelihood that the segment will persist for sufficient time to enable a return on the investment of developing a marketing mix for it.

- **Substantial**: the profits available will give an adequate return on capital employed.

- **Defensible**: there should be barriers to entry to allow the firm some measure of dominance.

Issues to consider include:

- How big is the market segment?
- How quickly is it growing?
- How many competitors are there and what is their market share?
- What are the main distribution channels?
- Are there any potential substitute products or services?
- What is the relative power of buyers/suppliers?
- What resources and competences does the company have?
- Can the segment be accessed through the deployment of internet technologies?

Target marketing tailors a marketing mix for one or more segments identified by market segmentation.

Targeting strategies can be:

- **Single segment** strategies (concentrated strategies): One market segment is served with one marketing mix – suitable for smaller organisations with limited resources.

- **Selective specialisation** (multi-segment strategies): Different market mixes are offered to different market segments. Proctor and Gamble provide Pampers disposable nappies to young families, cosmetics such as Calvin Klein to the youth market and Old Spice to the elder male.

- **Product specialisation**: The organisation specialises in a particular product and tailors it to suit different market segments. Dell makes computers targeted at homes and at businesses.

- **Market specialisation**: The organisation specialises in serving a particular market segment and offers that segment an array of different products. Harley Davidson aims at the older and born-again biker and sells a range of motorcycles, accessories, apparel and, with less success, cosmetics.

- **Full market coverage**: The organisation attempts to serve the entire market. This coverage can be achieved by means of either a mass market strategy in which a single marketing mix is offered to the entire market, such as Starbucks coffee houses, or by a multi-segment strategy in which sufficient separate marketing mixes are offered to cover the whole market. Many supermarket chains attempt the latter when they offer economy, standard, and premium ranges of own-label products in lines that include food, cleaning products, clothing and light bulbs.

2.5 Positioning

Positioning: The overall location of a product or service in the buyer's mind in relation to other competing products, services /brands.

Re-positioning: Changing the identity of a product or service, relative to the identity of competing products or services, in the collective minds of the target market.

A product or brand can be positioned in a number of ways, eg, via a price or emphasis on a particular characteristic or set of characteristics. In other words, positioning means giving a product a place relative to its competitors on factors such as quality, price, image, being exotic, providing status, etc.

Positioning can be facilitated by a graphical technique called perceptual mapping, various survey techniques and statistical techniques like multi-dimensional scaling and factor analysis.

One way of obtaining the information required to draw up this type of matrix would be to ask target consumers to rank the products on a five-point scale on quality. Values could then be attributed to the respective answers as follows: very good score: 5, good score: 4, reasonable score: 3, poor score: 2 and very poor score: 1. The information could be brought together as shown below.

Even such a rather simple product positioning matrix as shown above may give valuable insights in the relative positions of the various brands.

The first conclusion is that the position of brand B is rather precarious. It is more expensive than brand C, but considered to be of lower quality. C is considered to be of better quality, but sells at a lower price. There also appears to be a gap in the market in the middle segment at a price level between D and C.

In Chapter 7 we looked at Bowman's strategy clock as a model that can be used to analyse the position of a business relative to its competitors based on its chosen combination of price and perceived added value.

Worked example: Watches

Leading global watch brands are positioned to appeal to different buyer groups. Swiss brand Omega was founded in 1848, and its watches are largely targeted at business professionals and watch collectors. Omega is the producer of quality precision watches and prides itself on its long time association with the Olympic Games, having been nominated as the official time keeper on 21 occasions. Fellow Swiss brand TAG Heuer is classed as a luxury watch brand, targeted again at business professionals but also sports fans due to a long running partnership with the McClaren F1 team, and subsequently the Red Bull F1 team. Fossil watches by contrast was established in the USA in the 1980's. Its watches are targeted more as fashion items and are sold at considerably lower prices.

Interactive question 1: Rex Ltd

Rex Ltd is a UK-based nationalised car manufacturer that is going to be privatised in the next four years. It has suffered from years of poor management and under-investment. This has resulted in a poor public image and a diverse product range. Details of current models are given below.

Off-road division

Range Rex. A market leader with a strong image as being the off-road vehicle to be seen in around town. It enjoys a high profit margin but is starting to face increasing competition in a growing market.

Land Rex. A leader in the market of 'working' off-road vehicles. Has a huge market share and faces few competitors in a fairly static market.

Family division

Mindless. A revolutionary design – 30 years ago. This is the original small car. It is now competing against many larger models including Rex's Matchless in the small family hatchback market. The Mindless is not a hatchback and, as a result of nil investment over the last 20 years, is regarded as being an anachronism, bought only by enthusiasts. It is totally unprofitable.

Matchless. An economical and fun to drive small family hatchback. The car is well designed but poorly built. It has the potential to become market leader but is held back by its poor reputation. This is a growing but highly competitive market.

Hopeless and Hapless. Two models in the medium-size family market. They are both poorly designed, poorly built and have astonishingly bad reputations. Neither car has a market share of any significance. The market is not growing. It is, however, thought vital to have a car aimed at this market sector.

Executive division

The Rex. What was once a car synonymous with quality has had its reputation somewhat tarnished lately due to its unreliability. Its existing customer base is loyal but increasingly being persuaded to buy more reliable imported cars. This is a growing and highly profitable market.

Requirement

1.1 Explain what the terms 'product positioning' and 'market targeting' mean and how these might be applied in developing Rex's strategy.

See **Answer** at the end of this chapter.

3 Marketing research

Section overview

- The definition of marketing in paragraph 1.1 emphasises meeting customer requirements and also efficiency.

- Marketing research helps management identify needs that can be satisfied at a profit to the firm.

- It also helps evaluate the effectiveness of the component parts of the marketing effort to ensure marketing reaches it objectives efficiently.

3.1 Areas for marketing research

To be able meet the critical success factors in target segments and develop sustainable competitive advantage over competitors, information is needed.

Definition

Marketing research: is the systematic gathering, recording and analysing of information about problems relating to the marketing of goods and services.

Marketing research therefore includes not only market research but also the gathering of any data useful for formulating the seven 'P's marketing mix.

Market research involves looking at specific markets, their size, market trends, information re segmentation, customer characteristics, customer needs and wants, demand curves, competitors' products, etc.

Product research could include laboratory testing to analyse product safety, durability and shelf-life.

Pricing research could include attempts to generate more accurate figures to facilitate cost-plus pricing.

Promotional ('market communications') research might include contacting social media sites or the websites of online newspapers to determine how much they would charge for advertising.

Distribution research could include contacting potential retail outlets to determine what margins they would expect to make.

3.2 Stages in marketing research

A research programme will involve the following steps:

- Defining (and locating) problems, setting objectives
- Developing hypotheses
- Research – desk and field research
- Data collection
- Analysis and interpretation
- Conclusions and recommendations

3.3 Desk research

Definition

Desk research is the gathering and analysis of existing or secondary data. This may use existing company reports and other information from both internal and external sources.

Information from internal sources

Many companies develop internal databases. Information can come from many sources eg, accounts department, production records, orders etc. Supermarkets use loyalty cards, databases and the output from data analytics software to segment and target their customers.

Other often neglected sources of information are:

- Management accounts: Analysis of sales/profits by produce or region.
- Sales department: More sales analysis – customer complaints.
- R&D department: Information about technical developments.

Rules for successful desk research

- Assume that the work has already been done – it just needs to be located.
- Think laterally and keep an open mind.
- Follow up leads, however vague.
- Get behind the published data, since often what is published is just a summary.
- Avoid saying 'market research'.
- Avoid asking for 'statistics'.
- Use internal sources of data as this is often available in organisational databases.

3.4 Field research

Definition

Field research involves the collection of new (primary) information direct from respondents. As such it is usually more expensive than desk research and so is only performed if desk research fails to answer all questions asked.

3.4.1 Types of research

There are three basic types of field research.

- **Opinion research**: to determine people's opinions on general issues, eg, pollution.
- **Motivation research**: to determine why people do what they do, especially why they would buy one product rather than another. Their motives may be complex/subconscious.
- **Measurement research**: to quantify research so that sample results can be extrapolated to the target population, eg, how many people are planning a holiday to Italy next year?

Specific techniques

- In-depth interviews.
- Group interviews.
- Trial testing, eg, out of three chocolate bars which would you choose?
- Word association, eg, 'lager drinkers' – lout?

- Observation, eg, use cameras to determine how long on average it takes to serve customers in a restaurant.

- Questionnaires – very common.

- Online – internet surveys and focus groups (see later).

Sampling

- Ideally one should choose **random samples**, where each person in the target group has an equal likelihood of being selected. If large enough, a random sample will be representative of the target population in every respect, not just those considered important. Consequently extrapolation of results is more reliable and easier to quantify. Unfortunately it can be very difficult to be unbiased in a sampling technique.

- A popular alternative is **quota sampling**, where certain characteristics of the sample are predetermined. People are then chosen specifically to fill the required quotas within the sample.

  For example, suppose the target population is made up of 56% men and 44% women, a quota sample of 200 people would therefore contain 112 men and 88 women. Once 88 women had been questioned no more would be asked.

  The main problem with quota samples is that, while they may be representative as far as preselected criteria are concerned, they are likely to be biased in other respects. Consequently it is more difficult to predict how the population as a whole will behave.

- Opinion and motivation research tend to use small samples, whereas measurement research samples are much larger to facilitate more accurate extrapolation.

- In **panelling** the same sample is retained so that changes/trends in behaviour are easier to identify.

- Sampling may involve personal face-to-face contact (eg, door-to-door, intercepting people in shopping centres, etc), telephoning, mailshots and email shots or by putting questionnaires in magazines.

  The problems with surveys and questionnaires are, firstly, a low response rate and, secondly, that the sample picks itself, so may not be representative of the population as a whole as only those wishing to partake in the questionnaire will respond.

  In recent times it has become increasingly common for organisations to run surveys via their websites. In many cases this approach is directed to gain user feedback on using the entity's website, products or services. Companies such as Survey Monkey help businesses and individuals alike to run surveys on various issues through social media sites such as Facebook or Twitter.

Test marketing

Test marketing involves a trial run of a product in a typical segment of the market before proceeding to a national launch.

Worked example: Boohoo

In early 2018 it was reported that the online fashion company, Boohoo, had achieved a 97% jump in revenues on the previous year. Boohoo's products are targeted at 16 to 24 year old women. The company's success had been achieved in part by its approach to marketing. Known as 'test and repeat', Boohoo offers a large selection of clothes on its website, but only then re-stocks its warehouse with the best-selling lines (BBC, 2018).

Boohoo has shunned traditional approaches to marketing, instead preferring to maximise its appeal through attracting influential people to promote its brand via social media channels. Neate (2017) notes comments made by Neil Catto, Boohoo's Chief Financial Officer who, in

2017, said 'we work with a whole spectrum of influencers, celebrities and wannabe-bloggers – all people with a presence online – and we work with them so they can spread the word about Boohoo. It goes like wildfire on Instagram'. (Neate, 2017).

Sources:

Neate, R. (27 April 2017). Fashion retailer Boohoo nearly doubles profit after celebrity Instagram tie-ups. *The Guardian*. [Online]. Available from: www.theguardian.com [Accessed: 26 April 2018].

BBC, (2018) Boohoo online fashion chain sees sales and profits surge. [Online]. Available from: www.bbc.co.uk [Accessed: 26 April 2018].

Test marketing could involve just selling a product in selected locations. At the other end of the scale the test may incorporate all aspects of the marketing mix in a certain area of the country. Such a test market should have the following characteristics:

- Small
- Self-contained
- Representative
- Adequate promotional facilities

Experimentation

Users of the experimental method attempt to investigate only one variable at a time, keeping all other factors constant.

Examples of the experimental approach can be found in advertisement testing, where alternative advertisement designs can be assessed in otherwise identical marketing situations. It can also be found in package testing, where different packaging styles are used whilst other factors are held constant.

Theoretically, any marketing mix variable could be tested. The method for setting up a test would be similar to that set out below, which describes how to carry out a **sales area test**.

- Select areas which are as nearly identical as possible and which represent the market for the tested product.

- Ensure that all factors except that being tested are as nearly identical as possible. In a sales area test this means using similar distribution outlets in comparable positions within the area.

- Record sales in each area before the variable is introduced.

- Set up the new variable in all except one or two areas. These are the control areas, in which previous marketing mix settings are maintained.

- Measure sales while the tested variable is set up, and afterwards. Differences between the test-variable areas and the control areas are due to the effects of the test variable.

In practice it is difficult to find test areas which resemble each other closely, and non-tested variables tend to alter during the test due to factors beyond the control of researchers.

4 Branding and brand equity

Section overview

- Brands add value to products by making them recognisable and endowing them with associations attractive to the target segment.

- The ability of a brand to do this, to be the basis for future product launches, and to defend a product's market share against incursions makes a brand an asset because it generates future earnings.

- Although difficult to value precisely for balance sheet purposes it is conventional to describe this ability to create future value as brand equity.

4.1 Branding

Brands have three essential features:

- **Name**: this should be legally protected, memorable, and be consonant with the product itself if possible. The names of cosmetic brands like Obsession and Clinique do the latter well, whereas others like Estee Lauder and Helena Rubenstein as names say very little at all.

- **Livery**: designs, trademarks, symbols, and a range of visual features which should make it identifiable. Brands like Apple and Coca Cola are very recognisable.

- **Associations and personality**: this helps a brand distinguish a company's product from competing products in the eyes of the user. Drinks like Bacardi Breezer are fun drinks whereas Chivas Regal has gravitas.

4.2 Branding policy

There are different branding policies that an organisation can adopt:

- **Single company name**: Examples of companies which use a single label on all products, and describe individual items in a more or less factual way include Apple, Samsung, Crosse & Blackwell and Heinz. This policy has several advantages; the attributes possessed by one product are transferred to another and new product launch is simplified because there is no need to build up new brand awareness. (eg, Virgin and derivatives of easyJet).

- **Different brand names for each product**: This is where a company produces a number of products with significantly different positions in the market, or where the market is highly segmented, the brand strategy is often to use different brand names for each product. This policy is very common among manufacturers of soap powders, chocolate bars and breakfast cereals.

- **Own branding**: Many retailers sell grocery, clothing and hardware products under a brand name of their own to help create loyalty to the store rather than to the producer of the product.

4.3 Brand positioning

A basic perceptual map can be uses to plot brands in perceived price and perceived quality terms.

- Cowboy brands: excessively priced brand for the quality of the product.
- Premium brands: top of the range quality, but high-priced.
- Bargain brands: good quality for a relatively low price.
- Economy brands: cheap brands, low-priced and low quality.

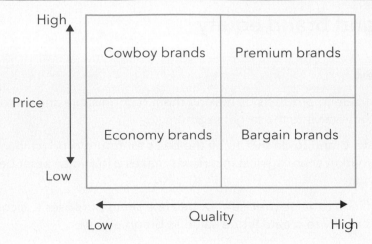

Price and quality are important elements in the marketing mix, but they will not, in the customer's opinion, be considered independent variables. A high price will usually be associated with high quality and equally low price with low quality. Thus, while everybody would like to buy a bargain brand, there is a problem to overcome. This is a question of belief: will customers accept that a high quality product can be offered at a low price? A key question is whether the quality of the product is readily discernible by the consumer.

4.4 Brand equity

Definition

Brand equity: An intangible asset that adds value to a business through positive associations made by the consumer between the brand and benefits to themselves.

- **Financial**: one way to measure brand equity is to determine the price premium that a brand commands over a generic product.

- **Brand extensions**: a successful brand can be used as a platform to launch related products. The benefits include raising brand awareness leading to reducing advertising expenditures and enhancing the core brand. These benefits are more difficult to quantify than are direct financial measures of brand equity.

- **Consumer-based**: a strong brand increases the consumer's attitude strength towards the product associated with the brand, leading to perceived quality, inferred attributes and eventually, brand loyalty.

The benefits of a strong brand equity include:

- A more predictable income stream.

- Increased cash flow by increasing market share, reducing promotional costs and allowing premium pricing.

- Having an asset that can be sold or leased.

- Reduced marketing costs because of high brand awareness and loyalty.

- More power in bargaining with distributors and retailers.

- Higher prices accepted by the market because the brand has higher perceived quality.

- Potential for launching extensions easily because the brand has high credibility.

- Defence against price competition.

5 The marketing mix

Section overview

- The marketing mix represents the tools marketers have to position products and to obtain sales.

- The traditional four Ps marketing mix was designed for tangible products and has been extended into the seven Ps to apply to service based businesses.

- The seven Ps were introduced in Business, Technology and Finance. The key themes are recapped here.

5.1 Seven marketing Ps

Definition

Marketing mix: The set of controllable marketing variables that a firm blends to produce the response it wants in the target market.

In the Business, Technology and Finance text you were introduced to the seven Ps of the marketing mix (Product, Price, Place, Promotion, People, Processes and Physical Evidence), the first four of which are primarily directed at tangible products. We recap this again here.

The tertiary sector of a developed economy will typically account for over half its economic activity. This is the service sector.

Services differ from products because of their intangibility and consequent need to provide reassurance to the customer through the visible aspects of service provision. This leads to the extended marketing mix for services and knowledge based businesses, known as the 7 Ps.

In practice, many manufacturing industries will pay attention to the service elements of their offering too as a form of differentiation eg, Car makers will pay attention to the showroom and after-sales service to enhance their brands and fast food providers likewise.

The three extra Ps with particular emphasis in service marketing are:

- **People**: The people working for an organisation often say more about that company than any product or service can. They must portray the values of that organisation whenever they contact customers – a restaurant could serve the finest food imaginable, but it counts for nothing if the waiter has poor personal hygiene.

- **Processes**: The way in which a good or service is delivered has an impact on the way in which customers perceive the organisation.

- **Physical evidence**: The elements of 'marketing mix' which customers can actually see or experience when they use a service, and which contribute to the perceived quality of the service, eg, the physical evidence of a retail bank could include the state of the branch premises, as well as the delivery of the banking service itself.

5.2 Characteristics of service

A service can include a haircut, an audit, a theatre presentation, the processing of a financial transaction in a bank account or an insurance policy.

There are some basic characteristics of services that distinguish them from purely physical products:

- **Intangibility**: A service is not a physical thing. A bank transaction is performed for you, you have evidence that it has been achieved, but in itself it is what someone does for you.

- **Inseparability**: The delivery of the service occurs often at the same time it is consumed. You do not store a haircut for consumption later. The service is produced by the barber/hairdresser and consumed by you at the same time.

- **Heterogeneity/variability**: Many services face problems in ensuring a consistent standard. For example, the friendliness of flight attendants on an aircraft can affect your enjoyment of the service. This is also true of business services such as auditing or the offering of financial advice: regulatory bodies and the firms themselves go to great lengths to ensure there are procedures in place to ensure consistency. Interestingly though, the increasing use of intelligent systems and virtual assistants (as discussed in Chapter 6) may help to address issues relating to the consistency of service customers receive.

- **Perishability**: A service cannot be stored. You cannot store a haircut for later consumption.

- **Ownership**: Typically, a service rarely results in a transfer of ownership. The purchase of a service sometimes only confers the right to use something.

Worked example: Disney

Disney theme parks are a good example of service delivery. The processes, including booking, queuing procedures at the attractions, operations of the attractions and design of the customers' walk through the park, are vital to its functioning. So too are the employees or the 'cast' as they are called; their job is to interact with customers. Physical evidence is clear in the branding and thematic coherence as well as the existence of souvenirs to take away, photographs of the people enjoying the ride and so on.

Interactive question 2: Services marketing

2.1 Identify four differences between services and products, giving a practical example for each, and discuss the problems that these differences present to the marketer.

2.2 Identify the extended marketing mix which a small service company, such as a management consultancy, would need to consider when marketing its services.

See **Answer** at the end of this chapter.

5.3 The extended marketing mix

Mix element	Comment
Product	Quality of the product as perceived by the potential customer. This involves an assessment of the product's suitability for its stated purpose, its aesthetic factors, its durability, brand factors, size, packaging, associated services, etc.
Price	Includes prices to the customer, discount structures for the trade, promotion pricing, methods of purchase, alternatives to outright purchase.
Place	Distribution channels, location of outlets, online sales, position of warehouses, inventory levels, delivery frequency, geographic market definition, sales territory organisation, intermediaries and logistics between the producer and the end consumer.

Mix element	Comment
Promotion	Covers the **communications mix** • Advertising (online and via social media) • Public relations • Personal selling • Sales promotions, eg, contests or limited special offers
People	Staff appearance, service training, technical and technological knowledge, manner etc.
Processes	Efficiency of the service. For example, the ease with which a well-designed online loan application form can be completed could be an important element in a bank's loan service.
Physical evidence	Refers to items that give physical substance, such as logos, staff uniforms and store layout/design. However, the purpose of evidence is that a service is intangible: physical evidence enforces the idea by giving something to show for it.

Interactive question 3: Marketing mix

Indicate the main characteristics of marketing mixes which would be appropriate for the following.

3.1   A large banking group
3.2   A company that manufactures electronic components for computer manufacturers

See **Answer** at the end of this chapter.

6   Product

Section overview

- Products are what the customer is physically buying and experiencing.

- Product strategy decides which features to add to a product, ranging from basic features to the augmented ones that may differentiate it from rivals.

- New product development is a part of this process and is the Product Development strategy identified by Ansoff. It is expensive and risky and so needs to be justified.

- Developing products for global markets, and whether to adapt them to different country markets, is reviewed in connection with Ansoff's Market Development strategy.

6.1   Defining and classifying products

Marketers consider products not as things with features, but as packages of benefits that satisfy a variety of consumer needs.

Products cover offerings that fall into one of the following categories:

- **Goods** – something tangible ie, something that is felt, tasted, heard, smelled or seen.

- **Services** –Unlike goods, services are not stored - they are only available at the time of use and the consistency of the benefit offered can vary from one purchaser to another (eg, not exactly the same hair cut each time).

- **Ideas** – the marketer attempts to convince the customer to alter their behaviour or their perception in some way. Marketing ideas are often a solution put forth by non-profit groups or governments to get targeted groups to avoid or change certain behaviour.

6.2 Components of a product

The total product offering is made up of three main elements:

- **Basic** (or core) product, eg, a mobile phone – at the very heart of all product decisions is determining the key or core benefits a product will provide. From this decision, the rest of the product offering can be developed.

- **Actual** product, eg, the latest iPhone – while the consumable product is, in most cases, the most critical of all product decisions, the actual product includes many separate product decisions including product features and technologies, branding, packaging, labelling, and more.

- **Augmented** product – goods and services that provide additional value to the customer's purchase. Eg the latest iPhone on a mobile contract, or an iPhone provided with insurance.

6.3 New product development

New product development (NPD) is a generic term which incorporates innovative products and modifications and improvements to existing products.

Not all NPD is blue-skies innovation.

Novelty to firm	Novelty to customer	
	Low	High
Low	Product refinement	Product repositioning
High	New product line	New to the world

The product development strategy of the company can:

- Develop new product features through adapting existing features
- Create different quality versions of the product
- Develop additional models and sizes

Reasons for product development

- The firm has high relative share of the market, strong brand presence and enjoys distinctive competitive advantages in the market.

- There is growth potential in the market. (The Boston Consulting Group recommends companies invest in growth markets.)

- The changing needs of its customers demand new products. Continuous product innovation is often the only way to prevent product obsolescence.

- It needs to react to or incorporate technological developments.

- It needs to respond to competitive innovations in the market.

However product development strategy carries considerable investment risk. A company typically has to develop many product ideas to produce one good one. Earlier in the study manual we explored the growing role that crowdsourcing has started to play in business. Crowdsourcing used conjunction with product development provides organisations with the opportunity to get feedback from groups such as customers on products and services. Feedback can be used as a way to suggest improvements to an organisation's offering, which in turn may help to reduce the associated cost and effort of new product development. Despite the increase in the use of crowdsourcing, new product development is very costly. Furthermore, even when a product is successful it might still suffer a short life cycle with rivals quick to 'copycat' in the market, but with their own innovations and improvements.

6.4 Global products: standardise versus adapt

Products can be classified according to their degree of potential for global marketing:

- Local products – seen as only suitable in one single market.

- International products – seen as having extension potential into other markets.

- Multinational products – products adapted to the perceived unique characteristics of national markets.

- Global products – products designed to meet global segments.

Factors encouraging standardisation	Factors encouraging adaptation
Economies of scale in production and marketing	**Differing usage conditions**. These may be due to climate, skills, level of literacy, culture or physical conditions.
Consumer mobility	**General market factors** – incomes, tastes etc.
Technology	**Government** – taxation, import quotas, non tariff barriers, labelling, health requirements. Non tariff barriers are an attempt, despite their supposed impartiality, at restricting or eliminating competition.
Image	**History**. Sometimes, as a result of colonialism, production facilities have been established overseas. Eastern and Southern Africa is littered with examples. These facilities have long been adapted to local conditions.
	Financial considerations. To maximise sales or profits the organisation may have no choice but to adapt its products to local conditions
	Pressure. Sometimes suppliers are forced to adapt to the regulations imposed on them (eg, the EU) if they wish to enter into the market.

Options available to an organisation wishing to launch a product in a foreign market are as follows:

- Introduce the product without any changes
- Alter the product to meet local conditions or preferences
- Create brand new products to meet the needs and exclusive conditions of the market

Whatever strategy is chosen the organisation also needs to consider adjusting its marketing strategy to meet local needs.

7 Place

Section overview

- The aim of distribution is to position the product where the target consumer can readily access it whilst at the same time maximising the earning to the firm.

- There are many distribution channels available to firms and they are selected on complex grounds including support, margin and market position.

- Distributing to overseas markets involves similar channel selection decisions.

7.1 Distribution channel

Organisations need to decide on the best way of getting their products to the customer. The distribution channels used by the organisation need to be consistent with its approach to price, product and promotion. The places where the product is available say a lot about its perceived quality and status. The channels of distribution must match the image of the product and the customer's perception of the product.

7.2 Points in the chain of distribution

Distribution functions are carried out through a **channel** of distribution which comprises all the institutions or people involved with the movement and exchange of products or services.

Retailers are traders operating outlets which sell directly to households. Retailers are increasingly using direct selling via the internet.

Wholesalers are intermediaries who stock a range of products from competing manufacturers to sell on to other organisations such as retailers.

Distributors and dealers are organisations which contract to buy a manufacturer's goods and sell them to customers. In addition to selling on the manufacturer's product, distributors often promote the products and provide after-sales service.

Agents purchase the manufacturer's goods, but earn a commission on whatever sales they make.

Franchisees are independent organisations which in exchange for an initial fee and (usually) a share of sales revenue are allowed to trade under the name of a parent organisation. Examples include Ikea, McDonald's and some Starbucks shops.

Direct selling includes:

- Mail order
- Telephone selling
- Personal selling (consumer/industrial)
- Online shopping

7.3 The choice of distribution channel

Distribution channels fall into one of two categories: direct and indirect channels.

- **Direct distribution** means the product going directly from producer to consumer without the use of a specific intermediary. Direct distribution methods generally fall into two categories: those using online sales channels, and other channels such as the press, leaflets and telephones to invite response and purchase by the consumer, and those using a sales force to contact consumers face-to-face.

- **Indirect distribution** refers to systems of distribution which make use of an intermediary; a wholesaler, retailer or perhaps both.

Considerations in developing efficient channels of distribution

- The reach of the distributor. Can they access the target markets?

- The degree of exclusivity that the channel will offer. Will the firm's goods be sold side by side with rivals?

- The amount of support given by the channel. It may be necessary for the channel to provide an efficient after-sales and repair service, or to agree to an immediate exchange of faulty products, advertising or sales promotion support.

- The economic costs of supplying such as number of delivery drops, the average order size and whether they can return unsold goods.

- Support for combined promotions.

Worked example: Insurance

Before the internet many car insurance sales were made through brokers, eg, the Automobile Association (AA) in the UK. With the internet there was the opportunity to sell direct, eg, Direct Line, via call centres. This led to the creation of online brokers to replace the traditional broker of the past, for example screentrade.co.uk.

7.4 Selling and distribution in overseas markets

There are a number of elements to consider when selling overseas. How the company's **sales presence** in export markets is organised is one of the key decisions.

Depending on the product, it may be sold directly. For example, over the internet or by exhibiting at local trade shows.

Many businesses look for a **partner** who already understands the local market. For example:

- They can sell to a **distributor** who then sells their products locally.

- They can use a **sales agent** who sells products on their behalf, or puts them into contact with potential customers on a commission basis.

- They can enter into a **joint venture** with a local business. This gives them a share of the management and profits of the joint venture, but is a more complicated and expensive option.

If an organisation wants complete control over sales, it can set up its own **local office**. This is the most expensive option.

8 Promotion

Section overview

- Promotion is more than advertising. It also involves public relations, personal selling and sales promotion. We consider the increasing use of social media as a means of promoting products and services along with the risks it brings in Chapter 14.

- Promotion does more than tell people the product and firm exists. It aims to influence the target customers' perceptions of the product so that they see it as a viable solution to their needs.

- Sales force selection, training and management are therefore as much part of this element of the mix as designing a poster.

8.1 Promotion mix

The promotion mix consists of four elements:

(a) **Advertising**: paid communications in the media (including online) which are designed to influence potential customers favourably regarding a company's products or services. Advertising is sometimes called above-the-line promotion.

(b) **Sales promotion**: non-media promotional activity aimed at increasing sales. Sales promotion includes a variety of techniques such as give-aways, competitions, trading stamps and exhibitions. It is sometimes called below-the-line promotion.

(c) **Public relations**: the creation of positive attitudes regarding products, services, or companies by various means, including unpaid media coverage and involvement with community activities.

(d) **Personal selling**: the techniques by which a sales force makes contact with potential customers.

The promotional mix is often described in terms of push and pull effects.

- A **pull effect** is when consumers ask for the brand by name, for example because they have been given a money-off coupon or offered a free gift.

  The demand from the consumer then induces retailers or distributors to stock up with the company's goods.

- A **push effect** is targeted on getting the company's goods into the distribution network. This could, for example, be by giving a special discount on volume or as a sales incentive to ensure that wholesalers and retail customers stock up with products that the company is promoting.

8.2 Sales promotion

Sales promotions are those marketing activities other than personal selling, advertising and publicity, that stimulate consumer purchasing and dealer effectiveness, such as displays, shows and exhibitions, demonstrations and various non-recurrent selling efforts not in the ordinary routine.

Examples of sales promotion activities are:

- Coupons to be redeemed against purchase or free gifts.

- Promotions directed to distributors such as 'listing allowances' paid by consumer goods firms to stores so that they will stock the good, or volume bonuses to car dealers.

- Sales force promotions aim to motivate the sales force to sell more. They might include contests.

8.3 Advertising

Advertising is an explicit invitation to buy the offering. It also seeks to reinforce the positioning of the product; for example UK department store John Lewis advertises its products with the tagline 'never knowingly undersold', which reinforces the company's brand image of quality and ethical trading. Advertising is often classed under one of three headings:

- **Informative advertising** – conveying information and raising consumer awareness of the product. Common in the early stages of the product lifecycle or after modification to the product.

- **Persuasive advertising** – concerned with creating a desire for the product and stimulating actual purchase. Used for well established products, often in the growth/maturity stages of the product life cycle. The most competitive form of advertising.

- **Reminder advertising** – reminding consumers about the product or organisation, reinforcing the knowledge held by potential consumers and reminding existing consumers of the benefits they are receiving from their purchase.

8.3.1 The objectives of advertising

The objectives of an advertising campaign will vary from organisation to organisation, but are likely to include:

- Communicating information about a product
- Creating an awareness among consumers of new products
- Highlighting specific features of a product such as the product's Unique Selling Proposition (USP)
- Increasing sales and profits (or increasing donations in the case of non-profit making organisations)

8.3.2 Advertising media

The principal media are:

- **Television**: this is developing into a targeted media as channels multiply with digital TV and viewers reveal product preferences through interactive TV such as responding to interactive polls.

- **Newspapers and magazines**: magazines in particular are targeted at specific customer groups.

- **Commercial radio**

- **Internet**: this is via websites, including social media platforms, promotion on search engines, and paying for banner advertising on associated websites.

- **Posters**

- **Direct mail**

Worked example: Use of Social Media Marketing

An article published on the *Forbes* website (2013) highlights the increasing use of social media marketing and information systems by businesses looking for a 'big return' on their investment in marketing activities. The article highlights a number of good reasons for organisations to turn to social media marketing.

Brand recognition

Social media can be used a means of brand-building. 'With consistent effort and great content, you can build a reputation for your brand around your company's values, benefits, and advantages.'

Community

Social media is particularly effective at creating a community. 'When your followers become part of your community, you gain instant access to them. That means you can find out what challenges they are facing and what they like and don't like about your offerings. You can engage in ongoing dialogue that can be more valuable than any kind of paid market research.'

Repeat Exposure

Forbes notes that social media provides organisations with the opportunity to 'remind followers over and over again about what companies have to offer, which can shorten the sales cycle dramatically'.

Influence

By building a social media following, this can create a 'snowball effect'. In essence, the greater the social media audience the greater scope for attracting new 'customers, media interviews, joint venture partnerships, and all kinds of other opportunities'. *Forbes* highlights that effective social media marketing through sharing posts, videos and other content can lead to an increased 'hit' rate on a company's websites.

Big Wins

'While many businesses large and small are trying to justify the cost and time investment for managing social media marketing, an important benefit often gets overlooked: Big Wins. For example, if someone from LindedIn connects your business with a significant government contract, then that would certainly qualify as a Big Win. If a major media outlet finds your business on Twitter and interviews the MD for a national article, then that is also a Big Win – one that you can't measure based on revenues directly generated.'

Adapted from:

Chandler, S. 'The hidden benefits of social media marketing'. *Forbes*, December 2013. Available at: www.forbes.com [Accessed 7 June 2016]

8.4 Public relations

Public relations has the aim of earning understanding and support and influencing opinion and behaviour eg, through corporate sponsorship. It is the planned and sustained effort to establish and maintain goodwill and mutual understanding between an organisation and the public. PR activities, such as press releases, are often part of an organisation's response during times of crisis management.

PR encompasses more than customers. It seeks to help the firm build relationships with:

- Customers
- Consumers
- Employees
- Influencers (such as government, regulators and investment advisers)
- Investors
- Suppliers
- Potential employees

8.5 Personal selling

The sales force engages in personal one-to-one selling, as compared with the non-personal activities of advertising and sales promotion. It will include the activities of:

- Delivery and repair staff who may also sell service agreements and upgrades.
- Sales staff within the premises of the sales organisation.
- Travelling sales representatives.
- Call centre staff.

Interactive question 4: Canal Cruises

Canal Cruises Ltd is 60% owned by Captain Salmon. The company has 60 narrow boats and is located just off a major boating canal in Southern England. There are 20 boats of each of the following lengths, 30ft, 50ft and 70ft. Boats are hired to families and parties of people during the cruising season, which is April to October.

The narrow boats are regarded generally as being of high quality and their hire charge reflects this. All boats have a microwave, stereo, Wi-Fi and a HD-TV on board. The boats are currently advertised in the *Waterways World* magazine and website.

Recently Canal Cruises has been approached by the directors of Welsh Cruisers Ltd who wish to sell their business. Welsh Cruisers Ltd is located on the largest boating canal in Wales and has 30 narrow boats. The boats are of a much lower quality than those of Canal Cruises and over recent years less than half of the boats have been hired out at any one time during the season.

Prepare briefing notes for Captain Salmon covering the following areas.

4.1 Assuming that Welsh Cruisers is to be acquired and using Ansoff's matrix, comment on the marketing strategies which the company can now pursue, and state with reasons that which you would recommend.

4.2 Suggest how the company may go about promoting the newly-acquired Welsh Cruisers and increase the number of boats hired.

See **Answer** at the end of this chapter.

9 Price

Section overview

- Pricing affects sales revenues and profits through affecting margin and volumes.

- Prices should be set with regard to **costs**, **customers** and **competitors**: the 3Cs.

- The sensitivity of volumes of demand and total earnings to price changes is assessed using the economic principles of the price elasticity of demand. The concept of price elasticity of demand was introduced during your Business, Technology and Finance studies.

- Although revenues must exceed costs so that a profit can be made it will be shown that basing price solely on costs is likely to be suboptimal.

- Basing prices on customer perceptions of value will establish the maximum prices that can be charged to a customer, but tends to overlook competition which may put a lower ceiling on maximum price.

9.1 Principles of pricing – the three Cs

Kotler presents the pricing decision as a balance between 3Cs

- Costs
- Customers
- Competitors

Prices must be supported by the remaining elements of the marketing mix. The ability of a firm to charge more than competitors depends on the ability to create differentiation.

A fourth C is corporate objectives.

Corporate objectives

Possible pricing objectives are:

- To maximise profits using demand, elasticity and cost information – the assumed objective in economic theory.

- To achieve a target return on investment (ROI or ROCE). This results in a cost-based approach.

- To achieve a target revenue figure (eg, sales maximisation below).

- To achieve a target market share (eg, using penetration pricing – see below).

- To match the competition, rather than lead the market where the market is very price sensitive.

9.2 Price elasticity of demand

Economics states that the market demand for a good will increase as the price falls.

Definition

Price elasticity of demand: measures how far demand for a good will change in response to a change in its price.

The price elasticity of demand is used in pricing decisions to:

- Forecast the impact on revenues of a change in the selling price.
- Forecast the impact on sales volumes of a change in the selling price.

9.2.1 Price elasticity of demand and sales revenue

Consider the following demand schedule which shows the effect of the price of this good on sales revenue the firm receives.

Price	Quantity demand	Total revenue
£10	50	£500
£5	150	£750

In this example the lower price permits a higher sales revenue to be obtained. This is because the fall in price has led to a significant rise in the volume of demand. Demand would be said to be **elastic**.

If at a price of £5 only 80 units were sold, then changing the price from £10 to £5 would mean that total revenue would fall from £500 to £400, and demand would be said to be **inelastic**.

(a) When demand is **elastic**, a change in price will lead to a change in total revenue in the opposite direction.

- If the price is lowered, total sales revenue would rise, because of the large increase in the volume demanded. This is the case in the example above.

- If the price is raised, total sales revenue would fall because of the large fall the volume in demanded.

(b) When demand is **inelastic**, total revenue moves in the same direction as the change in price.

- If the price is lowered, total sales revenue would fall, because the increase in sales volume would be too small to compensate for the price reduction.

- If the price is raised, total sales revenue would go up in spite of the small drop in sales quantities.

Information on price elasticity therefore indicates how consumers can be expected to respond to different prices.

9.2.2 Price elasticity of demand and sales volume

Management need to forecast the effects of changes in price on sales volume in two situations:

- Production planning: the level of production will need to be changed to avoid shortages, if the price is cut, or unsold stocks and slack capacity, if the price is raised.

- Rationing demand: where capacity is fixed and in excess demand the price can be raised to reduce the demand.

9.2.3 Influences on price sensitivity of demand

Price elasticity of demand is a measure of the price sensitivity of customers for a good.

Main influences making demand insensitive to price (ie, making demand price inelastic) are:

- The product is regarded as a necessity by buyers (eg, cigarettes).

- There are few close alternatives available from competitors (ie, a lack of **substitutes**).

- The product is highly differentiated and so the customer is brand loyal and will not switch even if prices rises.

- The time since the price changed is short. Therefore customers have not had a chance to notice the price change or to source alternatives.

- The price of the product is insignificant as a proportion of total spending.

9.3 Price discrimination

Definition

Price discrimination: Sometimes also referred to as differential pricing, involves setting different prices for a similar product in different parts of the market.

The economic principle behind not setting the same price for all is that it may be lower than the keenest (price inelastic demand) customer segments would pay, and so lose revenue, but also too high for less keen (price elastic demand) segments and so lose volumes. Charging high prices to the former and low prices to the latter will maximise revenues.

To be successful however there must be:

- Different elasticities in different markets

- Little 'leakage' between the markets where there are different prices so separation is maintained

Different methods of differential pricing are:

- **Market segment**: in many countries in the world there are discounts for students and young people for certain products and services (eg, cinema tickets, rail travel).

- **Product version**: many car models have 'add on' extras which enable one brand to appeal to a wider cross-section of customers. Final price need not reflect the cost price of the add on extras directly: usually the top of the range model carries a price much in excess of the cost of provision of the extras, as a prestige appeal.

- **Place**: theatre seats are usually sold according to their location so that patrons pay different prices for the same performance according to the seat type they occupy.

- **Time**: hotel prices vary according to season. These are all attempts to increase sales revenue by covering variable but not necessarily average cost of provision.

- **Dynamic pricing**: the price of the product varies according to present levels of demand compared with normal demand patterns. Budget airlines will initially set the prices of a future flight low and sophisticated computer programs will track cumulative sales volume and if it rises more sharply than normal the price will be increased.

9.4 New product pricing: market penetration and market skimming

Market penetration pricing is a policy of low prices when the product is first launched to gain sufficient penetration into the market. It is therefore a policy of sacrificing short-term profits in the interests of long-term profits.

- The firm wishes to **discourage rivals** from entering the market.

- The firm wishes to **shorten the initial period of the product's life cycle**, to enter the growth and maturity stages as quickly as possible. (This would happen if there is high elasticity of demand for the product.)

Market skimming: The aim of market skimming is to gain high unit profits very early on in the product's life.

- The firm charges high prices when a product is first launched (eg, a popular new book may first be published in hardback format, then only later in paperback).

- The firm spends heavily on advertising and sales promotion to win customers.

- As the product moves into the later stages of its life cycle (growth, maturity and decline) progressively lower prices will be charged. The profit is skimmed off in progressive stages until sales can only be sustained at lower prices (eg, newly released smartphones and computer games are launched at high prices initially, then the prices are lowered subsequently).

- The firm may lower its prices to attract more price-elastic segments of the market; however, these price reductions will be gradual. Alternatively, the entry of competitors into the market may make price reductions inevitable.

9.5 Prices and costs

With the exception of some not-for-profit organisations all organisations will require that in the long run sales revenues should exceed costs.

Therefore management often seek to set prices of each product on the basis of its costs to achieve a **mark-up** on the costs to attempt to earn a profit.

These approaches were covered in your earlier studies. Briefly they are:

- **Marginal cost based**: the price is set as a mark up on the variable costs of the product to give a contribution. This contribution should be sufficient to cover overheads with an additional amount for profit.

- **Full cost based**: the overheads are allocated to the product, eg, by absorption costing, and a mark-up added to this representing the profit.

- **Target return based**: the full cost is increased by an amount representing the rate of profit required on the assets used to make the product.

Basing price on costs may have several advantages:

- **Simplicity of operation for distributors**: stores with thousands of lines of stock and frequent changes will simply set mark-ups for each product class.

- **Control of sales discounting**: sales teams and distributors will be aware of the mark-up (more likely **margin** ie, % of full sales price that represents profit) and will ensure they do not drop price to uneconomic levels to win a sale.

- **Ease of budgeting**: systems of standard costing and budgetary control require that prices and costs be forecast more than a year in advance. It is easier to make assumptions based on costs and then use variance analysis and reporting to deal with exceptions.

- **Conformity with contracts**: an increasing number of commercial partnerships have followed state procurement methods of cost-plus contracts to ensure fair but not excessive profits for suppliers. Often the supplier is required to offer **open book accounting** so that partners can verify this.

The problems of cost-based pricing are that it:

- **Ignores the effect of prices on volumes**: most estimates of costs assume a forecast (standard) level of production. If this results in an excessive price then the firm will either not achieve these volumes, and so not recover fixed overheads, or it will suffer the costs of an increasing inventory of unsold goods. In both cases profits would be reduced.

- **Ignores the effect of volumes on costs**: stimulating demand by accepting low prices and margins on initial production may enable a firm to gain economies of scale over time and also to access a much larger market.

- **Is useless for very high fixed cost industries**: where variable cost per customer served is low or zero (eg, television broadcasting, cinemas, sports grounds and festivals, hotels), the objective of pricing must be to maximise sales revenue. This can only be accomplished by referring to the demand schedule and price elasticity of demand, and not by reference to costs.

- **May not suit positioning of the product**: successful differentiation will increase potential prices without increasing costs in the same proportion. There is a danger the firm could undersell its product and reduce profits.

- **Ignores competitive conditions**: where a product is sold in several markets, margins should vary. In less competitive markets margins can be higher, but lower in more competitive markets. Having the same price in all markets is unlikely to maximise profits (see differential pricing above).

- **Does not consider the implications for sales of other products made by the firm**: selling some products at low or negative margins may generate sales of associated purchases (a so-called **loss leader** approach).

- **Inherent problems in assessing costs**: the approach will focus on production costs and allocate other costs as overheads. The methods of attributing costs to products may not be sensitive enough and hence lead to some potentially profitable products to be priced out of the market.

- **Invites poor cost control**: increasing costs will be passed on as higher prices resulting in less sales and revenues.

In practice cost-based prices are taken as the starting point for prices but these are then adjusted for considerations of strategic advantage, competition etc, by the management of the firm or by the sales team in the field.

9.6 Basing prices on customer perceptions of value

Effective sales teams are able to negotiate prices to obtain the maximum price the customer is willing to pay. However setting list prices and deciding pricing points for product ranges requires a more general approach.

Recall the 3Cs (costs, customers, competitors) above. Prices should be set according to the perceived value differences between the product and its rivals.

Methods include:

- **Going rate approach**: where the product is being launched into an established market the existing market prices are taken as a ready guide to value. A firm launching a new chocolate bar would place its price close to the price of the most similarly positioned product. A house builder would look at the prices of similar established properties in the area.

- **Product comparison approach**: show a panel of target customers two products: a benchmark product which already has an established market price; and the new product for which a price is needed. Let the panel tell you how much more (or less) they would pay for the new product compared to the old.

- **Factor pricing approach**: some of the augmented features of a product can have known price potential, eg, car manufacturers can assess the price premium gained by having an automatic gearbox, sports styling kit, additional seating etc. Once the price of the basic car is set, the prices of the higher specification versions can be established by adding up the prices of the extra features.

- **Economic value to customer approach**: some products are bought for the value they give. In business-to-business marketing the price a supplier charges for its products must take account of the price that can be achieved for the finished product. Fleet cars may be sold at a premium if the supplier can show better residual values or lower running costs. In consumer markets prices may be increased to cover the benefits of interest free credit or extended warranties.

9.7 Special pricing decisions

- **Promotional prices** are short-term price reductions or price offers which are intended to attract an increase in sales volume. (The increase is usually short-term for the duration of the offer, which does not appear to create any substantial new customer loyalty.) Loss leaders and money off coupons are a form of promotional pricing.

- **Every day low prices** is a response to customer cynicism about many of the promotional prices being in fact the right price after highly promoted reductions to an artificially inflated price. Firms will maintain low prices on a number of benchmark products to restore customers' faith.

- **Product line pricing** refers to the situation where a firm produces ranges of products of different sizes and qualities. It is essential that appropriate **price differentials** be maintained to stop one product underselling another, say a smaller high specification car robbing customers from a larger low specification one, but also close enough to allow sales teams to trade some customers up to higher value versions.

- **Captive product pricing** refers to the situation where prices of accessories can be inflated because the customer already has the basic product. Examples include ink cartridges for printers, spares for cars, drinks and desserts in a restaurant selling an attractively-priced main product. In these situations the pricing decision is taken to maximise the total earnings from the customer, sometimes over a number of years, rather than the earnings from each particular product.

- **Predatory pricing** describes artificially low prices designed to drive competitors out of the market. In many countries this is regarded as an illegal anti-competitive action and the authorities will scrutinise the costs of the supplier in relation to the price to establish whether the margin being achieved is realistic or deliberately low. In cross-border trade this would be called **dumping**.

Interactive question 5: Pricing methods

The Managing Director of a small manufacturing company, specialising in industrial packaging tape, is worried that the cost-plus pricing method currently used is not necessarily the most appropriate.

Requirements

She asks you to provide a memorandum that:

5.1 Explains the role and importance of pricing to the marketing effort.

5.2 Suggests and explains the differences in both competitor-based methods and demand/market-based methods which could be considered as alternatives.

See **Answer** at the end of this chapter.

10 Relationship marketing

Section overview

- Repetitive purchases of a product create the potential for the firm to build a relationship with the customer.

- This leads to a distinction between transactions marketing, which sees product sales as a sequence of independent sales, and relationship marketing under which a transaction is another chance to maintain and deepen the relationship with the client.

- The change in focus has been driven by improvements in IT which enables better tracking of customers, and the need to retain and increase spend per customer in mature markets where winning new customers is an expensive *nil sum* game for the industry.

10.1 Transactions marketing and relationship marketing

Many marketers say that the marketing mix does not cross product/service boundaries whereas customers do. Customers expect firms to be consistent in how they treat them.

The regular client of a sandwich bar, railway station or hotel will perceive that they have a relationship with the firm. However to its staff the customer is just another transaction in a busy day. This disparity in perception can lead to difficulties when the customer believes their relationship has been breached by some action of staff.

Definitions

Transactions marketing: A management approach that focuses on the product, and develops marketing mixes for a product according to the needs customers satisfy when they buy it.

Relationship marketing: Management process that seeks to attract, maintain and enhance customer relationships by focusing on the whole satisfaction experienced by the customer when dealing with the firm.

The key characteristics of relationship marketing are:

- Every customer is considered an individual person or unit.

- Activities of the company or organisation are predominantly directed towards existing customers.

CHAPTER 8

- It is based on interactions and dialogues.

- The company or organisation is trying to achieve profitability through the decrease of customer turnover and the strengthening of customer relationships.

10.2 Developing relationship marketing

Building up customer relationships requires a change of focus from the 'transaction-based approach' to the relationship approach. The contrast is shown in the table below.

Transaction marketing (mainly one-way communication)	Relationship marketing (mainly two-way communication)
Focus on single sale	Focus on customer retention
Orientation on product features	Orientation on product benefits
Short time scale	Long time scale
Little customer service	High customer service
Limited customer commitment	High customer commitment
Moderate customer contact	High customer contact
Quality is the concern of production	Quality is the concern of all

Instead of one-way communication aimed solely at gaining a sale, it is necessary to develop an effective two-way communication process to turn a prospect into a lifetime advocate.

Payne shows this as a **relationship marketing ladder**. Only repeated good experiences of dealings with the firm will lead to a customer turning from a client into someone willing to tell others they should be buying from us. This is not uncommon in consumer markets such as automobiles, hairdressing, financial services etc.

Partners are principally found in business to business marketing and refers to situations where trust has grown to the point that our customers will seek to tailor their business to us and not to seek alternative suppliers. The exchange of technical information and consultation of design that goes between a major airline and an engine manufacturer is an example of this.

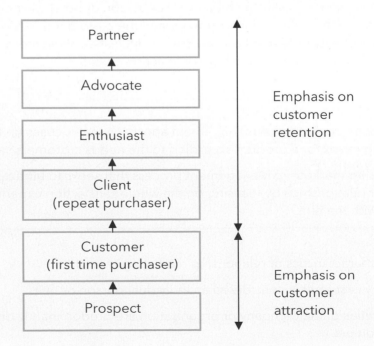

Stronger bonds to build loyalty and retention can be developed by:

- Loyalty schemes, eg, supermarket loyalty cards, frequent flier schemes, company clubs.

- Personalisation programmes, eg, Amazon.com suggesting films, books etc, which might suit returning customers.

- Structural ties, eg, providing customers with computer equipment to manage orders.

Relationship marketing has grown in response to several factors:

- **The increasing cost of attracting new customers**: it costs more to win new customers than to keep old ones. In mature markets encouraging customers to switch mobile telephone provider, credit card or home loan involves the firm in giving significant incentives which are readily matched and so the offer has to be raised.

- **Marketing strategies based on product development**: stores, utility providers and media owners seek to expand by selling wider ranges of products to their existing customers. Therefore the customer may deal with several parts of the business at once. A bad experience with one part could collapse sales in the rest.

- **Increased capabilities of information technology**: common databases and data analytics software used by organisations allow customer data relating to past dealings and also current transactions to be captured. These applications represent an important element in **Customer Relationship Management** (CRM).

10.2.1 Links to value chain and value system

Relationship marketing is a refocus of the traditional marketing approach, with a greater emphasis being placed on the creation of customer value. This requires a detailed understanding of the customer's value chain and an ability to identify whereabouts in that chain the opportunities for enhancing value arise.

Interactive question 6: Branding and relationship marketing

Your client is a large automobile manufacturer.

Requirements

6.1 Explain the concept and importance of branding to the company.

6.2 Explain the way in which relationship marketing can be used by the company to attract and retain its customers.

See **Answer** at the end of this chapter.

11 Marketing and ethics

Section overview

- The way that marketing is carried out may raise ethical concerns.

The way that marketing is carried out may raise ethical concerns. Ethical issues begin with questioning whether marketing exists to sell people things they don't need and so wastes resources and causes envy and dissatisfaction. The nature of products, the means by which they are promoted, the level of prices and the selective way they are made available are also ethical issues. There is also the key ethical question of honesty in marketing. These issues are examined in more detail in Chapter 16.

Summary and Self-test

Summary

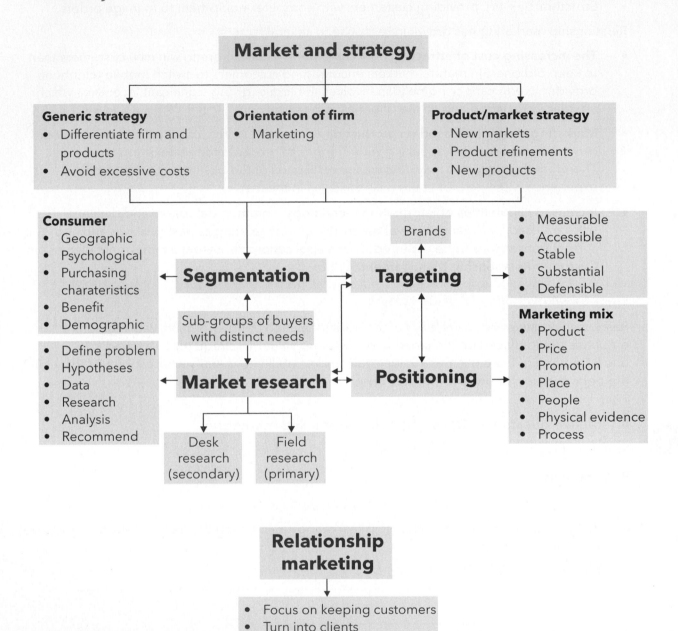

Market and strategy

Generic strategy
- Differentiate firm and products
- Avoid excessive costs

Orientation of firm
- Marketing

Product/market strategy
- New markets
- Product refinements
- New products

Consumer
- Geographic
- Psychological
- Purchasing charateristics
- Benefit
- Demographic

- Define problem
- Hypotheses
- Data
- Research
- Analysis
- Recommend

Segmentation

Sub-groups of buyers with distinct needs

Market research

Desk research (secondary)

Field research (primary)

Brands

Targeting

Positioning

- Measurable
- Accessible
- Stable
- Substantial
- Defensible

Marketing mix
- Product
- Price
- Promotion
- Place
- People
- Physical evidence
- Process

Relationship marketing
- Focus on keeping customers
- Turn into clients

Self-test

Answer the following questions.

1. What types of segmentation would a paint manufacturer segmenting the market in paint sold to other businesses use?

2. Why might demographic segmentation by itself not be a successful basis for car manufacturers targeting their customers?

3. Explain briefly market segmentation and market targeting, and the relationship between the two.

4. Describe, with examples, two ways in which a market can be segmented.

5. Give four differences between industrial and consumer markets.

6. Why is a brand name important to the following?

   (a) Purchasers
   (b) Manufacturers

7. Briefly describe the four elements of the promotion mix.

8. Give two reasons why most consumer good manufacturers choose not to distribute and sell their goods directly to the public.

9. Describe the use of targeting in marketing planning.

10. Show the marketing implications for two of the service characteristics.

11. Complete the table below describing the different relationships with a customer or client.

Relationship type	Description
Partner	
Advocate	
Supporter	
Client	
Purchaser	
Prospect	

12. Read the scenario of the **December 2014 Business Strategy and Technology** question entitled *Radar Traditional Radios Ltd*. Draft an answer for the requirement on market segmentation and the marketing mix.

13. Read the scenario of the **March 2016 Business Strategy and Technology** question in the Question Bank entitled *Outil plc,* referred to at the beginning of the chapter. Draft an answer to the requirement on test marketing.

Now, go back to the Learning outcomes in the Introduction. If you are satisfied that you have achieved these objectives, please tick them off.

Answers to Interactive questions

Answer to Interactive question 1

1.1 Positioning and targeting

Product positioning is a technique which carefully targets various product attributes of the (chosen) market segments.

Various factors of the product can be considered (eg, quality and price) and the company can in this way decide how to position its product. This will also help to focus on the competition and on what Rex will have to develop if it is to be successful.

Considering quality and price, this might be represented as follows.

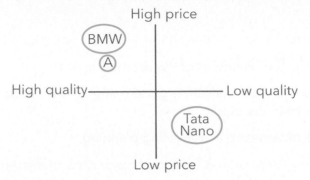

BMWs are regarded as high quality expensive cars; the Tata Nano, branded as the 'world's cheapest car', is regarded as a lower profit inexpensive vehicle. By focusing on the products in this way Rex Ltd can decide where it wants to position itself. As it enjoys a high reputation for its off-road vehicles, it might wish to try to move the whole business more upmarket. A possible position might therefore be at A, ie, quality to rival BMW but at a lower price.

Market targeting considers how markets can be split into different sectors and then each sector targeted with a specific product. There are three possible approaches.

- **Undifferentiated marketing**: One product, one market. No attempt is made to segment the market.

- **Differentiated marketing**: The market is segmented with products being developed to appeal to the needs of buyers in the different segments.

- **Concentrated marketing**: The market is segmented with the product being specifically targeted at a particular segment.

As Rex Ltd has different products aimed at different sectors, off-road, small, family hatchback, etc, it is obvious that it has adopted a differentiated approach. This might be developed further to produce a range of a particular model. For example, the new improved Matchless could be produced as a three-door, five-door, GTi etc. This will be necessary if Rex Ltd is going to win the market share it wants.

Answer to Interactive question 2

2.1 There are five characteristics of a service, which are described below:

- **Perishability**: A service cannot be stored or saved for later consumption. It has an immediacy that cannot be held over until sometime in the future. For example, a meal in a restaurant has to be eaten at the time it is paid for. This can cause problems with the utilisation of capacity as some occasions in the restaurant, eg, evenings and weekends, will be more popular than others, eg, lunchtimes. Marketers have to give incentives for customers to purchase at off-peak times to counter this eg, happy hour deals. Such tactics are often achieved through the use of internet technologies. Users of discount apps can download discount codes or QR codes which entitle them to reduced bills if redeemed at certain times of the day in participating restaurants.

- **Intangibility**: You cannot touch or feel the service offering as it has an abstract delivery. Unlike a product which you can touch (and smell and see) a service has no physical presence. It is only the paperwork that accompanies the service which has a tangible element, eg, an MOT certificate in the UK after the car has had its annual service and is deemed roadworthy. This can cause problems since customers cannot see what they are getting for their money and they can only make a judgement based on experience of the service.

- **Inseparability**: A key distinguishing feature of a service is that the provider and receiver of the service are inseparable in the sense that the customer has to be present for the service to take place – unlike a product, where you can buy a can of soft drink but the seller does not have to be present when it is consumed at a later date. This presents a problem for the marketer as they cannot always ensure that the process is enjoyable for the customer.

- **Heterogeneity**: The delivery of the service will vary each time to the customer. This is because a service is dependent on the unique interaction between the provider and the customer which will vary depending on the individuals. The variability is created by the influence of human behaviour in the transaction and consistency can become a difficult problem to manage. A meal in one Pizza Express restaurant may be a very different experience from a meal in the same restaurant in a different town.

- **Non-ownership**: With a product, eg, a computer, ownership is transferred at the point of sale. Ownership of a service typically remains with the provider and payment for the service just confers the right to use something. For instance, streaming a film under a rental agreement effectively allows the customer to watch the film during the rental period but the film itself is not physically owned by the customer.

These are the differences between a service and a product and their associated problems for the marketer.

2.2 The extended marketing mix

The extended marketing mix comprises People, Process and Physical Evidence and is to be applied to a small independent firm of management consultants to derive the following benefits.

- **People**

  There should be a strong emphasis on staff training to ensure a consistently high quality of provision. Poor customer service is the most commonly quoted reason for a change in sourcing services and is the most difficult problem to overcome to recover lost custom. The high level of people involvement in management consultancy demands that their customers are treated in a very professional manner throughout the delivery process. As their customers will judge the quality of the service by the conduct of the staff the close proximity of the staff working in a small business magnifies the need to adequately train all employees. This can include such areas as personal presentation, dealing with enquiries, providing quotations and maintaining knowledge of both technical and technological competencies in line with current developments.

- **Physical evidence**

  The image of the branches of the consultancy and any correspondence that is sent out in response to enquiries, including from the website and social media platforms, need to be consistent and include company brand identity such as logo or accreditation awards. This is crucial as it is one of the means that current or prospective clients will use to evaluate the consultancy.

Staff apparel, interior decoration of the branches, tidiness and signage should reflect a common and consistent quality image for the management consultancy. It should believe that the colour scheme and logo reflect its professionalism and trustworthy image which should be maintained to retain its fresh feel. All its literature and website and social media content should be regularly updated to provide an impression of current thinking for its clients that enhances quality perceptions for the offering.

- **Process**

  As part of customer service, efficient administrative processes underpin a high quality of provision. For instance if a client has spent an unnecessary amount of time trying to contact a management consultant they would become very frustrated and annoyed at the waste of their valuable time. It sends all the wrong messages concerning the offering and will become a source of friction between the two parties that will have to be recovered. The small business will need to consider putting procedures and resources into place to ensure these problems are carefully managed and that the client's expectations are at least achieved, if not surpassed. Processes here may involve the use of cloud-based client areas on the business's website, so that clients can send and receive documentation which may be too big to transfer to specific consultants via email. The use of digital asset management systems may also be appropriate.

  ### Conclusion

  Many companies, large and small, often treat these areas of the marketing mix with limited attention, which results in a poor perceived level of customer service. By paying due attention to the quality of all the people, the physical evidence and the process involved in the management consultancy operation will enhance the service marketing provision.

Answer to Interactive question 3

3.1 A large banking group

A large banking group, such as Barclays, has to focus on four key sectors.

- The consumer market
- The corporate market
- The small/medium business market
- The financial markets

In all these sectors both international and domestic considerations are necessary.

The bank, whilst essentially a service, offers its customers a range of products. Although some of these products are intangible, they are nevertheless perceived by customers as offering specific benefits and meeting specific needs. It is important for a large banking group to engage all the elements of the marketing mix for these sectors.

In the consumer market distribution has become a major issue, particularly with the advent of online banking. Service is an important element of the bank's response to an increasingly competitive marketplace. New products are being launched as the bank's marketing environment poses new opportunities and threats. Communication is critical both in terms of customer acquisition and retention. The heavy use of online and social media marketing are evidence of the importance attached to these components of promotion.

Within the corporate market a different range of tools will be utilised. In particular, relationship marketing and sponsorship become important elements of the mix. A range of financial services is offered to corporate clients particularly with investments. The product mix, communication and distribution structure will vary from the consumer market, with the sales function becoming more dominant.

For the small/medium business the role of the business adviser is important, along with the various online and in-branch services the bank provides to assist the business in managing its financial affairs more effectively. It is not uncommon to see TV and online advertising targeted at entrepreneurs. Each element has an important part to play in the bank's competitive position.

3.2 Electric component manufacturer

A company that manufacturers electronic components for computer manufacturers will focus its marketing activities on a relatively few number of customers in the business sector. The need for consumer marketing activity will therefore generally be unnecessary although organisations such as Intel have gained a strong market position in the supply of computer chips by building a strong brand reputation with consumers. The assumption in this case is that this manufacturer is focused upon its business customers.

The predominant marketing mix activities will focus upon product quality and delivery with strong sales force and technical support. It is likely that corporate entertainment and the building up of relationships throughout the customer's organisation will be important aspects of the company's marketing programme. The role of distribution is important particularly in terms of product availability and speed of delivery. There is a danger that this market can become price driven as technological change means new products are copied or become obsolete very quickly. A strong commitment must therefore be made to research and new product development.

Packaging and branding are less critical components as tools of communication, although they can play a role in supporting the manufacturer's overall positioning. Publicity, particularly in the trade press, and via online articles can be important tools of communication. The supply of support literature and price structure alongside easy to access order processes will enhance the competitive position of this company. With a focus on fewer customers, direct marketing techniques should predominate. The relationship that the manufacturer has with distributors in the supply chain will also be important to ensure wide availability of component parts.

Answer to Interactive question 4

Briefing notes

To   Captain Salmon
From   J Sayso, Chartered accountant
Date   Today
Subject   Marketing

4.1 Marketing strategies

If Welsh Cruisers Ltd is acquired, this will represent growth in the business of Canal Cruises. The information provided suggests that the quality of Welsh Cruisers' boats is much lower than that of Canal Cruises, as is the level of boat hiring. Four possible growth strategies could be adopted. These are discussed below.

Market penetration

Market penetration involves selling existing products in existing markets. The overall market of Canal Cruises is the narrowboat hire market and is restricted to those who read and use the *Waterways World* magazine and website. It targets the top end of this restricted market. To sell more of the existing product to this market it would have to convert the lower quality Welsh Cruisers' boats into those of a quality similar to its own (eg, installing Wi-Fi connectivity, HD-TVs, microwaves and stereos). Such conversion may be very expensive (complete boat refits and painting may be required) but the company would be operating in a market segment with which it is familiar. However, there may not be the demand for an extra 30 quality boats.

Market development

Existing products are sold in new markets. Again, conversion of Welsh Cruisers' boats is necessary and further expense will be incurred in developing new markets (market research, promotion etc). New markets can be developed by advertising, promotion via channels other than *Waterways World*.

Product development

Canal Cruises could leave the lower quality narrowboats as they are and target the lower end of its *Waterways World* market. Extra promotional expenses would be incurred as would marketing research costs (which would be necessary to gain information about the new stage segment).

Diversification

This involves leaving the lower quality boats as they are and selling to potential customers who are not already in the company's existing market. Marketing research and promotion costs would be incurred as for 'market development'.

Recommendation

Canal Cruises should pursue a diversification strategy, because Welsh Cruisers already has some business gained via its existing advertising and promotional channels; the business needs development. Restricting promotion to *Waterways World* (product development) may result in lower hirings. The other two strategies (converting the boats) are likely to be too expensive.

4.2 Promotion

The main promotional objective will be to increase hirings of Welsh Cruisers' boats to the same level as that of Canal Cruises. The promotional possibilities are discussed below.

Waterways World

The company could promote all its activities through the *Waterways World* channels (magazine and online) as it does presently. This policy has been very successful to date. Should the company adopt the diversification strategy above, it is doubtful whether the target market (those looking for a cheap boat) would read articles published by *Waterways World*, and the promotional objective would not be achieved.

Adverts could still be placed in the *Waterways World* magazine and online but other channels should also be used (see below). It is recommended that the name 'Welsh Cruisers' is maintained and separate advertisements used for the differing parts of the business, otherwise people may begin to associate the lower quality of Welsh Cruisers' boats with those of Canal Cruises.

Wider promotion

It has already been mentioned that Welsh Cruisers must have existing means of promotion and they should be examined carefully to see if they are reaching the target market.

An advertising message needs to be thought out – for example 'value for money' could be emphasised and this must be communicated to the target market. Advertisements could be placed in the larger circulation daily or Sunday newspapers (and including their online supplements), social media promotions could be used, travel agents could be approached to stock brochures and so on.

The possibility of online sales should be investigated. A website could be created (either for the company as a whole or for Welsh Cruises alone). Discounts could be offered for online booking, repeat purchases etc, to encourage market penetration and development. The site could be used to promote a particular image for the business and reinforce the brand.

Other promotional techniques

To increase sales and gain repeat hirings, various other 'non-advertising' techniques could be used. Examples are set out below.

- Welsh Cruisers could accept all male or female parties on 'social drinking' holidays (with the option for the customer of taking out damage insurance!)

- '20% off' coupons could be issued to customers for use later in the hiring season or '10% off next year's hire charge' coupons.

- Drivers could be provided at a small extra charge for those who are wary of taking out a boat for the first time and who would otherwise not hire.

Answer to Interactive question 5

5.1 Memorandum

To	Managing Director
From	Anne Accountant
Date	XX/XX/XX
Subject	Report on Pricing Methods

Introduction

I have been asked to produce a report detailing the importance of pricing in marketing terms and also to explain the differences in competitor-based methods and demand-based methods.

The importance of pricing in marketing terms

Pricing plays an essential role in the marketing of your product. First of all, you need to cover all of your costs, but the price will help to create an image of your product in the eyes of your customer.

As part of the marketing mix, price will help the perceived quality, value and image. If the price is high, then customers generally take the view that the product is of high standard and is good quality. This of course, needs to be backed up with the other elements of the marketing mix. If the price is low, there is a danger that the perception is of low quality and is 'cheap and cheerful'. This is only a danger, however, if you want to position your product as a high quality item. In general terms, price will help you to position your product in the market. This can be visualised with as 'perception map'.

The above map shows two dots, which demonstrate that in positioning your product by price, it will create an image to your customer.

Price can help to gain market share by using methods such as 'price skimming' or 'price penetration'. Penetration will gain a large marketing share as price is set very low, whereas skimming pricing is where the price is set high, usually for new products launched into a market with few competitors and a smaller market share is gained.

Key factors that concern pricing

There are four key factors that affect pricing decisions, also known as the 4 Cs:

- Cost - related to the actual costs involved.
- Consumer/customer - related to the price the consumer will pay.
- Competition - related to competitors prices for substitute or complimentary products.
- Company - related to the company's financial objectives.

Financial issues - cost

- This is the lower level of a price - often accountants use cost when deciding on the pricing structure. There are at least four different types of costs in regard to a product or service:

    - Fixed cost - a cost that does not change according to the increase in the number of units produced ie, rent and rates for the premises.

    - Variable costs - a cost that changes according to the number of units produced such as raw materials.

    - Total costs - a sum of fixed and variable cost times the quantity produced.

    - Average cost - this is the total cost divided by the number of units produced.

- Contribution - allows the accountant to analyse whether the product can be sold at less than cost for a period of time, but making a contribution to the costs.

- Break-even analysis - indicates the amount of units that must be sold at a given price to cover costs.

- Company's financial objectives - the company's objectives in terms of profitability also need to be taken into account when considering the price.

Economic issues

Economic issues such as the following also need to be taken into account:

- Customers' demand.

- Demand is considered and calculations on how much will be demanded at a certain price using the demand curve will be undertaken.

- It is useful to know the shape of the demand curve when setting prices as you can set a high price if your market is inelastic.

- Marketing communications serve to influence the demand curve to make it more inelastic.

- You must consider inflation year on year, affecting the cost of employment, raw materials and distribution.

- This is also a consideration for customers' disposable income.

Competitors

- Competitors must be taken into account.

- The marketer looks at competitors, macro environment, internal environment, stage in the product life cycle and sets a price at what the market will bear.

All of the above factors and perspectives play a key role in finalising a price.

5.2 Competitor-based pricing

This method is where the pricing policy is based upon competing prices in the market. This is different to cost-plus pricing in that it takes into consideration how the other competitors are pricing their products and how their products are perceived by their customers. Cost-plus pricing does not do this, and merely covers costs and leaves room for a little profit. The price does not necessarily have to be cheaper than competitors, as discussed before, it depends upon how you want your products to be perceived by your customers, and compared to your competitors.

Some of the methods used for competitor-based pricing include price matching, going rate pricing and predator pricing.

Price matching: This is where the company guarantees that the product cannot be bought for less anywhere. If it can be bought for less, they usually refund the difference. Therefore, the price is very much based on the competitors in the market place.

Going rate pricing: Here the pricing policy is determined by the competitors' pricing strategy and a similar price is set (but not guaranteed as above).

Predator pricing: This is where the pricing policy is set low so that the competition has problems in competing for market share.

Market/demand-based pricing

The final method is more suitable to take into account market needs and wants and relates to what is in demand. Compared to competitor-based pricing, it takes demand into consideration. As customers are becoming more demanding, this is a more suitable method of pricing. Economic issues and the elasticity of demand are considered here.

There are a number of methods such as penetration and skimming strategies, discount and allowance pricing, segmentation pricing and promotional pricing. I will explain a number of these methods below.

Skimming: This is where a high price policy is undertaken to 'skim the cream' of the market. This is more advisable if you have a product which is new into the market and there are few competitors. It is important that you are able to lower the price once you have established a customer base and need to gain more market share.

Penetration: This is where the price starts off low and market share is gained quickly. It is difficult however, to increase the price once this has been undertaken.

Segmented pricing: Companies will often adjust their basic prices to allow for differences in customers, products and locations. The company sells a product at two or more prices, even though the difference in price is not based on differences in costs. Examples may be where different customers pay different prices for the same product such as rail travel First Class and Standard fares. Another example is time pricing where prices vary by the day or the hour such as telephone companies and 'off-peak' calls.

Conclusion

I hope that this has helped in your consideration of the pricing policy to adopt for the industrial packaging tape. Please contact me should you require any further information.

Answer to Interactive question 6

6.1 Importance of branding

One of the most distinctive skills of professional marketers is their ability to create, maintain, protect, reinforce and enhance brands. A brand is a name or term like Toyota, General Motors or Ford, a symbol or design which is used to identify the goods or services of one seller to differentiate them from those of competitors. Thus the brand identifies the manufacturer and supplier of the product. Brands, unlike other forms of intellectual property, such as patents and copyrights do not have an expiry date and their owners have exclusive rights to use their brand name for an unlimited period of time.

A brand has value to the business, known as brand equity. They can reinforce customer loyalty as well as name awareness, perceived quality, strong brand associations and other assets such as channel relationships. Branding also increases innovation by giving producers an incentive to look for new features that can be protected against imitating competitors. Thus branding will result in more product variety and choice for consumers.

The use of branding

A brand conveys a specific set of features, benefit and services to the buyer. The brand has four different dimensions, which are described below.

Attributes

A brand first brings to mind certain product attributes such as build quality, power capability and so on. A large automobile manufacturer would use these attributes in its advertising and promotional activities.

Benefits

Customers do not purchase attributes, they purchase perceived benefits. Therefore, attributes must be translated into functional and emotional benefits. For example, the attribute 'well built' might translate into benefits demanded by our customers, such as reliability or high resale value.

Values

A brand also says something about the buyer's values. The brand marketer must identify the specific group of buyers whose values coincide with the delivered benefits package such as high performance, safety and prestige.

Personality

A brand also projects a personality. The brand will attract people whose actual desired self image match the brand's image. This would be important for the business customer who purchase from the large automobile manufacturer as well as the consumer purchasing an automobile.

A company must define its overall branding strategy which affects all of its products. It is necessary to consider how new products fit into the brand structure particularly as the large automobile manufacturer will have developed a series of marques that identifies each family of its products. Safeguarding the association of quality developed with the large automobile manufacturer's products will be paramount.

6.2 The concept of relationship marketing

Introduction

Customer relationship marketing is becoming increasingly more important owing to the increase in customer education and expectations. Many large firms now have a dedicated policy for this subject and we need to consider the implications.

Customer lifetime value

For any organisation, the sale should not be considered as the end of the relationship but instead the beginning of the process to retain that customer. Therefore, it is more efficient to keep existing customers happy and delighted with their experience rather than finding new customers. This process should be continued at each sale and be seen as part of a long-term relationship between ourselves and the customer.

Relationship marketing

This is a long-term approach to creating, maintaining and enhancing strong relationships with customers and other stakeholders. Organisations need to view each transaction as part of a long-term goal. If the customer is satisfied with the product or service they have received for the price they have paid, they are more likely to return. A short-term outlook on the other hand will consider only a quick profit and not the more important possibility of a repeat purchase.

There are five different distinguishable levels with the relationship that can be formed with customers who have purchased a product or service. These are:

- **Basic**

  Selling a product without any follow up.

- **Reactive**

  Selling a product with follow up encouraged on the part of the customer.

- **Accountable**

  Having sold a product, the follow up occurs a short time afterwards to confirm the customer's expectations have been met.

- **Proactive**

  The sales person contacts the customer from time to time with suggestions regarding improved products.

- **Partnership**

  The company works continuously with the customer to deliver improved levels of value.

Relationship marketing can contribute to an organisation in a number of ways. It can establish a rapport with customers creating trust and confidence. It allows an opportunity to interact and hence communicate the large automobile manufacturer's commitment to satisfying customer's needs and wants. It can help to improve their experience and adds that personal touch, which links the emotions of both parties. By creating a notional bond as one of its objectives relationship marketing strives to achieve a sense of belonging thereby making the customer feel part of the business. It attempts to tailor products and services to cater for specific needs of customers, therefore reducing the need to switch behaviour. The use of database management and information communication technology helps to address the customer needs in a focused manner and can be manipulated to the individual's requirements.

There are significant benefits that can be derived from relationship marketing. It can contribute to cost savings as it is up to five times more expensive to find a new customer than retain an existing customer. It can help to entice new customers away from competitors as a perceived added value activity. It will also make it more difficult for existing customers to switch, as there is an emotional bond that underpins loyalty to the customer and the company.

Answers to Self-test

1   A paint manufacturer segmenting the market in paint sold to other businesses might use the following types of segmentation:

- Type of business – potential customers may be divided into several different groups such as paint wholesalers, do-it-yourself retail outlets, specialist decorating outlets, housing developers, contracting decorators, and vehicle manufacturers.

- Usage, range and size are all means of segmenting the paint market. The size of container and packaging of the paint will vary according to the user needs of the customer. Contracting decorators may use large containers of a limited range of colours and not be particularly concerned about packaging, while do-it-yourself outlets and specialist stores may require a full range of colours and containers of various sizes with attractive decoration.

- Geographical area is an important segmentation variable for this type of industry. Customers may be domestic or overseas. Paint is exported to many different countries – each will need their own marketing strategies.

2   Reasons why demographic segmentation alone may not be a successful basis for car manufacturers targeting their customers include:

- A car manufacturer may use buyers' age in developing its target market and then discover that the target should be the psychologically young (young at heart) and not the young in age. (The Ford Motor Company used buyers' age in targeting its Mustang car in America, designing it to appeal to young people who wanted an inexpensive sporty car. Ford found to its surprise that the car was being purchased by all age groups.)

- Income is another variable that can be deceptive. One would imagine that working class families in the UK would buy a Vauxhall Astra and the managerial class would buy BMWs. However, many Astras are bought by middle-income people (often as the family's second car) and expensive cars are often bought by working class families (plumbers, carpenters etc).

- Personal priorities also upset the demographic balance. Middle-income people often feel the need to spend more on clothes, furniture and housing which they could not afford if they purchased a more expensive car.

- The upgrading urge for people trying to relate to a higher social order often leads them to buy expensive cars.

- Some parents although 'well off' pay large fees for the private education of their children and must either make do with a small car, or perhaps no car at all.

3   Market segmentation is the process of identifying groups of buyers with different buying desires or requirements. Market targeting is the firm's decision regarding which market segments to serve. Markets made up of buyers seeking substantially different product qualities and/or quantities are called 'heterogeneous markets'.

4   For example

- By geographical region   –   eg, North v South, different countries
- By demographic factors   –   eg, age, sex, social class, lifestyle, education, income
- By the way the product is used –   eg, professional builders or amateur DIY'ers
- By customer requirements   –   eg, tea granules, bags and leaves are a response to different levels of convenience required.

5   Industrial and consumer markets differ in the following ways.

Consumer markets	Industrial markets
Products purchased to satisfy personal needs	Products bought for use in firm's operations or to make other products
Buying decision may be complex and irrational: 'it caught my eye'	Buying motive linked to improving quality and/or profitability. Technical specifications are a very important element of the product definition
Likely to have many customers with low buying power	Likely to be fewer firms but each has greater spending power
Customers spread out	Customers concentrated, either geographically or by industry
Longer distribution channels	More likely to sell direct
Advertising is main promotional tool	Personal selling extremely important More negotiation involved with pricing

6   To the **purchaser** the brand name is important.

- It distinguishes the product from alternatives.

- It permits repurchase of a product which has proved satisfactory when previously bought.

- The purchaser is familiar with the attributes of each well-known brand.

- The problem of making a choice is reduced.

- The familiar brand name encourages a feeling of security about the purchase.

To the **manufacturer** the virtues of branding are somewhat different.

- It encourages repurchase (this is effectively the same as 'brand loyalty').

- The brand name is a merchandising asset: it is useful in persuading people to purchase at the point of sale.

- The brand name becomes associated with the product's intended attributes, thus positioning it in the customer's mind and the market.

- The brand name is used in all promotion effort, and tends to enhance the effectiveness of advertising.

7   The promotion mix consists of four elements.

- Advertising: paid communications in the media which are designed to influence potential customers favourably regarding a company's products or services. Advertising is sometimes called **above-the-line** promotion.

- Sales promotion: non-media promotional activity aimed at increasing sales. Sales promotion includes a variety of techniques such as give-aways, competitions, trading stamps and exhibitions. It is sometimes called **below-the-line** promotion.

- Public relations: the creation of positive attitudes regarding products, services, or companies by various means, including unpaid media coverage and involvement with community activities.

- Personal selling: the techniques by which a sales force makes contact with potential customers.

8   There are several reasons for using separate firms for getting goods to the consumer. These include the following.

- Market knowledge is far deeper in an established intermediary.

- Market coverage is larger for a firm with a distribution chain already running; set-up costs of a distribution network are large

- Distribution speed is likely to be much higher in an existing company specialising in this area.

- Distributors may cover a range of complementary products to enhance sales of the principal product.

9   Targeting involves selecting the most attractive market segments, and designing those elements of the marketing mix to fit the identified segment.

10   For any two characteristics:

Intangibility	Judgemental evaluation
Inseparability	Provider and client impact on quality of service
Variability	Consistency based on delivery process
Perishability	Instantaneous consumption that cannot be stored
Non ownership	Services are used and not owned

11

Relationship	Description
Partner	The most loyal business associate
Advocate	Active recommendation for business
Supporter	Some tacit approval for offering
Client	Some repeat activity
Purchaser	Completed at least one transaction
Prospect	Likely source of potential business

12   Refer to the answer to Radar Traditional Radios Ltd in the Question Bank.

13   Refer to the answer to Outil plc in the Question Bank.

CHAPTER 9

Strategy and structure

Introduction

Examination context

TOPIC LIST

Introduction

Learning outcomes

- Analyse the governance structure of an organisation, identifying strengths and weaknesses ☐

- Evaluate and recommend an appropriate organisational structure for a given strategy, taking into account the impact of changing technology and other factors ☐

- Identify the steps needed for a given organisation to develop its corporate governance to meet the needs of its stakeholders, strategic objectives and its compliance requirements ☐

Specific syllabus references for this chapter are: 1e, 3c, 3d.

Syllabus links

The rudiments of organisational structure and governance were covered in the syllabus for Business, Technology and Finance.

Examination context

The key element in this chapter is how structure links with strategy. Knowledge of organisational structures in isolation from strategy would not normally be examined. The idea that there is no one ideal structure is important, as it means that issues of structure will need to interact with the strategy according to the particular circumstances of the scenario. Organisations which are structured divisionally face particular issues including the extent of decentralisation, performance evaluation and transfer pricing. It is important to recognise the increasingly important role that outsourcing and internet technologies are having on organisational structures. Such developments have given rise to the concept of boundary-less organisations.

This chapter contains references to a number of named studies. It is desirable to attribute the source of these studies in describing them. However, for examination purposes it is not the intention that the names should be quoted or reproduced without application. Rather, it is intended that the implications and results of these studies can be applied appropriately to practical scenarios to inform applied strategy and organisational structure recommendations.

In Question 3 of the September 2016 exam (*Thistle Engineering Services Ltd*) the scenario focused on a Scottish company which specialised in the design, construction and installation of storage tanks and high-pressure steel pipelines for the oil and gas industry. One of Thistle's major customers, a global company, had asked Thistle to provide it with services for a major infrastructure project outside the UK, in Malta. Thistle was considering setting up a new base in Malta and had approached its UK bank for loan finance. The question requirements asked candidates to prepare different sections of a business plan, which explained why each section was important for the loan application, and identified any further information that would be useful in completing the section. As part of the business plan the final requirement asked candidates to suggest an:

'Appropriate organisational structure for international expansion.'

(7 marks)

The examiner noted that the 'requirement was generally well answered. Most candidates suggested some form of divisionalised structure for the new venture and discussed the need for local knowledge and input in deciding the degree to which decisions should be decentralised. Better candidates discussed the impact that the choice of structure could have on risk.' As these comments illustrate, it is your ability to apply your knowledge of organisational structures to the scenario which matters.

In Question 2 of the March 2017 exam (*Eclo Ltd*) the scenario featured a manufacturer of environmentally friendly corporate clothing, called Eclo. Eclo was a small company, set up by an entrepreneur, and it had a relatively flat organisational structure. Eclo's products were produced and printed in India, where Eclo had strategic partnerships with a few key suppliers. The first requirement asked candidates to:

'Discuss whether Eclo operates with a flexible organisational structure. Refer to relevant models.'

(7 marks)

Candidates were required to use their knowledge of relevant models in answering the question. Models such as Handy's shamrock and the work of Mintzberg (both discussed in this chapter) were appropriate. Better candidates made reference to those features of Eclo's organisational structure which are consistent with the newer types of flexible structure which have emerged in recent years.

1 Strategy and structure

Section overview

- The management team and staff of a firm must be organised to carry out the operations and strategy of the business.

- There is a debate about the direction of influence between strategy and structure. Does management build a structure once it has decided strategy or does the structure determine the strategy through its influence on the flows of information and managements assessment of what is possible?

- The most appropriate structure depends on the stage of development of the organisation and the nature of its competitive environment (**contingency approach**).

1.1 Structure needed to implement strategy

A strategy without effective organisation of the people required to carry it out is doomed. Strategies can only be implemented by, and through, people.

Developing an appropriate structure requires consideration of three areas:

- **Organisational configuration** – the primary groupings of staff into departments or divisions.

- **Centralisation/Decentralisation**– where the responsibility for decision making lies.

- **Management systems** – this includes the make-up of the senior management team, eg, the corporate board, and the methods they use to govern the organisation. This includes the processes used to monitor financial results, to arrive at strategic decisions and to manage risk.

1.2 Impact of strategic choices on structure and *vice versa*

The relationship between strategy and structure is a complex one.

Structure follows strategy

This **top-down approach** says that management decide the strategy then build or revise organisational structure to implement it.

The argument for structure following strategy was put forward by Chandler. He argues that the structure of the organisation must be adapted to fit the strategy adopted by management.

In his analysis any changes to organisation structure were a response to the organisation's stage of growth:

- Geographic expansion called for departmental offices to be set up to administer the new field units.

- Vertical integration required a central office and multi-departmental structure.

- Diversification required a general office to administer divisions operating in different industries.

Strategy follows structure

An alternative **bottom-up view** is that the strategy a firm follows emerges from, or depends on, its structure or that the structure limits the choice of strategy.

For example:

- Organisational structure and the interests of people within it shapes the flow of information to those responsible for strategic management. For example government ministers can only respond to issues they are told about and can select only from the options they are presented with.

- What actually gets done depends on power. The informal organisation may feature quite different power relations than suggested by the formal structure.

- Highly centralised structures tend to stifle innovative strategic solutions.

- Divisionalised structures restrict collaboration and 'joined up' strategies.

- Bureaucratic structures focus on maintaining the status quo.

Both the top-down and bottom-up views are extreme expressions. Managers recognise both forces will be at work:

- Management will restructure to implement new strategies.
- Management strategies will be partially unrealised because the structure worked against them.
- Structures will develop organically as teams and managers adapt to new challenges and initiatives.
- Restructuring will create new initiatives and possibilities at the same time as suppressing others.

1.3 Contingency approach to organisation structure

The modern contingency approach takes the view that there is no one best, universal structure. There are a large number of variables, or situational factors, which influence organisational design and performance. The contingency approach emphasises the need for flexibility.

The most appropriate structure for an organisation depends on its situation. It is an 'if then' approach, ie, **if** certain situational factors are present, **then** certain aspects of structure are most appropriate.

Typical situational factors include:

- Type and size of organisation and purpose
- Culture
- Preferences of top management/power/control
- History
- Abilities, skills, needs, motivation of employees
- Technology (eg, production systems)
- Environment (see below)

Burns and Stalker identified two (extreme) types of structure (and management style).

- **Mechanistic** – rigid structure, bureaucratic management structure/style, applicable in stable environments.

- **Organic** – more fluid appropriate to changing circumstances (ie, dynamic environments).

This links with the traditional/emergent approaches to strategy and structure. Both mechanistic and organic elements may exist side by side in any one organisation, eg, in a hotel 'production' departments like the kitchens may be suited to a mechanistic structure but 'service' departments like marketing/reception may work better with organic structures.

2 Mintzberg's organisational forms

Section overview

- Organisational structure sets out how the various functions within the organisation are arranged.

- Mintzberg suggested that all organisations can be analysed into six building blocks.

- The particular structure of the business will depend on which of the building blocks is more dominant.

2.1 Components of organisations

In Business, Technology and Finance you were introduced to Mintzberg's theory of organisational configuration (sometimes called **the structure of sixes**), characterised by five distinct components that operate within the sixth, the **ideology** of the organisation or **culture**.

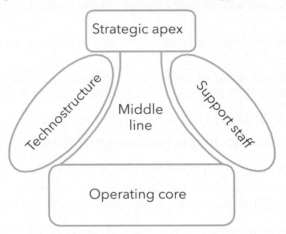

2.2 Configurations of organisations

Mintzberg suggests that each component of the organisation has its own **dynamic**. The precise shape (configuration) of the organisation will be determined by the degree of influence each exerts:

- The **strategic apex** is responsible to the organisation's owners and wishes to retain control over decision-making (centralisation).

- The **technostructure** consists of analysts whose reason for existence is the design of **procedures** and **standards** and wants an environment that is standardised and highly regulated.

- The members of the **operating core** work directly on the product or service. They prefer to work autonomously, achieving what other co-ordination is necessary by **mutual adjustment**.

- The managers of the **middle line** seek to increase their **autonomy** from the strategic apex, and to increase their control over the operating core.

- **Support staff** only gain influence when their expertise is vital.

2.3 Structure and environment

Mintzberg discusses five configurations, which stem from whichever building block is key. Each is characterised by different internal factors (size, type of work and complexity of tasks) and is appropriate in a different external environment (static/dynamic; simple/complex; single product/market or diverse).

These are outlined below.

Configuration	Key building block	Environment	Internal factors	Key co-ordinating mechanism
Simple structure (**entrepreneurial**)	Strategic apex	Simple Dynamic	Small Young Simple tasks	Direct supervision
Machine bureaucracy (**functional**)	Techno-structure	Simple Static	Large Old Regulated	Standardisation of work
Professional bureaucracy	Operating core	Complex Static	Professional Simple systems	Standardisation of skills
Divisionalised	Middle line	Simple Static Diverse	Very large Old Divisible tasks	Standardisation of outputs
Adhocracy/ Innovative (**matrix**)	Operating core	Complex Dynamic	Young Complex tasks	Mutual adjustment

Interactive question 1: Organisational configurations

Identify the organisation configurations suggested in the following cases.

1.1 Creation Ltd provides public relations services to clients. It is run by five partners, with a staff of copy editors, designers, party-throwers and people with contacts in the press. Clients contact one of the partners who assembles a team to solve a client's problem, though the partner does not direct the solution.

1.2 Smithers Ltd is a small family company. The Chief Executive and founder is a strong leader and tends to dominate decision making. He does not believe in discussing his decisions with staff.

See **Answer** at the end of this chapter.

We will now go on to consider the structures suggested by Mintzberg in more detail:

- Entrepreneurial
- Functional (or bureaucratic)
- Divisionalised
- Matrix

3 Types of business structure

Section overview

- Generally as a business grows, its structure progresses from entrepreneurial to functional to divisionalised.

- Matrix structures attempt to co-ordinate separate departments to serve joint goals such as particular customers or projects.

- A matrix structure can occur independently or within a functional or divisional structure.

3.1 Entrepreneurial structure (simple)

Typically a single owner-manager in a small business, who has specialist knowledge of the product or service and has total control over the running of the business.

This structure is flexible and quick to adapt to change, but dependent on the entrepreneur and limited in its ability to cope with expansion or diversification.

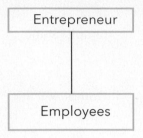

3.2 Functional structure (bureaucracy)

Functional structure leads to departments that are defined by their functions, that is, the work that they do. Specialism means the firm is more efficient and can benefit from economies of scale, but it can lead to conflict and the bureaucracy can hamper cross functional innovation and creativity. The rigid structure is unsuitable for changing environments.

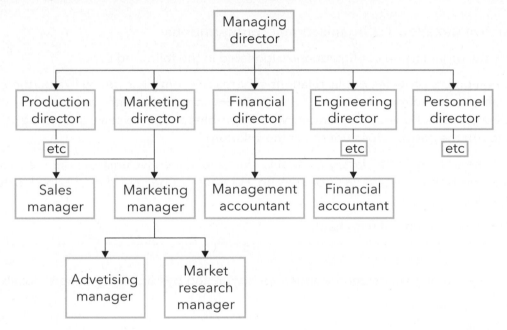

3.3 Divisional structure

The business can be divided into autonomous units based on geography, product or market. Divisionalised structures can be adapted for growth and diversification and are most suitable for larger diversified businesses.

3.3.1 Geographic structure

Some authority is retained at Head Office (organised, perhaps, on a functional basis) but day-to-day service operations are handled on a territorial basis. Within many sales departments, the sales staff are organised on this basis.

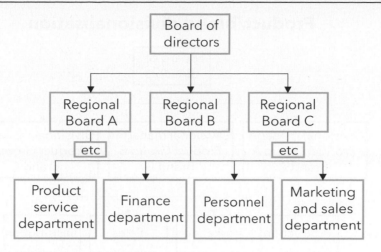

Advantages of geographic divisionalisation

*   Better and quicker local decision making at the point of contact between the organisation (eg, a sales executive) and its customers.

*   It may be less costly to establish area factories/offices than to run everything centrally (eg, costs of transportation and travelling may be reduced).

*   It might be essential for overseas operations to cope with different environments.

Disadvantages of geographic divisionalisation

*   Duplication of management effort (eg, a national organisation divided into 10 regions might have a customer liaison department in each regional office).

*   It struggles to cope with large clients who span the divisions.

3.3.2   Product/brand divisionalisation

Product divisionalisation: The elements of an organisation are grouped by products or product lines. Some functional divisionalisation remains (eg, manufacturing, distribution, marketing and sales) but a divisional manager is given responsibility for the product or product line, with authority over personnel of different functions.

Advantages

*   Individual managers can be held accountable for the **profitability** of individual products.

*   Specialisation can be developed. For example, some salesmen will be trained to sell a specific product in which they may develop technical expertise and thereby offer a better sales service to customers. Service engineers who specialise in a single product should also provide a better after sales service.

*   The different functional activities and efforts required to make and sell each product can be co-ordinated and integrated by the divisional/product manager.

*   It should be focused on how a business makes its profits.

The **disadvantage of product divisionalisation** is that it increases the overhead costs and managerial complexity of the organisation.

Brand: A brand is the name or design which identifies the products or services of a manufacturer or provider and distinguishes them from those of competitors. Brands may denote different products or, often, similar products made by the same firm.

C
H
A
P
T
E
R

9

Product/brand divisionalisation

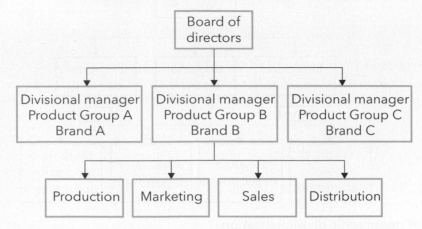

- Branding implies a unique marketing position. It becomes necessary to have brand divisionalisation. As with product divisionalisation, some functional divisionalisation remains (especially on the manufacturing side) but brand managers have responsibility for the brand's marketing and this can affect every function.

- Brand divisionalisation has similar advantages and disadvantages to product divisionalisation. In particular, overhead costs and complexity of the management structure are increased, the relationships of a number of different brand departments with the manufacturing department, if there is only one, being particularly difficult.

3.3.3 Customer or market segment divisionalisation

- Divisionalisation by customer is commonly associated with sales departments and selling effort, but it might also be used by a jobbing or contracting firm where a team of managers may be given the responsibility of liaising with major customers.

- Another example is where firms distinguish between domestic consumers and business customers, with different marketing and supply efforts for each.

3.4 Hybrid structures

Very few organisations divisionalise on one basis alone.

Many organisation hierarchies in practice combine elements of a number of these approaches. In the example below, research and development is centrally organised, but the operating activities of the firm are geographically arranged. This is an example of a **hybrid structure**.

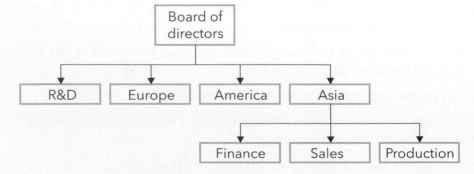

Interactive question 2: Erewhon Bank

The Erewhon Bank plc has branches in the UK, Eire, France, Germany and Denmark. It grew from the merger of a number of small local banks in these countries. These local banks were not large enough to compete single-handedly in their home markets. The Erewhon Bank hopes to attract both retail and corporate customers, through its use of home banking services and its heavily advertised Direct Bank service, which is a branchless bank. The Direct Bank service allows customers to conduct banking transactions using an online banking portal, and via a dedicated customer support telephone line. The bank also specialises in providing foreign currency accounts, and has set up a revolutionary service whereby participating customers can settle their own business transactions in euros.

Requirement

2.1 What sort of organisation structure do you think would be appropriate?

See **Answer** at the end of this chapter.

3.5 Matrix organisation

A matrix organisation structure provides for the formalisation of management control between different functions, whilst also maintaining functional divisionalisation. It can be a mixture of a functional, product and territorial organisation. The matrix structure is most suitable for complex/hi-tech industries.

The matrix organisation imposes the multi-disciplinary approach on a permanent basis.

	Production Dept	Sales Dept	Finance Dept	Distribution Dept	R&D Dept	Marketing Dept
UK director						
Netherlands director						
Sweden director						

The product managers may each have their own marketing team; in which case the marketing department itself would be small or non-existent.

In some cases the matrix structure involves the appointment of a special manager responsible for a project or customer. They are charged with ensuring that the necessary departments pull together to achieve what is needed.

Advantages of a matrix structure

- It offers greater **flexibility**. This applies both to **people,** as employees adapt more quickly to a new challenge or new task, and to **task and structure**, as the matrix may be short-term (as with project teams) or readily amended.

- It should improve **communication** within the organisation.

- Dual authority gives the organisation **multiple orientation** so that functional specialists do not get wrapped up in their own concerns.

- It provides a **structure for allocating responsibility to managers for end-results**. A product manager is responsible for product profitability, and a project leader is responsible for ensuring that the task is completed.

- It provides for **inter-disciplinary co-operation** and a mixing of skills and expertise.

- There are many geographic areas with distinct needs, but the firm wishes to exploit economies of scale.

Disadvantages of matrix structure

- Dual authority threatens a **conflict** between managers. To prevent this, the authority of superiors should not overlap and areas of authority must be clearly defined. A subordinate must know to which superior he is responsible for each aspect of his duties.

- One individual with two or more bosses is more likely to suffer **role stress** at work.

- It is sometimes more **costly** – eg, product managers are additional jobs which would not be required in a simple structure of functional divisionalisation.

- It may be **difficult for the management to accept** a matrix structure. A manager may feel threatened that another manager will usurp his authority.

- It requires consensus and agreement which may slow down decision-making.

Interactive question 3: Boxer plc

Boxer plc is a company which manufactures dried pasta, produces ready-to-eat meals and is about to start making specialist pasta sauces for distribution to independent delicatessen shops.

The dried pasta revenue and profits have been substantial and stable in the last few years, with sales of the Boxer brand to all large supermarket chains as well as to wholesalers.

The ready-to-eat meals are produced only for two major supermarket chains. Products are branded by the supermarkets under their own names.

Boxer has recently recruited Jake La Motta from Sauce Specialists Ltd. He has considerable knowledge of and contacts within the small delicatessen market. Boxer wishes to pursue a cautious approach to this new area, incurring only limited investment.

Requirement

3.1 Outline an appropriate structure for Boxer plc.

See **Answer** at the end of this chapter.

Worked example: Time for a new approach?

Findings from Deloitte's Human Capital Trends 2016 study highlighted that one of the biggest issues at the forefront of most business leaders' minds is how best to redesign organisational structures to meet the demands of the workforce and the business climate. Josh Bersin a contributor on the *Forbes* website commented that the conclusion from Deloitte's study is that 'today's digital world of work has shaken the foundation of organisational structure, shifting from the traditional functional hierarchy to one Deloitte calls a "network of teams"'.

Deloitte's research, which identifies the top 10 human capital trends, indicates that the most significant issues facing organisations are linked to new ways of working. Bersin notes that '92% of the companies Deloitte surveyed cited "redesigning the way of working" as one of their key challenges'.

According to the research, only 24% of larger organisations, those with 5,000 employees or more, claimed to operate a functional structure. As Bersin notes, finding a more flexible structure is not a challenge only facing those established organisations. He cites the innovative transportation company, Uber, which 'sets up city managers who run their local operations with local marketing, government relations, staffing and operations leaders.' However the problem such entities face is how best to 'co-ordinate and align these teams, how to get them to share information and work together'.

Bersin argues that this requires a new approach. Organisations increasingly need to rethink their leadership strategies, focus more on developing a strong culture supported through organisational learning and information centres, and to provide staff with digital HR tools to facilitate the sharing of information. Such characteristics are more akin to the concept of matrix management.

As Bersin notes, 'Many of us remember the old fashioned "matrix organisations" which were popular in the 1980's. Well today the "matrix" makes a company look more like a series of Hollywood movies, people come together and bring their skills and abilities to projects and programmes, they build and deliver the solution, and then many of them move on to the next "movie" later.'

Source:

Bersin, J . (2016) *New Research Shows Why Focus On Teams, Not Just Leaders, Is Key To Business Performance.* [Online]. Available from: www.forbes.com [Accessed 7 June 2016].

4 Span of control

Section overview

- Span of control refers to how many people report to one manager. This will influence the shape of an organisation.

- Wide spans of control create flat management hierarchies whereas narrow spans of control create tall organisational structures.

4.1 Introduction

- The span of control refers to the number of people reporting to one person.

- This influences the shape of the organisation:

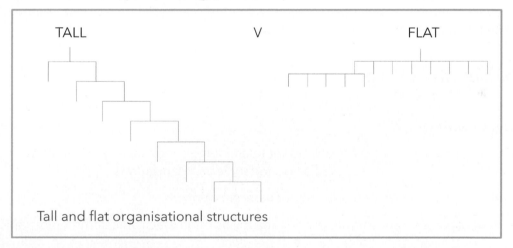

TALL   V   FLAT

Tall and flat organisational structures

- A determinant of whether the organisation is tall or flat is the use of delegation – 'the transfer of legitimate authority without passing on ultimate responsibility'.

Factors influencing span of control

- **Location of subordinates**: the more widely spread, the fewer that can be managed effectively.

- **Complexity/nature of the work**: as complexity increases (and the need for greater teamwork), so the span decreases.

- **Management personality and ability**: the better they are, the more people they can manage.

- **Subordinate ability**: the better they are, the more that can be delegated and therefore managed by the manager.

- **Level of organisational support**: personnel departments can remove the routine personnel tasks from a manager, enabling him to manage more people.

- **Level of 'danger' involved if delegation takes place**: the more dangerous, the less people that can be managed.

Effects of setting span of control incorrectly

Too wide (flat)

- Loss of contact between superior and subordinates – demoralised subordinates.
- Loss of control over subordinates.
- Subgroups form with unofficial leaders.

Too narrow (tall)

- Too many management levels and too much cost.
- Delays in decision-making (because of the length of the chain of command).
- Over-supervision and demoralised staff.

Span and IT

IT can have significant effects on organisational structure in terms of:

- New patterns of work
- Form and structure of groups
- Supervisory/management roles
- Changes in lines of authority
- Job design/descriptions
- Centralisation/decentralisation of decision making and control

New technology (eg, the internet) has often resulted in flatter structures (ie, wider spans) with fewer levels of management. Office-based technology can facilitate a greater range of functions and self-checking for staff.

5 Flexible structures

Section overview

- Flexible structures allow firms to adapt to changing circumstances. A number of flexible structures can also be classified as boundary-less organisations.

- Networks can exist within and between organisations.

- Virtual organisations operate predominantly through electronic communications.

- Hollow organisations are those in which all non-essential activities are outsourced.

- Modular organisations outsource the production of a particular component(s) to specialist outsourcers.

- Handy's shamrock structure or flexible firm captures the idea that modern organisations strive to be lean at the core but maintain access to other skills and activities through a variety of networks.

5.1 Boundary-less organisations

Boundary-less organisations are entities which are structured in such a way as to make it easier to collaborate with external parties. Such organisations remove the internal barriers that often exist between different functions and departments. Activities and processes regarded as bureaucratic and restrictive are removed to enable the organisation to concentrate on achieving its core objectives. Boundary-less organisations are focused on the creation of relationships with external groups including, customers, suppliers and even competitors. It is believed that being closer to such groups should enable the organisation to become more adaptable to change. Such structures effectively allow organisations to extend their value chains both forwards and backwards. Central to the creation of boundary-less organisations has been the increased use of outsourcing, and the establishment of virtual communication networks facilitated by internet technologies.

Organisational forms including network, virtual, hollow and modular organisations can be all regarded as being boundary-less organisations.

5.2 Network organisations

Network organisations were introduced in Chapter 6. The idea of a **network structure** is applied both within and between organisations.

Within the organisation, the term is used to mean something that resembles both the **organic** organisation discussed earlier in this chapter and the structure of informal relationships that exists in most organisations alongside the formal structure. Such a lose, fluid approach is often used to achieve innovative response to changing circumstances.

The network approach is also visible in the growing field of **outsourcing** as a strategic method. Complex relationships can be developed between firms, who may both buy from and sell to each other, as well as the simpler, more traditional practice of buying in services such as cleaning. These were discussed extensively in Chapter 6.

Writers such as Ghoshal and Bartlett point to the likelihood of such networks becoming the corporations of the future, replacing formal organisation structures with innovations such as **virtual teams**. Virtual teams are interconnected groups of people who may not be in the same office (or even the same organisation) but who:

- Share information and tasks
- Make joint decisions
- Fulfil the collaborative function of a team

Organisations are now able to structure their activities very differently:

- **Staffing**: certain areas of organisational activity can be undertaken by freelance or contract workers. Charles Handy's shamrock organisation (see below) is gaining ground as a workable model for a leaner and more flexible workforce, within a controlled framework. (The question is: how can this control be achieved?)

- **Leasing of facilities** such as machinery, IT and accommodation (not just capital assets) is becoming more common.

- **Production** itself might be outsourced, even to offshore countries where labour is cheaper. (This, and the preceding point, of course beg the question: which assets and activities do companies retain, and which ones do they 'buy-in'?)

- **Interdependence** of organisations is emphasised by the sharing of functions and services. Databases and communication create genuine interactive sharing of, and access to, common data.

Network structures are also discerned between competitors, where **co-operation on non-core competence matters** can lead to several benefits:

- Cost reduction
- Increased market penetration
- Experience curve effects

Typical areas for co-operation between **competitors** include R&D and distribution chains. The spread of the **Toyota** system of manufacturing, with its emphasis on JIT, quality and the elimination of waste has led to a high degree of integration between the operations of industrial **customers** and their **suppliers**.

5.3 Virtual organisation

In Chapter 6 we introduced the term virtual firm and above we considered the concept of the virtual team. Some of the main features of virtual organisations are considered in this section. The virtual organisation is closely linked to the concept of workforce flexibility which we discussed in Chapter 6.

The use of electronic communications, which have been facilitated by advancements in IT systems, is central to virtual organisations. The ability for employees within an organisation to communicate with one another through the use of email, extranets, intranets and e-conferencing has removed the need to physically bring individuals together in a single work location. This is one aspect of the virtual organisation concept, and has given rise to increased workforce flexibility. This is evident given the growing number of people now working from home. The need for such workers to visit a physical office has been removed by the widespread use of internet technologies.

Worked example: Home working

A 2016 article on the BBC website by Jessica Bown highlighted that the growth in the use of instant messaging and video conferencing technologies had given workers greater freedom to work from most places in the world. According to the article, more than four million Britons now work from home. Bown highlights comments made by Donna Sewell, the founder of a legal firm, who has been able to halve the amount of office space used by her team. Sewell highlighted that the move to home working meant that her firm was able to 'provide a better service using cloud-collaborative working tools such as Google's corporate suite and Google doc.' The use of free services such as WhatsApp have helped workers around the world keep connected, while the use of Dropbox software now means that workers can store and access their documents anywhere.

Source:

Bown, J. (2016) *The digital nomads making the world their office*. [Online]. Available from: www.bbc.co.uk [Accessed 27 April 2017].

It is important however, to recognise that the concept of the virtual organisation is not solely about home working. As discussed earlier in respect of virtual teams, the virtual concept is now being used to link customers and suppliers to the operations of the organisation. In the case of the customer relationship, the need to interact and sell goods or services to the customer via physical premises is removed. The need for customer-facing employees is also eliminated. Online retailer Amazon is a good example of a virtual organisation which operates without a physical store presence, as the majority of items sold are provided by partner organisations which use the Amazon website as a platform to reach customers.

5.4 Hollow organisations

Hollow organisations share some of the same features as network organisations, and in essence the use of outsourcing effectively enables an organisation to be hollowed out. In hollow organisations all of those activities and processes classed as being non-essential are outsourced to specialist providers. Commonly outsourced processes include HR and payroll. It is believed that by removing such activities the organisation is then free to focus on those activities deemed to be most value adding. For example, a company involved in the manufacture of innovative, cutting edge tablet computers may outsource the physical production of the devices to a third party, but would retain activities including R&D and marketing as these are deemed critical to the organisation's future success. The strong focus on outsourcing enables the organisation to reduce its costs by only retaining those workers considered to be essential.

5.5 Modular organisations

In much the same way as a hollow organisation, modular organisations also involve outsourcing. The concept of the modular organisation involves separating the organisation's production processes into individual modules. The activities undertaken by these modules are then outsourced to a number of different specialist parties which become responsible for producing one aspect or component used in the overall production process. For example, several outsourcers might each produce one of the technical components on behalf of a company which makes high speed trains. The core group of workers that remain with the company are then responsible for putting together all of the various component parts produced externally by the different outsourcers to manufacture a complete train. The benefits of this approach are that outsourcing allows the organisation to reduce its costs and gain access to specialist skills that would take a significant amount of time to develop in-house.

Historically car manufacturers would own subsidiary companies which produced components for use in manufacturing the final product, ie, a car. The growing use of the modular organisation model has helped to reduce the need for organisations to have burdensome ownership and reporting structures by removing the need for such subsidiary companies. Instead the modular model increases competition among the individual module outsourcers as they have to compete with other entities operating in the same market and providing the same services. This in turn helps to lower the component purchase price to the purchasing organisation.

5.6 The shamrock organisation

Largely driven by pressure to reduce personnel costs and to adapt to new market imperatives, there has been an increase in the use of part-time and temporary contracts of employment. These allow rapid down-sizing in times of recession or slow growth and can save on the costs of benefits such as pensions, holiday pay and health insurance. The growth in the proportion of the workforce employed on such less-favourable contracts has attracted political attention but continues. It has produced the phenomenon of the **flexible firm** or, as Handy calls it, the **shamrock organisation**.

Handy defines the **shamrock organisation** as a 'core of essential executives and workers supported by outside contractors and part-time help'. This structure permits the buying-in of services as needed, with consequent reductions in overhead costs. It is also known as the **flexible firm**.

The **professional core** are permanently employed staff who provide the core competencies and distinctive knowledge base of the organisation.

The **flexible labour force** are temporary and part-time workers who can be deployed, when required by peaks in demand (eg, seasonal tasks or projects).

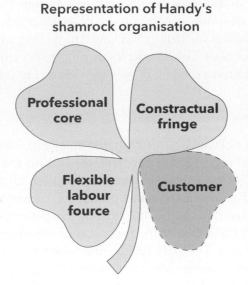

Representation of Handy's shamrock organisation

Professional core

Constractual fringe

Flexible labour fource

Customer

The **contractual fringe** are external providers (consultants, sub-contractors and freelancers) who can undertake non-core activities and/or provide specialist services more economically than the organisation could arrange internally. Many organisations now **outsource** activities such as IT, logistics, maintenance, call-centre management and so on.

Customers are a fourth cluster, to whom the organisation may be able to 'sub-contract' some tasks. Information and communication technology (such as the internet) has allowed sales, service and supply to be conducted on a 'self-service' basis: booking tickets, downloading music/books, getting online help and so on. (Even low-tech equivalents, such as home-assembly furniture, enable the organisation to devolve activities to customers and save costs.)

Organisations are increasingly seeking to be lean at the core – where activities are important to their competitive strategy – while maintaining access to a full range of flexibly deployed services at the periphery.

6 Issues for divisionalised organisations

Section overview

- An organisation is centralised when decision making authority is concentrated in its strategic apex.

- Centralisation offers greater control and coordination whereas decentralisation offers greater flexibility.

- Using financial controls necessitates the development of responsibility centres and the use of investment based control measures such as ROCE and residual income (RI).

- Divisional inter-trading requires the setting of appropriate transfer prices. The concept of transfer pricing is an area that candidates attempting the Business Strategy and Technology exam have struggled with. It is therefore particularly important that you take your time as you read through the next section.

6.1 Centralisation v decentralisation

Centralisation/decentralisation refers to how much authority/decision-making ability is diffused throughout the organisation.

- **Centralised structures**: upper levels retain authority to make decisions.

- **Decentralised structures**: ability to make decisions (ie, commit people, money and resources) is passed down to lower levels of the hierarchy.

Factors affecting amount of decentralisation:

- **Management style**: authoritarian = centralised.

- **Size of organisation**: as size increases, decentralisation tends to increase.
- **Extent of activity diversification**: the more diversified, the more decentralised.
- **Effectiveness of communication**: decentralisation will not work if information is not communicated downwards.
- **Ability of management**: the more able, the more decentralisation.
- **Speed of technological advancement**: lower managers likely to be more familiar with changing technology, therefore decentralise.
- **Geography of locations**: if spread, decentralise.
- **Extent of local knowledge needed**: if required, decentralise.

6.1.1 Advantages/disadvantages of decentralisation

Advantages

- Senior management is free to concentrate on strategy: day to day decisions are delegated to lower levels of management.
- Motivation for lower managers from increased delegation/responsibility.
- Local expertise of managers improves decisions based on local knowledge.
- Quicker and more effective responses to local conditions.
- Career paths for managers/employees.

Disadvantages

- More difficult to co-ordinate organisation as lots of people are making the decisions rather then just a few.
- Incongruent decisions, ie, different levels of management may pursue different objectives.
- Loss of control by senior management.
- Complicated structures.
- Problems with transfer prices.
- Evaluating divisional performance becomes difficult.
- Duplication of some roles (eg, administration).

6.2 Rules for successful divisionalisation

A divisionalised structure:

- Focuses the attention of subordinate management on business performance and results.
- Enables greater flexibility in business units to enable them to respond to local competitive challenges.
- Enables financial evaluation and comparison of performance of divisions, eg, by measures such as return on capital employed.

Three key considerations in successful divisionalisation are:

- **Autonomy**: divisional management should be able to run their businesses otherwise there is little to be gained from having separate divisions.
- **Controllability**: the factors against which divisional managers are evaluated should be within their control.
- **Corporate optimality**: divisions should follow courses of action that bring the best result for the corporation as a whole.

In practice there can be a tension between these three considerations, for example:

- Corporate centre wishes to implement **group-wide initiatives** on quality, risk management, human resource development or corporate branding which is irrelevant to, or conflicts with, the immediate business needs of a division.

- Inter-trading between divisions is important but there are disputes on the appropriate **transfer price** because each division want to maximise its own profits.

- Allocation of **head office costs** between divisions for central services such as IT, HRM, marketing, corporate treasury mean that many of the divisional costs are uncontrollable.

- **Local competitive conditions** seem to require different products and prices from those laid down by head office, eg, in a national marketing campaign.

Worked example: Leisure clubs

The following shows some of the problems that can occur where divisionalisation is operating inappropriately.

A major operator of health and leisure clubs has over 40 centres in a country. The centre manager has profit centre responsibility and is also evaluated on ROCE each year for the purposes of granting a bonus pool to the centre which is shared between the manager and staff. The clubs are ranked into grades according to their size and the range of activities offered. All exercise equipment and facilities are determined by the grade of club and the replacement of equipment is on a strict 5 year basis. Members join a particular centre and pay fees to it. The fees they pay are based on the grade of club they join. However membership of one club entitles them to use other clubs in the chain.

A number of problems have arisen:

- Managers of lower grade clubs situated near higher grade clubs have canvassed members by emphasising that their fees are lower but that members can still use the higher grade club if they choose.

- Some clubs face competition from smaller independent fitness clubs which are able to undercut the national pricing structure.

- Managers of older clubs are complaining that they are being forced to replace equipment that is still perfectly serviceable, and preferred by customers over newer versions which have slick but pointless features, and so are losing out on bonuses because the book value of assets leaps.

- Managers of established clubs are complaining that they get little benefit from the central re-charge for marketing because most marketing activity is being used to launch new clubs.

- Managers of new clubs complain that they are not getting bonuses because they have new equipment and membership numbers are still growing and this is causing staff to leave or become despondent.

6.3 Performance management of divisions

Responsibility centres

Control requires that managers are appointed with clear **domains of responsibility** such as range of activities, geographical scope and resources. As covered above, these are the basis of divisionalisation.

From a financial control perspective responsibility centres are:

- **Revenue centres**: responsible for revenues only such as a sales department
- **Costs centres**: responsible for keeping expenditure within limits such as a hospital ward or IT function
- **Profit centre**: responsibility for revenues and costs (and therefore profit) but not balance sheet
- **Investment centre**: a business within a business responsible for balance sheet and profit

Multi-divisional firms generally assign Investment Centre responsibility to divisions.

The nature of responsibility will influence the way in which performance is managed, since division managers must only be held to account for factors within their control. Divisional performance management is covered in Chapter 12.

6.4 Transfer pricing between divisions

Definition

Transfer price: The price at which one division in a group sells its products or services to another division in the same group.

Divisions buying and selling with each-other leads to transfer prices. Several situations may give rise to this:

- Transfer of finished goods between divisions, eg, a car manufacturer selling cars to its sales division.
- Transfer of components between divisions, eg, engine manufacturing plant selling engines to the car assembly plant.
- Transfer of staff or customers between divisions, eg, a professional practice seconding staff from one office to work on a project run by another office.
- Provision of central services, eg, the group IT function selling hardware, training and user support services to divisions.

Consider the following example:

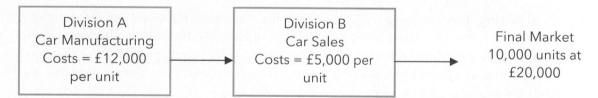

Transfer prices have several implications:

- **They determine the profits of divisions**: if the upstream (supplying) Division A charges Division B a higher price of £15,000 for its cars, then all of the final profit from the product (£30 million) will be enjoyed by it and none by the downstream Division B.
- **They affect performance evaluation**: if Division A takes all the profit its manager will look better.
- **They determine the tax to be paid**: if Division A is in a different country does take all the profit for itself then it will be taxed according to the tax rates in its country.
- **They determine the currency in which profits are made**: suppose Division B is in a country where dividends are subject to punitive withholding taxes. By charging a high price Division A is taking the money out of Division B's country as a payment for the cars and not as a dividend and so avoiding the withholding tax on dividends.

- **They may determine the price and final sales of the product**: suppose Division B decides to set its market price as a 15% mark-up on costs. If the cars are transferred by Division A at cost, the final price would be £19,550 ie, (£12,000 + £5,000) × 1.15. If the transfer price were £15,000 then the final price would be £23,000. This would clearly have a significant effect on volumes sold and therefore profits. Another situation is where the receiving division must pay an **import tariff** on its receipts of the components. Here charging a low transfer price will reduce the amount of the tariff and so avoid the final good being priced out of the market.

- **They can lead to dysfunctional decisions**: if either division believes it can get a better deal from the market it may take it. For example, if division B could obtain supplies of cars elsewhere, say from other dealers supplied by A, it might leave A with unsold stock. Conversely A might supply to alternative channels and leave B with empty showrooms and unabsorbed overheads.

Cost based methods of setting transfer prices

This leads to the inevitable problem of deciding which cost to use:

- **Full cost**: the variable costs plus an amount to cover overheads. This leaves the supplying division in a break-even situation.

- **Variable cost** (or marginal cost): this leaves the supplying division making nil contribution and so enduring losses equal to its fixed costs.

- **Opportunity cost**: the revenue foregone by not selling the item to highest bidder.

Optimal transfer pricing requires that divisions sell components at the higher of variable cost and opportunity cost.

Other methods of setting transfer prices

Managers of divisions will want to record a profit. For this reason the following transfer price setting methods have been identified:

- **Negotiated prices**: the transfer price is established by discussions between the divisional managers in a bargaining process.

- **Two-part transfer prices**: the transfer price is set at variable cost to ensure corporate optimality but in addition to this price the supplying division records an extra amount in its sales ledger to arrive at a profit figure for evaluation purposes.

- **Dual pricing**: the receiving division records the transfer at standard variable cost which may aid decision making. The transferring division reports the transfer at a higher value (eg, cost plus) to give a profit incentive. This should lead to goal congruence but may lead to poor cost control as profits are made more easily. The accounting problem makes this method unpopular.

Considerations in transfer pricing

- Impact on group profitability.

- Impact on product positioning: where the internal transfer price is also the price on external markets it will influence the positioning of the product.

- Costs of the system: month ends determining and recording inter-company charges ('chasing wooden dollars') is a non-value adding activity.

- Motivational impacts of the system: transfer prices affect evaluation of managers, bonuses for divisions and the purchasing decisions of the divisions.

Interactive question 4: Marble Makers Ltd

Marble Makers Ltd manufactures and sells high-end marble for use in domestic kitchens. The company's customers often pay a premium to purchase marble as part of bespoke kitchen designs.

The company has two divisions, the manufacturing division and the retail division. The manufacturing division is based in a factory in Kent, and it imports marble from overseas and finishes it to the customers' individual requirements. The retail division consists of four small shops located in wealthy areas across the UK. The Managing Director was keen to locate the shops as close as possible to those areas lived in by members of the target market. He believes that the shops act as a great showcase for Marble Makers' final product. The retail division is the manufacturing division's only customer.

The Head of Finance has provided the following projections for the two divisions for the next 12 months. These projections show external income and costs before any transfer price recharges:

	Manufacturing £m	Retail £m
Estimated retail sales	–	30
Variable costs	12	5
Fixed costs	7	3

Requirements

4.1 Calculate the expected profit or loss to be made by each division over the next 12 months. You should assume that transfer prices are based on the current arrangement of retail price less 40%.

4.2 Determine the transfer pricing formula (retail price less an appropriate %) which would enable the manufacturing division to break-even in the next 12 months. You should assume that costs are in line with the projections provided.

See **Answer** at the end of this chapter.

Interactive question 5: External offer

Unit costs	Division A £	Division B £
Variable	10.00	15.00
Transfer price	–	20.00
Fixed costs	5.00	10.00
Profit	5.00	25.00
Selling price	20.00	70.00

Division A can sell outside at £20 per unit or transfer internally to Division B at £20 per unit.

B receives an offer from a customer of £30 per unit for its final product.

Requirements

5.1 Will B accept the offer of £30 per unit given the existing transfer price?

5.2 Is this the right decision from the company's point of view if

-   A has surplus capacity?
-   A is at full capacity?

See **Answer** at the end of this chapter.

Interactive question 6: Full cost transfer price

A multi-product company has two divisions.

Unit costs for a particular product

	Manufacturing division £	Selling division £
Variable	20.00	15.00
Fixed (apportionment of costs incurred for all products)	11.00	–
	31.00	15.00

Transfers are at full cost.

Ultimate selling price = £40.00

Requirements

Are the transfers recommended from the point of view

6.1 Of the company?
6.2 Of the selling division?

See **Answer** at the end of this chapter.

Interactive question 7: Full or variable cost?

A corporate power plant serving divisions A and B:

Power plant

Budgeted fixed cost per month	£10,000
Standard variable cost	£1/kwh
Actual total cost in January	£18,000

Usage of power plant in January

	A	B
Budgeted usage (kwh)	4,000	6,000
Actual usage (kwh)	4,000	2,000

Requirements

How much are A and B charged if

7.1 The charge is based on full actual cost?
7.2 The charge is based on standard variable cost plus a share of budgeted fixed costs?

See **Answer** at the end of this chapter.

7 Organisational structures for international business

Section overview

- International business needs structures based on divisionalised structures but varied to reflect the national cultures of the countries where they are to be based.

- The steps in becoming an international (or transnational) organisation are outlined.

- The appropriate structure for an international business will depend on the stage of its international development and the trade of between local responsiveness and global coordination.

7.1 The development of overseas operations

With overseas operations, business structures are likely to be made complex by distance (geographical and cultural).

Organisational structures for international expansion often start by having a separate division for international activities. As growth occurs the business is often reorganised into divisions by geographical area or alternatively organised by worldwide product groupings. Eventually this may lead to a matrix structure.

The critical issue in devising an appropriate structure for an international business is the extent to which the need for local independence and responsiveness takes precedence over global coordination.

Thus international businesses can follow a **multi-domestic strategy** where activities are located in individual national markets and products/services tailored to local needs, or a **global strategy** where standardised products are developed and produced centrally.

7.2 Multi-national business structures

Bartlett and Ghoshal identify four possible structures for a multi-national business:

International division – a stand-alone division added on to the domestic structure, which draws on the products and technology of the home business. Often observed when a business first starts to internationalise.

Local subsidiary – geographically based and operate independently. Local management has a high degree of autonomy. Appropriate for a business following a **multi-domestic strategy**.

Global product division – typical for a company following a **global strategy,** which will have separate world-wide divisions for soft drinks, alcoholic beverages etc.

The transnational approach, which attempts to achieve high local responsiveness and high global coordination, has been used by some international companies to build in strategic and organisational flexibility. The transnational corporation (TNC) is like a matrix. It involves having dispersed and interdependent subsidiaries, integrated into a worldwide operation, with different parts of the organisation specialising in different areas.

The TNC:

- Co-ordinates **various stages** of the **production chain** between different countries

- Can take advantage of differences in geographical distribution in factors of production (eg, raw materials, skilled labour, access to capital) and government policies (eg, taxes, subsidies)

- Has geographical flexibility; it can switch resources and operations at an international and global scale

8 Governance

Section overview

- At its broadest, corporate governance would cover all aspect controlling the organisation including its structure and systems. Here it is restricted to a discussion of the role of the Corporate Board.

- Governance should take the overview of the direction of the business and consider the proper policies to deal with risk and the transparency of the appointment of directors etc.

- The governance of not-for-profit organisations requires greater transparency than the governance of businesses.

8.1 Introduction

Over the last two decades, in the wake of a series of major corporate scandals such as Enron and Worldcom, there has been a growing concern to make board stewardship of public companies more effective.

It is important when deciding on an appropriate structure that practical matters of corporate governance are not forgotten. Areas to consider include:

- The split between executive and non-executive directors.
- The possible establishment of an audit committee.
- The possible creation of an internal audit function.
- Building responsibility for risk management into job descriptions.
- Creating a framework for communication with external and internal stakeholders.

8.2 Strategy and governance

Definition

Corporate governance: The set of rules which governs the structure and determines the objectives of an organisation and regulates the relationship between the organisation's management, its board of directors and its shareholders.

- Corporate governance is about what the board of an organisation does and how it sets the values of the organisation, and is to be distinguished from the day-to-day management of operations by full-time business executives. The powers of executive managers to direct business operations are one aspect of governance, but management skills are not.

- Similarly, corporate governance is not concerned with formulating business strategy, although the responsibility of the board of directors and executive managers is for strategic decisions taken.

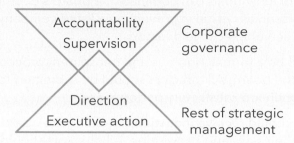

Corporate governance and strategic management

The diagram shows the distinction between governance and the rest of strategic management, with governance mainly concerned with accountability and supervision.

The **two-tier board form of governance** practised in Germany recognises this split. The upper, supervisory board is responsible for monitoring and overseeing the work of the executive board which runs the business, and has the power to hire and fire its members. The management body is responsible for direction and executive action. Thus the supervisory board is responsible for governance.

8.3 Structure of governance

The **UK Corporate Governance Code** (Financial Reporting Council, 2016) is a code of practice embodying a **shareholder-led approach to corporate governance.** The Code is a guide to a number of key components of effective board practice, based on the underlying principles of all good governance: accountability, transparency, probity (integrity) and focus on the sustainable success of an entity over the longer term.

The Code applies to all companies with a Premium Listing of equity shares on the London Stock Exchange, regardless of whether they are incorporated in the UK or elsewhere. Listing of shares is run by the UK Listing Authority (UKLA), which is part of the Financial Conduct Authority (FCA). The UKLA's Listing Rules require **all companies listed in the FTSE 350** to apply the Code's main Principles and to include in their annual reports **a statement of compliance** with the supporting principles and provisions of the Code or **an explanation of non-compliance** (which may be justified in certain circumstances provided good corporate governance is still achieved). **Other companies** can apply the Code more flexibly but are encouraged to follow it as an example of '**best practice**' and may experience pressure from their stakeholders if they do not adopt it.

The **key principles** set out in the five main sections of the Financial Reporting Council's (2016) Code are as follows:

1. **Leadership** – Every company should be headed by an **effective board** which is collectively responsible for the long-term success of the company. The board's role is to provide **entrepreneurial leadership** of the company **within a framework of prudent and effective controls** which enables risk to be assessed and managed.

   There should be a clear **division of responsibilities** at the head of the company between the **running of the board** and the executive responsibility for the **running of the company's business**. The roles of the Chairman and Chief Executive should **not be exercised by the same individual**. The Chairman is responsible for leadership of the board and ensuring its effectiveness in all aspects of its role.

   As part of their role as members of a unitary board, non-executive directors should **constructively challenge** and **help develop proposals on strategy**.

2. **Effectiveness** – The board and its committees should have the appropriate balance of skills, experience, independence and knowledge of the company to enable them to discharge their respective duties and responsibilities effectively.

The board should include an appropriate **combination** of **executive** and **non-executive directors** (and in particular **independent non-executive directors**) such that no individual or small group of individuals can dominate the board's decision taking. (The role of the non-executives is seen as critical in preventing a listed company from being run for the personal benefit of its senior executive directors.)

There should be a formal, rigorous and transparent procedure for the **appointment of new directors** to the board. All directors should be submitted for **re-election** at **regular intervals**, subject to continued satisfactory performance.

All directors should receive **induction** on joining the board and should regularly **update and refresh** their skills and knowledge. All directors should be able to allocate **sufficient time** to the company to discharge their responsibilities effectively.

The board should be supplied in a timely manner with **information** in a form and of a quality appropriate to enable it to discharge its duties.

The board should undertake a formal and rigorous annual **evaluation of its own performance** and that of its **committees** and individual **directors**, including an evaluation of the **balance** of skills, experience, independence and knowledge of the company on the board, its **diversity**, including gender, how the board works together as a unit, and other factors relevant to its effectiveness.

3. **Accountability** – The board should present a **fair, balanced** and understandable **assessment of the company's position and prospects.**

   The board is responsible for determining the nature and extent of the principal risks it is willing to take in achieving its strategic objectives. The board should maintain **sound risk management and internal control systems**.

   The directors should confirm in the annual report that they have carried out a robust assessment of the principal risks facing the company, including those that would threaten its business model, future performance, solvency or liquidity. The directors should describe those risks and explain how they are being managed or mitigated.

   The board should monitor the company's risk management and internal control systems and, at least annually, carry out a review of their effectiveness, and report on that review in the annual report. The monitoring and review should cover all material controls, including financial, operational and compliance controls. The board should establish formal and transparent arrangements for considering how they should **apply the corporate reporting and risk management and internal control principles** and for maintaining an appropriate relationship with the company's **auditors**. The board should establish an **audit committee** of at least **three** or, in the case of smaller companies, **two independent non-executive directors**.

   In annual and half-yearly financial statements, the directors should state whether they considered it appropriate to adopt the going concern basis of accounting in preparing them, and identify any material uncertainties to the company's ability to continue to do so over a period of at least 12 months from the date of approval of the financial statements.

4. **Remuneration** – Executive directors' remuneration should be designed to promote the long-term success of the company. Performance-related elements should be transparent, stretching and rigorously applied. There should be a formal and transparent procedure for developing policy on executive remuneration and for fixing the remuneration packages of individual directors. No director should be involved in deciding his or her own remuneration.

   A remuneration committee of independent non-executive directors should have delegated responsibility for setting remuneration for all executive directors and the Chairman, including pension rights and any compensation payments. This committee should determine an appropriate balance between fixed and performance-related, immediate and deferred remuneration. Performance conditions, including non-financial metrics where appropriate, should be relevant, stretching and designed to promote the long-term success of the company.

Remuneration incentives should be compatible with risk policies and systems. Upper limits should be set and disclosed. Performance-related schemes should include provisions that would enable the company to recover sums paid or withhold the payment of any sum, and specify the circumstances in which it would be appropriate to do so.

The remuneration committee should judge where to position their company relative to other companies. But they should use such comparisons with caution, in view of the risk of an upward ratchet of remuneration levels with no corresponding improvement in corporate and individual performance, and should avoid paying more than is necessary. They should also be sensitive to pay and employment conditions elsewhere in the business, especially when determining annual salary increases.

Levels of remuneration for non-executive directors should reflect the time commitment and responsibilities of the role. Remuneration for non-executive directors should not include share options or other performance-related elements. If, exceptionally, options are granted, shareholder approval should be sought in advance and any shares acquired by exercise of the options should be held until at least one year after the non-executive director leaves the board. Holding of share options could be relevant to the determination of a non-executive director's independence.

5. **Relations with shareholders** – There should be a **dialogue with shareholders** based on the **mutual understanding of objectives**. The board as a whole has responsibility for ensuring that a satisfactory dialogue with shareholders takes place.

    Nothing should override the general requirements of law to treat shareholders equally with regard to access to information. The board should use general meetings to communicate with investors and to encourage their participation.

8.4   Reward structures

The remuneration committee exists in public companies for the purpose of demonstrating to shareholders and any other interested parties that there is an objective process for determining the financial rewards of directors and any senior staff who are remunerated on a performance related system. The committee is composed of non-executive directors; members of the firm of external auditors have also sat on the remuneration committee.

The committee has delegated responsibility for setting remuneration (including pension rights and compensation payments) for all executive directors and the Chairman. The committee should also recommend and monitor the level and structure of remuneration for senior management. The board of directors implements the necessary recommendations.

Issues considered by the committee would be the following:

- Remuneration levels for non-executives
- Length of service contracts for executive directors
- Performance related systems of reward
- Pension contributions
- Compensation for loss of office
- Share option schemes

It is important to remember that the corporate governance issues on rewards extend to the entire reward package of individual directors, as well as to the reward policy generally. The package may consist of:

- Annual compensation (basic salary, pension contributions by the company for the individual, payments by the company into a personal pension scheme arrangement for the individual, a bonus (often a cash bonus) tied perhaps to the annual financial performance of the company and various perks, such as membership of the company's health insurance scheme, private use of company aircraft or boats, and so on).

- Long-term compensation, consisting of share option schemes or company shares or the award of additional options depending on long-term performance indicators.

- A severance payment arrangement, whereby the company is committed to giving the individual a minimum severance payment if he or she is forced to leave the company.

It is often useful to think of a reward package as a combination of fixed and variable elements:

- The fixed elements are the remuneration received by the director regardless of performance, such as fixed salary and salary-related pension.

- The variable elements are the performance-related elements (cash bonuses, awards of share options or shares depending on performance, etc).

8.5 Role of the board and non-executives

Boards of directors in the UK have five principal roles:

- **Accountability** – the liability to render account to someone else. A director is accountable to the shareholders, at common law or by statute, and the company's annual report and accounts, for example, should be presented to the shareholders for approval.

- **Supervision** – monitoring and overseeing management performance.

- **Direction** – formulating the strategic direction in the long term.

- **Executive action** – involvement in implementing and controlling strategy.

- **Risk assessment and management** – determining the nature and extent of the risks the company is willing to take to achieve its objectives and ensuring good practices in risk management.

The 'tone at the top' sets the pattern for the way in which a company conducts itself, and board members should give ethical leadership. A board of directors should have the necessary skills, experience and integrity, both individually and collectively, to govern the company effectively. A lack of collective experience among the board members will affect the quality of decision-making by the board.

The board of directors should exercise full control and monitor executive management.

- There should be a clearly accepted division of responsibility to ensure a balance of power. Where the Chairman is also the Chief Executive there must be a strong and independent element of the board.

- The board should recruit non-executive directors of sufficient calibre and number.

- The board should have a formal schedule of matters for decision to ensure that direction is firmly in its hands.

- All directors should take independent professional advice where necessary at the company's expense.

Non-executive directors (NEDs) should bring an independent viewpoint to the issues of strategy, performance, resources and standards of conduct. They should be independent of management and free of any responsibility that could materially interfere with the exercise of independent judgement apart from their fees and shareholding. Fees should be time-related and reflect responsibilities.

NEDs should be appointed by a formal selection process and appointment approved by the board for a specific term subject to re-election - their re-appointment should not be automatic.

Non-executive directors should scrutinise the performance of management in meeting agreed goals and objectives, and monitor the reporting of performance. They should satisfy themselves on the integrity of financial information and that financial controls and systems of risk management are robust and defensible. They are responsible for determining appropriate levels of remuneration of executive directors and have a prime role in appointing and, where necessary, removing executive directors, and in succession planning.

Directors' duties

You should be familiar with the duties of directors from your earlier law studies. As you will recall the UK Companies Act 2006 places the following 'general duties' on company directors:

Duty	Explanation
To act within powers (s171)	Directors must: • Act in accordance with the company's constitution. • Exercise powers only for the purpose for which they were conferred.
To promote the success of the company (s 172)	Directors must act in the way they consider, in good faith, would be most likely to promote the success of the company for the benefit of its members as a whole.
To exercise independent judgment (s 173)	It does not mean that they are not exercising independent judgment where they act in accordance with: • An agreement duly entered into by the company that restricts the future exercise of discretion by its directors; or • The company's constitution.
To exercise reasonable care, skill and diligence (s 174)	The care, skill and diligence that would be exercised by a reasonably diligent person with: • The general knowledge, skill and experience that may reasonably be expected of a person performing their functions as director. • Actual general knowledge, skill and experience.
To avoid conflict of interest (s 175)	A director must avoid a situation in which they have or could have a direct or indirect interest that conflicts or possibly may conflict with the interests of the company or another duty.
Not to accept benefits from third parties (s 176)	A director must not accept a benefit from a third party by reason of their: • being a director; or • doing (or not doing) anything as director (unless the acceptance of the benefit cannot reasonably be regarded as likely to give rise to a conflict of interest).

Duty	Explanation
To declare interest in proposed transaction or arrangement (s 177)	Provided the director is, or ought reasonably to be, aware of the situation, they must declare the nature and extent of any such interest (direct or indirect) to the other directors, unless it cannot reasonably be regarded as likely to give rise to a conflict of interest.

8.6 Cyber security and the board

In Chapter 6 we discussed the growing importance that cyber security plays in helping businesses protect the IT/IS infrastructures used in their supply chains. The concept of cyber security is explored in greater detail in Chapter 14, however it is worth highlighting the greater expectations that are now being placed on the board of directors in terms of managing cyber risks effectively.

ICAEW's 2015 *Audit insights: cyber security* report recommended a number of measures which corporate boards should instigate so that they are better able to respond to the threats posed by cyber risks. These recommendations included:

Greater awareness

The report suggested that boards should actively seek evidence throughout the organisation that managers are aware of the cyber risks which may affect the organisation's strategy and operations. It is the board's responsibility to ensure that management are responding to the risks identified by taking appropriate steps to mitigate these.

Non-executive directors

Non-executive directors should be far more prepared to challenge the executive management team about the measures put in place to address cyber risks. The report highlights the need for the non-executive directors to ensure that a coherent approach to managing cyber risks is in place across the organisation.

Build a security focused culture

The report recommends that boards need to demonstrate a commitment to developing a strong security-focused culture. This involves displaying the leadership needed to encourage behavioural change among the organisation's employees to make them more security conscious.

Protect information assets

Boards need to ensure that there are appropriate levels of responsibility and accountability in place to support the effective prioritisation of information assets. Part of this process involves identifying the critical information held by the organisation. This requires boards to consider where this information is held and who has access to it.

Reporting

Boards need to articulate the organisation's approach to managing cyber risks. The inclusion of such detail in the organisation's annual report should help to provide greater transparency over those mitigating actions, and places a stronger emphasis on accountability.

Learn from security breaches

The report highlights that boards need to accept the likelihood that the organisation's data security will inevitably be breached at some point. The key is that boards learn from specific incidents and should consider the level of breach the organisation is prepared to tolerate. To be prepared for such breaches it is recommended that the board encourages and participates in ad hoc IT breach simulations. Such activities can help to identify weaknesses in the organisation's response.

The recommendations mentioned here link closely to the concept of risk management, which is considered in greater depth in Chapter 10.

8.7 Risk profiles

An issue in corporate governance is that the directors of companies might take decisions intended to increase profits without giving due regard to the risks. In some cases, companies may continue to operate without regard to the changing risk profile of their existing businesses.

The **moral hazard** to shareholders from the increasing risk profile of a firm is greater than to its directors.

Shareholders stand to lose some or all of the value of their investment in the business. To shareholders, investment risk is important, as well as high returns.

Directors, on the other hand, are rewarded on the basis of the returns the company achieves, linked to profits or dividend growth, and their remuneration is not linked in any direct way to the risk aspects of their business. Risk assessment and risk management is now recognised, particularly in the UK, as an ingredient of sound corporate governance and greater emphasis has been placed on this in recent revisions to the Corporate Governance Code.

The duties of the board of directors include robustly assessing the principal risks facing the company, ensuring that there is an operative and effective framework of prudent controls which enables the risk to be assessed and managed. Shareholders should feel confident that the board is aware of the risks faced by the company, and that a system for monitoring and controlling them is in place.

The risk management cycle is an interactive process of identifying risks, assessing their impact, and prioritising actions to control and reduce risks.

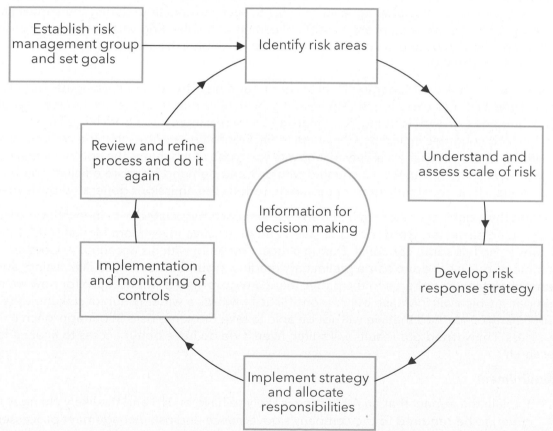

Source: 'The CIMA risk management cycle', taken from *Fraud risk management – A guide to good practice*

Once the risks have been identified and assessed, and the organisation's risk appetite has been set, strategies can be developed by the risk management group to deal with each risk that has been identified.

Strategies could include:

- Ignoring small risks (but ensuring that they remain under cyclical review)
- Contractual transfer of risk
- Risk avoidance
- Risk reduction via controls and procedures
- Transferring risks to insurers

Risk management is covered in more detail in Chapter 10.

Interactive question 8: Director's remuneration

8.1 Explain and assess the impact of various components of remuneration on a director's behaviour:

- Performance related bonuses
- Transaction bonuses
- Share options

See **Answer** at the end of this chapter.

Interactive question 9: Happy Harvester Ltd

Happy Harvester Ltd (HH) is a family-owned business, based in Norfolk, England. HH manufactures combine harvesters for use by farmers of grain crops. The widespread use of combine harvesters in global agriculture helps to save farmers time during the annual harvesting process. Combine harvesters are capable of cutting and collecting vast quantities of crops including wheat, oats and corn, which would otherwise be extremely labour intensive if performed manually.

Gordon Bennett is the Managing Director of HH, and he is the son of the original founder. In recent years HH has experienced significant growth in demand for the machines it manufactures. The company's growth is being heavily driven by increasing orders from large farms in developing countries including China and India. Gordon recognises that the continued success of HH lies in the company's ability to innovate the types of machines the company makes. Due to global environmental concerns coupled with growing demand for more efficient combine harvesters, HH is constantly under pressure to reduce the emissions generated by its machines.

To fund the significant research and development costs associated with innovating new models of combine harvester, Gordon is considering an Alternative Investment Market (AIM) listing. However, he has some concerns. During a recent meeting with his accountant, Gordon commented: 'I have done some preliminary reading around obtaining an AIM listing, and I know that if we offer some shares to the public there are governance implications for how we run the company, which will increase our responsibilities towards a wider group of stakeholders. I am particularly concerned that we will not be able to take the same risks in our approach to business. I'm worried our results will suffer, even if we do have better access to finance for research'.

Requirement

9.1 Explain the impact that an AIM listing is likely to have on HH and the likely changes that are going to be required to the company's governance and risk management processes.

See **Answer** at the end of this chapter.

8.8 Governance of government, public and non-profit organisations

This section applies to the following:

- **Government** – areas like defence and the law, which are the responsibility of the nation state.

- **Public** – the provision of health, transport, energy and other services which may be the responsibility of the state or may have been privatised, depending on the political views of the government.

- **Not-for-profit** – institutions that work for the common public good but are independent of the state – for example, charities, trusts and similar institutions.

In profit-oriented organisations, the board's minimum responsibilities are established by statute, regulation and case law. Many corporate boards also assume broader responsibilities in other key areas, such as health and safety or environmental practices. No similar set of legal minimum responsibilities exists for non-profit organisations' boards. Many of the issues are the same but there are some that are of specific importance to these sectors:

- **Accountability**: this is fundamental to the corporate governance of public bodies, and in recent years, the voluntary sector with regard to both the proper stewardship of public and donated funds and the increasing demand for service users to be involved in decision-making.

- **Stakeholders**: whilst commercial companies are primarily accountable to the shareholders, organisations in the public and voluntary sectors are accountable to a wide range of stakeholders, including service users, the general public, funders and national government. Issues of accountability are not clear-cut and conflicts can arise, eg, charity trustees have a legal duty to act in the interests of their beneficiaries, but if the charity is a membership body this may conflict with the wishes of members.

- **Openness and transparency**: there is a demand for open government and a distrust of decisions taken 'behind closed doors'. Voluntary organisations also face calls for transparency.

- **Governance/board structures**: the unitary board is not common in these sectors. Boards, or their equivalent, may be directly elected or appointed, and are often volunteer-based.

- **Monitoring performance**: in recent years a major emphasis in the public sector has been on performance measurement and evaluation. Increasingly voluntary organisations are beginning to look at ways of measuring outcomes.

Each group involved in a not-for-profit organisation – its board, management, staff, volunteers, donors and others – plays a part in its governance system. The board's role and activities can be examined in terms of five distinct areas:

1. **Responsibilities and mandate**: in profit-oriented organisations, the board's minimum responsibilities are established by statute, regulation and case law. No similar set of legal minimum responsibilities exists for NFP boards. The board bears the ultimate responsibility, though it usually delegates the authority to run the organisation to a CEO and a management team. The board's primary role is to oversee management and ensure that the NFP's affairs are being conducted in a way which achieves the organisation's objectives. NFP boards should have responsibility for:

   - strategic planning for the organisation;
   - risk identification and management;
   - management effectiveness and succession;
   - communications with stakeholders; and
   - internal control and management information systems.

2.   **Structure and organisation**: the structure and mandates of the board and each of its committees should be documented, to help ensure that board members, management and the NFP's stakeholders clearly understand the board's role. The board should also consider the qualifications it requires of individual board members to help them carry out the board's responsibilities.

3.   **Processes and information**: processes of decision-making and consultation should be open and will need to conform to procedures laid down in statute law (eg, planning applications) or in accordance with procedures laid down by the organisation itself. Information must be provided to interested parties and may be subject to various legal duties of disclosure.

4.   **Performance assessment and accountability**: boards of directors are accountable for their actions, and board members of all organisations are exposed to a growing personal liability resulting from the actions of the board and the organisation as a whole. Even though NFP board members are volunteers, their liability is the same as that of remunerated members of corporate boards. The responsibilities of board members include:

     *   Acting in good faith, in the best interests of the NFP
     *   Avoiding conflicts of interest
     *   Being diligent with regard to board meetings and obtaining information, and
     *   Obtaining a degree of confidence regarding the CEO's integrity and ability.

5.   **Organisational culture**

     A key development for the corporate governance of the UK public sector was the Nolan Committee on Standards in Public Life.

     The Nolan Seven Principles of Public Life include:

     *   **Selflessness**: holders of public office should take decisions solely in terms of the public interest. They should not do so to gain financial or other material benefits for themselves, their family or their friends.

     *   **Integrity**: holders of public office should not place themselves under any financial or other obligation to outside individuals or organisations that might influence them in the performance of their duties.

     *   **Objectivity**: in carrying out public business, including making public appointments, awarding contracts or recommending individuals for rewards and benefits, holders of public office should make choices on merit.

     *   **Accountability**: holders of public office are accountable for their decisions and actions to the public and must submit themselves to whatever scrutiny is appropriate to their office.

     *   **Openness**: holders of public office should be as open as possible about the decisions and actions that they take. They should give reasons for their decisions and restrict information only when the wider public interest clearly demands.

     *   **Honesty**: holders of public office have a duty to declare any private interests relating to their public duties and to take steps to resolve any conflicts arising in a way that protects the public interest.

     *   **Leadership**: holders of public office should promote and support these principles by leadership and example.

Summary and Self-test

Summary

Business Strategy

Structure follows strategy (Chandler)

Top down

Bottom up

Strategy emerges from and conditioned by structure

Governance ← **Organisation structure**

Consists of
- Staff roles
- Primary grouping into teams
- Departments and divisions
- Supervisory and management teans
- Control systems
- Corporate board and governance

Governance
- Constitution of board
- Reward structure
- Risk profiles

Divisionalisation

or
Hybrid
- Functional
- Geographic
- Product/brand
- Customer/market segment

Matrix

Fuctions

Markets

Centralisation

How authority/decision making diffused

Centralised
- Control
- Co-cordination

Span of control

Decentralised
- Motivation
- Quicker

Mintzberg organisations

Strategic apex

Technostructure

Middle line

Support staff

Operating core

Centralised
- Simple
- Machine bureaucracy
- Professional bureaucracy
- Divisionalised form
- Adhocracy

Divisionalised form

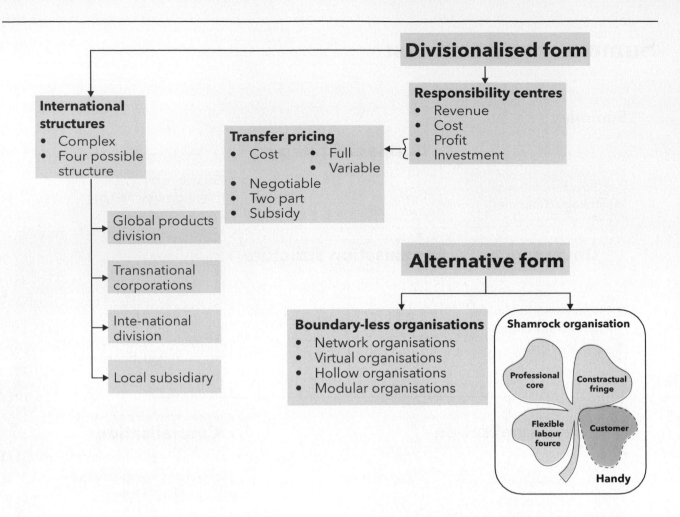

Divisionalised form

International structures
- Complex
- Four possible structure

Global products division

Transnational corporations

Inte-national division

Local subsidiary

Transfer pricing
- Cost
- Negotiable
- Two part
- Subsidy
- Full
- Variable

Responsibility centres
- Revenue
- Cost
- Profit
- Investment

Alternative form

Boundary-less organisations
- Network organisations
- Virtual organisations
- Hollow organisations
- Modular organisations

Shamrock organisation

Professional core

Constractual fringe

Flexible labour fource

Customer

Handy

Self-test

Answer the following questions.

1   Greenleaf Ltd has grown from a small entrepreneurial company of five staff to a larger organisation of 35. The growth, though welcome, has thrown Greenleaf into chaos. No-one is sure what they should be doing and mistakes are beginning to be made.

Recommend, with reasons, a suitable organisation structure and suggest the mechanism required to co-ordinate the various parts of the organisation.

2   Suggest two ways in which a company can ensure corporate governance processes are incorporated into the organisation structure.

3   What is a professional bureaucracy? Give two examples of organisations that would suit this form of structure.

4   What is meant by a matrix organisation structure?

5   Compare and contrast centralisation and decentralisation.

6   How do 'the location and complexity of the work' and 'the degree of delegation possible' influence the span of control?

7   Travel Fast Ltd is an established bus company. Its organisation chart shows a three-tier structure of directors, managers and drivers.

What factors will influence the span of control of the managers?

8   A substantial architectural practice designing and managing the construction of various buildings is likely to be best suited to a matrix organisational structure.

Why?

9   Within a manufacturing business an excerpt from the organisation chart is as follows.

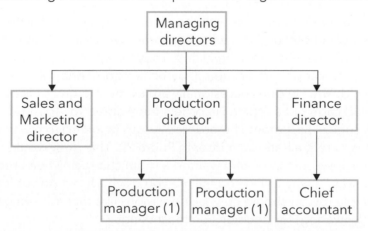

The Chief accountant is collating budget information for the coming year and the production managers (after reference to the chart) are unwilling to supply figures, saying they report to the production director.

Explain why the problem has arisen and how it can be solved.

10   In the context of international structures, explain the difference between a 'global product division' and a 'local subsidiary' and suggest when each might be appropriate.

11   **Byron Tuffin**

Byron Tuffin is the owner of four hotels. Three of these have been recently acquired; one is in London, one in the Lake District (Ambleside) and the third in the Clifton area of Bristol. The original hotel is the Imperial, outside Brighton. The Imperial has been in the Tuffin family for 50 years and was bequeathed to Byron by his father.

The Imperial has 40 rooms. Five of these are de-luxe suites with lounge/ante-room, bedroom and bathroom. 20 are double bedrooms and the remainder are single rooms. The hotel has a beautiful location in 10 acres of landscaped gardens and, being on a small hill, the rooms at the top command impressive views over Sussex. The hotel makes good returns and has good all-year-round occupancy rates. Much more comes from special events like weddings and as a stopover for honeymooning couples before departure elsewhere the next day.

The Regent in Clifton and The Orangery in the Lake District are similar to The Imperial. The former has 30 rooms while the latter has only 20 double rooms. The Serpentine hotel in London has 55 rooms, ie, 30 double, five de-luxe suites and 20 single rooms.

Byron bought the hotels from an old family friend. Each of the hotels needs some refurbishment. Byron has 10 years' experience in managing The Imperial but realises that a four-hotel group is a different matter. As a consultant brought in by his bankers (who helped in the acquisitions) you have been called in to assist Byron in developing the company. During the course of your investigations you conduct many interviews: details from some of these are given below.

Carolyn Reeder (Finance manager, The Imperial)

"I'm a bit overqualified for this job. I'm an ACA with four years' post-qualification experience. I've been here for two years and, although the job is fairly easy, the people here are great to work with. Byron is absolutely superb with customers: he checks their file (if they have one) before they arrive and he makes them feel really special. They love him. On the other hand he does not want to be concerned with detail. He forgets about decisions and he has trouble taking decisions without consulting everyone else first. He thinks about ''direction of the hotel'' etc, so I suppose he's more strategic. He does interfere sometimes though, by ordering my staff about or bypassing me to get information from them."

Rick Fowler (Facilities manager)

"There's a fair amount to do here with the hotel being a grade II listed building. This is a ''special'' occasion hotel and I love the ''pre-war'' feel to it. I've an excellent team of tradesmen under me who are all qualified. They take pride in their work but there isn't always enough to keep them occupied. Byron is a good enough man but on occasion he's difficult to pin down. He does occasionally annoy me. He gives his opinion on how one of my staff should carry out a repair. He orders them about too, overriding my authority. One instance will suffice. Last month he ordered Angus (a joiner) to repair his office door when I'd told Angus to refit a bathroom door in Room 22. This door would not close. We had a particularly stroppy customer who wanted a room change. When I remonstrated with Byron his response was ''...why didn't you tell me you'd scheduled Angus for elsewhere ...''. That's not the principle. Byron should only take decisions like that following consultation with me. I go to Peter (Unwaring) for decisions on most things."

Peter Unwaring (Operations manager)

"I look after the day-to-day operations of the hotel – bookings, staffing, etc. I only involve Byron if there is a problem. We have our weekly manager meetings which are fairly easy going. Byron is a good man to work for – he does think ''big'' though. He's always coming up with ideas for the hotel. He's also astonishing to watch with our regular customers. They adore him."

Alexandra Thorpe-Watson (Manager, The Regent)

"The acquisition was good news for us. The hotel needs some refurbishment – at the moment it has a little too much ''faded gentility''. Byron from The Imperial seems an enthusiastic person. We've agreed that this hotel needs to be re-positioned. I've been here a year, and before I joined the hotel was losing its direction."

Niall Gallagher (Manager, The Serpentine)

"This is a good hotel with a good occupancy rate. Our clients are mostly business people in London for a few days. We also get tourists, which we need to encourage as our weekend occupancy needs improving. Byron seems to be fairly open-minded in terms of ideas for the direction of the group. I'll be interested in what he comes up with."

Byron Tuffin (Group owner)

"I'm really excited about our future. The group now has different hotels. We now have different coverage geographically and in terms of markets. We'll need to invest in refurbishment, though. I have no problem with that. I fully understand and believe in the importance of the client. You have to make each guest feel that he is the most important person in the hotel."

Requirements

Prepare a memorandum covering the following.

11.1 An appropriate organisation structure for the group together with reasons for your recommendation and the advantages your structure would bring.

11.2 A review of Byron's management style and your reasoned suggestions for a new management structure, indicating the advantages of the new structure.

12 Goddess plc

Goddess plc is a manufacturer of kitchen appliances. The Chairman and Chief Executive is Barbara Best, whose father, Sid, originally set up the business 14 years ago. The company has a good reputation for the production of up-market refrigerators for built-in kitchens, following an invention by Sid of a fan to run at low speeds and keep food fresher for far longer than conventional products. The refrigerators have always sold at premium prices, but in the last 18 months demand has levelled off as the market sector has become saturated. The main customers have been department stores and electrical retailers. Due to Goddess plc being a relative newcomer to the kitchen appliances market, it has had to give retailers a 60% trade discount on the price sold to the consumer, to help obtain floor space in stores.

The company floated on the stock market five years ago. Initially the share price rose as sales exceeded expectations, but recently the price has fallen due to the decrease in demand for the fridges. Barbara and her family own 40% of the share capital, and a further 45% is owned by institutional investors, which have been critical of the underperformance of the share price. The institutional investors have also been unhappy about Barbara's domineering managerial style, and her refusal to allow non-executive directors on the board despite support for such a move from other executive directors.

Barbara feels that, as her father set up the company and developed many of the initial products, the board should always agree with her views. She does not believe that the other directors are as committed to the company as she is, and so insists on being involved in all decisions. She believes that she has always made the right decisions for the company as she has a vested interest arising from her shareholding. She has imposed her views by removing two of the directors in the past who have voted against her proposals. She is now aware that she needs the support of the other directors to help turn the company around.

The company has tried to counter criticisms regarding trading and the falling share price by entering a new market. The development has just been completed of a new style machine that washes twice the volume of a traditional washer, but in half the time. It has taken a lot of time and expense to create the new machine, called the Spin-King, but initial reaction by both retailers and consumers has been favourable. A new division will be set up to produce and market the Spin-King.

At a board meeting on 3 February 20X4 the finance director revealed the following projections for the Spin-King division.

	£
Annual factory rent	944,000
Material costs per unit	80
Production labour per unit	72
Advertising costs per annum	350,000
Initial investment in machinery	4,500,000

It is estimated that the Spin-King will be launched in April 20X4. The new machinery has an expected lifespan of five years with no residual value. Goddess plc does not have sufficient cash to buy the new production machinery, but the board is hoping to persuade institutional investors to support a new share issue that will raise funds to finance the capital expenditure. The manager of the new division will be paid a bonus based on the return on investment.

Market research analysis indicates that demand for Spin-Kings will be 60,000 units per annum at a trade price of £200 per unit, and 112,000 units per annum if the trade price is £160 per unit.

The purchasing director is confident that he can obtain a 15% discount on all material costs for the Spin-King if Goddess plc is buying materials for more than 100,000 units per annum.

Requirements

12.1(a) Spreading the cost of the new machinery evenly over the life of the asset, determine the annual output required for the Spin-King division to achieve break-even profit each year at both the suggested price points.

(b) Comment on the significance of these calculations to Goddess plc.

12.2 Discuss the merits of Goddess plc appointing non-executive directors. Explain the benefits of Barbara pursuing a less authoritarian role in the running of the company, and how as a consequence the board could be made a more effective group for decision making.

13 Read the scenario of the **September 2016 Business Strategy and Technology** question in the Question Bank entitled *Thistle Engineering Services Ltd*, referred to at the beginning of the chapter. Draft an answer to the requirement on organisational structure.

14 Read the scenario of the **March 2017 Business Strategy and Technology** question in the Question Bank entitled *Eclo Ltd*, referred to at the beginning of the chapter. Draft an answer to the requirement on organisational structure.

Now, go back to the Learning outcomes in the Introduction. If you are satisfied that you have achieved these objectives, please tick them off.

Answers to Interactive questions

Answer to Interactive question 1

1.1 Adhocracy
1.2 Professional bureaucracy

Answer to Interactive question 2

2.1 The bank basically serves two markets: the personal sector and the corporate sector. However, it would perhaps be ill advised to organise the bank **solely** on that basis because:

The banking needs of customers in the **personal sector** are likely to be quite distinct. This market is naturally segmented geographically. Despite the fact that most online and telephone banking services can nowadays be accessed globally, users of both services are still likely to require the online portal to be set out using their home language, home currency, with tech support being available from their home nation. Furthermore, different countries are likely to have different banking regulations which will need to be complied with, this reinforces the argument for geographic segmentation. In addition the telephone banking staff will need to able to speak the same language as customers, with staff available at all times of the day, this therefore lends itself to an organisational structure which takes account of local conditions.

For the personal sector, a geographic organisation would be appropriate, although with the centralisation of some common administrative functions, so that the bank gains from scale economies and avoids wasteful duplication.

For the **corporate sector**, different considerations apply. If the bank is providing sophisticated foreign currency accounts, these will be of most benefit to multi-nationals or companies which regularly export from, or import to, their home markets. A geographical organisation structure may not be appropriate, and arguably the bank's organisation should be centralised on a Europe wide basis, with the country offices, of course, at a lower level.

Answer to Interactive question 3

3.1

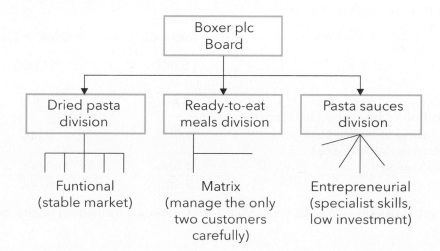

Answer to Interactive question 4

4.1 Profits and losses – Transfer price based on existing basis

	Manufacturing Division £m	Retail Division £m
Estimated retail sales	–	30
Estimate sales/purchases (at 60% of retail sales)	18	(18)
Variable costs	(12)	(5)
Fixed costs	(7)	(3)
Loss/profit	(1)	4

4.2 Transfer price set on break-even basis

Sales needed to break-even = £19m (£12m+£7m)

19m ÷ 30m = 0.633

Transfer price needs to be Retail price less 36.66%

Answer to Interactive question 5

5.1 Division B would **reject** the offer as there is a negative contribution of – £5 (30 – 20 – 15).

5.2 If A has **surplus capacity**, it is acceptable to the company, as contribution is £5 (30 – 15 – 10).

If A is at **full capacity**, there is a lost external sales contribution in A of £10.

Therefore, for the company, contribution = – £5, thus reject. (B may also lose contribution.)

Answer to Interactive question 6

6.1 **Company**: transfers recommended, as contribution = £5 (40 – 20 – 15).
6.2 **Selling division**: transfers not recommended, as contribution = – £6 (40 – 31 – 15).

Answer to Interactive question 7

	A	B	
7.1 Actual recharge	$\dfrac{£18,000}{6,000} \times 4,000$	$\dfrac{£18,000}{6,000} \times 2,000$	
	= £12,000	= £6,000	£18,000

Expected recharge (per kwh)

$£1 + \dfrac{£10,000}{10,000} = £2/kwh$

	A	B	
	4,000 × £2	2000 × £2	
	£8,000	£4,000	£12,000

	£	£	
7.2 Proportion of budgeted fixed cost according to budget usage	4,000	6,000	
Standard variable cost of actual usage	4,000	2,000	
	8,000	8,000	£16,000

In power plant £(18,000 – 16,000) = £2,000 adverse variance remaining uncharged due to inefficiency.

Answer to Interactive question 8

8.1 **Performance related bonuses**. Directors may be paid a cash bonus for improving the performance of the company. Performance related bonuses can be effective in aligning the interests of the directors with those of the shareholders, as improved company performance may help to trigger bonus payments. The danger with performance related bonuses is that if not adequately controlled, directors may be incentivised to take short term decisions to improve performance to the detriment of the company's longer term performance simply to trigger bonus payments. To guard against excessive payouts, some companies impose limits on bonus plans as a fixed percentage of salary or pay.

Transaction bonuses tend to be much more controversial. Some Chief Executives get bonuses for acquisitions, regardless of subsequent performance, possibly indeed further bonuses for spinning off acquisitions that have not worked out. The danger with such schemes is that it may encourage directors make acquisitions simply for the sake of it and not because it benefits the company. Again, such behaviour may be to the detriment of the company if bonuses are being paid in respect of acquisitions which do not workout.

Share options give directors the right to purchase shares at a specified exercise price over a specified time period in the future. If the price of the shares rises so that it exceeds the exercise price by the time the options can be exercised, the directors will be able to purchase shares at lower than their market value. Such schemes can be effective in encouraging directors to stay with the company over the longer term as share options act as an incentive for directors to work harder at improving the company's performance. It is likely that share options will influence the level of risk that the directors are prepared to take as the pursuit of high risk strategies may reflect negatively on the company's share price, which may diminish the potential return the directors may be able to realise when they exercise their options. Share options may also help to ensure that directors focus on the company's share price as opposed to focusing solely on profit measures.

[The UK Corporate Governance Code states that non-executive directors should not normally be offered share options, as options may impact upon their independence.]

Answer to Interactive Question 9

9.1 **Governance and risk management as a result of listing**

Happy Harvesters Ltd is currently 100% family-owned. By listing on AIM it will become a part publicly-owned company with a wider range of range of shareholders. This may give rise to possible agency issues as the owners and managers of HH will no longer necessarily be the same individuals.

Institutional shareholders are likely to have expectations concerning the corporate governance of HH – where corporate governance is about the relationship between the HH board and external stakeholders. Companies listed on the Alternative Investment Market are not required to comply with the UK Corporate Governance Code. However, pursuing good corporate governance practice will likely increase investor confidence.

HH may benefit by going beyond minimum regulatory requirements and adopting a positive approach to corporate governance, HH is likely to be more successful in satisfying the needs of stakeholders which may help to improve the company's competitive advantage especially if this helps to attract more investors.

As HH has been a growing business to date, it is likely that the company will have already put in place some form of internal controls and management information systems to help the company meet its objectives and create a culture of innovation. When HH lists the company should ensure that the corporate governance provisions surrounding the principles of leadership and effectiveness are adopted. Such provisions will require the separation of the roles of the Chairman and CEO. The Chairman should be solely responsible for running the board and the CEO responsible for running the company.

HH should also look to appoint some independent non-executive directors to ensure that the board has the necessary skills to govern the effectively.

Risk management

Gordon is concerned that by taking HH onto AIM that he will not be able to take the same types of risk. Clearly, to continue the company's success the directors will need to give consideration to the risks attached to the strategic decisions they make. External shareholders need to have confidence that the board is aware of the risks HH faces and have systems in place for monitoring them. As a result Gordon will need to ensure that there are systems in place to identify the strategic, operational, financial and hazard risks faced by the business. The scale of the risks can then be assessed, and appropriate priorities determined for risk mitigation. Risks can then be dealt with according to the TARA model – transfer, avoidance, reduction or retention.

For example HH could take steps to reduce the reputational risks that may arise as a result of the high levels of emissions that the company's combine harvesters currently emit.

Given the nature of HH's business the board and management will need to take into account any legal requirements such as health and safety in the manufacturing process.

Answers to Self-test

1   Recommendation – functional (bureaucratic)

Reasons:

- Formal job descriptions
- Clear reporting lines
- Formal procedures

Co-ordinating mechanism – standardisation of work.

2   - Appoint both executive and non-executive directors to the board
    - Establish an audit committee to oversee the board
    - Create an internal audit function

3   An organisation where the main building block is the operating core (professionally skilled staff) and the controlling mechanism is the standardisation of skills.

Suitable organisations:

- Solicitors' practice
- GP practice
- Accountants' practice

4   The matrix structure involves overlaying a second set of hierarchical connections over the first but at right angles to it. As an example consider a county council.

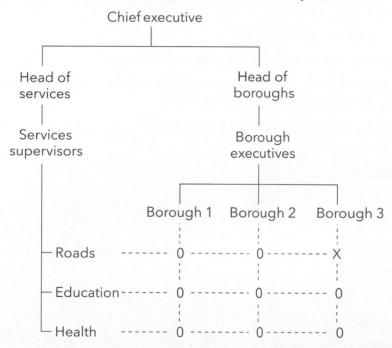

In this structure service supervisors for roads, education, health, etc in accounting, economics and marketing report to the head of services. Borough executives report to the head of boroughs. Each carries equal weight in terms of authority.

An individual (X above) who is part of Borough 3 may at the same time be part of the team responsible for roads. Thus the individual reports two ways – to the service supervisor and to the borough executive, and is subject to two lines of authority.

5   A centralised structure is a condition where the upper levels of an organisation's hierarchy retain the authority to make most decisions. The authority of lower levels to make decisions is very limited.

A decentralised structure is a condition where authority to make most decisions is passed down to lower levels of the hierarchy.

Upper levels of the hierarchy tend to set organisation objectives and strategies; lower levels are left to decide about detailed operational plans and take day-to-day decisions.

Decisions are taken quicker and are often better than in centralised systems as they are made by people with the relevant skills/knowledge. Delegation is part of decentralisation because authority must be delegated for decentralisation to occur.

6 • **The location and complexity of the work**: If the work is technically sophisticated, requiring a range of technical expertise or is physically widely distributed, then the smaller should be the span of control.

• **The degree of delegation possible**: The degree to which authority can be delegated to subordinates to carry out their tasks, which in turn is influenced by the ability of the subordinates. The less supervision required, the more the subordinates who can be controlled, eg, an audit team.

7 The following factors influence the span of control.

(a) Drivers should understand what is required of them without much guidance, eg, sticking to a set timetable with fixed stopping points.

(b) Face to face contact is not often necessary.

(c) Objective measures can be used to evaluate performance, eg,

- Bus mileage
- Takings per trip
- Customer complaints

The managers' span of control is likely to be fairly large.

8 A single design director or project management director is unlikely to be able to control all the projects of the practice at one point in time.

This overall directorship role would be allied with individuals or teams controlling individual jobs, eg:

Design director:

Project 1

• Designer A
• Manager B

Design director:

Project 2

• Designer C
• Manager D

9 The problem arises from two aspects of the organisation chart.

(a) It completely ignores the 'information flows' around a business – in this case budgets and management accounts.

(b) The chart can encourage staff to interpret their roles very narrowly; in reality the responsibilities of the production managers would necessarily include budget information.

The solution to the problem would be moving 'up' the organisation chart, and then back down again, ie, the Finance Director (and the Managing Director if necessary) ensuring that the production director explains the importance of budget information to the business as a whole.

A combination of organisation chart and detailed job description, one of which would be communicating budget details to the Chief accountant, would also be of assistance.

10　International businesses can follow a multi-domestic strategy where activities are located in individual national markets and products/services tailored to local needs, or a global strategy where standardised products are developed and produced centrally.

Thus international structures vary depending on the extent of global coordination and the amount of local independence/responsiveness required.

A **global product division** is typical for a company following a global strategy, which will have separate world-wide divisions for soft drinks, alcoholic beverages etc. This gives high global coordination but limited local responsiveness.

A **local subsidiary** is geographically based in the individual national market and operates independently. Local management has a high degree of autonomy, hence local responsiveness is high and global coordination is low. This is appropriate for a business following a **multi-domestic strategy**.

11　**Byron Tuffin**

Memorandum

To	The Imperial Hotel Group Ltd
Prepared by	ABC Consultants
Date	July 20X4
Subject	Management and organisation structure

11.1 Organisation structure

Current structure

The current structure is functional. This can be shown as follows.

This structure is perfectly suitable for a single hotel. However, despite the acquisitions being in the same area of business (hotels), this structure is no longer available for the following reasons.

(a)　Decision-making will take too long due to

– The sheer volume of information being made available
– Different geographical coverage

(b)　Centralised decisions will not make individuals react quickly enough to changes in the market.

(c)　It may stifle initiative and creativity of the individual hotel managers who may well have very good marketing ideas.

Recommended structure

For the reasons outlined above and below we would recommend the adoption of a divisional structure.

This would be as follows.

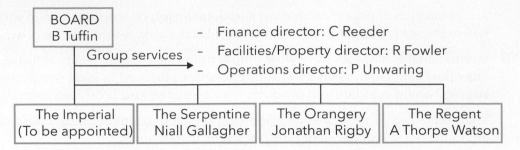

The following are the advantages of such a structure.

(a) It is now much easier to assess the performance of each hotel and its manager.

(b) Group services can set standards for the whole group

- In maintenance
- In service

(c) The group may benefit from purchasing economies, eg

- In cleaning services
- Laundry arrangements

(d) Individual managers feel more motivated because they are directly responsible for the performance of their hotel.

(e) They can adapt more quickly to any changes in their respective markets.

(f) Group services can usefully redirect and re-allocate funds to the hotel needing it most.

This structure will also facilitate any potential growth. With group support services in place, extra hotels could be added as new divisions.

11.2 Management style and structure

Current style of structure

Byron Tuffin's current management seems to vary between authoritarian and decentralised.

At times he interferes with decisions taken by individual managers (see the comments of R Fowler).

Conversely, he distances himself from detail and is only interested in top-level considerations and decisions.

This ambiguity leads to inconsistent attitudes. Staff need to know exactly to whom to report and the precise extent of their own authority.

Recommended style and management structure.

We recommend that Byron introduce a management structure as outlined in the diagram above, ie

- A board of directors comprising the group service directors and directors of the other three hotels plus at least one non-executive director.

- The adoption of a decentralised management style.

The advantages of these two simple changes are numerous and include the following.

(a) Clear and unambiguous reporting line – it is very important that the exact extent of the decentralisation is established. The limits should be defined in terms of spending limits, hire/fire of staff, etc.

(b) It allows individual hotel managers to exercise initiative in running the hotels.

(c) This delegation of authority will improve/maintain motivation of the hotel managers. They are aware that their performance is to be assessed on the basis of the performance of the individual hotel.

(d) It allows Byron to stay away from the 'detail' and thus to focus on group direction/strategy.

(e) The board is now responsible for group direction; this is preferable to having Byron dictate the direction and action of individual hotels. The Serpentine, for example, taps a different market from the other hotels in the group and so requires a knowledge of a different market. It is thus important that the board take decisions at this level. The non-executive directors will provide a check on the activities of the directors.

12 Goddess plc

12.1 (a) Break-even
Contribution per unit

	Price 1 £	Price 2 £
Sales price	200	160
Variable costs		
Labour	72	72
Materials	80	68
Contribution	48	20

Costs	£	£
Fixed costs		
Machinery depreciation	900,000	900,000
Advertising	350,000	350,000
Factory rent	944,000	944,000
Total	2,194,000	2,194,000
Break-even	2,194,000 ÷ 48	2,194,000 ÷ 20
	45,708 units	109,700 units

(b) Comments on significance of calculations

Benefit of bulk discount on higher sales volume outweighed by greater contribution at higher price.

At price of £200 the safety margin is far higher than at £160.

If the company adopts a low price strategy, then extra marketing may be required to obtain the significantly higher sales volumes required. This would further increase the advertising spending.

If lower volumes were produced, excess factory capacity could be used to produce other goods.

12.2 Merits of appointing non-executives

Improves the perception of independence between the board and the shareholders.

Removes the ability of directors to set their own pay and create an efficient executive remuneration scheme.

Acts as a buffer between the auditors and the board.

Brings experience to the board from other posts held by these non-executives.

Reduces the ability of a Chief Executive to dominate the board of directors.

Assists appointment of new directors on a merit basis.

Can also act as a voice piece for the interests of stakeholders.

Merits of less authoritarian role and improving board effectiveness

Barbara is reluctant to delegate any element of decision making and decisions are imposed.

Other directors are demotivated by threat of the sack. They may be choosing not to give their opinions as a result and decisions may be made by Barbara without all the knowledge held by individual directors.

Barbara is likely to lack the time and knowledge to make all decisions effectively.

By taking a less authoritarian role, Barbara could create a more participative environment and encourage discussion of issues. This is likely to lead to better decisions.

Such an environment would encourage open decision making, by removing fear of dismissal for disagreeing with Barbara's views.

Barbara should split the board into teams to work on individual tasks and projects.

She should encourage consensus decision making, rather than the use of votes of individual members of the board.

Institutional investors would welcome more openness and are likely to be reassured by the move.

Increased delegation/participation is likely to free up Barbara's time to concentrate on the strategic direction of the business and the relationships with key stakeholders.

13   Refer to the answer to Thistle Engineering Services Ltd in the Question Bank.

14   Refer to the answer to Eclo Ltd in the Question Bank.

CHAPTER 10

Risk management

Introduction

Examination context

TOPIC LIST

Summary and Self-test

Answers to Interactive questions

Answers to Self-test

Introduction

Learning outcomes

- Identify the risk attached to an organisation's present position, using all relevant qualitative and quantitative data, and considering attitudes to risk, security and cyber security ☐

- Identify the risks attached to proposed courses of action in a given situation, considering all relevant factors, stating all assumptions made and identifying strategies for managing risk ☐

- Choose for a given scenario, a strategy or combination of strategies which will best achieve the organisation's objectives, taking account of known constraints, including stakeholder risk preferences and developing technologies ☐

- Explain and demonstrate how an organisation can use management accounting approaches to evaluate its proposed strategies, while considering the value of information and the risk associated with forecasts ☐

- Identify and evaluate methods of further developing a specific organisation which adjust existing strategies or implement new strategies to take account of changing position and risk ☐

Specific syllabus references for this chapter are: 1f, 2d, 2g, 2j, 3e.

Syllabus links

Some of the risks associated specifically with IT/IS will be covered in Chapter 14. This chapter introduces the concept of cyber risk and the growing danger that it presents to organisations.

The concept of risk and risk management was introduced in your Business, Technology and Finance studies.

The concept of entity risk is discussed later in this chapter. A key component of entity risk is financial risk. While you need to be generally aware of financial risk management for Business Strategy and Technology, this topic is dealt with primarily in the Financial Management paper, which also deals in more detail with methods of handling risk and uncertainty in decision making.

Risk management is an important topic and is taken forward at Advanced level.

Examination context

The issues involved in analysing risk, for example in the context of the external environment, have already been discussed in previous chapters. This chapter discusses attitudes to those risks and how an organisation can manage such risks.

In Question 2 of the September 2015 exam (*Premier Paper Products plc*) the scenario focused on a company involved in the printing of banknotes and identity documents for a variety of central banks and governments. New technology meant that some central banks had recently decided to change from using paper banknotes to polymer notes, and the Premier Paper Products (PPP) board was unsure whether to invest in the new technology, which had already been adopted by one of its competitors. The second requirement in the question asked candidates to:

'Prepare a risk register, setting out what you consider to be **three** significant business risks facing PPP's Banknote division. You should present your answer in a three-column format, explaining, for each risk:

- The nature of the risk
- The possible impact of the risk and the likelihood of it occurring
- Risk management strategies'

(9 marks)

The examiner noted that 'the majority of candidates produced a well-structured table, identifying three risks facing PPP's banknote division, although weaker candidates did not always concentrate on the key ones. Some candidates limited their marks by not addressing all elements of the requirement comprehensively eg, focussing on the impact of the risk and its management, without considering its nature and likelihood. The strongest answers identified a range of key risks and used the TARA model to identify appropriate risk management strategies. A number of candidates wasted time and marks discussing risks facing PPP as a whole rather than the banknote division.' As these comments illustrate, carefully reading the requirement and giving due consideration to each aspect required is central to producing a good answer. Mastering these skills is essential if you are to ensure a pass mark in your exam.

Some questions may feature financial or other quantitative data which you are expected to use in assessing the types of risks facing an organisation featured in a scenario. Questions may require you to analyse the level of risk by conducting sensitivity analysis to determine an entity's break-even point.

In Question 1 of the June 2017 exam (*Holidays Direct plc*) the scenario focused on a UK-based, online holiday company, Holidays Direct (HD). The company sold package holidays (flights and accommodation) directly to UK customers via its website. The company operated two divisions: a Worldwide Division and a European Division. Holidays Direct chartered flights from three different airlines, making bookings under block contracts in the September of the year prior to travel. The exhibit in the scenario provided a significant amount of financial and operating data. The second requirement asked:

'Explain the operating and financial risks which arise for HD from the potential differences in quantities between:

- The number of flights and hotel stays that have been acquired through the block contracts; and
- Demand from consumers.'

The majority of candidates performed well, with many basing the discursive element of their answer around the issue of estimating demand. However, a number of candidates failed to make the most of the quantitative data provided. This resulted in weaker answers, and fewer marks being awarded. This example highlights the importance of ensuring that you make use of any quantitative data provided in the scenario as it has been provided for use in your answer. As highlighted in Chapter 1, the examiners have stressed the need for candidates to be comfortable using quantitative data when constructing their answers.

1 Risk and uncertainty

Section overview

- Risk arises when there may be a variety of possible outcomes.

- Risk management is concerned with the positive and negative aspects of risk. A business may look to minimise its downside risk while leaving open the potential to share in any upside.

- The term 'risk' is often muddled with 'uncertainty' which is strictly-speaking different because the latter cannot be quantified.

- Modern thinking suggests that all future outcomes are subject to uncertainty which ranges from a 'clear enough future' to one of 'true ambiguity'.

- Therefore risk management requires management to treat risks that it can forecast but also to take courses of action to cope with risks it cannot forecast.

1.1 What is risk?

It is usual to consider risk as negative, and in the field of safety this is certainly true since there is no gain if things go right- just a loss if they go wrong. As a result, safety risk management concentrates on the prevention or minimisation of harm. In most other spheres, however, risk implies variability which may work in the favour of the business (**an opportunity**) or against it (**a risk**).

Risk is more than probability. It includes consequences. The chances of flipping a coin and getting heads is 50%. It only becomes a risk if we gamble on the outcome. The larger the amount at stake, the bigger the risk, but the probability stays the same.

Risk is also different from uncertainty, which arises due to a lack of information about the future.

Definitions

Risk: The possible variation in outcome from what is expected to happen.

Uncertainty: The inability to predict the outcome from an activity due to a lack of information.

Downside risk (pure risk): The possibility that the outcome will be worse than expected ie, something will go wrong (the worst case scenario).

Upside risk (speculative risk or opportunity): The possibility that something could go better than expected (best case scenario).

Risk management is increasingly recognised as being concerned with both the positive and negative aspects of risk and looks to control risk from both perspectives.

For example, a person buying a house with a loan may decide to fix the interest rate for a period. They are eliminating two kinds of risk: the downside risk that their loan would become more expensive if the interest rate rose but also the upside risk that it could have become cheaper if the interest rate had fallen.

Businesses may look for ways to manage their downside risk, whilst at the same time leaving open the potential to share in any upside, although this flexibility may come at a price premium. In the context of our house purchase example, a capped rate loan would offer such an opportunity.

1.2 Risk and uncertainty

There is a technical distinction between risk and uncertainty:

- Risk is a quantification of the potential variability in a value based on past data (eg, when a coin is tossed the outcome will either be heads or tails).

- Uncertainty on the other hand, is non-quantifiable (whether a key customer will be retained for the next two years).

Strictly speaking, risk should therefore be defined as a measure of the variability in the value of a factor that is capable of statistical or mathematical evaluation.

For the purposes of risk management, risk can be defined as the combination of the likelihood of an event and its consequences:

The severity of a potential risk can be determined by considering the likelihood of the risk occurring in relation to its potential impact (likelihood × impact). When considering the financial impact of risks this can be stated as: likelihood × financial consequences.

In practice, the distinction between risk and uncertainty is blurred. Huge losses by insurance underwriting syndicates show that assessments of risk used in insurance have been compromised by unanticipated events such as flooding and hurricanes from climate change and claims for industrial injury resulting from asbestos and stress.

Despite using terms like risk, many business strategies are actually taking place in situations of uncertainty. A management team that only undertakes strategies in which the likelihood of success or failure can be precisely quantified would launch no new products, enter no new markets, and research no new technologies.

Courtney et al (*Strategy Under Uncertainty*) describe four classes of uncertainty.

1. **Clear enough futures**: The future can be assessed with reasonable accuracy because it follows on from the past without major change. Eg, the forecasts of bread sales made by management of a bakery.

2. **Alternative futures**: Outcomes depend on an event, eg, the value of rights to make national football team merchandise depends on whether they qualify for the World Cup or not.

3. **Range of futures**: Outcome varies according to a number of variables that interact, eg, hotel operator's forecasts of sales of holiday accommodation depend on level of temperature, prices of flights, levels of disposable income etc.

4. **True uncertainty**: Very high uncertainty due to the number and unpredictability of the variables influencing the outcome, eg, investment in emerging economies where the outcome will be determined by political events, global economic developments, natural and man-made disasters, cultural and religious change etc.

The first two of these could be quantified with tolerable accuracy perhaps. The second two are much more uncertain.

Therefore risk management requires management to treat risks that it can forecast but also to take courses of action to cope with risks it cannot forecast.

1.3 Why manage risk?

Corporate governance was covered in Chapter 9. Corporate governance standards encourage organisations and public sector bodies to adopt good practices in risk assessment and risk management. The board's role is to provide entrepreneurial leadership of the organisation within a framework of prudent and effective controls which enables risk to be assessed and managed.

A risk based management approach is required for all UK listed companies under the **UK Corporate Governance Code (Financial Reporting Council, 2016)**, which sets out the following principles on the management of risk:

- The board is responsible for determining the nature and extent of the principal risks it is willing to take in achieving its strategic objectives. The board should maintain **sound risk management and internal control systems**.

- The directors should confirm in the **annual report** that they have **carried out a robust assessment** of the principal risks facing the company, including those that would **threaten its business model, future performance, solvency or liquidity**. The directors should describe those risks and explain how they are being managed or mitigated.

- Taking account of the company's current position and principal risks, **the directors should explain in the annual report how they have assessed the prospects of the company**, over what period they have done so and why they consider that period to be appropriate. The directors should state whether they have a reasonable expectation that the company will be able to continue in operation and meet its liabilities as they fall due over the period of their assessment, drawing attention to any qualifications or assumptions as necessary.

- The board should **monitor the company's risk management and internal control systems and, at least annually**, carry out a review of their effectiveness, and report on that review in the annual report. The monitoring and review should cover all material controls, including financial, operational and compliance controls.

The Financial Reporting Council's (2014) Guidance on Risk Management, Internal Control and Related Financial and Business Reporting incorporates recommendations previously found in the **Turnbull Guidance** on **internal controls,** which emphasises that the Board of Directors must:

- Ensure the company has an effective system of internal control, covering financial, operational and compliance controls as well as risk management systems.

- Review the effectiveness of the internal control system in addressing the risks that the Board has identified face the company.

- Report on the internal control system every year (covered later in the chapter).

Shareholders of a company need to feel confident that the Board of Directors are aware of the risks facing the company and has a system in place to monitor and control them. Thus the Board should seek not only to adopt risk controls but also to make the deployment of such controls transparent and visible.

Whether a business thrives or fades is determined partly by how it manages risks and exploits opportunities. Thus risk management is not just a regulatory requirement or a defensive tactic to avoid losses but is integral to seeking and exploiting **competitive advantage.**

2   Introduction to risk management

Section overview

- Effective risk management should involve the implementation of a risk management policy involving all levels of management and staff in the identification, reporting and treatment of risk.

2.1 What is risk management?

Definition

Risk management: The process of identifying and assessing (analysing and evaluating) risks and the development, implementation and monitoring of a strategy to respond to those risks.

A risk management strategy involves the selection, implementation, monitoring and review of suitable risk treatments for each risk identified.

Effective risk management enables a business to:

- Reduce business threats to acceptable levels.
- Make informed decisions about potential opportunities.

This allows stakeholders (investors, lenders, customers, suppliers, employees etc) to have confidence in the business and its future prospects.

2.2 Risk management policy

In business, risk is unavoidable and the strategy must be to reduce risks to acceptable levels. The effect of risk management should be to reduce the probability and/or consequences of any failure whilst retaining, so far as possible, the benefits of successes.

Central to the risk management strategy, therefore, will be the organisation's risk management policy describing its approach to and appetite for risk, along with any legal requirements the business faces such as health and safety legislation.

When implementing any risk management strategy there will need to be an effective system for risk management, risk reporting and communication involving all levels in the business:

- **The board** – who are in a position to take an overall business view and have the authority to demand policies be implemented and adhered to.

- **Managers of the business units** – who are in a position to assess risks from a business unit perspective but also must ensure that risk management policies are implemented.

- **Individuals** – who may need to be aware of or be responsible for managing certain risks.

Risk management strategy needs to be a top-down process to ensure it is integrated across the entire business. In so far as it is possible, the risk treatments should be embedded within the businesses' culture and systems so that it becomes an integral part of the operations and financing of the business. Senior management must translate the risk management strategy into tactical and operational objectives, with managers and employees given the responsibility and authority to deal with such matters.

Examples of risk management policies for a large corporation would include:

- **Corporate codes of conduct**: regulates how managers and staff relate to each other and to outsiders and will seek to control risks from discrimination, bullying, bribery, anti-social behaviour.

- **Environmental policies**: issues such as energy use, emissions, recycling, waste disposal etc.

- **Health and Safety policies**: requiring health & safety officers at all levels, setting up committees, requirement for routine testing and risk assessments, fire procedures.

- **Financial controls**: budgetary control to safeguard earnings and spending, capital expenditure authorisation procedures, financial accounting systems, credit control procedures, cash management procedures, insurance of assets.

- **Information systems controls and cyber security measures**: creation of information officers at all levels, regulations on use by staff, password and access controls, requirements for back-ups and stand-by systems, institution of firewalls and other security programmes.

- **Personnel controls**: policies on identity and background checks on new recruits, discipline and grievance procedures, door entry controls and conventions on wearing of ID, attendance monitoring. Appraisals of staff and management can provide early warnings of stress or potential inability to perform vital tasks.

- **Internal audit processes**: in addition to its familiar role in assuring financial systems in relation to the requirement for a statutory audit, many internal audit functions have an expanded business assurance remit which will report on the adequacy of the controls above.

Many of these policies fulfil other functions too. Here we are concerned with how they are used to mitigate the danger of financial loss to the organisation.

Such financial loss can arise from:

- Litigation from persons injured by the activities of the organisation and its staff.

- Fines from regulatory bodies.

- Loss of assets due to theft or damage.

- Costs of making up for errors, eg, replacing lost data, apologising to injured parties, restoring lost corporate reputation.

- Revenues lost due to breakdowns, eg, factory burned down, operations temporarily grounded by authorities.

- Loss of reputation: customers, suppliers, investors etc lose faith in management.

2.3 Risk management models

The management of risk is an ongoing business process involving continuous identification, assessment, treatment, monitoring and review.

Risk management models are designed to show that risk management is continuous and that it is a logical process. They aim to demonstrate the **interaction and comparison** of risks, as well as the **assessment of individual risks**. Risks change and compliance must be continuous. The management of risk is an ongoing business process involving continuous identification, assessment, treatment, monitoring and review. Though it is most convenient to discuss it as a linear process, it is in reality a circular one with the results of any monitoring and review feeding back into the process to refine the identification, assessment and treatment processes:

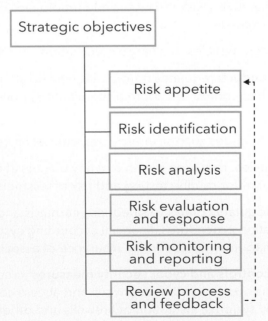

This framework will be used for the rest of this chapter.

3 Risk appetite

Section overview

- Risk appetite considers the extent to which an organisation is prepared to take on risk to achieve its objectives.

- Miles and Snow provide a useful characterisation of firms' attitudes to risk and how it influences their strategies (Defenders, Prospectors, Analysers and Reactors).

- Attitudes to risk will also be influenced by shareholder expectations, the regulatory framework and national and cultural factors.

3.1 What is risk appetite?

An organisation's risk management approach will depend on the appetite it has for bearing risks, which should link in with its business objectives and strategy.

Definition

Risk appetite: Is the extent to which a company is prepared to take on risks to achieve its objectives.

In broad terms we can distinguish **risk averse** attitudes, **risk neutral** attitudes and **risk seeking** attitudes.

Management responses to risk are not automatic but will be determined by their own attitudes to risk, which in turn may be influenced by shareholder attitudes and cultural factors.

3.2 The influence of managerial culture – Miles and Snow

Miles and Snow undertook an in-depth cross-industry analysis of a sample of large corporations from which they developed a theory that there are four strategic types of business, defined by the orientations of their management to strategic challenges.

(a) **Defenders**. Firms with this culture like low risks, secure markets, and tried and trusted solutions. These companies have cultures whose stories and rituals reflect historical continuity and consensus. Decision taking is relatively formalised. (There is a stress on 'doing things right', that is, efficiency.)

(b) **Prospectors** are organisations where the dominant beliefs are more to do with results (doing the right things, that is, effectiveness), and therefore prospectors take risks.

(c) **Analysers** try to balance risk and profits. They use a core of stable products and markets as a source of earnings to move into innovative prospector areas. Analysers follow change, but do not initiate it.

(d) **Reactors**, unlike the three above, do not have viable strategies. Arguably, they do not have a strategy at all, unless it is simply to carry on living from hand to mouth, muddling through. Unlike the other three, which may exhibit superior performance, the Reactor is sub-optimal in its performance.

Their findings suggest that to be superior, there must be a clear and direct match between the organisation's mission/values, the organisation's strategies, and the organisation's characteristics and behaviour.

C
H
A
P
T
E
R

10

3.3 Other influences on risk appetite

Miles and Snow indicate the role of managerial culture in determining a firm's attitude towards the risks of strategic ventures.

Management may be responding to other factors shaping the risk appetite of the organisation. These include:

- **Expectations of shareholders**: if a firm has a long history of stable and unremarkable performance it will attract investors requiring 'blue chip' performance rather than sudden lurches into the unknown.

- **Organisational attitudes:** management may be influenced by significant losses in the past, changes in regulation and best practice, or even changing views of the benefits risk management can bring.

- **National origin of the organisation**: some national cultures exhibit uncertainty avoidance. Surveys suggest that attitudes to risk vary nationally according to how much people are shielded from the consequences of adverse events. National culture is a matter to consider when trying to establish an organisation-wide risk culture: a highly procedural approach, say, that is quite acceptable in the country where the head office is based, may be difficult to implement in other countries.

- **Regulatory framework**: investment firms and banks are required to maintain prudent reserves to display capital adequacy to their regulators. They cannot afford to get involved in too many gambles.

- **Nature of ownership**: the management of state-owned enterprises stand to gain little from successful but risky ventures but they will lose much from unsuccessful ones. Similarly a family firm may be prevented from risk taking by the influence or dependence of family members on the 'family firm' and the potential shame of failure.

- **Personal views**: surveys suggest that managers acknowledge the emotional satisfaction from successful risk-taking, although this is unlikely to be the most important influence on appetite. This has been attributed in part to the fact that, unlike shareholders, they will not suffer a loss of their investment if the decision doesn't pay off.

4 Risk identification

Section overview

- Risk can be categorised in a number of ways, including into strategic, operational, hazard and financial risks. It is important to recognise that such classifications form the overarching term 'entity risk' which is concerned with all risks (controllable and uncontrollable) that affect the organisation.

- Risks may be identified by reference to **risk sources**, ie, risk factors which can lead to variability of outcomes, or **risk events**, ie, events which are known in the industry and for which the contributory factors can be identified and treated.

- A risk description should be prepared for each risk to which the firm is subject.

Risk identification sets out to identify an organisation's exposure to risk.

This requires knowledge of the organisation, the market in which it operates and the legal, social, political and cultural environment in which it exists.

4.1 Types of risk

Before we explore the different types of risk that organisations face it is important to distinguish how the Business Strategy and Technology module classifies the concept of risk when compared to other Professional level modules. In particular the Business Strategy and Technology module defines financial risk more widely than the definitions that you may have seen in your Financial Management studies. Risk can be classified in a number of different ways depending on the perspective from which it is viewed. The list of risks set out below provides a number of possible definitions of risk as it relates to the entity. As we shall see the term 'entity risk' is the overarching umbrella term used to describe all of the possible risks that an organisation may face.

At this point is useful to make the distinction between controllable and uncontrollable risk.

Controllable risks are those risk factors which are within the ability of management to control to some extent. Often controllable risks relate to factors internal to the organisation and may be easy to manage directly, however, this may not always be the case. By contrast, **uncontrollable risks** are outside of the organisation's direct control and tend to be driven by external changes; factors include changes in economic conditions and advances in technology. You need to recognise that controllable and uncontrollable risks are the forms which various risks can take, and are not types of risk themselves.

Entity risks is all of the risks that affect an entity, how it trades, the markets and countries it operates in, the decisions that management make, the operational, strategic, hazard, financial and compliance risks the entity faces. It is important to recognise that 'entity risk' is wider than the term 'business risk'. All of the risks listed below make-up an organisation's entity risk:

- **Business risk** is the variability of returns due to how a business trades or operates, its exposure to markets, competitors, etc.

- **Strategic risk**: Risks associated with the long-term strategic objectives of the business, potential variability of business returns arising as a result of the company's strategy and its strategic position with respect to competitors, customers, reputation, legal or regulatory change, political change. Strategic risk also encompasses knowledge management, ie, the effective management and control of the knowledge resources including key personnel, intellectual property and production technology.

  Note: The risks associated with information systems and knowledge management are dealt with in more detail in Chapter 14.

- **Operational risk**: Variability arising from the effectiveness of how the business is managed and controlled on a day to day basis, the accuracy and effectiveness of its information/accounting systems, its reporting systems and its management and control structures. Operational risk also encompasses compliance with issues such as health and safety, consumer protection etc.

- **Hazard risk**: The exposure a business may have to natural events and their impacts. Such risks may arise from factors outside of the control of the entity. They may also arise from factors that would ordinarily be within the control of the organisation, such as the actions of employees, the consequences of accidents etc, be it on the business, its trading partners or customers.

- **Financial risk** comprises controllable and uncontrollable considerations. The controllable element of financial risk is concerned with how the business chooses to finance itself. Issues cover the entity's choice of finance structure including the level of gearing or leverage, its exposure to credit risk and liquidity risks. The uncontrollable element of financial risk is likely to relate to factors beyond the entity's control such as interest and exchange rates, taxes and the state of economy. These factors may contribute to the risk of business failure; though they can be managed to some extent they cannot be controlled as such by the entity.

Financial risk tends to amplify inherent business risk at low levels of gearing, and at higher levels may directly contribute to the risk of business failure. Uncontrollable elements of financial risk will bear more heavily on firms with operations limited to one country than they will upon a transnational operator.

- **Compliance risk** is the risk arising from non-compliance with laws or regulations. This includes breach of laws/regulations by the company, or breaches by a stakeholder (eg, customer or supplier) which may have consequences for the company. It may relate to financial laws/regulations (eg, contracts, tax, financial reporting, pensions and social security, company law etc) or to non-financial laws/regulations (eg, health and safety, employment law etc).

- **Cyber risk** is any risk of financial loss, disruption or damage to the reputation of an organisation from some sort of failure of its information technology systems.

  The increase in the use of IT in business exposes organisations to a range of threats in which both internal and external groups might attempt to steal confidential data or damage IT infrastructures. Common risks here include hackers, viruses and denial of service attacks. In Chapter 14 we consider the increasing importance of cyber security in tackling these risks.

The tools discussed in earlier chapters for analysing the internal position of a business and its external environment (SWOT, PESTEL, Porter's 5 forces) may be useful in identifying risk.

4.2 Risk identification techniques

Management must identify the types of risk faced by its business. Risk identification must be a continuous process so that management can quickly identify new risks and changes that affect existing risks.

There are two broad approaches:

- **Risk sources**: the cause of potential problems, things (people/activities/events) that may give rise to risk that may trigger an event. These risk sources may be either internal or external to the business as discussed above. Management deals with the source.

- **Risk events (problems)**: specific identified threats or events themselves. Management can attempt to deal with the problem.

 Worked example: Print works

A printing company is conducting a risk assessment of its operations. A fire officer is looking at the machine room:

- Risk source approach: the fire officer sees machine minders smoking and also sees piles of loose discarded paper. Both are risk sources.

- Risk event approach: the fire officer knows that fires in machine rooms are a major cause of loss.

Seeing risks from both ends is complementary. It is obvious that an employee carelessly discarding a cigarette butt into a pile of paper may cause a fire. Using both approaches together will yield insights that neither alone would:

- **Risk source**: there are more risks arising from smoking than just fire. For example to the health of the employee and to passive smokers, using machines one-handed, triggering respiratory attacks in colleagues. Firms could face litigation from the effects of any of these. In fact, in the UK and many other European countries it is now illegal to smoke in any work place or public place. Similarly, loose paper or can cause people to slip over, conceal health hazards, offer potential for good work to be thrown out along with scrap in a hasty tidy-up.

- **Risk event**: fires are caused by more than physical sources and their effects depend on how they are handled. The officer might consider whether evacuation procedures are in place, whether extinguishers are regularly tested, whether smoke vents have been fitted to the roof. This assessment would enable management of risks arising from more than smoking such as electrical faults causing fires or poisonous fumes from chemical spillages.

4.3 Risk register

Organisations should have formal methods of collecting information on risk and response. A risk register **lists and prioritises the main risks** an organisation faces, and is used as the basis for decision-making on how to deal with risks. The register may also detail **who is responsible for dealing** with risks and the **actions taken**. The register may show the risk levels **before** and **after** control action is taken, to facilitate a cost benefit analysis of controls.

A risk register can be used to facilitate the identification and assessment of risks and may include:

- Description of the risk.

- Scope of the risk – description of the events giving rise to the risk, their likelihood and the possible impacts of the risk.

- Nature of the risk – ie, financial, strategic, operational, hazard.

- Parties affected – both internal and external parties and how they will be influenced.

- Quantification of the risk – the probability and scale of any losses or gains, possibly including Value at Risk assessments.

- Risk tolerance/appetite – level of risk considered acceptable for this matter.

- Risk treatment and control – the means by which the risk is managed at present and an assessment of the current risk controls in force.

- Potential action for improvement – recommendations about further risk reduction options.

- Strategy and policy developments – identification of function responsible for developing strategy and policy.

Note: Only the first four of these can be completed at this risk identification stage, the remainder are completed as the process continues.

5 Risk analysis

Section overview

- Once risks have been identified, the organisation needs to understand and assess the scale of the risk. This can be done by risk assessment and profiling.

- The organisation's likely exposure to loss can be assessed by quantitative or non-quantitative methods for risk assessment and prioritisation.

- The result of this should be a risk profile of the firm which management can use to set priorities for risk mitigation.

5.1 Risk assessment

Definition

Risk assessment: Involves establishing the financial consequences of each risk event (severity) and its likelihood of occurrence (frequency).

In many cases the financial consequences are easy to measure, eg, the value of lost inventories or the cost of rebuilding premises, although it may not be until after an event that the full cost of a loss can be recognised.

Some consequences may be more awkward, particularly where loss of life is concerned.

The assessment of the probability of occurrence is often more problematic, particularly for the less likely events such as natural disasters.

Risk estimation can be quantitative, semi-quantitative or qualitative in terms of the probability of occurrence and the possible consequence.

Quantitative risk assessment involves the determination of measured figures for probabilities and consequences producing a specifically quantified measure of likelihood and of impact.

Some types of risk lend themselves to this process. Insurance companies have detailed statistical information on the occurrence of many risk events. They also have detailed estimates of the cost of repairing the insured loss, of say a car or house.

Others are very difficult to assess. For example, the impact of an event on the reputation of a business is much harder to quantify, and from this perspective risk assessment is more subjective.

Worked example: Buying new aircraft

The decision to purchase new aircraft is a major decision for an airline. In recent years, many transnational airlines have needed to replace or expand their fleets. The investments were worth billions of pounds and the lifetime of the aircraft they were buying was 25 years. The airlines have faced a number of developments which could affect their decisions, including:

- National carbon taxes on airlines according to the CO_2 emissions from the planes.

- The possibility that they could buy or sell licences to pollute.

- Locally decided restrictions on noise where each airline would get a certain number of noise units per airport.

- The possibility that surplus noise units could be bought and sold.

However, there was uncertainty over the likelihood of these developments being introduced, and about their potential impact. Different countries could choose different policies and rates of charges, and some could even vary from airport to airport within a country according to the power of local stakeholders.

The planes the airlines were evaluating differed in their noise, fuel use and emissions. Choosing the wrong plane could impose financial risk from fewer flights, increased costs, lost opportunities to sell permits, defection of ecologically concerned passengers and exclusion from some countries.

One major airline based its decision on an NPV calculation into which the cost increases and savings etc, of each potential risk had been entered based on a subjective assessment of the likelihood of its occurrence in each country, its timing, and its potential financial impact. This was constructed as a model on an Excel spreadsheet with cost lines for each of the 120 destinations the airline intended to serve, reflecting the assumptions the airline had made about the likelihood and impact of the carbon and noise taxes at that destination.

It conducted the same exercise for its 150 existing planes to decide which to phase out first. Taking a systematic approach based on informed assumptions helped the airline to assess the risks that it faced.

5.2 Risk profiling

The result of the risk analysis process is an overall risk profile detailing each of the risks along with an estimate of the risk to the company. This risk profile ranks each identified risk so as to give a view of the relative importance, forming the primary tool for prioritising and addressing risks.

One way of doing this is to use a severity/frequency matrix (also known as a likelihood/consequences matrix).

		Severity	
		Low	High
Frequency	Low	Loss of small suppliers	Loss of senior or specialist staff Loss of sales to competitor Loss of sales due to macroeconomic factors
	High	Loss of lower-level staff	Loss of key customers Failure of computer systems

This profile can then be used to set priorities for risk mitigation. Clearly risks categorised as high frequency and high severity should be prioritised and dealt with first.

The risk profile will

- Describe the risk and the business area affected.

- Describe the primary control procedures in place.

- Indicate areas where the level of risk control investment might be increased, decreased or reapportioned.

The similarity of this to the techniques used in auditing a company's accounts will be obvious to you. This is because audit risk is an example of the sorts of more general risks discussed in this chapter.

Interactive question 1: Identification of risks facing an airline

As a consultant specialising in risk management, you have been appointed by the Director of Corporate Development (DCD) to undertake a comprehensive review of the risks facing SkyWays Airlines (SWA) as a precursor to the latest strategic planning process.

You are told that the extended supply chain of SWA makes it reliant on suppliers of fuel, aircraft parts, air traffic control etc. SWA has increased its borrowings this year and its liquidity ratio has fallen below one and it has negligible retained earnings. It has also experienced increased dissatisfaction from employees as a result of voluntary redundancies arising from moving to a new more efficient terminal and, apparently, the loss of control over them by the decline in influence of the trade unions.

Requirement

1.1 From the information provided and your knowledge of the industry, prepare a report identifying the range of externally driven risks to which SWA is subject and any internally driven risks. Suggest appropriate improvements to controls for the risks you identify.

See **Answer** at the end of this chapter.

6 Evaluating and addressing risk

Section overview

- Risks are evaluated according to significance. The most significant and most probable risks will be prioritised for treatment.

- The possible strategies for dealing with a risk are avoidance, reduction, transfer or retention.

- The chosen response is likely to depend on the significance of the risk and the specific risk appetites of management.

6.1 Risk evaluation

Definition

Risk evaluation: The process by which an organisation determines the significance of any risk and whether those risks need to be addressed.

Risk evaluation should be carried out both for:

- New business proposals and changes to operations
- Existing business operations

Once risk analysis has been completed for these operations and the businesses risk tolerance established and accounted for, management should compare the identified risks to the risk criteria established by the business. This will allow them to make decisions about the significance of the risks to the organisation and whether each specific risk should be accepted or treated.

This risk criteria is liable to include a consideration of such factors as costs and benefits, legal requirements, socioeconomic and environmental factors, concerns of stakeholders, etc.

Interactive question 2: Risk assessment of outsourcing cleaning

The management of a state-funded hospital is considering outsourcing the cleaning of its premises. This will mean private firms taking over as employers of existing cleaning staff and assuming responsibility for the cleaning of the areas around beds, corridors and communal spaces.

Increases in incidents of infections during hospital stays by patients, some resulting in death, has been widely attributed by the media to poor hospital hygiene. Several legal cases for compensation have been decided against hospitals on the grounds of negligence by management.

Requirement

2.1 What factors should management consider in evaluating the proposal to outsource its cleaning?

See **Answer** at the end of this chapter.

6.2 Addressing risk

Addressing risk involves the selection of procedures to monitor, control and mitigate the effects of risk. The possible approaches to the treatment of risk are:

- Avoidance (Abandon)
- Reduction
- Transfer
- Retention (Accept)

The ideal use of these strategies may not be possible, however, as some of them may involve trade-offs that are not acceptable to the business making the risk management decisions.

Risk response can be linked into the severity/frequency matrix, discussed earlier and also the organisation's **appetite** for risk-taking.

Severity

		Low	High
Frequency	Low	**Retain or accept** Risks are not significant. Keep under view, but costs of dealing with risks unlikely to be worth the benefits.	**Transfer** Insure risk or implement contingency plans. Reduction of severity of risk will minimise insurance premiums.
	High	**Control or reduce** Take some action, eg, enhanced control systems to detect problems or contingency plans to reduce impact	**Avoid or abandon** Take immediate action, eg, changing major suppliers or abandoning activities.

6.2.1 Risk avoidance

Risk avoidance means not undertaking or terminating an activity that carries risk. Examples of this would be not entering a contract with many contingencies, or not buying a business to avoid any potential tax consequences. Avoidance may seem to be the obvious answer to all risks, but avoiding risks also means losing out on the potential return or profit associated with it.

6.2.2 Risk reduction

Risk reduction means retaining the activity in the business whilst undertaking actions to constrain the risk to acceptable levels, establishing systems and procedures to mitigate the effects or probability of any risk. Risk reduction examples include alarm systems to warn of a fire or sprinkler systems to reduce its effects.

Mitigating controls include:

- **Preventative controls**: controls designed to minimise the probability of occurrence of an undesired event. Many of the usual business internal controls such as segregation of duties, authorisation limits etc, fall into this category. A non-financial example is that no smoking rules reduce the probability of fires.

- **Corrective controls**: controls designed to correct the effects of an undesired event, such as the fire sprinkler system.

- **Directive controls**: controls designed to ensure a particular outcome is achieved, especially in the context of security or Health and Safety. For example protective clothing may be obligatory when undertaking certain tasks.

- **Detective controls**: detective controls are designed to identify the occurrence of risk events. Examples would include alarm systems for fire and security purposes, financial reconciliations, inventory checks.

6.2.3 Risk transfer

Risk transfer is the transfer of the risk to a third party either contractually or by hedging. Insurance is a contractual method of transferring risk as are many outsourcing contracts. Financial risks, on the other hand, tend to be hedged through the use of offsetting derivatives positions or contractual arrangements.

6.2.4 Risk retention

Risk retention involves tolerating the loss when it arises. All risks that are not avoided or transferred fall into this category. Many risks are tolerable without any further action being taken. Risk retention is a viable strategy for small risks where the cost of insuring against the risk would be greater than the total losses sustained over time. This may be described as **self-insurance**.

Risk retention is also the only treatment for some uninsurable risks such as the effects of war. In this situation, the decision to tolerate the risk may, however, be supplemented by contingency planning to mitigate its effects.

Furthermore, for most insured risks there is an excess which counts as a retained risk, as would any amount of a potential loss in excess of the insured sum

6.2.5 Other considerations

Any system of risk treatment should, as a minimum, provide:

- Effective and efficient operation of the organisation
- Effective internal controls
- Compliance with laws and regulations

The effectiveness of an internal control can be assessed based on the degree to which it will either reduce or eliminate the associated risk. It is important, however, that the control put in place is proportional to the risk. The cost effectiveness of internal control, therefore, relates to the cost of implementing the control compared to the risk reduction benefits expected.

Compliance with laws and regulations is not optional; legal or regulatory breaches may result in severe penalties for a business. An organisation must understand the applicable laws and must implement a system of controls to achieve compliance.

Interactive question 3: Managing risks in an oil company

A multinational oil company is considering exploiting the gas and oil reserves in a country where the national government has a history of suddenly seizing control of foreign assets and of introducing taxes to ensure all the profits are taken away.

Requirement

3.1 Prepare a risk register for what you consider to be the **three** most significant political risks to the oil company. Use a table with three columns, for each risk which explains:

- The nature of the risk
- The possible impact of the risk and likelihood of it occurring
- Possible risk management procedures

See **Answer** at the end of this chapter.

7 Risk monitoring, reviewing and reporting

Section overview

- The nature of risks and the adequacy of the risk management strategies will change over time.

- For this reason management should not treat risk management as a one-off exercise but instead set up systems to regularly monitor, review and report on risk (embedded risk management).

- Managing risk requires that organisations have procedures to detect lessons and to learn from them.

7.1 Systems to monitor, review and report on risk

Management must establish systems for the monitoring and review for two important reasons:

- To monitor the effectiveness of the current risk management processes.
- To monitor whether the risk profile is changing or not.

Processes should be put in place to review whether risks still exist, whether new risks have arisen or whether the likelihood or impact of a risk has changed. These processes should report significant changes that impact on risk priorities. These should be embedded into the normal reporting procedures of the company so risk management is regularly reported alongside other reporting practices such as monthly management accounting reports (embedded risk management).

In addition, the overall risk profile should be reviewed on a regular basis to give assurance that there are appropriate controls in place for the organisation's current activities and that the controls are understood and followed.

7.2 Examples of risk monitoring processes

Examples of risk monitoring processes include:

- Regular review of projects against specific costs and completion milestones.

- Systems of notification of incidents (eg, accidents at work, near misses of aircraft).

- Internal audit functions (eg, financial, systems security, compliance with health and safety).

- Employment of compliance monitoring staff.

- Skills assessment and medical examinations of staff and managers to assure competence and fitness to work.

- Practices and drills to confirm readiness (eg, fire drills, evacuations, disruption to operations).

- Use of embedded IT 'intelligent agents' to monitor risks (eg, bad debts, unusual costs or revenue entries, attempts to access restricted files).

- Intelligence gathering on occurrences elsewhere (eg, experiences of frauds, equipment failures, outcomes of legal cases).

- Monitoring of the regulatory framework of the industry to ensure compliance.

The monitoring and review process should also establish whether:

- The controls adopted achieved the desired result.

- The procedures adopted and information gathered for undertaking the assessment were appropriate.

- Improved knowledge would have helped to reach better decisions, identifying what lessons could be learned for future assessments.

Interactive question 4: Risk monitoring in a fast-food restaurant

4.1 What risk monitoring systems should be established by the management of a global fast-food restaurant chain?

See **Answer** at the end of this chapter.

7.3 Feedback, communication and learning

Organisations are dynamic and operate in dynamic environments. Changes in the organisation and the environment in which it operates must be identified and appropriate modifications made to systems. Thus communication and learning is not a separate stage in the risk management process, rather it is something that must be in place and operating effectively at every stage of the process.

- **Learning from experience**: it is important that the effectiveness or otherwise of the planned risk management process is thoroughly reviewed and critically appraised so that risk plans can be revised as necessary in the light of anything learned, eg, an IT department learning from restoring systems after a breakdown, an office learning from regular fire drills, emergency services learning from actual or simulated call-outs.

- **Constant updating**: in a dynamic business the risks will be in a state of continuous flux. Management must ensure systems exist to identify any new risks or changes in risks As a result, the risk management process must be a continuous ongoing one where risks are continuously being assessed and plans continuously refined (especially in light of the occurrence of any risk events) eg, money laundering practices change continuously as do the penalties for infringement of the law. The experiences of different divisions or offices must be shared.

Effective and efficient communication is vital for the business as it is essential that:

- Everyone in the risk management process is fully familiar with its importance to the business, the risk priorities of the business and their role within the process. Without this, risk priorities may be misinterpreted and risk controls may not be correctly integrated into business systems.

- Knowledge gleaned from any new risks identified by one area of the business or any lessons learnt from risk events is transferred to all other areas of the business in a considered and consistent manner, so that it can be correctly incorporated into the business-wide risk management strategy.

- All levels of management are regularly updated about the management of risk in their areas of responsibility, to enable them to monitor the adequacy and completeness of any risk plans and controls.

- There are procedures in place for escalation of any issues arising.

7.4 External considerations

No organisation operates in isolation; they all have trading partners/customers/suppliers.

Communication of risk issues with business partners is essential, especially when one business is dependent on another. Differing risk priorities mean that a partner may not have the requisite policies and systems in place to satisfy our own risk appetite. Management must gain assurance that its major partners have implemented an adequate and appropriate risk management strategy.

All business stakeholders are concerned by risk and so it is important that the business communicates the way it is managing risks. It is equally important that any business manages stakeholders' expectations on the subject of risk management through regular communication.

7.5 Reporting on risk management

The Financial Reporting Council's (2014) Guidance on Risk Management, Internal Control and Related Financial and Business Reporting states that the board has responsibility for an organisation's overall approach to risk management and internal control. The board should report in the annual report and accounts on its review of the effectiveness of the company's risk management and internal control systems. In its statement the board should, as a minimum, acknowledge: that it is responsible for those systems and for reviewing their effectiveness.

Section 2 of the Financial Reporting Council's (2014) Guidance entitled 'Board Responsibilities for Risk Management and Internal Control' highlights that the board's responsibilities include:

- The design and implementation of appropriate risk management and internal control systems that identify the risks facing the company and enable the board to make a robust assessment of the principal risks.

- Determining the nature and extent of the principal risks faced and those risks which the organisation is willing to take in achieving its strategic objectives (determining its "risk appetite").

- Ensuring that appropriate culture and reward systems have been embedded throughout the organisation.

- Agreeing how the principal risks should be managed or mitigated to reduce the likelihood of their incidence or their impact.

The assessment and processes set out in the Financial Reporting Council's (2014) Guidance should be used coherently to inform a number of distinct but related disclosures in the annual report and accounts.

These are set out in section 6 of the Financial Reporting Council's (2014) Guidance:

- Reporting on the principal risks facing the company and how they are managed or mitigated (as required by the Companies Act 2006 (the "Companies Act") and the Code.)

- Reporting on whether the directors have a reasonable expectation that the company will be able to continue in operation and meet its liabilities as they fall due (as required by the Code.)

- Reporting on the going concern basis of accounting (as required by accounting standards and the Code.)

- Reporting on the review of the risk management and internal control system (as required by the Code), and the main features of the company's risk management and internal control system in relation to the financial reporting process (as required under the UK Listing Authority's Disclosure and Transparency Rules.)

The purpose of such reporting is to provide information about the company's current position and prospects and the principal risks it faces. It helps to demonstrate the board's stewardship and governance, and encourages shareholders to perform their own stewardship role by engaging in appropriate dialogue with the board and holding the directors to account as necessary.

The system recommended by the FRC's (2014) Guidance is notable because of the following.

- It is forward looking.

- It is open, requiring appropriate disclosures to all stakeholders in the company about the risks being taken.

- It does not seek to eliminate risk. It is constructive in its approach to opportunity management, as well as concerned with 'disaster prevention'. To succeed companies are not required to take fewer risks than others but they do need a good understanding of what risks they can handle.

- It is strategic, and driven by business objectives, particularly the need for the company to adapt to its changing business environment.

- It should be re-evaluated on a regular basis.

- It should be durable, evolving as the business and its environment changes.

- To create shareholder value, a company needs to manage the risks it faces and communicate to the capital markets how it is carrying out this task. Communication of risks helps shareholders make informed decisions – remember shareholders are prepared to tolerate risk provided they receive an acceptable level of return. It will also provide more confidence in the company and hence lower the required return of shareholders and lenders. However this will be balanced against the need to avoid excessive disclosures to competitors.

Interactive question 5: Ferry

You are a senior manager in the internal audit department of Ferry.

In July 20X0, Ferry purchased exclusive rights to operate a car and passenger ferry route until December 20X9. This offers an alternative to driving an additional 150 kilometres via the nearest bridge crossing. There have been several ambitious plans to build another crossing but they have failed through lack of public support and government funds.

Ferry refurbished two 20-year old roll on, roll off ('Ro-Ro') boats to service the route. The boats do not yet meet the emission standards of Environmental Protection Regulations which come into force in two years' time, in 20X6. Each boat makes three return crossings every day of the year, subject to weather conditions, and has the capacity to carry approximately 250 passengers and 40 vehicles. The ferry service carried 70,000 vehicles in the year to 31 December 20X3 (20X2: 58,000 vehicles; 20X1: 47,000 vehicles).

Hot and cold refreshments and travel booking facilities are offered on the one hour crossing. These services are provided by independent businesses on a franchise basis.

Ferry currently receives a subsidy from the local transport authority as an incentive to increase market awareness of the ferry service and its efficient and timely operation. The subsidy increases as the number of vehicles carried increases and is based on quarterly returns submitted to the authority. Ferry employs 20 full-time crew members who are trained in daily operations and customer-service, as well as passenger safety in the event of personal accident, collision or breakdown.

The management of Ferry is planning to apply for a recognised Safety Management Certificate (SMC) in 20X5. This will require a ship audit including the review of safety documents and evidence that activities are performed in accordance with documented procedures. A SMC valid for five years will be issued if no major non-conformities have been found.

Requirements

5.1 Identify and explain the risks facing Ferry which should be assessed.

5.2 Describe the processes by which the risks identified in 5.1 could be managed and maintained at an acceptable level by Ferry.

See **Answer** at the end of this chapter.

8 Risk and uncertainty in decision-making: sensitivity, break-even analysis and relevant cash flows

Section overview

- Business decisions are based on estimates and forecasts which are subject to varying degrees of uncertainty.

- The business can increase its confidence in a decision by trying to reduce uncertainty, using techniques such as sensitivity analysis and break-even. Techniques such as these could easily be examined in the Business Strategy and Technology exam, as a result you should ensure that you spend sufficient time when going through the content in this section.

- Scenario building can be used to develop contingency plans to cope with risks and as a prediction technique.

- Cash flows provide an alternative approach to addressing uncertainty when making business decisions as they more closely reflect the impact on shareholders' wealth than traditional profit related measures. Relevant cash flows are those which are affected by the decision. Opportunity costs reflect the cash foregone as a consequence of using resources.

8.1 Techniques for dealing with uncertainty

A business can build confidence into its decisions by reducing uncertainty.

Techniques for dealing with decision making under situations of risk and uncertainty include:

- Making prudent estimates of outcomes to assess the worst possible situation, eg, at what level of sales would the business become loss-making (break-even).

- Assessing the best and worst possible outcomes to obtain a range of outcomes: thus, in assessing a business plan received from a company seeking finance, the bank or investor may want to consider the best and worst possible scenarios.

- Using sensitivity analysis to measure the impact of changes in forecast estimates eg, by considering for example how much fixed costs could increase before the business failed to meet its profit target, or by measuring the margin of safety associated with the current level of operations (see below).

8.2 Sensitivity analysis

In its simplest form sensitivity analysis involves changing the value of one variable to test its impact on the final result. The sensitivity could be with respect to the break-even position, but this need not be the case.

Sensitivity analysis is an attempt at priority setting. By looking at how sensitive results are to changes in assumptions, it allows an organisation to ascertain which parameters will have the biggest impact on a decision and therefore which ones need to be forecast most accurately.

Various mathematical techniques exist for performing sensitivity analysis. Eg, in Financial Management you will look at sensitivity in the context of project evaluation and net present values.

On a practical level however, sensitivity analysis can be seen as a technique that allows an organisation to consider the range of possible outcomes by asking 'what if?' type questions. For example:

- What will happen to profits if the price of components increases by 10%?
- What would happen to demand and profit if the selling price were to be increased by 15%?
- What would happen to sales revenue if the business's market share drops by 5% etc?

Using sensitivity analysis a business can only consider changes in one variable or parameter at a time and therefore it does not allow for the interaction between variables. Techniques such as simulation remedy some of the shortcomings of sensitivity analysis by allowing the simultaneous change of values for key variables in the decision.

In determining whether to go ahead with a new product, or whether to create a new overseas subsidiary, the business may want to consider how much margin of safety exists between planned and break-even sales.

Worked example: Sensitivity analysis

Sensivite Ltd has estimated the following sales and profits for a new product which it may launch on to the market.

	£	£
Sales (2,000 units)		4,000
Variable costs: materials	2,000	
labour	1,000	
		3,000
Contribution		1,000
Less incremental fixed costs		800
Profit		200

Requirement

Analyse the sensitivity of the project.

Solution

(a) If incremental **fixed costs** are more than 25% above estimate, the project would make a loss.

(b) If **unit costs of materials** are more than 10% above estimate, the project would make a loss.

(c) Similarly, the project would be sensitive to an **increase in unit labour costs** of more than £200, which is 20% above estimate, or else to a drop in the **unit selling price** of more than 5%.

(d) The **margin of safety**, given a break-even point of 1,600 units, is (400/2,000) × 100% = 20%.

Management would then be able to judge more clearly whether the product is likely to be profitable. The items to which profitability is most sensitive in this example are the selling price

(5%) and material costs (10%). Sensitivity analysis can help to **concentrate management attention** on the most important factors.

Weaknesses of sensitivity analysis include:

- It only examines the risks relating to one variable at a time. Changes in more than one variable are likely to occur simultaneously, particularly where they are interrelated.

- It measures the extent of the change needed before break-even is reached, but not the probability of this occurring. In the above example, to reach break-even it would take a 20% movement in sales volume, but only a 10% movement in material cost. Nevertheless, a 20% movement in sales volume may be far more likely to occur than the 10% movement in material cost and may therefore be the greater risk.

8.3 Break-even analysis and margin of safety

The examiner has highlighted the need for candidates attempting the Business Strategy and Technology exam to be comfortable with break-even and margin of safety calculations as they could easily form the basis of a question requirement in the exam.

A simple method of evaluating one aspect of risk is break-even analysis. This technique is, in essence, a measure of the sensitivity of profit to changes in output.

The break-even point occurs where total sales revenue equals total costs. The below chart shows the relationship between the different kinds of costs, revenue, profits and losses.

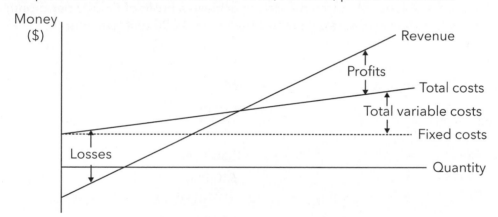

$$\text{Break-even point:} \quad \frac{\text{Fixed costs}}{\text{Sales revenue per unit - variable costs per unit}}$$

The bottom part of this formula, sales revenue-variable costs, is known as the **contribution per unit.**

The **margin of safety** is the extent to which the planned volume of output or sales lies above the break-even point.

The relationship between contribution and fixed costs is known as **operational gearing**. An activity with high fixed costs compared with its variable costs is said to have high operational gearing. Increasing the level of operational gearing makes profits more sensitive to changes in the volume of activity.

The calculations are derived as follows:

Total contribution – Total fixed costs	=	Profit
Total contribution	=	Contribution per unit × output

At the break-even point:

Total contribution	=	Total fixed costs

Thus:

Contribution per unit × output   =   Total fixed costs

Therefore:

break-even output $= \dfrac{\text{Total fixed costs}}{\text{Contribution per unit}}$

To achieve a required level of profit (say £10,000) then:

Required output $= \dfrac{\text{Total fixed costs} + £10,000}{\text{Contribution per unit}}$

Margin of safety $= \dfrac{\text{Planned output} - \text{Break-even output}}{\text{Planned output}}$

The greater the margin of safety, the less sensitive the profits to a sudden fall in volume.

Worked example: Break-even

Selling price per unit	£10
Variable cost per unit	£6
Fixed costs	£10,000 per month

Requirements

(a) Calculate the break-even volume per month.
(b) Calculate the volume of output needed to achieve a profit of £2,000 per month.
(c) Calculate the margin of safety if planned sales are 4,000 units per month.

Solution

(a) Contribution per unit   =   £4

Break-even $= \dfrac{£10,000}{£4}$

=   2,500 units

(b) Output $= \dfrac{£10,000 + £2,000}{£4}$

=   3,000 units

(c) Margin of safety $= \dfrac{4,000 - 2,500}{4000}$

=   37.5%

8.3.1 Popularity and weaknesses of break-even analysis

Break-even analysis provides useful insights into the relationship between an organisation's fixed costs, variable costs and level of activity. It is a widely-used and popular planning tool.

There are, however, three main problems associated with break-even analysis.

- **Non-linear relationships**. Break-even assumes linear (straight line) relationships. This is unlikely in real life.

- **Stepped fixed costs**. Most fixed costs are not fixed over **all** volumes of activity and are more likely to be stepped.

- **Multi-product businesses**. Most businesses offer more than one product or service. It may be hard to identify which fixed costs belongs to which product, and the effect that the sale of one product may have on the sales of another.

8.4 Scenario building

Scenario planning was discussed in Chapter 4.

Scenarios are used in two situations.

1. **To develop contingency plans** to cope with the arrival of threats or risks which, although they may arise at any time, are of indeterminable probability. For example, a chemicals company may develop a scenario of a major spillage at one of its plants and then set up emergency routines to cope with it. They cannot assess how likely the spillage is to occur in actual practice.

2. **As a prediction technique**: a series of alternative pictures of a future operating environment are developed which are consistent with current trends and consistent within themselves. The impact of each different scenario upon the business is assessed and specific risks highlighted. Contingency plans are drawn up to implement in the event of a given scenario coming true, or to implement now to give protection against the scenario.

Approaches to choosing scenarios as a basis for decisions are as follows:

Assume the most probable: this would seem common sense but puts too much faith in the scenario process and guesswork. Also, a less probable scenario may be one whose failure to occur would have the worst consequences for the firm.

Hope for the best: a firm designs a strategy based on the scenario most attractive to the firm. Wishful thinking is usually not the right approach.

Hedge: the firm chooses the strategy that produces satisfactory results under all scenarios. Hedging, however, is not optimal for any scenario. The low risk is paid for by a low reward.

Flexibility: the firm plays a 'wait and see' game. This means that the firm waits to follow others. It is more secure, but sacrifices first-mover advantages.

Influence: a firm will try to influence the future, for example by influencing demand for related products so that its favoured scenario will be realised in events as they unfold.

8.5 Relevant cash flows

In the Business Strategy and Technology exam you will not be required to prepare a net present value (NPV) calculation. You may however be required to evaluate whether the organisation featured in a question should undertake a proposed business strategy, eg, whether or not to enter into a proposed contract. Part of your evaluation may require you to consider the relevant cash flows of the contract to decide on its viability.

Definition

Relevant cash flows: Future, incremental, cash flows arising from the decision being made.

Relevant cash flows provide management with an alternative approach to making business decisions. Relevant cash flows can assist management in better understanding the uncertainty relating to different courses of action.

The relevant cash flow is the difference between:

*   the cash flow if the course of action is taken
*   the cash flow if it is not

The assessment of relevant cash flows needs to be done from the point of view of the business as a whole and not individual divisions or departments.

Typical items which are **excluded** from the analysis as irrelevant are discussed below:

- **Sunk costs** – money already spent eg, when trying to determine whether an existing machine which cost £250,000 three years ago should be used on a new project, the analysis should ignore the £250,000 as nothing can be done about it; instead, the machine's current worth (either scrap value or cash benefits from retention) should be included.

- **Accounting entries that do not have a cash flow impact** – eg, depreciation is not a cash flow.

- **Unavoidable costs** – money already committed eg, a non-cancellable lease or **apportioned** fixed costs. As far as fixed costs are concerned it is the total amount of cash expenditure which is important (not any attempt to spread the fixed cost ie, apportionment). If the **total** changes, then this is relevant; if not, the fixed costs are ignored as they are unaffected by the decision. For example, if a firm can make a new product within its existing rented factory, then any share of the rent apportioned to the new product should be ignored as the **total** rent bill is unchanged. However, if a new factory needs to be rented, then the **additional** rent is relevant in the appraisal of the new product.

- **Finance costs** – eg, interest. If the firm has undertaken a discounted cash flow (DCF analysis), the discount rate will already reflect the cost of capital, including interest costs.

Specifically **include**:

- all opportunity costs and revenues

8.6 Opportunity costs and revenues

Definition

Opportunity cost: The cash flow foregone if a unit of the resource is used on the contract/project instead of in the best alternative way.

If there are scarcities of resources to be used on contracts/projects (eg, labour, materials, machines), then consideration must be given to revenues which could have been earned from alternative uses of the resources.

- Shareholders are concerned with the cash flows generated by the whole organisation in terms of assessing their impact on their wealth.

- The cash flows of a single department or division cannot therefore be looked at in isolation. It is always the cash flows of the whole organisation that must be considered.

- **For example**, the skilled labour needed for the new contract/project may have to be withdrawn from normal production, causing a loss in contribution. This is obviously relevant to the contract/project appraisal.

Worked example: Relevant cost of material

A new contract requires the use of 50 tonnes of metal ZX 81. This metal is used regularly on all the firm's projects. At the moment there are in inventory 100 tonnes of ZX 81, which were bought for £200 per tonne. The current purchase price is £210 per tonne, and the metal could be disposed of for net scrap proceeds of £150 per tonne.

With what cost should the new contract be charged for the ZX 81?

Solution

The use of the material in inventory for the new contract means that more ZX 81 must be bought for normal workings. The cost to the organisation is therefore the money spent on purchase, no matter whether existing inventory or new inventory is used on the contract.

Assuming that the additional purchases are made in the near future, the relevant cost to the organisation is current purchase price ie, 50 tonnes × £210 = £10,500.

Interactive question 6: Material with no alternative use

Suppose the organisation has no alternative use for the ZX 81 in inventory.

6.1 What is the relevant cost of using it on the new contract?

See **Answer** at the end of this chapter.

Interactive question 7: Material with a scrap value

7.1 Suppose again there is no alternative use for the ZX 81 other than a scrap sale, but that there are only 25 tonnes in inventory.

See **Answer** at the end of this chapter.

Worked example: Relevant cost of labour

A mining operation uses skilled labour costing £8 per hour, which generates a contribution of £6 per hour, after deducting these labour costs.

A new project is now being considered which requires 5,000 hours of skilled labour. There is a shortage of the required labour. Any used on the new project must be transferred from normal working.

Requirement

What is the relevant cost of using the skilled labour on the project?

Solution

What is lost if the labour is transferred from normal working?

	£
Contribution per hour lost from normal working	6
Labour cost per hour which is not saved	8
Cash lost per hour as a result of the labour transfer	14
The relevant cost of skilled labour is 5,000 × £14	£70,000

Interactive question 8: Relevant cost of surplus labour

8.1 Facts as in the previous Worked Example, but there is a surplus of skilled labour sufficient to cope with the new project. The idle workers are being paid full wages.

See **Answer** at the end of this chapter.

8.7 Deprival value of assets

When an asset which is currently owned by the business is required for another specific contract/project, the existing activity is to be deprived of that asset. The loss to the business from the existing activity being deprived of use of the asset is the deprival value. The value to be used in quantifying the financial impact of the contract/project is the asset's deprival value.

This can be summarised as follows:

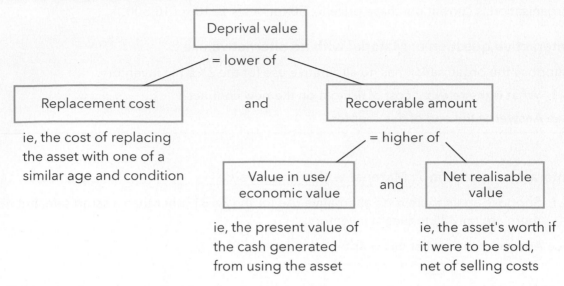

- If the asset has a net realisable value in excess of its economic value it should be sold ie, it is better to sell it than keep on using it. If the economic value is higher than the net realisable value, it is worth keeping and using. At this point, therefore, were the firm to be deprived of the asset, the best alternative foregone is the higher of the net realisable value or economic value (the 'recoverable amount').

- However, if the recoverable amount is less than the replacement cost, then the recoverable amount is the deprival value ie, the asset would not be replaced were the firm to be deprived of its use. If the recoverable amount exceeds the replacement cost, the asset should be replaced as the latter represents its deprival value.

Interactive question 9: Deprival value

JX Ltd. owns a machine purchased two years ago for £2,000. A similar machine would now cost £1,000. The machine could be sold for £1,000 after spending £100 on advertising. The machine has two years of life remaining, and over this period the cost of renting the machine instead would be a present value of £800.

Requirement

9.1 What is the deprival value of the machine?

See **Answer** at the end of this chapter.

9 Probability, expected values and decision trees

Section overview

- Probability is a measure of likelihood, and expected values are weighted average values based on probabilities. These calculations and values are incorporated into decision trees to illustrate the possible choices and outcomes of decisions.

Decision trees can be very helpful tools for making strategic and operational decisions. Each branch of the tree represents the different outcomes that may occur. For the decision tree to be useful, each outcome should be assigned a probability and an expected value. This is so that we can evaluate how likely each outcome is to occur, and what will be achieved should that outcome actually occur. Let us first recap the basic concepts of probability and expected values before we go on to look at how these can assist decision making by incorporating them into decision trees.

9.1 Probability

Probability is a measure of **likelihood** and can be stated as a percentage, a ratio, or more usually as a number from 0 to 1. It is a measure of the likelihood of an event happening in the long run, or over a large number of times.

$$\text{Probability of achieving the desired result} = \frac{\text{Number of ways of achieving desired result}}{\text{Total number of possible outcomes}}$$

Mutually exclusive outcomes are outcomes where the occurrence of one of the outcomes excludes the possibility of any of the others happening, for example, you can't roll one dice and score both five and six simultaneously.

The probability of mutually exclusive events occurring can be calculated by adding the probabilities together. For example, the probability of rolling a dice once and scoring either a five or a six can be determined by adding together the probability of rolling five and the probability of rolling six.

1/6 + 1/6 = 2/6

Independent events are events where the outcome of one event in no way affects the outcome of the other events. For example, simultaneously rolling a dice and tossing a coin. The probability of both throwing a five and getting heads on the coin can be found by multiplying the probabilities of the two individual events.

$1/6 \times 1/2 = 1/12$

The **general rule of addition** for two events, A and B, which are not mutually exclusive, is as follows.

Probability of (A or B) = P (A∪B) = P(A) + P(B) – P(A and B)

For example, in a standard pack of 52 playing cards, what is the probability of selecting an ace or a spade?

Ace = 4/52

Spade = 13/52

Ace of spades = 1/52

Therefore the probability of selecting an ace or a spade is:

4/52 + 13/52 – 1/52 = 16/52 = 4/13

Dependent or **conditional** events are events where the outcome of one event depends on the outcome of the others. The probability of two dependent events occurring is calculated by **multiplying** the individual probabilities together. **Contingency** tables can be useful for dealing with conditional probability.

For example, the probability of rolling a six, followed by another six is:

$1/6 \times 1/6 = 1/36$

Probability is used to help to calculate **risk** in decision making. The higher the probability of an event occurring, the lower the associated risk will be.

Risk involves situations or events which may or may not occur, but whose probability of occurrence can be calculated statistically and the frequency predicted.

Uncertainty involves situations or events whose outcome cannot be predicted with statistical confidence.

A popular quote that illustrates an element of the distinction between risk and uncertainty was given by the United States ex Secretary of Defence, Donald Rumsfeld:

'There are known knowns; there are things we know that we know.
There are known unknowns; that is to say there are things that we now know we don't know.
But there are also unknown unknowns – there are things we do not know, we don't know.'

9.2 Expected values

An **expected value** (or **EV**) is a weighted average value, based on probabilities. The expected value for a single event can offer a helpful guide for management decisions.

Although the outcome of a decision may not be certain, there is some likelihood that probabilities could be assigned to the various possible outcomes from an analysis of previous experience.

If the probability of an outcome of an event is p, then the expected number of times that this outcome will occur in n events (the expected value) is equal to n × p.

The concepts of probability and expected value are vital in **business decision-making**. The expected values for single events can offer a helpful guide for management decisions.

- A project with a positive EV should be accepted.

- A project with a negative EV should be rejected.

- When choosing between options the alternative which has the **highest EV of profit** (or the **lowest EV of cost**) should be selected.

Where probabilities are assigned to different outcomes we can evaluate the worth of a decision as the **expected value**, or weighted average, of these outcomes. The principle is that when there are a number of alternative decisions, each with a range of possible outcomes, the optimum decision will be the one which gives the highest expected value.

Expected values can be built into decision trees to aid decision making. The amount of expected profit is likely to be conditional on the result of various decisions. We will look at this in more detail below. First, let us briefly consider some limitations of using expected values as a basis for decisions.

9.2.1 Limitations of expected values

Evaluating decisions by using expected values has a number of limitations.

(a) The **probabilities** used when calculating expected values are likely to be estimates. They may therefore be **unreliable** or **inaccurate**.

(b) Expected values are **long-term averages** and may not be suitable for use in situations involving one-off decisions. They may therefore be useful as a **guide** to decision making.

(c) Expected values do not consider the **attitudes to risk** of the people involved in the decision-making process. They do not, therefore, take into account all of the factors involved in the decision.

(d) The **time value of money may not be taken into account**: £100 now is worth more than £100 in 10 years' time.

Probabilities and expected values can be represented diagrammatically using **decisions trees** to aid decision making.

9.3 Structure of decision trees

Decision trees are diagrams which illustrate the choices and possible outcomes of a decision.

A **decision tree** is a pictorial method of showing a sequence of interrelated decisions and their expected outcomes. Decision trees can incorporate both the probabilities of, and values of, expected outcomes. It is important to note that in the Business Strategy and Technology exam you will not be required to draw complex decision trees, but you may need to set out conditional probability calculations in the form of a table, or interpret a decision tree provided in the question scenario.

Decision trees provide a clear and logical approach to problem solving by:

- Showing all possible **choices** as **branches** on the tree (squares)
- Showing all possible **outcomes** as **subsidiary branches** on the tree (circles)

Decision trees begin with a decision point, usually represented by a **square**, and the various choices branch off from this, flowing from left to right.

If the outcome for any of those choices is certain, then the branch of the decision tree for that alternative is complete.

If the outcome of a particular choice is uncertain, then the various possible outcomes must be shown. This is done by inserting an **outcome point** on the branch. This is symbolised by a **circle**. Each possible outcome will then branch out from that outcome point. These are known as **subsidiary branches**.

The **probability** of each outcome occurring should be written on the branch of the tree that represents that outcome.

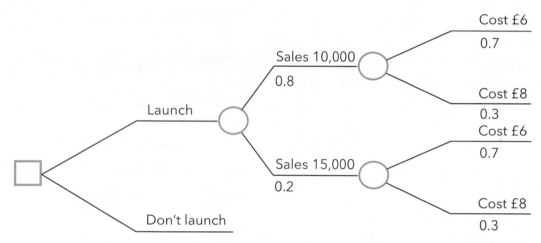

Sometimes a **decision taken now** will lead to **other decisions** being taken in the future. When this situation arises, the decision tree can be drawn as a **two-stage tree**, as shown below.

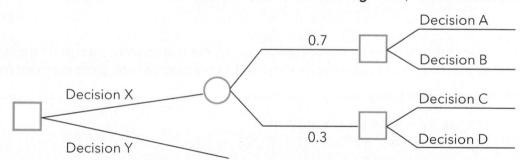

In this tree, either a choice between A and B or else a choice between C and D will be made, depending on the outcome which occurs if Decision X has previously been chosen.

The decision tree should be in chronological order from left to right.

9.3.1   Evaluating decisions with a decision tree

The EV of each decision option can be evaluated, using the decision tree to help with keeping the logic properly organised. Once the basic decision tree (ie, choices, outcomes and probabilities) has been drawn from left to right chronologically, the basic rules for attaching values to the decision process are as follows.

(a) We start on the **right hand side** of the tree and **work back** towards the left hand side and the current decision under consideration. This is sometimes known as the **'rollback' technique** or **'rollback analysis'**.

(b) Working from **right to left**, we calculate the **EV of revenue, cost, contribution or profit** at each outcome point on the tree.

Consider the decision tree below which has been prepared for a new product that has been developed. The decision is whether the new product should be test marketed or abandoned. The outcomes are high, medium or low demand and are dependent on whether the result of the test marketing is positive or negative.

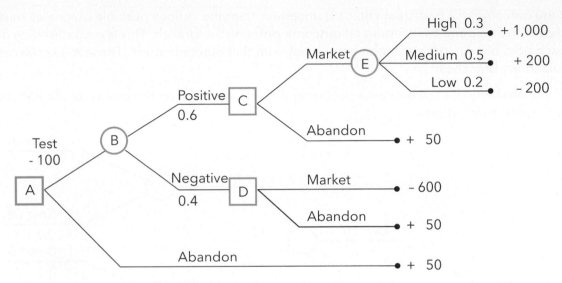

The right-hand-most outcome point is point E, and the EV is as follows.

	Profit X £'000	Probability p	pX £'000
High	1,000	0.3	300
Medium	200	0.5	100
Low	(200)	0.2	(40)
		EV	360

This is the EV of the decision to market the product if the test shows a positive response. It may help you to note the EV on the decision tree itself, at the appropriate outcome point (point E).

(a) **At decision point C**, the **choice** is as follows.

(1) Market, EV = +360 (the EV at point E)
(2) Abandon, value = +50

The choice would be to market the product, and so the EV at decision point C is +360.

(b) **At decision point D**, the **choice** is as follows.

(1) Market, value = – 600
(2) Abandon, value = +50

The choice would be to abandon, and so the EV at decision point D is +50.

The second stage decisions have therefore been made. If the original decision is to test market, the company will market the product if the test shows positive customer response, and will abandon the product if the test results are negative.

The evaluation of the decision tree is completed as follows.

(a) **Calculate the EV at outcome point B.**

0.6×360 (EV at C)
$+0.4 \times 50$ (EV at D)
$=216 + 20 = 236$.

(b) **Compare the options at point A**, which are as follows.

(1) Test: EV = EV at B minus test marketing cost = 236 – 100 = 136
(2) Abandon: Value = 50

The choice would be to test market the product, because it has a **higher EV of profit**.

Evaluating decisions by using a decision tree has a number of limitations:

- The time value of money may not be taken into account.

- Decision trees are not suitable for use in complex situations (eg, probabilities could be continuous in the form of a normal distribution, rather than only two possible outcomes).

- The outcome with the highest EV may have the greatest risks attached to it. Managers may be reluctant to take risks which may lead to losses.

- The probabilities associated with different branches of the tree are likely to be estimates, and possibly unreliable or inaccurate.

The following Interactive Question brings together a number of the key themes discussed in this chapter so far. It is based on a question which appeared in the Business Strategy and Technology exam, and requires you to evaluate the financial and non-financial aspects of a business decision. As such, you are strongly advised to take the time to attempt it.

Interactive question 10: Safe Storage Ltd

Safe Storage Ltd (SS) provides secure storage units to customers who are unable to store all of their personal belongings at their home. Many customers use the company's services during the process of moving house as an easy way of securely storing items until a new home purchase is completed. On average, customers store their items for a period of six to nine months. The company operates a number of storage sites around the country. At present, the direct costs of storing customers goods are £202 per customer per annum.

SS is unique as it provides a delivery service to its customers of items held in storage. Customers can have their goods delivered to any UK location without charge for up to the first three deliveries. Customers pay a £50 subscription per month for the use of the storage service. The company currently has 28,000 customers on average per year which generates revenue of £11 million.

SS has recently been approached by a large retailer, Furniture World plc, to enter into a contract to store furniture for the company over the next 12 months, after Furniture World's main depot was recently destroyed in a fire. Furniture World has requested a fixed price arrangement which would see SS hold inventories of furniture, with up to three deliveries over the course of the year being made to each of its 1,050 UK stores. Each store is to be treated as an individual customer as part of the arrangement. Although unlikely, in the event that more than three deliveries per store are needed Furniture World has agreed that its own fleet of trucks will collect furniture from SS and arrange delivery to store. Furniture World is renowned for driving a hard bargain and wants to receive a discount on all contracts it enters into, usually at 25% of the standard prices charged.

SS currently has spare capacity at some of its storage sites to hold furniture for Furniture World. The MD of SS has estimated that the probability of deliveries being needed over a 12 month period to Furniture World stores would be:

Number of requests	0	1	2	3
Probability	5%	10%	40%	45%

At present SS's average delivery costs are £32 per delivery made. Each delivery attracts an administration cost of £10, this relates to the processing of the delivery at the respective storage site. SS's current fixed costs amount to £143,000, however this would increase by £162,000 to £305,000 should the company accept the contract with Furniture World as additional storage sites would need to be rented at locations where SS has no spare capacity.

Requirement

10.1 Discuss how the discount requested would affect the profitability of the Furniture World contract. Show supporting calculations including a break-even price.

See **Answer** at the end of this chapter.

10 Risk management and business continuity planning

Section overview

- Risk can be mitigated by management having plans to deal with problems if they occur.

Definition

Business continuity planning: A process through which a business details how and when it will recover and restore any operations interrupted by the occurrence of a rare, but massive, risk event.

Because all businesses must accept some level of residual risk, business continuity planning has been developed to deal with the consequences of any realised residual risks. These are likely to be the unpredictable one-off events such as building fires, acts of terrorism, regional incidents like earthquakes, or national incidents like pandemic illnesses.

Factors that must be considered include:

- Securing interim management and staff
- Inventory replacement
- Restoration of data and other IT systems
- Securing interim premises
- Management of the PR issues

Though events bringing a business's existence into jeopardy do not arise on a regular basis, they do, nevertheless, arise occasionally and business continuity planning is concerned with crisis management and disaster recovery if an event of this magnitude occurs.

Summary and Self-test

Summary

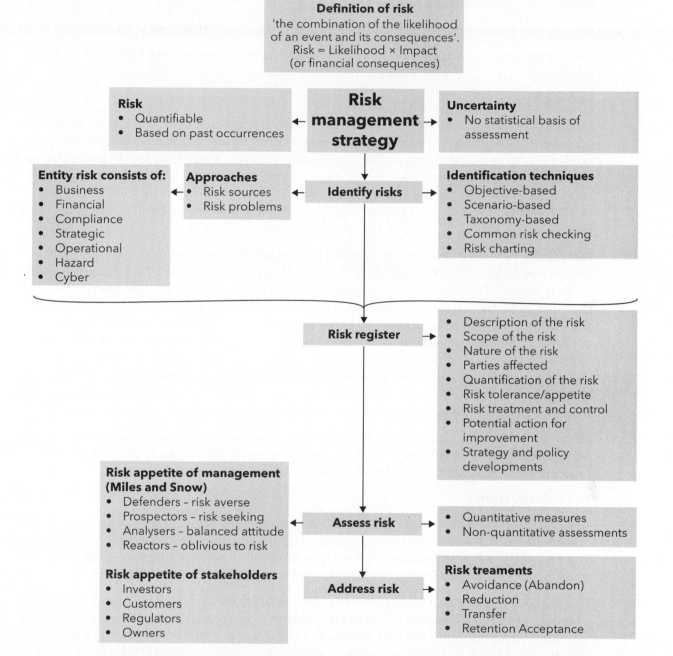

Definition of risk
'the combination of the likelihood of an event and its consequences'.
Risk = Likelihood × Impact
(or financial consequences)

Risk
- Quantifiable
- Based on past occurrences

Risk management strategy

Uncertainty
- No statistical basis of assessment

Entity risk consists of:
- Business
- Financial
- Compliance
- Strategic
- Operational
- Hazard
- Cyber

Approaches
- Risk sources
- Risk problems

Identify risks

Identification techniques
- Objective-based
- Scenario-based
- Taxonomy-based
- Common risk checking
- Risk charting

Risk register
- Description of the risk
- Scope of the risk
- Nature of the risk
- Parties affected
- Quantification of the risk
- Risk tolerance/appetite
- Risk treatment and control
- Potential action for improvement
- Strategy and policy developments

Risk appetite of management (Miles and Snow)
- Defenders – risk averse
- Prospectors – risk seeking
- Analysers – balanced attitude
- Reactors – oblivious to risk

Assess risk
- Quantitative measures
- Non-quantitative assessments

Risk appetite of stakeholders
- Investors
- Customers
- Regulators
- Owners

Address risk

Risk treaments
- Avoidance (Abandon)
- Reduction
- Transfer
- Retention Acceptance

Self-test

Answer the following questions.

1 Distinguish between risk and uncertainty.

2 Explain the two general approaches to risk identification.

3 Identify four general strategies for risk management.

4 Identify two sources of risk to which multinational firms in particular are exposed.

5 Identify the four descriptions of management attitudes to strategic risk identified by Miles and Snow.

6 **Ferien plc**

Ferien plc is a small listed company based in a developed European country which is outside of the Eurozone. The currency in Ferien's country is the dollar. The company sells country cottage and camping holidays in France and Italy. It was founded 17 years ago and floated on its domestic stock exchange 7 years later, much of the additional capital then raised being used to purchase camp sites abroad. The company has no long term fixed interest debt, and 55% of the equity is still in the hands of the three families which set up the business.

After flotation the company's revenue and pre-tax profits grew steadily, reaching $100 million and $10 million respectively in the year ended 31 December 20X4. However, with three quarters of the revenue coming from sales of holidays in France, pre-tax profits declined to $7 million in 20X5, when fine summer weather in Ferien's home country, the high value of the euro relative to the dollar, and a decline in the popularity of French country cottage holidays adversely affected trading. Performance in 20X6 showed some recovery but was still disappointing, notwithstanding a steady weakening of the euro against the dollar, with pre-tax profits totalling $8 million. Early bookings in 20X7 have shown little improvement and the board has recently met to consider various strategies that might be pursued to maintain the growth momentum experienced in the early 20X0s.

Ferien plc purchases its country cottage holidays in advance each year and, under an agreement with the agents representing cottage owners, the company pays half the amounts due on 1 February and the balance six months later on 1 August.

The industry profile

About half the 24 million foreign holidays taken by citizens from Ferien's country each year are sold as packages, of which two thirds are supplied by three companies ('the Big Three'). The remainder are sold by some 100 independent (and overwhelmingly privately owned) firms, many of which specialise in particular types of holiday.

The dominant position of the Big Three is reinforced by vertical integration, eg, as owners of hotels, charter airlines and cruise liners, through their control of the three leading travel agencies, which together sell well over half of all package holidays, and through the included tied holiday insurance contracts as part of the package deals. The commission structure of the travel agencies has led to accusations that they unfairly promote packages offered by their associated operators. After an extensive study of the situation, the competition regulator decided that they should make clear to customers their relationships with the operators.

Profits are not only determined by the volume of holidays sold, but also by avoiding having to sell off surplus holidays at knock-down prices. Another factor is a growing tendency for customers to put together their own packages from flight and accommodation offers made via direct selling organisations. Other key variables are the changing preferences of customers, and shifts in taxes and exchange rates. In particular, it is desirable for travel companies to immunise themselves from the latter as prices are set some months in advance of the actual travel dates. This is usually done by currency hedging and by charging supplements to reflect costs at the date of travel.

It is also necessary for companies selling package holidays to be able to forecast annual sales volumes with some accuracy – which will depend on the sensitivity of demand to both prices and customer incomes – otherwise they can find themselves overcommitted. To the extent that companies get their budgets wrong, reported profits will tend to be highly volatile; this is evident from the records of the largest operators, as well as from the experience of their smaller counterparts.

Another feature of the industry is the need to manage cash flows and the highly seasonal patterns of business. With respect to the former, it is necessary to pay deposits up front to hoteliers, air charter and ferry companies. This in turn means that operators ask customers for deposits on booking to minimise the strain on their working capital requirements. As for seasonal patterns of trading, there are clearly advantages in trying to spread business over 12 months, eg, by offering skiing holidays, short breaks and long-haul packages, as well as popular summer holidays at European destinations.

Clearly the largest companies have the advantage of diversification, backed up by vertical integration, which reduces their exposure to risk and smoothes demand on working capital. Nevertheless, even the biggest operators can overreach themselves, and at the smaller end of the market there is a steady stream of failures, some 5-10 independent companies collapsing each year. However, customers paying deposits in advance are generally protected by the existence of industry-backed guarantees, although such schemes may encourage reckless operators to offer cut-price deals in the hope of generating sales volume, but with a reduced risk of losing customers. On the other side, in seeking to unload surplus holidays the big operators usually publicise massive discounts (often recouping some of the lost revenues through tied insurance and 'hidden' supplements), knowing full well that around 30% of bargain-hunting customers book at the last minute.

The options facing Ferien plc

At the board meeting convened to consider the strategic options facing Ferien plc, the Managing Director argued that it was necessary to try to reduce the volatility of profits and cash flows. In particular, he felt it would be helpful to diversify the interests of the company. He suggested that the company should try to arrange villa and camping holidays in Spain and Portugal; and villa holidays further afield in Greece and Cyprus.

The Marketing Director generally agreed that this strategy should be pursued, but he felt it would also be useful to reduce dependence on sales and summer holidays and on camping and cottage and villa holidays. He argued that the company should offer skiing holidays in the French and Italian Alps and the Pyrenees, while at the same time entering the long-haul holiday market.

The Finance Director was in general agreement with his fellow directors, but he suggested that the expansion envisaged would require considerable new investment. He was aware that the founding families would find it difficult to subscribe to a share issue to finance such expansion and still retain majority control of the company. A debt issue was a possibility but, apart from the camp sites, the company could offer few assets as security and, given the risks inherent in the travel business, he would anticipate high interest rates. In the circumstances he felt that it would be necessary for the diversification strategy to be phased in gradually.

Requirements

As an assistant to the finance director, prepare a memorandum to the board of Ferien plc which examines the strategic options available to the company. It should deal only with the following matters.

- Risks inherent in the travel and overseas holiday industry

- Risks specific to Ferien plc

- The advantages and disadvantages to Ferien plc of diversifying the types and locations of holidays offered to customers

7 Read the scenario of the **September 2010 Business Strategy and Technology** question in the Question Bank entitled *e-Parts Ltd (amended)*. Draft answers for the requirements on risk management and the key IT risks (including cyber risk) arising from the company's reliance on IT.

8 Read the scenario of the **September 2015 Business Strategy and Technology** question in the Question Bank entitled *Premier Paper Products plc*. Draft an answer for the requirement on risk and risk management strategies.

9 Read the scenario of the **June 2017 Business Strategy and Technology** question in the Question Bank entitled *Holidays Direct plc*. Draft an answer for the requirement on operating and financial risk.

Now, go back to the Learning outcomes in the Introduction. If you are satisfied that you have achieved these objectives, please tick them off.

Answers to Interactive questions

Answer to Interactive question 1

1.1 Report

To	Director of Corporate Development, SkyWays Airlines
From	Financial Analyst
Date	XX/XX/XXXX
Subject	Risks faced by SWA

Terms of reference

This report has been commissioned by the Director of Corporate Development to illustrate the risks facing SWA and to identify appropriate controls.

Introduction

Risk has been defined as 'a condition in which there exists a quantifiable dispersion in the possible outcomes from any given activity'. This report does not attempt to quantify the risks faced by SWA. Rather it seeks to identify the origins of such risk and, for each, suggest suitable controls to manage that risk.

Financial risks

Interest rate risk: A change in the interest rate can affect the cash flows of the company where there are debts owed by the company at variable rates. Similarly any incomes related to interest rates, such as from short-term deposits or where passenger or freight volumes are affected by interest rates, will also be subject to risk.

This risk can be managed in a variety of ways:

- Avoidance of floating rate debt by switching funding to equity or fixed rate debt or interest hedging. (It might be noted however that fixed rate debt changes the type of risk but may not eliminate it altogether. Hedging avoids the cash flow risk in future interest payments but transfers risk into a fair value risk in term of the susceptibility of the value of the bond to market interest rate changes.)

- Deliberate purchase of floating rate debt such that the fall in earnings from business operations as rates rise can be offset by the increase in returns from the investments.

- Development of lines of business where earnings are negatively co-variant to those of SWA with respect to interest rates, ie, internal diversification.

Foreign exchange risk occurs when exchange rates change and affect the cost of servicing debts denominated in foreign currency, the receipts from payments denominated in foreign currency and the changes in the volumes of business as the foreign currency costs of tickets changes.

Methods of managing this risk include:

- Denomination of debts and sales in domestic currency where possible.

- Exchange rate hedging.

- Development of streams of earnings and expenditures that are matched for each currency. For example if SWA needs to pay sterling for meals supplied on return journeys from London it should consider using the ticket revenues from sales in UK to pay this. If these are insufficient then a sterling denominated airline shop should be considered.

- Diversification of operations across several currency zones.

Credit risk is the disruption to revenue streams by delayed payments from debtors or from bad debts.

This risk can be managed by:

- Credit control procedures
- Debt factoring

Operational risks

Regulation risk refers to the costs of complying with changes in aviation regulations, fines for non-compliance and of disruption to operations if aircraft are grounded.

This risk can be managed by:

- The creation of mechanisms for consultation and advance warning with regulators. The experience and contacts of SWA's Engineering Director will be an important part of this.

- Compliance with regulations. SWA will need to have robust procedures for all operations that can be inspected and verified by regulators.

- Transfer of sensitive operations outside the business. Outsourcing maintenance, staffing, catering etc, means that the expertise of the provider may reduce some of the risk but also that they will bear the costs of changes to regulation or fines for non-compliance. Loss of earnings due to disruption of these activities can be recovered by SWA through legal action.

Culture risk deals with the danger of commercial failure, reputation damage, or disruption to operations due to mismanagement of cultural interfaces in the business. Examples include the adverse effects of staffing or advertising decisions, poor product or service provision. At the highest level it can include the fall-out from national cultural clashes for the firms in those nations.

This risk can be managed by:

- **Taking appropriate advice on cultural issues**: many consultancies will provide SWA with practical advice on doing business in particular countries to avoid damaging cultural sensibilities.

- **Business partnerships with local operators**: these will be more experienced in dealing with differences.

- **Diversity policy**: SWA could take deliberate action to ensure that the breadth of cultures that it deals with are represented within its staff at all levels. Staff could also be given culture awareness training such as BA did with cabin staff to make them aware of the variability of dietary conventions, body language, name conventions, forms of address etc, that will be encountered by a global airline.

- **Organisational development**: SWA could take the decision to shift from a national to a global organisation by a transformational change involving restructuring, recruitment and changing the perspective of existing staff towards persons from other cultures.

Board composition: to avoid operational risks the board should have representatives of main operational areas such that the operational implications of board decisions receive proper consideration and that operational concerns receive a proper airing.

This risk can be managed by key operations having board representation.

Hazard risks

Contracts: the extended supply chain of SWA makes it reliant on suppliers of fuel, aircraft parts, air traffic control etc. Particular contract risks in SWA's present situation are its employment contracts with staff, and potential contracts with the makers of new aircraft. Risks arise where a counterparty is unable or unwilling to fulfil their obligations under the contract, such as a threat to strike or to withdraw service, or where SWA wishes to vary the terms of the contract but cannot without penalties.

Management of this risk can be assisted by:

- Proper procedures for supplier selection
- Development of dedicated procurement and contracts function within SWA
- Multi-sourcing of inputs to avoid excessive reliance on one
- Financial redress for non-performance of contract such as penalty payments

Relationship building with counterparties to develop trust and commitment. Regular meetings to air concerns and address grievances will assist and will also provide SWA with early warnings of potential risk from the contracts.

Natural events: for airlines this includes hurricanes, snow, rain and fog. These lead to cancellations and diversions of flights resulting in displaced passengers and aircraft with subsequent costs of relocation (buses, alternative flights, empty flights), compensation and lost revenue. Such events can also affect demand for air services such as a lack of snow reducing demand for flights to skiing resorts or the tragedy of a Tsunami making tourists unwilling to visit island and low lying coastal resorts.

Management controls that can be used include:

- Contingency plans for dealing with disruptions such as alternative schedules, stand by arrangements with other transport providers and airports.

- Advance warning such as use of weather forecasts.

- Contractual clauses limiting SWA's liability for costs of losses due to natural events and *force majeure*.

- Risk assessment of airports used to assess vulnerability to fog, flood etc.

Suppliers: these are risks arising from the collapse or poor performance of suppliers or aggressive action on their part such as levying of increased prices.

Many of the management controls for contract risk discussed above apply here too. Additional controls would include:

- Engagement of suppliers in long-term contracts.

- Creation of parallel sourcing strategies to ensure suppliers remain competitive and sourcing approach (eg, a sole reliance on agents or e-trading) is not an additional source of risk.

Management controls include:

- Development of relationship with key stakeholders (eg, governments, environmental groups, local warlords etc).

- Improvement of physical security of operations.

- Improvement of information available by environmental scanning and creation of knowledge management within SWA.

Strategic risks

Competition: This imposes the commercial risk of reduced profits through lower prices and volumes and increased costs of participation in the industry (service quality, promotion etc).

Management controls include:

- Competitor monitoring and analysis

- Development of competitive advantage such as brand or unique access or technology

- Pre-emptive action such as developing 'flanker' businesses. Faced with challenges from low cost airlines many full service airlines developed cheaper second brands (eg, in 2013 Aeroflot the Russian national carrier announced plans to launch Dobrolet, a low cost airline offering flights from St Petersburg to other Russian cities). Ryanair moved in the opposite direction by seeking to acquire the Irish long-haul operator Aer Lingus. In 2013 Ryanair's bid to acquire Aer Lingus was blocked by European competition authorities

- Diversification of business to reduce expose to particular competitors

- Negotiation of understandings with competitors (potentially unethical and illegal)

- Acquisition of competitors

Customer changes includes loss of key customers, failure of key target customers, or sharp changes in customer demand patterns. An example is the successful publicity by economy airlines to name and shame corporations who refuse to use them and hence expend shareholders' money on flying staff with expensive full-service airlines.

Management controls include:

- Operation of a flexible fleet able to be adapted to serve a variety of customer types and destinations.

- Provision of a portfolio of ticket prices and service levels (eg, BA offer First, Business, Premium economy and economy classes).

- Avoidance of reliance on one or a few main clients or destinations.

- Good quality customer information to detect changing tastes or defections to rivals.

Industry changes: this includes the arrival of new competition, merger of rivals and the failure of rivals. These change the nature of competitive pressure. For example a merger may create greater economies of scale for the larger firm, a threat to SWA, but may also reduce capacity in the industry and so relieve price pressure, an opportunity for SWA.

Management controls include:

- Environmental information on potential industry changes.

- Ability to launch pre-emptive action such as appeals to regulatory authorities or to mount counter-bids.

- Leasing some aircraft to enable reduction or changes in fleet composition.

Customer demand refers to fluctuations in demand. These are inevitable for airlines as a consequence of the strategic choice to be an airline. Their profits and survival will depend on developing strategies to cope with these changes in demand. Management controls include:

- Use of flexible staffing (part-time, contract etc,) to cope with peaks and troughs in passenger volumes.

- Dynamic pricing to raise or lower prices to shift demand towards unfilled seats.

- Flexible service and maintenance schedules which allow planes to be pressed into service during peaks and rested during troughs.

- Variety of plane sizes to enable low demand routes to have small planes and so re-deploy larger planes to busy routes.

- Multi-skilled staff able to cope with changes of aircraft on their route (in particular pilots who must be able to switch flight decks) or being asked to work a different route and so be familiar with passenger demands and able to give information on customs formalities etc.

Internally driven risks

These are ones that result from the operations of management. Some of these risks are incurred as a response to particular external risks, such as the investment of funds in R&D to gain strategic advantage to reduce strategic risk. Other internal risks leave the firm exposed to external risk, such as poor liquidity and cash flow leaving a firm exposed to the financial risks from higher interest rates or banks withdrawing credit. The internally driven risks that can be identified in SWA are discussed below.

Liquidity and cash flow: borrowing increased during the latest financial year. SWA has a liquidity ratio below 1. This means that any interruption to its business and cash flows could potentially leave it unable to pay its creditors. Moreover it has insufficient retained earnings to meet its present operating capital needs, hence the increased borrowing in the last year despite a modest increase in business activity, and so may not be able to repay any loans falling due in the near future. Any fall in liquidity may make SWA unable to maintain its dividend and hence jeopardise its share price.

Employees and supply chain: both internal risk drivers are present with the increased dissatisfaction of employees with the voluntary redundancies resulting from the new terminal and, apparently, the loss of control over them by the decline in influence of the Trades Unions.

Public access is an inherent risk for all airlines. Admitting passengers and relatives to airport buildings, airplanes etc, also means admitting potential illnesses (such as the avian flu virus) or terrorists.

Intellectual capital: the customer and flight information held by SWA is of high commercial value, yet under the codeshare arrangement, is sometimes shared with potential rivals. The board should remember the scandal that engulfed BA when it was revealed that its seat reservation system, leased to other airlines for their use too, was being used to break into the passenger details held by Virgin Atlantic for the purposes of poaching customers – the so-called 'dirty tricks' campaign. The damage to BA's reputation and the commercial damage to Virgin Atlantic from this episode illustrates the risks inherent in high dependence of IT/IS.

Conclusions

This report has identified the range of risks present in SWA's environment and also those to which it is subject from its own internal structure and operations. It has been noted that at present there is no board position responsible for implementing and monitoring a risk management strategy at SWA. Some appropriate management controls have been suggested.

Recommendations

SWA should establish a role at board level for risk management by creating a new post or by extending the portfolio of an existing director. The first task of this role holder should be to assess internal controls at SWA and, on the basis of this, present a risk analysis to the board.

Tutorial note

The solution to Interactive question 1 is more detailed than you would be expected to produce in light of the limited information provided in the question. It is included here as a learning tool.

Answer to Interactive question 2

2.1 The list of factors will be very large. It will include:

Costs and benefits from outsourcing

- Fees charged by contactors

- Cost presently incurred by using own staff

- Financial returns from transfer of assets to contractor (floor polishing machines, vacuum cleaners etc)

- Potential redundancy costs of staff not transferred

- Costs of writing and agreeing suitable contracts and service level agreements

- Costs of monitoring compliance of contractors with service agreements

Risks from outsourcing

- Financial stability and robustness of the contractor

- Track record of contractor in delivering suitable service elsewhere

- Availability of controls over performance (eg, whether staff will take instructions from hospital managers, performance indicators, regular meetings, legal redress mechanisms)

- Potential staff and media criticism of decision

- Extent of proof of link between hospital cleanliness and acquired infections

- Extent of public hostility to outsourcing as a source of increased infections

- Will legal liability for negligence claim pass to the contractor or stay with the hospital?

Risks from continuing to provide cleaning in-house

- Operational risks from cleaners not being available (eg, strike action)

- Employment risks of having own staff (eg, claims for industrial injury, discrimination etc)

- Rising wages and other employment costs

- Legal costs of negligence claims resulting from poor cleaning

- Potential fines for inadequate monitoring of staff (work permits, benefit fraud, health and safety)

Risk environment and appetite

- Potential changes in government policy resulting in contract penalties

- Extent of pressure on hospital to cut costs

- Management's previous experience of outsourcing agreements

- Relative risks of other cost-cutting measures under consideration

- Degree of support management enjoys from influential stakeholders (eg, media, governors, doctors, nurses)

- Potential personal consequences for management of bad decision (eg, personal liability, career impact, stress of dealing with problems)

Answer to Interactive question 3

3.1

Risk	Impact and likelihood	Risk management
Loss of profits due to government seizing assets or imposing stringent taxes:	Potentially high significance (however will be determined by the size of the oil company's operations). High likelihood due to government's past behaviour of taking over assets belonging to privately owned companies.	Risk avoidance. Don't invest in the country Risk reduction. Insist on written assurances from the government that they will not intervene or tax.
Loss of expensive resources (drilling equipment, pipelines leading out of the country and knowledge) if government takeover the company's assets.	High significance and likelihood as the government is unlikely to reimburse the oil company for any resources assumed.	Risk reduction. Retain as many of the venture's assets as possible outside the country. Or, invest small amounts incrementally.
A government takeover of the company's assets or operations may put the organisation as a whole under financial distress possibly causing bankruptcy.	Potentially highly significant with high likelihood depending on the global spread and size of the oil company's operations.	Risk transfer. Set up the venture as a separate company with own sources of finance. Or, use local sources of financing the assets (preferably government sources where possible). Sell the rights to the oil to third parties as soon as possible so they adopt the risk.

Other risk management strategies which you could have mentioned include:

Risk reduction

- Ensure the firm has other sources of oil and gas and of earnings
- Seek to influence the policy of the government by political lobbying
- Invite the government to be part owner of the venture

Risk transfer

- Insure the assets
- Invite involvement and investment from other oil firms or pipeline owners
- Obtain assets using lease arrangements
- Sell the rights to the oil to third parties as soon as possible so they adopt the risk
- Enter into joint ventures

Risk retention

Accepting the remaining loss if and when it occurs

Note: This solution deals with only the political risks from the project. It has not dealt with other risks such as explosions, fall in the price of oil and gas, unexpected cost overruns, poor weather hampering production, industrial action, laws being passed to discourage use of fossil fuels to quote some of numerous examples.

Answer to Interactive question 4

4.1 At store level risk monitoring should be established for:

- Temperature of chilled and frozen foods such as alarm bells or luminescent strips that are activated if temperatures rise

- Compliance with food hygiene procedures such as visual inspections and questions to staff

- Compliance with customer service standards such as by mystery shoppers

- Financial integrity such as by close reconciliations between ingredients supplied and totals from sales data and wasted stock

- Staff integrity such as by existence checks on names and personal tax references, confirmations of employment from past employers

At national level risk monitoring should be established for:

- Compliance with laws on hygiene, employment, food labelling

- Impact of the competitive strategies of rivals

- Changes in the costs of ingredients, staffing or premises costs

- Impact of potential legislation

- Social attitudes towards the firm, its activities and its products

- Stability and performance of business partners

At global level monitoring should be established for:

- Changes in cost of capital resulting from market sentiments or interest rate movements

- Development of new country markets

- Developments in trading relations between host and home country that may affect access and earnings repatriation

- International pressure group activity aimed at the industry or firm

Answer to Interactive question 5

Ferry

5.1 **Risks**

Rights to operate

The exclusive rights to operate are **only effective until 20X9**. Depending on the likelihood of these rights being renegotiated this raises questions about the ongoing viability of the business.

The right to operate may have been granted provided that **certain conditions** are met. If Ferry does not continue to satisfy these terms its operational existence may be called into question.

Future competition

Profitability could be affected by **future competition**. This might be the case if a new bridge is constructed or if the rights were no longer exclusive to Ferry.

Age of the ferries

It is likely that **running costs** will be higher than those for newer ships.

Fuel consumption is likely to be **higher** as the engines will be less efficient. This is of particular concern in periods when **fuel prices are volatile**. Ongoing maintenance is also more likely to be required.

Emission standards

The company will be required to meet the emission standards which come into force in 20X6. If the necessary modifications are not made the company could incur **substantial penalties**.

Custom may be lost due to the potential disruption caused to services during the period in which the modifications are made to the ferries.

Surplus capacity

The ferries are currently only operating at **40% capacity**

2 boats × 40 vehicles × 6 crossing × 365 days = 175,200

70,000/175,200 = 40%

As a high proportion of the cost of each trip is likely to be fixed (ie, fuel), consideration needs to be given as to whether the business is **viable** at this level. The company is also likely to be sensitive to any downturn in business (for example, due to general economic conditions).

Franchise arrangements

The **quality of outsourced services** are outside the direct control of Ferry. Ferry may receive complaints and ultimately lose customers if services are poor.

Subsidy

Ferry may **depend on the subsidy** to continue in business. Cash flow problems could arise if the subsidy stopped (ie, it may only be awarded for a given period or be dependent on certain quality standards being maintained.)

If sufficient controls are not in place returns may be **submitted late** or may include **inaccurate information**. **Cash flow problems** could result due to late or non-payment.

There is a risk that details on the return might be **deliberately inflated** to increase the payment received.

Health and safety

Ferry may **not be awarded its Safety Management Certificate** if it fails to meet the performance and documentation standards.

Ferry will find it difficult to **find and retain staff** if working conditions do not comply with health and safety regulations.

Litigation

Ferry may be **sued by customers** for personal injury and damage to, or loss of, property. In the case of serious injury or death damages could be substantial.

Serious incident

A catastrophic incident could lead to a **loss of assets** which may threaten the operations in the short and long term.

5.2 **Rights to operate**

It is unlikely that the business is in a position to change the situation regarding the period for which the rights have been granted and therefore is a risk that the **business has to accept**. Management should be aware of any **conditions** which will affect the renewal of rights and take steps to ensure that these are complied with.

Relevant staff should be made aware of any **contractual conditions** and their responsibility for ensuring that these are met. Compliance should be **reviewed** and **monitored** by an appropriate level of management.

Future competition

Management should **monitor any plans** which would introduce new competition, for example the building of a new bridge. Management should also consider how it can **maintain its competitive advantage** by ensuring that its service meets the needs of its customers.

Age of the ferries

Running costs should be **adequately budgeted** for and **cash flows monitored** to ensure that these can be met.

Price structures should be **flexible** to allow increased fuel costs to be passed on to the customer.

Forward contracts could be **used to hedge** against the effect of changing oil prices.

Emissions standards

Management should **familiarise** themselves with the **Environmental Protection Regulations**. Funds should be made available and the work scheduled to ensure that the deadline for compliance is met.

Plans should be made to **minimise the inconvenience** to **the customer** eg, changes in the schedule should be advertised, the work should not be planned for peak periods in the year.

Surplus capacity

Management need to be aware of the **capacity** required to ensure that revenue at least covers costs (ie, break-even point). This should be **reviewed and monitored** on a continual basis.

Marketing strategies should be used to **encourage bookings and maximise revenues**, for example discounts for regular users and different price structures for peak and off peak travel.

Franchise arrangements

The **performance of other businesses/franchisees should be monitored** by Ferry through the press, observation etc.

Franchise agreements should stipulate **minimum quality standards** and should include **penalties/termination clauses** for consistent unsatisfactory performance.

Subsidy

Management should be aware of the conditions attached to the payment of the subsidy and ensure that **these targets** are met. If the subsidy is available for a limited period plans should be made to ensure that the business can remain viable by a long-term review of revenues and benefits.

Controls such as checking by other staff should be implemented to ensure that **returns are accurate** and completed on time. Checks by **Internal audit** may provide management with added assurance.

Fraudulent completion of returns is likely to be performed with the knowledge of management. The **seriousness of this risk depends** largely on the **integrity** of the individuals involved.

Health and safety

Management should **monitor activities** and the **completion of safety documents**. This function could be performed by internal audit.

Litigation

Liability should be limited where possible (eg, telling passengers they leave valuables in unattended vehicles at their own risk).

Staff training should emphasise public safety. Safety drills should be practised regularly.

The company should have adequate public liability insurance.

Serious incident

The ships should be maintained to a high standard and regular checks should be made to ensure that safety equipment is in working order, eg, life boats.

The ships should be fitted with up to date equipment to prevent or deal with serious incidents. This equipment should be tested and maintained regularly.

Answer to Interactive question 6

6.1 Now the only alternative use for the material is to sell it for scrap. To use 50 tonnes on the contract is to give up the opportunity of selling it for 50 × £150 = £7,500. The relevant cost of the material is therefore this amount.

Answer to Interactive question 7

7.1 The relevant cost of 25 tonnes is £150 per tonne. The organisation must then purchase a further 25 tonnes and, assuming this is in the near future, it will cost £210 per tonne.

The relevant cost of materials is:

	£
25 tonnes @ £150	3,750
25 tonnes @ £210	5,250
	9,000

Answer to Interactive question 8

8.1 What revenue is lost if the labour is transferred to the project from doing nothing? Nothing.

The relevant cost is zero.

Answer to Interactive question 9

9.1 The recoverable amount is the £900 NRV (which is higher than the £800 economic value). As this is lower than the £1,000 replacement cost, £900 is the deprival value.

Answer to Interactive question 10

10.1 Factors affecting profitability

Calculation of the contract price:

Number of deliveries	0	1	2	3
Probability	5%	10%	40%	45%
Prob x number of deliveries	0	0.1	0.8	1.35

EV deliveries per store = 2.25
Incremental costs:

	£
Direct storage costs (£202 × 1,050 stores)	£212,100
Delivery costs (£32 per delivery × 1,050 stores × 2.25)	£75,600
Administration costs (£10 admin charge × 1,050 × 2.25)	£23,625
Additional fixed costs	£162,000
Total costs	£473,325

Therefore, assuming that costs for the contract are comparable to those for existing customers, SS needs revenue of £473,325 to break-even on the contract.

The break-even contract price = £473,325. This equates to break-even prices of £450.79 per annum per store (£473,325/1,050 stores) or £37.57per month per store.

SS's normal standard price for individual customers is £50 per month or £600 per annum.

Therefore, if SS charged £50 per store per month, SS would receive £630,000 per year from Furniture World, making £156,675 profit on the contract (£630,000 – £473,325). The maximum discount SS could offer on the standard price would be £156,675/£630,000 = 24.9%, but it would then only break-even.

Furniture World has asked for a discount of 25%, ie, a charge of £37.50 would result in revenue of £472,500, which based on original costs would result in a loss of £825 (being £472,500 – £473,325).

On the balance of the information provided it would be advisable for SS to not enter into a contract with Furniture World on the terms currently being requested.

Answers to Self-test

1   **Risk**: the possible variation in outcome from what is expected to happen

    Uncertainty: the inability to predict the outcome from an activity due to a lack of information

2   **Risk sources**: the cause of potential problems, things (people/activities/events) that may give rise to risk that may trigger an event. These risk sources may be either internal or external to the business. Management attempt to deal with the source.

    Risk events (problems): specific identified threats or events themselves. Management can attempt to deal with the problem.

3   • Risk avoidance – not undertaking the relevant activity
    • Risk reduction – taking steps to reduce the severity of the impact
    • Risk transfer – passing the risk to a third party through hedging or insurance
    • Risk retention – accepting the loss, if and when it occurs

4   Two of:

    • Political risk
    • Currency risk
    • Cultural risk
    • Trading risk

5   • Prospectors
    • Defenders
    • Analysers
    • Reactors

6   **Ferien plc**

    Memorandum

To	Board of directors, Ferien plc
From	Assistant to the Finance Director
Date	Today
Subject	The strategic options available to Ferien plc

    Risks inherent in the travel and overseas holiday industry

    The risks inherent in the industry in which Ferien plc operates include the following.

    • Risk of fewer people holidaying overseas due to better weather in Ferien's domestic country (global warming?), a recession in Ferien's home economy and/or fluctuations in exchange rates, especially a weakening of the dollar. A company could reduce its exposure here by selling domestic holidays as well.

    • Risk of wrongly estimating demand for different destinations and having to cut prices to sell off surplus holidays. As tastes become more sophisticated and costs lower, customers want increasingly exotic holidays. Companies can limit their exposure here by offering holidays to destinations all around the world.

    • Risk of wrongly estimating costs and hence mispricing holidays. Costs may vary due to inflation in different countries and to exchange rate fluctuations. Some of these variations can be limited by fixing prices with suppliers in advance and some can be recovered through supplements charged to customers.

    • Risk due to high fixed costs. Vertically integrated firms in particular will have a high proportion of fixed costs.

    • Risk of reduced revenue due to more and more customers delaying their purchase to the last minute to get discounts.

- Risk of further intervention by the competition regulator.

- Risk of more people deciding not to go via travel/holiday companies but choosing to design their own holidays. With the increase in availability of information on figures, hotels, etc, and the ease with which these can be booked, for example, over the internet, this is a significant threat to the long-term future of the industry.

- Risk of cash flow problems due to having to pay most costs up front before the bulk of income is received. This structure, coupled with the very seasonal nature of the business has resulted in many firms going into liquidation.

Risks specific to Ferien plc

Of the risks detailed in section 1, Ferien plc is particularly exposed to the following.

- Given that Ferien plc sells holidays only in France and Italy it is particularly vulnerable to people deciding to holiday at home rather than overseas and to people switching between different countries (eg, Turkey rather than Italy).

- Selling only cottage and camping holidays exposes Ferien plc to the problem of customers becoming more sophisticated and not wanting what could be perceived as old-fashioned holidays.

- Selling summer holidays only in Europe makes the volatility of Ferien plc's cash flow much greater than that of companies offering holidays through the year.

- Owning camp sites presumably gives Ferien plc more control of these costs but it is still exposed to changes in travel costs and cottage costs.

- The increased ease with which people can travel around Europe may leave Ferien plc increasingly exposed to the risk of customers choosing the 'DIY' alternative.

Diversification

The advantages and disadvantages of diversifying the types and locations of holidays offered to customers include the following.

Advantages	Disadvantages
• Diversification of risk, ie, not all of the eggs in one basket. • Reduces the impact of customers switching to other countries. • Ferien plc has experience of offering cottage and camping holidays. This could be used to develop similar in Spain, Portugal, Greece and Cyprus. • Winter holidays will smooth out Ferien plc's cash flow. • Ferien plc already uses French and Italian speaking reps who could also be employed for the winter season.	• Merely extending the range of summer holidays offered would place even greater demands on cash flow. • Ferien plc has little or no experience of the skiing holiday market. It is unlikely to be able to match the low costs of the Big Three or the knowledgeable personal service of specialised skiing operators. Without expenditure to get such expertise, Ferien plc would be left without a competitive advantage. • People who go skiing are not necessarily going on cottage or camping holidays in the summer. Thus the Ferien plc brand name is unlikely to count for much in this market. • Problems with finance. • The best villas and hotels in new locations are probably already booked up by other operators. This could be a significant barrier to expansion.

Conclusion

Ferien plc operates in a highly competitive, high-risk industry. Due to its narrow focus and hedging policies it is more exposed to some of these risks than many other firms so it is critical to Ferien plc's survival that these risks be reduced.

To obtain the greatest benefits of diversification, Ferien plc should look to winter holidays as well as expanding summer camping and cottage/villa deals.

Unfortunately this is the area where it is most difficult for the company to extend its existing competitive advantage. A possible solution would be to look to take over or merge with a specialist skiing company that is also looking to diversify.

7   Refer to the answer to e-Parts Ltd in the Question Bank.

8   Refer to the answer to Premier Paper Products plc in the Question Bank.

9   Refer to the answer to Holidays Direct plc in the Question Bank.

CHAPTER 10

CHAPTER 11

Methods of development

Introduction

Examination context

TOPIC LIST

Introduction

Learning outcomes

Tick off

- Identify, describe and evaluate in a given scenario the alternative strategies available to an organisation ☐

- Choose for a given scenario, a strategy, or combination of strategies, which will best achieve the organisation's objectives, taking account of known constraints, including stakeholder risk preferences and developing technologies ☐

- Identify and evaluate methods of further developing a specific organisation which adjust existing strategies or implement new strategies to take account of changing position and risk ☐

Specific syllabus references for this chapter are: 2a, 2g, 3e.

Syllabus links

The concept of different forms of business alliance will be familiar to you from your Business, Technology and Finance studies. The discussion of acquisition and mergers here complements the studies you will be taking in Financial Management concerning business valuations.

Examination context

Having decided on a strategy for growth, an organisation must consider how that growth is to be achieved. This chapter considers the options available to a business that wishes to expand. In the exam you will be expected to apply the knowledge covered in this chapter to the scenario, to advise an organisation on the most appropriate method of expansion. This is a popular exam topic.

Earlier in the study manual we mentioned that some exam questions may specify the models candidates are expected to use when attempting particular questions. It is also important to understand that some questions may not specify which models to use at all, instead asking for 'appropriate' or 'relevant' models to be used. This illustrates the importance of being able to identify how the information in a scenario lends itself to a particular model or theory.

In Question 1 of the December 2014 exam (*Confo plc*) the scenario focused on a company involved in the manufacture of confectionery items (sweets). Sweets were sold through the company's owned and franchised stores. In recent times the company had struggled and had subsequently appointed a new board of directors. Since this time, the company had started selling its products to commercial customers and started exporting products to overseas retailers. The third requirement asked:

'As part of the appraisal of the first year of the recovery plan, write a report which:

(a) Reviews the strategies adopted by the Export Division and the Commercial Division, and evaluates their performance. Include any relevant strategic models in your appraisal.'

The requirement provided no specific guidance as to the models to use in answering the question. This question scenario lends itself nicely to the use of both Ansoff's matrix and the work of Lynch (discussed later in this chapter). As ever the key thing to remember is to apply your knowledge of the various methods of expansion to the scenario itself, as marks are limited otherwise.

It is worth noting, however, that some question requirements may not require the use of a model at all, with the focus being wholly on making practical points drawn from the scenario detail.

In Question 1 of the September 2017 exam (*Blakes Blinds Ltd*) the scenario focused on a company involved in the manufacturing and installation of high-quality door and window blinds for corporate customers. In response to falling profits, the company's board were considering the acquisition of one its suppliers, a Chinese firm named RX. The first part of the third requirement asked:

'In relation to the proposal to acquire RX:

- Discuss the advantages and disadvantages of the acquisition.'

Simply listing the general advantages and disadvantages of acquisitions would not have been sufficient to earn the marks on offer. Candidates were expected to consider the advantages and disadvantages of this specific acquisition, noting that RX was a supplier and therefore the acquisition was an example of backwards vertical integration. This again highlights the importance of ensuring that your answers are applied to the scenario detail.

1 Methods of growth

1.1 What is growth?

An organisation's growth may be expressed in a number of ways, for example:

- Sales revenue (a growth in the number of markets served)
- Profitability (in absolute terms, and as a return on capital)
- Number of goods/services sold
- Number of outlets/sites
- Number of employees
- Number of countries

Chapter 7 looked at Ansoff's four directions (or vectors) of growth available to the business. Growth may be achieved by a number of mechanisms:

- Develop the business from scratch
- Acquire or merge with an already existing business
- Co-operate in some way with another firm

The main issues involved in choosing a method of growth are these.

- A firm may not be able to go it alone, or it may have plenty of **resources** to invest.

- Two different businesses might have **complementary skills.**

- Does a firm need to **move fast**?

- A firm might wish to **retain control** of a product or process.

- Is there a potential acquisition target or joint venture partner with compatible **people and organisation culture**?

- **Risk**: a firm may either increase or reduce the level of risk to which it is subject.

1.2 Expansion method: Lynch

Lynch summarised possible expansion methods in the matrix below.

Company → New location ↓	Internal development	External development
Home country	Internal domestic development	Joint venture Merge Acquisition Alliance Franchise/licence
Abroad	Exporting Overseas office Overseas manufacture Multinational operation Global operation	Joint venture Merger Acquisition Alliance Franchise/licence

2 Organic growth

Section overview

- **Organic growth** is expansion by use of internal resources (internal development).
- Its advantages are the maintenance of overall control, and the fact that managers can concentrate on product-market issues, rather than concerns of organisation structure.
- Its drawbacks are that it can be slow and there may be barriers to entry preventing organic growth.

Definition

Organic growth: Involves the expansion of a firm's size, profits, and activities through the use of its own resources and capabilities without taking over other firms.

2.1 Benefits of organic growth

Firms pursue organic growth for a number of reasons.

- The **process of developing** a new product gives the firm the best understanding of the market and the product.
- It might be the only sensible way to pursue **genuine technological innovations.**
- There is **no suitable target for acquisition.**
- It can be planned and financed easily from the company's **current resources** and the costs are spread over time.
- The same **style of management** and corporate culture can be maintained so there is less disruption.
- **Hidden or unforeseen losses**, common in acquisitions, are less likely with organic growth.
- It provides **career development** opportunities for managers otherwise plateaued in their present roles.
- It could be **cheaper** because assets are being acquired without additional payments for goodwill (eg, future earnings foregone by the persons selling their business or shares).
- It is **less risky**. In acquisitions the purchaser may also take on liability for the effects of decisions made by the previous owners (eg, underpaid tax, liability to employees for health and safety breaches and so on).

2.2 Drawbacks of organic growth

- It may **intensify competition** in a given market compared to buying an existing player.
- It is too **slow** if the market is developing very quickly.
- The firm does **not gain access to the knowledge and systems** of an established operator so it can be more risky.
- It will initially lack economies of scale/experience effects.
- There may be prohibitive barriers to entry in new markets.

3 International expansion

3.1 Reasons for international expansion

Some of the reasons management cite for expanding internationally are the following:

- **Chance**: a company executive may recognise an opportunity while on a foreign trip or the firm may receive chance orders or requests for information from potential foreign customers.

- **Life cycle**: home sales may be in the mature or declining stages of the product life cycle. International expansion may allow sales growth since products are often in different stages of the product life cycle in different countries.

- **Competition**: intense competition in an overcrowded domestic market sometimes induces firms to seek markets internationally, where rivalry is less keen.

- **Reduce dependence**: many companies wish to diversify away from an over-dependence on a single domestic market. Increased geographic diversification can help to **spread risk**.

- **Economies of scale**: technological factors may be such that a large volume is needed either to cover the high costs of plant, equipment, R&D and personnel or to exploit a large potential for economies of scale and experience. For these reasons firms in the aviation, ethical drugs, computer and automobile industries are often obliged to enter multiple countries.

- **Variable quality**: international expansion can facilitate the disposal of discontinued products and seconds since these can be sold abroad without spoiling the home market.

- **Finance**: many firms are attracted by favourable opportunities such as the following:

  - The development of lucrative emerging markets (such as China and India)
  - Depreciation in their domestic currency values
  - Corporate tax benefits offered by particular countries
  - Lowering of import barriers abroad

- **Familial**: many countries and companies trade because of family or cultural connections.

- **Aid agencies**: countries that benefit from bilateral or unilateral aid often purchase goods which normally they would not have the money for.

3.2 International expansion

- **Reasons supporting international expansion**

  - **Profit margins** may be higher abroad.

  - Increase in **sales volume** from foreign sales may allow large reductions in unit costs.

  - The **product life cycle** may be extended if the product is at an earlier stage in the life cycle in other countries.

  - **Seasonal fluctuations** may be levelled out (peak periods in some countries coinciding with troughs in others).

  - It offers an opportunity of **disposing of excess production** in times of low domestic demand.

- International activities **spread the risk** which exists in any single market (eg, political and economic changes).

- **Obsolescent products** can be sold off to international customers without damage to the domestic market.

- The firm's prestige may be enhanced by portraying a **global image**.

- **Reasons for avoiding international expansion**

- Profits may be unduly affected by factors outside the firm's **control** (eg, due to fluctuation of exchange rates and foreign government actions).

- The **adaptations** to the product (or other marketing mix elements) needed for international success will diminish the effects of economies of scale.

- Extending the product life cycle is not always **cost effective**. It may be better to develop new products for the domestic market.

- **Opportunity costs** of investing abroad – funds and resources may be better utilised at home.

- In the case of marginal cost pricing, **anti-dumping duties** are more quickly imposed now than in the past.

3.3 Issues for management to consider

3.3.1 Strategic issues

- Is the venture likely to yield an acceptable financial **return**?

- Does it fit with the company's overall **mission** and objectives?

- Does the organisation have (or can it raise) the **resources** necessary to exploit effectively international opportunities?

- What is the impact on the firm's **risk** profile?

- What **method of entry** is most suitable?

3.3.2 Tactical issues

- How can the company get to **understand customers' needs** and preferences in foreign markets?

- Does the company know how to **conduct business** abroad, and deal effectively with potential partners there?

- Are there **foreign regulations** and associated hidden costs?

- Does the company have the necessary **management skills** and experience?

Such tactical issues may mean international expansion is more easily achieved through some form of acquisition or shared arrangement, rather than by organic growth.

4 Mergers and acquisitions

Section overview

- A merger is the integration of two or more businesses. An acquisition is where one business purchases another. This offers speedy access to new technologies and markets, but there are risks: only about half of acquisitions succeed.

- The mechanics of financing and undertaking a merger or acquisition are essential to its success and will be covered in the Financial Management syllabus.

4.1 The motives for acquiring companies

Definitions

A **merger** concerns the joining of two separate companies to form a single company.

An **acquisition** is the purchase of a controlling interest in another company.

Some acquisitions are dressed up to look like mergers (ie, a combination of equals) because it suggests agreement and may ease the integration of cultures.

In financial reporting, IFRS do not permit the concept of a merger. Nevertheless, strategically and in terms of financial arrangements, a merger may best describe a business combination, rather than being forced to identify an acquirer.

The classic reasons for mergers/acquisitions as a part of strategy are as follows.

Reason	Effect on operations
Marketing advantages	• New product range • Market presence • Rationalise distribution and advertising • Eliminate competition
Production advantages	• Economies of scale • Technology and skills • Greater production capacity • Safeguard future supplies • Bulk purchase opportunities
Finance and management	• Management team • Cash resources • Gain assets • Tax advantages (eg, losses bought)
Risk-spreading	• Diversification
Retain independence	• Avoid being taken over by acquiring predator by becoming too big to buy
Overcome barriers to entry	• Acquired firm may have licences or patents
Outplay rivals	• Stop rival getting the target

4.2 Diversification

Diversification means a change of both products and markets from the company's present base. Because of the extent of the change there is clearly more risk involved than in expansion, so we must consider the reasons why firms nevertheless diversify:

- **Objectives can no longer be met without diversification**. This would be identified by the gap analysis. The reason for the dissatisfaction with the present industry might be due to poor return caused by product decline, with little chance of technological innovation in the same field, or due to a lack of flexibility, eg, unavoidable dependence on a single customer or a single product line.

- **The firm has more cash than it needs for expansion.** Whether it prefers to invest this outside the business or to seek opportunities for diversification will depend on the relative rates of return obtainable (in general the return from operations exceeds the return from outside investments, but of course more risk is involved) and management preference (management have to balance the internal flexibility achieved by keeping reserves in liquid form with external flexibility offered by diversification).

- **Firms may diversify even if their objectives are being or could be met within their industry**, if diversification promises to be more profitable than expansion.

Related and conglomerate diversification were covered in detail in Chapter 7.

4.3 Porter's attractiveness tests

An acquisition at a bargain price is unlikely to make up for a long-run lack of profits due to a flawed industry structure. For reasons of cost, the ideal acquisition is in an industry not yet attractive but capable of being made attractive.

Porter proposes two tests:

1. **The 'cost of entry' test**

   Unfortunately attractive industries tend to have high costs of entry. Premiums likely to be paid for the acquisition of companies are an important consideration.

2. **The 'better off' test**

   The acquisition must do something for shareholders that they cannot do for themselves. Diversification for its own sake will not increase shareholder wealth. Asset stripping brings only one-off benefits and is not a sound basis for long-run investment.

4.4 Acquisitions and risk

Acquisitions provide a means of entering a market, or building up a market share, more quickly and/or at a lower cost than would be incurred if the company tried to develop its own resources.

Corporate planners must however consider the level of **risk** involved. Acquiring companies internationally is more risky, for a number of reasons.

The acquirer should attempt an evaluation of the following:

- The prospects of technological change in the industry
- The size and strength of competitors
- The reaction of competitors to an acquisition
- The likelihood of government intervention and legislation
- The state of the industry and its long-term prospects
- The amount of synergy obtainable from the merger or acquisition

Worked example: Apple and Shazam

The following example focuses on Apple's bid to acquire the music app Shazam. Apple's bid is aimed at exploiting the potential technological synergies between the two companies.

In December 2017 it was reported that Apple had agreed to purchase the music recognition app Shazam. According to BBC (2017) the deal was believed to be worth $400 million (£300 million). The Shazam app allows a user to play a piece of music through their smartphone and other devices, and it then identifies the music and artist. Having identified a particular song, users are then able to 'purchase' the music via a streaming service such as Apple's iTunes Store. Shazam generates revenue from 'commissions paid on referrals to Apple's iTunes Store'. (BBC, 2017).

In February 2018, Gibbs (2018) reported that the proposed deal was being investigated by the European Commission amid fears raised by member states that the acquisition would undermine competition. Kottosova (2018) noted that the European Commission was particularly concerned that 'the deal could give Apple access to commercially sensitive data about customers of its competitors, and that Apple could use it to hurt its rivals.'

At the time of writing the Commission had not concluded its investigation into the deal.

Sources:

BBC, (2017) *Apple 'buy Shazam for $400m'*. [Online]. Available from: www.bbc.co.uk [Accessed: 27 April 2018].

Gibbs, S. (7 February 2018). EU to review Apple's reported $400m purchases of music app Shazam. *The Guardian*. [Online]. Available from: www.theguardian.com [Accessed: 27 April 2018].

Kottasova, I.(2018) *EU hits pause on Apple's deal to buy Shazam*. [Online]. Available from: http://money.cnn.com [Accessed 27 April 2018].

4.5 Synergy as a motive for acquisitions

Definition

Synergy: The benefits gained from two or more businesses combining that would not have been available to each independently. Sometimes expressed as the 2 + 2 = 5 effect. Synergy arises because of complementary resources which are compatible with the products or markets being developed and is often realised by transferring skills or sharing activities.

Worked example: Marriott group

The US-based Marriott group provides a good example of skill transfers. The group initially began in the restaurant business. One of its major skills was the use of standardised menus and hospitality routines. Much of its initial business was in the sale of takeaways to customers on the way to the airport. Accordingly it diversified in turn into airline catering, in-house catering, family restaurants, gourmet restaurants, hotels, cruise ships, travel agents and theme parks. Interestingly some areas, such as gourmet restaurants and travel agents, where skills were not easily transferred, were subsequently divested.

Synergies arise from four sources:

1. **Marketing and sales synergies**

   - Benefits of conferring one firm's brands on products of another.
   - Use of common sales team and advertising.
   - Ability to offer wider product range to the client.

2. **Operating synergies**

   - Economies of scale – in purchasing of inputs, capital equipment etc.
   - Economies of scope – including use of distribution channels and warehousing.
   - Rationalisation of common capacity (eg, logistics, stores, factories).
   - Capacity smoothing (eg, one firm's peak demand coincides with the other's slack time).

3. **Financial synergies**

   - Risk spreading allows cheaper capital to be obtained.
   - Reduction in market competition if firms in similar industry.
   - Shared benefits from same R&D.
   - Possibly more stable cash flows.
   - Sale of surplus assets.

4. **Management synergies**

   - Highly paid managers used to fix ailing firm rather than administer successful one.
   - Transfer of learning across businesses.
   - Increased opportunity for managerial specialisation in a larger firm.

4.6 The mechanics of acquiring companies

Management will wish to assess the value of an acquisition since the price to be paid is critical in determining whether the acquisition is worthwhile. A number of share valuation techniques are available and there are different ways of paying for an acquisition (cash, shares, loan stock). These topics will be covered in your Financial Management syllabus.

Broadly speaking, there are two types of acquisition approaches:

1. **Agreed bids**: here there have been discussions beforehand between the boards of the two companies and their significant investors and a price and management structure agreed. The bid is announced and the board of the target recommends acceptance to the shareholders.

2. **Hostile (contested) bids**: the predator has either been turned down by the board in discussions or did not approach them to begin with, preferring to build a shareholding over the months beforehand at lower prices before announcing a bid to the market through the financial media.

4.7 Reasons for failure of acquisitions

Takeovers benefit the shareholders of the acquired company often more than the acquirer. According to the Economist Intelligence Unit, there is a consensus that fewer than half of all acquisitions are successful, if seen from the point of view of the buyer's shareholders.

The reasons for the poor performance of acquisitions include:

- Acquirers conduct financial audits but, according to research by London Business School, only 37% conducted anything approaching a management audit.

- Some major problems of implementation relate to human resources and personnel issues such as morale, performance assessment and culture. If key managers or personnel leave, the business will suffer.

- A further explanation may be that excessive prices are paid for acquisitions, resulting in shareholders in the target company being rewarded for expected synergy gains.

- Lack of actual strategic fit between the businesses.

- Failure of new management to retain key staff and clients.

- Failures by management to exert corporate governance and control over larger business.

4.8 Reasons acquisitions still occur

- Many acquisitions and mergers are successful.

- Evidence of a loss of value resulting from a merger doesn't consider whether a worse outcome might have occurred if the firms had not combined.

- Vested interests of corporate financial advisors in pressing for the acquisition, ie, commissions and fees.

- Weak corporate governance allows domineering CEOs or boards to pursue personal agendas with shareholder funds (eg, 'empire building').

- Short-term need for boards to give impression of strategic action to convince investors that business is growing.

Worked example: Expedia

The following example illustrates the mixed fortunes that Expedia has endured following its recent programme of acquisition.

In March 2016, Expedia - one of the world's largest online travel services companies - reported a quarterly profit following a number of acquisitions during 2015. Reuters (2016) noted that shares in the company rose 11.7% and also saw the company beat its revenue expectations.

The news followed Expedia's acquisition spending spree during 2015 in which it purchased rival firms Orbitz Worldwide and Travelocity for $1.3 billion and $280 million respectively. Chowdhry (2016) noted the comments made by Exepdia's then CEO Dara Khosrowshahi following the acquisition of Travelocity, 'Travelocity is one of the most recognised travel brands in North America, offering thousands of travel destinations to more than 20 million travellers per month'. At the end of 2015 Expedia completed the purchase of holiday rental site, HomeAway Inc for $3.9 billion. Expedia plans to use HomeAway as a means of competing with Airbnb which offers rental accommodation.

In February 2018 it was reported that Expedia's share price had fallen following the announcement of disappointing quarter results, with the company forecasting that its 'selling and marketing costs would outpace revenue growth as it battles rivals for market share'. (Ajmera and Shivdas, 2018). Prior to releasing its quarterly results Expedia had announced that its 'investments in its core business and in vacation rental site HomeAway […], as well as higher-cloud spending' would impact its results in 2018. (Ajmera and Shivdas, 2018).

Sources:

A.Chowdhry. (2016) *Expedia has acquired Travelocity for $280 million in cash*. [Online]. Available from: www.forbes.com [Accessed 7 June 2016]

Reuters. (2016) *Expedia posts surprise profit as acquisitions pay off*. [Online]. Available from: www.reuters.com [Accessed 7 June 2016]

Ajmera, A. and Shivdas, S. (2018) *Expedia shares sink after disappointing 2018 forecast*. [Online]. Available from: www.reuters.com [Accessed 27 April 2018].

5 Joint ventures, alliances and franchising

Section overview

- These are other types of arrangement whereby businesses pool resources.

5.1 Choosing business partners

The following factors should be considered in choosing business partners for joint ventures, alliances and franchising.

Drivers	What benefits are offered by collaboration?
Partners	Which partners should be chosen?
Facilitators	Does the external environment favour a partnership?
Components	Activities and processes in the network.
Effectiveness	Does the previous history of alliances generate good results? Is the alliance just a temporary blip? For example, in the airline industry, there are many strategic alliances, but these arise in part because there are legal barriers to cross-border ownership.
Market-orientation	Alliance partners are harder to control and may not have the same commitment to the end-user.

5.2 Joint ventures

Definitions

Consortia: Organisations that co-operate on specific business prospects.

A **joint venture:** is a contractual arrangement whereby two or more parties undertake an economic activity which is subject to joint control.

Joint ventures are especially attractive to **smaller or risk-averse firms**, or where very expensive new technologies are being researched and developed. Other advantages of joint ventures are:

- They permit coverage of a **larger number of countries** since each one requires less investment.
- They can reduce the risk of **government intervention**.
- They can provide close **control** over operations.
- A joint venture with an indigenous firm provides **local knowledge**.
- They can also be a **learning exercise**.
- They provide funds for expensive **technology and research** projects.
- They are often an alternative to seeking to buy or build a wholly owned manufacturing operation abroad.
- Core competences, which are not available in one entity can be accessed from another venturer.

The major disadvantages of joint ventures are:

- Major **conflicts of interest** over profit shares, amounts invested, the management of the joint venture, and the marketing strategy.
- Problems in each party protecting **intellectual property** such as proprietary product designs, process methods.
- Danger that a **partner may seek to leave joint venture** if its priorities change (eg, shortage of funds) or it is acquired by another firm.
- **Lack of management interest**: the JV will be seen as a secondment outside of the main career hierarchy of the parent firms.
- Exit routes may be unclear, including sharing of the assets generated in the venture.
- Contractual rights may be difficult to enforce across geographical borders or regulatory boundaries.

Worked example: Alphabet and Aramco

In early 2018 it was reported that Alphabet, the parent company of Google, had entered into preliminary talks with Saudi Arabia's state-owned oil company, Aramco, with a view to establishing a joint venture to build a network of data centres in Saudi Arabia. DiChristopher (2018) noted that Saudi Arabia 'is embarking upon an ambitious plan, led by […] Crown Prince Mohammed bin Salman, to diversify the nation's oil-dependent economy'.

Source:

DiChristopher, T. (2018) *Google parent Alphabet and Aramco are in talks to build a tech hub in Saudi Arabia'.* [Online]. Available from: www.cnbc.com [Accessed: 27 April 2018].

5.3 Alliances

Some firms enter long-term **strategic alliances** with others for a variety of reasons:

- They share development costs of a particular technology.

- The regulatory environment prohibits take-overs (eg, most major airlines are in strategic alliances because in most countries there are limits to the level of control an 'outsider' can have over an airline).

- Complementary markets or technology.

Such alliances tend to be a looser contractual arrangement than a joint venture and no separate company is formed. There may be less commitment than to a joint venture so the benefits whilst similar, may not be so great. Strategic alliances only go so far, as there may be disputes over control of strategic assets.

Alliances have some **limitations**:

- **Core competence**: each organisation should be able to focus on its core competence. Alliances may not enable it to create new competences.

- **Strategic priorities**: if a key aspect of strategic delivery is handed over to a partner, the firm loses flexibility. A core competence may not be enough to provide a comprehensive customer benefit.

5.3.1 Information systems based alliances

The cost of major Information system (IS) based methods of working, combined with their inherent communications capability have made alliances based on IS a natural development. There are four common types:

- **Single industry partnerships**: for example, UK insurance brokers can use a common system called IVANS to research the products offered by all of the major insurance companies.

- **Multi-industry joint marketing partnerships**: some industries are so closely linked with others that it makes sense to establish IS linking their offerings. A well-known example is holiday bookings, where a flight reservation over the internet is likely to lead to a seamless offer of hotel reservations and car hire.

- **Supply chain partnerships**: greater and closer co-operation along the supply chain has led to the need for better and faster information flows. Electronic data interchange between customers and suppliers is one aspect of this improvement, perhaps seen most clearly in the car industry, where the big-name manufacturers effectively control the flow of inputs from their suppliers. However, as we discussed in Chapter 6, linking the information systems of customers and suppliers presents new challenges especially around data protection.

- **IT supplier partnerships**: a slightly different kind of partnership is not uncommon in the IT industry itself, where physical products have their own major software content. The development of these products requires close co-operation between the hardware and software companies concerned.

5.4 Licensing agreements

A licence grants a third-party organisation the rights to exploit an asset belonging to the licensor.

Licences can be granted over:

- The use of brands and recipes (eg, Nestle selling Starbucks coffee 'under licence' .)

- A patent or technology (eg, an IT firm may be licensed to install and maintain some given software application.)

- A particular asset (eg, a drinks firm may buy a license to exploit a mineral water source or a media firm will license the rights to produce and sell a particular film, book or recording in its country.)

Licensees will pay an agreed proportion of the sales revenue to the licensor for the right to exploit the license in a given geographical area or for a given range of products.

Licence agreements will vary considerably in the constraints the place on the licensee. Some will dictate branding, pricing and marketing issues. Others will leave there decisions to the licensee.

A very common form of licensing is the franchise.

5.5 Franchising

Franchising is a method of expanding the business on less capital than would otherwise be possible. Franchisers include IKEA, McDonald's, Starbucks and Pizza Hut.

Franchising can be a method of financing rapid growth without having to raise as much capital as conventional business structures. The International Franchising Association provides prospective franchisors with a directory of current global franchise opportunities. Companies including American car repair business AAMCO offer franchises in Africa, while Dairy Queen are looking for investors in their domestic US market.

The mechanism

- The franchiser grants a licence to the franchisee allowing the franchisee to use the franchiser's name, goodwill, systems.

- The franchisee pays the franchiser for these rights and also for subsequent support services which the franchiser may supply.

- The franchisee is responsible for the day-to-day running of the franchise. The franchiser may impose quality control measures on the franchisee to ensure that the goodwill of the franchiser is not damaged.

- Capital for setting up the franchise is normally supplied by both parties. The franchiser may help the franchisee in presenting proposals to suppliers of capital; presenting a business plan based on a successful trading formula will make it easier to obtain finance. Thus far, the franchiser needs less equity capital than other business structures.

- The franchiser will typically provide support services, including national advertising, market research, research and development, technical expertise, and management support.

Advantages for the franchiser

- Rapid expansion and increasing market share with relatively little equity capital, since franchisees will put in some capital. Strategically, the franchiser will be able to pursue an aggressive expansion policy to cover all geographical areas and establish brand dominance which otherwise could not be afforded.

- The franchisee provides local knowledge and unit supervision. The franchiser specialises in providing a central marketing and control function, limiting the range of management skills needed.

- The franchiser has limited capital in any one unit and therefore has low financial risk.

- Economies of scale are quickly available to the franchiser as the network increases. Hence supply of branded goods, extensive advertising spend are justifiable.

- Franchisee has strong incentives.

The advantages for the franchisee are mainly in the set-up stages, where many new businesses often fail. The franchisee will adopt a brand name, trading format and product specification that have been tested and practised. The learning curve and attendant risks are minimised. The franchisee usually undertakes training, organised by the franchiser, which should provide a running start, thus further reducing risk.

Disadvantages

- A franchisee is largely independent and makes personal decisions about how to run his operation. In addition, the quality of product, customer satisfaction and goodwill is under his control. The franchiser will seek to maintain some control or influence over quality and service from the centre, but this will be difficult if the local unit sees opportunities to increase profit by deviating from the standards which the franchiser has established.

- There can be a clash between local needs or opportunities and the strategy of the franchiser. For example, in the late 1980s McDonald's pursued a strategy of widening the usage of outlets, in particular by encouraging breakfast trade and family groups in the evenings. As part of this it was determined that ideal locations would be in pedestrian areas, near to schools, hospitals, office centres. A franchisee in an industrial town may disagree with this strategy and want to locate on a busy approach road to an industrial estate.

- The franchiser may seek to update/amend the products/services on offer, while some franchisees may be slow to accept change or may find it necessary to write off existing inventory holdings.

- The most successful franchisees may break away and set up as independents, thereby becoming competitors.

5.6 Agency arrangements

These can be used as the distribution channel where local knowledge and contacts are important, eg, exporting. The agreements may be restricted to marketing and product support. Other situations where agents are used include:

- Sales of cosmetics
- Holidays
- Financial services, eg, insurance

The main problem for the company is that it is cut off from direct contact with the customer.

Interactive question: Ponda

Ponda plc is the second largest vehicle manufacturing firm in Europe. The board was recently concerned about the lack of 'infant' products in the firm's portfolio, and so decided to launch an electric car – the Greencar. Early research has shown that the demand is expected to be much higher in the US market initially than in the European market.

For the initial trial launch Ponda has decided to distribute the car using the American dealer Envirofriend Inc. The firm was keen to participate in the venture to bolster its environmental credentials in the market. If the launch proves to be successful, the arrangement will be reviewed. If the new product proves to be as popular as the board of Ponda hopes, it may be necessary to enlist additional distribution networks. However, the Managing Director has assured Envirofriend that the networks will include Envirofriend (so long as the Greencar continues to be sold in American markets).

Ponda had originally wanted to invoice Envirofriend in sterling, but reluctantly agreed to do so in dollars, on the understanding that all the cars would be paid for, whether sold or not. Envirofriend accepted this risk, as the car's remarkable technical properties were expected to result in near certain sales (according to research).

If the car is popular in the initial market, Ponda has decided to penetrate the mass market as quickly and efficiently as possible by setting up a manufacturing subsidiary in the US. It has never been the intention of the firm to distribute its own products; Ponda will continue to do so via third parties. Franchising is currently being considered as part of the distribution mix.

Ponda's strategic planning department has investigated the possible effect of US Government policy on the Greencar venture. You have been given a rough draft of the research.

(1) It is likely that indigenous firms will be awarded preferential taxation treatment, such as 100% capital allowances, on research-related expenditure.

(2) Government grants for the purchase of the robotic machinery required for the manufacture of the electric cars are to be awarded to firms buying from US companies.

(3) Legislation is currently being planned to increase redundancy payments required in the hi-tech manufacturing industries. It is felt that this may lead to firms investigating ways in which to utilise their spare capacity.

(4) Unfortunately for Ponda the potential competitors are all government suppliers.

(5) The regulatory bodies in the US are likely to bring severe pressure to bear on Ponda – particularly with regard to price and environmental performance indicators.

(6) The Government has already decided to buy a large number of electric motorbikes for the state education sector, to provide free transport to children from low income families (as an alternative to public transport). The scheme has proved extremely popular in rural areas. The US supplier has profited considerably from the deal, and is considering diversification into related areas.

(7) Import tariffs are to be levied on all 'environmental' goods manufactured by firms which are not resident in the US.

(8) A network of 'recharging points' is to be set up by the US Government, designed for use by all types of 'electric vehicle'. The government is keen to set up the system as quickly as possible, and is therefore planning to develop a system ensuring compatibility with the first firm offering marketable vehicles.

(9) Output tax is to be levied on petrol, but not on electricity obtained from the 'recharging network'.

Apart from political research Ponda has also commissioned research into the environmental movement in the US. There is a board consensus in favour of electrically-powered vehicles, particularly in urban areas. The main lobby against such products argues that the switch from petrol engines to electrical engines merely transfers the pollution problem from the car to the power station. Ponda is finding it difficult to judge which lobby will win the greater support in the long term.

The technology associated with the Greencar is far superior to that developed by other manufacturers to date: the electric car is no longer the poor relation of the petrol car. In fact, the Greencar has consistently outperformed its 'petrol using' rivals in respect of:

- Miles per $ of 'fuel'
- Top speeds
- Quietness inside the car
- Reliability of the engine
- Servicing frequency required
- Environmental pollution

Ponda is concerned about the expected speed of competitive reaction if the car causes the revolution in the industry which its performance specification would merit. Unfortunately, a patent could not be obtained for the design, so Ponda is expecting its rivals to introduce 'copycat' versions a year or so after the initial launch. One strategy, currently under serious consideration, would be to sell the manufacturing technology to allow production of the Greencar under licence. In any case the directors are sure of the need to establish a strong brand image as quickly as possible, so that the generic product – the electric car – becomes strongly identified in the mind of the consumer with the brand name Greencar, rather as the generic product 'vacuum cleaner' is strongly associated with the brand 'Hoover'.

Requirements

Write a memorandum to the Managing Director of Ponda concerning the strategic aspects of the Greencar project.

Your memorandum should include the following.

- US Government policy

- A discussion on whether the manufacturing plant should be constructed by Ponda or acquired or whether manufacturing should be licensed

- Consideration of the appropriateness of franchising as a distribution strategy for the Greencar

See **Answer** at the end of this chapter.

Summary and Self-test

Summary

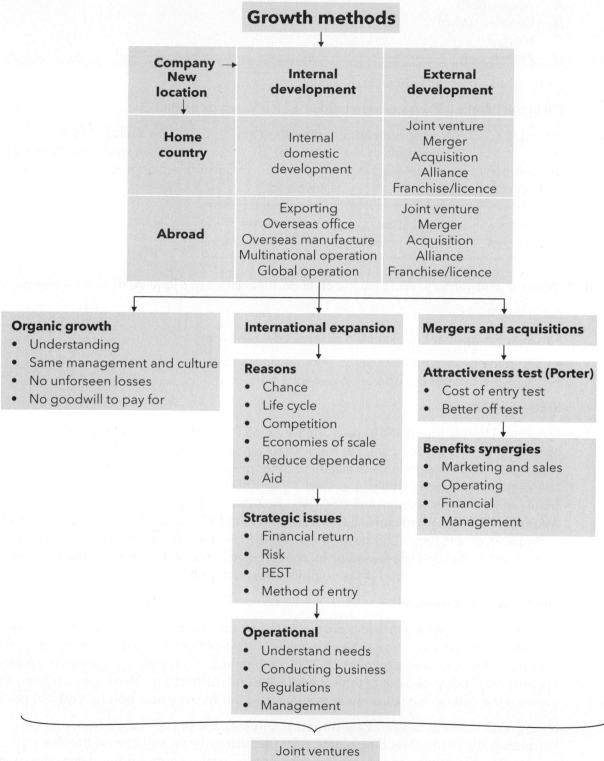

Growth methods

Company → New location	Internal development	External development
Home country	Internal domestic development	Joint venture Merger Acquisition Alliance Franchise/licence
Abroad	Exporting Overseas office Overseas manufacture Multinational operation Global operation	Joint venture Merger Acquisition Alliance Franchise/licence

Organic growth
- Understanding
- Same management and culture
- No unforseen losses
- No goodwill to pay for

International expansion

Reasons
- Chance
- Life cycle
- Competition
- Economies of scale
- Reduce dependance
- Aid

Strategic issues
- Financial return
- Risk
- PEST
- Method of entry

Operational
- Understand needs
- Conducting business
- Regulations
- Management

Mergers and acquisitions

Attractiveness test (Porter)
- Cost of entry test
- Better off test

Benefits synergies
- Marketing and sales
- Operating
- Financial
- Management

Joint ventures
Alliances
Franchises/licences

Self-test

Answer the following questions.

1   What is the primary method of growth for most organisations?

    A   Acquisitions
    B   Organic growth
    C   Merger
    D   Franchising

2   Distinguish a merger from an acquisition.

3   **Fill in the blanks** in the statement below, using the words in the box.

(a) .... provide a means of entering a (b) .... or building up a (c) .... , more quickly and at a lower (d) .... than would be incurred if the company tried to develop its own (e) .... Corporate planners must however consider the level of (f) .... involved.

• risk	• cost	• market
• market share	• resources	• acquisitions

4   Define a joint venture. What are the chief disadvantages of a joint venture for a company?

5   Fill in the blanks.

Particularly important questions in a buyout decision are:

- Can the buyout team .... to pay for the buyout?
- Can the bought out operation generate enough ....?

6   **Kultivator Ltd**

Kultivator Ltd was founded 10 years ago by Jamie Dimmock and Charlie Oliver, when they opened their first garden centre in Hampshire. Since then the business has grown, both organically and through the acquisition of other privately-owned businesses. The largest acquisition took place in the year ended 31 July 20X0, following an injection of capital by a small number of institutional investors, who now own 15% of the company's share capital. As a result, Kultivator Ltd currently operates a chain of 25 garden centres across the south of England, employing 1,250 staff. To expand further, it is now considering raising more capital, either through borrowing or by converting to a plc and floating on the London Stock Exchange to obtain a full listing or floating on the AIM.

The industry background

Over the past 15 years a growing proportion of consumer spending in the UK has been devoted to gardening. This has been matched by a rapid growth in the number of garden centres and an increasing number of TV programmes and 'lifestyle' magazines dedicated to the pastime. Today, two out of three people in Britain admit to gardening as a hobby, which makes it the country's most popular pastime, and the industry now employs 60,000 people.

Most garden centres are privately-owned businesses, usually operating from one site. Frequently they buy in bedding plants and specialist services, sometimes franchising retailers to offer particular services (eg, mower repairs and garden equipment sales; garden furniture; fencing; greenhouses and huts; fountains and water garden facilities; etc). Others have developed expertise in growing certain types of plants and trees, which has enabled them in part to capture a niche in the market and partially integrate their production activities into one or more retailing outlets.

Despite the rapid growth in this part of the consumer market, amongst large companies only a few DIY chains have ventured into the field. A major inhibiting factor appears to have been the general lack of horticultural skills amongst potential employees. Such skills, however, are often possessed by the owners of smaller, locally-based businesses. Some of these – such as Kultivator Ltd – have been able to expand successfully, either growing organically by opening up new outlets, or – more usually – by acquiring other ready-made family businesses. This has enabled them to take advantage of economies of scale in retailing (eg, in providing deliveries), and their buying power when dealing with larger specialist suppliers (eg, of plants and trees and of garden equipment).

The flotation option

A merchant bank consulted by Kultivator Ltd has estimated the most likely flotation value of the business, once it has converted to become a plc, would be £94,200,000. This is based on the estimated 20X0/20X1 pre-tax profit growing at 4% per annum over the next three years and thereafter at 2% per annum.

The bank has proposed that the company should either be floated on The London Stock Exchange to obtain a full listing or be floated on the AIM. This means that Jamie Dimmock and Charlie Oliver will together receive over £20 million for part of their holding in the business, but still leave them with a controlling interest of 63%.

The views of the owners of Kultivator plc

Jamie Dimmock is disappointed with the merchant bank's advice. He believes that it is unduly pessimistic to assume that the growth rate in pre-tax profits will be as low as 4% per annum over the next three years, falling thereafter to a mere 2%. After all, in recent years profits have grown faster than the increase in revenue, reflecting the company's ability to reap the rewards of economies of scale, while at the same time being able to exercise greater bargaining power when negotiating with suppliers. He believes that the merchant bank's rather pessimistic forecasts are based on an unrealistic assumption that the large DIY groups will take a growing share of the market at the expense of independents such as Kultivator Ltd. Already they face an effective barrier to entry in as much as they are having difficulty in employing skilled horticulturalists. Customers are increasingly anxious to have appropriate advice, and the existing well-rewarded staff at Kultivator Ltd have the appropriate expertise. In the circumstances, he would prefer either to rely on further bank borrowing or to seek advice from another merchant bank.

Charlie Oliver does not entirely agree. She is not so sure that the barriers to entry facing the large DIY groups are that high, and anyway she cannot quite see what competitive edge companies such as Kultivator Ltd have over these groups when it comes to recruiting skilled personnel. Equally, she would favour growth by pursuing an alternative production strategy rather than only by expanding retail sales. This could be achieved if Kultivator Ltd were to grow its own plants and shrubs or sought a tie-up with a nursery or seed merchant. Capital could also be used to increase holdings of inventories and reduce short-term borrowings, thus strengthening the company's working capital position.

Requirements

As an assistant to a partner in the firm of accountants which advises Jamie Dimmock and Charlie Oliver, draft a memorandum for them which deals briefly with the following issues:

- An assessment of how floating the company might affect the objectives of the company, even though Jamie Dimmock and Charlie Oliver would still control the business.

- The validity of the assumptions which appear to underlie the growth projections implicit in the merchant bank's calculation of the company's flotation value, dealing in particular with:

    - Barriers to entry and the threat of competition from large DIY groups
    - Whether growth should be via vertical integration or horizontal expansion

- Whether organic growth should be preferred to expansion via acquisition.

Note: Ignore taxation.

7   Read the scenario of the **September 2010 Business Strategy and Technology** question in the Question Bank entitled *Marcham plc (amended)*. Draft an answer to the requirement on organic growth versus acquisition.

8   Read the scenario of the **December 2014 Business Strategy and Technology** question entitled *'Confo plc'*. Draft an answer to the third requirement which asks for a review of the strategies adopted by the Export Division and the Commercial Division.

9   Read the scenario of the **September 2017 Business Strategy and Technology** question entitled *'Blakes Blinds Ltd''*. Draft an answer to the requirement which asks for a discussion of the main advantages and disadvantages of the acquisition.

Now, go back to the Learning outcomes in the Introduction. If you are satisfied you have achieved these objectives, please tick them off.

Answer to Interactive question

Answer to Interactive question

Ponda plc

Memorandum

To	The Managing Director, Ponda plc
From	F Smith
Date	Today
Subject	The strategic aspects of the Greencar project

Government policy

According to research present policy favours the US firms over foreign competition. Import tariffs for non-resident companies in the sector, preferential taxation treatment relating to R&D expenditure, grants to aid the purchase of equipment from US firms, and heavy government expenditure on Ponda's competitors all mean that Ponda has an inherent disadvantage compared to the US competition. The extent of the government support is well illustrated by the government contract to buy electric motorbikes for the state sector. This has resulted in the supplier making large profits, and thus being able to finance new developments internally, which may include the production of a Greencar-like product.

The planned legislation concerning increasing the redundancy payments in the high-technology sector effectively acts as an exit barrier, as firms will incur high costs if they attempt to close down manufacturing plant. Therefore, excess capacity in the industry is to be expected. Some firms may use this spare capacity to produce rival products to the Greencar. Alternatively, Ponda can use this resource to 'contract out' its productions.

The output tax treatment of electricity from the recharging network (at 0%) gives the electric car product an advantage over its petrol-engine rivals. This is an advantage for the entire industry, but is most significant for Ponda, which, as the pioneering manufacturer, will be the first to realise the benefits. Similarly, the government-funded recharging network will prove advantageous to Ponda, particularly as the technical capability (with Ponda) will inevitably force Ponda's rivals to alter their designs.

The manufacturing plant

The manufacturing facility, whether acquired or constructed, will only be required if the initial sales go well. This is expected because of the extraordinary technical specification of the Greencar. Therefore, given a successful result in the test market, the company should proceed with a 'fast growth' strategy to capture the mass market before the competition has a chance to enter the market. Ponda could achieve this by

- Buying an existing manufacturing firm (bearing in mind that the process of adoption may be onerous and lengthy)

- Allowing other firms to manufacture the Greencar under licence (essentially a joint venture)

- Setting up its own plant

The case in favour of Ponda setting up its own plant is weak: to build up the necessary capacity quickly by internal means could be difficult. However, the overwhelming case against Ponda setting up its own plant is found in the US Government policy of favouring US firms. Because of increased redundancy payment legislation, many suitable firms will have spare capacity that they are anxious to use. It should be possible to enter into a very favourable joint venture with a US firm. (It is assumed that if a US firm were taken over by Ponda, it would lose its favoured position as a US firm.)

Franchising as a possible distribution strategy

Assuming that the test market is a success, the firm should attempt to reach the mass market as soon as possible. Assuming that Ponda has arranged sufficient production capacity to achieve this, distribution networks must be set up quickly. The main choice appears to be between established dealers and franchisees (since Ponda has expressed an intention not to set up its own networks). There is an additional constraint: under either scenario Envirofriend must be included in the distribution mix.

Franchising is an arrangement whereby a company distributes products – usually of a 'famous' brand type (as Greencar is expected to become). For the privilege the franchisee pays a capital sum (at the start of the arrangement) plus a stream of royalty payments, dependent on the success of the franchise.

Franchising would be a suitable component of distribution for Ponda for the following reasons.

- The arrangement typically involves tight control over the marketing elements of the business such as brand name, unique selling points to employ, in-store promotions, etc. A unified marketing effort across the outlets is essential for the firm to penetrate the market, and this is arguably easiest to achieve by franchising.

- The franchisees are strongly motivated to sell a high volume of cars (since their success depends on it).

- Ponda does not have to invest in any capital (this is provided by the franchisee), thus the strategy is low risk (for Ponda) if the project fails no capital has been wasted, whereas if the project succeeds the franchisees suffer (and Ponda is not affected).

- Franchise systems have been associated with a high rate of growth – ideal for Ponda.

The disadvantages include the following.

- Selection of the franchisees may be difficult (given the new type of products).

- Since the Greencar has no track record, setting the balance between the initial fixed capital and the variable royalty payments could be difficult.

- The time spent in training the franchisees could result in a drain on resources.

Nevertheless, these disadvantages are not insurmountable, and therefore the franchising strategy is to be recommended.

Answers to Self-test

1 B Most organisations expand via organic growth. This involves the use of internal resources.

2 A merger is the joining of two separate companies to form a single company.
An acquisition is the purchase of a controlling interest in another company.

3 (a) Acquisitions (b) market (c) market share (d) cost (e) resources (f) risk

4 A joint venture is an arrangement where two firms (or more) join forces for manufacturing, financial and marketing purposes and each has a share in both the equity and the management of the business. The major disadvantage of joint ventures is that there can be conflicts of interest.

5 Particularly important questions in a buyout decision are:

- Can the buyout team afford to pay for the buyout?

- Can the bought out operation generate enough earnings to pay the interest on the borrowings?

6 **Kultivator plc**

Memorandum

To	AN Other & Co
From	Assistant to A Partner, AN Other & Co, Chartered Accountants
Date	Today
Subject	Objectives, assumptions and growth

An assessment of how floating the company might affect the objectives of the entity, even though the existing majority shareholders would still control the business.

Clearly at the present time Jamie Dimmock and Charlie Oliver, as controlling shareholders of Kultivator Ltd, can run the business in a way which suits their own private objectives.

These might include maximising revenue, expanding the business, and/or maximising their directors' salaries.

However, as soon as outside shareholders take a stake in the company the interests of Jamie Dimmock and Charlie Oliver will be constrained to some degree, even if they retain a controlling stake in the business.

In fact, Jamie Dimmock and Charlie Oliver will almost certainly already be constrained to some extent, given that institutions have taken a 15% stake in the business.

It is unlikely that they will have done this without having some say in the way in which the company is managed eg, by appointing a director to the board.

It is also probable that the bank will also have placed restrictions on the way in which the directors may operate if it has lent money to the business.

However, in the absence of any contractual constraints, in company law the fact that Jamie Dimmock and Charlie Oliver would still own more than 50% of the share capital of Kultivator plc would effectively mean that they could do very much as they pleased.

This follows from the 'majority rule' principle established in *Foss v Harbottle* in 1843.

The main constraint imposed by company law is that Dimmock and Oliver will no longer have a 75% majority of votes, which would enable them to pass a special resolution.

But once a company becomes a plc there is an implied assumption that the directors must run a business in the best interests of all the shareholders, presumably meaning that the overriding goal is to maximise the value of the company.

This is now formally recognised with respect to quoted companies in the Corporate Governance Code (2016).

Nevertheless, despite the introduction of the Code on corporate governance of listed companies, the majority owners of a business exercise considerable power.

Consequently one could regard the overriding goal of shareholders' wealth maximisation as being severely constrained in the case of Kultivator plc by the fact that Jamie Dimmock and Charlie Oliver would still in large part be able to pursue their own private objectives, even if this might lower the value of the business to the detriment of the minority of shareholders.

However, Dimmock and Oliver will no longer be able to determine their directors' salaries immune from criticism.

The validity of the assumptions which appear to underlie the growth projections implicit in the merchant bank's calculation of the company's flotation value.

Barriers to entry and the threat of competition from large DIY groups

With respect to the growth rates assumed, these depend on a number of factors.

These include the growth in demand in the industry and the level of competition (which will affect both the volume of sales and the prices and profit margins that can be charged).

Estimates of the former will depend in part on the forecasts for the economy as a whole and on consumer tastes and habits.

The level of competition, however, will depend on a number of factors (eg, the rate of technological change and how easy it is for rivals to enter the industry if it appears to be profitable).

It is the latter issue that is to be addressed here, ie, are there significant barriers to entry?

Jamie Dimmock apparently takes the view that the merchant bank's assumption that the growth rate in pre-tax profits over the next three years will only be 4% per annum and thereafter 2% per annum is far too pessimistic.

He bases this assessment on the fact that in recent years profits of Kultivator Ltd have grown faster than the increase in revenue reflecting the company's ability to reap the rewards of economies of scale as it has expanded, while at the same time using its greater bargaining power when negotiating with suppliers.

Nevertheless, he believes that there is still potential for further profitable growth.

This is because he does not believe that the large DIY groups will take a growing share of the (expanding) market at the expense of independents because they face an effective 'barrier to entry'.

In particular, they do not possess one of the key 'core competences' possessed by Kultivator, namely horticultural expertise. Moreover, these groups are finding it difficult to employ personnel with the necessary skills, which is a severe disadvantage when customers are anxious to have appropriate advice.

Further, he believes independents (such as Kultivator) have an in-built advantage here because they pay well qualified staff appropriately.

However, as Charlie Oliver seems to be suggesting, there is nothing to stop the large DIY groups matching these pay scales, so that alone is unlikely to be an effective 'barrier'.

Only if there is some other factor that enables independents to hold on to the scarce supply of skilled labour will such a 'barrier' be effective.

(And then presumably only in the short term as the labour market adjusts, more individuals train as horticulturalists or where appropriately trained personnel are recruited from abroad.)

In fact, there are several other possible barriers to entry that may thus far have prevented DIY firms entering the industry, quite apart from the fact that they may not anticipate growth prospects to be sufficiently attractive.

These include:

- The fact that existing garden centres have strong bargaining power with suppliers and/or are vertically integrated, giving them a competitive edge.

- Garden centres enjoy the maximum economies of scale, so DIY firms could not beat them on efficiency grounds.

- DIY stores are typically located at relatively expensive city centre or edge-of-town sites, whereas garden centres are usually to be found out in the country.

Another difference is that DIY stores typically use the 'shed' format, as this facilitates rapid throughput and the use of JIT inventory replenishment systems. By contrast, garden centers tend to carry large ranges of plants, shrubs and trees, many of which will be slow moving.

Garden centres also often emphasise their ambience, tending to focus on a positive 'shopping experience' (eg, by offering refreshment facilities). In other words, DIY stores and traditional garden centres appear to be catering for different markets.

On the other hand, DIY firms enjoy certain advantages, suggesting that there would be synergies if they decided to expand their garden centre activities (eg, they already stock garden furniture, decking, huts, tools and garden equipment).

Whether growth should be via vertical integration or horizontal expansion

Charlie Oliver appears to think that independents such as Kultivator may enjoy another competitive advantage, namely through vertical integration by growing their own plants and shrubs or seeking a tie-up with a nursery or seed merchant.

If this is so, it would provide an alternative means of expanding to horizontal integration, where more and more garden centres are set up or are acquired.

(However, it should be recognised, of course, that the two means of growth are not mutually exclusive.)

The main disadvantage of vertical integration is that it reduces flexibility and tends to increase operational gearing.

On the other hand, there should be opportunities to cut costs (eg, by reducing the levels of inventories of plants, shrubs and trees held at individual garden centres, although such savings are likely to be minimal).

Another potential advantage, which may be important for Kultivator, is that it should be easier to exercise quality control (potentially important where customers are likely to want plants which grow vigorously and flower profusely).

The main benefits of horizontal integration are that it should provide opportunities to exploit economies of scale, while at the same time slightly reducing risk exposure as a result of diversification.

More generally, if Jamie Dimmock and Charlie Oliver really feel that the merchant bank has undervalued their business, they could raise finance to expand the business in other ways.

Whether organic growth should be preferred to expansion via acquisition

In a perfect market there should be little to choose between expansion via organic growth rather than via acquisition, regardless of whether the proposal involves horizontal or vertical integration.

The additional costs that will be incurred setting up a business from scratch, including the greater risks being taken, should be matched by the higher price one might expect to pay to acquire a 'going concern' where someone has already taken those risks.

In practice, however, other strategic considerations are likely to determine which option will be preferred.

Thus, for instance, if speed is of the essence to secure a competitive advantage in a market, expansion via acquisition is likely to be preferred.

Indeed, sometimes two independent entities will see it as being in their mutual interest to engage in a defensive merger, in which case both sides should benefit by sharing the potential synergistic gains.

However, at other times, where speed is not of the essence, it may be preferable for a business to grow organically, particularly where it has an in-built competitive advantage (eg, because it has a technological superiority, backed up by patents).

In the circumstances relating to Kultivator, the main justification for opting for expansion via acquisition, rather than via organic growth, would be to establish a strong position in the market.

Given the fact that the DIY groups are an ever-present threat, there may be a strong case for trying to expand as quickly as possible via acquisition, even though this may mean that a large part of the potential synergistic gains may have to be paid for 'up front'.

7   Refer to the answer to Marcham plc in the Question Bank.

8   Refer to the answer to Confo plc in the Question Bank.

9   Refer to the answer to Blakes Blinds Ltd in the Question Bank.

CHAPTER 12

Evaluating performance and strategies: data analysis

Introduction

Examination context

TOPIC LIST

Introduction

Learning outcomes

- Analyse an organisation's current position and performance from both financial and non-financial perspectives, using management information and data presented in different formats ☐

- Explain and demonstrate how an organisation can capture and analyse qualitative and quantitative data, presented in different formats, to provide relevant information for decision making at an appropriate level within the organisation ☐

- Identify the implications for stakeholders, including shareholder value, of choice between strategies ☐

- Show, in a given scenario, how an organisation chooses from competing strategies in order to maximise the achievement of its key objectives, including those relating to technology, corporate responsibility and sustainability ☐

- Choose, for a given scenario, a strategy or combination of strategies which will best achieve the organisation's objectives, taking account of known constraints, including stakeholder risk preferences and developing technologies ☐

- Explain and demonstrate how an organisation can use management accounting approaches to evaluate its proposed strategies, while considering the value of information and the risk associated with forecasts ☐

- Explain and demonstrate how qualitative and quantitative data, including forecasts, budgets and other management information presented in a range of formats, can be analysed to monitor the performance of an organisation's projects, divisions and other strategic units ☐

Specific syllabus references for this chapter are: 1g, 2b, 2c, 2e, 2g, 2j, 3h.

Syllabus links

The techniques covered in this chapter were introduced in your Business, Technology and Finance and Management Information studies at Certificate Stage.

Earlier chapters in this text have looked at a variety of techniques that can be used to analyse data for risk analysis and other purposes. This chapter attempts to draw these techniques together and to provide guidance on how to tackle data analysis requirements in the exam. In the Business Strategy and Technology exam there is coverage of both quantitative (often financial) and qualitative (often non-financial) data analysis. It is important to recognise that the inclusion of qualitative data in a question scenario is intended to provide you with a different source to use when considering how the featured organisation has performed, beyond simply looking at financial quantitative data. Qualitative data in questions may take the form of customer feedback or comments made on social media about an organisation's products or services. Such data should be used in conjunction with any quantitative data to explain why an organisation has performed as it has. The analytical skills covered at Professional level will help you to develop necessary skills in preparation for Advanced level.

Examination context

This chapter looks at two key technical areas: evaluation of strategies and performance measurement. It also looks at a key skills element in the exam: data analysis.

At least one of the exam questions will include data analysis. Data may be presented in different forms (not always presented as a separate exhibit) and may appear in more than one question.

When you are presented with data in a question you are expected to use it in forming your answer. It is particularly important that you draw upon this data even if you are not presented with a separate numbers requirement. In the Business Strategy and Technology exam there are effectively three types of data analysis requirement. The first of these may require you to carry out specific calculations. For example, you may be expected to calculate the break-even point in relation to a business proposal.

The second type of requirement you may encounter may require you to evaluate a strategy or business decision with supporting calculations.

The third type of requirement may require you to consider the financial/quantitative and non-financial/ qualitative aspects of organisational performance.

The key issue is that the data analysis you perform should be linked to the wider strategy, position or issue in the scenario. Numbers will form part of the analysis but it is important to recognise that the numbers are a peg on which to hang discussion: you must demonstrate an understanding of the story behind the numbers. Being selective about what numerical analysis to undertake and then explaining your numerical analysis is thus an important element of data analysis. The examiners have repeatedly highlighted that those candidates which struggle with the data analysis questions tend to make the same mistakes. These include only calculating the numbers provided with little or no attempt to interpret the results, solely focusing on the issue of profitability with no consideration of liquidity or investment, failure to adopt a methodical approach (the so-called What-How-Why-When-SoWhat analysis) when interpreting the results of any financial analysis (see later in this chapter), failing to present calculations in tables.

It is important to note at the beginning of this chapter that the data analysis requirement could examine more than your ability to carry out ratio analysis as questions could involve the analysis of forward-looking information in the form of forecasts (as opposed to analysing historic information). You also need to be alert to the fact that not all data provided will necessarily be for a whole year as a question could provide you with quarterly or even monthly trend data to review.

In Question 1 of the September 2017 exam (*Blakes Blinds Ltd*) the scenario focused on a company involved in the manufacturing and installation of high-quality door and window blinds for corporate customers. The scenario information included extracts from Blakes Blinds' (BB's) management accounts. The second requirement asked:

'Using the data in the Exhibit and the other information provided, analyse BB's financial performance to:

- Explain the key reasons for the differences in performance between 20X5 and 20X6
- Assess the likelihood of achieving the 20X7 budget, highlighting any areas of concern.

Identify specific further information that would assist your analysis.'   **(20 marks)**

This was a fairly typical 'data analysis' requirement, in which candidates were provided with a lot of numbers to review, and were required to make comparisons between two periods in time, and to use their judgement when considering whether a budget was realistic and achievable. As mentioned earlier, to produce a good answer, candidates need to be selective about the calculations performed. The examiner commented that 'many candidates identified and calculated additional relevant data (such as exchange rate movements and analysis by product) and presented their figures in a structured table with appropriate columns. Weaker candidates often reproduced all the data already given in the question, which simply wasted time without scoring marks. Some weaker candidates only considered percentage changes in data.' In such requirements it is fairly common that candidates will be asked to identify further information which would be useful when conducting such analysis. The ability to recognise any limitations in the data provided (in terms of either content or accuracy) is an important skill.

In Question 1 of the March 2015 exam (*Rocket Co*) the scenario focused on an accountancy practice with a single office based in a European country. The scenario information included an extract from the firm's balanced scorecard report for two years. The first requirement asked:

'Using the balanced scorecard in the Exhibit and the other information available, analyse and evaluate the performance of Rocket between 20Y3 and 20Y4.' **(18 marks)**

The examiner reported that 'the fact that a balanced scorecard of performance indicators was provided in the Exhibit seemed to discourage a surprising number of candidates from undertaking any further numerical analysis. Better candidates provided some additional up-front calculations in a reasonably well structured table to help explain some of the changes in the scorecard (fee income per service stream, billable hours, market size, profit per partner). Weaker candidates were very poor in this regard, merely reiterating the KPIs that had been given or at most providing occasional calculations of changes in figures, within their narrative.'

1 Choice of strategic options

Section overview

- Strategic choices are evaluated according to their suitability (to the organisation and its current situation), their feasibility (in terms of usefulness or competences) and their acceptability (to relevant stakeholder groups).

- Using these criteria a strategy can be selected and then be broken down into functional strategies to be implemented.

1.1 Recap of the rational approach

The rational model was described in Chapter 2.

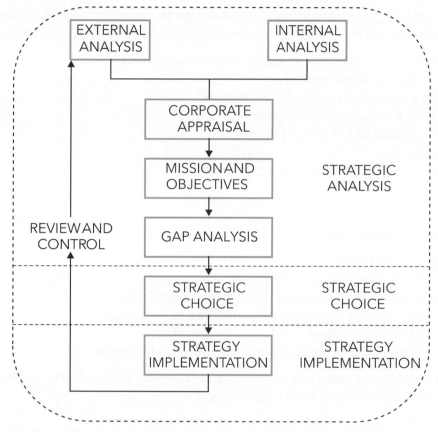

(Diagram: The rational planning model)

If the business is facing a gap, then devising strategies to fill the gap is a two-step process:

1. Option generation: creative thinking to generate options.

2. Evaluation and selection: assessment of options against goals of the business and commitment to some and not to others.

In Chapters 7 and 11 we considered how a business might develop strategic options, using models such as Ansoff.

Evaluation of these options to decide which of the options to implement occurs as the second phase of **strategic choice**.

In the next section we will look at how the business can use strategic control systems to monitor the success of the strategy and its impact on performance, once implementation has taken place.

1.2 Evaluation criteria: SFA

Johnson, Scholes and Whittington (in *Exploring Corporate Strategy*) provide a checklist for assessing options:

- **Suitability**: is this option appropriate considering the organisation's strategic position and outlook?

- **Feasibility**: does the organisation have the resources and competences required to carry the strategy out? Are the assumptions of the strategy realistic?

- **Acceptability**: will this option gain the support of the stakeholders essential for the success of the strategy and the organisation as a whole? Will the option antagonise significant powerful stakeholders that could thwart its success or that of management as a whole?

1.3 Suitability

Suitability relates to the **strategic logic** and **strategic fit** of the strategy. The strategy must fit the organisation's operational circumstances and strategic position. Does the strategy:

- **Exploit** company strengths and distinctive **competences**?
- Rectify company **weaknesses**?
- **Neutralise** or deflect environmental **threats**?
- Help the firm to seize **opportunities**?
- **Satisfy the goals** of the organisation?
- **Fill the gap** identified by gap analysis?
- Generate/maintain **competitive advantage**?

1.4 Feasibility criteria

Feasibility asks whether. the strategy can in fact be implemented:

- Is there enough **money**?
- Is there the **ability** to deliver the goods/services specified in the strategy?
- Can we deal with the likely **responses that competitors** will make?
- Do we have access to **technology, materials and resources**?
- Do we have enough **time** to implement the strategy?
- Will the strategy deliver results within an appropriate timeframe?

Strategies which do not make use of the existing competences, and which therefore call for new competences to be acquired, might not be feasible.

- Gaining competences via organic growth takes time.
- Acquiring new competences can be costly.

1.5 Acceptability (to stakeholders)

The **acceptability** of a strategy relates to people's expectations of it and its expected performance outcomes. This includes consideration of:

- Returns – the likely benefits that stakeholders will receive; and
- Risk – the likelihood of failure and its associated consequences.

It is here that stakeholder analysis, described in Chapter 3, can also be brought in.

- **Financial considerations**: strategies will be evaluated by considering how far they contribute to meeting the dominant objective of increasing shareholder wealth, using measures such as:

    - Return on investment
    - Profits
    - Growth

- EPS
- Cash flow
- Price/Earnings
- Market capitalisation

- **Customers** may object to a strategy if it means reducing service, but on the other hand they may have no choice.

- **Banks** are interested in the implications for cash resources, debt levels etc.

- **Government**: a strategy involving a takeover may be prohibited under monopolies and mergers legislation. Similarly, the environmental impact may cause key stakeholders to withhold consent.

Considerations of **ethics and corporate responsibility** are included here.

1.6 Strategy selection and implementation

After evaluating the various strategic options for suitability, feasibility, acceptability, the business must make a decision as to which strategy (or strategies) to implement. It may be the case that some of the strategies are mutually exclusive. Others may be implemented in parallel.

To implement the chosen strategy, it needs to be broken down into the relevant functional strategies (marketing, operations, human resources, finance etc). This is considered further in Chapter 13.

2 Strategic control

Section overview

- A business's planning and control cycle is designed to ensure its mission and objectives are met by setting plans, measuring actual performance against plans, and taking control action.

- Control at a strategic level means asking the question: 'is the organisation on target to meet its overall objectives, and is control action needed to turn it around?'

- The existence of an annual budgeting process compels planning and enables the establishment of a system of control by comparing budgeted and actual results.

2.1 Strategic control systems

Steps in setting up formal systems of strategic control:

Step 1
Strategy review: review the progress of strategy.

Step 2
Identify milestones of performance (**strategic objectives**), both quantitative (eg, market share) and qualitative (eg, quality, innovation, customer satisfaction):

- Milestones are identified after critical success factors have been outlined.

- Milestones are short-term steps towards long-term goals.

- Milestones enable managers to monitor actions (eg, whether a new product has been launched) and results (eg, the success of the launch).

Step 3

Set **target achievement levels**. These need not be exclusively quantitative:

- Targets must be reasonably precise.
- Targets should suggest strategies and tactics.
- Competitive benchmarks are targets set relative to the competition.

Step 4

Formal **monitoring** of the strategic process. Reporting is less frequent than for financial reporting.

Step 5

Reward: for most systems, there is little relationship between the achievement of strategic objectives and the reward system, although some companies are beginning to use measures of strategic performance as part of the annual bonus calculations.

2.2 Budgets and budgetary control

2.2.1 Short-term planning and budget preparation

A budget is a plan expressed in financial terms. Short term plans attempt to provide short-term targets within the framework of longer-term strategic plans. This is generally done in the form of a budget.

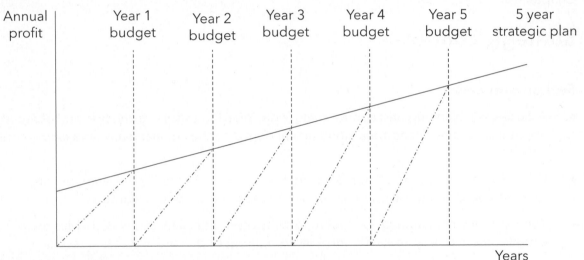

The diagram shows that the five-year strategic plan is to grow annual profits. This gives annual profit milestones and these are taken as the starting point for each annual budget.

2.2.2 Budgets, long term plans and corporate objectives

Budgets are an important planning tool for the organisation and are directly related to the mission, objectives and business strategy of an organisation.

A budget is a business plan for the short term, usually one year. It is likely to be expressed in financial terms and its role is to convert the strategic plans into specific targets. It therefore fits into the strategic planning process as follows:

- The mission sets the overall direction.

- The strategic objectives illustrate how the mission will be achieved.

- The strategic plans show how the objectives will be pursued.

- The budgets represent the short-term plans and targets necessary to fulfil the strategic objectives.

These budgets will then have to be **controlled** to ensure the planned events actually occur and is therefore a key element in assessing the effectiveness of the business strategy. This is as much a part of the budgeting process as actually setting the budget.

A budget is a **plan** not a forecast. You plan to meet the targets in the budget, a forecast is a prediction of future position. Forecasts are helpful to budget setters and planners.

A **periodic budget** is a budget covering a period, eg, a year.

A **continual**, or **rolling budget**, is continually updated.

Different budgets are prepared for each specific aspect of the business, and the contents of the individual budgets are summarised in **master budgets**. The contents of each of the individual budgets affect, and are influenced by, the contents of the others; they are linked together.

The sales budget is usually the first budget prepared as the level of sales determines the overall level of activity for the period and therefore most of the cost budgets.

Planning (including budgeting) is the responsibility of managers, not just accountants. Although management accountants help by providing relevant information to managers and contributing to decision making.

2.2.3 Benefits of budgets

There are five main benefits of budgets:

1. **Promotes forward thinking.** Potential problems are identified early, therefore giving mangers time enough to consider the best way to overcome that problem.

2. **Helps to co-ordinate the various aspects of the organisation.** The activities of the various departments and sections of an organisation must be linked so that the activities complement each other.

3. **Motivates performance.** Having a defined target can motivate managers and staff in their performance. Managers should be able to relate their own role back to the organisational objectives, seeing as the budgets are based on these objectives.

4. **Provides a basis for a system of control.** Budgets provide a yardstick for measuring performance by comparing actual against planned performance.

5. **Provides a system of authorisation.** Allows managers to spend up to a certain limit. Activities are allocated a fixed amount of funds at the discretion of senior management, thereby providing the authority to spend.

These five uses may however conflict with each other. For example, a budget used as a system of authorisation may motivate a manager to spend to the limit even though this is wasteful. This is particularly likely where the budget cannot be rolled over into the next period. In addition to this, budgets have some other limitations that could potentially arise:

(1) Employees may be **demotivated** if they believe the budget to be unattainable.

(2) **Slack** may be built in by managers to make the budget more achievable.

(3) Focuses on the **short-term results** rather than the underlying causes.

(4) Unrealistic budgets may cause managers to make decisions that are **detrimental** to the company.

2.2.4 Using budgets for control

Budgets are useful for exercising **control** over an organisation as they provide a yardstick against which performance can be assessed. This means finding out where and why things did not go to plan, then seeking ways to put them right for the future.

If the budget is found to be unachievable, it may need to be revised. Only realistic budgets can form the basis for control, and therefore they should be adaptable.

Budgets enable managers to manage by exception, that is focus on areas where things are not going to plan (ie, the exceptions). This is done by comparing the actual performance to the budgets to identify the **variances.** We will look at variances later in this chapter.

2.2.5 Making budgetary control effective

Successful budgetary control systems tend to share the same common features.

- **Senior management** take the system seriously. They pay attention to, and base decisions on, the monthly variance report. This attitude cascades down through the organisation.

- **Accountability.** There are **clear responsibilities** stating which manager is responsible for each business area.

- **Targets** are **challenging but achievable**. Targets set too high, or too low, would have a de-motivating effect.

- **Established data collection, analysis and reporting routines** which involve looking at actual versus budgeted results to calculate and report variances. This should be done automatically on a monthly basis.

- **Targeted reporting**. Managers receive specific rather than general purpose reports so that they do not have to wade through information to find the relevant sections.

- **Short reporting periods**, usually a month, so that things can't go too wrong before they are picked up.

- **Timely reporting.** Variance reports should be provided to managers as soon as possible after the end of the reporting period. This is so they can take action to prevent the same problems occurring in the next reporting period.

- **Provokes action.** Simply reporting variances does not cause change. Managers have to act on the report to create change.

2.2.6 Behavioural aspects of budgets

Budgets can be very effective in motivating managers. In particular, budgets have been found to:

- Improve performance.

- Be most effective when they are demanding, yet achievable. Though if they are unrealistically demanding performance may deteriorate.

- Are most effective when the managers have participated in the setting of their own targets.

2.2.7 Informal control

Many companies do not define explicit strategic objectives or milestones that are regularly and formally monitored as part of the ongoing management control process:

- Choosing one objective (eg, market share) might encourage managers to ignore or downgrade others (eg, profitability), or lead managers to ignore wider issues.

- Informality promotes flexibility.

- Openness of communication is necessary.

- Finite objectives overlook nuances especially in human resource management. In other words, an objective like 'employee commitment' is necessary for success, but hard to measure quantitatively.

Informal control does not always work because it enables managers to skate over important strategic issues and choices.

2.3 Guidelines for a strategic control system

The characteristics of strategic control systems can be measured on two axes.

- How formal is the process?
- How many milestones are identified for review?

As there is no optimum number of milestones or degree of formality, Goold and Quinn (*Strategic Control*) suggest these guidelines.

Guideline	Comment
Linkages	If there are linkages between businesses in a group, the formality of the process should be low, to avoid co-operation being undermined.
Diversity	If there is a great deal of diversity, it is doubtful whether any overall strategic control system is appropriate, especially if the critical success factors for each business are different.
Criticality	Firms whose strategic stance depends on decisions which can, if they go wrong, destroy the company as a whole (eg, launching a new technology) need strategic control systems which, whether formal or informal, have a large number of milestones so that emerging problems in any area will be easily and quickly detected.
Change	Fashion-goods manufacturers must respond to relatively high levels of environmental turbulence, and have to react quickly. If changes are rapid, a system of low formality and few measures may be appropriate, merely because the control processes must allow decisions to be taken in changed contexts.
Competitive advantage	• Businesses with few sources of competitive advantage – control can easily focus on perhaps market share or quality with high formality. • Businesses with many sources of competitive advantage – success over a wider number of areas is necessary and the firm should not just concentrate on one of them.

2.4 Using CSFs for control

In Chapter 6 we considered Critical Success Factors (CSFs) as the areas that are vital if the business is to achieve competitive advantage. CSFs focus management attention on what is important. The advantages of building a control system based around CSFs are:

- The process of identifying CSFs will help alert management to the things that need controlling (and show up the things that are less important).

- The CSFs can be turned into Key Performance Indicators (KPIs) for periodic reporting in the same way as conventional budgetary control might focus on, and report costs against standard costs.

- The CSFs can guide the development of information systems by ensuring that managers receive regular information about the factors that are critical to their business.

- They can be used for benchmarking organisational performance internally and against rivals (benchmarking was also discussed in Chapter 6).

3 Measuring performance

Section overview

- Effective performance measurement helps a business ascertain whether it has achieved its strategic and operational objectives.

- This section reminds you of some of the key performance measures you will have seen in your previous studies:
    - Profitability, liquidity and gearing
    - Economy, Efficiency, Effectiveness (the 3 Es)
    - CSFs and KPIs

- Performance measurement is only effective if there are yardsticks against which to compare.

- The 3 Es is an approach widely used in the public sector and by NFP organisations to measure Value for Money.

- Sections 8 and 9 of this chapter give guidance on how to approach performance measurement in the context of a data analysis question in the exam.

3.1 Measuring performance

Actual performance follows on from setting objectives and developing plans and targets.

Performance measurement is a fundamental part of the control process as it allows the business to consider how it has performed in comparison to those plans and to take corrective action where necessary.

Performance can be measured in different ways:

- **Financial performance** can be measured in terms of growth, profitability, liquidity and gearing.

- **Resource use** can be measured in terms of effectiveness, economy and efficiency.

- **Competitive advantage** can be measured by identifying critical success factors (CSFs) and then measuring achievement via appropriate key performance indicators (KPIs).

You should be familiar with some of these approaches from your Certificate level studies.

Remember that a performance measure is only useful if it is given meaning in relation to comparatives such as budgets or targets, trends over time and benchmarks from within or outside the business.

3.2 Measures of financial performance

3.2.1 Measures of growth

An organisation's growth may be expressed in a number of ways, for example:

- Sales revenue (a growth in the number of markets served)
- Market share
- Profitability
- Number of goods/services sold
- Number of outlets/sites
- Number of employees
- Number of countries in which the business operates (sales and/or production)

3.2.2 Measures of profitability

A company should be profitable, and there are obvious checks on profitability:

- Whether the company has made a profit or a loss on its ordinary activities.
- By how much this year's profit or loss is bigger or smaller than last year's profit or loss.

It is probably better to consider separately the profits or losses on exceptional items if there are any. Such gains or losses should not be expected to occur again, unlike profits or losses on normal trading.

Common measures of profitability include **gross profit margin** and **net profit margin** (measured in relation to revenue) and **gross profit mark up** (measured in relation to cost of sales). Profitability can also be measured in terms of return, via the **return on capital employed**.

3.2.3 Measures of liquidity and gearing

These are used to consider the financial health of the business.

The availability of short term cash and working capital can be considered using the **current ratio** and ratios such as **inventory turnover** and **receivable/payable days**.

The longer term financial structure can be assessed by considering **gearing ratio** and **interest cover**.

These measures of performance are covered in more detail in Management Information and Financial Management.

3.3 Economy, efficiency and effectiveness

Organisations need to ensure that the resources they employ are put to optimum use and that they are achieving an effective ratio of outputs to inputs. One way of doing this is to consider the 3 Es:

1. **Economy** – is a measure of the actual resources used (inputs) eg, cost of labour per employee or the rent per square metre.

2. **Efficiency** – is a measure of productivity. It considers the relationship between the goods or services produced (outputs) and the resources used to produce them (inputs) eg, output per person or per £ of labour, sales per square metre.

3. **Effectiveness** – is a measure of the impact achieved and considers outputs in relation to objectives. It looks at the extent to which the processes used by the business deliver the right results, eg, percentage of products delivered without faults, market share.

The 3Es can be used to measure performance of support functions eg, when assessing the performance of the IT department, the organisation could consider:

- Economy – the total cost of the IT function.

- Efficiency – the amount spent on IT per user.

- Effectiveness – the competence of the users (measured for example by a survey or via an online assessment.)

- The 3Es are often used as an approach for measuring 'Value for Money' (VFM) in the public and not-for-profit sectors.

3.4 Critical success factors and KPIs

Once the business has identified its CSFs, it must set performance standards to be achieved in these areas. This is done by identifying appropriate KPIs. For example if quality is important, the business first needs to ascertain the quality expected by customers and then set appropriate targets which might include the percentage of products returned; the amount spent on warranties etc.

Some examples of KPIs which can be used to measure the effectiveness of different areas of the organisation and which cover both financial and non-financial criteria are outlined below.

Activity	Key performance indicators
Marketing	Sales volume Market share Gross margins
Production	Capacity utilisation Quality standards
Logistics	Capacity utilisation Level of service
New product development	Trial rate Repurchase rate
Sales programmes	Contribution by region, salesperson Controllable margin as percentage of sales Number of new accounts Travel costs
Advertising programmes	Awareness levels Attribute ratings Cost levels
Pricing programmes	Price relative to industry average Price elasticity of demand
Management information	Timeliness of reports Accuracy of information

3.5 Strategic performance measures

Desirable features of strategic performance measures are shown below.

Role of measures	Comment
Focus attention on what matters in the long term	For many organisations this might be shareholder wealth.
Identify and communicate drivers of success	Focus on how the organisation generates shareholder value over the long term.
Support organisational learning	Enable the organisation to improve its performance.
Provide a basis for reward	Rewards should be based on strategic issues not just performance in any one year.

Characteristics of strategic performance measures:

- Measurable
- Meaningful
- Defined by the strategy and relevant to it
- Consistently measured
- Re-evaluated regularly
- Acceptable

4 Divisional performance measurement

Section overview

- Return on Capital Employed and Residual Income are two methods of measuring divisional performance.

4.1 Return on Capital Employed (ROCE)

ROCE is also called Return on Investment (ROI or Return on Net Assets (RONA). This divisional performance target is calculated as:

$$\frac{\text{Profit for the period} \times 100\%}{\text{Average capital employed during the period}}$$

The economic principle behind this measure, developed by Du Pont in the early 1900s, is that the return derived should be in excess of the cost of capital of the firm to provide a suitable return to investors.

In practice this measure has achieved popularity because:

- It can **lead to a desired group ROCE** ie, if all divisions return a 15% ROCE then, assuming all central costs and assets are charged back to divisions, the group as a whole will make 15%. Improvements in group ROCE can also feed into the EPS of the group and so into the share price.

- It **enables comparisons** to be made between divisions of different sizes for the purposes of identifying where group value is being created or destroyed and also for the identification of high and low performing divisional managers.

- It is **readily understood by management** due to its similarity to an interest rate or other yield on assets.

- It is **cheap to calculate** given that the financial reporting system will be calculating profits and asset values already.

4.2 Residual Income (RI)

This measure was developed in 1950s by GE to avoid a dysfunctional consequence of ROCE/ROI, namely that managers who are evaluated and rewarded against ROCE improvements may choose to forego investments which are actually in the investor's interest.

Worked example: XYZ Corporation 1

XYZ Corporation has a cost of capital of 10% which is the rate that all new investments are expected to achieve as a minimum (the 'hurdle' rate), and so is the minimum benchmark for divisional performance.

Division A presently has profits of £158 million on assets of £610 million.

A proposed capital investment of £60 million will yield net cash flows of £13 million pa for the next 10 years after which the asset will be worthless.

Will management of Division A undertake the project?

According to the NPV approach to project appraisal they should:

ie £13m for 10 years at 10% = £13 × 6.145 = £79.89m

NPV = (£79.89m – £60m) £19.89m

But the division's present ROI is £158/£610 = 26% whilst the project has an ROI of only £13/£60 = 22%

It will drag the divisional ROI down to (£158 + £13)/(£610 + £60) = 25.5%.

So managers who are evaluated against ROI targets may decide against it.

The board of XYZ Corporation would not know that this valuable project had been foregone. The decision is dysfunctional and so potentially is the use of ROI as a divisional performance measure.

Definition

Residual income (RI) is a divisional performance measure. It is calculated as:

Divisional profit – (Net assets of division × required rate)

Worked example: XYZ Corporation 2

Returning to the example of XYZ Corporation above:

Present divisional residual income is:

	£m
Profit	158
Cost of assets (£610 × 10%)	(61)
Residual income	97
Divisional residual income with new project	
Profit (£158 + £13)	171
Cost of assets (£610 + £60) × 10%	(67)
New residual income	104

Residual income is theoretically superior to ROI for the reasons shown above. However it is not widely used because:

- It is conceptually more complex than a simple percentage yield.
- It doesn't allow easy comparison of divisions of different sizes.
- It requires that a required rate be assessed and this may be different between divisions according to risk.
- It lacks the clear link to the ROCE of the group. Although **in financial theory** the market capitalisation of the firm will be the NPV of all its business units rather than being influenced by one year's ROCE and EPS, the fact remains that, for all its shortcomings, ROCE is still closely monitored by the investment analysts who determine share prices with their buy/sell recommendations.

4.3 Problems of using ROCE/RI

Problems of both ROCE/ROI and RI in the evaluation and control of business divisions are:

- **Short-termist**: being based on annual profit figures both disregard the future earnings of the division. Using BCG terminology from Chapter 6, a cash cow might present a high ROI and a star a low one, which would be a misleading guide to their true financial value if assessed as the NPV of future earnings.
- **Discourage investment in assets**: to boost ROI or RI, assets with low book values will be used in preference to new assets. This could reduce the prestige of the organisation (eg, shabby fittings) or lead to risk (eg, leaking vessels). It may also lead to inappropriate outsourcing to avoid having the assets required to provide the service on the division's balance sheet.

- **Lack of strategic control**: unless the corporation is acting merely as a super financial controller (eg, as defined by Goold and Campbell) it will wish to co-ordinate and integrate operations of its divisions to gain group synergies. Financial control measures alone cannot do this.

Interactive question 1: ROI

An asset costs £100,000, has a life of four years, and no scrap value. It generates annual cash flows of £34,000. Depreciation is calculated on the straight-line basis.

Requirements

1.1 Calculate annual ROI using opening carrying amount.
1.2 Calculate annual ROI using historic cost.
1.3 Comment on any problems identified by these calculations.

See **Answer** at the end of this chapter.

Interactive question 2: Asset disposal

A manager has the following data.

	Year 1	Year 2	Year 3	Year 4
Profit (£'000)	20	15	10	5
Historic cost (£'000)	100	100	100	100
ROI	20%	15%	10%	5%

Manager's target ROI = 12% per annum.

Requirements

2.1 When would the manager dispose of the asset and what problem might this cause?

See **Answer** at the end of this chapter.

Interactive question 3: ROI or RI?

A division manager has the following data.

Target ROI	20%
Divisional profit	£300,000
Capital employed	£1m

Requirements

3.1 Would the division manager accept a project requiring capital of £100,000 and generating profits of £25,000, if the manager were paid a bonus based on ROI?

3.2 Would the decision change if the manager's pay were based on RI?

See **Answer** at the end of this chapter.

Interactive question 4: Comparing divisions

A company has two divisions.

Target ROI = 20%

	Division 1	Division 2
Capital	£1m	£100k
Profits		
Year 1	£200k	£20k
Year 2	£220k	£40k

Requirements

4.1 Which division is performing better

    (a) Using RI?

    (b) Using ROI?

See **Answer** at the end of this chapter.

4.4 Other considerations in divisional assessment

When assessing divisional performance, the following issues must also be considered:

- The division manager should only be held accountable for factors within their control. The divisional profit figure may be distorted by arbitrarily allocated head office costs and thus performance measurement should focus on traceable profit.

- Where there is inter-divisional trade, careful consideration should be given to any transfer pricing mechanism in place, which may under or over-state the profits of a particular division.

- Divisions operating in different marketplaces and facing differing levels of competition cannot be expected to produce similar returns. Thus in addition to comparing one division against another, external comparisons should be made via benchmarking, eg, to industry leader.

- Wider strategic issues need to be taken into account such as any interdependence between divisions eg, shared distribution systems, shared customers, the impact that a division has on the portfolio of the business and its brand.

- In assessing the future strategic direction of the business it is not just the historic performance of the division but also its future potential that is relevant.

- Focus on a narrow set of financial measures is unlikely to give a true picture of performance (see section 5 below).

5 Balanced scorecard

Section overview

An approach that tries to integrate the different measures of performance is the balanced scorecard, where key linkages between operating and financial performance are brought to light. This offers four perspectives:

- Financial
- Customer
- Innovation and learning
- Internal business processes

5.1 Financial measures of performance

There are a number of limitations where management rely solely on financial performance measures.

- **Encourages short-termist behaviour**: focusing on hitting monthly, quarterly and annual targets may be inconsistent with longer term strategic business development.

- **Ignores strategic goals**: financial control cannot enable senior management to affect other important determinants of commercial success such as customer service and innovation.

- **Cannot control persons without budget responsibility**: operative and other staff cannot be controlled by financial targets if they have no responsibility for financial results.

- **Historic measures**: financial measures of performance are essentially **lagging indicators** of competitive success ie, they turn down after competitive battles have been lost. Management needs **lead indicators** of where problems are occurring to avoid losing such battles.

- **Distorted**: financial measures can be distorted by creative accounting. Also some of the conventions of financial reporting mean that internal financial control measures are of limited value for decision-making, eg, lack of valuation of intangibles such as brands, failure to value inventory and transactions at opportunity cost and so on.

In section 4, we discussed divisional performance measures. The research of Goold and Campbell revealed the practice by the boards of divisionalised firms to utilise a **strategic control style** that combined financial and non-financial performance measures.

5.2 The origins of the balanced scorecard

Kaplan and Norton's **balanced scorecard** (BSC) was developed in the early 1990s following research into performance measures in high-performing US firms, notably in the IT industries of Silicon Valley, Northern California.

According to their research these firms conducted regular assessments of **four different perspectives**, as follows.

Perspective	Question	Explanation
Customer	What do existing and new customers value from us?	Gives rise to targets that matter to customers: cost, quality, delivery, inspection, handling and so on.
Internal business	What processes must we excel at to achieve our financial and customer objectives?	Aims to improve internal processes and decision making.
Innovation and learning	Can we continue to improve and create future value?	Considers the business's capacity to maintain its competitive position through the acquisition of new skills and the development of new products.
Financial	How do we create value for our shareholders?	Covers traditional measures such as growth, profitability and shareholder value but set through talking to the shareholder or shareholders direct.

Performance targets are set once the key areas for improvement have been identified, and the balanced scorecard is the **main monthly report**.

Kaplan and Norton claimed that the scorecard is **balanced** in the sense that managers are required to think in terms of all four perspectives, to **prevent improvements being made in one area at the expense of another**.

A decade later and the BSC was being proposed as more than a performance measurement system. In *The Strategy Focused Organization*, Kaplan and Norton state that the setting of performance measures in the four areas can drive strategic change (a topic returned to in Chapter 15).

5.3 Developing a balanced scorecard

Kaplan (*Advanced Management Accounting*) offers the following 'core outcome measures'.

Perspective	Core outcome measure
Financial	Return on Investment Profitability Revenue growth/revenue mix Cost reduction Cash flow
Customer	Market share Customer acquisition Customer retention Customer profitability Customer satisfaction On-time delivery
Innovation and learning	Employee satisfaction Employee retention Employee productivity Revenue per employee % of revenue from new services Time taken to develop new products
Internal business	Quality and rework rates Cycle time/production rate Capacity utilisation

Kaplan and Norton suggest the following process for setting the BSC:

1. Senior executives decide strategy.

2. Budgets and information systems are linked to the measures in the BSC. This allows divisional and operational management to monitor the performance of their areas of responsibility.

3. Personal scorecards are developed and, through performance management become the basis for staff development and incentive payments. (These are discussed in Chapter 13).

4. Collaborative working occurs as many targets require team work to achieve.

5. Therefore strategy is 'operationalised' through being turned into day-to-day operations.

Kaplan and Norton recognise that the four perspectives they suggest may not be perfect for all organisations: it may be necessary, for example, to add further perspectives related to the environment or to employment.

A balanced scorecard for a computer manufacturing company

PERFORMANCE EVALUATION

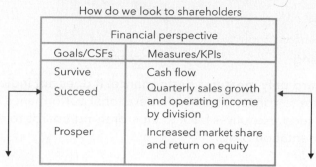

How do we look to shareholders

Financial perspective	
Goals/CSFs	Measures/KPIs
Survive	Cash flow
Succeed	Quarterly sales growth and operating income by division
Prosper	Increased market share and return on equity

How do customers see us?

Customer perspective	
Goals/CSFs	Measures/KPIs
New products	% of sales from new products % of sales from proprietary products
Responsive supply	On-time delivery (defined by customers)
Preferred supplier	Share of key accounts purchases
	Ranking by key accounts
Customer partnership	Number of co-operative engineering efforts

What must we excel at?

Internal business perspective	
Goals/CSFs	Measures/KPIs
Technology capability	Manufacturing geometry v Competition
Manufacturing excellence	Cycle time Unit cost Yield
Design productivity	Silicon efficiency Engineering efficiency
New product information	Actual introduction schedule v Plan

Innovation and learning perspective	
Goals/CSFs	Measures/KPIs
Technology leadership	Time to develop next generation
Manufacturing leadership	Process time to maturity
Product focus	% of products that equal 80% of sales
Time to market	New product introduction v competition

Can we continue to improve and create value?

5.4 The vertical vector

Kaplan and Norton's original perspectives may be viewed as hierarchical in nature, with a **vertical vector** running through the measures adopted, indicating that an organisation's financial performance is underpinned by its performance in the other three perspectives.

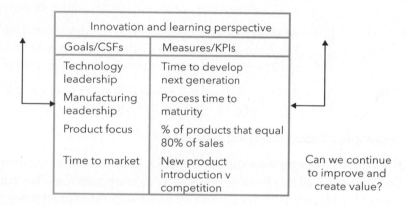

Perspective	Measures
Financial	ROCE ↑
Customer	Relationships and loyalty ↑

CHAPTER 12

Perspective	Measures
Internal business	Quality, efficiency and timeliness ↑
Innovation and learning	Skills and processes

The balanced scorecard only measures performance. It does not indicate that the strategy is the right one. 'A failure to convert improved operational performance into improved financial performance should send executives back to their drawing boards to rethink the company's strategy or its implementation plans.'

5.5 Problems

As with all techniques, problems can arise when it is applied.

Problem	Explanation
Conflicting measures	Some measures in the scorecard such as research funding and cost reduction may naturally conflict. It is often difficult to determine the balance which will achieve the best results.
Selecting measures	Not only do appropriate measures have to be devised but the number of measures used must be agreed. Care must be taken that the impact of the results is not lost in a sea of information. The innovation and learning perspective is, perhaps, the most difficult to measure directly, since much development of human capital will not feed directly into such crude measures as rate of new product launches or even training hours undertaken. It will, rather, improve economy and effectiveness and support the achievement of customer perspective measures.
Expertise	Measurement is only useful if it initiates appropriate action. Non-financial managers may have difficulty with the usual profit measures. With more measures to consider, this problem will be compounded.
Interpretation	Even a financially-trained manager may have difficulty in putting the figures into an overall perspective.

Worked example: Tesco steering wheel

In May 2015, shortly after he was appointed CEO, Dave Lewis, announced plans to cease the use of Tesco's own version of the Balanced Scorecard, known as the 'The Steering Wheel'. The Steering Wheel had been used for almost 20 years and measured store performance from five perspectives; community, operations, people, finance, and customer. Each perspective was formed of a number of elements which supported the overarching perspective, for example, the people perspective focused on offering employees 'an interesting job' and opportunities for career progression, while the community perspective focused on the need for Tesco to 'be a good neighbour'.

The rationale behind the decision to stop using the Steering Wheel was that it had become increasingly complex for staff to use, due to the number of different elements against which their performance was being measured. In response, Lewis introduced a set of principles known as 'The Big Six'.

A post on the Tesco (2015) website, highlighted that by performing well in the areas which are important to stakeholders such as its customers, staff, suppliers and communities, Tesco should then be able to achieve its financial performance targets in key areas such as sales, profit and cash flow.

The Big 6:

- Customers recommend us and come back time and again
- Colleagues recommend us as a great place to work and shop
- We build trusted partnerships
- Grow sales
- Deliver profit
- Improve operating cash flow

Tesco's annual report for 2017 highlighted that the company had improved its performance in respect of its big six key performance indicators on the previous year. (Tesco, 2017).

Sources:

Tesco. (2015) *The Big 6* [Online]. Available from: https://www.ourtesco.ie/2015/06/03/the-big-6/ [Accessed 7 June 2016].

Tesco. (2017) Annual Report and Financial Statements 2017. Tesco.

5.6 Using the balanced scorecard

- Like all performance measurement schemes, the balanced scorecard can influence behaviour among managers to conform to that required by the strategy. Because of its comprehensive nature, it can be used as a wide-ranging driver of organisational change.

- The scorecard emphasises **processes** rather than **departments**. It can support a competence-based approach to strategy, but this can be confusing for managers and may make it difficult to gain their support.

- Deciding just what to measure can be particularly difficult, especially since the scorecard **vertical vector** lays emphasis on customer reaction. This is not to discount the importance of meeting customer expectations, purely to emphasise the difficulty of establishing what they are.

- The scorecard should be used **flexibly**. The process of deciding **what to measure** forces a business to clarify its strategy. For example, a manufacturing company may find that 50% – 60% of costs are represented by bought-in components, so measurements relating to suppliers could usefully be added to the scorecard. These could include payment terms, lead times, or quality considerations.

The scorecard can be used both by profit and not-for-profit organisations because it acknowledges the fact that both financial and non-financial performance indicators are important in achieving strategic objectives.

5.7 Developments in the balanced scorecard

The original balanced scorecard of Kaplan and Norton was initially developed as a measurement and control tool for managers. Essentially, its focus was 'strategic control' rather than 'management control'. It has, however, been developed over time in terms of both its design and application.

The **second generation** balanced scorecard attempted to develop further the guidance on how the measures should be selected (filtered) and linked to the overall objectives of the organisation. It also began to look at more complex linkages and causality between the perspectives (sometimes called a 'strategic linkage model'). As a consequence, the balanced scorecard evolved from an improved measurement system to a core management system.

More recently, what has been termed a **third generation** balanced scorecard, has been developed. This involves enhancing the links between the balanced scorecard and the strategic objectives to be achieved within a given timeframe. This has been reflected in a 'destination statement' which sets out in some detail what the organisation is trying to achieve. Its purpose is to check the extent to which the objectives, targets and measures chosen, have been attained after a given period of time. It has also supported the development of multiple balanced scorecards in complex organisations.

6 Measuring performance in NFP organisations

Section overview

- Measuring the performance of not for profit organisations (NFPs) can be challenging.
- Traditional financial measures of performance may not apply and outcomes and outputs may be harder to measure or quantify.

Measuring the performance of NFPs can be more challenging because they tend to have a more diverse set of stakeholders and therefore a wider set of objectives. Also the traditional financial measures of performance may not apply in the absence of a meaningful bottom-line profit figure. Thus the outcomes or outputs may be harder to measure or quantify.

If we consider a school for example, performance at a very basic level could be measured by considering the pass rates in external examinations.

However if the school is felt to have a wider role, eg, in developing non-academic talents, or in preparing children for independent lives, then progress towards these objectives also need to be measured.

Since many NFP organisations have to deal with limited resources, the concept of 3Es is particularly relevant.

7 Types of data

Section overview

- It is important that you understand the key differences between quantitative and qualitative types of data as both are mentioned in the Business Strategy and Technology syllabus and could easily appear in your exam. You need to be prepared to use both types of data in order to understand an organisation's performance.
- Data analysis requirements in the exam may require you to consider data presented in a range of different formats.

Definition

Qualitative data: is fundamentally concerned with trends in opinions, thoughts and motivations, as a result it tends to be subjective. Qualitative data cannot be calculated or computed.

Quantitative data: is focused on numerical data which can be calculated and computed.

7.1 Qualitative and quantitative data

Feedback received from customers about an organisation's new product which allows them to express their opinion is an example of qualitative data. Such feedback may be captured through the use of customer surveys, discussion groups or social media posts: as a result it is likely to be of an unstructured nature. Qualitative data is of a non-financial nature.

Quantitative data is presented in numerical form. The quantity of products sold in the year is an example of quantitative data. Quantitative data is likely to be easier to structure than qualitative data. It is typically financial but can also include operating data eg, the number of customer returns.

Worked example: Quantitative and qualitative data in action

Euro-Shop is a low price supermarket chain which operates in a number of developed European countries across much of central Europe. It mainly sells a narrow selection of grocery and household products. Customer choice is limited to one or two lines per product as this allows greater quantities of inventory to be stored on the shop floor. Many of the items sold are well-known brands in Eastern European countries which are not as well known in central Europe. Inventory is stacked on wooden pallets on the shop floor for customers to access. Each store only operates with the minimum number of staff required by European law. This is part of Euro-Shops strategy to keep running costs low.

Two years ago Euro-Shop established a number of stores in Country X, a European country in which it had previously not operated. Customers in Country X expect a high degree of personalised service when they visit the supermarket, and demand lots of choice in the products available for them to purchase. Euro-Shop's Managing Director in Country X has gathered the following data based on the first two full years of trading:

	20X4	20X3
Sales (€)	8,294,000	8,513,000
Profit for period (€)	531,000	596,000

Using social media analytics tools Euro-Shop's Marketing Manager in Country X has collated the most frequently used words that customers use when tweeting on the Euro-Shop Country X Twitter feed. He has specifically looked at the terms used when customers tweet complaints, and those words which signify what customers most value when shopping at Euro-Shop:

Most common complaints between 20X3 and 20X4: poor customer service/lack of product choice

What customers value the most between 20X3 and 20X4: low prices

Types of data

In this example the sales and profit figures represent quantitative data as they are in numeric form. 'Poor customer service', 'lack of product choice' and 'low prices' are examples of qualitative data as they embody the opinions of Euro-Shops customers. Although, the use of social media analytics makes capturing and collating the tweets easier, it is likely that less reliance can be placed on these findings, as it will only be based on those comments made by shoppers using the Euro-Shop Twitter account.

Based on the limited scenario detail and data provided we can make the following assessment of Euro-Shops performance over the period.

Firstly, it is evident that there has been a fall in sales between the two years of 219,000€ (or 2.6%), and a reduction in profitability of 65,000€ (10.9%) over the period. This may reflect the fact that customers in Country X have not responded as well as may have been hoped when Euro-Shop first set up operations two years ago. This is likely to have been caused by the fact that customers expect a higher degree of personalised service when they go shopping whereas Euro-Shop operates its stores using the minimum of workers required by law. This point is supported by the fact that one of the most common complaints between 20X3 and 20X4 related to poor customer service. The drop in sales and profits potentially indicates, that after the initial novelty of Euro-Shops arrival in Country X, shoppers are now gradually returning to the supermarkets that they used prior to Euro-Shops entry in the market. This may in part be supported by the fact that customers are unwilling to sacrifice the lack of choice of products available when shopping at Euro-Shop. This point is reinforced by the complaint made via Twitter that there is a lack of choice in Euro-Shop's stores. Despite this, it is evident that Euro-Shops Twitter users do value the opportunity to complete their shopping at lower prices.

Clearly, more detail would be needed in order to make a full assessment of Euro-Shops performance.

7.2 Format of data in the exam

In the Business Strategy and Technology exam you need to be prepared for the fact that quantitative and qualitative data may be presented in a range of formats. Examples may include:

- Extracts from financial statements
- Extracts from balanced scorecards
- Extracts of posts on social media
- Data dashboards
- Diagrams (eg, value chain, BCG matrix)
- Graphs
- Pie charts (eg, analysis of sales revenue by product)

You must ensure that you are comfortable analysing and interpreting data, regardless of the format in which it is presented. A key part of this involves not solely focusing on financial data to the detriment of other non-financial or operating data which may also appear.

7.2.1 Use all relevant data

If qualitative data in the form of posts on social media are provided in the question scenario then the examiner is expecting you to use it when constructing your answer. Extracts from social media should be used in conjunction with the other detail provided in the question scenario and any relevant financial data to give your answers greater depth and insight. Adopting this approach is likely to be useful when, for example, explaining why an organisation may have performed better or worse than had been expected in a given period. The last worked example which featured Euro-Shop, the discount supermarket chain, illustrated this interaction.

7.2.2 Follow question requirements carefully

It is worth noting that some exam questions may only provide operating data with no corresponding financial information. The December 2014 question, Norgate Bank plc, focused on a bank providing services to customers in the UK and France via its two telephone call centres (one of which was based in the UK and the other based in Vietnam). Three key performance indicators were used by the bank to assess the performance of its call centres. One of the requirements asked candidates to explain the benefits and problems of Norgate using benchmarking to evaluate its performance. Candidates were expected to refer to different types of benchmarking, and were directed to use the operational data provided in the form of a data dashboard:

Exhibit: Data for the year ended 30 November 20X4

	UK call centre (UK customers)		Vietnam call centre (French customers)	
	Business	**Individuals**	**Business**	**Individuals**
Number of calls in the year ('000s)	120	1,200	90	600
Number of call operators	20	100	12	30
Time to answer a call (minutes)	2	2	1	1.2
Length of call (minutes)	10	4	8	3
Average customer satisfaction score	3.9	4.1	3.1	3.3

Here, candidates were expected to draw upon their knowledge of the different types of benchmarking when discussing advantages and disadvantages, and to comment on the operational data provided in relation to its applicability to different types of benchmarking. Failure to use the data provided, especially when it is specified in the requirement, will cost you marks when attempting your exam.

7.2.3 Understand the interaction between strategy models and data

Some exam questions may require you to combine your data analysis skills with knowledge of key strategy models. Past exam questions for example, have required candidates to construct a BCG matrix using product sales data provided in the question scenario (and the sales data for the organisation's largest competitor) in order to determine the market share of the products sold by the featured organisation.

This was the case in a March 2014 exam question (Tai Ltd and Jelk plc) where candidates were provided with the following data relating to the products sold by two separate companies which were considering a merger:

Exhibit 1: Market data UK and China

UK market (figures stated in £ millions)

	Jelk sales	Largest competitor	UK market Annual growth rate
Elevators	£54m	£260m	-2%
Travelators	n/a	£182m	Nil
Stairlifts	£96m	£80m	8%

Chinese market (figures stated in US$ millions)

	Tai sales	Largest competitor	Chinese market Annual growth rate
Elevators	n/a	$4,550m	19%
Travelators	$19.6m	$342m	15%
Stairlifts	n/a	$12m	30%

Note: Assume an exchange rate of US$1 = £0.65

Using the sales and market growth data, candidates were required to identify the product portfolio benefits in the event that the merger went ahead. The data provided coupled to the fact that candidates were told to 'refer to relevant models where appropriate' was a clear indication that preparing a BCG matrix was required.

Once again this illustrates the importance of reading the question requirements carefully and ensuring that you are comfortable with applying your knowledge of key models to the scenario data.

7.2.4 Interpreting graphs, charts and diagrams

Some exam questions may present data in a visual format such as a pie chart or a graph. The March 2017 exam featured a company called Ignite plc, which made a range of products including cigarette lighters, multi-purpose lighters, and lighter fuel. Candidates were provided with a line graph (in addition to company background information and financial performance data) which showed the sales performance of Ignite's luxury cigarette lighters over a 60-year period:

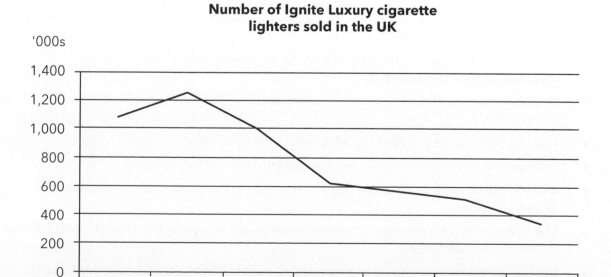

Number of Ignite Luxury cigarette lighters sold in the UK

Candidates were required to use the graph, alongside the other data in the question to identify the key changes in demand for Ignite's products over the period. The graph clearly shows the downward trend in the sales volumes of Ignite's luxury cigarette lighters, from their peak in the 1960s. This analysis could be extended further by drawing upon the additional information provided in the scenario which highlighted the growing health concerns of smoking cigarettes. Reduced demand for cigarettes had in turn reduced demand for cigarette lighters. As this illustrates you need to be comfortable combining data presented in a visual format with the supporting narrative in the question, to produce a good answer.

7.2.5 Developing data analysis skills

Developing your skills in analysing and interpreting data in different formats will be of particular importance as you progress to the Advanced Level of your ACA studies. The Business Strategy and Technology Question Bank contains a variety of questions with data presented in a range of different formats for you to attempt. As such you are strongly advised to attempt as many of these as possible in the lead up to sitting your exam.

In the following section we explore a very useful approach that you can use when faced with data analysis requirements in the exam.

8 The data analysis element of the exam

Section overview

- At least one of the questions in the exam will include data analysis.

- These questions may include financial data or alternatively they may include some management data which may require analysis and some supporting argument or judgement to comment on the situation.

- The key issue is that the data analysis should be linked to the scenario and the strategy.

- This section looks at the types of requirement you may have to deal with, the key skills you need to develop and the mistakes to avoid to be successful.

8.1 What does data analysis involve?

A key requirement in the Business Strategy and Technology exam is to be able to interpret financial and other data provided in the question (such as non-financial performance indicators) and relate it to the business's strategy, its environment and others factors that may have influenced the scenario.

Typically this analysis may cover:

- The financial position of the business eg, basic groups of key financial ratios (profitability/liquidity/gearing.)

- The performance of the business – financial and non-financial (eg, KPIs/balanced scorecard.)

- The use of resources – economy, efficiency, effectiveness.

- Product/market positioning eg, market growth/share/BCG/life cycle.

- Risk eg, break-even calculations, best and worst case scenarios, sensitivity analysis, expected values.

- The financial impact of a new project or strategy eg, analysing the effect by considering incremental contribution.

- Evaluating the overall impact of a strategy in both quantitative and qualitative terms.

- Operational and resource data over time (eg, units of output, number of branches, floorspace, number of employees.)

- Forecasts and budgets – forward looking data which, for example, may reflect the expected impact of a strategy or be used to monitor a strategy after implementation.

8.2 Data analysis skills required

The examiners are looking for you to demonstrate the following skills:

- Choosing analytical tools that are appropriate in the context of the question eg, financial ratios, KPIs, BCG analysis, break-even calculations.

- Identifying analysis that would be appropriate/useful and carrying out the relevant calculations.

- Interpreting the resulting information to demonstrate an understanding of the story behind the numbers and communicating that analysis succinctly.

- Exercising judgement to draw conclusions and/or produce sensible recommendations. The examiners are looking for you to justify any conclusions or recommendations that you provide. This means avoiding just stating your recommendations, as you should be confident in briefly explaining why you have recommended a particular course of action.

- Looking beyond the information provided at what additional information may be useful to generate a better analysis/understanding and at any reservations regarding the data/techniques/assumptions applied. Central to this is the need for a degree of professional scepticism when analysing the data provided in a question. You should recall from your Audit and Assurance studies that professional scepticism requires a questioning mind and to not simply accept information at face-value. When detailing additional information that you could request, you need to ensure such information could be realistically obtained.

- Linking different pieces of data to explain trends or outcomes.

- Highlighting weaknesses or omissions in the data provided.

- Analysing cause and effect relationships – eg, identifying underlying causes of changes in the data.

- You need to be mindful of the advice given in Chapter 1 concerning the use of the exam software when presenting your numerical and narrative answers. Remember that the examiner can only see your answers as they appear on the screen. The examiners cannot see the formulae that you have used nor can they make the window larger to view narrative answers which extend beyond the view of the screen. It is therefore important that you present your numerical workings in an appropriate format ie in an easy to follow table with appropriately labelled rows and columns, and ensure that all text is clearly visible so that the examiners can fully review your answer. Furthermore, you will not be expected to reproduce calculations and figures already provided in the question scenario. Failure to follow this advice may cost you marks in the exam.

8.3 Key weaknesses in candidate scripts

The following list highlights the weaknesses most commonly identified in exam answers and suggests ways to address these:

1   Restating facts or numbers without applying them to the context of the question. A common failing is to explain **what** has happened rather than **why**, eg, stating that sales have grown by 15% in the period but not indicating why they have done so.

   Solution: use the **'because rule'** to add value.

In most cases a good answer passes the 'because' test, eg, 'Market share has fallen from 35% to 29% **because** of the entry of a new lower-cost competitor.'

Including the word 'because' in your answer changes the 'what' into a 'why'.

The 'why' should be related to specific information in the scenario, demonstrating that you have understood the relationship between the financial/quantitative information and the business issues.

2   Failure to use the additional information from the scenario in formulating answers resulting in generic answers that could apply to any company rather than the one in question.

Solution: Make specific points, focusing on the particular organisation and relating to the circumstances in the scenario.

Eg, 'falling R&D expenditure may be a problem for XYZ Ltd because it has built market share on the basis of innovative products.'

3   Interpreting figures/results in isolation

Solution: link the figures/analysis, eg, if market share has increased but gross margins have decreased, the company may have made a decision to reduce the selling price as part of a market penetration strategy.

Eg, a company is considering outsourcing production as a result of rising raw material prices. This might be expected to lead to a decrease in gross margin if the company is unable to pass on the price increase to customers or a loss in sales/market share if, as a result of passing on the price increase, the company's product is no longer competitive. Outsourcing may also lead to a reduction in fixed costs and hence lower operating gearing (risk), but this would depend on the nature of the outsourcing contract.

4   Focusing on a narrow range of measures

Financial measures alone will not provide the full picture and are often the result of other factors, not the cause.

Solution: in addressing performance issues your answer should, where possible, address a variety of performance indicators. Consider using the balanced scorecard headings to help you cover a wider range of measures. Remember that these measures will often help you understand what is causing the strategy to succeed or fail.

5   Failure to use numerical analysis elsewhere to support your answer

Often the data analysis element is one of the first requirements. Conclusions that you draw from this will help in answering later parts of the question.

Solution: consider where else in your answer the analysis may be relevant/how you can 'make the numbers talk'.

Eg, if you have been asked in another requirement to assess the suitability/feasibility/acceptability of a strategy being considered, you can refer to earlier calculations of profitability and other measures in your assessment of returns and/or break-even calculations when looking at risk.

Eg, if the data analysis shows that the business is currently loss making and that sales and profitability are forecast to decline further, then the business cannot afford to do nothing. Any new strategy that is expected to address this decline or increase returns should be acceptable to the shareholders.

6   Failure to explain trends in the data by identifying **cause and effect relationships**. This may, for example, include analysing information into ratios or percentages based on the data provided.

Eg, where sales revenues are growing by (say) 10% per year but the number of branches/outlets is growing by 15% per year then calculating the sales per branch/outlet will show that sales per branch are, on average, falling. Growth in overall sales revenue may therefore be due to greater investment (ie, more outlets) rather than generic growth in sales per branch because of improved efficiency or stronger market conditions

Eg an alternative analysis of sales revenue growth might be in relation to volume growth, changes in selling prices and changes in sales mix. Analysis of this data may reveal the relative causes (quantitatively) of sales revenue growth from each of these underlying factors.

7 Failure to get a **reasonable balance** between numerical analysis and descriptive analysis. Some weak answers are almost entirely descriptive, while other weak answers go to the opposite extreme, producing reasonable numbers but descriptive analysis that is little more than briefly stating which numbers have gone up and which have gone down.

Solution: both numerical and descriptive analysis are important and need due emphasis. Two approaches by candidates in this respect are:

(1) To set out a comprehensive numerical analysis at the beginning of the answer with workings (eg, in a table) then produce the descriptive interpretation of these numbers; or

(2) To mix the numerical analysis with the descriptive analysis by producing calculations as each issue arises.

In general approach (1) tends to produce better answers with a more systematic evaluation of the issues. Specifically, with approach (1) the numerical analysis tends to be more comprehensive and better thought out with clearer workings.

8.4 Additional information required

The examiner may ask you to highlight any additional information that might be necessary for a more meaningful analysis and on occasion you may be required to specify possible data sources. Even if this is not part of the requirement, a comment about the limitations of your analysis and any additional information required will demonstrate higher skills. It is important however that requests for additional data are realistic, relevant and obtainable.

- Information in the scenario is likely to be in the form of a summary.

  More detailed information may be required, eg, a breakdown by product, country, business unit. If you have been provided with historic information for analysis purposes, eg, at five-yearly intervals, data for the years in between would help assess the trend more accurately. If average figures have been given, then actual prices/volumes/data would be necessary to properly identify which products/business units are under-/over-performing for instance.

- The source of information can be both external as well as internal.

  To properly interpret performance it is necessary to make comparisons. Comparisons may be made between:

  - Current results and past results/budgets
  - One business unit and another
  - Industry/sector information
  - Market leader/other competitors

  Thus any data obtainable on the industry and competitors will help benchmark the performance of the business.

- Set out any assumptions made and explain any limitations of these.

  To carry out break-even analysis for example you will have to make certain assumptions about the split of costs between fixed and variable, and about the sales price and costs remaining constant.

9 Developing an approach to data analysis questions

Section overview

- To help you develop an approach and a range of skills for exam questions, this section leads you through a sample question 'The Legume'. The intention is to demonstrate the thought processes to be adopted when tackling such a question and the attributes of an answer that will score well in the exam.

- Once you have worked through this section, you should attempt the question Waltex at the end of this chapter.

- You will find further examples of data analysis questions contained in the Business Strategy and Technology revision Question Bank.

9.1 Recommended approach to data analysis

The following is a suggestion for the approach to adopt when tackling questions:

Step 1: initial review (of scenario and requirements.)
Step 2: decide on appropriate analysis to undertake.
Step 3: produce the necessary calculations (to form the appendix.)
Step 4: interpret your analysis.
Step 5: identify additional information required.

9.1.1 What-How-Why-When-SoWhat analysis

The parts that cause most problems are Steps 3 and 4. It is difficult to produce a universal approach but one tool which draws together many of the issues already noted above is: **What-How-Why-When-SoWhat analysis** (WHWWsW), which includes both numerical and descriptive elements.

- **What** – looks at WHAT has happened overall (eg, revenue has increased by 10.5%).

- **How** – attempts to analyse the available data in more detail to obtain a better understanding of HOW the WHAT element occurred (eg, sales prices have risen by 10% and monthly sales volumes have risen by 10% following the price change).

- **Why** – looks for the underlying causes of the HOW element, which may be part of the story or strategy provided in the question (eg, there have been significant product improvements introduced during the year with additional features compared to competitors which has enabled a higher price to be charged but also an increase in demand despite this increased price).

- **When** – in assessing the impact of changes in strategy over time or in making comparisons it is important to know WHEN changes occurred. Thus, for example, in assessing the impact of a price change it is important to know when during the year the price change took place. If the price change occurred, for example, half way through the year, then the impact on the current year may be reduced, but may be more significant on next year's trading. For example, using the above numbers if the change in the product, the price and the sales volumes only occurred half way through the year it would only impact on two of the four quarters resulting in a sales revenue increase of only 10.5%, rather than the 21% that might be expected for a full year.

- **So What** – the above steps analyse and interpret the nature of the data provided and attempt to identify and explain the underlying causes of any changes in the data. This step goes to the next stage by attempting to ask the question 'SO WHAT are the consequences of our analysis for deciding on the future business strategy'? (Eg, what are the consequences for profit of the 10% increases in sales price and sales volume after considering the variable cost increases arising from the product improvements and volume increases? How have competitors responded with price changes and improvements in their own products which may make the consequences next year different from those which occurred this year?)

Worked example: Snowdon Ltd

This is an example with a very simplified application of WHWWsW analysis.

Snowdon Ltd is the sole UK importer of a branded cast iron cooker. To penetrate the market it reduced its selling prices by 5% on 30 June 20X5. There have been no changes in total fixed costs or variable costs per unit. Prior to the change in price, monthly demand had been constant for some time. The Snowdon board is attempting to assess the impact of this change in strategy for the year ended 31 December 20X5 and provides the following data:

	20X5 £'000	20X4 £'000
Sales	21,400	20,000
Cost of sales	(11,000)	(10,000)
Gross profit	10,400	10,000

Requirement

Analyse the change in performance of Snowdon in 20X5.

Solution

What: gross profit has increased by £400,000 in absolute terms, but gross margins have fallen from 50% in 20X4 to (10,400/21,400) = 48.6% in 20X5.

How: sales revenues have risen by 7%. This includes a 5% price reduction so there must have been a significant increase in sales volumes to compensate and cause an overall increase in sales revenue.

Note: There is only one product, so sales mix is not a factor in explaining HOW the change occurred. Also, see the **when** question below, as the price change only occurred halfway through the year.

Why: sales prices have been reduced to sell greater volumes to pursue a strategy of penetrating the market.

When: as the price change only occurred half way through the year the impact is restricted to this period. Given we are told that the first half of the year was similar to 20X4 we could do some analysis to isolate the second half effect in 20X5. If we take the first half of 20X5 as similar to half of 20X4 and strip this out we obtain the following:

	Actual full year 20X5 (A) £'000	Half of 20X4 (ie first half of 20X5) (B) £'000	Imputed second half 20X5 (A) – (B) £'000
Sales	21,400	10,000	11,400
Cost of sales	11,000	5,000	6,000
Gross profit	10,400	5,000	5,400

This table enables us to compare the two half years of 20X5. This shows that sales revenues have risen by 14% from £10m for six months to £11.4m. Given prices have fallen by 5% this implies that sales volumes have risen by 20% (ie 1.14/0.95 = 1.2). This 20% is consistent with the increase in cost of sales. (**Note:** This is because Snowdon is a retailer and hence cost of sales are variable costs. If Snowdon had been a manufacturer then cost of sales would not increase in a linear relationship with output as there would an element of fixed costs.)

So What: more information is needed to assess the impact of this strategy in the longer term (eg, market share). The response of competitors needs to be assessed. Snowdon's price reduction may not have been immediately followed but if the company is taking market share then competitors may decrease prices after a delay. In extrapolating the consequences of the price change forward care therefore needs to taken in allowing for different market conditions. Also price penetration is a temporary policy, but if competitors follow the price decrease of Snowdon it may be more difficult to increase them in future.

Summary

It is too early to judge the new strategy yet but in terms of short term financial performance there appears to have been a benefit in higher absolute profit despite the fall in percentage margin.

Note however that any tool needs to be used flexibly. In this case the HOW and WHEN questions could have been dealt with jointly.

The following is a longer question with more detailed analysis and shows that an understanding of the issues is needed and that any tool needs to be applied to purpose. It should not dominate thought and application to the scenario.

Worked example: The Legume

The business profile

'The Legume' is a prize-winning vegetarian restaurant located near the centre of Barchester, a cathedral city with a population of 100,000.

The restaurant was opened in January 20X0 by its proprietors, John and Eleanor Bold, who share responsibility for preparing the food and managing the restaurant. The staff comprises a full time chef, a kitchen assistant, four full-time and two part-time waiting staff.

'The Legume' seats 60 customers and is open six days a week, both at lunchtimes and in the evenings. It is licensed to sell alcohol and has established a reputation for having good wines.

Business is traditionally best at weekends, but activity is seasonal. Sales are above average in the four weeks in the year when there are meetings at the local racecourse, and the restaurant is equally busy before Christmas and during the summer tourist season.

The history of the business

John Bold commenced the business after investing £50,000 that he had inherited from his parents. Located on the ground floor of a Georgian building near the cathedral close, the restaurant attracted customers from among the many tourists visiting the city, but in addition its clientele included a small core of regular customers, local business people and shoppers.

Up until 20X5 the business was doing well, turning in good profits. However in 20X6 there was a 20% decline in the number of overseas tourists visiting Barchester as a result of a strong UK pound. In addition the local economy suffered when one of the city's largest employers decided to move its production overseas and was forced to lay off sizeable numbers of staff.

Although there was some revival in the number of overseas tourists visiting Barchester in 20X7, this coincided with a gradual erosion of the popularity of 'The Legume' amongst its local clientele. This was largely because rival restaurants and pubs had begun to include vegetarian dishes on their menus, but also because a new and inferior chef had been appointed, the decor was becoming rather faded, and the novelty value of the restaurant had worn off. Another factor, however, was the closure of the city's two cinemas, which were replaced by two multi-screen complexes sited in new out-of-town shopping centres.

As a result, there was a further sharp fall in trade in 20X7, forcing John Bold to turn to the bank for increased funding in the form of an increased overdraft facility. Initially support was forthcoming, since it was widely assumed that the setback would be temporary, and the bank took a second mortgage on the Bold's home as security. However, results in 20X8 were only slightly better and the Bolds were forced to cut their drawings significantly to keep the overdraft within reason.

Extracts from the management accounts for 'The Legume' restaurant over the last four years:

	20X5	20X6	20X7	20X8
	£	£	£	£
Sales				
Food	170,000	149,750	155,400	154,000
Drink	85,000	74,875	81,400	87,500
Total	255,000	224,625	236,800	241,500
Cost of sales				
Food	68,000	59,900	62,160	61,600
Drink	42,500	35,940	36,630	35,000
Total	110,500	95,840	98,790	96,600
Gross profit				
Food	102,000	89,850	93,240	92,400
Drink	42,500	38,935	44,770	52,500
Total	144,500	128,785	138,010	144,900
Other costs				
Wages	74,000	71,000	74,000	76,000
Rent	14,000	15,000	15,000	15,000
Depreciation	3,000	3,000	3,000	3,000
Interest	0	3,000	4,000	2,000
Other expenses	17,000	22,000	20,000	24,000
Total	108,000	114,000	116,000	120,000
Net profit	36,500	14,785	22,010	24,900
Average spend per customer				
Food	£10	£10	£10.50	£11
Drink	£5	£5	£5.50	£6.25
	£	£	£	£
Non-current assets at NBV	21,000	18,000	15,000	12,000
Bank overdraft	1,000	14,000	18,000	10,000
Drawings	33,000	30,000	25,000	20,000

The Bolds' dilemma

Somewhat belatedly the Bolds have begun thinking about how they might turn the business round. John Bold has been considering various options, each of which would be feasible under the existing 25-year rental agreement for the premises and under the current licensing arrangements:

Options

1. The restaurant could be converted into a wine bar serving hot and cold vegetarian and fish dishes. This might attract a younger clientele which at present largely patronises the local pubs and fast food restaurants.

2. By redesigning the layout a fast food, but vegetarian, menu could be offered at lunchtimes, while in the evenings the restaurant could revert to its more traditional role. However, to try to increase the volume of trade, prices would be cut and further discounts offered for regular customers, those eating midweek, and those starting their meals before 7pm.

As part of the reorganisation, the restaurant would have to be redecorated and new kitchen equipment installed. Option 1 would make it possible to dispense with full-time waiting staff and – apart from the chef – only employ part-time staff. Likewise, Option 2 would make it possible to dispense with one of the full-time waiting staff and instead employ two part-timers at lunch times.

The Bolds estimate that their pre-tax joint income in alternative employment would total £35,000 a year.

Any additional finance requirement would be provided by a loan from Eleanor Bold's family.

Requirements

You are a business consultant. The Bolds have asked for your help in assessing the current situation and deciding on a new strategic direction for The Legume:

(a) Using the data and other information provided, explain how the business has performed since 20X5;

(b) State what additional information would be useful to provide a more detailed assessment of performance; and

(c) Evaluate the risk and potential rewards associated with the strategic options being considered.

Solution

Step 1: Initial review

Read the requirements and then read through the question. As you read, you should be thinking about:

* Context
* Requirements
* Key issues
* Purpose of analysis
* Additional information

Context

You have been employed as a business consultant by the owner managers of the restaurant.

Requirements

Part (a) requires an analysis of performance since 20X5. The phrase 'using the data and other information provided' indicates the need to include both quantitative analysis and information drawn out of the scenario (see key issues) in formulating your answer.

In part (b) you are required to state additional information that might be useful to you. Jot down anything that comes to mind as you read through the scenario.

Part (c) asks for an evaluation of the strategic options being considered under the heading of risks and rewards. This evaluation will need to be undertaken in the light of your answer to (a). Thus if your performance analysis identifies issues such as a lack of sales volume or high fixed costs then it will be important to evaluate whether the options address this.

Key issues

- As a prize-winning vegetarian restaurant The Legume appears to be operating a focused differentiation strategy.

- Whilst initially profitable it now appears to lack competitive advantage (inferior chef, faded décor, other competitors offer vegetarian food etc).

- The business is highly seasonal and also very dependent on the state of the economy and the level of tourist trade.

- The high level of fixed costs, combined with falling sales volumes, have led to deteriorating profitability.

- The two key stakeholders could earn more elsewhere (£35k) than they are currently earning from the business. Also their home is at risk as a result of the bank taking a second mortgage.

- A new strategy is urgently needed for the business to survive.

- As a small business, sources of finance are presumably limited and if Eleanor's family are unable/unwilling to provide the necessary funds, the bank will need convincing of the Bolds' ability to turn the business round.

Purpose of analysis

Here we are told in the scenario, and we can see clearly from the accounts extracts, that in terms of profitability, the business performance has deteriorated since 20X5. The analysis should seek to address the underlying reasons for the decline and identify areas that need to be addressed by the new strategic proposals.

Additional information

The information provided is mainly financial, in the form of an income statement and a few highlights from the statement of financial position. We also have figures for average spend by customer.

There is little by way of non-financial performance indicators and no external information on competitors/the market sector.

Step 2: Decide on appropriate analysis to undertake

Much of the WHAT analysis is already provided in the question but in answering the HOW question and in deciding on what analysis to undertake and which calculations to perform it is important to consider the following:

- How does the analysis help to identify the issues the company is facing?
- How does the analysis demonstrate an understanding of the scenario?

If we look at the information from the income statement extract, the following analysis should help to confirm the reasons behind the declining performance:

- Sales mix
- Sales volumes (using the information on average customer spend)
- Sales growth
- Margins
- Operating gearing (level of variable costs in relation to fixed costs)

We might also want to analyse the other financial information provided:

- Non-current assets
- Drawings
- Bank overdraft

Finally there is sufficient information to undertake a break-even analysis, which would help to quantify the risk of the business becoming loss making. Operating gearing is also a good measure of risk; if a high proportion of total costs are fixed, any reduction in activity takes the business closer and closer to being loss-making.

Step 3: Produce the necessary calculations

This will form the appendix to your answer.

Appendix 1:

	20X5 %	20X6 %	20X7 %	20X8 %
Sales mix				
Food	66.7	66.7	65.6	63.8
Drink	33.3	33.3	34.4	36.2
Sales growth				
Food	n/a	-11.9	+3.8	-0.9
Drink	n/a	-11.9	+8.7	+7.4
Total	n/a	-11.9	+5.4	+2.0
Gross profit margin				
Food	60	60	60	60
Drink	50	52	55	60
Total	56.9	57.5	58.4	60.0
% Increase in fixed costs	n/a	5.6	1.8	3.4
Net profit margin	14.3	6.6	9.3	10.3
Operating gearing %	49.4	54.3	54.0	55.4
Other analysis				
No. of customers served (Sales/average spend)	17,000	14,975	14,800	14,000
Reduction in customers		11.9%	11.7%	5.4%
Average contribution per customer (GP/no of customers)	£8.50	£8.60	£9.33	£10.35
Break-even number of customers (Other costs/average contribution)	12,706	13,256	12,440	11,594

When faced with a requirement which asks you to perform some type of data analysis it is important to not only focus on the financial figures provided, as these will only tell part of the story. There are three ways in which ratios and calculations can be considered when attempting questions which require some form of data analysis:

1 **Using two financial figures** together, for example, the sales and gross profit figures, to determine the gross profit margin for a period. As the appendix above illustrates 'The Legume' has seen its gross profit margin rise from 56.9% in 20X5 to 60% in 20X8. This has been caused by annual rises in the gross profit margin of drink.

2   **Comparing one financial and one operating figure** with one another, for example, the average contribution per customer, which could be determined using the gross profit figure divided by the number of customers served by the organisation. Over the period the average contribution per customer has risen from £8.50 in 20X5 to £10.35 in 20X8. This is promising, especially as the number of customers has in fact fallen over this period.

3   **Comparing two operating figures**, for example, the number of customers served per year. As mentioned above the number of customer served between 20X5 and 20X8 has fallen each year. This would match the detail provided in the scenario.

Performance analysis requirements provide you with the opportunity to show that you are confident in using all types of data in constructing a well-balanced answer. In the following section we consider the importance of interpretation in greater detail.

Step 4: Interpretation

In conducting the WHY analysis it is important to look at the reasons behind the performance. Here are a number of areas that you might find it useful to consider:

- Trend in revenue – mix/volume/price. How achieved if rising /cause if falling?

- Pattern of costs against revenue – rising or falling; are they fixed or variable?

- Is the business seasonal? Does this place a strain on cash flow or lead to periods of under-capacity and a lack of recovery of fixed overheads?

- What is the level of operating gearing? Is this an issue for the business, eg, because of the seasonality of sales or in view of falling demand?

- Is the level of profit satisfactory/stable/increasing/decreasing?

- Is the company earning an appropriate return for its stakeholders? Is it paying this out in the form of dividends?

- What is the organisation's long-term finance strategy and is it appropriate for the business?

- What are the strategic implications of the level of investment in R&D/HR and training, marketing and non-current assets? Is this consistent with the organisation's generic strategy, eg, if a company is following a differentiation strategy it is likely to need to invest in at least some of these areas.

Interpreting the analysis from Step 3

This will form the text of your answer to requirement (a).

Sales growth/volumes

Sales growth figures indicate that sales have fallen by almost 12% between 20X5 and 20X6 and then risen by 5% and 2% respectively in the following two years. It is important to recognise that these movements could be the result of a price or volume change or a combination of the two.

Here we can use the figures provided on average spend per customer to deduce that the drop in revenue between 20X5 and X6 must be due to a loss of customers, because the average spend in the period remained constant.

In fact we can go a step further and calculate the number of customers served in the year, which allows us to see that the number of people served fell from 17,000 to 14,975. This is consistent with the information in the scenario which explains that there was a 20% decline in the number of overseas tourists visiting Barchester as a result of a strong UK pound. In addition the redundancies at the large local company are likely to have had an impact on the volume of local business.

The growth in sales in the following two years came at a time when the number of customers continued to fall. Although the volume of tourists increased, The Legume is unlikely to have benefited because of a loss of its competitive edge/differentiating factors (faded décor/inferior chef etc). It will also have suffered as a result of the reduction in customers due to the new out-of-town cinemas. Thus the overall increase in revenue in this period must be down to an increase in the average spend per customer.

Pricing and margins

Average food spend per customer, which was constant in 20X5 and 20X6, increased by approx 5% pa in each of 20X7 and 20X8. This could be because customers were buying more eg, having a starter or dessert in addition to a main course, or it could be that the Legume is now charging more for the same food. If this has led to The Legume charging more than other restaurants in the town it could explain some of the loss of business.

Food margins have remained constant at 60%, which could be a result of good control of purchasing/ wastage etc. Alternatively it may be that The Legume's pricing policy is to charge a fixed mark up on costs incurred.

The average spend on drinks has followed a similar trend although the increases have been higher at 10% and 14% respectively. Again this could be that the price of the drinks has increased or that, attracted by the reputation of The Legume's wines, customers are buying higher quality bottles of wine.

The margins on drinks have increased from 50 to 60% over the period. This may be because the more expensive wines can be sold at higher margins or might reflect better purchasing policies which have led to reduced costs.

The sales mix appears to have remained relatively constant over the period, with a marginal increase in the significance of drinks sales (33% in 20X5, increasing to 36% in 20X8).

In 20X8 the margins on both products were the same at 60% so the sales mix is irrelevant to profitability. However if the trend for increasing margins in the drinks side of the business continues, then increasing the sales mix in favour of drinks will have a positive effect on profits.

Other costs

The fixed costs have been increasing both in total and as a proportion of the total cost base.

This means the business has high and increasing operating gearing (moved from 49.4% fixed costs in 20X5 to 55.4% in 20X8) and as a result has profits that are more risky.

The restaurant is open twice a day, six days a week, and can seat 60 people.

Hence the maximum number of people eating per week is 720 which, assuming it is open 50 weeks of the year, amounts to a total potential volume of 36,000 customers pa.

Clearly with 14,000 customers in 20X8 it is operating significantly below capacity but despite the downturn in business, the restaurant is unable to reduce its cost base significantly, since it only has two part-time staff.

There are other clues in the question that operating gearing might be an issue:

- The seasonality of trade.

- The new suggestions for reducing the number of full-time staff and increasing the level of part-timers, thus attempting to make the cost base more flexible. (**Note:** In other questions companies may be attempting to do this by outsourcing either production or services.)

Investment in the business/returns to the owners

The question states that the Bolds could together earn £35k pa in alternative employment.

The profits of the business in all but 20X5 have been considerably less than this, forcing the owners to overdraw in both 20X6 and 20X7, presumably to maintain their personal lifestyle. The total drawings taken over the four year period amount to £108k which exceed the £98,195 profits made.

Thus none of the profits have been reinvested in the business and after the initial £50k investment it does not appear that the Bolds have provided any further capital. This may explain the state of the restaurant and the lack of investment in non-current assets.

As a small business, sources of finance are presumably limited. If the Bolds are unable to invest further in the business and if Eleanor's family are unwilling to provide the necessary funds, then the bank will need convincing of the Bold's ability to turn the business round.

Any new strategy will need to generate better returns or the Bold's might be advised to consider closing the restaurant. Having said that, It may be that the owners are prepared to sacrifice some of this alternative income as a result of the benefits they perceive from being their own boss, so it would be useful to ascertain the minimum level of income they need to live off.

Risks

Having signed a second mortgage the Bold's house is at risk if the business fails or the bank withdraw the overdraft facility.

The break-even analysis indicates that a further 17% drop in sales (14,000 – 11,594/14,000) would cause The Legume to become loss making.

Conclusions

The high level of fixed costs, combined with the fall in the volume of business, has sharply cut into profits so that earnings are below what the owners could earn outside.

The reduction in the volume of business is not just a result of reduced consumer spending but appears to be a result of a change in the competitive environment. Other restaurants now offer similar food to the Legume, which appears to have lost its competitive advantage by not maintaining its differentiating factors.

In addressing the SO-WHAT question we can conclude that, if the business is to survive, it urgently needs to improve performance by:

- Reducing fixed costs or finding ways to convert these to variable costs
- Increasing the volume of trade
- Addressing the finance requirement

Note: In applying WHWWsW analysis, the WHEN question is implicit here in the wide time span of the data provided, so intra-year analysis is not really required.

Step 5: Additional information

This will form the text of your answer to requirement (b).

The following is indicative of the type of information that might help better assess the performance to date and indicate which of the proposals are likely to be more successful:

- Split of sales revenue by midweek/weekend/month/lunchtime/evening and between food and drink at these times. Also mix of meals and drinks served (eg, sales of wine split by price range: under £10/bottle; £10 – £15; over £20). This may help identify which of the new proposals is more suitable; for example it may be that the lunchtime trade is typically food only, whereas in the evenings more drink is sold.

- Analysis of capacity utilisation/throughput of customers, ie, covers served v available tables at different times in the week and at different points in the year. The Bolds might be able to save money by closing the restaurant on certain days or at certain times of the year when trade is normally slow. Alternatively this may indicate when to implement special offers.

- The figures quoted are for average spend per customer. This is likely to vary between lunchtime and evening and by type of customer, eg, business v tourist. A breakdown of the average spend by lunchtime and evening would be helpful, as well as details of any discounts offered at off-peak times.

- Whether the spend per customer has increased as a result of Legume increasing prices or whether they are trading up the sales eg, by persuading more customers to buy a coffee at the end of the meal.

- Competitor information regarding prices charged, average spend per customer, number of customers (although not all of this will be easily available).

- Data regarding the total potential customers, their demographics and spending habits eg, number of tourists visiting the town's restaurants each year, number of business customers, average age of local population, to help assess market share and suitable target markets.

- Minimum income level required for the Bolds to live off.

- Maximum overdraft limit.

- Cash flow showing the pattern of receipts/payments during the year to help better assess the short- and long-term financing requirement.

Step 6: Sample answer for (c)

This will form the text of your answer to requirement (c).

Strategic options for the business

Option 1: Conversion to a wine bar

Rewards

- Will capitalise on the good name built up for the wine cellar and it may be harder for others such as pubs to compete with this strategy

- May increase profitability since margins earned on wines have increased to 60% in 20X8

- The addition of fish to the menu may increase trade by attracting non-vegetarian customers

- The business will not be totally reliant on vegetarian meals. However there will be still no meat dishes on the menu

- It may reduce reliance on the tourist trade and lessen the effect of uncontrollable factors such as the exchange rate

- Only having part-time waiting staff should reduce operating gearing and hence profit volatility

Risks

- If Barchester has an ageing population then this approach may not generate more trade ie, without cinemas etc, there may be nothing to attract young people to Barchester in the first place

- The Legume may alienate its existing clientele by changing the décor/music/menu etc to appeal to young people

- This strategy may simply replace one type of clientele with another, rather than generate additional trade. Alternatively it may increase the sales of drinks but reduce the sales of food as customers purchase snacks to go with their wine, rather than full meals

- The wine bar image may be more suitable to evening trade only and still leave the restaurant empty at lunchtimes during the week

- The Legume may not be able to change its image sufficiently to appeal to its target clientele

- Running a successful wine bar rather than a restaurant may require different skills

- The strategy may lead to a loss of the good name built up amongst its existing clientele

Option 2: Offering fast food at lunchtime and varying prices

Rewards

- There should be little impact on the existing trade, which is likely to be mainly evening based

- It is consistent with the existing reputation for vegetarian food and the Bolds have the necessary experience

- It is in line with business customers need for fast food at lunchtime

- By varying the pricing some attempt is made to address the seasonality and offering discounts may increase the trade at off-peak times

- There will be some reductions in staffing levels and by employing part-timers more of the costs become variable

Risks

- There is a possibility that their evening clientele may not approve of the lunchtime operations

- The fast food concept may be seen as cheaper and detract from the image of a prize winning restaurant

- The business will be entering a highly competitive lunchtime market, one it knows little about

Conclusion

The additional information noted in (b) above will help identify whether it is appropriate to increase lunchtime/evening trade and which food and drinks items on the menu are more profitable.

The Bolds should undertake some market research to assess the size of the potential customer base for each option and the forecast returns, before a decision can be made.

Whichever option is chosen, The Legume need to replace the inferior chef and improve the décor of the restaurant so that it addresses its current lack of competitive advantage.

Summary and Self-test

Summary

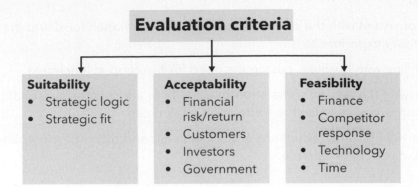

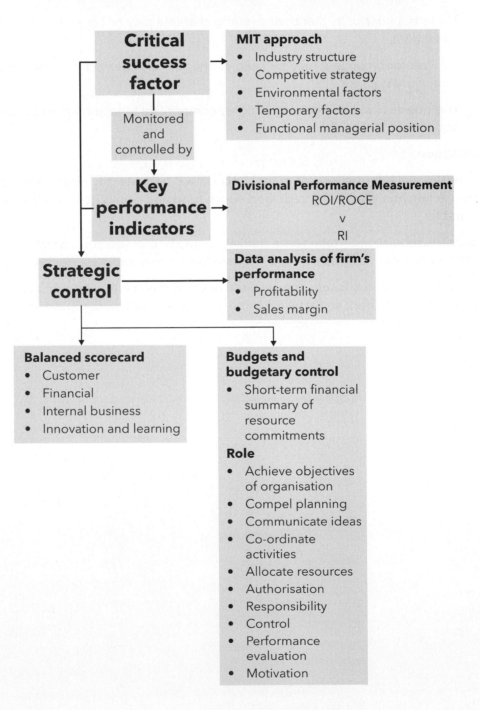

Evaluation criteria

Suitability
- Strategic logic
- Strategic fit

Acceptability
- Financial risk/return
- Customers
- Investors
- Government

Feasibility
- Finance
- Competitor response
- Technology
- Time

Critical success factor

Monitored and controlled by

MIT approach
- Industry structure
- Competitive strategy
- Environmental factors
- Temporary factors
- Functional managerial position

Key performance indicators

Divisional Performance Measurement
ROI/ROCE
v
RI

Strategic control

Data analysis of firm's performance
- Profitability
- Sales margin

Balanced scorecard
- Customer
- Financial
- Internal business
- Innovation and learning

Budgets and budgetary control
- Short-term financial summary of resource commitments

Role
- Achieve objectives of organisation
- Compel planning
- Communicate ideas
- Co-ordinate activities
- Allocate resources
- Authorisation
- Responsibility
- Control
- Performance evaluation
- Motivation

DATA ANALYSIS

- Financial position
- Performance
- 3Es
- Product/market positioning
- Impact of strategy/projects
- Risk
- Data

TYPES OF DATA

- Qualitative data
- Quantitative data

SKILLS

- Choosing analytical tools
- Calculations
- Interpreting results
- Conclusions/recommendations
- Looking beyond the information given
- Linking data/explaining trends
- Highlighting weaknesses/omissions in the data provided

APPROACH

1 Initial review
2 Decide on appropriate analysis
3 Perform calculations
4 Interpret your analysis
5 Additional information required

AVOID COMMON MISTAKES

- Use 'because'
- Relate to scenario
- Be specific
- Link the figures/analysis
- Use financial AND non-financial indicators
- Identifying cause and effect relationships

ADDITIONAL INFORMATION REQUIRED

- More detailed information
- Data for prior years
- Missing data
- Actual figures (if given estimates)
- Other data from the industry
- Market leader data
- Think of all information you may need, from internal and external sources

To interpret data properly, you need to make comparisons

CHAPTER 12

Self-test

Answer the following questions.

1 What do the 3 Es stand for?

2 What are the four perspectives of the balanced scorecard?

3 What are Johnson, Scholes and Whittington's three criteria for evaluating individual strategies?

4 Identify the role that CSFs can play in strategic control and performance measurement.

5 A firm's ROCE is the product of which two ratios?

6 Define four liquidity ratios.

7 List four limitations of relying on financial measures alone to manage divisional performance.

8 Greens Ltd is a growing firm providing organic fruit and vegetables for delivery via phone or internet order. It has decided to measure performance for the coming year using the balanced scorecard approach.

Requirement

Suggest two measures in each of the four areas covered by the scorecard.

9 **Maysize Ltd**

Maysize Ltd owns a department store located in a prime site in a regional city in the UK. The store has 16 different departments, selling such diverse items as shoes, fabrics and children's toys, and it has an accounts office for administration. The store is run by a store manager and there is a manager for each department within the store. Selling margins are set by the store manager, although there is scope to flex the margin after consultation with departmental managers. All suppliers are paid by the accounts office. Each departmental manager is responsible for product sales, employee costs and any sale events (eg, the January sales).

Management reporting

The management reporting system is very simple. The accounts office prepares a monthly cash flow statement, balance sheet and cumulative income statement. The income statement and balance sheet are compiled from the 16 departmental income statements and balance sheets. The departments prepare their income statements by calculating cost of goods sold by reference to the selling margins.

Maysize Ltd is now in the process of changing to a computerised management reporting system. This system will be able to generate reports in as much detail as is necessary for management.

The managing director has come to you for advice about the new reporting system. She would like to know what financial and non-financial performance indicators should be generated by the new reporting system so that she can monitor in more detail and improve the profitability and liquidity of the department store.

Requirements

Prepare a memorandum for the managing director suggesting the six most useful performance indicators that the new system should generate for the departments. For each performance indicator which you recommend, specify what information it should contain, its frequency and why it would be useful for the managing director.

10 Old and New

In 20X2 the divisional manager of the household products division of Rogers Industries plc, George Old, announced to the board of directors that he intended to retire at the end of 20X4. In view of this an assistant manager, Ian M New, was recruited in 20X3 with the intention that he should take over when Old retired. As part of his responsibilities New was given the task of preparing the budget for 20X4 onwards. It was felt that this would allow him to become acquainted with the way in which the division operated and introduce him to one of the jobs he would have to do when he became divisional manager.

As a divisionalised company Rogers Industries plc gives each division a fair degree of autonomy. Divisional budgets are reviewed by the central finance committee but rarely amended. Any capital investment decisions are made jointly by the finance committee and divisional manager; it is the responsibility of the divisions to implement the investment programmes. Rogers Industries plc assesses performance of divisions and their managers by reference to return on capital employed. Cash is controlled centrally. The figures below show the performance of the household products division for the years 20X3 to 20X5 and the budgets for 20X5 and 20X6. These budgets have been approved by the finance committee which agreed with New that there was no need to amend the 20X6 budget in the light of 20X5 performance.

Household products division

	Actual			Budget	
	20X3	20X4	20X5	20X5	20X6
	£'000	£'000	£'000	£'000	£'000
Sales	2,000	3,000	3,600	4,000	4,800
Variable costs					
Materials	200	300	360	400	480
Labour	300	450	540	600	720
Overheads	40	60	70	80	96
Repairs	100	150	90	200	240
Divisional fixed costs					
Staff training	60	70	40	80	90
Advertising	10	15	10	20	24
Maintenance	100	110	90	120	140
Depreciation	240	320	310	400	410
Rent	160	205	220	250	250
Other costs	20	25	30	30	35
Total divisional costs	1,230	1,705	1,760	2,180	2,485
Net profit	770	1,295	1,840	1,820	2,315
Divisional net assets					
Non-current assets	3,200	5,180	5,500	6,700	7,550
Receivables	200	300	350	400	480
Inventory	400	600	550	800	960
Payables	(300)	(450)	(750)	(600)	(720)
Divisional investment	3,500	5,630	5,650	7,300	8,270
Return on capital employed	22%	23%	32.5%	25%	28%

Requirements

10.1 Comment on the performance of Ian M New during 20X5, calculating those extra ratios you feel are important and including a note on the areas of Mr New's responsibility for the household products division.

10.2 Suggest what changes might be made in either the responsibilities of the divisional managers or the method of assessing their performance.

10.3 Set out possible reasons why Rogers Industries plc might wish to be organised on divisional lines and the possible disadvantages of such a corporate structure.

11 Waltex

Assume that the current date is December 20X7

Waltex Ltd (Waltex) is a large, unlisted company which manufactures watches. Its shares are held equally by three groups: the Waltex family, venture capitalists and employees. Customers are jewellers shops which are located throughout Europe and the Far East, although 90% of Waltex's sales are in the UK.

Company history

Waltex was established in Wales in 1924 as a manufacturer of watches, positioned in the low to medium price range. It has maintained a good reputation as a manufacturer of traditional style mechanical watches. Waltex has not copied many of the larger watchmakers which have moved to making quartz watches and have adopted sports or fashion stylings. Moreover, Waltex does not try to compete with the major watchmakers of international quality and reputation, which use precious metals and support their brands with significant advertising. The brand image that Waltex has tried to promote has been a good value, classic style and traditional mechanical mechanism that appeals mainly to the over 45s age group.

All watches are currently sold under the Waltex brand name. There are 59 different product lines (ie, types of watch) which are sold to retailers in the price range £35 to £100. Retailers normally have a 30% mark-up on cost when selling to the public.

The UK watch market

The UK watch market generates retail sales of around £1,100 million per year. Wrist watches dominate the market, but there are three main types: quartz digital, quartz analogue and traditional mechanical watches. There is very high market penetration with around 70% of adults in the UK owning a watch.

There is a trend in the UK market for consumers to buy cheaper watches. This is partly due to 'watch wardrobing', whereby consumers own different watches for different occasions. This has given rise to the role of watches as accessories. The success of cross-branding (a marketing approach to enhance two brand names of different companies by associating them with each other) and seasonal collections from the major suppliers have encouraged this trend.

The market for watches is fragmented, with a significant number of suppliers and retailers. In watch retailing, the entry of large market participants (for example supermarkets and clothing chains) has increased the competition in recent years for traditional retailers such as jewellers and, as large retailers, supermarkets have significant buying power. The internet, through online sales of watches, has created competition for traditional retailers and has also generated greater transparency in the market, as it is easier for consumers to make comparisons before buying.

The UK market for watches, in sales value terms, will probably experience a decline in the next few years, caused by continuing selection of cheaper watches; slower growth in the UK economy; and competition from other products in the leisure and consumer electronics markets.

Strategies for change

The poor performance of Waltex in recent years has caused some concern amongst shareholders and in September 20X7 some of the executive directors, who did not own shares, resigned, with a new Chief Executive and Finance Director being appointed almost immediately. After a period of evaluation, several strategies for change were identified. These are not mutually exclusive.

Strategy 1

Increase the advertising expenditure from £1 million in 20X7, to £2 million in 20X8, to promote the brand and increase sales.

Strategy 2

Launch a new range of watches with a new brand name. These would be ladies' quartz watches, branded with the name *Splash!* They would have a fashion orientation and a distinctive pink and yellow striped design. This would be part of a joint venture with a well-known fashion company, Kuchi plc, who would adopt the same design for their matching *Splash!* range of women's clothes. The *Splash!* watches and clothes would be jointly marketed to the same retailers, which would be fashion clothing and accessories shops, none of which have been previously used by Waltex. No separate joint venture company would be set up, but contractual obligations would be entered into to produce adequate volumes to match approximately the other venturer's production. Additional joint advertising obligations would also be needed to support the cross-branding (this would be independent of the £2 million commitment in strategy 1). The *Splash!* watches are expected to retail at £90, while the matching Kuchi clothing would retail at an average of around £250. Initial cash costs of £10 million would be incurred by Waltex to set up a quartz watch production line. Incremental annual fixed costs (in addition to the initial cash outlay) of £3 million would be incurred in manufacture. Variable costs are expected to be £40 per watch in the expected range of output, although sales volumes are very uncertain.

Strategy 3

Accept an offer from a large UK supermarket, Yarmack plc, to buy 40,000 watches in 20X8 with the possibility there would be a further contract in 20X9 if sales went well. These watches would normally have a price to jewellers of £45, but Yarmack is only willing to pay Waltex £36 per watch. Yarmack would then sell the watches for about £46. Yarmack is not currently a customer, but this contract would make it Waltex's largest customer.

The board meeting

A meeting of the new board was held to discuss the proposed strategies for change.

The **Marketing Director** spoke first: 'I would undertake all three of the strategies for change. From a marketing perspective we need to grow sales volumes and all three of these proposals achieve that.'

The **Finance Director** responded: 'The company has performed poorly in the past few years, as shown in the preliminary data I have provided for the UK market and the company (see **Exhibits 1 and 2**). However, I am not yet sure whether the poor performance is because of a difficult market or because there has been internal mismanagement. I agree that there needs to be change, but we first need to establish what has been going wrong. I have provided some information from a marketing survey to help us (**Exhibit 3**). However, it is not just about making sales, we need to look carefully at our costs.'

The **Production Director** also expressed some concerns: 'There is some spare capacity in the factory at the moment, but we need to make sure that we can supply all these new sales initiatives. I reckon our annual capacity is currently 1.2 million units. If we set up the quartz production we will probably lose factory floorspace and cut annual production capacity of existing mechanical watches to around 1.1 million units.'

Exhibit 1

UK Watch Market data

	20X3 £m	20X4 £m	20X5 £m	20X6 £m	20X7 £m (Estimate)
Total UK retail sales	998	1,049	1,112	1,125	1,100
UK media advertising expenditure on watches	26.5	27.2	28.9	27.0	26.5

Exhibit 2

Waltex data

	20X3 £m	20X4 £m	20X5 £m	20X6 £m	20X7 £m (Estimate)
Revenue	49.5	44	42.5	42.75	45
Fixed operating costs	20	20	20	20	21
Total variable operating costs	27	24	25.5	28.5	30
Operating profit/(loss)	2.5	0	(3)	(5.75)	(6)
UK media advertising expenditure	0.8	0.8	0.90	0.96	1.0
Units sold (watches millions)	0.90	0.80	0.85	0.95	1.00
Number of product lines	45	47	53	57	59

Exhibit 3

Marketing survey (in 20X7)

	Waltex	UK Industry Average
Age (percentage of sales to over 45s)	62%	29%
Higher Socioeconomic groupings (percentage of sales to groups A and B)	19%	24%
Gender (women's watches as a percentage of total sales)	54%	51%
Gender (percentage of watch purchases made by females, including gifts)	60%	53%
Average wholesale price	£45	£50

Requirements

11.1 (a) Using the data in Exhibit 1 and Exhibit 2, prepare a memorandum which provides a preliminary analysis to help explain the performance of Waltex over the period 20X3-20X7. Show supporting calculations where appropriate.

(b) Indicate any further data that you would reasonably require for a more detailed performance report, including any additional breakdown of the existing data. Ignore the proposed strategies for change and the marketing survey.

11.2 With respect to **Strategy 1** explain:

(a) The types of advertising that would be appropriate to each of the market segmentation groups (ie, age, socioeconomic and gender) identified in the market survey in Exhibit 3.

(b) How you would evaluate the impact of the proposed advertising campaign (assuming that the evaluation would take place in January 20X9). Use the data provided to support your arguments.

Note: Ignore the other proposed strategies for change.

11.3 For each of **Strategy 2** and **Strategy 3**, identify the potential risks and benefits, and give a reasoned recommendation of whether the strategy should be undertaken in each case.

12 Read the scenario of the **March 2015 Business Strategy and Technology** question in the Question Bank entitled *Rocket Co*. Draft an answer to the question which requires an evaluation of Rocket's performance using the Balanced Scorecard.

13 Read the scenario of the **December 2014 Business Strategy and Technology** question in the Question Bank entitled *Confo plc*. Draft an answer to the question which requires an analysis and evaluation of the performance of the Manufacturing Division and the Retail Division.

14 Read the scenario of the **September 2017 Business Strategy and Technology** question in the Question Bank entitled *Blakes Blinds Ltd*. Draft an answer to the question which requires an evaluation of performance between 20X5 and 20X6, and an assessment of the likelihood of achieving the 20X7 budget.

Now go back to the Learning outcomes in the Introduction. If you are satisfied you have achieved these objectives, please tick them off.

Answers to Interactive questions

Answer to Interactive question 1

1.1 ROI using opening carrying amount:

Year 1 £34k – £25k ÷ £100k = 9%
Year 2 £34k – £25k ÷ £75 = 12%
Year 3 £34k – £25k ÷ £50 = 18%
Year 4 £34k – £25k ÷ £25k = 36%

ROI improves despite constant annual profits thus divisional managers might hang on to assets for too long.

(RI would also improve, giving the same problem.)

1.2 ROI using historic cost:

Years 1– 4 £34k – £25k ÷ £100k = 9%

(RI would also be constant under these circumstances.)

1.3 ROI using historic cost overcomes the increasing return problem of using the carrying amount. However, it is not perfect.

Answer to Interactive question 2

2.1 The manager would dispose of the asset after two years, ie, she might get rid of the asset too quickly. (The same problem occurs with RI with interest at 12%.)

Answer to Interactive question 3

3.1

Divisional ROI pre-project	=	£300k
		£1m
	=	30%
Divisional ROI post-project	=	£325k
		£1.1m
	=	29.5%

Although the project ROI is acceptable to the company, the manager would not be motivated to accept a project which lowers divisional ROI.

3.2 In this particular circumstance, RI would lead to the right decision as the absolute figure for the division would increase.

RI pre project 300,000 – 20% (1m)   =   £100k
RI post project 325,000 – 20% (1.1 m)   =   £105k

Answer to Interactive question 4

4.1 (a) Residual income

	Division 1	Division 2
Year 1		
£200k – 20% (£1m)	–	
£20k – 20% (£100k)		–
Year 2		
£220k – 20% (£1m)	20k	
£40k – 20% (£100k)		20k

(b) Return on investment

	Division 1	Division 2
Year 1		
£200k/£1m	20%	
£20k/£100k		20%
Year 2		
£220k/£1m	22%	
£40k/£100k		40%

It is much easier for the larger division to generate a further £20k of residual income; hence using RI to compare divisions of different sizes is misleading. ROI gives a better indication of performance.

Answers to Self-test

1 Economy, Efficiency, Effectiveness

2 • Financial
  • Customer
  • Innovation and learning
  • Internal business processes

3 Suitability, feasibility and acceptability.

4 CSFs identify the areas that an organisation must excel at if it is to gain competitive advantage. Having identified its CSFs a business can determine suitable KPIs to measure the achievement of those CSFs. These can be used as part of the strategic control system and for performance measurement.

5 Profit margin × asset turnover = ROCE

6 Current ratio: current assets/current liabilities
  Quick ratio: (current assets less inventories)/current liabilities
  Receivable days: trade receivables/revenue × 365
  Payable days: trade payables/cost of sales × 365

7 Four of:

  • Encourages short-termist behaviour
  • Ignores strategic goals
  • Cannot control persons without budget responsibility
  • Historic measures
  • Distorted

8 **Financial perspective**
  Increase in revenue
  Market share

  Customer perspective
  Time taken from order to delivery
  Freshness of products (measured in terms of days since harvesting)

  Internal business process perspective
  Time taken to process an individual order
  Speed with which product availability updates register on the website

  Innovation and learning perspective
  Number of different products in the range offered
  Geographical areas covered by delivery teams

9 **Maysize Ltd**

  Memorandum

To	Managing director, Maysize Ltd
From	A Consultant
Date	1 January 20X2
Subject	Departmental performance indicators

  This memorandum considers the new computer management reporting system for Department Store X. As requested six specific performance indicators for departments are identified as being of critical importance.

  The relative importance of each of these indicators will vary over time as organisational priorities change (eg, if liquidity were to become more important than profitability).

The specific indicators identified are, as requested, local in nature. Global considerations, such as market share and capital expenditure, will also be of relevance but are not discussed in this report. In each instance the reporting system should incorporate information on prior period and (flexed) budgetary comparatives, and be analysed between individual departments and the store as a whole. Where possible, appropriate industry averages should also be incorporated (eg, in margin analysis or area utilisation).

Suggested indicators are as follows.

Customer feedback summaries

Content

A summary of customer feedback, including details of the number and nature of complaints. These should include feedback received at the customer service desk, and a log of matters noted by store and department managers.

Frequency

Periodically (monthly – depending on the extent and gravity of matters arising).

Benefits

Levels of service quality will be critical to the success of the store. Weaknesses in customer relations management need identification to ensure that the appropriate client culture is adopted.

Sales margins

Content

Gross profit margins should be calculated, expressing gross departmental profitability as a percentage of departmental revenue.

Frequency

Margins should be calculated periodically (probably weekly). In the event of specific queries, further detailed analyses could be provided on demand (eg, a summary of exceptional margins for product lines relating to a specific department).

Benefits

Since authority to fix margins is delegated to the store manager (and in some cases department managers), some control will be vital.

Weak margins may indicate poor purchasing policies, or highlight high or low profitability for specific departments that may warrant a reallocation of resources.

Margins will also be relevant when considering strategic pricing policies (eg, price wars). High level review should also facilitate overall goal congruence, eg, one area targeting economy purchases (low margin), with another targeting the other end of the market.

Area utilisation

Content

A measure of departmental revenue against space occupied should be prepared. [If possible a more elaborate measure of departmental profitability by floor space would provide further benefit.]

Frequency

Periodically (monthly) or even as sales seasons change.

Benefits

Store space is a key scarce resource; maximising returns from available space will be critical to success.

Measures yielding higher utilisation of existing space, once identified, could also be replicated within other departments.

Potential improvements in profitability from devoting more space to areas yielding the highest return will need to be balanced with interdependencies between the departments. Shoppers may, for example, be using the store primarily for convenience food shopping, but may make additional impulsive purchases while on the premises.

Staffing

Content

A simple calculation of departmental turnover against head count should be performed.

Frequency

This should be produced on a periodic basis (monthly).

Benefits

Staff costs will represent a significant determinant of profitability. Given the extent of delegation of responsibilities, they are also an important resource.

The measure should highlight areas of possible over/under staffing and may assist in staff planning.

An 'equitable' allocation of the workload should also avoid demotivating the staff and reduce staff turnover (training costs, etc).

Inventory holding

Content

Average inventory holding days by department calculated as

$$\frac{Average\,inventory\,of\,finished\,goods}{Annual\,cost\,of\,sales} \times 365$$

Frequency

Periodically (possibly monthly) with fuller analyses of individual product lines available on demand in the event of exceptional inventory holdings.

Benefit

Inventory will be the key element of working capital. Inventory levels may also have a direct impact on sales levels (eg, if shelves are bare).

A simple comparison of inventory levels between departments will identify excessive or minimal inventory levels, assisting in the review of purchasing policies, or handling of slow moving inventory lines and the use of sales.

Inventory counts may also be modified to allow investigation of unusual inventory levels, which may have been a result of inventory losses or inaccuracies in the recording of inventory movements.

Purchasing efficiency

Content

Value of trade and settlement discounts, in both absolute and relative (as a percentage of purchases) terms.

Frequency

Periodically (monthly), with the option of specific exception reporting (eg, discounts over £1,000).

Benefits

The ability to purchase quality goods at a reasonable price will be a key factor in the success of the store.

The organisation of purchasing responsibilities between departments and a central purchasing department will be particularly relevant.

A review of discounts obtained may assist in consideration of strategic purchasing policy (central buying from key suppliers giving rise to potential economies of scale) and a consideration of payables management issues.

Conclusion

The new system offers the opportunity for a review of the full range of operational and tactical management information. The six indicators suggested have considered measures that may have more strategic relevance. I would be happy to offer further advice on other information enhancements at your instruction.

10 Old and New

10.1 Performance evaluation

It would appear at first sight that Mr New has achieved much in his first year as divisional manager. Return on capital employed has risen by nearly 10% on the previous year and is well up on budget. The growth in net profit seen under Mr Old's management has been sustained under Mr New and the division's net profit percentage has cleared 50%. However, when one examines how this has been achieved, Mr New's performance looks less spectacular, in particular with respect to the following points.

- Sales are down on budget (down £400,000 or 10% on budget and the chances of achieving the 20X6 budget seem remote).

- Repair costs are down (other variable costs have maintained their normal relation to sales but repair costs have dropped off markedly) .

- Discretionary fixed costs are below budget (previously-made commitments to staff training, advertising and maintenance have been cut by 25% or even 50%).

- Depreciation is below budget (perhaps as a result of reduced investment – see below).

- Non-current assets are £1.2 million below budget (capital investment programmes have not been carried out).

- Receivables and inventory levels are down on budget (the first could be attributable to the low level of sales, the latter to efficient working capital management, though there could be problems of meeting future sales).

- Payables have increased dramatically (this could be called good credit management or perhaps an attempt to manipulate figures used for divisional assessment).

Each of these items, of which items two to seven are controllable by Mr New, have moved in such a way as to improve the division's reported return on capital employed. However, in the case of most of the controllable items, they could be said to have changed in a way that has improved short-term profitability whilst seriously jeopardising longer-term performance. The fall in repair costs, training and maintenance must put a question mark over whether the division can continue to be run efficiently. The cuts in non-current assets, inventory and advertising make it unlikely that sales will be maintained, even at their current level.

10.2 Changes in responsibility and evaluation

Although the responsibilities that appear to have been assigned to Mr New, particularly the responsibility for producing regular budgets, are in line with what one would expect of a divisional manager, some changes need to be implemented.

- There is a need for managers' budgets to be more critically reviewed. Questions should be asked as to how certain budgetary targets can be attained.

- Divisional managers must be fully committed to any capital investment programmes following joint discussions with the finance committee.

Major improvements, however, can be made in the method of appraising divisional performance.

- The extent to which a division might contribute towards the company's profit would be better measured by residual income (an absolute measure of profitability) rather than by return on capital employed (a relative measure).

- Subsidiary ratios should be used such as asset/turnover; gross profit percentage; inventory, receivables and payables periods – though these may be open to the sort of 'window-dressing' carried out by Mr New.

- Other performance measures could be introduced to establish whether discretionary costs have been cut back too far. Examples would be machine downtime and staff turnover ratios.

- Using a balanced scorecard approach would involve assessing success from a financial, customer, innovation and learning and internal business perspective. Other useful measures might then include market share, dissatisfied customer orders, number of new products launched.

The important steps are to change the main evaluation measure used and to support it with other measures that aim to examine every facet of 'performance'.

10.3 Reasons for and disadvantages of decentralisation

Reasons why Rogers Industries plc might wish to be organised along divisional lines might include the following.

Size – it is useful to split a large organisation into smaller manageable units.

Specialisation and complexity – central management may not have sufficient skills to be responsible for the day-to-day control of certain specialised tasks.

Uncertainty and unpredictability – in uncertain trading conditions local management will be able to react to changes more quickly than central management.

Motivation – by assigning responsibility for a section of the business to one divisional manager, that manager might be encouraged to ensure that the division's performance is enhanced. The division also presents the manager with a degree of independence and acts as a training ground for him to develop his management skills.

Economic – a geographical separation of divisions might allow advantage to be taken of local investment grants and favourable tax rates. Such geographical dispersion also allows a firm to be closer to markets or sources of supply.

Freeing central management – being released from day-to-day responsibilities for some operations of the business allows central management to concentrate more on longer-term strategic planning and control.

Though these may be valid reasons for a firm decentralising, there are certain disadvantages of such a policy.

Interdependencies – complete separation of divisions is probably impossible, since divisions may be engaged in supplying each other with goods or services or selling complementary or substitute products. Each makes demands on centralised resources, especially cash.

Cost – the advantages gained from economies of scale may well be lost by decentralisation, with divisions each requiring certain types of assets or other resources which might otherwise be shared.

Loss of goal congruence – divisional managers may make decisions which, whilst in the best interest of their own division, are not in the best interest of the organisation as a whole.

Loss of control – central management will need to learn to delegate responsibility, co-ordinate divisional activities and control their performance.

11   Waltex

Memorandum

To   Board of Waltex Ltd
From   Accountant
Date   Today
Subject Analysis of data

11.1 (a)   Analysis of basic data

	20X3	20X4	20X5	20X6	20X7
Average price per unit	£55	£55	£50	£45	£45
Market share (revenue × 90%)/ industry sales	4.5%	3.8%	3.4%	3.4%	3.7%
Advertising expenditure as % of industry	3.0%	2.9%	3.1%	3.6%	3.8%
Average variable cost per unit	£30	£30	£30	£30	£30
Break-even (units)	0.8m	0.8m	1m	1.33m	1.4m
Contribution per unit	£25	£25	£20	£15	£15

Sales revenues

The volume of sales has increased by 100,000 units (11.11%) over the period 20X3-20X7 while, at the same time, sales revenues have fallen by £4.5 million (9.09%) over the same period.

The sharp fall in the average selling prices of £10 (18.2%) appears to explain at least some of this difference. However more information is needed to determine the cause of the underlying fall in selling prices. Specifically, each of the following factors may be relevant:

Prices of individual items may have been reduced to maintain or increase the volume of sales.

The selling prices of individual items may not have changed substantially but there may have been a **change in the mix of sales**, with an increase in the proportion of lower priced items being sold within the price range of £35 to £100. This explanation is consistent with the 'trend in the market for consumers to buy cheaper watches'. The new product lines introduced may also have been at the bottom end of the product range.

A less important effect may also be a change in exchange rate on overseas sales, but these only make up 10% of sales.

Sales volumes

As already noted, sales volumes have increased significantly (11.1%) although not enough to compensate for the reduction is sales prices.

While more information is needed, the possible reasons for the increase may be:

- The reductions in selling prices may have increased demand.

- There may have been a change in the market desire to purchase traditional mechanical watches in general, and Waltex watches in particular.

- Increased advertising in absolute terms has increased. This may be important as watches are competing with 'other products in the leisure and consumer electronics markets'. However the levels of advertising in these industries would need to be assessed to provide evidence of whether the increase is sufficient to persuade customers to buy watches in preference to other consumer products.

- Increased advertising relative to the industry average. This is important to improve market share. However, despite the increased advertising compared to the industry average, the market share of Waltex has fallen. Care needs to be exercised here however as market share is in sales value terms, where Waltex has not performed well. Market share in volume terms may have increased, and more information is needed in this respect.

In terms of profitability, the company has performed poorly over the period 20X3-20X7 with a £2.5 million operating profit turning into a £6 million operating loss. Other costs such as financing costs may make these figures worse, although tax effects may moderate the decline.

Revenue factors have already been considered but costs are relevant to any analysis of performance.

Costs

Variable costs per unit have remained constant over a long period. A number of factors might have caused variable costs to change but may have acted in opposite directions.

- Variable costs might have been expected to fall as output increased with longer production runs (this would depend however on how much of the new output was due to the new product lines).

- Fixed costs remained constant, except in 20X7 when they increased to £21 million.

- Inflation may have been expected to increase costs (eg, wage inflation).

(b) **Further information**

Further information that is needed in respect of sales and marketing would be:

- Analysis of sales volumes for each type of product to evaluate whether there has been a shift in the mix from high value to low value

- A listing of selling price changes on individual products

- Prices of the new product lines compared to existing product lines

To assess the performance on costs the following information would be needed:

- Detailed analysis of costing for each product

- Split of overseas and UK costs to examine if overseas sales, at only 10% of the total revenue (and made to many different countries) are viable

- Impact of inflation of costs compared to underlying efficiency gains
- Identification of cost drivers to consider activity based costing and the viability/ performance of each of the 59 different product lines

11.2(a) Demographic – age

- Advertising in magazines that are read mainly by over 45s
- Radio and TV – day-time slots are cheaper and a proportion of over 45s may be retired and not working
- TV advertising during programmes which are popular with the over 45s
- Use of actors and images which are recognised and valued by over 45s age group
- Appearance of shops, packaging and staff that would appeal most to over 45s

Socioeconomic

- Advertising in newspapers and magazines read by middle income groups
- Direct mail – to occupations known to be in middle to low income ranges
- Selective use of Satellite TV for programmes popular with middle income groups
- Public transport – is used disproportionately by low-middle income groups
- Internet – identify commonly used web sites for middle income groups

Gender

- While females make up the largest proportion in this group, the male purchasers are also substantial and target marketing on a gender basis may not be sufficiently focused on a significantly large majority of customers
- Segmentation in this case may mean (rather than focusing on one gender group) advertising to each gender in different ways to attract consumers to the different features of male/female watches
- There is a difference between the consumer (male/female watches) and the customer (the retailers in the case of Waltex and for the retailers themselves it is the person who buys the watch)
- Promoting a female image of the watches to excess may make the watches less attractive to male customers
- To the extent that market segmentation is followed, then this may be similar to the above but on the basis of gender:
  - Female magazines
  - TV and radio programmes popular with females
  - Packaging and shop appearance that would have a feminine preference (but not at the cost of putting off male customers/consumers)

(b) Identifying the impact of the advertising campaign would depend on the type of advertising and its objectives. Any evaluation should therefore be in comparison to the related objectives.

If the objective of advertising is to promote long term recognition of the brand, or a particular image of the brand, then the effects in terms of sales may not be noticed by January 20X9. Additional market research may therefore be needed to assess the impact in terms of customer recognition (eg, questionnaires, interviews etc). This may determine whether there is increased recognition of the brand before advertising (pre test) and after advertising (post test) or, more directly the extent to which people can remember the advert or other form of promotion.

If the objective is more short term, such as promotion of a particular offer, or to stimulate sales of a particular product line, then sales figures could be examined before and after the adverts. The problem is that other factors are also changing (eg, price, fashions etc,) so changes in sales may not be entirely due to advertising.

In addition, retailers could be asked to give customer feedback on why they purchased a watch (eg, as part of filling in the guarantee on the watch which is then submitted to Waltex).

Notes

1   In each case significant sales are made outside the segmental target groups and it may be appropriate not to ignore these entirely.

2   The above are single variable segmentations. It may be appropriate to identify multivariable segmentation eg, females over 45.

11.3 Strategy 2 – Cross-marketing Joint Venture

Risks

- This is a new venture that requires a new investment of £10 million. If the venture fails then there is a risk that exit costs may be high. However, as the investment is mainly in machinery to manufacture quartz watches, they are not specific to this venture and may be utilised in alternative product and market strategies in manufacturing quartz watches.

- There is a core competence in mechanical watch making. It is not clear that this competence could be readily transferred to quartz technology. It is the same watch market but largely a different industry, or at least a different production technique.

- Break-even. The higher fixed costs may mean that break-even will increase annually. The annual break-even is £3m/(£90 – £30) = 50,000 units (or £450,000 or revenue). However, this ignores the depreciation on the initial outlay which will increase the break-even.

- The contractual joint venture depends on a new partner Kuchi. Waltex is therefore at risk from the actions of the partner in terms of reputation, fulfilment of contract terms and acting reasonably in dealing with Waltex.

- The venture is based on a particular fashion design which may be short term. There is therefore a risk of sustainability of the market which is the subject of the joint venture.

- There is a risk that in focussing on ladies' watches in the new venture that the Waltex brand will be identified as a feminine brand and lose sales of men's watches.

- The contractual obligations of the joint venture may give rise to problems of meeting supply requirements under the arrangements.

- The selling price of £90 is low in comparison to the joint partner's average revenue of £250. The costs of the JV should therefore be considered on this basis of disproportionate benefits. If the cost are shared equally then this would present an additional risk.

- Even if break-even can be attained in the short term, there needs to be a sustainable revenue to recover the initial outlay of £10 million over the life of the project.

- Some customers may switch from traditional to quartz watches, thus sales could be replacement rather than incremental.

- The Production Director appears to be concerned that the new production line might have a negative impact on existing capacity.

- As this is a new venture it is likely to require significant management time which could cause them to take their eye off the core business.

- As well as the extra operating gearing, funding the investment is likely to result in increased financial gearing. In addition there may be further WC requirements beyond the initial £10 million, particularly if the business is expanding.

Benefits

- The venture may change the image of the company as well as that of the specific products in the venture.

- It diversifies out of mechanical watches, which have particular market attributes. Quartz watches may appeal to a different market.

- This is a high margin product at £60 per unit. If sales exceed the break-even level then additional profits will be made. The break-even level needs to be assessed as to whether it is attainable using market research but, at 50,000 units, it is low by comparison to existing output.

Recommendation

There are some concerns which need to be addressed before entering into the agreement. These include the following:

- The terms of the joint venture need to be established clearly so Waltex does not incur a disproportionate share of the costs.

- Market research needs to be completed to establish whether the break-even is likely to be attained over the life of the project.

- The reputation and benefits of the joint venture partner need to be considered in terms of the benefits of cross marketing. Any alternative partners who can deliver a better package of benefits and costs of cross marketing may be considered.

Subject to these concerns there seems to be merit in investigating the venture further.

Strategy 3 – Yarmack offer

Risks

- Additional fixed costs may be incurred in addition to the variable costs.

- There may be some opportunity costs in terms of lost sales to the extent that people buy Waltex watches from Yarmack rather than other retailers. To the extent that this occurs, then there is a lost contribution of £9 per watch (see working) for each item purchased in this manner.

- The contract is short term and thus may fail to deliver benefits in the long term.

- The contract may reinforce the downmarket image of Waltex.

- If the contract is undertaken alongside Strategy 2, then there is no spare capacity in the factory to benefit from increased output – particularly if additional advertising is undertaken in Strategy 1.

- As a large and powerful buyer Yarmack may put further pressure on Waltex eg, delayed payment, more stringent quality requirements.

Benefits

- Potential additional sales of 40,000 watches generating a contribution of £240,000.

- Yarmack may improve the exposure of Waltex and thus improve the promotion of the product.

- The contract may be renewed, perhaps at an increased volume, in future years if they sell well in the first year of the contract.

Recommendation

The benefit of the increased sales needs to be weighed against the lower margin and the risk to existing sales from lost sales and lowering of reputation.

Subject to these concerns, there seems to be merit in entering into the contract this year provided there is minimal substitution of sales, since there is a contribution of £6 and the potential increase in volume is 4% of existing output.

WORKING

Sales to jewellers:

	£
Original sales price	45
Less VC per unit	(30)
Contribution	15
Sales price to Yarmack	36
Less VC per unit	(30)
Contribution	6

Thus contribution lost by Waltex if customers buy from Yarmack instead of jeweller = £9

12 Refer to the answer to Rocket Co in the Question Bank.

13 Refer to the answer to Confo plc in the Question Bank.

14 Refer to the answer to Blakes Blinds Ltd in the Question Bank.

CHAPTER 13

Business planning and functional strategies

Introduction

Examination context

TOPIC LIST

Summary and Self-test

Answers to Interactive questions

Answers to Self-test

Introduction

Learning outcomes

- Evaluate how an organisation's overall strategy can be achieved by implementing appropriate functional strategies ☐

- Draft a simple business plan, or extracts, which will achieve given or implied objectives ☐

- Evaluate the form and content of an organisation's business plan ☐

Specific syllabus references for this chapter are: 3a, 3f, 3g.

Syllabus links

The development of operational plans to implement corporate strategy received brief coverage in your Business, Technology and Finance exam.

Examination context

There are two key elements in this chapter. Firstly, in the exam you might be expected to draft elements of a business plan for a client or to identify weaknesses and omissions in a given business plan and suggest improvements. Secondly, the chapter looks at functional strategies. These would normally be examined in the context of the overall objectives and strategy of an organisation. So for example you might be expected to look at how the organisation could develop its functional strategies to achieve its objectives.

It is therefore important that you are comfortable analysing the issues affecting the functional strategies of those organisations featured in exam questions.

In Question 2 of the September 2017 exam (*Air Services UK Ltd, ASU*) the scenario focused on a company responsible for providing airspace management systems to all airports and aircraft using UK airspace. The company was owned partly by the UK government and partly by private shareholders, who consisted of several UK-based airlines as well as Air Services UK employees. Following some recent difficulties, the company appointed a new CEO (Joan Louli), who set a new organisational vision to make the company 'the global leader in innovative airspace management.' The second requirement asked candidates to:

'Explain the following two functional strategies that ASU could implement to achieve Joan Louli's stated vision:

- Human Resources (HR); and
- Research and Development (R&D)'

(10 marks)

To produce a good answer, candidates were expected to make use of the scenario detail, including the new vision as set out by the CEO. It is perfectly acceptable to draw upon your own work experiences as they may help you to make practical points when attempting questions such as this. It is, however, crucial that you link the points you make to scenario detail, and failure to apply your answer will cost you valuable marks.

1 Business planning

Section overview

- Business planning converts longer-term business strategies into actions to be taken now.

- Business plans are also used to apply for funding and are a critical document for a potential investor.

- In the exam you must be able to critically appraise a business plan provided by a client, recognising weaknesses and omissions and making recommendations for improvement.

1.1 Planning

Chapter 2 covered strategic planning as a way of determining the long-term success of the business.

This chapter looks at planning as an activity concerned with implementation of strategy.

The long-term corporate plan serves as the long-term framework for the organisation as a whole, but for operational purposes it is necessary to **convert the corporate plan into a series of short-term plans relating to sections, functions or departments**, perhaps covering one year.

Business planning may assist with:

- Co-ordinating the activities of different functions behind the achievement of the strategic goals for the year.

- Putting the case for finance to funding sources (eg, small businesses may approach a bank with a business plan or a charitable organisation will approach potential donor organisations.)

- Gaining the approval of the Board (eg, a national car dealership requires the manager of each showroom to submit an annual business plan for its approval.)

- Winning contracts where the potential client wishes to be convinced that the firm will fully support the product or service being offered.

- The development of the annual budget.

Worked example: Planning at an airline

A major global airline operates two levels of planning.

Strategic planning: this considers the development of the business over the coming 10 to 15 years, a long period coinciding with the lifespan of its major capital investments. Here management will consider the development of emerging markets, the airline's market position, issues such as carbon and noise pollution and consolidation in the airline industry.

Business planning may concern the coming 12 months and is driven by route planning, ie, which planes will fly which routes and where route schedules will be increased or cut-back. From this route-planning will come estimates of staffing needs, the number of aircraft required, fuel and maintenance requirements and the number of passengers, and the promotional activity to be undertaken. These will then form the basis of the annual budget of costs and revenues.

The annual business plan is in effect an annual instalment of the airline's strategic plan. Of course, given the inherent uncertainties of the industry, the strategic plan is very flexible.

CHAPTER 13

1.2 Creating the business plan

The process of creating a business plan from a bigger picture strategy leads to questions being asked, and issues raised, which require detailed resolution.

Frequently business plans are created using a pro-forma supplied by the approving body, say a bank or government development agency.

Worked example: Small business plan template

The following is a suggested outline for a business plan.

Elements of a business plan

1. Cover sheet
2. Statement of purpose
3. Table of contents

    (i) The business

        (a) Description of business
        (b) Marketing
        (c) Competition
        (d) Operating procedures
        (e) Personnel
        (f) Business insurance
        (g) Financial data

    (ii) Financial data

        (a) Loan applications

        (b) Capital equipment and supply list

        (c) Statement of financial position

        (d) Break-even analysis

        (e) Pro-forma income projections (forecast income statements)

            - Three-year summary
            - Detail by month, first year
            - Detail by quarters, second and third years
            - Assumptions upon which projections were based

        (f) Pro-forma cash flow

            - Follow guidelines for letter (e)

    (iii) Supporting documents

        • Tax returns of the business and owners for last three years

        • Personal financial statement (all banks have these forms)

        • In the case of a franchised business, a copy of franchise contract and all supporting documents provided by the franchisor

        • Copy of proposed lease or purchase agreement for building space

        • Copy of licences and other legal documents

        • Copy of resumes of all owners and senior managers

        • Copies of letters of intent from suppliers, etc

Small businesses frequently request the help of their accounting advisers in the preparation of these business plans.

Interactive question 1: Aldine Computers & Training

A new client, Aldine Computers & Training (Aldine), has approached you for assistance in preparing a business plan to obtain bank funding. Aldine have drafted the following business plan and have requested your comments on its viability and on how it might be improved to maximise the chance of the bank giving them funding.

Requirements

1.1 Draft a report assessing the viability of the business proposal and making recommendations on how the document may be supplemented to improve the chances of Aldine securing funding.

BUSINESS PLAN

for

Aldine Computers & Training

May 20X0

For South East Bank plc

INDEX

1 Summary of Business Plan

    (a) Introduction to Aldine Computers & Training & Co
    (b) Product: Computer Sales
    (c) Product: Training Services
    (d) Critical success factors which will make Aldine succeed
    (e) Financial Summary

2 Management

    (a) Proprietor: Employment Record
    (b) Junior Partners: Brief Summary
    (c) How and Why the Business Started

3 Product/Service

    (a) Computers Sales
    (b) Printer Sales
    (c) Training Sales

4 Marketing

    (a) The Market Size
    (b) Future Growth
    (c) Market Sector
    (d) Expected Client Profile
    (e) Competitors

5 Sales

    (a) Advertising
    (b) Promotion
    (c) Who will Sell
    (d) The Unique Selling Points
    (e) Setting the Price

6 **Operational**

    (a)   Location
    (b)   Equipment and Costs To-date
    (c)   Equipment Required
    (d)   Staff

7 **Short-Medium Term Trading**

    (a)   Objectives Short and Medium-term
    (b)   What if ? – contingency plans

8 **Financials**

9 **Contact Details**

Summary of Business Plan — Page 1

Introduction to Aldine Computers & Training

Aldine Computers & Training (Aldine) was established in March to trade on a regional basis. There are currently two partners: Peter Stone (37) and Kate Schofield (26). Both have extensive experience of computers and training.

Product: Computer Sales

Peter Stone has been building computers for five years for the well-known firm PCNow.com and can use his contacts from there to obtain computer parts at favourable prices. Aldine will aim its computers at the corporate market and will aim to sell them with service contracts as an add-on. They may also offer leasing facilities.

Product: Training Services

Kate Schofield has spent the past five years in computer training with the last two years as an independent consultant. Kate's area of expertise is in the most modern cutting edge technology. The planned courses will run for two – three days, with quarterly one-day progress and update courses to keep those under training up to date with the latest technology. Advanced update courses will include training in the fields of intelligent system design, and digital asset management. It is intended that corporate clients will pay for an initial training course for a group of employees with an annual fee payable to entitle members of this group to attend update courses and also to receive technical e-bulletins.

Critical success factors which will make Aldine succeed

Peter and Kate will make a good team. Peter worked for the family manufacturing firm for four years as an office manager in a small company and has demonstrated strong managerial skills. These will compliment Kate's ability to easily master new technology and her proven skills in technology training. Further, both bring existing business and network contacts and both believe that they could increase their own business areas by 200% within 6 – 12 months if they could delegate some of the more day-to-day activities in their current work schedules to a team within the expanded Aldine business.

Financial Summary

Initial forecasts suggest mark-up will be 40% and will yield expected profits of £90,000 in the first year. Peter and Kate have, between them, £20,000 capital to invest in the company. They require a further £40,000 in funds from a lender – secured on Peter's home. An overdraft facility of £15,000 is also required to finance larger than expected growth if cash flow is limited due to increased costs.

Proprietor: Employment Record

Peter Stone – CV attached

Aged 37, Peter holds a City & Guilds qualification in Computer Studies, and has always held responsible positions in his past career. Peter worked for his family's manufacturing company as office manager for five years where his interest in computers began. Since then Peter worked for PCNow.com as Computer Services Manager. He gained much experience of 'blue chip' requirements. Peter has been married for four years and has two young children.

Kate Schofield – CV attached

Aged 26, Kate has three A Levels in English, History and Art. Kate has always sought positions that allow her to use her skills as a communicator and organiser. Kate worked for the leading firm APB Training Systems for three years before branching out as a successful independent training consultant for the past two years.

Other: Brief Summary

Peter Stone's father, Andrew Stone, will be assisting with the initial setup of the manufacturing outlet. He retired four years ago after running his own successful manufacturing business for 40 years. He has promised to be available as an ongoing source of help and advice.

Two other suitable individuals have been sounded out for management positions and are keen to be involved with this venture.

How and Why the Business Started

Peter and Kate met about a year ago whilst working for the same client. Peter later used Kate's services on an in-house training need at PCNow.com. Both came to believe that actively sourcing business for each other as a combined service will give them 'first sight' of opportunities.

Computer Sales

Three models of all-in-one touchscreen computers will be built:

- RS 01 2.6 GHz 6MB 8GB 23.8" Screen
- RS 02 2.7 GHz 6MB 8GB 23.8" Screen
- RS 03 2.8GHz 8MB 8GB 25" Screen

Each machine can have a number of specified add-ons: CD-RW, DVD-RW, WiFi, Network Card, extra USB ports, and Memory Card readers. The machine will built in Aldine's own manufacturing unit, with service for the first year at the client's site. Thereafter an additional service contract will be offered which will feature a back-to-base repair service.

Servers will be purchased externally, as required to the specifications of the client.

Printer Sales

A number of leading laser and ink jet printers will be available, with the anticipated service contracts as a major source of continuing income.

Training Sales

Four levels of training will be available:

1	Trainee:	Up to 8 persons with no, or little, computer experience
2	Basic:	Up to 8 persons with basic computer skills
3	Intermediate:	Up to 8 persons who have a good working knowledge of computer systems
4	Advanced:	Up to 4 persons who understand technical computer systems

Market Outlook

Corporate computer sales are rising at 8% per quarter. It is expected to continue at that rate for another two years at which point the forecast economic slowdown may reduce sales growth to 4%. This will also be affected by the availability of new applications requiring corporations to upgrade their IT equipment. The ability to configure and give service support to virtual networks of computers to facilitate remote (home) working will be an important requirement.

Future Growth

The growth of PCs took place over the last two decades to a point that penetration of the UK corporate market is complete. The market is saturated. However new applications require larger memory capacity and higher processing (and co-processing) speeds. It seems likely that concerns over data security will make future applications less PC based and instead require much greater reliance on access to corporate 'cloud' networks for data and applications.

This will create a further wave of PC spending as corporations upgrade to the new 'portal' technologies.

Market Sector

Based in Runcorn, North-West England, the need for computer hardware and training is always available. SME Office space is increasing by 10% per annum. There are currently 95,000 SME's within a 50 mile radius of Runcorn.

Expected Client Profile

- Small Medium Enterprise (SME) Computer Sales
- Medium to Large Companies for Training Services
- Commerce and Industry
- Revenue £2m +
- Initially: Manchester and Districts
- Prefer client to be computer literate

Competitors

Computers

Three main companies have been identified as true competitors ie, computer and peripheral sales and service direct to corporate clients on-site.

- **PowerShed Computers (Liverpool):** established six years, revenue £0 (not known), six staff, no growth in past two years

- **Kato & Son PCs (Cheadle):** established four years, revenue £2 million, 10 staff, specialist computer systems, steady growth

- **Solutions.com (national company):** established two years, revenue £7.5 million, 40 staff, mainly top end clients, always stretched

Summary

Service complaints are common with all competitors, and hardware upgrades are long overdue. Solutions.com is looking to revamp their national operation in the spring.

Training

Two companies currently service the above client profile in computer training.

- **TrainOnline (Runcorn):** established 15 years, revenue £900,000, computer training staff four, no plans for rapid growth

- **SolutionsTraining.com (National Company – sister firm to Solutions.com):** established eight years, revenue £6.5 million, computer training staff 35, no local office

Summary

At present demand exceeds resources. No effective competition is challenging the top companies, who offer only limited cutting edge technology training skills.

Sales

Advertising

An advert has been placed in:

- The *Computer Sales* and *Training* sections of local telephone directories

- The Tuesday business section of the syndicated regional newspapers covering Runcorn, Manchester and Liverpool (this appears each week and is booked to the end of the present calendar year)

- *Computing* magazine – classified advertisement for Aldine in each issue of this weekly trade newspaper for IT specialists (available on free subscription). The advertisements have also been posted on the *Computing* magazine website and social media platforms.

Promotion

- Targeted mail shot within three months of receipt of funding to SMEs within 50 miles radius of Runcorn

- Telesales company to start promotion within one month of receipt of funding

- Two regional computer shows booked – 1st in two months, 2nd in six months

Who will Sell?

Both Peter and Kate are competent sales negotiators

The Unique Selling Points (USPs)

- Dual capability of hardware supplier and training provider
- Latest technology training package
- Availability within seven working days

Setting the Price

Computers

PC computers:

Prices include one year on-site total cover

- RS 01 2.6 GHz 6MB 8GB 23.8" Screen   £699.00
- RS 02 2.7 GHz 6MB 8GB 23.8" Screen   £999.00
- RS 03 2.8 GHz 8MB 8GB 25" Screen   £1,199.00

PC Service contracts are:

- £150 per annum for one PC and then £85 for each additional PC

Printers will be leased and serviced:

- £50 per annum for one, then £30 for each additional unit. This excludes consumables (paper, cartridges etc) which will be sold at cost + 30%

Training

- £110 Per Day **Trainee**:   Up to 8 persons with no, or little, computer experience
- £135 Per Day **Basic**:   Up to 8 persons with basic computer skills
- £180 Per Day **Intermediate**: Up to 8 persons, a good working knowledge of computer systems
- £295 Per Day **Advanced**:   Up to 4 persons who understand technical computer systems

20% reduction for in-house training

Location

New office-warehouse development on Industrial Estate located three miles from Runcorn town centre. Development has three meeting/conference rooms of high standard.

Three-year lease – no payment for first three months, then £3,000 per quarter in advance.

Equipment and Costs To-date

	£
Office	
4 × Tables	475
4 × Chairs	350
4 × Filing cabinet	210
2 × Computer (at cost)	875
1 × Laser printer	375
1 × Ink jet printer	300
1 × Photocopier	1,450
1 × Answer phone	100
2 × Phone lines (installation)	150
Stationery and printing	1,100
Sub Total	5,385
Warehouse	
4 × Work bench	2,000
6 × Stack shelving	1,500
Lighting	750
Sub Total	4,625
Inventory	
Computer parts	3,750
Total	13,860

Staff

A mature office manager, and a trainee computer assembler will be sufficient for the initial three months – between three and nine months two training staff (to cover Trainee and Basic training) and a junior office clerk will be employed. At nine months a review of staff will need to take place.

Short – Medium Term Trading

Objective Short-term

Computers

An average of five computer sales per week, and two service contracts. The trainee assembler to be competent at assembly within six months, and to service a computer on site within 9 months.

Training

Kate training for average of three days per week within three months. New training staff to be working an average of four days per week by nine months.

At the 12 month plus period, a number of Kate and Peter's tried and tested ex-colleagues and friends will be approached to join the company with equity available.

Financials

Page 8

Monthly Statement of Profit or Loss – projected for two years

- 20X1 to 20X2 Net Profit £90,000
- 20X2 to 20X3 Net Profit £175,000

As you can see from the Statement of Profit or Loss the business is expecting to make a net profit of £90,000 in the first year. The figures include the salary of the full complement of staff as outlined on page 6 above. The second year shows a net profit of £175,000: if this does happen they will purchase their own premises for £180,000. The total complement of staff at the end of 20X2 is 25.

Statement of financial position projected for two years

- 20X1 to 20X2 Net Assets £130,000
- 20X2 to 20X3 Net Assets £260,000

The projected figures show the anticipated reinvestment of all profits for the first two years: this trend will continue. Inventory at the end of the second year is high but the discounts on bulk purchase is a profitable option in the computer industry, if technology allows.

Monthly Cash Flow Forecast for two years

- 20X1 to 20X2 Year-end Net Cash Flow £25,000
- 20X2 to 20X3 Year-end Net Cash Flow £120,000

In the first year the cash flow will remain positive unless an opportunity to buy bulk computer parts presents itself. Likewise the entire second year is planned to be in the black and consideration will be given at that time as to the purchase of assets.

Contact Details

Peter Stone		Kate Schofield
0XXXX 9876543	**Office** Unit 3 The Trading Estate The Avenue Runcorn WA7 4SA	0XXXX 9876543
019671 3546387	**Home**	01234 1234567
09876 1234567	**Mobile**	017790 9876544
96 Avenue Hill Runcorn WA7 5RR	**Home Address**	12 High Road Runcorn WA7 3AA

See **Answer** at the end of this chapter.

C H A P T E R 13

2 Implementing strategy

Section overview

- Implementation requires the corporate strategy to be broken down into functional strategies and operational plans.

- The business's choice of competitive strategy (cost leadership or differentiation) has implications for its functional strategies.

To implement the chosen corporate strategy, the business's competitive, investment and financial strategies need to be broken down further into functional strategies and operational plans.

The operational plan sets out what is expected of each function of the business and how actions will be taken to meet those expectations.

2.1 The finance department and strategic planning

The role of finance is three-fold:

1 Finance is a resource, which can be deployed so that objectives are met.

2 A firm's objectives are often expressed in financial or semi-financial terms.

3 Financial controls are often used to plan and control the implementation of strategies. Financial indicators are often used for detailed performance assessment.

As a planning medium and tool for monitoring, financial management makes a variety of strategic contributions.

- Ensuring that resources of finance are available. Issues of raising equity or loan capital are important here. The amount of resources that the strategy will consume needs to be assessed, and the likely cost of those resources established. Cash flow forecasting will also be necessary.

- Integrating the strategy into budgets for revenues, operating costs and capital expenditure over a period. The budgeting process serves as a planning tool and a means of financial control and monitoring.

- Establishing the necessary performance measures, in line with other departments for monitoring strategic objectives.

- Establishing priorities, if, for example, altered conditions make some aspects of the strategy hard to fulfil.

- Assisting in the modelling process. Financial models are simplified representations of the business. It is easier to experiment with models, to see the effect of changes in variables, than with the business itself.

2.2 Functional strategies and competitive advantage

In Chapters 6 and 7 we considered how competitive advantages can be gained by a business. We examined the concept of the value chain and discussed how a business can create and sustain competitive advantage using cost or value drivers. The business's choice of competitive strategy determines whether the focus of the chain should be cost (cost leadership) or value (differentiation).

This has implications for the organisation when it is implementing its functional strategies.

The rest of this chapter will discuss functional strategies for:

- Marketing
- Human resources
- Research and development, and innovation planning
- Operations/production
- Purchasing

Strategies for information and technology are considered in Chapter 14. In Chapter 6, we considered the emergence of workforce flexibility and the increasing use of developing technologies (such as artificial intelligence). Both of these trends can have a significant impact on the strategies that organisations implement to achieve their objectives.

3 Marketing planning

Section overview

- Marketing planning is one way by which corporate strategy is implemented.

- This requires a detailed plan of implementation and also of control.

3.1 The marketing plan

The main concepts and tools of marketing received detailed coverage in Chapter 8.

The implementation and control of the marketing effort might take the form of a **marketing plan**:

Section	Content
The executive summary	This is the finalised planning document with a summary of the main goals and recommendations in the plan.
Situation analysis	This consists of the SWOT (strengths, weaknesses, opportunities and threats) analysis and forecasts.
Objectives and goals	What the organisation is hoping to achieve, or needs to achieve, perhaps in terms of market share or 'bottom line' profits and returns.
Marketing strategy	This considers the selection of target markets, the marketing mix and marketing expenditure levels.
Strategic marketing plan	<ul><li>Three to five (or more) years long</li><li>Defines scope of product and market activities</li><li>Aims to match the activities of the firm to its distinctive competences</li></ul>
Tactical marketing plan	<ul><li>One-year time horizon</li><li>Generally based on existing products and markets</li><li>Concerned with marketing mix issues</li></ul>
Action plan	This sets out how the strategies are to be achieved. The Marketing mix strategy should cover the 7 Ps discussed in Chapter 8. The mix strategy may vary for each segment.
Budgets	These are developed from the action programme.
Controls	These will be set up to monitor the progress of the plan and the budget.

3.2 Corporate strategy and marketing strategies

So, what is the relationship between marketing and overall strategic management? The two are closely linked since there can be no corporate plan which does not involve products/services and customers.

Corporate strategic plans aim to guide the overall development of an organisation. Marketing planning is subordinate to corporate planning but makes a significant contribution to it and is concerned with many of the same issues:

- The **strategic** component of marketing planning focuses on the direction which an organisation will take in relation to a specific market, or set of markets, to achieve a specified set of objectives.

- Marketing planning also requires an **operational** component that defines tasks and activities to be undertaken to achieve the desired strategy. The **marketing plan** is concerned uniquely with **products** and **markets**.

The process of corporate planning and the relationship with marketing strategy is shown in the following table.

	Corporate	Marketing
Set objectives	For the firm as a whole: eg, increase profits by X%.	For products and market: eg, increase market share by X%; increase revenue.
Internal appraisal (strengths and weaknesses)	Review the effectiveness of the different aspects of the organisation.	Conduct a marketing audit: a review of marketing activities. Does the firm have a marketing orientation?
External appraisal (opportunities and threats)	Review political, economic, social, technological, ecological factors impacting on the whole firm.	Review environmental factors as they affect customers, products and markets.
Gaps	There may be a gap between desired objectives and forecast objectives. How to close the gap.	The company may be doing less well in particular markets than it ought to. Marketing will be focused on growth.
Strategy	Develop strategies to fill the gap: eg, diversifying, entering new markets.	A marketing strategy is a plan to achieve the organisation's objectives by specifying: • Resources to be allocated to marketing • How those resources should be used. In the context of applying the marketing concept, a marketing strategy would: • Identify target markets and customer needs in those markets • Plan products which will satisfy the needs of those markets • Organise marketing resources, so as to match products with customers.

	Corporate	Marketing
Implementation	Implementation is delegated to departments of the business.	The plans must be put into action, eg, advertising space must be bought.
Control	Results are reviewed and the planning process starts again.	Has the firm achieved its market share objectives?

The following diagram summarises the relationship of marketing planning to the corporate plan.

Marketing and corporate planning

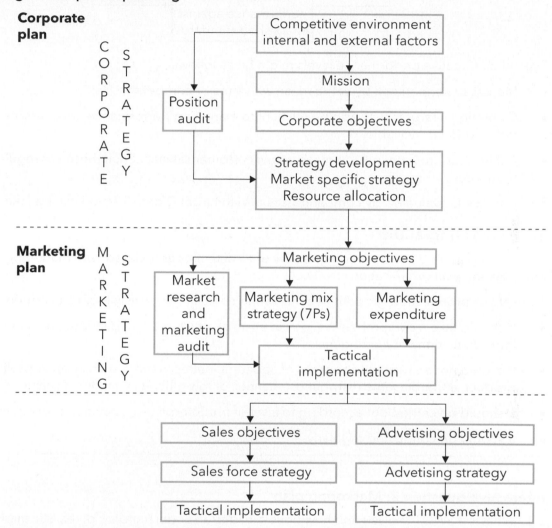

3.3 Controlling marketing activities

Once marketing strategies are implemented, there needs to be **control** and **performance measures** in place to support the purpose of the plan. **Marketing strategies** are developed to satisfy corporate objectives and may reflect the results of the marketing audit.

The **marketing control process** can be broken down into four stages.

- Development of objectives and strategies
- Establishment of standards
- Evaluation of performance
- Corrective action

Part of the corrective action stage may well be to adjust objectives and strategies in the light of experience.

The marketing control process

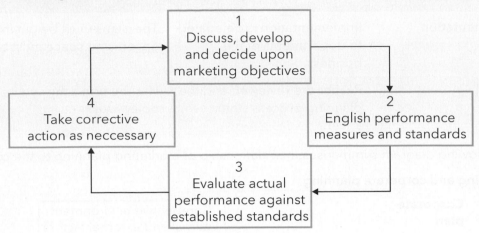

Typical quantitative performance levels might be as follows.

- Market share, perhaps by comparison with a major competitor.

- Operational targets may also be relevant to marketing performance, for example having the right products available.

- Other measures can include measures of customer satisfaction, if these are regularly monitored.

Performance is evaluated by comparing actual with target. Control action can be taken.

3.4 The marketing audit

A marketing audit is a wide ranging **review of all activities associated with marketing** undertaken by an organisation.

To exercise proper strategic control a marketing audit should satisfy four requirements:

- It should take a comprehensive look at every product, market, distribution channel and ingredient in the marketing mix.

- It should not be restricted to areas of apparent ineffectiveness such as an unprofitable product, a troublesome distribution channel, or low efficiency on direct selling.

- It should be carried out according to a set of predetermined, specified procedures.

- It should be conducted regularly.

Interactive question 2: Marketing plan

2.1 What is a SWOT analysis and how does it lead to an understanding of realistic market opportunities?

2.2 Explain the importance of marketing planning for a new consumer product to be launched in your country.

2.3 Using examples, identify the main steps involved in the marketing planning process.

See **Answer** at the end of this chapter.

4 Human resources planning

Section overview

- **Human resource management (HRM)** is the process of evaluating an organisation's human resource needs, finding people to fill those needs, and getting the best work from each employee by providing the right incentives and job environment – with the overall aim of helping achieve organisational goals.

- This requires planning resource needs for the future and succession planning for existing staff.

- Staff appraisals are a vital part of this process.

- The increased use of technology in the workplace raises some interesting considerations in respect of human resource planning.

4.1 Scope of human resource management (HRM)

Definition

Human resource management (HRM): 'A strategic and coherent approach to the management of an organisation's most valued assets: the people working there who individually and collectively contribute to the achievement of its objectives for sustainable competitive advantage.' (Armstrong)

4.1.1 Goals of strategic HRM

- Serve the **interests of management**, as opposed to employees
- Suggest a **strategic approach to personnel issues**
- Link **business mission to HR strategies**
- Enable **human resource development to add value** to products and services
- Gain **employees' commitment** to the organisation's values and goals

The HR strategy has to be related to the business strategy.

Worked example: HR issues in the airline industry

Most airlines are trying to become global companies to avoid dependence on one country.

Business strategy	HR implications	Airline example
What business are we in?	What people do we need?	Air transportation requires pilots, cabin crew, ground crew etc.
What products/markets, level of output and competitive strategy, now and in future.	Where do we need people, what are they expected to do, and how many? Location and size of workforce? Productivity expected and output?	The airline is going global and therefore it needs cabin crew who are skilled in languages and are sensitive to cultural differences.
What is the culture and value system? Is it the right one?	The need to change culture and values.	A cultural change programme; recruiting people to fit in with the right value system; attitudinal assessments.
Tomorrow's strategies, demands and	Tomorrow's personnel needs must be addressed **now**,	Recruitment, training, cultural education.

Business strategy	HR implications	Airline example
technologies.	because of lead times. New technology requires training in **new skills**.	
Critical success factors.	How far do these depend on staff?	Service levels in an aircraft depend very much on the staff, so HRM is crucial.

4.2 Human resources planning

HR must keep a **balance** between the **forecast supply** of human resources in the organisation and the organisation's **forecast demand** for human resources.

Forecast internal supply

- Numbers of people
- Skills/competences
- Experience
- Age/career stage
- Aspirations
- Forecast natural wastage

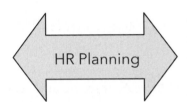

Forecast demand

- New skills required
- New attitudes needed
- Growth/contraction in jobs/roles
- New technologies

Assessed from:

- Human resource audits
- Staff appraisals
- Historical records of staff turnover
- Forecasts of economic outlook (lose staff in boom)

Derived from:

- Business strategy
- Technological developments
- Competitor behaviour
- Outlook for the industry

4.3 Closing the gap between demand and supply: the HR plan

The HR plan is prepared on the basis of personnel requirements, and the implications for productivity and costs. The HR plan breaks down into subsidiary plans.

Plan	Comment
Recruitment plan	Numbers; types of people; when required; recruitment programme
Training plan	Numbers of trainees required and/or existing staff needing training; training programme
Redevelopment plan	Programmes for transferring, retraining employees
Productivity plan	Programmes for improving productivity, or reducing manpower costs; setting productivity targets
Redundancy plan	Where and when redundancies are to occur; policies for selection and declaration of redundancies; re-development, re-training or re-location of redundant employees; policy on redundancy payments, union consultation
Retention plan	Actions to reduce avoidable labour wastage

The plan should include budgets, targets and standards. It should allocate responsibilities for implementation and control (reporting, monitoring achievement against plan).

4.4 Succession planning

Succession planning should be an integral part of the HR plan and should support the organisation's chosen strategy. The developed plan should also be compatible with any changes that that are foreseen in the way the organisation operates. It is likely that strategic objectives will only be obtained if management development proceeds in step with the evolution of the organisation.

4.4.1 Benefits of succession planning

- The development of managers at all levels is likely to be improved if it takes place within the context of a succession plan. Such a plan gives focus to management development by suggesting objectives that are directly relevant to the organisation's needs.

- Continuity of leadership is more likely, with fewer dislocating changes of approach and policy.

- Assessment of managerial talent is improved by the establishment of relevant criteria.

4.4.2 Features of successful succession planning

- The plan should focus on future requirements, particularly in terms of strategy and culture.

- The plan should be driven by top management. Line management also have important contributions to make. It is important that it is not seen as a HR responsibility.

- Management development is as important as assessment and selection.

- Assessment should be objective and preferably involve more than one assessor for each manager assessed.

- Succession planning will work best if it aims to identify and develop a leadership team rather than merely to establish a queue for top positions. A pool of talent and ability is a flexible asset for the organisation.

4.5 The human resource (HR) cycle

A relatively simple model that provides a framework for explaining the nature and significance of HRM is Devanna's human resource cycle.

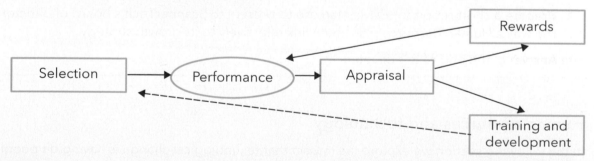

Selection is important to ensure the organisation obtains people with the qualities and skills required.

Appraisal enables targets to be set that contribute to the achievement of the overall strategic objectives of the organisation. It also identifies skills and performance gaps, and provides information relevant to reward levels.

Training and development ensure skills remain up-to-date, relevant, and comparable with (or better than) the best in the industry.

The **reward system** should motivate and ensure valued staff are retained.

Performance depends upon each of the four components and how they are co-ordinated.

4.5.1 The role of staff appraisals

The setting up of a systematic approach to staff appraisal (otherwise called a performance review) is essential to good human resources management. It has the following benefits.

- A forum for agreeing objectives for the coming year that ensure the individual pursues goals that are congruent with the business strategy

- An opportunity to outline or respond to difficulties affecting the individual's performance

- Provision of feedback will motivate and develop the individual

- Identifies personal development needs of the individual, eg, for future roles

- Identifies candidates for succession and development

Interactive question 3: ScannerTech

ScannerTech is a fast growing hi-tech company with expertise in electronic scanners. It has 100 employees and aims to double in size over the next three years. The company was set up by two researchers from a major university who now act as joint Managing Directors. They are intend leaving ScannerTech once the growth objective is achieved and it is large enough to be sold.

ScannerTech makes sophisticated imaging devices used by the airline security and health industries. These two markets are very different in terms of customer requirements but use the same basic technology. Because of growing sales from exports the current strategic plan anticipates a foreign manufacturing plant being set up within the next three years. Present managers are staff who joined in the early years of the company and have their expertise in research and development. Further growth will require additional staff in all parts of the business, particularly in manufacturing and sales and marketing.

Olivia Marcuse is HR manager at ScannerTech. She is annoyed that HR is the one management function not involved in the strategic planning process shaping the future growth and direction of the company. She feels trapped in a role traditionally given to HR specialists, that of simply reacting to the staffing needs brought about by strategic decisions taken by other parts of the business. She feels it is time to make the case for a strategic role for HR at ScannerTech to help it face its challenges.

Requirement

3.1 Prepare a short report for Olivia Marcuse to present to ScannerTech's board of directors on the way a Human Resource plan could link effectively to its growth strategy.

See **Answer** at the end of this chapter.

4.6 Human resources and technology

In the following section we explore the impact that technological change is having on people working within organisations and its implications for human resource planning.

4.6.1 Human resources and big data

In Chapter 6 we discussed the emergence of big data and developing technologies, and the role that they are starting to play in organisations. It is important to note that advances in wearable data capturing technologies are now being used by organisations as way of improving the work life balance of employees. Wearable data capturing technologies are clothing accessories which incorporate computer and electronic technologies, such as sensors. They can be used to track and monitor the physical movements of the wearer.

Worked example: Wearable technologies in the workplace

A growing number of organisations have taken to offering employees the option of using wearable technologies while at work, and in some cases allowing users to take them home. Devices, including Fitbits, enable employers to monitor the physical symptoms that workers experience during a typical working day. Metrics covered by such devices enable the employer to monitor an employee's heart rate, physical location and even internet browsing habits.

There is a current school of thought among large organisations that deploying such technology should enable them to better understand the factors which affect employees' work performance and if needed implement practices to help make the work environment healthier. For example, if an employee's personal data indicates that they are experiencing symptoms of stress, then it may be possible for the employer to take steps to change the individual's workload or work activities.

Wild (2017) highlighted research from marketing firm ABI Research which suggested that 202 million wearable devices were issued to employees in 2016, with this number expected to rise to 500 million by 2021.

The rise in the usage of wearable technologies in the workplace does, however, raise some interesting considerations. One of the biggest issues facing organisations deploying wearable technology concerns the ethical issues that it raises. 'HR professionals, lawyers and unions say that this creates an ethical quandary and that employers should act quickly to develop codes of conduct about how they collect, store and use data about their workers'. (Wild, 2017). Employers have a duty of care to ensure that any employee data they hold does not contravene their legal obligations under the General Data Protection Regulations. Employers need to ensure that personal data is not used in an unfair or discriminatory way.

Sources:

Wild, J. (28 February 2017) Wearables in the workplace and the dangers of staff surveillance. *The Financial Times*. [Online]. Available from: www.ft.com [Accessed 30 April 2018].

4.6.2 Human resources and home working

Earlier in the Study Manual we explored the concept of the virtual organisation and the growth in workforce flexibility. The drive among employers to allow their employees to work from home has provided many obvious benefits, including reductions in the amount of physical office space required and the costs associated of running premises, whilst also giving workers greater flexibility. Home working however is not without its challenges.

Worked example: The perils of home working

An article in *the Guardian* by Jowit (2016) highlighted the findings from research which indicated that home working can take a 'heavy psychological toll' where workers are encouraged to adopt an 'always on' mentality, where the lines between work and home life are increasingly blurred. Jowit (2016) highlighted that 'working away from the office can isolate employees from social networks and career opportunities while fostering a "grazing" instinct that keeps dangerous stress hormones at persistently high levels'.

"Grazing" is the term used to describe the compulsion to work outside of normal office hours. The article highlighted that working ever longer days increased stress and depression, and led to poor diet and sleep among home workers. Jowit (2016) noted comments made by Professor Gail Kinman from the University of Bedfordshire: 'work has become more intense as new technology enables, and even forces, people to work faster, do more, and multi-task'. This in turn has led to 'presenteeism' where people continue to work even when they are off ill. According to an Ofcom report, on average adults in the UK now 'spend more time using technology than sleeping each day'. (Jowit, 2016).

According to Wild (2017) some countries have started passing legislation directed at protecting workers affected by workplace digitisation. 'One example of this pressure bearing fruit is a French law enacted in January [2017] that gives employees the right to ignore emails out of office hours'. (Wild, 2017).

As this example has highlighted, the current situation presents s some challenges for employers in determining appropriate working arrangements which suit workers in providing an improved work-life balance, while also addressing the health implications.

Source:

Jowit, J. (2 January 2016) Work-life balance: flexible working can make you ill, experts say. *The Guardian*. [Online]. Available from: www.theguardian.com [Accessed 28 April 2017].

Wild, J. (28 February 2017) Wearables in the workplace and the dangers of staff surveillance. *The Financial Times*. [Online]. Available from: www.ft.com [Accessed 30 April 2018].

5 Research and development, and innovation planning

Section overview

- Research and development is essential for product and process improvement.
- The need to ensure that R&D has a commercial application forms a link between R&D and other disciplines such as Marketing, Operations and Finance.
- Closely connected to the need for R&D planning is the need for innovation planning.

5.1 Product and process research

Research may be intended to improve **products** or **processes**. R&D should support the organisation's strategy, be properly planned and be closely co-ordinated with marketing.

Many organisations employ **specialist staff** to conduct research and development (R&D). They may be organised in a separate functional department of their own. In an organisation run on a product division basis, R&D staff may be employed by each division.

There are two categories of R&D.

Product research - new product development

The new product development process must be carefully controlled; new products are a major source of competitive advantage but can cost a great deal of money to bring to market. A screening process is necessary to ensure that resources are concentrated on projects with a high probability of success.

Process research

Process research involves attention to how the goods/services are produced. Process research has these aspects.

- **Processes** are crucial in service industries (eg, fast food), as part of the services sold.
- **Productivity**: efficient processes save money and time.
- **Planning**: if you know how long certain stages in a project are likely to take, you can plan the most efficient sequence.
- **Quality management** for enhanced quality.

R&D should be closely co-ordinated with marketing

- Customer needs, as identified by marketers, should be a vital input to new product developments.

- The R&D department might identify possible changes to product specifications so that a variety of marketing mixes can be tried out and screened.

5.2 Strategic role of R&D

Despite the evident costs and uncertainties of R&D expenditure its strategic importance can be understood by reference to some of the strategic models discussed earlier:

- **Porter's generic strategies**: product innovation could be a source of **differentiation**. Process innovation may enable differentiation or **cost leadership**.

- **Porter's value chain**: R&D is included within the support activities of **technology development**. It can be harnessed in the service of lower costs or improved differentiation.

- **Ansoff matrix**: R&D supports all four strategic quadrants. Strategies of Market Penetration and Market Development can be served by product refinement. Product Development and Diversification will require more significant innovations to product.

- **Industry and product lifecycles**: the obsolescence of existing products can be accelerated by product R&D and so R&D is required to provide the firm with replacements.

5.3 Innovation planning

Definition

Innovation: Is concerned with the generation of new ideas of how to do business. It is primarily a creative activity.

Closely linked to the need for R&D planning is the need for innovation planning. The desire to reduce costs and build a basis for differentiation are key drivers for innovation. Generating and maintaining a creative environment within the organisation is a key feature of innovation, establishing such an environment can be created through a number of dimensions:

- **Leadership:** Senior management need to set and communicate a vision which encourages the exploration of new ideas which challenges existing ways of doing things. Leadership is important in giving direction.

- **Culture:** Encouraging a creative culture requires managers to change their ways of thinking, for example viewing failure as an important learning process to be expected. 'Learning organisations' don't view failure as something negative, but instead they learn from their mistakes.

- **People:** Organisations need to encourage a team-based approach that creates a sense of ownership and encourages participation.

- **Structure:** Managers need to embrace new ways of working, part of which may involve developing increasingly flexible organisational structures which encourage innovation.

- **Communication:** Management need to encourage greater openness in communication between workers so that ideas can be shared more freely.

6 Operations planning and management

Section overview

- Operations management is concerned with the transformation of 'inputs' into 'outputs' that meet the needs of the customer.

- It is characterised by the four Vs of volume, variety, variation in demand, and visibility.

- Capacity planning and some of the modern IT/IS applications supporting them are reviewed.

- Quality assurance and TQM are essential components of many modern manufacturing approaches.

6.1 Formulating operations strategy

Definition

Operations management is concerned with the **design**, **implementation** and **control** of the **processes** in an organisation that transform inputs (materials, labour, other resources, information and customers) into output products and services.

In broad terms, operational planning will include many of the following concepts.

- Setting **operational objectives** that are consistent with the overall business strategy of the organisation.

- Translating **business strategy** or **marketing strategy** into **operations strategy**, by means of identifying key competitive factors (referred to perhaps as order-winning factors or critical success factors).

- Assessing the relative importance of different **competitive factors**.

- Assessing current operational performance by **comparison** with the performance of **competitors**.

- Using the idea of a 'clean-slate' or 'green-field' approach to strategy selection. Managers are asked to consider how they would ideally design operations if they could **start again from scratch**. The ideal operations design is then compared with actual operations, and important differences identified. Strategy decisions are then taken to move actual performance closer towards the ideal.

- Formulating strategy could be based on other types of **gap analysis**, such as comparing what the market wants with what the operation is actually achieving, and taking decisions aimed at closing the significant gaps.

- Emphasising the iterative process of strategy selection: Strategies should be **continually reviewed, refined and re-developed** through experience and in response to changes in the environment.

Six items that should be incorporated into an organisation's operations strategy:

Item	Comment
Capability required	What is it that the organisation wants to 'do' or produce?
Range and location of operations	How big does the organisation want to be – or can it be? How many sites and where should they be located?
Investment in technology	How will processes and production be performed?
Strategic buyer-supplier relationships	Who will be key strategic partners?
New products/services	What are the expected product life-cycles?
Structure of operations	How will staff be organised and managed?

6.2 Operations: the four Vs

In Business, Technology and Finance you will have learnt about the **four Vs** of operations: **volume**, **variety**, **variation** in demand and **visibility**. These affect the way in which an operation will be organised and managed.

	High	Low
Volume	A high volume operation lends itself to a capital-intensive operation, with specialisation of work and well-established systems for getting the work done. Unit costs should be low.	Low-volume operations mean that each member of staff will have to perform more than one task, so that specialisation is not achievable. There will be less systemisation, and unit costs of output will be higher than with a high volume operation.
Variety	When there is large variety, an operation needs to be flexible and capable of adapting to individual customer needs. The work may therefore be complex, and unit costs will be high.	When variety is limited, the operation should be well defined, with standardisation, regular operational routines and low unit costs.
Variation in demand	When the variation in demand is high, an operation has a problem with capacity utilisation. It will try to anticipate variations in demand and alter its capacity accordingly. For example, the tourist industry takes on part-time staff during peak demand periods. Unit costs are likely to be high because facilities and staff are under-utilised in the off-peak periods.	When demand is stable, it should be possible for an operation to achieve a high level of capacity utilisation, and costs will accordingly be lower.

	High	Low
Visibility	Many services are highly visible to customers. High visibility calls for staff with good communication and inter-personal skills. They tend to need more staff than low-visibility operations and so are more expensive to run.	When visibility is low, there can be a time lag between production and consumption, allowing the operation to utilise its capacity more efficiently. Customer contact skills are not important in low-visibility operations, and unit costs should be low.
	When visibility is high, customer satisfaction with the operation will be heavily influenced by their perceptions. Customers will be dissatisfied if they have to wait, and staff will need high customer contact skills. Unit costs of a visible operation are likely to be high.	Some operations are partly visible to the customer and partly invisible, and organisations might make this distinction in terms of front office and back office operations.

6.3 Capacity planning

Various types of capacity plan may be used.

- **Level capacity plan** is a plan to maintain activity at a constant level over the planning period, and to ignore fluctuations in forecast demand. In a manufacturing operation, when demand is lower than capacity, the operation will produce goods for inventory. In a service operation, such as a hospital, restaurant or supermarket management must accept that resources will be under-utilised for some of the time, to ensure an adequate level of service during peak demand times. Queues will also be a feature of this approach.

- **Chase demand plan** aims to match capacity as closely as possible to the forecast fluctuations in demand. To achieve this aim, resources must be flexible. For example, staff numbers might have to be variable and staff might be required to work overtime or shifts. Variations in equipment levels might also be necessary, perhaps by means of short-term rental arrangements.

- **Demand management planning**: reduce peak demand by switching it to the off-peak periods such as by offering off-peak prices. Price discrimination is discussed in Chapter 8.

- **Mixed plans**: capacity planning involving a mixture of level capacity planning, chase demand planning and demand management planning.

6.4 Capacity control

Capacity control involves reacting to actual demand and influences on actual capacity as they arise. IT/IS applications used in manufacturing operations include:

- **Materials requirements planning (MRP I)**: converts estimates of demand into a materials requirements schedule.

- **Manufacturing resource planning (MRP II):** a computerised system for planning and monitoring all the resources of a manufacturing company: manufacturing, marketing, finance and engineering.

- **Enterprise resource planning (ERP)** software: includes a number of integrated modules designed to support all of the key activities of an enterprise. This includes managing the key elements of the supply chain such as product planning, purchasing, stock control and customer service including order tracking.

6.5 Just-in-time systems

Definition

Just-in-time manufacturing: An approach to planning and control based on the idea that goods or services should be produced only when they are ordered or needed. Also called lean manufacturing.

Interactive question 4: Lean manufacturing at Toyota

Japanese car manufacturer Toyota was the first company to develop JIT (JIT was originally called the Toyota Production System). After the end of the world war in 1945, Toyota recognised that it had much to do to catch up with the US automobile manufacturing industry. The company was making losses. In Japan, however, consumer demand for cars was weak, and consumers were very resistant to price increases. Japan also had a bad record for industrial disputes. Toyota itself suffered from major strike action in 1950.

The individual credited with devising JIT in Toyota from the 1940s was Taiichi Ohno, and JIT techniques were developed gradually over time. The *kanban* system for example, was devised by Toyota in the early 1950s, but was only finally fully implemented throughout the Japanese manufacturing operation in 1962.

Ohno identified wastes and worked to eliminate them from operations in Toyota. Measures that were taken by the company included the following.

(a) The aim of reducing costs was of paramount importance in the late 1940s.

(b) The company should aim to level the flow of production and eliminate unevenness in the work flow.

(c) The factory layout was changed. Previously all machines, such as presses, were located in the same area of the factory. Under the new system, different types of machines were clustered together in production cells.

(d) Machine operators were re-trained.

(e) Employee involvement in the changes was seen as being particularly important. Team work was promoted.

(f) The *kanban* system (production on demand) was eventually introduced, but a major problem with its introduction was the elimination of defects in production.

Requirement

4.1 Can you explain how each of the changes described above came to be regarded as essential by Toyota's management?

See **Answer** at the end of this chapter.

6.5.1 Three key elements in the JIT philosophy

Element	Comment
Elimination of waste	Waste is defined as any activity that does not add value. Examples of waste identified by Toyota were: • Overproduction, ie, producing more than was immediately needed by the next stage in the process. • Waiting time: measured by labour efficiency and machine efficiency. • Transport: moving items around a plant does not add value. Waste can be reduced by changing the layout of the factory floor so as to minimise the movement of materials. • Waste in the process: some activities might be carried out only because there are design defects in the product, or because of poor maintenance work. • Inventory: inventory is wasteful. The target should be to eliminate all inventory by tackling the things that cause it to build up. • Simplification of work: an employee does not necessarily add value by working. Simplifying work reduces waste in the system (the waste of motion) by eliminating unnecessary actions. • Defective goods are quality waste. This is a significant cause of waste in many operations.
The involvement of all staff in the operation	JIT is a cultural issue, and its philosophy has to be embraced by everyone involved in the operation if it is to be applied successfully. Critics of JIT argue that management efforts to involve all staff can be patronising.
Continuous improvement	The ideal target is to meet demand immediately with perfect quality and no waste. In practice, this ideal is never achieved. However, the JIT philosophy is that an organisation should work towards the ideal, and continuous improvement is both possible and necessary. The Japanese term for continuous improvement is *kaizen*.

6.5.2 JIT purchasing

With JIT purchasing, an organisation establishes a close relationship with trusted suppliers, and develops an arrangement with the supplier for being able to purchase materials only when they are needed for production. The supplier is required to have a flexible production system capable of responding immediately to purchase orders from the organisation.

6.5.3 JIT and service operations

The JIT philosophy can be applied to service operations as well as to manufacturing operations. Whereas JIT in manufacturing seeks to eliminate inventories, JIT in service operations seeks to remove queues of customers.

Queues of customers are wasteful because:

• They waste customers' time.
• Queues require space for customers to wait in, and this space is not adding value.
• Queuing lowers the customer's perception of the quality of the service.

The application of JIT to a service operation calls for the removal of specialisation of tasks, so that the work force can be used more flexibly and moved from one type of work to another, in response to demand and work flow requirements.

Worked example: JIT in a postal service

A postal delivery has specific postmen or postwomen allocated to their own routes. However, there may be scenarios where, say, Route A is overloaded whilst Route B has a very light load of post.

Rather than have letters for Route A piling up at the sorting office, when the person responsible for Route B has finished delivering earlier, this person might help out on Route A.

Teamwork and flexibility are difficult to introduce into an organisation because people might be more comfortable with clearly delineated boundaries in terms of their responsibilities. However, the customer is usually not interested in the company organisation structure because he or she is more interested in receiving a timely service.

In practice, service organisations are likely to use a buffer operation to minimise customer queuing times. For example, a hairdresser will get an assistant to give the client a shampoo to reduce the impact of waiting for the stylist. Restaurants may have an area where guests may have a drink if no vacant tables are available immediately; such a facility may even encourage guests to plan in a few drinks before dinner thereby increasing the restaurant's revenues.

6.6 Quality management

Definitions

Quality assurance focuses on the way a product or service is produced. Procedures and standards are devised with the aim of ensuring defects are eliminated (or at least minimised) during the development and production process).

Quality control is concerned with checking and reviewing work that has been done. Quality control is focused on detecting defects in the output produced, as a result it has a narrower focus than quality assurance.

6.6.1 Cost of quality

The **cost of quality** may be looked at in a number of different ways. For example, some may say that producing higher quality output will increase costs – as more costly resources are likely to be required to achieve a higher standard. Others may focus on the idea that poor quality output will lead to customer dissatisfaction, which generates costs associated with complaint resolution and warranties.

The demand for better quality has led to the acceptance of the view that quality management should aim to **prevent** defective production rather than simply detect it because it reduces costs in the long run.

Most modern approaches to quality have therefore tried to assure quality in the production process, (quality assurance) rather than just inspecting goods or services after they have been produced.

6.6.2 Total Quality Management (TQM)

Total Quality Management (TQM) is a popular technique of **quality assurance.** Main elements are:

- **Internal customers and internal suppliers**: All parts of the organisation are involved in quality issues, and need to work together. Every person and every activity in the organisation affects the work done by others. The work done by an internal supplier for an internal customer will eventually affect the quality of the product or service to the external customer.

- **Service level agreements**: Some organisations formalise the internal supplier-internal customer concept by requiring each internal supplier to make a **service level agreement** with its internal customer, covering the terms and standard of service.

- **Quality culture within the firm**: Every person within an organisation has an impact on quality, and it is the responsibility of everyone to get quality right.

- **Empowerment**: Recognition that employees themselves are often the best source of information about how (or how not) to improve quality.

7 Purchasing

Section overview

- Purchasing is a major influence on a firm's costs and quality.

- Sourcing strategy is developing from the use of many suppliers to get a better price to the fostering of strategic procurement relationships with just a few.

- E-procurement systems can help to improve the efficiency of the process and reduce costs.

Definition

Purchasing is the acquisition of material resources and business services for use by the organisation.

7.1 The importance of purchasing

Cost: raw materials and subcomponents purchases are a major cost for many firms.

Quality: the quality of input resources affects the quality of outputs and the efficiency of the production function.

Strategy: in retailing, buying goods for resale is one of the most important activities of the business.

7.2 The purchasing mix

The purchasing manager has to obtain the best purchasing mix.

7.2.1 Quantity

The size and timing of purchase orders will be dictated by the balance between two things:

- Delays in production caused by insufficient inventories

- Costs of holding inventories: tied up capital, storage space, deterioration, insurance, risk of pilferage

A system of inventory control will set optimum reorder levels (the inventory level at which supplies must be replenished so as to arrive in time to meet demand) to ensure economic order quantities (EOQ) are obtained for individual inventory items.

7.2.2 Quality

The production department will need to be consulted about the quality of goods required for the manufacturing process, and the marketing department about the quality of goods acceptable to customers. Purchased components might be an important constituent of product quality.

7.2.3 Price

Favourable short-term trends in prices may influence the buying decision, but purchasing should have an eye to the best value over a period of time – considering quality, delivery, urgency of order, inventory-holding requirements and so on.

7.2.4 Delivery

The lead time between placing and delivery of an order can be crucial to efficient inventory control and production planning. The reliability of suppliers' delivery arrangements must also be assessed.

7.3 Sourcing strategies

There are a range of possible strategies open to an organisation when deciding who they will purchase their supplies from.

Supply sourcing strategies	
Option	Comment
Single supplier	**Advantages** • Stronger relationship with the supplier. • Possible source of superior quality due to increased opportunity for a supplier quality assurance programme. • Facilitates better communication. • Economies of scale. • Facilitates confidentiality. • Possible source of competitive advantage. **Disadvantages** • Vulnerable to any disruption in supply. • Supplier power may increase if no alternative supplier. • The supplier is vulnerable to shifts in order levels.
Multiple suppliers	**Advantages** • Access to a wide range of knowledge and expertise. • Competition among suppliers may drive the price down. • Supply failure by one supplier will cause minimal disruption. **Disadvantages** • Not easy to develop an effective quality assurance programme. • Suppliers may display less commitment. • Neglecting economies of scale.

Supply sourcing strategies	
Option	Comment
Delegated	A supplier is given responsibility for the delivery of a complete sub-assembly. For example, rather than dealing with several suppliers a 'first tier' supplier would be appointed to deliver a complete sub-assembly (eg, a PC manufacturer may delegate the production of keyboards). **Advantages** • Allows the utilisation of specialist external expertise. • Frees-up internal staff for other tasks. • The purchasing entity may be able to negotiate economies of scale. **Disadvantages** • First tier supplier is in a powerful position. • Competitors may utilise the same external organisation so unlikely to be a source of competitive advantage.

Interactive question 5: PicAPie Ltd

PicAPie Ltd employs a total quality management program and manufactures 12 different types of pie from chicken and leek to vegetarian. The directors of PicAPie are proud of their products, and always attempt to maintain a high quality of input at a reasonable price.

Each pie has four main elements:

• Aluminium foil case
• Pastry shell made mainly from flour and water
• Meat and/or vegetable filling
• Thin plastic wrapping

The products are obtained as follows.

• The aluminium is obtained from a single supplier of metal related products. There are few suppliers in the industry resulting from fall in demand for aluminium related products following increased use of plastics.

• The flour for the pastry shell is sourced from flour millers in four different countries – one source of supply is not feasible because harvests occur at different times and PicAPie cannot store sufficient flour from one harvest for a year's production.

• Obtaining meat and vegetables is difficult due to the large number of suppliers located in many different countries. Recently, PicAPie obtained significant cost savings by delegating sourcing of these items to a specialist third party.

• Plastic wrapping is obtained either directly from the manufacturer or via an internet site specialising in selling surplus wrapping from government and other sources.

Requirements

5.1 Explain the main characteristics of a Total Quality Management (TQM) programme.

5.2 Identify the sourcing strategies adopted by PicAPie and evaluate the effectiveness of those strategies for maintaining a constant and high quality supply of inputs. Your answer should also include recommendations for changes you consider necessary.

See **Answer** at the end of this chapter.

7.4 Strategic procurement

The traditional supply chain model (see diagram below) shows each firm as a separate entity reliant on orders from the downstream firm, commencing with the ultimate customer, to initiate activity.

The disadvantages of this are:

- It slows down fulfilment of customer order and so puts the chain at a competitive disadvantage.

- It introduces possibility of communication errors delaying fulfilment and/or leading to wrong specification products being supplied.

- The higher costs of holding inventories on a just-in-case basis by all firms in chain.

- The higher transactions costs due to document and payment flows between the stages in the model.

Strategic procurement is the development of a true **partnership** between a company and a supplier of strategic value. The arrangement is usually long-term, single-source in nature and addresses not only the buying of parts, products, or services, but product design and supplier capacity.

This recognises that increasingly, organisations are recognising the need for and benefits of establishing **close links** with companies in the supply chain. This has led to the **integrated supply chain** model (the second model in the following diagram) and the concept that it is **whole supply chains** which compete and not just individual firms.

Traditional and integrated supply chain models

Traditional supply chain

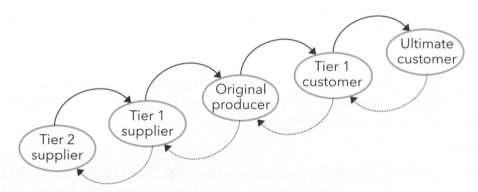

Integrated supply chain

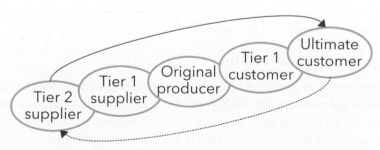

The integrated supply chain shows that the order from the ultimate customer is shared between all the stages in the chain and that the firms overlap operations by having integrated activities as business partners. This is consistent with the idea of a **value system** and the concept of **supply chain networks** discussed in Chapter 6.

Interactive question 6: Beau Ltd

Beau Ltd is a medium sized maker of specialised components which are used in the manufacture of tablet computers. It has three major customers, each of which are major players in the global personal tablet market. The three customers are very demanding, and constant advances in tablet technology mean that Beau Ltd invests heavily in R&D to keep the components it produces at the cutting edge of technology.

Beau Ltd purchases the parts it uses in production from a supplier in China, Xu Co. Xu Co sends deliveries from its factory in China to Beau Ltd's production facility in the UK. Xu Co is in daily communication with Beau Ltd's procurement staff regarding quantities. Recently, there have been delays in supply, so Beau Ltd has taken to holding 20 days worth of parts in inventory. Xu Co charges high prices; the company's MD explains that this reflects Xu Co's focus on improving product quality and service delivery.

Beau Ltd is currently in the process of updating the main component that it sells, the POD52. The POD52 is regarded as being 'state of the art' technology. The updated version will be launched next year and is expected to be highly sought after by the three customers.

Beau Ltd has identified two issues in respect of its procurement and supply chain management:

Issue 1: Beau Ltd is unsure whether to procure parts for the mass production of POD52 from (i) one supplier, Xu Co; or (ii) a range of seven new suppliers, producing similar parts for the POD52 component. One of the suppliers would be Xu Co, three would be American, and three would be German.

Issue 2: POD52 is constructed from 37 individual parts. In a bid to reduce costs, Beau Ltd is undertaking an assessment of its procurement activities. It is looking to review all of its direct 'Tier 1' suppliers to improve efficiencies. The Head of Procurement at Beau Ltd has mentioned the need to review the company's own supplier's suppliers (Tier 2) to ensure that they are being cost efficient.

Requirements

6.1 Issue 1

Outline the main advantages and disadvantages to Beau Ltd of using one supplier or more than one supplier for the components needed to manufacture POD52. You should recommend a course of action.

6.2 Issue 2

Review the Head of Procurement's comment that Beau Ltd should conduct a Tier 2 inspection of its supplier's suppliers. You should recommend whether a Tier 1 or Tier 2 supplier review would be most appropriate.

See **Answer** at the end of this chapter.

7.5 Suppliers and e-procurement

E-procurement involves using technology to conduct business-to-business purchasing over the internet. As we explored earlier in Chapter 6, organisations need to carefully consider cyber security issues when linking their own computer systems to those of suppliers. A key aspect of this concerns whether a supplier's systems are sufficiently robust enough to securely store and handle sensitive data. This issue is further compounded when data breaches occur, as it may be difficult to determine which party (ie, the organisation or supplier) is responsible for resolving the matter. This issue is particularly topical as organisational supply chains are becoming increasingly global.

There are however huge savings to be had, especially for large corporate organisations with vast levels of procurement. Siemens believes that, since it embarked on its fully-integrated e-procurement system, this purchasing strategy saved $15 million from material costs and $10 million from process costs in the one year alone, close to a 1,000% increase in savings from the previous year and only the second year into implementation.

7.5.1 Advantages of e-procurement for the buyer:

- Facilitate cost savings
- Easier to compare prices
- Faster purchase cycle
- Reductions in inventory
- Control indirect goods and services
- Reduces off-contract buying
- Data rich management information to help reduce costs and predict future trends
- Online catalogues
- High accessibility
- Improved service levels
- Control costs by imposing limits on levels of expenditure

7.5.2 E-procurement from a supplier's perspective

Traditionally the business of supplying goods has been about branding, marketing, business relationships, etc. In the expanding e-procurement world the dynamics of supplying are changing and, unlike the expectations of companies implementing e-procurement systems for cost savings, suppliers are expecting to feel profit erosions due to the e-procurement mechanism.

Nevertheless, there are obvious advantages to suppliers:

- Faster order acquisition
- Immediate payment systems
- Lower operating costs
- Non-ambiguous ordering
- Data rich management information
- 'Lock-in' of buyers to the market
- Automate manufacturing demands

7.6 Ethical aspects of purchasing and procurement

Many firms seek to fulfil their own CR commitments by demanding similar commitments from their suppliers. This gives rise to **ethical procurement** which is examined in more detail in Chapter 16.

Summary and Self-test

Summary

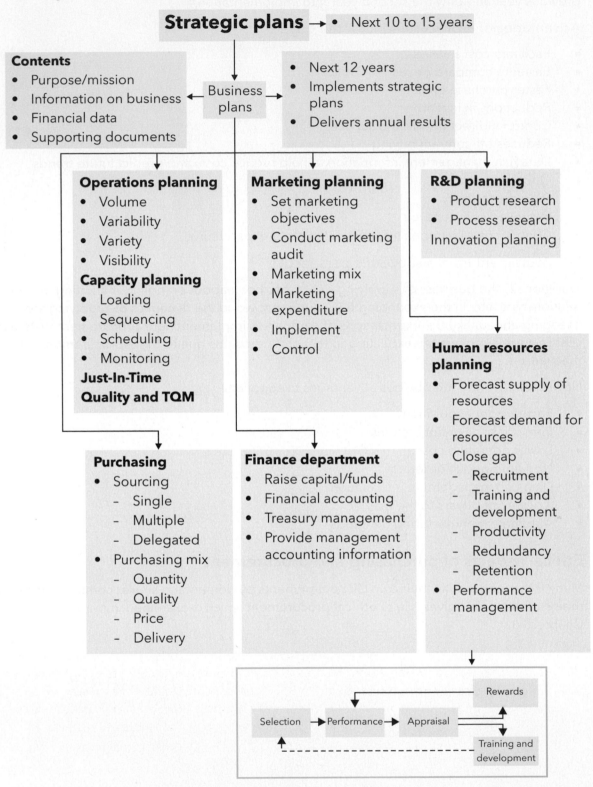

Self-test

Answer the following questions.

1   Here are four characteristics of long-term planning information. List the corresponding characteristics of short-term planning information.

    A   Used by top management
    B   Broad in scope rather than deep in detail
    C   External
    D   Looks to the future and lacks certainty

2   List the 10 purposes of using budgets.

3   Which of the following is not a use of budgetary control?

    A   To define the objectives of the organisation as a whole
    B   To ensure that resources are used as efficiently as possible
    C   To provide some central control when activities are decentralised
    D   To provide the basis for the preparation of future budgets

4   What is the main intention behind R&D?

5   What are the elements of the purchasing mix?

6   What is the role of the production function?

7   Define marketing.

8   How does the finance function relate to strategic planning?

9   What are the four main objectives of HRM?

10 Six factors that should be taken into account when devising an operations strategy are:

- Capacity
- Range and location of operations
- Investment in technology
- Strategic buyer-supplier relationships
- New products/services
- Structure of operations

Requirements

Briefly describe what each of the six factors identified above mean in the context of operations strategy.

Illustrate your answer with examples related to a retail supermarket chain.

11 The recently appointed HR manager in a medium sized accounting firm is struggling. The Senior Partner of the firm is unconvinced about the benefits of appraisal systems. He argues that accountants, through their training, are self-motivated and should have the maximum freedom to carry out their work. His experience of appraisal systems to date has shown them to lack clarity of purpose, be extremely time consuming, involve masses of bureaucratic form filling and create little benefit for the supervisors or their subordinates. He refuses to have his own performance reviewed through an appraisal system.

The HR manager is convinced that performance management and an appraisal system are integral elements in helping the firm achieve its ambitious strategic growth objectives. This reflected her experience of introducing an appraisal system into the corporate finance unit for which she was responsible. The unit had consistently outperformed its growth targets and individual members of the unit were well motivated and appreciative of the appraisal process.

Requirements

11.1 Evaluate the extent to which an effective appraisal system could help the accounting firm achieve its goals.

11.2 Assess the contribution of performance management to the strategic management process.

12 Defence Lamination Ltd

Defence Lamination Ltd (DLL) has been trading for many years making specialist glass products for military uses. Its main customers have been manufacturers in the defence sector which need glass that can withstand special conditions, such as windscreens in jet fighter aeroplanes. By 20X2 annual sales had grown to £22 million with net profits of around 9% after tax.

The current position

Over the past two years DLL has found its customer base eroded by reductions in defence spending by national governments. Sales have fallen significantly in 20X6 and, although some cost savings have been possible, the company lost £500,000 in 20X5.

DLL has the advantage of using very modern automated intelligence-controlled equipment which allows it great flexibility and enables the company to pursue new markets by applying expertise gained in the (now rapidly shrinking) defence sector.

Staff and management have become very anxious but are loyal and keen to change the direction of the company. Managers see themselves as experienced, yet modern.

The industry environment

Customers are historically defence based but, as DLL has realised, these are fewer in number. New customers would include private sector firms such as high street banks, which need security glass. Major customer potential exists overseas, but here the twin problems of bad debt risk and uncertain cash flow are key factors.

Rivals are largely niche operators, except for a few big companies such as Pilkington, but tend to be small because each customer has a unique problem to solve. Product quality and innovative design are crucial elements but branding is not important.

Technology is continually evolving but pricing is not a major problem because customers value quality above all, and are prepared to pay a premium for new technology that can (for example, with bomb-proof glass) save them a fortune.

Suppliers are plentiful, except that key skilled staff are highly sought after.

The increased threat of terrorism around the world means that many opportunities exist for DLL globally.

The proposal

The Managing Director of DLL, Peter Hobbs, has proposed to the board that a bold, global expansion programme is implemented. He believes that DLL has the skills to enter the global private sector for financial services and the diplomatic protection market. To fund the sales team and working capital, he proposes to use National Factors plc (NF) which should advance up to 80% of current receivables, yielding about £2.8 million, which will be adequate to fund growth. He also proposes to change the company name to Security Glass Ltd.

The board's response

DLL has a non-executive director, James Greening, who convinces the board that a proper business plan is needed. He argues that NF will only agree to the proposal if such a plan is produced. However, he is unsure how to go about this and advises that DLL's accountants become involved.

Requirement

As a member of staff of DLL's accountants, write a memorandum to Peter Hobbs which explains the steps required to create, implement and review a business plan. You need not specify detailed strategies but must identify the critical factors for successful implementation of the plan.

13   Read the scenario of the **September 2017 Business Strategy and Technology** question in the Question Bank entitled *Air Services UK Ltd (ASU)*. Draft an answer to the requirement which asks for an explanation of the two specified functional strategies ASU could implement to achieve the CEO's vision.

14   Read the scenario of the **December 2013 Business Strategy and Technology** question in the Question Bank entitled *The Foto Phrame Company (FPC)*. Draft an answer to the requirement which asks for an explanation of the factors which FPC should consider in relation to the procurement and supply chain issues.

15   Read the scenario of the **September 2016 Business Strategy and Technology** question in the Question Bank entitled *Thistle Engineering Services Ltd*. Draft an answer to the entire question. The focus of this is on the creation of a business plan.

Now, go back to the Learning outcomes in the Introduction. If you are satisfied you have achieved these objectives, please tick them off.

Answers to Interactive questions

Answer to Interactive question 1

1.1 Report

To   Aldine Computers & Training
From   An Accountant
Date   Today
Subject   Evaluation of business plan and application for funding

Terms of reference

We have been asked to comment on the viability of the business proposal by Aldine Computers & Training (Aldine) to secure funding for an extension to its business and to propose improvement to the proposal document.

Disclaimer

This report is based on the information given us by the management of Aldine and its accuracy is restricted to the accuracy of that data. No opinion is expressed on the accuracy of that data. This report is intended solely for the management of Aldine and is not for any third parties. The authors cannot be held liable for any loss incurred by third parties relying on this report.

Introduction

Aldine has been established three months and is trading. We understand that some initial capital investment has taken place and that premises have been secured. The business plan therefore is to secure funding for the expansion of the business.

The business model

Business proposals should be evaluated according to the criteria of suitability, acceptability and feasibility.

Suitability concerns the strength, weaknesses, opportunities and threats of the business and the industry in which it operates.

The **strengths** of Aldine include:

- Relevant experience of management in the proposed areas of business

- Industry links with suppliers and corporate customers

The **weaknesses** of Aldine are:

- Very high reliance on its principal managers, Peter and Kate for both direct making and provision of training and also for business development and client prospecting

- Relatively small size will deny Aldine economies of scale in the purchasing of components compared to larger PC makers like PCNow and Dell

- Its inability to offer a national coverage for servicing and training means it will not be able to gain access to national corporate clients

- Low brand and business profile compared to established PC providers

- Many aspects necessary to run its business have not been considered in its business plan (see Section 3 below)

The **opportunities** for Aldine include:

- Continued sales of PCs encouraged by new applications and the desire by firms to encourage flexible working

- The perceived service failings and backlogs of rival providers

The **threats** facing Aldine include:

- Competition in the PC construction market from larger firms able to access cheaper manufacturing resources overseas

- Development of more sophisticated computer-based training and virtual learning which will reduce demand for the face to face training proposed by Aldine

- Increased outsourcing of IT by firms will reduce the demand for Aldine's services

- Forecast economic slowdown in two years will reduce demand for PCs and hence leave Aldine with excess capacity and costs.

In summary its business model poses significant risks to Aldine. By focusing on SMEs it is possible that it may access a market segment overlooked by larger rivals but at the expense of high marketing to sales costs and it will be serving markets where low IT literacy will necessitate considerable and costly support.

Acceptability means that the business proposal should meet approval from key stakeholders.

Kate and Peter are clearly in favour of the business proposal. There is no research presented to help us form a judgement about client attitudes to the services proposed and to dealing with Aldine. The remaining key stakeholder will be the bank. The present report will need some modification before it will secure the banks agreement to lend the money (see Section 4 below).

Feasibility means the ability of the business to carry out its strategic initiatives. This will depend on a combination of internal resources and external factors.

The production plan seems well-thought through. However questions must be raised over the feasibility of the 40% mark-up behind the forecast first year profit of £90,000 which implies a revenue of £225,000 (100/40 × £90,000) supporting the two founders, the mature office manager and the trainee assembler as well as the actual costs of production and service provision. Margins in a competitive industry like IT are likely to be lower and it is an industry with a high failure rate amongst start-ups like Aldine.

The other issue of feasibility seems to be Aldine's reliance on supplier relations built up by Peter whilst at PCNow. Faced with competition from Aldine there is a danger that PCNow would pressurise its suppliers for preferential terms over Aldine.

In summary the business model is potentially viable but the founders need to satisfy themselves, and the bank, on the issues above.

Critique of the business plan

The main omissions from the business plan are:

- A statement of the legal entity: It is not clear whether Aldine is to be a company or a partnership.

- Detailed financial workings to back up the ambitious forecasts on page 8: The business mix between sales, service and training is not clear and nor are the volumes and costs of each. These should be included as an appendix together with a sensitivity analysis of profits against price, costs and volumes.

- The purposes for which the money is required: The initial equipment has been detailed and purchased. What is not clear is what the further £40,000 is required for inventory, working capital, marketing etc. It is not clear. A bank will wish to ensure it is adequate and will not be impressed by the £15,000 additional commitment it is being asked to pledge.

- Any evidence of demand for its services or the preferential supply terms: These are key elements in the business model and so letters of reference and indications of willingness to buy/supply should be included.

- Job roles: Aldine intends to employ office staff, trainees etc. It is not clear what they will do.

- Security: Details of the assets to be pledged by Peter should be included.

- Market information: It is not appropriate to leave details of competitors at the level they are. Evidence is needed of their size, strengths and weaknesses and also their likely responses to Aldine's arrival in the market.

- The proposals for the loan: The business plan does not indicate the likely timing for take-up of the borrowing nor the repayment proposals.

- Plans beyond 20X3: The plan ceases at the year the economic slowdown is forecast to begin. There is no indication on how Aldine intends to develop its business then. Most business plans will be for five years.

- Detailed operational information such as how clients will be prospected and dealt with.

Suggested improvements to the business plan

As indicated above, there are several elements of the business plan that need improvement.

As a minimum Aldine should include:

- A cash flow forecast broken down by month indicating the likely timing for take-up of the borrowing and the repayment proposals.

- Evidence of supplier and client intentions.

- Details of the security being offered for the loan.

- A better strategic analysis utilising the SWOT analysis in Section 2 of this report and indicating how the weaknesses and threats may be addressed.

- Better competitor analysis.

- Job descriptions for the roles being recruited and also how work will be allocated to cover the manufacture and servicing of the PCs.

Conclusions

Providing the above issues are addressed we believe that Aldine will be successful in business and in the application for its loan.

If there are any questions on this report, or further assistance is required, please revert to the author.

Answer to Interactive question 2

2.1 A **SWOT analysis** identifies the strengths and weaknesses of the organisation relative to the opportunities and threats it faces in its marketing environment. The SWOT analysis leads to an understanding of **realistic market opportunities** through the process of a detailed **marketing audit**, covering market and environment analysis, competitor and supplier analysis, customer analysis and internal analysis.

This analysis will highlight potential market gaps, new customer needs, marketing channel developments, competitor strategies and their strengths and weaknesses. The organisation can evaluate market opportunities against its strengths and weaknesses and identified threats and determine what actions to take to exploit the opportunity.

2.2 To successfully launch a new customer product into the UK market the organisation needs to have clear and realistic **objectives**, and identification and understanding of its **target market segment**. Its channel of distribution, branding, packaging and communications activity need to be in place to support the launch. Forecasts of future demand, and return on investment need to be assessed and projected.

A formalised **marketing planning system** that involves all departments, customers, agents and suppliers, the complexity and timing of activities is required to support the launch to prevent lack of coordination, resource and ultimate failure. A **monitoring system** is also required to evaluate the effectiveness of the launch and take actions as required. A successful launch requires a planning process that pulls all the people and activities together, co-ordinates what is done, by who, when and with what resource.

2.3 Marketing planning involves the following stages.

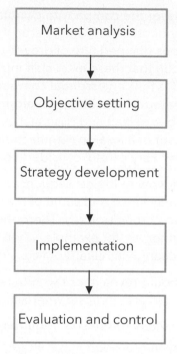

Market analysis: This phase involves establishing an audit process that assesses the macro and micro market environment, market segment analysis, customers, competitors and development strategy. Without a clear understanding of these issues it is difficult to set objectives and develop strategy.

Objective setting: Once the issues arising from market analysis have been understood, objectives can be set. Objectives should be consistent with the overall mission of the organisation and goals, and they must be realistic.

Strategy development: This phase can begin once the objectives have been agreed. In this process alternative strategic options will be evaluated to determine the best way forward for the organisation. Strategy evaluation should consider the organisation's current strengths and weaknesses, market attractiveness, resource requirements, and profitability.

Implementation: This is frequently the hardest part of the marketing planning process. Effective implementation requires co-ordination between different organisations, people and departments. An organisation structure and culture should support this co-ordination, provide good communication and access to information and appropriate levels of resources. In reality, many issues, conflicts and trade-offs occur within organisations that act as barriers to effective implementation.

Evaluation and control: The final phase of the process involves setting an effective system of monitoring and control to measure and evaluate performance.

Answer to Interactive question 3

3.1 Report

From Olivia Marcuse: HR Manager, ScannerTech
To Board of Directors: ScannerTech
Date Today

Human resource planning and strategy

ScannerTech's strategy calls for the company to double in size over the next three years. This will require the employment of extra staff, particularly in marketing, sales and manufacturing. The ambitious planned rate of growth and the high technology base of ScannerTech's business mean that these extra staff must be of very high quality. Human resource (HR) management is thus an **essential component** of the company's business strategy and so should be **integrated with its development**. The alternative is increased potential for serious shortages of staff and mismatches between job requirements and staff availability. The establishment of a foreign manufacturing plant will complicate all HR issues significantly and will demand very careful consideration.

Human resource planning follows a logical sequence, echoing the rational model of strategy. This is not necessarily linear and some of the activities involved in establishing a satisfactory plan can overlap chronologically. There will also be occasions where the various activities influence one another, as, for example, when the persistence of staff shortages in important areas leads to a change in reward policy.

An **audit of existing staff** should reveal those with potential for promotion or employability in new specialisations. It would also indicate where shortages already exist.

Concurrently, an analysis of **likely future staff requirements** could be carried out. We anticipate the need to employ more staff in the areas already mentioned, but we do not really know how many will be required, whether other functions will need to be increased in size or if more support and administrative staff will be needed. There are also the related and sensitive issues of **management succession** and **internal promotion** to consider. In particular, we must consider the eventual replacement of our existing joint Managing Directors, who are likely to leave once the current growth objective has been achieved.

These two studies should enable us to identify the gaps that we need to fill if we are to have the staff required for our overall strategy.

Recruitment, in the sense of attracting applicants, and **selection** from within the pool of applicants are the logical next steps. This work is often **outsourced** and it will be necessary to decide whether the **expertise** and **economies of scale** offered by outsourcing outweigh the need for deep familiarity with our operations on the part of the recruiters.

Reward policy must be considered. At the moment, ScannerTech's staff profile is heavily biased towards people with a background in research and development. Different types of people will be required in the future and their expectations must be expected to show some differences. A doubling in size to, say, 200 employees is likely to take the company into an area of HR complexity in which a formal reward policy and structure is required. Informal decisions about pay and benefits will not be satisfactory. It may be necessary to establish a more formal scheme of **employee relations**, possibly along the lines of a works council.

Increasing size is also likely to require the establishment of a policy on **appraisal and performance management**. This should be linked to a programme of **training and development**. No doubt ScannerTech will continue to hire well-qualified technical staff, but there will be a need for development of staff in other functions and for management development in particular.

Answer to Interactive question 4

4.1 (a) **Cost reduction**: Toyota was losing money, and market demand was weak, preventing price rises. The only way to move from losses into profits was to cut costs, and cost reduction was probably essential for the survival of the company.

(b) **Production levelling**: Production levelling should help to minimise idle time whilst at the same time allowing the company to achieve its objective of minimum inventories.

(c) The **change in factory layout** was to improve the work flow and eliminate the waste of moving items around the work floor from one set of machines to another. Each cell contained all the machines required to complete production, thus eliminating unnecessary materials movements.

(d) With having **cells of different machines**, workers in each work cell would have to be trained to use each different machine, whereas previously they would have specialised in just one type of machine.

(e) A **change of culture** was needed to overcome the industrial problems of the company. Employee involvement would have been an element in this change. Teamwork would have helped with the elimination of waste: mistakes or delays by one member of a team would be corrected or dealt with by others in the team. The work force moved from a sense of individual responsibility/blame to collective responsibility.

(f) The *kanban* system is a 'pull' system of production scheduling. Items are only produced when they are needed. If a part is faulty when it is produced, the production line will be held up until the fault is corrected. For a *kanban* system to work properly, defects must therefore be eliminated.

Answer to Interactive question 5

5.1 In a nutshell, **Total quality management** (TQM) is a management philosophy, aimed at **continuous improvement** in all areas of operation.

A TQM initiative aims to achieve continuous improvement in quality, productivity and effectiveness. It does this by establishing management responsibility for processes as well as output.

Principles of TQM

- **Prevention**
  Organisations should take measures that prevent poor quality occurring.

- **Right first time**
  A culture should be developed that encourages workers to get their work right first time. This will save costly reworking.

- **Eliminate waste**
  The organisation should seek the most efficient and effective use of all its resources.

- **Continuous improvement**
  The Kaizen philosophy should be adopted. Organisations should seek to improve their processes continually.

- **Everybody's concern**
  Everyone in the organisation is responsible for improving processes and systems under their control.

- **Participation**
  All workers should be encouraged to share their views and the organisation should value them.

- **Teamwork and empowerment**

    Workers across departments should form team bonds so that eventually the organisation becomes one. Quality circles are useful in this regard. Workers should be empowered to make decisions as they are in the best position to decide how their work is done.

Note: This is a question that may appear daunting at first, but if you go through and deal with each element in turn it should not prove too difficult to earn a pass. Ensure you provide justification for the changes you recommend.

5.2 **Aluminium foil** is obtained from a single supplier – a sourcing strategy termed '**single sourcing**'. The advantages of this strategy include:

- Easy to develop and maintain a relationship with a single supplier – which is especially beneficial when the purchasing company relies on that supplier.

- A supplier quality assurance program can be implemented easily to help guarantee the quality of products – again mainly because there is only one supplier.

Economies of scale may be obtained from volume discounts.

However, the **disadvantages** of this strategy are:

- PicAPie is dependent on the supplier – providing significant supplier power. Issues such as quality assurance may not be addressed quickly because the supplier is aware that there are few alternative sources of supply.

- PicAPie is vulnerable to any disruption in supply.

Given that there are few suppliers in the industry this strategy may be appropriate. However, there is no guarantee that the current supplier will not go out of business so the directors of PicAPie could look for alternative sources of supply to guard against this risk.

The **pastry shell flour** is obtained a number of suppliers – a strategy known as **multi-sourcing**. The advantages of this strategy include:

- Ability to switch suppliers should one fail to provide the flour. Having suppliers in different countries is potentially helpful in this respect as poor harvests in one country may not be reflected in another.

- Competition may help to decrease price.

Disadvantages include:

- It may be difficult to implement a quality assurance program due to time needed to establish it with different suppliers.

- Suppliers may display less commitment to PicAPie depending on the amount of flour purchased making supply more difficult to guarantee.

PicAPie appears to have covered the risk of supply well by having multiple sources of supply. The issue of quality remains and PicAPie could implement some quality standards that suppliers must adhere to keep on supplying flour.

A third party is given the responsibility for obtaining **meat and vegetables** – this is termed **delegated sourcing**. Advantages of this method include:

- Provides more time for PicAPie to concentrate on pie manufacture rather than obtaining inputs. Internal quality control may therefore be improved.

- The third party is responsible for quality control checks on input – again freeing up more time in PicAPie. Where quality control issues arise, PicAPie can again ask the third party to resolve these rather than spending time itself.

- Supply may be easier to guarantee as the specialist company will have contacts with many companies.

Disadvantages are:

- Quality control may be more difficult to maintain if the third party does not see this as a priority.

- There will be some loss of confidentiality regarding the products that PicAPie uses, although if there are no 'special ingredients' then this may not be an issue.

Given the diverse sources of supply, PicAPie are probably correct using this strategy.

The **plastic film** is obtained from two different sources utilising two different supply systems. This is termed **parallel sourcing**. The advantages of this method include:

- Supply failure from one source will not necessarily halt pie production because the alternative source of supply should be available.

- There may be some price competition between suppliers.

Disadvantages include:

- PicAPie must take time to administer and control two different systems.

- Quality may be difficult to maintain, and as with multiple sourcing, it will take time to establish supplier quality assurance programmes. Given that some stock is surplus to requirements from other sources, quality control programmes may not be possible anyway.

The weakness in the supply strategy appears to be obtaining film from the internet site – in that quality control is difficult to monitor. Changing to single sourcing with a supplier quality assurance programme would be an alternative strategy to remove this risk.

Answer to Interactive Question 6

6.1 Issue 1

The key issues:

(1) Whether to have one supplier or many
(2) Whether to continue solely with a current supplier or to engage with new suppliers

One supplier: Xu Co

- The arrangement with Xu Co represents strategic procurement.

- This relationship can be beneficial as Beau Ltd and Xu Co can establish close links in the supply chain through introducing EDI facilities to reduce the need for daily communication.

Advantages to Beau Ltd from single sourcing from one supplier:

- Consistent parts from a sole supplier

- Should make monitoring quality easier

- Xu Co may be dependent on Beau Ltd for income, and therefore more responsive to Beau Ltd's needs

- Collaboration in working together on new components is mutually beneficial

- Beau Ltd already has a relationship with Xu Co

Disadvantages to Beau Ltd from single sourcing from one supplier:

- Disruption to Xu Co's output will impact on Beau Ltd. Could damage relations with the three highly demanding customers if orders are not fulfilled on time. Furthermore, Beau Ltd is already having to hold higher levels of inventory than it might otherwise hold to overcome current problems.

- Xu Co may not to be able to support increases in demand.

- Xu Co may attempt to exploit relationship with Beau Ltd by increasing prices if a long-term supply agreement is entered into.

Advantages to Beau Ltd of having seven suppliers:

- Beau Ltd can encourage competition among suppliers to reduce prices.

- The costs of switching supplier are reduced.

Disadvantages to Beau Ltd of having seven suppliers:

- Increased scope for suppliers to lack commitment to supply as less revenue is generated per supplier from serving Beau Ltd

- Increase in costs and management time of communicating with seven suppliers

- Reduced economies of scale

- Still have long lead times if parts are being delivered from China and the US in particular. Increases the uncertainty of delivery

Recommendation

Beau Ltd is advised to continue using existing supplier Xu Co due to the relationship that the two have already established. This approach helps increase Beau Ltd's buying power as the company will be better placed to negotiate on price. The threat of losing Beau Ltd altogether to other suppliers may incentivise Xu Co to improve its current terms of supply.

6.2 Issue 2

An integrated supply chain approach highlights that the supply chain of an organisation and it's suppliers should be viewed as a whole. The desire for information about Beau Ltd's own suppliers (Tier 1) and its supplier's suppliers (Tier 2) is a feature of this approach.

In theory, if Tier 2 suppliers can find efficiencies and reduce costs these can be passed onto Tier 1 suppliers, which should result in lower purchase prices for customers, in this case the likes of Beau Ltd. Sound supply chain management is needed to attain such benefit.

Beau Ltd's supply chain review is focused on upstream supply chain management as there is no focus on its own customers, with the main emphasis being on realising cost efficiencies.

Beau Ltd as a customer does not have a legal right to request an inspection of its suppliers processes. However, it should be noted that such a review may help to improve transparency and the degree of openness between the parties. Suppliers for whom Beau Ltd is a major customer may be more inclined to participate in the review for fear of damaging existing relations.

Tier 2 suppliers have no legal obligations to participate in Beau Ltd's review as the two parties do not have any direct contractual obligations to one another. However, Tier 2 suppliers may be motivated to allow Beau Ltd to investigate their own operations due to the fact that Beau Ltd could cease to make purchases from a Tier 1 supplier, which in turn would result in fewer purchases from Tier 2 suppliers.

Recommendation

Attempts to manage costs throughout the supply chain are in line with best practice in supply chain management. A focus on Tier 1 suppliers is most likely to be more value adding to Beau Ltd as these are the third parties which most closely interact with the company's own value chain.

Answers to Self-test

1   A   Used at a lower level by those who implement plans
       B   Detailed
       C   Internal
       D   Definite

2
- Ensure the achievement of the organisation's objectives
- Compel planning
- Communicate ideas and plans
- Co-ordinate activities
- Allocate resources
- Authorisation
- Provide a framework for responsibility accounting
- Establish a system of control
- Provide a means of performance evaluation
- Motivate employees to improve their performance

3   C   To provide some central control when activities are decentralised.

4   To improve products or processes and so support the organisation's strategy.

5
- Quantity
- Quality
- Price
- Delivery

6   To control the necessary activities to provide products (or services) creating outputs which have added value over the value of inputs.

7   'The management process which identifies, anticipates and satisfies customer needs profitably'. *Chartered Institute of Marketing*

8
- Ensuring that resources of finance are available
- Integrating the strategy into budgets
- Establishing the necessary performance measures
- Establishing priorities
- Assisting in the modelling process

9
- To develop an effective human component for the company
- To obtain, develop and motivate staff
- To create positive relationships
- To ensure compliance with social and legal responsibilities

10
- **Capability required**: Any operations strategy will be influenced by what it is that the organisation does.

  For example, a supermarket chain sells food and other items to consumers.

- **Range and location of operations**: The operations strategy will be affected by the scale and geographical spread of the organisation's operations.

  For example, a supermarket chain with say 10 outlets in one region of a country will face different operation strategy issues than a nationwide chain.

- **Investment in technology**: Technology will impact upon operations and therefore operations strategy as it has the potential to change the processes associated with operations.

For example, a supermarket chain operating using an EFTPOS system linked to their stock (logistics/warehousing systems will operate differently to a chain relying on less-automated systems).

- **Strategic buyer-seller relationships**: Who key strategic partners are will affect operations strategy.

  For example, a supermarket may have a preferred supplier for canned food items. Operations may then be designed to help facilitate this relationship. Relationships with 'buyers' (consumers) may be developed using loyalty card schemes – and operations changed based on what the scheme reveals.

- **New products/services**: This relates to how long the business will be able to do what it is currently doing (in the same way).

  A supermarket may find it also needs to offer online shopping and home delivery. It could also decide to move into non-traditional areas such as consumer electronics – or even consumer insurance or finance. These types of changes require changes to operations strategy.

- **Structure of operations**: Operations strategy will also be influenced by how staff are organised and managed.

  For example, will 'regional managers' have responsibility and complete control over all stores in one region – or will one national strategy apply?

  Issues such as staff levels, shift patterns and human resources policies will also affect operations strategy. For example, will stores be open 24 hours – and if so how will this be staffed?

11.1 The Senior Partner and the HR manager emphasise the aspects of appraisal schemes that **support their own favoured policies**. Such schemes should support the organisation's overall objectives without incurring excessive administrative and management costs.

In an organisation such as an accounting practice, the professional staff should indeed be highly **self-motivated**, able to judge the effectiveness of their own performance and bring to their work a commitment to high professional standards. On the other hand, it is inevitable that their **talents and performance will vary** and they will need **guidance and help with their future development**. Dealing with these issues would be the role of an appraisal scheme.

The overall aim of such a scheme would be to **support progress toward the achievement of corporate objectives** and it would do this in three ways: performance review, potential review and training needs review.

Performance review: Performance review should provide employees with an **impartial and authoritative assessment of the quality and effect of their work**. Individuals should have personal objectives that support corporate goals via intermediate objectives relevant to the roles of their work groups. A reasoned assessment of performance can have a **positive motivating effect**, simply as a kind of positive, reinforcing feedback. It can also provide an opportunity for analysing and addressing the **reasons for sub-optimal performance.**

Potential review: Any organisation needs to make the best use it can of its people; an accountancy practice is typical of many modern organisations in that its people are its greatest asset and its future success depends on managing them in a way that makes the best use of their skills and aptitudes. An important aspect of this is **assessing potential for promotion and moves into other positions of greater challenge and responsibility.**

Training needs review: A further aspect of the desirable practice of enabling staff to achieve their potential is the provision of training and development activities. The appraisal system is one means by which **training needs can be assessed** and training provision initiated.

The appraisal system: An appraisal system must be properly administered and operated if it is make a proper contribution to the organisation's progress.

The appraisal cycle: Formal appraisal, with interviews and written assessments, is typically undertaken on an **annual cycle**. This interval is commonly regarded as too long to be effective because of the speed with which individual roles can evolve and their holders can develop, so the annual appraisal is often supplemented with a less detailed review after six months. Sometimes the procedure is sufficiently simplified that the whole thing can be done at six monthly intervals. Much modern thinking on this topic is now suggesting that any frequency of periodic appraisal is unsatisfactory and that it should be replaced by a **continuous process of coaching and assessment**.

Objectivity and reliability: Appraisal involves an element of direct personal criticism that can be stressful for all parties involved. If the system is to be credible its outputs must be seen to be objective and reliable. This requires proper **training for appraisers**, the establishment of appropriate **performance standards** and, preferably, input into each appraisal from **more than one person**. Having reports reviewed by the appraiser's own manager is one approach to the last point; 360 degree appraisal is another.

Setting targets: Past performance should be reviewed against **objective standards** and this raises the question of the type of objective that should be set. Objectives set in terms of **results** or outcomes to be achieved can encourage **creativity** and **innovation** but may also lead to **unscrupulous**, **unethical** and even **illegal choice of method**. On the other hand, objectives designed to maintain and improve the quality of output by **encouraging conformity** with approved procedure and method may stifle the creativity and innovation widely regarded as a vital source of continuing competitive advantage.

11.2   **Performance management** involves the establishment of clear, agreed individual **goals and performance standards**, continuous leadership action to both **motivate and appraise subordinates** and a **periodic review** of performance at which the goals and performance standards for the next cycle are set.

Performance management is an application of the **rational model** of strategic management, in that individual goals are intended to form the lowest echelon of a **hierarchy of objectives** that builds up to support the **overall mission** of the organisation. It is an essential aspect of the system that individual goals should be **agreed and internalised** so that true **goal congruence** is achieved.

This overall approach was first described (as is so often the case) by Peter Drucker, in 1954, and is seen most clearly in the system of **management by objectives** (MbO). MbO as a management system has fallen somewhat from favour with the rise of quality management methods that emphasise processual and procedural conformance rather than the attainment of overall performance goals. Nevertheless, it has much to offer.

Under a formal MbO system, the process of setting goals is part of the **implementation phase** of strategic management and follows consideration of resources, overall objectives and SWOT analysis. Top level subordinate goals are agreed for heads of departments, divisions or functions: these goals should be specific, measurable, attainable, relevant and time-bounded (SMART). It is particularly important that the achievement of a goal can be established by objective **measurement**. There may be different timescales for different objectives, with short-term goals supporting longer-term ones.

Departmental heads then agree SMART goals for their subordinates in discussion with them, that support their own personal goals, and so on down the hierarchy to the level of the individual employee. All members of the organisation thus know what they are expected to achieve and how it fits into the wider fabric of the organisation's mission.

Periodic **performance review** is based on the objective appraisal of success against agreed goals, the agreement of goals for the next period and an assessment of the resources, including training, that the reviewee may require to reach those goals. The MbO system thus closes the **feedback loop** in the corporate control system.

12 Defence Lamination Ltd

Memorandum

To	Peter Hobbs Esq, Managing Director, Defence Lamination Ltd
From	A Smith, on behalf of Taylor & Co, Chartered Accountants
Date	31 October 20X6
Subject	Proposed business plan

The planning process

Broadly this covers

- Creation
- Implementation
- Review

Creating the plan involves a position analysis for DLL which would include the following.

- The company mission, which could be changed to include civilian private sector markets. The name change will help this.

- Shareholder analysis, which would highlight the anxiety of staff and the need to return DLL to profit.

- Internal strengths and weaknesses of DLL such as its high product quality. See below for critical success factors.

- External pressures and future events, including rivalry, political changes, new technology, and economic forecasts.

Implementing the plan involves two steps.

- Setting objectives that are measurable, specific and realistic. You need targets at which to aim, but these will presumably include sales and profit measures, as well as cash flow. In addition, I suggest qualitative targets such as customer satisfaction and product quality.

- Deciding on a strategy. This is up to you, although it will involve debt factoring. It would be helpful to have a unique selling proposition to put to National Factors plc (NF) and I imagine sales and language expertise must form part of this. You should also set a timetable for implementation.

Reviewing the plan means that you must assess three factors.

- Is the plan consistent? Does it fit in with the position analysis that you have completed?
- Is the plan sufficient? Does it meet your objectives previously set?
- Is the plan feasible? Do you possess the resources necessary?

It would be sensible for the review to be done independently, perhaps by James Greening.

Critical success factors

I believe that success depends on six factors.

(1) DLL's ability to adapt to new markets. This should be possible, given that you have high quality, flexible and automated production facilities. If you can make any type of glass in any size, then you should penetrate new markets.

(2) Finding new customers in the non-defence sector. Your brand name counts for very little and potential customers must be convinced that you are serious. Your ability to meet their exact requirements will evidence this, but you have to diversify into a new customer base or face closure.

(3) Providing top quality and specific solutions. Each customer is a new challenge and, if you are to compete with other niche rivals, you must offer excellent quality and innovation. Do you have product testing facilities?

(4) Retention of key employees as your rivals perceive a threat and try to poach them.

(5) DLL's willingness to tackle overseas markets. If you are to be successful, you need to be prepared to travel, employ interpreters and take some risks in unknown markets.

(6) Bad debt and foreign exchange risks. If you achieve overseas sales, you will be exposed to these risks, but NF may provide some stability and credit insurance for a fee.

13 Refer to the answer to Air Services UK Ltd in the Question Bank.

14 Refer to the answer to The Foto Phrame Company in the Question Bank.

15 Refer to the answer to Thistle Engineering Services Ltd in the Question Bank.

CHAPTER 14

Strategies for information

Introduction

Examination context

TOPIC LIST

Introduction

Learning outcomes

	Tick off

- Identify the risk attached to an organisation's present position, using all relevant qualitative and quantitative data, and considering attitudes to risk, security and cyber security ☐

- Identify the risks attached to proposed courses of action in a given situation, considering all relevant factors stating all assumptions made and identifying strategies for managing risk ☐

- Explain and demonstrate how qualitative and quantitative data, including forecasts, budgets and other management information presented in a range of formats, can be analysed to monitor the performance of an organisation's projects, divisions and other strategic units ☐

- Explain and demonstrate how an organisation can capture, analyse and interpret data, including big data, to provide management with information that enables it to implement, monitor, and modify a strategy and to create or sustain competitive advantage ☐

Specific syllabus references for this chapter are: 1f, 2d, 3h, 3i.

Syllabus links

You will have been introduced to the provision and use of financial information in your Management Information and Business, Technology and Finance studies.

The strategic value of IT/IS and big data is a relatively new topic that complements earlier chapters on strategy. In Chapter 10 we explored the different types of risks that organisations are exposed to, one of the most significant of these concerned the threats now presented by cyber risks. The growing global dependency on information technology systems has increased the focus on cyber security. In this chapter we explore the implications of this in greater detail.

Examination context

In the examination you are unlikely to get a whole question focusing on information systems. Instead you may be required to comment upon the information/data available for decision making in a scenario question – is there enough information available? What other information is needed? Where might the organisation source relevant information? Is the information system adequate to fulfil the functions required of it by the organisation? How can the organisation use information to generate competitive advantage?

In the context of the exam, a key aspect of information strategy is that it should provide the appropriate type and amount of information needed by management to select, implement and control its chosen overall strategy. The information strategy therefore needs to match the organisation's overall strategy in terms of the types of information available. Also, the level of detail, the form of the information and its timing should be appropriate to the role of the person(s) who receive it.

In Question 3 of the March 2017 exam (*Gighay Ltd*) the scenario focused on a company (Gighay) which provided IT services. The scenario included information about two potential new clients for Gighay. The second client, Feltar, specialises in selling coffee to individual customers and independent cafes. Feltar uses a basic website through which to make its online sales. Feltar's Managing Director has approached Gighay for assistance concerning the use of data analytics.

The second requirement in the question asked:

'Explain how Feltar can use data analytics to achieve competitive advantage. Address the Managing Director's concerns about the practical implications of implementing a big data strategy.'

(9 marks)

To produce a good answer, candidates needed to make active use of the scenario detail, as this provided some clear indicators about how data analytics could be used at Feltar to achieve a competitive advantage. Areas relevant to Feltar here related to marketing, inventory and pricing. The use of the 4Vs of big data, discussed in Chapter 6, was highly appropriate when applied to the scenario facing Feltar.

The Business Strategy and Technology exam may also test your understanding of issues related to cyber security and cyber risk. Therefore you need to ensure that you are comfortable with identifying potential cyber security issues, and providing recommendations as to how these could practically be addressed.

Question 2 in the September 2017 exam (*Air Services UK Ltd, ASU*) focused on a company responsible for providing airspace management systems to all airports and aircraft using UK airspace. The scenario highlighted that one of ASU's operational centres had recently been targeted by hackers, resulting in the immediate shut down of ASU's systems. The third requirement asked:

'Explain the cyber security risks that ASU faces, and how these risks can be managed.'

(9 marks)

When faced with a requirement such as this it is important that you deal with each part in turn. Firstly, identify the cyber-security risks by stating what they are and their significance to the featured entity, which in this case was ASU. Secondly, recommend how the risks can be managed. It is important that any recommendations you make are realistic and appropriate for the featured entity. Central to producing a good answer here was recognising the significance of IT infrastructures to ASU.

1 The role of information

Section overview

Information takes many forms and has many roles within the organisation. It comes from **internal** and **external** sources.

Organisations require information for a range of purposes.

- Planning
- Controlling
- Recording transactions
- Performance measurement
- Decision making

Organisations require different types of information system to provide different levels of information in a range of functional areas, supporting the distinction between strategic, tactical and operational decision making.

1.1 Why do organisations need information?

A modern organisation requires a **wide range of systems** to hold, process and analyse information. Organisations require different types of information system to provide different **levels of information** in a range of functional areas. **Strategic planning**, **management control** and **operational control** may be seen as a hierarchy of decisions. This is sometimes called the Anthony hierarchy, after the writer Robert Anthony. One way of portraying this concept is shown on the following diagram.

Types of information systems

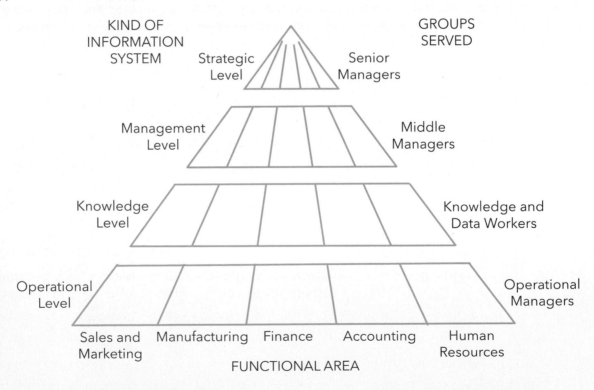

The point to note from the above diagram is that the higher level applications such as managerial information depend to a great extent on skimming data from the operational systems maintained by the different functional departments for their own purposes.

Strategic information	Tactical information	Operational information
Derived from both internal and external sources	• Primarily generated internally (but may have a limited external component)	• Derived from internal sources
• Summarised at a high level	• Summarised at a lower level	• Detailed, being the processing of raw data
• Relevant to the long term	• Relevant to the short and medium term	• Relevant to the immediate term
• Concerned with the whole organisation	• Concerned with activities or departments	• Task-specific
• Often prepared on an *ad hoc* basis	• Prepared routinely and regularly	• Prepared very frequently
• Both quantitative and qualitative	• Based on quantitative measures	• Largely quantitative
• Uncertain, as the future cannot be accurately predicted		

1.2 Information requirements in different sectors

Sector	Information type	Example(s)	General comments
Manufacturing	Strategic	Future demand estimates New product development plans Competitor analysis	The information requirements of commercial organisations are influenced by the need to make and monitor profit. Information that contributes to the following measures is important:
	Tactical	Variance analysis Departmental accounts Inventory turnover	• Changeover times • Number of common parts • Level of product diversity • Product and process quality
	Operational	Production reject rate Materials and labour used Inventory levels	
Service	Strategic	Forecast sales growth and market share Profitability, capital structure	Organisations have become more customer and results-oriented over the last decade. As a consequence, the difference between service and other organisation's information requirements has decreased. Businesses have realised that most of their activities can be measured, and many can be measured in similar ways
	Tactical	Resource utilisation such as average staff time charged out, number of customers per hairdresser, number of staff per	

Sector	Information type	Example(s)	General comments
		account Customer satisfaction rating	regardless of the business sector.
	Operational	Staff timesheets Customer waiting time Individual customer feedback	
Public sector	Strategic	Population demographics Expected government policy	Public sector (and non-profit making) organisations often don't have one overriding objective. Their information requirements depend on the objectives chosen. The information provided often requires interpretation (eg, student exam results are not affected by the quality of teaching alone). Information may compare actual performance with: • Standards • Targets • Similar activities • Indices • Activities over time as trends
	Tactical	Hospital occupancy rates Average class sizes Percent of reported crimes solved	
	Operational	Staff timesheets Vehicles available Student daily attendance records	
Non-profit/ charities	Strategic	Activities of other charities Government (and in some cases overseas government) policy Public attitudes	Many of the comments regarding public sector organisations can be applied to not-for-profit organisations. Information to judge performance usually aims to

Sector	Information type	Example(s)	General comments
	Tactical	Percent of revenue spent on admin	assess economy, efficiency and effectiveness.
		Average donation	A key measure of efficiency for charities is the percentage of revenue that is spent on the publicised cause (eg, rather than on advertising or administration).
		'Customer' satisfaction statistics	
	Operational	Households collected from/approached	
		Banking documentation	
		Donations	

1.3 The qualities of good information

Regardless of the type of information or the sector in which an organisation operates it is important that organisational information has certain qualities.

The **qualities of good information** can be summarised by the mnemonic **Accurate**: **A**ccurate, **C**omplete, **C**ost-beneficial, **U**ser-targeted, **R**elevant, **A**uthoritative, **T**imely and **E**asy to Use.

Interactive question 1: Strategic decision making

Decision making at the strategic level in organisations needs to be supported by information systems that are flexible and responsive.

Requirements

1.1 Describe the characteristics of information flows at the strategic level.

1.2 Describe the sources of information required for strategic decision making and the characteristics of an information system used to provide strategic information.

See **Answer** at the end of this chapter.

2 The strategic value of information technology

Section overview

- Business analysis views the information system in the context of the organisation's operations and strategy.

- As the importance of big data and information has increased, organisations have realised the role that IT/IS can play in achieving a competitive advantage.

Definitions

Information management strategy: Strategy specifying who controls and uses the technology provided.

Information systems strategy: Strategy specifying how hardware, software and telecommunications can achieve delivery of the information systems strategy.

Information technology strategy: Strategy specifying the systems that will best enable the use of information to support the business strategy.

2.1 The benefits of a proposed information system

The benefits from a proposed information system should be evaluated against the costs. To quantify the benefits, several factors need to be considered.

- **Increased revenue**

  Improved data collection, storage and analysis tools may indicate previously unknown opportunities for sales. Such tools may include **data-mining and data analytics** software which allow relationships to be discovered between previously unrelated data. Later in this chapter we consider how big data and data analytics can help organisations achieve a competitive advantage.

- **Cost reduction**

  In Chapter 6 we explored the impact that new developing technologies are having on organisations' ability to automate previously manually intensive work. Increasing automation saves staff time and may result in a smaller workforce being required.

  Systems such as inventory control can benefit as losses from obsolescence and deterioration are reduced.

- **Enhanced service**

  Computerised systems that create a more prompt and reliable service will increase customer satisfaction. Earlier in the Study Manual we considered the increasing use of 'chatbot' technologies to handle customer queries. As discussed in Chapter 6, the use of computer systems isn't solely restricted to improving the customer experience, as they can also help to enhance the productivity of the workforce, through the use of digital asset management systems.

- **Improved decision making**

  Providing decision makers with the most accurate and up-to-date information that is possible can have substantial benefits. The main areas of benefit are:

  - **Forecasting**

    Predictive data analytics can be used to forecast sales trends, and their effect on costs. Organisations that can make accurate forecasts are in a better position to plan their structure and finances to ensure long-term success.

  - **Developing scenarios**

    Organisations facing uncertain times, or those which operate in dynamic, evolving environments, need to make complex decisions (often quickly) to take advantage of opportunities or to avoid threats. Scenario planning models enable a wide range of variables to be changed (such as inflation rates or sales numbers), the overall effect on the business to be identified and a business plan to be constructed.

  - **Market analysis**

    Modelling can be extended into the market that the organisation operates in. Trends such as sales volumes, prices and demand can be analysed. Relationships between price and sales volume can be identified. These can be used by an organisation when deciding on a pricing strategy. Setting the best price for a product can help drive up sales and profitability. The use of information systems to identify trends in social media posts is becoming common practice in business, particularly in relation to pricing decisions.

  - **Project evaluation**

    Organisations will benefit from improved decision making where systems can accurately evaluate a wide range of projects. Investment decisions often involve large capital outlays and if the system prevents bad decisions it can prevent the organisation wasting large sums of money.

Systems can also prevent an organisation agreeing 'bad' deals. Tenders for suppliers or other long-term contracts can prove costly if the wrong choice is made.

2.2 Strategic implications

When formulating an overall IS/IT strategy the following aspects should be taken into consideration:

- What are the key business areas which could benefit most from an investment in information technology, what form should the investment take, and how could such strategically important units be encouraged to use such technology effectively? Will maintenance of the new system be provided in-house or be outsourced?

- How much would the system cost in terms of software; hardware; management commitment and time; education and training; conversion; documentation; operational manning; and maintenance? The importance of lifetime application costs must be stressed – the costs and benefits after implementation may be more significant than the more obvious initial costs of installing an information technology function.

- What criteria for performance should be set for information technology systems. Two areas can be considered: the technical standard the information system achieves and the degree to which it meets the perceived and often changing needs of the user.

- What are the implications for the existing work force – have they the requisite skills; can they be trained to use the systems; will there be any redundancies? The decision to automate existing processes through the use of IT and intelligent systems often underlines the need for business leaders to possess effective change management skills. A good change management process is likely to be critical in overcoming any resistance that may arise from those individuals affected by the introduction of a new IT system.

2.3 Earl's systems audit grid

Earl suggests a **grid** to analyse an organisation's current use of information systems

		Low Technical quality	High Technical quality
Business Value	High	Renew	Maintain, enhance
	Low	Divest	Reassess

- A system of poor quality and little value should be **disposed of** (divest).

- A system of high business value and low technical quality should be **renewed** (invested in). An important system of low quality carries a high risk.

- A system of high quality but low business value should be **reassessed**. Is the system meeting an information need? Why is it under-utilised?

- High quality systems with a high business value should be **maintained** to preserve the high quality, and if possible **enhanced** in the quest for competitive advantage.

Establishing where to place systems on the grid is the difficult part. Consultation with system users and those for formulating and implementing information system strategy would be undertaken to form an opinion of each system. Again, judgements are subjective.

2.4 Information systems and competitive advantage

Porter identified three generic strategies that an organisation can use to compete and depending on the chosen strategy, IT can be used in different ways to enhance the business's competitive advantage.

This if the business has chosen cost leadership, IT can be used within the supply chain to improve scheduling and thus reduce the costs of inventory.

A differentiator may use IT to make the customer ordering process as easy and flexible as possible.

A business that focuses on a particular niche market may use IT to capture data electronically via a loyalty card and use it to generate information about customer preferences and buying habits.

Value chain analysis, also covered in Chapter 6 can be used to assess the impact of IS/IT, and to identify **processes where IT could be used to add value**.

IT can be used to **automate** and improve physical tasks in the **manufacturing** sector. It also provides **extra information** about the process.

2.4.1 Operations

- **Process control**: computer systems enable tighter control over production processes.
- **Machine tool control**: machine tools can be automated and, it is hoped, be made more precise:
    - **Numerical control**: information to operate the machine tool is prepared in advance to generate a set of instructions.
    - **Computer numerical control** is where the computer produces the instructions.
    - **Direct numerical control** is where the computer is linked directly to the machine tool.
- **Robots** can automate some of the process.
- **Computer aided manufacturing** (CAM) involves a variety of software modules such as:
    - Production control, supervisory systems.
    - Materials requirement planning (MRP 1) and Manufacturing Resources Planning (MRP II). These are automated component ordering and automated production scheduling systems respectively.
    - Capacity requirements planning.
- **3D printing** involves producing a three-dimensional object using a 3D printer. This technique uses a robotic printer laying successive layers of material on one another, and these are then etched into a three dimensional shape using light. The increasing publicity surrounding the commercial benefits of using 3D printing has attracted interest from various industries, including clothing manufacturers and even the construction industry.
- **Computer Integrated Manufacturing** (CIM) integrates all aspects of an organisation's manufacturing activities. 'IT cannot solve basic organisational problems, but the essence is the use of the IT to provide integration though communication, effectiveness and efficiency'. Flexible manufacturing systems include:
    - Machine tools
    - Materials handling conveyor sets
    - Automatic guided vehicles
- **Enterprise Resource Planning** (ERP) systems take MRP II systems a step further, and are not restricted to certain types of organisation. ERP systems are used for identifying and planning the **enterprise-wide** resources needed to record, produce, distribute, and account for customer orders.

2.4.2 Logistics

In both **inbound** logistics and **outbound** logistics IT can have an impact.

- The use of IT in **inbound logistics** includes stock control systems such as MRP, MRPII, ERP and IT.

- **Warehousing**: the use of barcodes can increase knowledge about the quantity and nature of stock in hand.

- It is possible to create computer models, or **virtual warehouses**, of stock actually held at **suppliers**. For example an organisation with several outlets might have each connected to a system which indicates the total amount of stock available at different sites.

2.4.3 Marketing

Marketing activities can be made more effective by the use of **customer databases** and the use of **social media**:

- Many large organisations have redirected their marketing effort through **social media** ie, Facebook and Twitter, as a means of achieving competitive advantage. Organisations are increasingly using social media to find out what their customers are saying about their products or services, and to respond to complaints.

- Buying data about **customer purchasing habits** and interrogating it is providing a more precise method of targeting particular groups of consumers than television advertising.

- A variety of market research companies use IT/IS as a way of **interacting** with consumers. Examples include: the use of online viral marketing campaigns and online questionnaires.

- Supermarkets can use automated **EPOS** (electronic point of sale) systems to have precise real time data about how products are selling to enable speedy ordering and replenishments.

However, as the following worked example illustrates, organisations need to take special care when embracing social media.

Worked example: When social media goes wrong

In recent years there have been numerous memorable examples of companies which have failed to manage their online and social media communications effectively.

American Apparel

In 2014, US clothing manufacturer and retailer, American Apparel, posted an image of the 1986 Challenger space shuttle disaster on its Tumblr stream. The image was accompanied by the hashtags #smoke and #clouds. The individual who made the post mistook the image of the exploding space shuttle for a firework. The post was intended to form part of the company's advertising promotions during the Fourth of July celebrations. The company apologised.

Coca-Cola

In early 2016 it was reported that Coca-Cola's new year's message to its Russian customers had been met with anger and indignation. The message posted on the VK social media platform was supposed to show a snowy map outline of the Russian Federation, accompanied with seasonal greetings. The image did not include the Crimea ,the Kuril Islands or the Kaliningrad regions of Russia. The company faced a barrage of criticism from Russian customers which led to a revised image being posted that included the missing regions. This in turn caused anger in Ukraine as Crimea, which had previously been part of Ukraine, was controversially annexed by Russia in 2014. Agence France-Presse writing in *The Guardian*, noted that the outcry forced Coca-Cola to drop its message. Coca-Cola responded with the following post 'Dear friends! Thank you for your attention. It has been decided to delete the item which caused the upset'.

Sources:

Kemp, J. (2014) *American Apparel apologises for posting picture of Challenger disaster as 'clouds.*[Online]. Available from: www.nydailynews.com [Accessed 8 June 2016]

France-Presse, A. (5 January 2016) Unhappy new year for Coca-Cola as it upsets first Russia, then Ukraine. *The Guardian* [Online]. Available from: www.theguardian.com [Accessed 5 May 2017].

2.4.4 Service

Customer relationship management (CRM) describes the methodologies, software, and usually internet capabilities that help an enterprise manage customer relationships.

For example, an enterprise might build a database about its customers that described relationships in sufficient detail so that management, salespeople, service staff, and maybe the customer, could access information, match customer needs with product plans, remind customers of service requirements and know what other products a customer had purchased.

CRM consists of:

- Helping an enterprise to identify and target their best customers, manage marketing campaigns with clear goals and objectives, and generate quality leads.

- Assisting the organisation to improve telesales, account, and sales management by **optimising information shared**, and streamlining existing processes (for example, taking orders using mobile devices).

- Allowing the formation of relationships with customers, with the aim of improving customer satisfaction and maximising profits; identifying the most profitable customers and providing them with the highest level of service.

- Providing employees with the information and processes necessary to know their customers, understand their needs, and effectively build relationships between the company, its customer base, and distribution partners.

2.4.5 Support activities

As far as **support** activities are concerned IT has some impact.

- **Procurement**. IT can automate some purchasing decisions. Paperwork can be saved if the organisation's purchase systems are linked directly to the sales order systems of some suppliers (eg, by electronic data interchange) and costs can be reduced through the use of internet based marketplaces (see following worked example).

- **Technology development**. Computer automated design (**CAD**) is, in a number of areas, an important influence.

  - **Drafting**: CAD produces engineer's drawings, component design, layout (eg, of stores, wiring and piping) and electronic circuit diagrams in complex systems.

  - **Updating**: it is easy to change design in CAD systems and to assess ramifications of any changes. Some CAD systems have archive data (eg, for reference).

  - CAD enables modelling to be **checked** without the necessity of producing working prototypes. Some 'stress testing' can be carried out on the model.

- As we explored earlier in the study manual IT has had an impact on **human resources** as it has changed the way in which people in certain industries now work. This is evident given the rise in workforce flexibility, which has resulted in growing numbers of people now working from home. In addition there are now a number of HR applications which organisations can use to assist in managing their human resources these include: the maintenance of a skills database, staff planning (eg, using network analysis), computer based training, time attendance systems, payroll systems, pension systems.

Worked example: Alibaba

Alibaba is the world's largest e-commerce company which predominantly operates in China. According to the company's website its mission is to 'make it easy to do business anywhere'. (Alibaba, 2018).

Alibaba was set up in 1999 by a Chinese English teacher (Jack Ma), with the aim of helping small Chinese businesses trade globally. As Yueh (2013) explains, Alibaba is effectively a 'combination of eBay and Amazon. It is an online company with multiple revenue streams that are more conventional than a social network site. Alibaba.com is a B2B, or business-to-business, website. It links up businesses around the world looking for suppliers. For instance, they link wholesalers to distributors around the world, from the UK to China to the US'. Businesses can trade almost anything from olive oil to computer components.

Sources:

Alibaba. (2018) *About Alibaba*. [Online]. Available from: www.alibaba.com [Accessed 30 April 2018]

Yueh, L. (2013) *Alibaba: The next facebook?* [Online]. Available from: www.bbc.co.uk [Accessed 7 June 2016]

2.5 Strategic importance of big data

So far in this chapter we have explored some of the more general ways in which IT systems can help organisations. You may recall that in Chapter 6 we introduced the concept of big data, and the increasingly important role that data plays in business. We explored the growth in the so-called 'internet of things' whereby organisations embed sensor technologies into their operations to collect data on a range of activities, including gathering data about their customers. In the next section we consider through the use of real life examples how organisations can analyse and use the data they collect. Consideration is also given to how big data and data analytics can help organisations to monitor performance and modify strategies in order to achieve a competitive advantage.

A report by the McKinsey Global Institute 'Big data: The next frontier for innovation, competition and productivity' highlighted that there five broad ways in which big data and data analytics can help organisations to compete in increasingly competitive environments:

- Enhanced data transparency
- Enhanced performance
- Market segmentation and customisation
- Improved decision-making
- New products and services

Each of these points is considered in more detail in the following section.

2.5.1 Enhanced data transparency

Big data can create value by making the meaning held within the data more transparent and usable. For example, new insights might be gained by data which was previously too expensive or complex to process. Transparency may also add value especially if data generated by other parts of the organisation can be integrated with externally obtained data. Improved transparency should assist the organisation to achieve its corporate objectives.

For example, consider a company which operates in a highly competitive industry. Product innovation and being first to market are both highly desired by customers. As a result, continual product development is critical to success. Integrating data obtained from the marketing department about customer requirements and demand, with data from the R&D team about the feasibility of new products could help the company to meet customer needs and reduce the time to market.

Worked example: Social media analytics

The following worked example explores how organisations are increasingly able to use social media analytics to measure qualitative data.

For large organisations, social media analytics is no longer solely focused on measuring simple quantitative metrics such as the number of times its Facebook account has been 'liked'. Today there is far greater focus on identifying and measuring qualitative data. The widespread use of social media analytics tools now means that organisations can capture the key words used by customers when posting about the organisation's products and services online. Feedback or comments posted on sites such as Twitter allow organisations to perform 'sentiment analysis' which provides a useful insight into how end users perceive the organisation's offering. Sentiment analysis is helping organisations to co-ordinate operations in response to both positive and negative trends. For example, complaints posted on Twitter about a product can now be directed through to the organisation's customer service teams to help limit the potential negative publicity generated.

2.5.2 Enhanced performance

The availability of vast quantities of transactional data provides organisations with a large amount of detailed, 'real time' performance data. This data can then be analysed to identify fluctuations in performance, and take corrective action in 'real time' where performance deteriorates. The following worked example focuses on the steps taken by UK supermarket chain Tesco to improve the efficiency of its in-store refrigeration units using real time performance data.

Worked example: Tesco and big data

In 2013 It was reported that UK retailer Tesco had installed a state-of-the art energy management system into its stores. The move was aimed at helping the retailer reduce the carbon footprint of its stores and to reduce its energy costs. As Thorpe (2013) highlighted, one of Tesco's three carbon reduction targets was to reduce emissions from its stores by 50% between 2006 and 2020. Thorpe (2013) noted that 'the company recognised that meeting its energy targets would not come from investments in infrastructure alone; it would also need to find ways to improve energy efficiency on a day-to-day basis'.

As a result, Tesco introduced a new energy management system which connected each of its stores to its data analysis facility. This facility is staffed with 13 analysts and tracks data obtained from electricity meters. The meters monitor store lighting, refrigeration, heating and cooling results. As Thorpe (2013) notes the new system produces 'half-hourly reports on energy consumption which allow the team to immediately identify hotspots or irregularities in consumption and notify Tesco's maintenance team. Noticing that lights were on all night at Cradley Heath Extra, for instance, prompted a response from the maintenance team that saved the store £4,554'.

Source:

Thorpe, L. (17 May 2013) Tesco cuts energy use with 24-hour monitoring system. *The Guardian*.[Online]. Available from: www.theguardian.com [Accessed 7 June 2016]

2.5.3 Market segmentation and customisation

Big data should help organisations to further segment their market in 'real time', allowing for the customisation of promotions and advertising to more effectively attract customers to the organisation's product/service offering. The concept of tailored promotions is covered in more detail in the next worked example.

Worked example: Mobile apps and customer data

The following case study highlights the links between data and the customisation of promotions.

An increasing number of companies around the world are turning to the widespread use of mobile technologies to collect data about their customers. American firm Relevant Mobile specialises in the development of mobile phone app software which is used by major restaurant chains to enhance their approach to customer engagement.

Relevant Mobile customises its app software to meet the needs of major restaurant chains in the US. The app is integrated with the point of sale technologies used by restaurant chains to allow them to capture data about customers and to build a relationship which encourages the customer to make return visits. As highlighted by the Relevant Mobile (2018) website, this approach works by customers downloading the restaurant's customised app, which enables them to 'place orders, pay with their phone in store, send gift cards, provide […] feedback, and stay in touch with [the] brand socially'. (Relevant Mobile, 2018).

A key feature of Relevant Mobile's (2018) app is that it incorporates a push marketing approach which allows restaurant chains to send customers notifications of special offers 'tailored by location, time, event or purchase history' (Relevant Mobile, 2018). The company prides itself on helping its clients to create relationships with customers, as opposed to simply viewing a purchase decision as a one-off transaction.

Source:

Relevant Mobile (2018), *About Us.* [Online]. Available from: https://relevant mobile.com [Accessed 30 April 2018].

2.5.4 Improved decision-making

The use of big data should create value by improving the organisation's approach to decision-making. For example an online retailer could flex the prices it charges for its products using 'real time' sales and inventory data to influence the customer's purchasing behaviour. Such an approach may enable the retailer to entice customers to purchase a slow selling inventory line by reducing the price while the customer is still online.

Worked example: Big data and the supermarkets

The following worked example illustrates how leading UK retailers collect, analyse and use data obtained about customers to inform their competitive strategies.

The use of in-store loyalty cards as a means of capturing data about customers and their shopping habits to enable the effective targeting of shoppers with promotions, is nothing new. Tesco's loyalty card, the Clubcard, was introduced in 1995. The Clubcard scheme operates by collecting data about a customers' shopping habits when items are purchased either in-store or via the retailer's website. The data held is then analysed to provide customers with 'money off' vouchers based on previous purchases and to earn points which can be used to reduce future shopping bills.

BBC (2018) highlights that the use of loyalty cards enables retailers to build up 'an accurate picture of when, where and how people do their shopping.' Retailers are also able to use the services offered by data brokers to enhance the customer data that they have captured themselves. 'These third-party companies amass information from a variety of sources to create "profiles" of people with information about habits, patterns and personality. Retailers can then match their loyalty card data to these profiles, producing a clearer picture of shoppers'. (BBC, 2018).

Ferguson (2013) highlights many large retailers are now using the vast amounts of data available to them to decide which products their stores should stock. Ferguson (2013) cites the example of supermarket chain Sainsbury's which 'discovered that a cereal brand called Grape-Nuts was worth stocking – despite weak sales – because the shoppers who bought it were extremely loyal to Sainsbury's, and were often big spenders'. Furthermore, following extensive data analysis, Sainsbury's purchased the remaining 50% of Sainsbury's bank, which it did not own, after it discovered that customers who used the bank's services 'become more loyal and spend more in-store'. (Ferguson, 2013).

Some retailers have taken to sharing data about customers with their retail partners. 'Nectar, […] can share data with at least 49 companies including Argos and EasyJet, according to consumer group Which?' (BBC, 2018).

Source:

Ferguson, D. (8 June 2013) How supermarkets get your data – and what they do with it. *The Guardian*. [Online]. Available from: www.theguardian.com [Accessed 7 June 2016]

BBC (2018) *How do companies use my loyalty card data?* [Online]. Available from: www.bbc.co.uk [Accessed 30 April 2018].

2.5.5 New products and services

The use of big data obtained from customer shopping habits can also help organisations to develop new and existing products and services to meet customer needs. For example, in response to growing demand from customers wanting to pay lower insurance premiums a number of insurance companies have started to monitor the way in which car policy holders drive their vehicles. Data is collected on how the car is been driven through the use of mobile apps or in some cases through the use of GPS devices. The data obtained then enables the insurance company to monitor the safety of the driving and adjust the car insurance premiums to reflect the level of risk that the insurer is exposed to.

2.6 Criticisms of big data and data analytics

While big data and data analytics offer a number of potential benefits it is important to appreciate some of the criticisms levied at them.

2.6.1 Latest buzzword

Some critics argue that big data simply represents the latest buzzword to have made it into the business press and suggest that there are insufficient examples to illustrate how analysing larger data sets have revealed anything significant beyond what was already known.

2.6.2 Correlation and causation

It has also been argued that too much of the focus on big data to-date has centred on the identification of correlations in data sets with little consideration given to the causes of such correlation. Failing to understand those elements which cause a correlation to exist between data variables ultimately means that analysts have no understanding of those factors or circumstances which could force a correlation to end.

Worked example: Correlation and causation

In 2013 Google's Flu Trends program failed. It was meant to be able to track the spread of flu in the US. Using specially designed algorithms the program was capable of identifying correlations between symptoms searched for using the Google search engine and actual reported cases of flu in particular parts of the country.

Having championed the power of the program, Google embarrassingly overstated the spread of flu across the US as its algorithms were not designed to understand what linked the online searches for symptoms with actual reported cases. The program was engineered to look for correlations in data sets not the factors causing them.

It is believed that the failure of the program was due in part to a number of news stories about influenza over the winter period, which prompted people to search for the symptoms of flu even if they themselves were not actually ill.

2.6.3 Data overload

Critics also argue that capturing and analysing all of the available data about a particular subject does not automatically create value for the organisation. For data to be value adding it needs to provide an insight or some meaning that was previously unknown. Failure in this regard simply means the organisation has a lot of data which it cannot do anything with.

2.6.4 Ability to verify

Data captured from external sources increases the difficulty of verifying whether it is suitable as a basis for decision-making. This ultimately reduces any reliance that can be placed on the conclusions drawn from using such data.

2.6.5 Sustainable competitive advantage

Whether or not big data can provide organisations with a sustainable long-term competitive advantage remains to be seen. As the earlier worked example illustrated, many supermarkets now operate loyalty card schemes and therefore have access to similar types of customer data.

2.6.6 Representative data

Finally, it is important to recognise that analysing a lot of data does not necessarily mean that it is fully representative of the whole data population. For example, asking customers via the organisations Twitter feed which of its products they value most, and analysing the customers tweets would not represent the views of all of the organisation's customers. It is likely that the responses received will largely represent the opinions of younger, urban customers as research suggests that it is this group which tend to use Twitter the most.

2.7 Barriers to introducing big data and data analytics

An article published by accounting firm EY titled *'Ready for take-off?'* focusses on the main strategic challenges organisations face when introducing a big data strategy (some of these points were introduced in Chapter 6). The article highlights 8 significant barriers:

2.7.1 The unknown destinations

The majority of larger organisations are already aware that they possess useful data, but do not really understand which questions they should be asking of the data they hold to extract meaning from it.

2.7.2 The underlying technology challenges

Many organisations are unable to cope with the amount of data that they have access to. The volume of data flowing into the organisation can be intimidating. Management can be intimidated by the concept of establishing 'real time' data analytics systems, a problem which is further compounded by a lack of knowledge around which technological tools best meet their needs.

2.7.3 The lack of a holistic approach

Particularly in larger organisations the introduction of a big data strategy often occurs on a project-by-project basis, within distinct departments in the organisation. Organisations need to take a more holistic approach when introducing big data. Management need a better understanding of how the value created from big data in one department can be used throughout the organisation. Promoting a holistic approach needs to be driven by senior management.

2.7.4 The shortage of talent

To extract meaning from captured data requires organisations to have employees with specialist skills. Job roles needed are likely to include data scientists, visualisation experts, business intelligence analysts, data warehousing professionals, and data privacy experts. Developing the skills needed in the short term can be particularly difficult, and the cost of buying in such expertise can be prohibitive.

2.7.5 The fear of cyber attack

Later in this chapter we discuss the concept of cyber security. The growing dependence on data and data analytics increases the potential exposure to cyber-attack. The reputation damage and potential regulatory risks caused by such a breach may deter the management in some organisations from introducing a big data strategy.

2.7.6 The difficulty of building the business case

While senior management in an organisation may accept the general argument supporting the need for big data initiatives, they often want to understand the potential benefits of specific projects before authorising the related investment needed to improve the IT infrastructure. In cases where a business has undertaken very few big data projects quantifying the benefits can often prove difficult.

2.7.7 The need for legal and regulatory compliance

Organisations need to understand the data privacy issues surrounding the introduction of a big data strategy. Failure to address the legal and regulatory risks could potentially be very costly from both a financial and reputation perspective.

2.7.8 The need for customer data

There is also a growing concern among customers that any data they provide to organisations will be misused or that their privacy will suffer. This presents a challenge for organisations in determining how best to address their customers' concerns, and to comply with the provisions of the General Data Protection Regulations (GDPR).

Worked example: Facebook and Cambridge Analytica

In early 2018 it was widely reported that Cambridge Analytica, a UK based data analytics and political consulting firm, had improperly gained access to the data of millions of Facebook users. BBC (2018) reported that the number of people affected by the scandal could be as high as 87 million. Greenfield (2018) highlighted that the allegations against Cambridge Analytica centred around the alleged use of data from millions of Facebook users 'without permission to build a system that could target US voters with personalised political advertisements based on their psychological profile'. (Greenfield, 2018). Amid claims that Facebook had been aware of the data breach for a number of years, Facebook's CEO Mark Zuckerberg, explained that 'clearly we should have done more, and we will going forward' (BBC, 2018). It is believed that the data breach occurred when Facebook users installed an app which captured (harvested) their data, which was subsequently sold onto Cambridge Analytica. In the weeks following news of the scandal Facebook's share price fell, and Mark Zuckerberg appeared before the influential US House of Commerce Committee to answer questions relating to the allegations. In May 2018 it was widely reported that following the scandal Cambridge Analytica had ceased trading.

Source:

BBC (2018). *Facebook scandal 'hit 87 million users'.* [Online]. Available from: www.bbc.co.uk [Accessed 30 April 2018].

Greenfield, P. (26 March 2018). The Cambridge Analytica files: the story so far. *The Guardian.* [Online]. Available from: www.theguardian.com [Accessed 30 April 2018].

3 Knowledge management

Section overview

- Knowledge management is a key element in this chapter. Effective use of information requires knowledge. In Chapter 6 we explored the increasingly important role that human capital plays in business, where the knowledge of workers is increasingly being viewed as a strategic asset.

- Organisation-specific knowledge, which has been built up over time, is a core competence that cannot easily be imitated.

- Knowledge management (KM) refers to the process of harnessing IT and other systems to develop and disseminate relevant knowledge throughout the organisation.

- KM is a source of competitive advantage because it encourages process improvement and innovation and helps the organisation identify ways to meet customer needs better than the competition. The concept of knowledge management is an area that candidates attempting the Business Strategy and Technology exam have struggled with. It is therefore particularly important that you take your time as you read through the next section.

- Capturing the knowledge is insufficient. Competitive advantage is achieved by acting on the knowledge and using it to make effective decisions.

3.1 Knowledge management programmes

Definitions

Knowledge is the potential for action based on data, information, intuition and experience.

Explicit knowledge is knowledge that the company knows that it has. This includes facts, transactions and events that can be clearly stated and stored in management information systems.

Tacit knowledge is personal knowledge and expertise held by people within the organisation that has not been formally documented.

> **Knowledge management** describes a range of strategies and tools that capture all the knowledge that is valuable to an organisation, and deliver it to the people in such a way that it can be acted on quickly, to the competitive advantage of the business.

As we have seen during our discussions of big data, organisations now operate in an age of information. Faced with increasing environmental change, organisations have begun to focus on the importance of exploiting their **intangible assets**, one of which is knowledge. The **effective use of information** requires knowledge.

Knowledge management programmes extend beyond any particular piece of IT/IS and embrace changing the attitudes of management and staff towards sharing information. They concern:

- Designing and installing techniques and processes to create, protect and use **explicit knowledge**.

- Designing and creating environments and activities to discover and release **tacit knowledge**.

- Capturing good quality information from outside the business as well as within eg, intelligence on competitors.

Tacit knowledge is a difficult thing to manage because it is **invisible** and **intangible**. We do not know what knowledge exists within a person's brain, and whether he or she chooses to share knowledge is a matter of choice. Tacit knowledge may be difficult to express or communicate to others but is also invaluable because it is a unique asset that is very hard for other organisations to copy.

Collaboration between employees helps to transform tacit knowledge into explicit knowledge.

The **motivation to share** hard-won experience is sometimes low; the individual is 'giving away' their value and may be very reluctant to lose a position of influence and respect by making it available to everyone.

Organisations should encourage people to share their knowledge. Electronic tools such as online bulletin boards, web logs (blogs) and wikis (editable web pages designed for groups of users) all facilitate knowledge sharing.

However, whilst technology can help unlock knowledge, corporate culture is more important. Collaboration can be encouraged through a culture of openness and rewards for sharing knowledge and information.

3.2 Systems that aid knowledge management

Information systems play an important role in knowledge management, helping with **information flows** and helping formally **capture** the knowledge held within the organisation.

Interactive question 2: Information and knowledge management

Increasingly the management of information sharing and group working ventures is a fundamental part of business management.

Requirements

2.1 Discuss how the management of information might differ from the management of knowledge.

2.2 How can an organisation develop a knowledge strategy?

See **Answer** at the end of this chapter.

3.3 Knowledge management as a source of competitive advantage

The resource based view of strategy, discussed in Chapter 2, is one of a successful organisation that acquires and develops resources and competences over time and exploits them to create competitive advantage.

The ability to capture and harness corporate knowledge has become critical for organisations as they seek to adapt to changes in the business environment, particularly those businesses providing financial and professional services.

Knowledge is seen as a strategic asset and organisation-specific knowledge, which has been built up over time, is a core competence that cannot easily be imitated.

Knowledge management can help promote competitive advantage through:

- The fast and efficient exchange of information
- Effective channelling of the information to:
    - Improve processes, productivity and performance.
    - Identify opportunities to meet customer needs better than competitors.
    - Promote creativity and innovation.

In Chapter 6 we discussed benchmarking. The process of identifying the outstanding qualities and practices of competitors allows an organisation to capture knowledge that can then be used internally to make improvements that will further its competitive advantage.

If knowledge management is about making sure that information flows efficiently through a company, competitive advantage is achieved by making sure that the knowledge is translated into decisions and actions.

Knowledge must be delivered in a form that can be quickly interpreted and acted on. There must also be a processes for learning from past experiences (successes or failures) and identifying opportunities to improve.

Thus competitive advantage is not necessarily achieved by those who have the best knowledge, but by those who use knowledge best.

Interactive question 3: Kid A Ltd

Kid A Ltd (KA) is a company that runs four pre-school nurseries for children aged two to four years old, and is planning to expand the business.

Industry background

Demand for pre-school nurseries has grown substantially in the UK since the start of the 19X0s. Changes in the labour market have resulted in a rise in the number of working women with dependent children. In 20X8, 52% of women whose youngest dependent child was under five years of age were working, compared to only 31% 10 years earlier. During this period unemployment in the UK fell significantly.

This has, however, coincided with a change in demographics in the UK and a drop in the birth rate, resulting in a falling population of children of pre-school age.

There has been an increased emphasis by the Government on the role of childcare and education in raising educational standards and enhancing children's social development. In the UK over the last 10 years, the number of day nursery places more than doubled as more nurseries were opened. Day nurseries are one form of pre-school childcare available in the UK, the other main ones being playgroups, childminders and the use of domestic nannies.

Most day nurseries operate independently from one another and are, in the main, owner managed. Demand for nursery places normally outstrips supply.

Since 20X1, all nurseries have been subject to government registration and inspection, and the inspectors' reports are available on the internet for viewing by interested parties.

Company background

KA was formed in 20X2 by Thom Yorke, a former IT engineer, and Debra Curtis, who previously worked as a manager for another nursery. Both Thom and Debra have a close involvement in the day to day running of the nurseries, which have a maximum of 48 children on each of the premises at any one time.

The company has utilised modern technology to help address concerns of parents. All the children at the nurseries are given GPS (global positioning satellite) wristbands that are linked wirelessly to a series of webcams. Parents can call up the webcams from their workplaces to see the activities of their children.

Parents who have busy work commitments can also utilise a collect and return service whereby KA will pick up children and return them to their homes outside the normal nursery hours of 8am-6pm. This service, although popular with some parents, has attracted criticism from some commentators, who believe it results in disruption to the lives of children.

The KA nursery has a far greater emphasis on learning, especially via computers, than children of the same age-groups at other nurseries, and this has proved to be very popular with some parents. Parents can review the computer-based games and work undertaken by their children remotely via the internet. These innovations have been praised in the government inspector reports on KA.

KA operates on a staff-to-child ratio that is far higher than the industry average, to ensure the children are given a more structured environment and personal attention. All staff members are NNEB (National Nursery Examining Board) qualified, unlike other nurseries which have a mixture of qualified and unqualified staff. Staff are paid a premium over the salaries of other nurseries. They are expected to have an understanding of the technology that is used within the nurseries and are given a list of tasks each day that they are expected to carry out. Tasks are reviewed by Thom and Joy each week to ensure they have been completed.

KA charge about 40% more than other nurseries, to reflect the extra services provided, but this has not prevented the nurseries being permanently full with a waiting list. Despite extra costs being incurred, KA has a higher profit margin than most other nurseries.

Latest developments

KA is now considering an expansion of the business and opening four more nurseries, with a view to opening additional nurseries if this proves to be a success. Thom and Debra have previously controlled the individual nurseries themselves. They now want to appoint managers to run the nurseries and to set budgets to ensure that they generate a return on the initial investment made, without compromising the standards of care and education offered to children. They are uncertain as to how to assess the managers in terms of how well they are running the individual nurseries.

Thom and Debra will dictate the initial layout of the individual nurseries in terms of building sizes and fixtures and fittings. The nursery managers would be responsible for advertising, bookings, staff, communication with parents and day-to-day running expenses.

Requirements

3.1 Prepare a Porter's Five Forces model for the nursery industry as a whole.

3.2 Identify and explain the critical success factors that operate within the business of KA. Discuss how KA has used information systems and technology to add value and give competitive advantage.

3.3 As an external consultant, prepare a report to Thom and Debra that

    (a) Explains the risks that may arise as a result of expanding the business.

    (b) Suggests how they could implement an effective budgeting process for the nurseries.

(c) Explains the strategic, tactical and operational information that Thom and Debra will need to assist in decision making and control.

See **Answer** at the end of this chapter.

4 Risks associated with IT/IS

Section overview

- The risks of IT/IS can be summarised as:

    - The **risk of inadequacy**: the failure by the firm to utilise IT/IS as effectively as its rivals will lead to loss of competitive advantage, eg, inferior service, poorer products, excess costs.

    - The **risk of breakdown**: where the firm depends on IT/IS a breakdown in its operations threatens the business.

    - The **risk of excess expense**: IT/IS is a significant budget item. Botched projects, expensive contracts, inappropriate systems or non-adoption presents a direct financial risk.

- Risks are present at the system specification stage, and they carry through to implementation. There is also the risk of systems failure.

4.1 Development and implementation – what can go wrong

Problems that occur when implementing a new information system can usually be traced to deficiencies in the development and specification process. Some of these issues involve change management which is covered in Chapter 15.

The following table outlines some common mistakes that adversely affect the implementation process.

Stage/activity	Problems
Analysis	The problem the system is intended to solve is not fully understood.
	Investigation of the situation is hindered by insufficient resources.
	User input is inadequate through either lack of consultation or lack of user interest.
	The project team is unable to dedicate the time required.
	Insufficient time spent planning the project.
Design	Insufficient user input.
	Lack of flexibility. The organisation's future needs are neglected.
	The system requires unforeseen changes in working patterns.
	Failure to perform organisation impact analysis. An organisational impact analysis studies the way a proposed system will affect organisation structure, attitudes, decision making and operations. The analysis aims to ensure the system is designed to best ensure integration with the organisation.
	Organisational factors sometimes overlooked include:
	• Ergonomics (including equipment, work environment and user interfaces)

Stage/activity	Problems
	• Health and safety • Compliance with legislation • Job design • Employee involvement
Programming	Insufficient time and money allocated to programming. Programmers supplied with incomplete or inaccurate specifications. The logic of the program is misunderstood. Poor programming technique results in programs that are hard to modify. Programs are not adequately documented.
Testing	Insufficient time and money allocated to testing. Failure to develop an organised testing plan. Insufficient user involvement. User management do not review and sign-off the results of testing.
Conversion	Insufficient time and money allocated to data conversion. Insufficient checking between old and new files. The process is rushed to compensate for time overruns elsewhere.
Implementation	Insufficient time, money and/or appropriate staff mean the process has to be rushed. Lack of user training increases the risk of system under-utilisation and rejection. Poor system and user documentation. Lack of performance standards to assess system performance against. System maintenance provisions are inadequate.

A recurring theme when examining the reasons for information system failure is user resistance. Users may be management and staff, but for outward-facing systems equally could involve customers, suppliers and other partners.

The three types of theories to explain user resistance are explained in the following table.

Theory	Description	Overcoming the resistance
People-oriented	User-resistance is caused by factors internal to users as individuals or as a group. For example, users may not wish to disrupt their current work practices and social groupings.	User training. Organisation policies. Persuasion. User involvement in system development.
System-oriented	User-resistance is caused by factors inherent in the new system design relating to ease of use and functionality. For example, a poorly designed user-interface will generate user-resistance.	User training and education. Improve user-interface. Ensure users contribute to the system design process. Ensure the system 'fits' with the organisation.

Theory	Description	Overcoming the resistance
Interaction	User-resistance is caused by the interaction of people and the system. For example, the system may be well-designed but its implementation will cause organisational changes that users resist eg, reduced chance of bonuses, redundancies, monotonous work.	Re-organise the organisation before implementing the system. Redesign any affected incentive schemes to incorporate the new system. Promote user participation and encourage organisation-wide teamwork. Emphasise the benefits the system brings.

4.2 Risks from IT systems

There are a range of general risks which IT systems are exposed to. Common risks include:

- **Natural threats**: Fire, flood, electrical storms.

- **Non-compliance with regulations**: The use of IT systems, and the data they contain, is subject to close legal supervision in most countries. In the UK relevant legislation includes the General Data Protection Regulations which can result in large financial penalties where personal data is wrongly held and used.

- **Data systems integrity**: These may include incorrect entry of data, use of out-of-date files, loss of data through lack of back-ups.

- **Accidents:** Staff are a physical threat to IT installations, accidents including spilling a cup of coffee over a desk, or tripping and falling, thereby doing some damage to an item of office equipment.

- **Cyber security risks**: Hackers and malicious attacks on computer systems represent an increasingly complex threat to organisational IT systems. This is discussed in greater detail in the next section.

5 Cyber security and IT controls

Section overview

- The issue of cyber security has become an increasingly important issue for most organisations. Controls are therefore needed to protect data and information.

Definition

Cyber security: The protection of systems, networks and data in cyberspace. (*ICAEW Strategic Business Management, Study Manual*).

This definition can be extended to include the protection of data from unauthorised modification, disclosure or destruction, and the protection of the information system from the degradation or non-availability of services – in other words, system failure.

In Chapter 6 we introduced the concept of cyber security in relation to the supply chain. In this section we consider in more detail the need for organisations to have in place adequate cyber security measures.

The widespread use of IT/IS throughout the world presents organisations with the increasingly complex challenge of keeping the systems and data they hold safe from a range of constantly evolving risks. This has made cyber security a major issue for most organisations. Cyber security is directed towards protecting IT systems from risks which predominantly feature some degree of human involvement.

Although by no means definitive, the list below details some of the most significant cyber risks an organisation's IT systems might encounter:

- **Human threats**: Hackers may be able to get into the organisation's internal network, either to steal data or to damage the system. Political terrorism is a major risk in the era of cyber-terrorism.

- **Fraud**: The theft of funds by dishonest use of a computer system.

- **Deliberate sabotage**: For example, commercial espionage, malicious damage or industrial action.

- **Viruses and other corruptions** can spread through the network to all of the organisation's computers.

- **Denial of Service (DoS) attack**: A denial of service attack is characterised by an attempt by attackers to prevent legitimate users of a service from using that service.

In recent years, there has been an alarming rise in the number of so called 'cyber attacks' carried out by hackers and saboteurs, intent on causing maximum disruption to organisational IT systems.

Worked example: LinkedIn

In 2016 it was reported that millions of user IDs of business-focused social network, LinkedIn, had been stolen by hackers. The BBC (2016) reported that hackers had advertised the details of more than one million LinkedIn logins as being for sale. Concerns were raised that criminals could make use of the stolen information with a view to identifying whether LinkedIn account users had used the same passwords on other online sites.

It was reported that the data breach had actually occurred four years earlier. At the time LinkedIn believed that the number of account details stolen were considerably fewer, which led the company to only reset the accounts of those users that they believed had been compromised.

In response to the developments in 2016, LinkedIn announced plans to reset the accounts of a far greater number of users. Experts claim that the company should have done this when the breach was first identified. A LinkedIn spokesman speaking at the time said 'we are taking immediate steps to invalidate the passwords of the accounts impacted, and we will contact those members to reset their passwords'.

Source:

BBC, (2016) *Millions of hacked LinkedIn IDs advertised for sale*. [Online].*BBC*, 2016. Available at: www.bbc.co.uk [Accessed 14 July 2016]

Worked example: Risks of cloud computing

In Chapter 6 we introduced the term cloud computing and explored some of the advantages that this relatively new approach to data storage may bring to organisations. The following worked example explores some of the main risks associated with cloud-based services.

An article by Wall (2016) highlights comments made by Gavan Egan, the Managing Director of cloud and IT solutions for global telecoms company, Verizon. 'The biggest risk is giving up control of your data to someone else, using different data centres in remote places. What happens in the event of disaster? You are also putting your data next to someone else's.' Wall (2016) comments that in such situations 'data can be lost, wiped, corrupted or stolen'.

Amichai Shulman, Chief Technology Officer of cyber security at Imperva, notes that 'most of the major data breaches that have taken place over the last five years, from Sony to Ashley Madison, Talk Talk to Target, have been from internal, not cloud-based, databases' (Wall, 2016).

However, as Shulman highlights there is always a real danger posed by the inherent threat that employees working for the cloud-based service provider could access or meddle with a company's data stored on its servers.

However, it is not just conventional human threats which pose a danger to data stored on cloud-based architectures. Bearne (2016) highlights the perils that exist when companies sign up with cloud-based storage service providers. 'Web hosting firm 123-reg recently deleted a number of its customers' websites after a "clean-up" operation of its virtual private servers went wrong following a coding error' (Bearne, 2016).

Bearne (2016) highlights comments made by Mark McArdle a director with PwC 'I've heard nightmare stories of companies setting themselves up with software-as-a-service with renewal based on a credit card, which subsequently expired and the account was deleted with all data lost. It's important to remember that you're licensing services, so the moment you stop paying, you lose access' (Bearne, 2016).

Sources:

Wall, M. (2016) *Can we trust cloud providers to keep our data safe?* [Online]. Available from: www.bbc.co.uk [Accessed 2 May 2017].

Bearne, S. (2016) *From wetsuits to wine: Small firms embrace the cloud* [Online]. Available from: www.bbc.co.uk [Accessed 2 May 2017].

5.1 Cyber security and boundary-less organisations

In Chapter 9 we explored the ways in which traditional organisation structures have evolved, including the rise of boundary-less organisations. Boundary-less organisations are structured to make it easier for them to collaborate with external parties, and often involve the removal of barriers (including IT network barriers) that exist between different internal departments, as well as external groups. The creation of these organisations has primarily occurred as a result of outsourcing, and the establishment of virtual communication networks facilitated by internet technologies.

Although, the removal of IT network barriers between organisations has brought significant benefits in terms of data sharing, it has also created significant challenges from a cyber security perspective. Organisational data, which traditionally would have been held privately in databases, is now being accessed by employees dispersed all around the world, and by various external groups including customers and suppliers. The interconnectedness of data which can be accessed by various groups has resulted in the creation of a greater number of access points to organisational networks. It is the weaknesses in these access points which criminal groups are keen to exploit.

The removal of such barriers to this data raises some interesting considerations: which party should be deemed ultimately responsible for protecting the data accessed which is in fact owned by another organisation? In the case of data which is accessible from a number of locations around the world, under which countries legal jurisdiction should a data breach be dealt?

Worked example: The boundary-less network

The following worked example focusses on the challenges presented by the rise of the boundary-less network.

An article by Watkins (2017) published on the *Computer Weekly* website notes that the interconnected nature of data and IT systems has led to the creation of the 'boundary-less corporate network'. Watkins (2017) suggests that the notion of 'my network and your network' has effectively been made obsolete by the creation of the boundary-less corporate network. Watkins (2017) notes that 'the logical boundary has gone, and along with it the physical – users might be safe and snug within corporate buildings, but are more likely to work at home, on the move, [or work] from someone else's premises entirely. [...] Even the information boundary is going – integration and sharing with customers – mash-ups are blending our information with internet sources, with staff pumping corporate information onto the internet.'

These developments have left organisations with increasingly less control over their own data and IT systems. In responding to the challenges that this brings, Watkins (2017) highlights the need for the development of effective policing of the internet, 'an effective international legal framework would be nice, but is probably well beyond the capability of our politicians. Our laws, particularly on personal data, need to catch up with the technology, without killing the creativity and flare the internet has unleashed.'

The article highlights that the loss of traditional boundaries has created uncertainty among organisations as to which data should be made available to share, as well as determining which external data sources they themselves should trust.

Source:

Watkins, B. (2017) *The boundary-less network*. [Online]. Available from: www.computerweekly.com [Accessed 15 May 2017].

5.2 The cyber gap

ICAEW's 2015 *Audit insights: cyber security* report highlights that many organisations suffer from a so-called 'cyber gap', between the organisations' capabilities to protect their IT infrastructures and the ability of attackers to do damage. The report suggests that to combat these risks effectively, organisations need to make cyber security central to everything they do:

> *In spite of significant efforts from businesses to improve their cyber security practices, most of them are struggling to close the 'cyber gap'. In some cases auditors are even seeing businesses going backwards in their practices, as management considers the business has achieved compliance with basic security measures and sees no further value in further investment. Many of the steps taken are exposing a much deeper gap in understanding about how cyber security fits into a business. To close this 'cyber gap', businesses need to put cyber security at the heart of their business model and focus on becoming a trusted partner in a digital environment. The need for this shift is made all the more urgent by the growing influence of disruptive technology and the pressure on organisations to innovate and respond quickly to new technology trends, business models and ways of working. However, businesses must manage this in a considered way to ensure that they respond in a proportionate, pragmatic and timely manner which manages the associated risks.*

5.3 Challenges and recommendations

In Chapter 9 we introduced some of the key findings from the ICAEW's report in relation to the role of the board and combating cyber risk. In this section consideration is given to those challenges identified by the ICAEW's report that organisations face when trying to understand cyber risks, and provides some insights as to how organisations can combat these challenges:

- **Communication is a key barrier to common understanding and discussion**. The language of cyber security is often highly technical and difficult for the layperson to fully understand. As a result it is becoming increasingly important for organisations to install a Chief Information Security Officer (CISO) to translate such language into a form which is accessible for employees to understand. Organisations need to work with security professionals to build better communication about the articulation and management of cyber risks, and the value of associated security spending.

- **Organisational structures need to define responsibility and accountability for cyber security**. Particularly in larger organisations, in recent years there has been a growth in the number of entities operating information security functions. The challenge for these departments is finding individuals with the specialist skills and expertise to help the organisation protect itself against cyber-attacks.

- **Board level accountability for cyber risks needs to be determined**, but at present in many organisations it is unclear who is ultimately responsible for managing cyber risks. Accountability for such activity could be assigned to a number of roles including the CEO, Chief Risk Officer, Chief Information Officer and even the HR Director. Equally important is the need to ensure that clear lines of responsibility for cyber security are embedded in day-to-day operations throughout the organisation. Furthermore, the board need to regularly consider the organisation's risk tolerance and risk appetite in relation to cyber security and reflect this in risk management strategies.

- **Non-executive directors and audit committees also need to play a part** in tackling cyber security, by ensuring that the executive management put in place adequate provisions to safeguard the organisation. For non-executive directors to be effective they need to have sufficient knowledge and confidence to hold the board to account in a meaningful way.

5.4   Small and medium sized enterprises

It is however important to note that the points outlined above in the ICAEW's report do present some challenges for small and medium sized enterprises. Creating new positions such as the Chief Information Security Officer role and introducing dedicated information security teams is very often unviable for smaller entities. Due to their size, and simpler business models, the associated costs involved in pursuing best practice in the field of cyber security often mean that smaller organisations lag behind their larger counterparts. Smaller organisations are unlikely to have dedicated IT departments or in-house experts monitoring their exposure to cyber risk. It is common for such organisations to rely on external third parties such as outsource firms providing IT services to put in place measures to address the threats posed by cyber risk. As a result it is likely that to some degree a 'cyber gap' will remain.

5.5   IT security controls

Security can be subdivided into a number of aspects.

- **Prevention**: practical measures such as the use of passwords and securing IT assets by keeping doors leading to servers locked when not in use may help to prevent unauthorised access. In practice it is impossible to prevent all threats cost-effectively.

- **Detection**: detection techniques are often combined with prevention techniques: a log can be maintained of unauthorised attempts to gain access to a computer system.

- **Deterrence**: as an example, computer misuse by personnel can be made grounds for dismissal.

- **Recovery procedures**: if the threat occurs, its consequences can be contained.

- **Correction procedures**: these ensure the vulnerability is dealt with (for example, by instituting stricter controls).

- **Threat avoidance**: this might mean changing the design of the system.

CHAPTER 14

It is interesting to note that the ICAEW's 2015 *Audit Insights: Cyber security* report highlighted that there has been a gradual shift in focus among many organisations in relation to IT security. Traditionally many organisations focussed their efforts on taking steps to defend an IT system from breaches, however this would appear to be changing. As the ICAEW highlight there is increasing emphasis on analysing IT systems to detect when and where specific breaches may occur:

> *Analysis focuses on specific preventative actions. However, organisations are increasingly widening their focus to include intelligence, monitoring, detection and response activities. The profile of security spending is therefore changing to reflect this broader range of operational activities, resulting in different discussions about the value and return on spending.*

The following worked example focuses on the emergence of cyber security firms which have embraced the focus on analysis.

Worked example: Darktrace

Darktrace was set up in 2013 by mathematicians and machine learning specialists from the University of Cambridge together with input from world-leading intelligence experts from MI5 and GCHQ (the British intelligence services), to bring transformative technology to the challenge of cyber security.

Darktrace's Enterprise Immune System offers a new approach to cyber defence. A video on the company's website highlights that organisations are gradually moving away from the old model of attempting to define cyber threats and trying to defend the perimeter of the organisation's IT systems, to addressing threats from within.

The company suggests that the threat posed by individuals working for large organisations intent on causing disruption to IT systems has become a major problem. As the video explains, 'insider threat' has historically been difficult to detect, 'How do you find something if you don't know what you are looking for?'

The Enterprise Immune System is based on a similar principle to that of the human immune system. The company's website notes, 'cyber threats take many forms and are increasingly difficult to predict – like viral DNA, they mutate and evolve constantly to survive within their chosen environment. The human body deals with this problem through its immune system, which continually learns about what is normal for our individual bodies and can identify outliers which do not fit that evolving pattern of normality'.

In essence the program is able to learn 'what normal looks like' in terms of an organisation's IT system usage and data flows. It works by automatically modelling the behaviour of every device used throughout an organisation.

The system is then able to identify system anomalies in real time by comparing any deviations detected against normal device usage and prioritise those threats deemed to be most serious. Identification in real time allows threats to be dealt with whilst they are in progress, as a result the organisations IT experts can then take action to investigate and stop these anomalies before they cause significant disruption.

Source:

Darktrace, (2016). *Darktrace*. [Online]. Available from: www.darktrace.com [Accessed 8 June 2016].

5.6 Combating IT risks and IT security

There are a number of practical measures that organisations can take in combating IT risks.

- **Business continuity planning**: this means that there should be measures to ensure that if major failures or disasters occur, the business will not be completely unable to function.

- **Systems access control**: this includes protection of information, information systems, networked services, detection of unauthorised activities and security when using the systems.

- **Systems development and maintenance**: this includes security measures and steps to protect data in operational and application systems and also ensuring that IT projects and support are conducted securely.

- **Physical and environmental security**: measures should be taken to prevent unauthorised access, damage and interference to business premises, assets, information and information facilities and prevention of theft.

- **Compliance** with any relevant legal requirements and also with organisational policies in standards. There is no point in having them if they are not enforced.

- **Personnel security**: this covers issues such as recruitment of trustworthy employees, and also reporting of security-related incidents. Training is particularly important, with the aim that users are aware of information security threats and concerns and are equipped to comply with the organisation's security policy.

- **Security organisation**: it should be clear who has responsibility for the various aspects of information security. Additional considerations will apply if facilities and assets are accessed by third parties or responsibility for information processing has been outsourced.

- **Computer and network management**: this includes ensuring continuity of operations and minimising the risk of systems failures, also protecting the integrity of systems and safeguarding information, particularly when exchanged between organisations. Particularly important is protection from viruses.

- **Asset classification and control**: information is an asset, just like a machine, building or a vehicle, and security will be improved if information assets have an 'owner', and are classified according to how much protection they need.

- **Security policy**: a written document setting out the organisation's approach to information security should be available to all staff.

Strategies for identifying and managing other risks faced by a business were discussed in Chapter 10.

5.7 Blockchain

Definition

Blockchain: is a technology that allows people who do not know each other to trust a shared record of events. *Bank of England.*

We mentioned blockchain in Chapter 6 when we explored the growing use of cryptocurrencies, and how the increasing use of blockchain technologies looks set to dramatically change the way in which people and organisations trade with each other. The major benefit offered by blockchain is its enhanced security over the recording of transactions. Blockchain provides an effective control mechanism which addresses some of the fundamental cyber risks associated with using IT systems and the internet.

A blockchain is a type of distributed ledger. It is effectively a form of collective bookkeeping. Transactions are recorded between a number of participants using an network which operates via the internet. Unlike traditional bookkeeping records held by a business, which are closed to outsiders and are solely controlled by the organisation, all records in the blockchain are publicly available and are distributed across everyone connected to the network. All transactions between participants are recorded in identical records (ledgers) held by each user throughout the network. When a transaction between participants (ie, selling and purchasing items) occurs, the details of the transaction are logged in all of the blockchain ledgers simultaneously, recording the time, date, value of the deal, and the details of the participants. The blockchain records are only updated when those parties in the network have reviewed and verified that the transaction details are correct. This verification process is carried out by the computers which make up the network. The central benefit offered by blockchain is that all participants in the network have access to updated records, in which each individual transaction has effectively been audited by the computers in the network.

It is this control aspect of blockchain technology which holds the greatest relevance for addressing cyber security concerns. Any attempt by a participant to interfere with a transaction, for example by attempting to post incorrect details to the ledger, will be rejected by the network parties assigned to verify the transaction. Failure to achieve consensus will lead to the transaction not being recorded in the ledger in the blockchain.

Worked example: Blockchain in action

The potential uses of blockchain are extremely far reaching. An article by Oscar Williams-Grut (2016) highlighted the key points outlined in a report titled *Blockchain: Putting Theory into Practice,* issued by Goldman Sachs. The report suggested the potential practical applications that blockchain technology offers.

Building trust

The report highlights the potential security benefits that blockchain offers in protecting the online identities of internet users. Goldman Sachs highlight that the use of blockchain could have far reaching implications for organisations like Airbnb, the peer-2-peer lodging site which enables individuals (hosts) to let out their home to potential guests. Storing a person's identity on the blockchain should mean that 'that identity is then linked to reviews and scores on the sharing economy and other marketplace sites – a little like with Facebook. People can easily check to see if you're a trusted host by checking your ID number. Unlike Facebook, people can't simply delete accounts and re-register if they get a bad reputation, as records on the blockchain can't be tampered with or duplicated. Your identity is your identity.' (Williams-Grut, 2016).

Reducing costs

The report suggests that the administrative costs associated with transactions between individuals could be significantly reduced through the use of blockchain. Williams-Grut (2016) notes that items such as property records could be recorded on blockchain so that 'prospective buyers can quickly, easily and cheaply verify that the owner of a house really does own the place. At present, this process is done manually. Not only is that costly, there's also a greater chance of errors, which could add to costs' (Williams-Grut, 2016).

Improving money laundering procedures

Goldman Sachs also envision a time when the data stored on a blockchain could be used to help financial institutions verify the identity of new clients which is required by money laundering regulations. 'Know your customer' requirements could be met quickly by the use of blockchain as it effectively provides a firm of accountants or a bank with access to a new clients tamper-proof 'digital passport'. (Williams-Grut, 2016).

Source:

Williams-Grut, O. (2016) *Goldman Sachs: 5 practical uses for blockchain – from Airbnb to stock markets.* [Online]. Available from: http://uk.businessinder.com [Accessed 3 May 2017].

Summary and Self-test

Summary

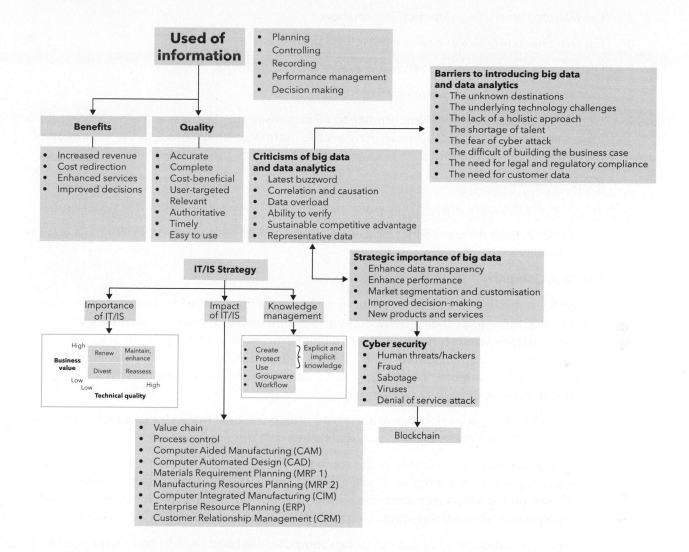

Used of information
- Planning
- Controlling
- Recording
- Performance management
- Decision making

Benefits
- Increased revenue
- Cost redirection
- Enhanced services
- Improved decisions

Quality
- Accurate
- Complete
- Cost-beneficial
- User-targeted
- Relevant
- Authoritative
- Timely
- Easy to use

Criticisms of big data and data analytics
- Latest buzzword
- Correlation and causation
- Data overload
- Ability to verify
- Sustainable competitive advantage
- Representative data

Barriers to introducing big data and data analytics
- The unknown destinations
- The underlying technology challenges
- The lack of a holistic approach
- The shortage of talent
- The fear of cyber attack
- The difficult of building the business case
- The need for legal and regulatory compliance
- The need for customer data

IT/IS Strategy

Importance of IT/IS

Business value: High / Low
Technical quality: Low / High
- Renew
- Maintain, enhance
- Divest
- Reassess

Impact of IT/IS

Knowledge management
- Create
- Protect
- Use
- Groupware
- Workflow
  } Explicit and implicit knowledge

Strategic importance of big data
- Enhance data transparency
- Enhance performance
- Market segmentation and customisation
- Improved decision-making
- New products and services

Cyber security
- Human threats/hackers
- Fraud
- Sabotage
- Viruses
- Denial of service attack

Blockchain

- Value chain
- Process control
- Computer Aided Manufacturing (CAM)
- Computer Automated Design (CAD)
- Materials Requirement Planning (MRP 1)
- Manufacturing Resources Planning (MRP 2)
- Computer Integrated Manufacturing (CIM)
- Enterprise Resource Planning (ERP)
- Customer Relationship Management (CRM)

Self-test

Answer the following questions.

1 List five uses of information.

2 List five characteristics of strategic information.

3 List five characteristics of tactical information.

4 List five characteristics of operational information.

5 Distinguish between explicit knowledge and tacit knowledge.

6 Identify four controls for assuring IT security.

7 Computer security is of vital importance to all organisations. Security is the means by which losses are controlled and therefore involves the identification of risks and the institution of measures to either prevent such risks entirely or to reduce their impact.

Requirements

7.1 Identify the main areas of risk which may arise in relation to a computer system.

7.2 Describe the different forms of control which should be instituted to safeguard against computer security risks.

8 **The SFA Company**

The SFA Company manufactures clothing and operates from one location in a major city. It purchases cotton and other raw materials and manufactures these into garments of clothing, such as sweatshirts, T-shirts and similar articles in its factory. There are approximately 20 administration staff, 30 sales staff and 300 production workers. Although the company is profitable, three major concerns were raised at a recent board meeting about the operations of the company:

(1) The company does not always appear to obtain the best prices for raw materials, which has decreased gross profit in the last few years of trading.

(2) Many garments are made to order for large retail shops, but the company has spare capacity and so it maintains an active salesforce to try to increase its total sales. However, the salesforce does not seem to be making many sales because of lack of information about the garments in production and stocks of finished garments.

(3) Some production is carried out using Computer Assisted Design and manufacture although the company has found limited use for this application to date. The system was purchased in a hurry two years ago with the objective of keeping up with competitors who had purchased similar systems. The board believes that greater use could be made of this technology.

The Value Chain model produced by Porter provides a good summary of the primary and support activities of the company. An adaptation of Porter's general model follows.

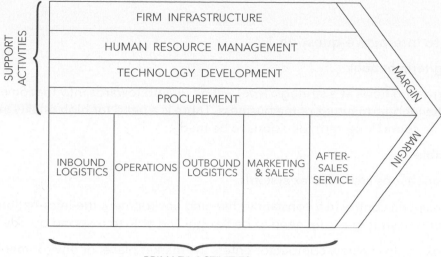

The board of SFA is currently considering introducing some form of information system or systems, such as a MIS, into the company for all staff to use. Because of the perceived weaknesses in the current systems already mentioned, the directors are particularly interested in the areas of:

(1) Inbound logistics
(2) Marketing and sales
(3) Technology development

Requirements

8.1 Explain what inputs will be needed for the information systems designed to support the operations of the business in the three areas mentioned above.

8.2 Explain what outputs will be required from those information systems.

Note: Do **not** describe Porter's general model.

9 Read the scenario of the **September 2014 Business Strategy and Technology** question in the Question Bank entitled *Forsi Ltd*. Draft an answer to the requirement on knowledge management.

10 Read the scenario of the **March 2013 Business Strategy and Technology** question in the Question Bank entitled *Mayhews Ltd (amended)*. Draft an answer to the requirement which asks for a discussion of the advantages and disadvantages of investing in information technology. You need to ensure that your answer refers to the use of data analytics.

11 Read the scenario of the **Septmeber 2010 Business Strategy and Technology** question in the Question Bank entitled *Marcham plc (amended)*. Draft an answer to the requirement which asks for a discussion about the benefits of data analytics and the creation of a competitive advantage.

12 Read the scenario of the **March 2017 Business Strategy and Technology** question in the Question Bank, entitled *Gighay Ltd*. Draft an answer to the requirement which asks for a discussion about the of use data analytics and implementing a big data strategy.

13 Read the scenario of the **September 2017 Business Strategy and Technology** question in the Question Bank, entitled *Air Services UK Ltd*. Draft an answer to the requirement which asks for an explanation of the cyber security risks facing the company.

Now, go back to the Learning outcomes in the Introduction. If you are satisfied you have achieved these objectives, please tick them off.

Answers to Interactive questions

Answer to Interactive question 1

1.1 **Long-term outlook**

Information flows at a strategic level will be geared towards information expected to impact on the long-term future of the business. There is a need for high quality information to enable sound long-term decisions to be made.

Flexible

Organisations are complex systems.

To maintain control in a constantly changing environment the information flows and systems at strategic level need to be flexible and able to respond quickly to new demands.

For example, if a new competitor enters the market place, or environmental legislation is introduced affecting production processes or a trading opportunity arises in an overseas territory, then strategic decisions will be required to formulate the most appropriate response.

Good decisions can only be made when all the implications can be quantified with an acceptable degree of certainty. Management information systems must be flexible enough to provide concise, accurate and timely information relevant to the new environment.

Multi-directional

In a business organisation information flows both vertically and horizontally. The familiar pyramid hierarchy of an organisation sets out three levels of control and information.

Information flows at the strategic level facilitates decision-making that will affect the whole organisation and provide the framework for long term strategic plans. Internal information will flow from middle management up to senior management and *vice versa*.

Information also flows horizontally between different activities in a business. For instance overtime hours provided by the payroll section may be used by the production department, delivery lead times from warehouses may be used by the sales team and the level of future orders from the sales department will be used to forecast turnover and cash flows by the accounts department. The quality of these information flows will dictate both the efficiency of the business operations and will impact on the type and quality of information received by senior management.

The complex nature of strategic decisions makes information sharing vital.

An external component

Strategic level information flows will include information from external sources (eg, government, suppliers, media etc). Strategic decisions are generally non-routine and require a high degree of judgement. The quality of information is critical at the strategic management level.

1.2 Information used at a strategic level is often *ad hoc* – strategic decision making is non-routine and potentially risky.

Strategic information comes from both internal and external sources.

Internal sources

Most management information systems are now computer-based because of processing speed, accuracy and the ability to process large volumes of data. Internal data needs to be captured from day-to-day operations, processed into relevant information and made available in a suitable form at a strategic level.

Senior management information requirements should play a part in the development of information systems to ensure that the information required for strategic decision making is able to be produced.

Centralised systems are relatively powerful and usually controlled at senior level. However, a flexible response to non-routine problems may be lacking.

Decentralised systems may provide more flexibility, however central control and standard formats are often lacking.

Currently, popular solutions revolve around **networked and distributed** processing systems. These can provide information to different levels of management – often from the same database. They combine the advantages of local control, speed and ease of use with flexibility and the potential for standardised presentation of information.

Executive Support Systems (ESS) can be particularly useful in this area, providing summarised high-level information with the ability to view the underlying data if required.

The introduction of an ESS will also encourage senior management to consider which type of information is really relevant to the business.

An **intranet** may also be appropriate to encourage the sharing of knowledge and opinions relevant to strategic decisions (eg, bulletin boards).

External sources

External information may be in the form of official reports, tax leaflets, technical updates, press updates and often just word of mouth.

Much of this information is now available via the **internet**. **Intelligent agents** and **newsclipping services** can also be utilised on the internet, to find user-defined information and forward it – usually via email.

Some organisations are able to access external information through an **extranet** – allowing them to enter certain parts of another organisation's intranet.

Answer to Interactive question 2

2.1 **Information management** entails identifying the current and future information needs, identifying information sources, collecting and storing the information and facilitating existing methods of using information and identifying new ways of using it. It should also ensure that the information is communicated to those who need it and not to those who are not entitled to see it.

Mayo defines **knowledge management** (KM) as 'the management of the information, knowledge and experience available to an organisation – its creation, capture, storage, availability and utilisation – so that organisational activities build on what is already known and extend it further'.

More specifically, **knowledge** is interpreted in terms of **potential for action** and distinguished from **information** in terms of its more immediate link with performance. This interpretation is consistent with what the information systems philosopher and professor Charles West Churchman observed three decades ago in his pioneering work *The Design of Inquiring Systems*: 'knowledge resides in the user and not in the collection of information… it is how the user reacts to a collection of information that matters'.

Databases, or more correctly **knowledge bases**, need to be designed and developed to store the organisation's knowledge. This will be particularly difficult because of the **tacit** nature of much of the knowledge and also because it is largely inside the heads of individuals. Recording this knowledge will be very different to recording the fields and records of a traditional database. An **expert system** seems one way forward as this has a knowledge base made up of facts, rules and conditions. But much of this knowledge may have to be represented pictorially as images and 'knowledge maps'. An intranet that lends itself to full multimedia representation and intelligent searching may therefore be the way forward.

Knowledge-based companies will vary from industry to industry but there are some broad common principles about where knowledge resides and how to capture its value. The intellectual capital can be divided between human capital (the bodies that go home at night), and structural capital. Structural capital includes innovation capital (intellectual property), customer capital (address lists and client records), and organisational capital (systems for processing policies and claims). A number of organisations are creating knowledge management programmes for **protecting and distributing knowledge** resources that they have identified and for discovering new sources of knowledge.

- One such programme is the identification and development of informal networks and communities of practice within organisations. These self-organising groups share common work interests, usually cutting across a company's functions and processes.

- Another means of establishing the occurrence of knowledge is to look at knowledge-related business outcomes eg, product development and service innovation. While the knowledge embedded within these innovations is invisible, the products themselves are tangible.

- Every day companies make substantial investments in improving their employees' knowledge and enabling them to use it more effectively. Analysis of these investments is a third way of making KM activities visible. For example how much technical and non-technical training are individuals consuming? How much is invested in competitive and environmental scanning, and in other forms of strategic research?

The process by which an organisation develops its store of knowledge is sometimes called **organisational learning**. A **learning organisation** is centred on the people that make up the organisation and the knowledge they hold. The organisation and employees feed off and into the central pool of knowledge. The organisation uses the knowledge pool as a tool to teach itself and its employees.

There are dozens of different approaches to KM, including document management, information management, business intelligence, competence management, information systems management, intellectual asset management, innovation, business process design, and so on. Many KM projects have a significant element of information management. After all, people need information about where knowledge resides, and to share knowledge they need to transform it into more or less transient forms of information.

2.2 A **knowledge management strategy** might take the form shown in the diagram below.

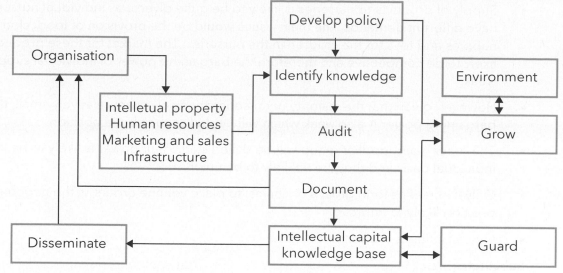

The stages may include the following.

- Develop and determine a policy for owning, growing and sharing knowledge within the organisation.

- Identify critical knowledge functions within each department.

- Audit knowledge to determine its type, location, longevity and whether it is explicit or tacit.

- Document knowledge in a medium that best suits the purpose for which it will be used.

- Store it in a repository where it can be easily updated and retrieved.

- Determine ways in which it can be grown and tracked.

- Decide how the knowledge will be disseminated inside the organisation and possibly outside.

- Ensure this valuable organisational asset is kept secure.

Answer to Interactive question 3

3.1 **Porter's five forces**

Customers

- Parents individually have very little power/influence over the industry.

- This is because they have low buying power in relation to the size of the industry.

- Because demand exceeds supply of childcare places even if parents take their children elsewhere, it is unlikely to cause any problems for the industry as others will take their places.

- However, if there were a series of damaging reports into the industry, then parents may decide to use alternative forms of childcare. Their children are very precious to them and they would not be prepared to accept substandard levels of service.

- Switching costs are low in terms of money; however parents would have to consider issues such as distress to the children involved and the problem of finding a better alternative in the local vicinity due to the lack of supply.

- Overall influence: Low.

Suppliers

- Supply of products to nurseries is likely to be quite diverse as individual nurseries will have different demands. The main issues would be the provision of food, clothing, nappies and toys for the children in the nurseries. The market for these products is likely to be competitive and therefore the bargaining power of individual suppliers is weak.

- However, given that the majority of nurseries themselves are relatively small, their bargaining power is also weak which will neutralise the above position.

- The other main supplier group will be skilled staff. Their power is likely to be low on an individual basis and they are unlikely to be unionised.

- Only if nurseries form groups or chains, to place volume orders, is the negotiating position likely to improve.

- Overall influence: Low.

Substitutes

- Demand currently exceeds supply within the childcare industry. Substitutes exist in the form of domestic nannies, playgroups and childminders.

- These competitors individually have little power, although they may offer a service which is more convenient and local to that of nurseries, especially in the form of domestic nannies and childminders.

- Considerations such as the level of service offered by the competition would have an influence on whether they could take market share away from nurseries. Parents would be concerned about the level of regulation over the substitutes, due to the importance of high quality childcare to them.

- Overall influence: Medium.

Competitors

- The majority of entities in the industry are small, owner managed businesses. As such competitors' power is low, as one nursery will not be able to significantly influence the behaviour of others.

- Even if individual nurseries set up close to one another, because demands outstrips supply there is potentially room for both to survive.

- If there were a number of chains of nurseries then they might be able to demonstrate some power, but there seems to be little evidence of this.

- Overall influence: Low/Medium.

New entrants

- Set up costs are relatively low, as demonstrated by the large number of owner managed nurseries in existence. The main costs to be incurred would be premises and equipment, along with ensuring that staff were appropriately qualified and trained.

- The excess demand for childcare is likely to attract new entrants to the market. This may come from existing nursery staff who decide to set up businesses themselves.

- Government regulation and red tape may however act as a deterrent to new entrants.

- The other main restraint on new entrants would be the ability to find suitable premises from which to operate.

- Overall influence: High.

3.2 Critical Success Factors

Innovation

KA has a range of services and tools that distinguish it from competitors due to the company embracing modern technologies and applying them to the nursery model. This will help to attract new children as parents will be keen to take advantage of being able to see the activities their children undertake during the day.

This is coupled with flexibility in terms of offering services such as the collect and return service, which puts KA in a position of offering unique services that competitors are either unable or unwilling to provide.

This is likely to result in fewer children being removed from the nursery, and customers being willing to accept the higher pricing structure charged by KA.

Compliance with regulations

KA has a good reputation in the form of the positive feedback from the government reports. Independent approval from a third party is one of the considerations that parents would take when deciding where to send their children. This will keep parents satisfied that the level of care given to their children is appropriate.

Quality of staff

KA offers a more personal level of service to children, through having a higher staff-to-child ratio, with staff being qualified to a degree in excess of competitors. In addition one of the owners of the company has extensive experience of working in the industry and knows the concerns of customers. This will be a comfort factor to parents.

Use of information systems and technology

In relation to Porter's generic strategies Kid A is operating a differentiation strategy. Parents are prepared to pay a premium for the factors noted above and as a result KA can charge 40% higher fees and still have full nurseries with waiting lists.

Porter's value chain can be used to identify areas where IT could be used to add value.

KA makes use of IT in the following areas:

- The use of GPS wristbands linked to webcams allays parents concerns regarding the safety and welfare of their offspring. This may make them more likely to choose KA over other nurseries.

- Computers are used within the nursery for learning purposes. In addition parents are able to get feedback via the internet on the computer based games and work that their children have been involved in. These have helped KA gain a good reputation in government reports which is likely to increase demand and retention rates.

- Staff are expected to have knowledge of the systems used and are paid more highly as a result. This may encourage better quality nursery nurses who are more able to communicate with parents.

3.3 Report

To: The Directors of Kid A Limited
From: XYZ Consultants
Date: 21 June 20X8
Re: Expansion plans

(a) **Risks caused by expansion**

Loss of control

As the number of nurseries increases you will have to take a more strategic and hands off approach to running the business. This will require developing a new range of skills and provide new problems.

The managers recruited must be competent at the tasks that are being delegated to them. If not, the business could suffer damage to its reputation that would be difficult to repair.

Given the sensitive nature of the business, one poorly performing nursery could have a detrimental impact on the reputation of the whole business. There is also the potential conflicts that would arise between yourselves and new managers

Financial/economic risks

Fresh finance will be required to expand the business. Because you are running a small business this will have to come from your own savings or new borrowings. If you borrow money then the lenders will require security, either over the nursery properties themselves (if purchased as opposed to rented) or in the form of personal guarantees.

Interest on borrowings will eat into profit and is a fixed cost. If demand for nursery spaces falls then there is a risk that the interest payments may not be fulfilled.

To attract good nursery managers you may have to increase salaries, which will also have an impact on profitability.

A downturn in the economy could have a significant impact on the business. Higher unemployment could result in more families where both parents are not working, and therefore demand for nursery spaces may fall. Financial insecurity amongst the working population may mean that fewer families are willing to pay the premium prices charged by KA.

(b) **Budget issues**

There are a variety of budget elements that could be adopted to make the process more effective:

Profit centres

Because you want to transfer responsibility for each individual nursery to the managers, consider making each nursery a profit centre. Here the managers are responsible for both revenues and costs within the nursery.

Controllable costs

Budgets and income statements should be produced for you to review on a regular (say monthly) basis for each nursery.

These should focus on controllable issues over which managers have influence (local advertising, recruitment, pay and day-to-day expenses). It is not appropriate to assess them on costs over which they have no control.

Delegation/participation

Managers should be involved in the budget setting process, rather than it being imposed by you. This is because managers will be motivated by the increased responsibility and their knowledge of local conditions may improve the budget.

Authorisation

Care must be taken however that managers do not build in slack into their budgets to make them too easy. It may therefore be useful to compare the different budgets prepared by individual managers and adopt one of them as the approved model.

Once the budget has been approved this will act as authorisation to the manager to incur expenditure. Budgets should be created by computer, as this will allow for greater sensitivity analysis.

Evaluation of performance

Actual performance should be compared to the budget plan, feedback provided to the managers and any necessary action taken. The budgets should be flexed to allow you to compare the performance of different sized nurseries operated by KA.

Rewards

Managers should be given rewards for achieving and exceeding budgets. This could be extended to their staff too.

(c) **Information for control and decision making**

Strategic information

Thom and Debra will require strategic information to help with long term planning and assess whether objectives are being met. This information will be both external and internal:

- Information about the external environment would be useful to assess the future political, economic, social and technological changes that may impact on KA eg, proposed changes to health and safety regulations, the government's inspection process.

- Market information to estimate future demand eg, demographic information regarding the local population for each nursery - number of working parents with pre-school age children living or employed locally who might choose to use the nursery.

- Data about competitors might provide a benchmark against which the performance of individual nurseries and the business as a whole might be assessed. This should consider financial and non-financial factors eg, the fees charged, government ratings, range of services offered, opening hours etc.

- Financial information to assess the overall profitability of the business and each nursery

- Information regarding fixed asset investments eg, premises and capital structure/financing

Tactical information

This might focus on key performance indicators such as the utilisation of resources by each nursery, particularly in relation to staff requirements eg, ratio of children to staff, fees earned per staff member, staff turnover rates, expenditure as a percentage of fees earned.

Thom and Debra should monitor customer satisfaction, eg, by asking parents to complete a survey online.

They should monitor the number of parents who switch from them to other nurseries, the number of parents they attract from competitors.

They could monitor utilisation of capacity by considering nursery places filled as a percentage of places available and the waiting lists at each nursery. They can also monitor the ability of individual managers to convert enquiries into bookings.

It would be useful to monitor the take up of some of the additional services offered eg, the number of parents who actually use the webcam, the number of times work is reviewed by parents on the internet. This will help assess the demand for these services and the value being ascribed to them by parents.

KA should ensure that they generate and monitor performance indicators for the areas that the government inspection focuses on.

Operational information

This should be prepared very frequently to help track the specific day-to-day activities of the nursery:

- Staff timesheets to monitor hours worked and sickness
- Weekly task completion sheets
- Weekly running costs in comparison to budget
- Weekly attendance record for children
- Fees invoiced/collected

Answers to Self-test

1   Planning, controlling, recording transactions, measuring performance and making decisions.

2   Five of:

- Derived from both internal and external sources
- Summarised at a high level
- Relevant to the long term
- Concerned with the whole organisation
- Often prepared on an *ad hoc* basis
- Both quantitative and qualitative
- Uncertain, as the future cannot be predicted accurately

3   Five of:

- Primarily generated internally (but may have a limited external component)
- Summarised at a lower level
- Relevant to the short and medium term
- Concerned with activities or departments
- Prepared routinely and regularly
- Based on quantitative measures

4   Five of:

- Derived from internal sources
- Detailed, being the processing of raw data
- Relevant to the immediate term
- Task-specific
- Prepared very frequently
- Largely quantitative

5   Explicit knowledge is knowledge that an organisation already stores in formal systems. It includes facts, transactions and events that can be clearly stated and stored in information systems.

   Tacit knowledge is expertise held by people within the organisation that has not been formally documented.

6   Four from:

- Business continuity planning
- Systems access control
- Systems development and maintenance
- Physical and environmental security
- Compliance
- Personnel security
- Security organisation
- Computer and network management.
- Asset classification and control
- Security policy

7.1   The main areas of risk to which a computer system is exposed, and some of the factors which may lead to the exposure are as follows.

   Accidental destruction or **loss of data** by operator or software error. The auditors should pay particular attention during their audit to recovery procedures. In addition the possibility of accidental destruction of programs or hardware, particularly the dropping of a disk pack, by an operator, and the consequences thereof, should not be overlooked.

The **acceptance of inaccurate input data** due to inadequate edit or other checks is another frequent cause of loss of data.

A **complete systems failure** can lead to loss of data and may be caused by a failure in the power supply or possibly a failure of the air conditioning or other environmental controls.

Theft of data from a **batch processing system** by an operator copying or removing data files, particularly where these are on easily transportable media such as magnetic tapes.

Theft of data from an **online or real time system** by a person obtaining unauthorised access to the system via a remote terminal and either using passwords illegally or alternatively using a 'piggyback system' (in which a valid transmission is intercepted and the final 'logging off' operation stopped in transmission to permit the illegal operator to continue in operation masquerading as the authorised user).

Theft of software either by operators copying or removing the program file, and in the latter case possibly demanding a ransom from the rightful owner, or alternatively by programming staff copying and attempting to sell the source documentation, with or without the object program.

Deliberate destruction of the hardware has been known to occur, and where adequate protection has not been provided, such acts have also led to the simultaneous destruction of software and data. Similar results may occur as a result of fire or explosion either in the computer room or adjoining premises.

7.2 The different forms of control which should be instituted may be sub-divided into three main headings.

Physical security

Strict control of access to the computer area, using such devices as magnetic keys and alarm systems.

Effective precautions against **fire** or other **natural disruption** including alarm systems, automatic extinguishing systems and regular inspections.

Established and well-practised **emergency procedures** in the event of fire or other disorder and alternative power supply.

Location of the computer so that it is difficult for unauthorised personnel to have access with the minimum of entrances and exits.

Possibility of **remote storage of security copies of data**.

Location of the computer room so that it is, if possible, **situated away from known** hazards such as flooding, radiation from X-ray equipment and radio systems and fire/explosion risks in adjoining premises.

Software security

Effective control over the **preservation of information** contained on files by ensuring that before a file is to be overwritten a check is made on the file version.

Prevention of unauthorised access by the use of devices such as passwords.

Systems security

Strict control and verification of all **input data**, where possible with control totals prepared outside the computer department.

All input should pass through an **'edit' program** as the first stage in being entered on to the computer files. This program clearly indicates all items accepted and rejected, the latter to be investigated by the user department.

Adequate controls should be in force to ensure that **amendments to programs** are properly **authorised, checked out** and **validated** before use.

There should be **adequate recovery, restart and standby procedures** in the event of power failure or machine breakdowns, which can be facilitated by a 'log' of all work performed and by frequent dumping of files.

Controls should be instituted to ensure that **computer output** is **properly distributed**, especially confidential print-outs, payments and so on.

Proper control over **storage and issue of electronic media** with manual records being kept of physical maintenance performed. Such records frequently also record current status of the media and the details of the file(s) currently stored upon it.

8.1 The SFA Company

Introduction

As a result of concerns raised at the recent board meeting a new Management Information System (MIS) is currently being considered. Output from the main transaction processing systems will form the input of the MIS.

The MIS manipulates this data into summary level information for control and decision-making purposes to support the monitoring and control of the key functions of the organisation. The MIS will require inputs relating to the three key primary activities of inbound logistics, marketing and sales and technology development.

Inbound logistics

The inbound logistics function aims to ensure **the right materials are available at the right price and at the right time**. A key element of this involves ensuring the best possible price for raw materials of the required quality is negotiated. Output from the Computer Assisted Design (CAD) and Computer Assisted Manufacture (CAM) systems will become inputs into the MIS. The MIS will manipulate and summarise this data, resulting in information that will enable the purchasing department to **plan** and meet its responsibilities in the most efficient manner. For example, negotiations with suppliers can be faced with **improved knowledge** of the quantities of raw materials required in the medium term which should help win **improved prices**.

Marketing and sales

The MIS can provide information on the activities of customers and salespeople, showing who is buying and selling what. Over time, useful **trends** should become apparent. The links with the CAM system will enable customers to be given accurate information relating to both orders in progress and finished goods. Forecast demand can be made available via the feeder systems to the MIS, and when matched with production scheduling information, instances of **spare capacity** should be able to be established and appropriate action taken.

Technology development

The new MIS should provide information that will allow the increased use of **Computer Assisted Design** (CAD) and **Computer Assisted Manufacture** (CAM). Use of CAD and CAM techniques will **improve efficiency**, resulting in the faster production of garments, and **improved garment quality**. **Prototypes** can be produced rapidly allowing customer feedback to be acted on at the design stage.

The MIS can **monitor sales and production** information and when necessary provide **control information** to ensure orders are delivered on time. One difficult area to predict in the clothing industry is future demand levels for fashion items, as a change in consumer taste can often be rapid and on the surface unpredictable. The MIS will therefore require information feeds from **'outward looking'** sources such as fashion show trends and market research.

8.2 Outputs required

Outputs from the CAD/CAM systems should include **performance measures** that show whether the design, development and production activities are **achieving their targets**, and how these functions are contributing to the overall performance of SFA. The performance measures should be available for on-screen viewing, and be included in control reports that highlight areas in need of corrective action.

Reports from the MIS should also show supplier and buyer **performance**, including information on price, quantity and quality (including service quality). Marginal cost information should feed from the accounting system to the MIS, as this information is vital when negotiating prices relating to 'extra' production runs to utilise any spare capacity.

Conclusion

The proposed MIS will consolidate information from the main transaction processing systems. It will 'pull-together' information from the separate functions of SFA, allowing the **overall picture** to be seen more clearly. This will enable SFA to identify and respond quickly to circumstances that require action. The MIS will enable SFA to operate more **efficiently and effectively** and should be implemented as soon as possible.

9   Refer to the answer to Forsi Ltd in the Question Bank.

10 Refer to the answer to Mayhews Ltd in the Question Bank.

11 Refer to the answer to Marcham plc in the Question Bank.

12 Refer to the answer to Gighay Ltd in the Question Bank.

13 Refer to the answer to Air Services UK Ltd in the Question Bank.

CHAPTER 15

Strategies for change

Introduction

Examination context

TOPIC LIST

Summary and Self-test

Answers to Interactive questions

Answers to Self-test

Introduction

Learning outcomes

- Identify in a given situation the key issues which should be addressed by the management of an organisation during the planning and implementation of change

The specific syllabus reference for this chapter is 3j.

Syllabus links

This chapter involves the implementation of the strategies discussed in the preceding chapters. It has not been covered in the syllabus of previous examinations.

Examination context

Previous chapters concentrate on identifying the need for, and the direction of change if an organisation is to remain successful. This chapter looks at the issues which need to be addressed by an organisation during the planning and implementation of such changes.

In exams so far, most candidates have demonstrated a reasonable knowledge of change management but a common mistake has been to provide a generic answer, repeating elements by rote from the learning materials. As we have mentioned throughout this Study Manual, your ability to apply your knowledge to the question scenario will be vital in earning you marks.

The scenario for Question 2 in the June 2017 exam (*Jason Smyth Textiles (JST) Ltd*) focused on a UK-based manufacturer of soft furnishings. The company's business model was based on pursuing a competitive strategy of cost leadership. However, this model was starting to become difficult to sustain, and a new business model had therefore been proposed. This involved a move upmarket, by producing better quality soft furnishings in a new range of higher priced fabrics. The second part of the second requirement asked:

'With respect to JST's proposed new business model, explain the change management issues for JST'.

Although, the requirement did not mention the use of a theoretical model it would have been relevant to use one provided you applied the model to the scenario. When attempting this requirement, structuring your answer around the work of Lewin/Schein's three-stage model of change, or the Gemini 4R's model would have been appropriate. Both of these models are covered in this chapter, and they are particularly helpful as they provide a structure when attempting change management questions.

It is worth noting that a significant driver of change concerns the growing use of technology in organisations, and the rapid speed with which technological change can affect long-standing business models. Exam questions could very easily test your ability to pick out technological drivers of change in a scenario, and require you to suggest appropriate strategies in addressing such developments.

1 The need for change

Section overview

- The sources of change are both internal and environmental.

- The range of impacts of a 'change trigger' will be felt as shock waves through the organisation and will affect staff and management at all levels.

- Change must be handled carefully to avoid the organisation being overwhelmed.

1.1 The need for an organisation to change or develop

The need for an organisation to change or develop could be caused (or 'triggered') by a number of factors:

- **Changes in the environment**: these could be changes in what competitors are doing, what customers are buying, how they spend their money, changes in the law, changes in social behaviour and attitudes, economic changes, and so on.

- **Changes in the products the organisation makes, or the services it provides**: these are made in response to changes in customer demands, competitors' actions, new technology, and so on.

- **Changes in technology and changes in working methods**: these changes are also in response to environmental change such as the advent of new technology and new laws on safety at work.

- **Changes in management and working relationships**: for example, changes in leadership style, and in the way that employees are encouraged to work together. Changes could also be triggered by the growing flexibility in workplace arrangements. Also changes in training and development.

- **Changes in organisation structure or size**: these might involve creating new departments and divisions, greater delegation of authority or more centralisation, changes in the way that plans are made, management information is provided and control is exercised, and so on. **Organisation re-structuring** will be made in response to changes of the types discussed above.

- **Post-acquisition**: incoming management will wish to improve and integrate the firm into the new parent's structure and systems. This will involve visible change to names and signage but also deeper changes to organisational structures, culture, job roles, staff numbers and management systems.

Worked example: The gig economy

In Chapter 6, we explored the concept of workforce flexibility and considered some of the impacts that it is having on the relationships which exist between organisations and workers.

Advances in technology have been key facilitators of the so-called gig economy in the UK. However, as the following worked example illustrates a number of legal challenges are likely to lead to significant changes in how this 'economy' operates in the future.

Wilson (2017) highlights that the gig economy is a term used to describe a labour market in which work is undertaken by freelancers and people on short-term contracts, as opposed fully employed workers. Proponents argue that the gig economy provides workers with flexibility around the hours they work, whilst critics suggest that it is fundamentally exploitative by nature, as individuals are not eligible to receive standard employment benefits or trade union representation. In recent times a number of firms operating in the gig economy have been accused of deliberately attempting to misclassify workers as independent subcontractors in order to get around legal requirements governed by employment law.

Companies including taxi-firm, Uber, and food delivery firm, Deliveroo, have become synonymous with the gig economy. Both companies operate through the use of internet technologies including apps. On its website Uber (2018) claims that it is a 'technology platform' which connects 'driver-partners and riders' via its smartphone app. Drivers are effectively freelancers who use the Uber app as a means of picking up fares. Uber then collects a percentage of the fare charged, as commission. Deliveroo operates in a similar manner, whereby customers use the company's homepage to order food from a selection of local restaurants. As Deliveroo (2018) highlight this is then couriered by its team of independent contractors by bicycle from the selected eatery to the end customer. Deliveroo riders are paid a standard rate per hour with an additional amount per delivery made.

In recent times a number of high profile cases have made the news as groups working for the likes of Deliveroo and Uber have claimed that the nature of their relationships entitles them to certain employment rights including: sick and holiday pay and the right to receive the minimum wage.

In late 2017 it was widely reported that the Independent Workers Union of Great Britain (IWGB) had lost a case against Deliveroo. The IWBG had hoped to force Deliveroo to officially recognise the union and meet its demands that the company's couriers should be afforded employment rights. According to the BBC (2017) the Central Arbitration Committee (CAC) ruled that Deliveroo's couriers 'were self-employed because of their freedom to "substitute" – allowing other riders to take their place on a job' (BBC, 2017). The IWGB's defeat in this case followed contrasting news that Uber had lost an appeal against a previous ruling which claimed that the company should recognise its drivers as workers, and afford them employment rights – including holiday pay and a right to receive the national minimum wage.

The debate over whether an individual should be classified as employed or self-employed has important ramifications for the gig economy and the legal entitlement of workers alike. The case of Pimlico Plumbers v Smith illustrates the importance of this distinction. Mr Smith was a plumber who paid tax on a self-employed basis, but also worked for Pimlico Plumbers for a six year period up to April 2011. An article by Russell (2018) highlighted that following a heart attack in January 2011 Mr Smith asked if he could reduce his working week with Pimlico Plumbers from five days to three. Mr Smith claimed that Pimlico Plumbers turned down his request, removed his branded van and subsequently dismissed him. Mr Smith claimed due to the nature of his relationship with Pimlico Plumbers that he should in fact be treated as a worker per the definition set out in the Employment Rights Act 1996. Despite subsequent appeals by the company, Mr Smith's claim was upheld by the Court of Appeal. (Russell, 2018).

In February 2018, Pimlico Plumbers' latest appeal reached the Supreme Court. It was widely reported in June 2018 that the Supreme Court had found in favour of Mr Smith's claim, thereby awarding him workers rights.

Sources:

Deliveroo (2018) *About Deliveroo*. [Online]. Available from: https://deliveroo.co.uk/faq [Accessed 1 May 2018].

Uber (2018) *What is Uber?* [Online]. Available from: https://help.uber.com [Accessed 1 May 2018].

Wilson, B. (2017) *What is the 'gig' economy?* [Online]. Available from: www.bbc.co.uk [Accessed 28 April 2017].

BBC. (2017) *Deliveroo claims victory in self-employment case*. [Online]. Available from: www.bbc.co.uk [Accessed 1 May 2018].

Russell, E. (2018) *Pimlico Plumbers: Worker or Self-employed? Supreme Court decision expected imminently* [Online]. Available from: www.crane-staples.co.uk [Accessed 1 May 2018].

1.2 Types of change

Change itself may be divided into two types, **incremental** and **transformational**, and so may the management approach to change be divided into **reactive** and **proactive**.

Definitions

Incremental change is characterised by a series of small steps. It is a gradual process.

Transformational change is characterised by major, significant change being introduced relatively quickly.

Step change describes an unexpected jump (upwards) or drop (downwards) in the pace of change. The step is caused by an unexpected event (eg, environmental disaster, unexpected change in government etc).

Planned change involves following a series of pre-planned steps.

Emergent change views change as a series of continuous open-ended adjustments to the environment.

Johnson, Scholes and Whittington suggest the model of change shown below:

Nature of change

	Incremental	Transformational
Pro-active	Tuning	Planned
Reactive	Adaption	Forced

Management role

The importance of **proactive management** is that it implies that organisational change may be undertaken **before** it is imposed by events. It may, in fact, result from the process of forecasting and be a response to expected developments. **Forced change** is likely to be both painful and risky.

Interactive question 1: Types of change

1.1 Classify and explain the following changes using Johnson, Scholes and Whittington model.

(a) An international car maker undertaking a turnaround strategy in response to external pressures following years of underperformance

(b) A nationwide UK supermarket retailer announcing its entry into a large and profitable foreign market. It is anticipated that the change will have a far reaching impact on the retailer's current business model.

See **Answer** at the end of this chapter.

1.3 Levels at which change efforts may focus

There are three main levels to which organisational development and change efforts may be directed:

- **Individual level** where the focus is on improving individual skill levels, attitudes and motivation. Techniques employed could include education and training, management development, coaching and counselling, team building activities, inter-group activities, role analysis, job re-design, planning and objective setting activities and process consultation.

- **Organisation structure and systems level**: The characteristics of the organisational situation in which people work (eg, job redesign, reward systems, setting clear objectives) that help achieve organisational goals.

- **Organisational climate and interpersonal style levels**: The improvement of social and other informal processes among organisation members by creating a system with a wide climate of high interpersonal trust and openness and a reduction in the negative consequences of excessive social conflict and competitiveness.

2 Strategic change in organisations

Section overview

- Change management involves management of people's expectations and attitudes. This can range from the willingness of an operative to learn a skill or change a shift up to the willingness of the Board to authorise the necessary resources.

- Therefore most change models seek to describe stages of psychological transition.

- These stages may be the focus of planned change management initiatives.

2.1 Change processes

For an organisation to be innovative, and continually responsive to the need for change, a systematic approach should be established, for planning and implementing changes.

Although each situation should be considered individually, the following general steps can be identified in a major change initiative:

Step 1
Determine need or desire for change in a particular area.

Step 2
Prepare a tentative plan. Brainstorming sessions are a good idea, since alternatives for change should be considered.

Step 3
Analyse probable reactions to the change.

Step 4
Make a final decision from the choice of alternative options. The decision may be taken either by group problem-solving (participative) or by a manager on his own (coercive).

Step 5
Establish a timetable for change.

- 'Coerced' changes can probably be implemented faster, without time for discussions.

- Speed of implementation that is achievable will depend on the likely reactions of the people affected.

- Identify those in favour of the change, and perhaps set up a pilot programme involving them. Talk with any others likely to resist the change.

Step 6
Communicate the plan for change. This is really a continuous process, beginning at Step 1 and going through to Step 7.

Step 7
Implement the change.

Step 8
Review the change. This requires continuous evaluation.

2.2 The three-stage approach (iceberg model)

The Lewin/Schein three-stage **model of change** identifies key steps as **unfreeze**, **move** and **refreeze**.

UNFREEZE		MOVE		REFREEZE
Existing behaviour	→	Attitudinal/behavioural change	→	New behaviour

Step 1

Unfreeze is the most difficult (and in many cases neglected) stage of the process, concerned mainly with selling the change, with giving individuals or groups a motive for changing their attitudes, values, behaviour, systems or structures.

Unfreezing processes require four things:

- A trigger
- Someone to challenge and expose the existing behaviour pattern
- The involvement of outsiders
- Alterations to power structure

Step 2

Move is the second stage, mainly concerned with identifying what the new, desirable behaviour or norm should be, communicating it and encouraging individuals and groups to 'own' the new attitude or behaviour. This might involve the adoption of a new culture. To be successful, the new ideas must be shown to work.

Step 3

Refreeze is the final stage, implying consolidation or reinforcement of the new behaviour. Positive reinforcement (praise and reward) or negative reinforcement (sanctions applied to those who deviate from the new behaviour) may be used.

2.3 Adaptive change approach

Adaptive change occurs when an organisation's environment changes slowly. It is **change implemented in little stages**, and thus has the advantage of minimising the resistance faced at any one time.

2.4 Coercive change approach

Coercive change is enforced without participation. Change of culture and power structures is left to the end of the change process. There are several problems with a coercive approach:

- Underestimation of the forces of resistance
- Failure to muster forces in favour
- Failure to attack root causes of resistance
- Management shift their attention too quickly elsewhere
- Failure to ensure implementation

This approach is necessary in situations of **crisis** where there simply is no time to consult, or where decisions need to be taken quickly. Crisis has the effect of inducing panic – which managers must do what they can to minimise – but **it can also promote an immediate willingness to change**: it can be the necessary 'unfreeze' process before an organisational change.

An example is a sudden environmental shock that endangers the company's survival.

Most of the time, a **mixed approach between coercive change and adaptive change** is suitable. Adaptive change may be too slow, whereas coercive change is often resented and therefore not accepted.

2.5 Change agents

A change agent is an individual (sometimes called a **Champion of Change**), a group or external consultancy with the responsibility for driving and 'selling' the change.

The role of the change agent varies depending on the brief they are given. It may include:

- Defining the problem
- Suggesting possible solutions
- Selecting and implementing a solution
- Gaining support from all involved

To be effective a change agent should have the following skills and attributes:

- Communication skills
- Negotiation and 'selling' skills
- An awareness of organisational 'politics'
- An understanding of the relevant processes

The **champion of change model** recognises the importance of change being led by a **change agent**, who may be an individual or occasionally a group.

Step 1
Senior management are the change strategists and decide in broad terms what is to be done. There is a need for powerful advocacy for change at the strategic apex. This will only occur if senior management are themselves agreed on the need for change. This is a role requiring a clear vision of what the change is to achieve.

Step 2
They appoint a change agent to drive it through. Senior management has three roles:

- Supporting the change agent, if the change provokes conflict between the agent and interest groups in the organisation.

- Reviewing and monitoring the progress of the change.

- Endorsing and approving the changes, and ensuring that they are publicised.

Step 3
The change agent has to win the support of functional and operational managers, who have to introduce and enforce the changes in their own departments. The champion of change has to provide advice and information, as well as evidence that the old ways are no longer acceptable.

Step 4
The change agent galvanises managers into action and gives them any necessary support. The managers ensure that the changes are implemented operationally, in the field. Where changes involve, say, a new approach to customer care, it is the workers who are responsible for ensuring the effectiveness of the change process.

It is important to realise that successful change is not something exclusively imposed from above. There is a sense in which middle and junior managers are **change recipients** in that they are required to implement new approaches and methods. However, they are themselves also **change agents** within their own spheres of responsibility. They must be committed parts of the change process if it is to succeed.

Worked example: Fitbit

The following worked example focuses on the changes being introduced at wearable technology company, Fitbit.

In March 2017 wearable technology firm Fitbit announced changes to its leadership team. A press release issued by the company announced that Jeff Devine, an expert with 25 years' experience in 'scaling global technology brands including Cisco, Nokia, and Hewlett-Packard' had been appointed as Executive Vice President of Operations. (Fitbit, 2017).

An article by Pressman (2017) highlighted that Devine's appointment was part of a 'multi-pronged strategy' by Fitbit's CEO, James Park to help turn the business around. The announcement followed tough trading conditions in 2016 in which profits fell and sales flat-lined as the company suffered from excess inventory holdings. In January 2017, Fitbit announced that it was laying off 6% of its workforce in response to the company's deteriorating performance. Pressman (2017) noted that 'in Fitbit's view, the sales slump was due to the fact that the market for trackers among early adopters had been saturated' with mainstream buyers, the so-called late adopters, failing to show sufficient interest in the company's offering. Pressman (2017) highlighted 'with over 50 million devices sold in the past three years, and over 23 million active users, the company must now reach more casual, less tech savvy buyers'. (Pressman, 2017).

Pressman (2017) likened the appointment of Jeff Devine to Steve Jobs hiring of Tim Cook (the current CEO of Apple), who was brought in 'from Compaq Computer to overhaul Apple's operations in 1998'. Central to Devine's role will be improving Fitbit's gross margins and improving the quality of the company's products. The changes at Fitbit would also appear to be part of CEO James Park's desire to enter the smartwatch category, with a view to taking on Apple and Samsung.

Pressman (2018) highlighted that, in April 2018, Fitbit agreed a deal with Google to 'use Google's recently announced health data standards for apps, […] to connect its wearable devices to the electronic medical records systems used by doctors and hospitals'. It is Fitbit's intention that, in time, doctors will be able to access patient health data from their Fitbit device.

Sources:

Pressman, A. (2018) *Fitbit Strikes Deal With Google That Could Lead to Wearables Collaboration* [Online]. Available from: http://fortune.com [Accessed 1 May 2018].

Pressman, A. (2017) *Fitbit CEO Offers Turnaround Strategy After a Tough Year.* [Online]. Available from: http://fortune.com [Accessed 28 April 2017].

Fitbit (2017) *Fitbit Announces Changes to Leadership Team.* [Online]. Available from: https://investor.fitbit.com [Accessed 28 April 2017].

2.6 The Gemini 4Rs framework for planned strategic change

Management consultants Gouillart and Kelly describe a four-dimensional process for business transformation in their book *Transforming the Organisation*. Known as the Gemini 4Rs framework, this approach aims to cover all the important components of the organisation's identity.

Reframing involves fundamental questions about what the organisation is and what it is for:

- **Achieve mobilisation**: create the will and desire to change.
- **Create the vision** of where the organisation is going.
- **Build a measurement system** that will set targets and measure progress.

Restructuring is about the organisation's structure, but is also likely to involve cultural changes:

- **Construct an economic model** to show in detail how value is created and where resources should be deployed.

- Align the physical infrastructure with the overall plan.

- Redesign the work architecture so that processes interact to create value.

Revitalising is the process of securing a good fit with the environment:

- Achieve market focus.
- Invent new businesses.
- Change the rules of competition by exploiting technology.

Renewal ensures that the people in the organisation support the change process and acquire the necessary skills to contribute to it:

- **Create a reward system** to motivate.
- **Build individual learning**.
- **Develop the organisation** and its adaptive capability.

Worked example: National Mail Group

The following worked example sets out the difficulties faced by the National Mail group (National Mail) at two points in its history. National Mail was a previously-state owned postal service provider in a developed European country. You should assume that the current date is June 20X9.

May 20X0

In May 20X0 the government announced that from 1 January 20X1 any licensed operator would be allowed to deliver mail to business and residential customers, effectively ending the state-owned business's monopoly:

'National Mail [17 May 20X0] today announced a record €537 million profit on its operations for the last 12 months with quality of service to customers now hitting the highest levels in a decade.

National Mail's then Chairman, Jennifer Smith, said: 'Postmen and women have achieved a fantastic turnaround. They will now deservedly each get a 'Share in Success' payment of €1,074, amounting to €218 million of the company's profit. It's one of the biggest profit shares with employees in European corporate history.'

But Mrs Smith warned: 'There is still a huge amount to do. Transforming our operations, cutting our costs and, above all, winning the support of our people for the modernisation plan with its top priority being to improve customer service, has been National Mail's greatest achievement in decades.

But competing successfully in an open mail market is going to be even more difficult. We've a mountain to climb and we've only reached the base camp.

The greatest challenge now is to bring about a complete culture change in National Mail. We need everyone in the company focused on ensuring that we consistently deliver high quality, value-for-money services that customers need and want. Competition has arrived and customers have a choice; so we need to prove that National Mail is the best and our people are key to that' said Mrs Smith.

The company, she said, was also facing other daunting hurdles:

National Mail will have to generate sufficient profit to pay millions of pounds into its pension fund to tackle the €2.5 billion deficit, the 14,609-strong network of Letter and Parcel Office (LPO) branches made a loss on its operations last year of €110 million. Its rural network of 8,037 branches is fundamentally uneconomic and needs an injection of €3 million a week to survive. However, with the current annual Government funding of €150 million due to end in 20X3, Letter and Parcel Office Ltd cannot be expected to absorb extra costs at this level.

National Mail lags behind its major rivals in automated sorting technology. It needs to make a several billion euro investment if it is to compete successfully and that means being more profitable to invest. However, the 8.6% return on its domestic letters business last year compares with the 16.4% Fast Post (a major postal service in another European country) makes in its home market, and 22.2% made by RNT Post Group (a commercial postal service).

National Mail's Chief Executive at the time, Craig Thomas, also stressed the challenges ahead.

'The huge task now facing National Mail is to make the cultural change needed to succeed as a commercial business and to become the postal operator of choice for customers in an open competitive market.

Our vision remains to be demonstrably the best and most trusted mail company in the world. With the dedication and commitment of our people, we are confident we can achieve our goal.

October 20X8

'Since 20X0 the National Mail has undergone some significant changes. In October 20X8, the government controversially sold off the National Mail for €3.3 billion. The flotation saw a significant number of National Mail employees (15,000) purchase shares in the company. In May 20X9, it was reported in the press that National Mail was embroiled in a row with the postal regulator over the company's ability to meet its obligations to provide a 'universal postal-delivery service'. National Mail's commitment to the universal postal-delivery service requires it to deliver post to all addresses in its country six days a week.

It was also reported that at the same time as she unveiled a 12% rise in full-year operating profits to €671 million, National Mail's Chief Executive, Sandra Khan, warned that there is a prospect that National Mail will not be able to sustain a commercial rate of return if it maintains its commitment to deliver mail to all of the country's homes six days a week.

A spokesman for the regulator commented 'we do not believe there is presently a threat to the financial sustainability of the universal postal service. National Mail should take appropriate steps to respond to the challenge of competition, including improving efficiency'.

When the government sold off the National Mail in 20X8 it guaranteed that it would continue with its universal six day service.

A press release concerning the National Mail's 20X8/X9 financial results noted the following comments made by Sandra Khan.

'Our performance was in line with our expectations. We delivered 2% revenue growth, controlled operating costs and drove strong free cash flow. We are facing a couple of key issues. The competitive environment on the parcels side is more intense. We are taking steps to remain the leader in this growing market. On the letters side, the main issue is direct delivery and we have strategies in place to counter its adverse financial impact. However, without timely regulatory action, direct delivery could undermine the economics of the universal service and our ability to generate sustainably a 5-10% EBIT margin in our reported business .

Our key value drivers of single digit revenue growth, margin expansion and underlying free cash flow growth remain the objectives for the Group for the 20X8-X9 financial year'.

Below are a selection of key highlights from the National Mail's press release:

- 'Group revenue increased by 2%, due to parcel revenue growth. Parcels are the largest contributor to Group revenue, accounting for 51%.

- Group operating profit before transformation costs grew to €671 million.

- Transformation costs of €241 million for the year include a provision of €104 million in relation to the management reorganisation programme, announced on 25 March 20X9, which will be implemented post 20X9.

- The Board has recommended a final dividend of 13.3 cents per share, subject to shareholder approval at the Annual General Meeting, to be held on 24 July 20X9.

- Based on our estimates of the impact of RNT Post's publicly-stated plans, direct delivery could reduce National Mail revenue by over £200 million in the next 10 years.

Summary outlook

We are facing increasing challenges in the parcels and letters markets.

National Mail's annual report 20X8/X9 highlighted a number of initiatives the company has undertaken to boost its performance. It has acknowledged the decline in the number of letters now being posted, and has moved to streamline its operations, with plans to reduce the number of people it employs by 1,300 over the coming year.

In May 20X8, the company unveiled an agreement it has entered into with the Letter and Parcel Office (LPO) to offer retailers and customers the option of having parcels delivered to a local LPO branch ready for collection. The 'local click and collect' service has led National Mail to modernise a number of its operations.

National Mail also invested €70 million in the year on improving its business mail operations. And it intends to introduce barcode technology to allow business customers to track their parcels prior to delivery.

Interactive question 2: Transforming the National Mail

Consider the cultural change described in the final paragraphs of the National Mail press release from 20X0 and the steps taken to respond to the deregulation of the postal service.

Requirement

2.1 Apply the activities of the Gemini 4Rs approach to this change. Refer to the information provided in respect of the period 20X8/X9, where relevant, for evidence of how successfully the various elements of the 4 Rs framework have been applied.

See **Answer** at the end of this chapter.

3 Change and the individual

Section overview

- Understanding the implications of change for the individual is essential to a change agent or other would-be 'midwife' of change.

- The way the individual views the change will be influenced by the manner of its introduction and the forces driving it and restraining it.

3.1 How change affects individuals

Change may affect individuals in several areas.

- **Physiological** changes: pattern of shift-working, location of place of work

- **Circumstantial** changes: unlearning previous knowledge and learning new ways of doing things, new work-mates, using new IT/IS

- **Psychological** changes: feelings of disorientation, insecurity, changing relationships etc

3.2 Reactions to proposed change

The importance of staff support during a change programme should not be underestimated. We look here in more detail at the barriers to change they may cause to arise.

3.2.1 Cultural barriers

Structural inertia is the cumulative effect of all the systems and procedures the organisation has installed over the years to ensure consistency and quality. These act as barriers to change. For example, selection processes systematically select certain kinds of people; promotion processes regularly reward certain kinds of people.

Group inertia may block change where changes are inconsistent with team/departmental norms, or where they threaten to make skills and expertise of a particular professional or skill group less important or even redundant.

Power structures may be threatened by the redistribution of decision-making authority or resources, or the re-routing of lines of communication.

3.2.2 Personnel barriers

In addition to cultural barriers, there are also barriers which affect individuals and result in them seeing the change as a threat.

- Habit, because habitual ways of work are hard to change, and the new and unknown is often uncomfortable.

- Security is almost inevitably threatened – job security and the security of familiarity.

- Effect on earnings may be considerable: impact on promotion and income.

- Fear of the unknown reduces people's willingness and interest in learning new skills and processes; they may lack the confidence to take on a new challenge.

- Selective information processing results in employees choosing what to hear and what to ignore; they can then use their selected information to justify their position and ignore management argument for change.

3.2.3 The psychological contract

The psychological contract is the 'deal' between employer and employee. It covers the full set of expectations each party has of the other.

On either side of the contract, there are offers and wants.

EMPLOYER		EMPLOYEE
OFFERS:		**WANTS:**
Certain pay levels.		Certain pay levels.
Certain benefit levels.		Certain benefit levels.
Job design which offers particular opportunities for responsibility and learning.	Match	Particular opportunities for responsibility and learning.
Availability of promotion.		Access to promotion/or not.
Working conditions of a certain quality.		Desire for particular level of conditions.
Opportunities for close relationships.		Desire for close working relationships.
Style of management.		Style of being managed.
WANTS:		**OFFERS:**
Particular skills, experience, attitudes.	Match	Particular skills, experience, attitudes.
Particular level of commitment.		Capacity level of commitment.
Particular quality of contribution.		Capacity for contribution.

The contract works if offers and wants match. The selection process is the means both parties use to assess the initial match. The promotion process is the means used to check the ongoing match. In addition, both parties continuously monitor the match. The model is dynamic, any change in one part triggers changes in others. If a change programme threatens any item listed under employer offers, the employee will reconsider what they offer as their part of the deal. If the employee believes that their offers will be made wholly or partially redundant by the changes, they will anticipate that their wants will no longer be satisfied.

3.2.4 Identification of pressure points

Two important pressure points can develop in the psychological contract during times of change.

- **Lack of appropriate skill levels**: this can happen if the employer fails to reconsider how employee wants will alter as a result of changes, or if the employer fails to redesign their offers to ensure these attract and encourage the right kind of people needed in the new set-up.

- **Declining staff morale**: the driver of employee performance is the human emotions which underlie employee wants. These wants express personal motives, desires, ambitions and needs and determine people's commitment to the changes.

A change programme must be preceded by a review of:

- New competences and qualities required
- Selection processes to ensure they identify the above
- Promotion processes to ensure they identify the above

A change plan must include a staff development plan covering:

- Communication of implications for jobs
- Communication of required skills
- Discussions about individual development needs/options
- Learning and training opportunities
- Opportunities for making a contribution to changes

Worked example: Teachers' performance-related pay

It is interesting to set side by side the comments made by a Department of Education spokesperson and the General Secretary of the National Union of Teachers in a developed country regarding the introduction of performance-related pay. It isn't difficult to tell which is which!

- 'There is strong support from teachers across the country for our plans to let schools pay good teachers more. This year schools will be able to reward the most effective teachers who get the best out of their pupils with higher pay. We already have the best generation of teachers ever, and the changes that we are making to teachers' pay arrangements will further raise the status of the profession and encourage more great people into teaching'.

- 'Despite the spin, this research proves again that teachers oppose the government's new performance-related pay measures. Historically movement up the pay scale was linked to seniority and increasing professional skills and competence. It is hardly surprising, therefore, that teachers continue to favour the previous system, which is transparently fairer and less open to biased judgements. While effective appraisal linked to professional development is useful, provided it encourages collaboration, this will not be achieved by the new pay system'.

3.3 Introducing the change

Three factors for managers to consider when dealing with resistance to change.

- The **pace** of change
- The **manner** of change
- The **scope** of change

3.3.1 Pace

Given time, people can get used to the idea of new methods – can get acclimatised at each stage, with a consequent confidence in the likely success of the change programme, and in the individual's own ability to cope.

- Presenting the individuals concerned with a *fait accompli* may short-circuit resistance at the planning and immediate implementation stages. But it may cause a withdrawal reaction (akin to 'shock'), if the change is radical and perceived as threatening, and this is likely to surface later, as the change is consolidated – probably strengthened by resentment.

- **Timing** will also be crucial: those responsible for change should be sensitive to incidents and attitudes that might indicate that 'now is not the time'.

3.3.2 Manner

The manner in which a change is put across is very important: the climate must be prepared, the need made clear, fears soothed, and if possible the individuals concerned positively motivated to embrace the changes as their own.

- **Resistance should be welcomed and confronted**, not swept under the carpet. Talking through areas of conflict may lead to useful insights and the adapting of the programme of change to advantage. Repressing resistance will only send it underground, into the realm of rumour and covert hostility.

- **There should be free circulation of information** about the reasons for the change, its expected results and likely consequences. That information should appear sensible, clear, consistent and realistic: there is no point issuing information which will be seen as a blatant misrepresentation of the situation.

- **The change must be sold to the people concerned**: People must be convinced that their attitudes and behaviours need changing. Objections must be overcome, but it is also possible to get people behind the change in a positive way. If those involved understand that there is a real problem, which poses a threat to the organisation and themselves, and that the solution is a sensible one and will solve that problem, there will be a firm rational basis, for implementing change. The people should also be reassured that they have the learning capacity, the ability and the resources to implement the plan. It may even be possible to get them really excited about it by emphasising the challenge and opportunity by injecting an element of competition or simply offering rewards and incentives.

- **Individuals must be helped to learn**, that is, to change their attitudes and behaviours. Few individuals will really be able to see the big picture in a proposed programmed of change. To put across the overall objective, the organisation should use **visual aids** to help conceptualise. Learning programmes for any new skills or systems necessary will have to be designed according to the abilities of the individuals concerned.

- The effects of **insecurity**, perceived **helplessness**, and therefore **resentment**, may be lessened if the people can be **involved** in the planning and implementation of the change, that is, if it is not perceived to have been imposed from above.

3.3.3 Scope

The scope of change should be carefully reviewed. Total transformation will create greater insecurity – but also greater excitement, if the organisation has the kind of innovative culture that can stand it – than moderate innovation. There may be hidden changes to take into account: a change in technology may necessitate changes in work methods, which may in turn result in the breaking up of work groups. Management should be aware of how many various aspects of their employees' lives they are proposing to alter – and therefore on how many fronts they are likely to encounter resistance.

3.4 Force field analysis

There is a technique developed by Lewin to visualise the change process called **force field analysis** It is based on the idea that in any group or organisational situation there is an **interplay of restraining and driving forces that keeps things in equilibrium**.

Lewin's **force field analysis** maps the forces that are pushing **toward the preferred state** and the restraining forces, which are **pushing back to the current state**. They can then be presented in a chart.

The example below describes a public sector organisation whose management are introducing a performance review system. A group of workers are producing at 70% of the efficiency that might be expected on purely technical grounds. Their output can be visualised as a **balance** between two opposing sets of forces, ie, **driving forces** which are propelling their output upwards and **restraining forces** which are preventing it from going beyond the 70% level.

The role of change management is to help

- Weaken the resisting forces
- Strengthen the driving forces

The Lewin/Schein three-step (unfreeze-move-refreeze) approach is one way to do this.

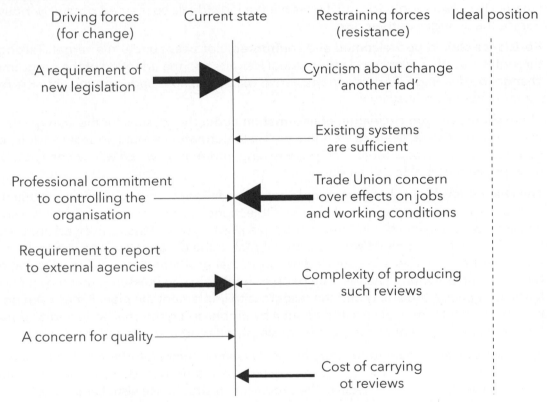

Arrow sizes denote the relative strength of the forces.

(Diagram: Illustration of the force field analysis model)

Interactive question 3: Gerrard, Dudek & Smicer

Gerrard, Dudek & Smicer are a small long established firm of solicitors. They have recently appointed Eva, a new business development manager. She has suggested that the firm introduce electronic diaries as staff often don't know where to find each other. Secretaries also struggle to book meetings as the partners often keep their agendas with them, which has annoyed some key clients. However, the partners are extremely reluctant to consider such a departure from their current methods.

3.1 Using Lewin's force field model, analyse the above situation and suggest how the new manager could bring about the change she wants.

See **Answer** at the end of this chapter.

3.5 Communicating change

Stakeholder	Their needs	What they want to know	How to communicate
Shareholders	Reassurance	That there is well thought-through strategy. How the strategy will benefit them	The press Financial statements AGM Website
The press	A good story	What is happening, the rationale, and whether the changes are under control	Briefings
Suppliers	Information	How the changes will affect their working relationship	Meetings face-to-face with major suppliers Letters/email to small suppliers
Customers	Motivation	That the service will continue uninterrupted	The press Advertisements
Senior managers	Acknowledgement and involvement	How they will be involved and opportunities in the new structure. Reassurance over employment positions	One-to-one meetings
Staff	Help to adapt	Training and support Job security	Briefings One-to-one with line manager
Line managers	Involvement	Opportunities to be involved and opportunities to learn	Briefings One-to-one with senior manager/HR

Interactive question 4: Burgermania

Company background

Burgermania plc (hereafter Burgermania) is the world's largest fast food chain. The company has 30,000 restaurants in over 100 countries, and has been committed to opening over 700 new restaurants each year in recent times. The company has benefited from consumers wanting quick and filling foodstuffs, and has met this need with its style of product for both adults and children. The company has also had many tie-in arrangements with sports and films, to encourage consumers to buy its product range. The range is very limited, focussing mainly on burgers, fries and soft drinks. There are occasional variations in some countries. This approach has proved popular with consumers who have conservative tastes and are happy to know that the food will be of a consistent quality wherever it is sold.

The company operates mainly via a combination of owned and franchised restaurants. Franchisees sign a 15-year deal in which they are given the right to use Burgermania trademarks, restaurant decor designs, formulae and specifications for menu items, use of Burgermania's inventory control systems, bookkeeping, accounting, marketing and the right to occupy the restaurant premises.

In return the franchisee agrees to operate the business in accordance with Burgermania's standards of quality, service, cleanliness and value. The company is anxious to avoid any negative publicity, so it employs 'secret shoppers' who randomly visit and assess restaurants on the above criteria. The company pays relatively low wages and has high staff turnover; this has prevented Burgermania being able to recruit high calibre staff, as the image of the jobs offered is poor.

Recent events

The company has had stagnant profits and sales growth in the last two years. The main reasons for this are increased health concerns in its major geographical markets. The company's products are high in both fat and carbohydrate content, and stories in the media about preventable obesity, heart disease, diabetes and cancer have caused turnover to falter. Furthermore, new style diets, whilst promoting meat consumption, have discouraged many consumers from eating bread or fries due to their high carbohydrate content. Initially Burgermania claimed that its products were nutritious and healthy, but this policy was deemed to be a failure as it did not reverse the stagnation of sales. Some high profile legal claims against the company from consumers claiming that Burgermania products caused health problems have also had a negative impact on the company's image.

The company has decided at board level to respond to this deterioration in its financial performance by introducing and promoting a healthier menu, with options that include burgers but no burger buns, chicken and fish based products, grilled rather than fried meats, salads, fruit and healthier drinks, as well as phasing out extra large portions of food on its menu. The directors want to give more autonomy to individual restaurant managers to offer a wider range of products that will vary between different locations.

In addition, the board intend to change the company name to 'Eatwise' to move away from the association with burgers and fries. The cost of changing all the company, logos, livery, advertising campaigns and cooking equipment is expected to be massive. Staff will also will have to be trained to use the new equipment and promote healthy eating to customers. The company is uncertain how the public and franchisees will respond to these changes in the business. Moreover, Burgermania is under pressure to deliver improved financial performance as its share price has underperformed that of the overall stock market by 20% in the last 18 months.

Requirements

4.1 Identify the type of change that Burgermania is considering.

4.2 Outline the potential barriers to the proposed changes from:

   (a) Franchisees
   (b) Restaurant staff
   (c) Customers

4.3 Prepare a draft blueprint for submission to the board of directors of Burgermania that details how the company will deal with the changes of menus and name.

4.4 Suggest ways in which the company can communicate successfully the changes to customers, franchisees and shareholders.

See **Answer** at the end of this chapter.

Summary and Self-test

Summary

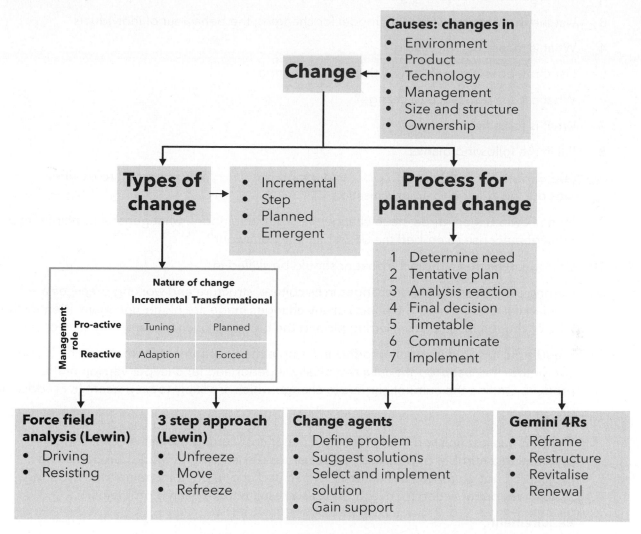

Change ← **Causes: changes in**
- Environment
- Product
- Technology
- Management
- Size and structure
- Ownership

Types of change →
- Incremental
- Step
- Planned
- Emergent

Nature of change

	Incremental	Transformational
Pro-active	Tuning	Planned
Reactive	Adaption	Forced

(Management role)

Process for planned change

1 Determine need
2 Tentative plan
3 Analysis reaction
4 Final decision
5 Timetable
6 Communicate
7 Implement

Force field analysis (Lewin)
- Driving
- Resisting

3 step approach (Lewin)
- Unfreeze
- Move
- Refreeze

Change agents
- Define problem
- Suggest solutions
- Select and implement solution
- Gain support

Gemini 4Rs
- Reframe
- Restructure
- Revitalise
- Renewal

Self-test

Answer the following questions.

1   List the three levels at which organisational development/change efforts may focus.

2   'An organisation enjoying good profitability should not consider change.' TRUE or FALSE?

3   List the three stages of Lewin's model for changing the behaviour of individuals.

4   What is meant by 'refreezing'?

5   List three possible problems with coercive change.

6   What causes resistance to change?

7   What is force field analysis?

8   Fill in the following blanks.

(a)C..................., (b)c................... and (c)c................... play important roles when introducing change to an organisation.

9   In the Lewin/Schein three-stage change management model, what general principle does management use to embed the desirable new behaviour?

10   List four areas that a project manager should be skilled in.

11   Herring plc is in crisis. Major changes in its culture, structure and working practices are needed if it is to survive. The effects of any changes made are highly uncertain. Identify the type of change involved for Herring plc and the best approach to managing such change.

12   Freddis plc has sold its single product in a single market segment for many years. It's only competitor has just brought out a technically superior and far cheaper version of the product. Outline the cultural barriers to change which are likely to be present in Freddis plc.

13   **Plant Ltd**

Plant Ltd has just finished implementing a major cost cutting project which involved automating a number of previously paper processes across the whole company. The project did not go as well as had been hoped and at one point the telephone ordering system was out of action for over a week as a result of unexpected problems.

Requirement

Explain how this type of change could be categorised. What kind of investigation is likely to be instigated as a result of the problems that occurred?

14   **Timbermate Ltd**

After a difficult few years trading, a new Chief Executive, Brian Parsons, has been appointed to the board of Timbermate Ltd. A large divisionalised company, it specialises in the production of wood-based products, from plywood and chipboard, to kitchens and conservatory windows.

Parsons in his initial press interview made it clear that the costs incurred by the business were far too high and that efficiency and productivity were unacceptably low. He has made clear his intention to turn the business around. However, there have already been rumblings from the union to which most of the workers belong. They are not prepared to negotiate over wages or working conditions.

Timbermate is a major importer of wood. Russian and Scandinavian joinery redwood, together with spruce from North America, make up a high percentage of imports. They also import from the Baltic States. Although sterling is strong against the dollar it has been struggling lately against the other currencies. There have been signs that some of Timbermate's overseas suppliers are considering expanding into the UK directly. There has also been an increase in the popularity of UPVC alternatives in a number of Timbermate's core business areas.

A number of operational issues need addressing. Recently, complaints about quality and product specification have become more common. Additionally the delivery fleet has become less reliable and several key customers have been let down. However many of the senior managers do not seem unduly concerned. They often talk about historic problems in the timber trade and how these problems are just part of the nature of the industry. They rarely stay at their desks after 5pm. There is little in the way of knowledge sharing and it is unusual for staff in any one division to even know the names of staff in the others.

One key pillar of Parson's plan is to introduce a fully integrated information system, covering (amongst others) inventory control and e-procurement, computer aided design and manufacture, resource planning and management accounting. The system is to operate across all the divisions and allow potential cross-selling and better customer management.

Requirements

14.1 Analyse the forces for and against change at Timbermate Ltd.
14.2 Recommend to Brian Parsons how he might best manage the change process.

15 Read the scenario of the **March 2013 Business Strategy and Technology** question in the Question Bank entitled *Chiba*. Draft an answer to the requirement on change management issues.

16 Read the scenario of the **March 2015 Business Strategy and Technology** question in the Question Bank entitled *Rocket Co*. Draft an answer to the requirement which asks for a discussion of best practice in change management.

17 Read the scenario of the **June 2017 Business Strategy and Technology** question in the Question Bank entitled *Jason Smyth Textiles Ltd (JST)*. Draft an answer to the requirement which asks for an explanation of the change management issues for JST.

Now go back to the Learning outcomes in the Introduction. If you are satisfied you have achieved this objective, please tick it off.

Answers to Interactive questions

Answer to Interactive question 1

1.1 (a) **International car maker**

Forced: The car maker is reacting to external competitive and environmental changes. Such a change may result in significant changes in the way the company is structured.

(b) **Supermarket retailer**

Planned: It is proactive, aimed at seizing an opportunity. Furthermore, the change is anticipated to have a far reaching impact on the existing business model. The large size of the foreign market will change the character of the retailer in terms of size but also its global profile.

Answer to Interactive question 2

2.1 **Reframing**

The major reframing is the term 'commercial business' which implies making profits as the primary goal, or at least providing as good a service as competitors in a de-regulated environment.

The ensuing strong emphasis on profits and termination of loss-making activities underlines this.

The challenge for management would be to make this a goal that staff wished to support. The government's decision in 20X8 to sell off National Mail appears to have been well received by employees, with 15,000 choosing to purchase shares. This change in the ownership structure of the National Mail is likely to be positive in aligning the aims of the company with its employees.

Restructuring

Although not obviously stated in the 20X0 press release, references to automated sorting suggest changes were required here. The points raised from the 20X8/X9 annual report indicate that National Mail is attempting to automate and enhance its current operations in response to changes in the demand for its services.

Revitalising

In 20X0, Jennifer Smith recognised the challenge of adapting to the new competitive environment: 'Competing successfully in an open mail market is going to be even more difficult. We've a mountain to climb and we've only reached the base camp.' The 20X8/X9 annual report explains how National Mail is looking to increase it's use of technology to respond to the change in the nature of the marketplace and the increasing competition.

Renewal

The statements from 20X0 are clearly inclusive and emphasise the importance of gaining staff commitment... "with the dedication and support of our people''. The offer of shares to employees as part of the 20X8 flotation might be seen as a further attempt to gain support from staff.

Answer to Interactive question 3

3.1 Driving forces for change: Technological developments raising customer expectation, irritated customers, new innovative staff member.

Restraining forces: Partners' habits and possible fear of the unknown, possible concerns over expense.

Eva should strengthen the driving forces by stressing to the partners the level of clients' concerns and gain the support of the secretaries in encouraging the partners to consider the system.

The restraining forces should be weakened by producing costings, and explaining clearly how the system would work and what benefits would arise.

Answer to Interactive question 4

4.1 Type of change

Burgermania is undertaking a change in the business that would be deemed revolutionary in terms of impact on the business. Both the process and the underlying paradigm of the company will have to change. The retraining and rebranding of the business suggests a low degree of predictability, as it will be difficult to anticipate the reaction of stakeholders, especially customers, to the proposed changes.

4.2 Barriers to change

(a) **Franchisees**

- Franchisees will fear that new system is too radical and may have detrimental impact on revenues of restaurants.

- They may fear that costs of changing name and livery of the restaurants will be recovered by Burgermania in the form of higher franchise fees.

- Franchisees will be reluctant to change to a new system of delivering food if they are happy with current products and procedures.

- They may lack initiative when it comes to introducing new products that they can add to the menu.

(b) **Restaurant staff**

- Staff in fast food restaurants tend to be poorly paid and have short periods of employment. Therefore they may be reluctant to be retrained or adopt a pro-active policy with customers in terms of promoting the new healthier food lines.

- Staff may feel that if Burgermania is suffering then jobs may be lost – likely to cause demotivation.

- Staff may fear that management will use the change as a means of introducing new working practices that could reduce income, overtime, bonuses etc.

- Staff may lack the skills to adapt to the new nature of the business.

- The decision is likely to be enforced by coercion if necessary due to Burgermania's poor recent results, potential for conflict and resentment by staff.

(c) **Customers**

- Customers are more concerned with being fed quickly than with the quality of what they eat, so may choose to go elsewhere. Many people have conservative tastes and so will be reluctant to try the new products on offer.

- They may feel that the new products are being forced on them and again vote with their feet by eating at other fast food restaurants.

4.3 Draft blueprint

To   Board of directors, Burgermania plc
From B. Cowie, consultant
Date Today

Subject Blueprint for menu and name changes

Action required

- Introduction of healthier menus and local autonomy
- Launch of new name/brand for the company

Purpose

- The objective of the changes is as follows.

    - To reverse the decline in the company's performance.
    - To adapt to changes in consumer demands and tastes.
    - To promote the company as a family-friendly and healthy eating place.

Timing of changes

- Given the nature of the company's products and positioning in the market, a national change will have to be launched if it wants to maximise publicity for the changes. The company could try introducing the new menus on a trial basis in selected restaurants.

- The transformation will be very time-consuming given the global nature of the company and its products.

Responsibilities

- A committee needs to be formed to co-ordinate the changes, headed by a senior manager/director.

Evaluation

- Market research needs to be undertaken to establish public reaction to both the menu and name changes.

- Performance data can be produced to determine the popularity of the new food products on a trial basis in selected stores.

4.4 Communication of changes

- Franchisees could be invited to a conference to see the new 'Eatwise' logos and product range.

- A major PR campaign, with TV, radio and press adverts should take place to coincide with the changes to advise customers. Perhaps special promotions relating to the new products could be used to encourage customers to try them out.

- Shareholders could be briefed via email and the company's website, together with press releases in the financial media.

Answers to Self-test

1 Individual; organisation structure and systems; organisation climate and interpersonal style.

2 FALSE. Organisations should embrace change, and not wait until the obsolescence of their current practices leads to crisis.

3 Unfreeze, change (or move) and refreeze.

4 The final stage of the Lewin/Schein three-stage approach in which the desired new behaviour is consolidated.

5 Underestimating resistance; not coercing hard enough or long enough; failure to ensure implementation.

6 Attitudes, beliefs, loyalties, habits and norms, politics.

7 Lewin's analysis of the driving and restraining forces which underlie any group or organisational equilibrium.

8 (a) Commitment, (b) co-ordination and (c) communication.

9 Reinforcement – both positive and negative.

10 Four of:
- Leadership
- Team building
- Organisation
- Communication
- Technical expertise
- Personal qualities

11 Revolutionary change

Approach – emergent, ie, flexibility is essential.

12 Structural inertia – systems and procedures are likely to have been in place for many years.

Group inertia – production and marketing departments, for example, may resist change (probably used to doing things in the same way for many years).

Power structures – lack of pressure to change in the past may have resulted in clear lines of decision making authority and/or control over resources.

13 **Plant Ltd**

The change could be categorised as reconstruction – it affects the entire organisation, but does not appear to require a paradigm shift.

A post-project audit would be required. It would be carried out by an independent team who would review all elements of the project process in detail to identify why the problems arose.

14 **Timbermate Ltd**

14.1 **Forces for and against change**

Forces for change

The forces for change in Timbermate appear to be both external and internal.

External factors would include:

- Overseas competitors: current suppliers may be able to undercut Timbermate if they set up their own operations in the UK. It will be essential for them to bring down their own cost base to survive.

- Exchange rates: weakening sterling will make imports more expensive, putting up Timbermate's costs still further.

- Growth in plastic alternatives may reduce demand in a number of key areas. Unless they can fight back, share will be lost, reducing economies of scale and brand strength.

Internal factors would include:

- Brian Parsons' determination to make the changes needed.

- Customers: increasing dissatisfaction with the current standard of service has already given rise to complaint and may, if not addressed, lead to loss of current customers and brand image.

- Shareholders: a period of poor results cannot have been satisfactory for the shareholders which is presumably why they have appointed Parsons.

Forces against change

- Attitude of managers: the managers lack a sense of urgency and are therefore likely to resist any major change programme as unnecessarily disruptive.

- Attitude of staff: it is likely that the laid back culture permeates the whole organisation and staff may not understand the need for change. They will undoubtedly also be fearful for their jobs.

- Unions have already expressed their intention to resist any changes to wages or working conditions. This could lead to walk-outs and strikes.

14.2 Managing change

A useful method of managing change was proposed by Lewin. This divides the process of change into three stages, unfreezing, changing and refreezing.

Unfreezing

The forces for change must be used to encourage the change, and the forces against it must be weakened. Methods might include:

Carrying out a PEST analysis to identify the exact nature of the threats from the outside environment (issues such as deforestation may also have potential impact and have been overlooked).

These issues and their consequences should then be stressed to the managers. Forecasts of market performance (and its impact on bonuses) if no change is made should be communicated. Workshops to involve senior managers in the process may help them to appreciate the urgency of the situation.

Consultation and negotiation with the unions will have to be entered into. They will need to be persuaded of the importance of change now to protect jobs in the future.

Change

The new information system must be introduced. Training in all aspects will be required – not just in how to use the system, but in its potential benefits, so that staff start to identify ways in which it could further improve business.

New working practices will need to be introduced. Some processes may need re-engineering.

Greater collaboration between different divisions needs to be encouraged.

Efforts must be made to change the culture of the organisation. Stories about problems being caused by economic cycles that can be ignored, rituals such as leaving work on the dot, and an organisation structure so rigid that there is little or no horizontal communication suggests a 'jobs worth' paradigm where bureaucracy has taken on all its worst characteristics. Whilst education may start the process, it may be necessary to remove those managers who are unwilling or unable to change.

Refreezing

This is the process of trying to ensure planned changes become the norm.

Reward systems should be developed to focus on issues such as cost management, customer satisfaction, productivity and innovation.

Continual training: The staff should be given regular training updates to deepen their understanding of the new system.

Communication: Interdivisional meetings should be scheduled on a monthly basis. The agenda should be shared problem solving and sharing of best practice. It may be that major customers should be provided with a single point of contact, who will then liaise with all divisions on their behalf (a matrix structure within the divisional one).

15 Refer to the answer to Chiba in the Question Bank.

16 Refer to the answer to Rocket Co in the Question Bank.

17 Refer to the answer to Jason Smyth Textiles Ltd in the Question Bank

CHAPTER 16

Ethics, sustainability and corporate responsibility

Introduction

Examination context

TOPIC LIST

Introduction

Learning outcomes

- Analyse for a given situation the external factors which may impact upon an organisation's performance and position, identifying significant issues in areas such as sustainability, including natural capital and stakeholder impact ☐

- Explain the ethical factors to be considered in determining the scope and nature of an organisation's objectives and its strategic analysis, having regard to the legitimate interests of all stakeholder groups ☐

- Show, in a given scenario, how an organisation chooses from competing strategies in order to maximise the achievement of its key objectives, including those relating to technology, corporate responsibility and sustainability ☐

- Evaluate the ethical implications of an organisation's strategies and operations for the organisation and for individuals (including the accountant in business and others), including ethical considerations in the use of data ☐

- Evaluate the ethical implications of how an organisation chooses to implement and modify its strategies, suggesting appropriate courses of action to resolve ethical dilemmas that may arise ☐

Specific syllabus references for this chapter are 1b, 1h, 2e, 2f, 3k.

Syllabus links

Some coverage was given in your Business, Technology and Finance studies to the policies that can be used to help ensure an organisation acts ethically, in addition to issues of sustainability and corporate responsibility. The knowledge from Business, Technology and Finance is developed further in Business Strategy and Technology and applied in the context of different business scenarios. At Advanced Stage sustainability and corporate responsibility are integrated into the technical areas of the syllabus.

This chapter also considers how best to apply knowledge of ethics, sustainability and corporate responsibility in the exam, in the context of a specific scenario. This is an approach which will help you in developing the necessary skills to make ethical judgements at Advanced Stage.

Examination context

Ethics

At least one of the exam scenarios is likely to include an ethical issue or dilemma, possibly in the context of the ethics of an organisation or in relation to a professional accountant working in business. Between 7 and 10 marks of the exam will be allocated to the appropriate discussion of such ethical issues, but they are often not clear cut. The important skills here are for you to develop a balanced argument, use appropriate ethical language and have regard to any relevant professional principles.

Scenarios might include topics such as:

- Conflict between the accountant's professional obligations and their responsibilities to the organisation.

- Lack of professional independence eg, personal financial interest in business proposals.

- Conflicts of interest among stakeholders.

- Attempts to intentionally mislead key stakeholders (by disclosure or non-disclosure of information.)

- Doubtful accounting or commercial business practice.

- Facilitation of unethical strategies.
- Inappropriate pressure to achieve a result.
- Actions contrary to law, regulation and/or technical and professional standards.
- The ethical usage of data or technology.

In Question 1 of the September 2016 exam (*Guayaporto Ltd*) the scenario contained information about a company based in South America, which manufactured discs (CDs and DVDs) for businesses in the entertainment and education sectors. As a result of technological developments, the market for discs was declining, and the company's financial performance had deteriorated. Customers provided the company with confidential data files from which a master-disc template was created. The company outsourced the production of the master-disc to an Asian supplier. Two proposals to improve performance had been outlined in the scenario including one from the Sales Director. The Sales Director was keen to establish alternative revenue streams and had one specific proposal. Guayaporto Ltd produced a range of revision guides for Alegre, an educational publisher. A college had suggested that the company use Alegre's master-disc to produce its "own-brand" version of Alegre's material which the college would then buy directly from Guayaporto Ltd, at a lower price. The fourth requirement asked candidates to:

'Discuss the advantages and disadvantages of the proposals made by the Production Director and the Sales Director.'   **(12 marks)**

Identifying and explaining the ethical issues when presented with a scenario and requirement such as this is vitally important. To produce a good answer, you need to ensure that you give sufficient consideration to the proposals outlined in the scenario, and to highlight the ethical, and potential legal considerations which may be pertinent to your analysis of the proposals. Consideration of legal aspects was highly appropriate in this case, especially given the nature of the Sales Director's proposal.

In Question 2 of the December 2016 exam (*Zeter Domestic Chemicals plc*) the scenario focused on a manufacturer of domestic cleaning products, which had acquired a distribution company. The scenario featured an ethical issue relating to the CEO who had failed to disclose during the acquisition that his niece worked for the acquired entity. In response, the CEO has attempted to intimidate the Marketing Director not to disclose the situation to the rest of the board. The third requirement asked:

'Explain the ethical issues for David Xuan [CEO] and Kevin Hilton [Marketing Director] arising from their conversation. Set out the actions that they should each now take.'   **(8 marks)**

It is important when faced with requirements such as this that you clearly identify and explain the ethical issues raised by the scenario detail. To produce a good answer here you would need to ensure that you made use of appropriate ethical language including reference to honesty, transparency, objectivity and conflict of interest. Once you have considered the ethical issues it is then important that you build upon your answer by outlining the practical actions that both individuals featured should now take in response to the issues.

The requirements from the September 2016 and December 2016 exams highlight that ethics will always be set in the context of the scenario. Although the question may indicate clearly that there is an ethical issue, it can be tricky to tease out the exact nature of it. The key to a good answer is also to appreciate that ethical issues are unlikely to be black and white and that a balanced argument rather than a definitive 'right or wrong' answer is required. It is also worth noting that although the transparency, effect and fairness framework (discussed in greater detail in this chapter) may provide a structure for an answer, you need to exercise caution in trying to apply it to every scenario as it may cause you to overlook or omit important issues.

Corporate Responsibility and sustainability

Scenarios may consider how organisations create, embed and monitor a corporate responsibility (CR) strategy. Areas that might be examined in the context of sustainability and CR include:

- The involvement of key stakeholders in identifying objectives, conflicts of interest, and communication with such stakeholders

- The development of appropriate strategy and governance structures to implement CR

- Determination of appropriate KPIs to measure performance of the CR strategy

The examiners have noted that a significant number of candidates attempting the Business Strategy and Technology examination in recent sittings appear to specifically lack knowledge surrounding the concept of sustainability and sustainable enterprise. In Question 3 of the September 2014 exam (*Water On Tap*), the scenario focussed on a small social enterprise operating in central London which aimed to provide a cheaper and more sustainable alternative to bottled water. The first requirement asked candidates to:

'Discuss the extent to which Ontap is a sustainable enterprise.'   **(7 marks)**

When faced with question requirements like this it is important that your answer highlights those features which indicate a sustainable approach to conducting business. Sustainability with regard to Ontap does not just refer to social and environmental considerations but might also be extended to cover the financial sustainability of the venture and whether this is likely to be viable in the long term.

1 Strategy and ethics

Section overview

- Morals and ethics involve doing the 'right' thing. This may not always be the same as 'best for the individual manager' or 'best for the organisation as a whole'.

- Some ethical imperatives may be enshrined in laws but ethics and law are not the same thing.

- Ethical issues exist at the level of the individual, the business and, at its widest, corporate responsibility.

- A professional accountant is required to comply with the five fundamental principles of the ICAEW Code of Ethics.

- The Code provides guidance for the professional accountant working in business on how to identify, evaluate and address any threats to those fundamental principles and the safeguards to implement.

- The desire by management to act ethically affects the scope of strategies adopted but also requires that management keep an eye on the ethical consequences of its operations.

- Section 8 of this chapter gives guidance on how to approach ethics in the context of an examination question.

1.1 Ethics and morals

The meanings of the words 'ethics' and 'morals' are intermingled and difficult to distinguish. For example, the Concise Oxford Dictionary offers the following two definitions:

- **Morals** are 'standards of behaviour or principles of right and wrong'
- **Ethics** are 'the moral principles governing or influencing conduct'

Morals or ethics will also differ depending on the beliefs, value systems and norms of a particular society or culture. So ethics might be considered as:

Definition

Ethics: A system of behaviour which is deemed acceptable in the society or context under consideration.

Another area in which ethics can be invoked is Corporate Responsibility (CR) which is discussed in more detail later in this chapter.

For present purposes the field can be simplified by suggesting that business ethics exist at three levels.

1. **Personal ethical behaviour**

   This relates to the way you as an individual conduct yourself. Bad behaviour would include bullying, stealing, discrimination against a colleague and giving away business secrets to a rival.

2. **Business ethics**

   This is the way a firm as a whole behaves. Bad conduct here would include offering bribes to win contracts, distorting the accounts, victimisation or discrimination against certain workers and telling lies to regulators.

3. **Corporate responsibility**

    This is the belief that a firm owes a responsibility to society and its wider stakeholders, as well as to shareholders. Examples of bad behaviour would include pollution, mass redundancies and dangerous products.

1.2 Ethical stance of corporations

An organisation can adopt a range of ethical stances:

- Meet minimum legal obligations and concentrate on short-term shareholder interests.

- Recognise that long-term shareholder wealth may be increased by well-managed relationships with other stakeholders (corporate governance approach which was discussed in Chapter 9.)

- Go beyond minimum legal and corporate governance obligations to include explicitly the interests of other stakeholders in setting mission, objectives and strategy. In this context issues such as environmental protection, sustainability of resources, selling arms to tyrannical regimes, paying bribes to secure contracts, using child labour etc, would be considered.

- Public sector organisations, charities, etc, where the interests of shareholders are not relevant.

The ethical stance taken by an organisation is often reflected in its mission statement.

Worked example: Innocent Drinks

The following statement about ethics was taken from the Innocent Drinks website in 2016:

We sure aren't perfect, but we're trying to do the right thing.

It might make us sound a bit like a Miss World contestant, but we want to leave things a little bit better than we find them. We strive to do business in a more enlightened way, where we take responsibility for the impact of our business on society and the environment, and move these impacts from negative to neutral, or better still, positive. It's part of our quest to become a truly sustainable business.

Our Strategy

| brand | ingredients | production | packaging | legacy |

Source:

Innocent Drinks,(2016). *Innocent Drinks*. [Online]. Available from: www.innocentdrinks.co.uk [Accessed 8 June 2016].

1.3 Regulating ethical behaviour

Ethical business regulation operates in two ways:

1. **Forbidding or constraining certain types of conduct or decisions**: eg, most organisations have regulations forbidding ethically inappropriate use of their IT systems. Similarly many will forbid the offering or taking of inducements to secure contracts.

2. **Disclosure of certain facts or decisions**: eg, because the board sets its own pay they disclose it, and sometimes the reasons behind the awards, to shareholders in final accounts.

In other Professional Stage exams you will have been introduced to the following codes potentially binding on you as a trainee Chartered Accountant.

The Financial Reporting Council's (2016) Ethical Standard

You should recall from your Audit and Assurance studies that auditors are expected to comply with the Financial Reporting Council's (2016) Ethical Standard, which covers:

- Introduction and scope
- Part A: *Overarching Principles and Supporting Ethical Provisions*
- Part B:
  - Section 1: *General Requirements and Guidance*
  - Section 2: *Financial, Business, Employment and Personal Relationships*
  - Section 3: *Long Association with Engagements and with Entities Relevant to Engagements*
  - Section 4: *Fees, Remuneration and Evaluation Policies, Gifts and Hospitality, Litigation*
  - Section 5: *Non-Audit / Additional Services*
  - Section 6: *Provisions Available for Audits of Small Entities*

The ICAEW Code of Ethics for members

Five fundamental principles:

1. **Integrity**: straightforward and honest in business and professional relationships.

2. **Objectivity**: not allow bias, conflict of interest or influence of others to override professional or business judgement.

3. **Professional competence and due care**: be aware of all prevailing knowledge necessary to give professional service and apply the same diligently to affairs of the client in accordance with technical and professional standards.

4. **Confidentiality**: respect the confidentiality of information acquired as a consequence of professional or business engagements and not use the same for personal advantage or that of third parties.

5. **Professional behaviour**: comply with laws and regulations and not to discredit the profession.

Interactive question 1: Why have ethical standards?

1.1 The Codes of the ICAEW and of the FRC above seek to regulate the behaviour of accountants. Why do the bodies have these?

See **Answer** at the end of this chapter.

In the next section we explore in more detail how the ICAEW Code applies to both professional accountants working in business and those working in public practice.

1.4 ICAEW Code of Ethics for Professional accountants working in business

Investors, creditors, employers, the business community, government and the public may **rely** on the work of professional accountants in business in the context of:

- Preparation and reporting of financial and other information.
- Providing effective financial management.
- Competent advice on a variety of business-related matters.

The more senior the position held, the greater the ability and opportunity to influence events, practices and attitudes.

A professional accountant in business is expected to **encourage an ethics-based culture** in an employing organisation, that emphasises the importance that senior management places on ethical behaviour.

1.4.1 Threats

The Code outlines areas where there may be **conflict** for the professional accountant between furthering the legitimate aims of their organisation and their absolute duty to comply with the fundamental principles:

(a) **Self-interest** – financial interests, loans or guarantees; incentive compensation arrangements; inappropriate personal use of corporate assets; concern over employment security; commercial pressure from outside the employing organisation.

(b) **Self-review** – business decisions or data being subject to review and justification by the same professional accountant in business responsible for making those decisions or preparing that data.

(c) **Advocacy** – when furthering the legitimate goals and objectives of their employing organisations, professional accountants in business may promote the organisation's position, provided any statements made are neither false nor misleading. Such actions generally would not create an advocacy threat.

(d) **Familiarity** – a professional accountant in business in a position to influence financial or non-financial reporting or business decisions having an immediate or close family member who is in a position to benefit from that influence; long association with business contacts influencing business decisions; acceptance of a gift or preferential treatment, unless the value is clearly insignificant.

(e) **Intimidation** – threat of dismissal or replacement of the professional accountant in business or a close or immediate family member, over a disagreement about the application of an accounting principle or the way in which financial information is to be reported; a dominant personality attempting to influence the decision making process, for example with regard to the awarding of contracts or the application of an accounting principle.

1.4.2 Safeguards

To comply with the Code, professional accountants are required to consider whether their actions or relationships might constitute **threats** to their adherence to the fundamental principles and where these are significant, to implement **safeguards.**

These safeguards might be generic, created by the profession or regulation or developed in the working environment by the individual or their organisation.

If effective safeguards are not possible, they are required to **refrain** from the action or relationship in question.

The Code sets out the types of safeguards in the **work environment** which might be applied to overcome these threats:

- The employing organisation's systems of corporate oversight or other oversight structures.

- The employing organisation's ethics and conduct programs.

- Recruitment procedures in the employing organisation emphasising the importance of employing high calibre competent staff.

- Strong internal controls.

- Appropriate disciplinary processes.

- Leadership that stresses the importance of ethical behaviour and the expectation that employees will act in an ethical manner.

- Policies and procedures to implement and monitor the quality of employee performance.

- Timely communication of the employing organisation's policies and procedures, including any changes to them, to all employees, and appropriate training and education on such policies and procedures.

- Policies and procedures to empower and encourage employees to communicate to senior levels within the employing organisation any ethical issues that concern them without fear of retribution.

- Consultation with another appropriate professional accountant.

1.4.3 Action required in unethical circumstances

In circumstances where a professional accountant in business believes that unethical behaviour or actions by others will continue to occur within the employing organisation, they should consider seeking **legal advice**.

In extreme situations where all available safeguards have been exhausted and it is not possible to reduce the threat to an acceptable level, a professional accountant in business may conclude that it is appropriate to **disassociate** from the task and/or **resign** from the employing organisation.

1.5 Other ethical codes

Other ethical codes impacting on businesses include the *Sarbanes-Oxley Act* requirement, policed by US Securities and Exchanges Commission (SEC), that public corporations filing returns in the US have a Code of Ethics and that this should be detailed in their annual filings. It is described by SEC as **A codification of standards that is reasonably necessary to deter wrongdoing and to promote:**

1. Honest and ethical conduct, including the ethical handling of actual or apparent conflicts of interest between personal and professional relationships.

2. Avoidance of conflicts of interest, including disclosure to an appropriate person or persons identified in the code of any material transaction or relationship that reasonably could be expected to give rise to such a conflict.

3. Full, fair, accurate, timely, and understandable disclosure in reports and documents that a company files with, or submits to, the Commission and in other public communications made by the company.

4. Compliance with applicable governmental laws, rules and regulations.

5. The prompt internal reporting of code violations to an appropriate person or persons identified in the code; and accountability for adherence to the code.

Many firms use these headings to develop their own internal code of ethics for management.

1.6 ICAEW Code of Ethics for Professional accountants working in public practice

The following paragraphs are based on the ICAEW's Code of ethics for **accountants working in public practice**. They outline some of the threats that professional accountants may experience. It is important to note that the following section is not exhaustive but gives an indication of the types of issue that may arise in a Business Strategy and Technology exam question scenario.

1.6.1 Threats

(a) **Self-interest** – a firm or professional accountant having a financial interest in an assurance client; a firm which has undue dependence on fees from a client or fears losing a significant client; a firm which enters into a contingent fee arrangement with a client; a member of the firm enters into employment negotiations with a client; a firm which develops a significantly close relationship with a client; a professional accountant discovers a significant error when evaluating the results of professional services carried out in the past by a member of the firm.

(b) **Self-review** – a firm designs a financial reporting system and is then asked to issue an assurance report on the effectiveness of the same system, a firm which has prepared the original data used to produce records that are reviewed as part of an assurance engagement; a member of the assurance team has been a director of the client; a member of the assurance team has been employed by the client and is now able to significantly influence the subject matter of the engagement.

(c) **Advocacy** – the firm promotes shares in an audit client; the professional accountant acts as an advocate on behalf of a client in litigation.

(d) **Familiarity** – a member of the engagement team having an immediate or close family member who is a director or officer of the assurance client; a member of the engagement team having a close or immediate family member who is employed by the client who is in a position to significantly influence the subject matter of the engagement; a director or officer of the client or employee is in a position to exert significant influence over the subject matter having recently been the engagement partner at the firm providing assurance services; the acceptance by a member of the engagement team of gifts or preferential treatment from a client, unless the value is inconsequential; members having a long association with the assurance client.

(e) **Intimidation** – a firm which is threatened with dismissal by a client; an audit client indicating that it will not award non-assurance related work to the firm if the firm disagrees with the client's accounting treatment; a firm being threatened with legal action by a client; a firm being pressured to reduce fees; a professional accountant being pressured to agree with a member of the client's staff due to the employee's level of expertise on a particular matter.

1.6.2 Safeguards

The Code details the following **safeguards** relating to the professional accountant's work environment to overcome the threats explored above, these include:

- Leadership of the firm that stresses the importance of compliance with the fundamental principles.

- Leadership of the firm that establishes the expectation that members of an assurance team will act in the public interest.

- Documented policies regarding the need to identify threats to compliance with the fundamental principles, evaluate the significance of those threats, and apply safeguards to eliminate or reduce the threats to an acceptable level or, when appropriate safeguards are not available or cannot be applied, terminate or decline the relevant engagement.

- Policies and procedures that will enable the identification of interests or relationships between the firm or members of engagement teams and clients.

- Policies and procedures to monitor and, if necessary, manage the reliance on revenue received from a single client.

- Using different partners and engagement teams with separate reporting lines for the provision of non-assurance services to an assurance client.

- Policies and procedures to prohibit individuals who are not members of an engagement team from inappropriately influencing the outcome of the engagement.

- Timely communication of a firm's policies and procedures, including any changes to them, to all partners and professional staff, and appropriate training and education on such policies and procedures.

- A disciplinary mechanism to promote compliance with policies and procedures.

- Published policies and procedures to encourage and empower staff to communicate to senior levels within the firm any issue relating to compliance with the fundamental principles that concerns them.

The Code also sets out a number of engagement-specific safeguards which a firm can employ:

- Having a professional accountant who was not involved with the non-assurance service review the non-assurance work performed or otherwise advise as necessary.

- Having a professional accountant who was not a member of the assurance team review the assurance work performed or otherwise advise as necessary.

- Consulting an independent third party, such as a committee of independent directors, a professional regulatory body or another professional accountant.

- Discussing ethical issues with those charged with governance of the client.

- Disclosing to those charged with governance of the client the nature of services provided and extent of fees charged.

- Involving another firm to perform or re-perform part of the engagement.

- Rotating senior assurance team personnel.

Interactive question 2: Ethical dilemmas

This next question should serve as a refresher from your earlier studies as to how ethics and professional standards impact the work of accountants in different settings.

Russell Ltd

Your company has been acting as consultants to Russell Ltd providing advice about the need to cut costs and restructure the company's manufacturing operations. In a recent meeting with the Production Director of Russell Ltd you are made aware that the entire consulting team will be invited to the company's Christmas celebrations which run over the course of a weekend and are being held at an expensive Castle-Keep Hotel.

Ravencroft White plc

You are a manager in the audit firm of Swain Brothers. Mr Bootle has been the engagement partner for a client Ravencroft White plc for the last 11 years. He has excellent knowledge of the client and knows all of the directors of Ravencroft White exceptionally well.

Sole Records Ltd

Mr Minus, the principal consultant in the advisory firm for which you work, has been assisting a client Sole Records Ltd to help improve the company's performance. Mr Minus's son, David, recently joined the finance department of Sole Record's largest competitor.

Requirement

2.1 Explain the ethical threats which may affect the independence of the accountants/consultants featured in the three scenarios.

For each threat explain how it might be reduced.

See **Answer** at the end of this chapter.

1.7 Simple ethical tests for a business decision

Compliance with codes of conduct will be mandatory for members and employees subject to the codes.

Ethical tests enable managers to consider ethical consequences of decisions where:

- The wording of codes may be imprecise;
- Situations arise that are not covered in the codes.

Initially at least the situation should be evaluated as to:

1. The facts of the situation and whether all relevant information is available for making the decision; and

2. Whether there is any possibility of illegality – if there is then seeking legal advice should be considered.

The *Institute of Business Ethics* offers three tests to then apply to situations to assess whether they raise ethical issues:

1. **Transparency**: Is the situation characterised by integrity, openness and honesty? Would a third party construe it as honest and straightforward?

2. **Effect**: Whom does the situation potentially affect or hurt? Have the interests of all stakeholders been considered?

3. **Fairness**: Would the situation or proposed course of action be considered fair by those affected and by third parties?

The examiners have stressed that all too often when presented with an ethical dilemma in exam questions a significant number of candidates seem to rely very heavily on the *Institute of Business Ethics* three tests for assessing the situation, but do not apply it coherently. Answers often fail to apply the three tests to the scenario information, and fail to use ethical language, such as honesty and integrity (candidates only seem to refer to such terms when the question scenario involves a chartered accountant). It is important that you recognise that the three tests seek to identify whether general ethical values apply. Heavily relying on the three tests increases the scope to overlook other relevant issues featured in the scenario information. As such care should be taken when using it to answer question requirements. You are strongly advised to review the following interactive question as this considers how ethical values could be examined in a broader business setting.

Interactive question 3: Pay to stay

You are a supply chain manager working for Happy Foods, a leading food production company renowned for making a range of well known household food brands including cakes, bread and custard. A significant part of your day-to-day work involves dealing with the company's many suppliers to ensure Happy Foods pays the best possible price for the ingredients needed in its operations. Earlier in the year tough trading conditions required the company to approach shareholders and request a fresh injection of funds to support the business. Shortly after this the Happy Foods board issued a profit warning.

A week ago your line manager called you into a confidential meeting. During the meeting he explained that the board had recently decided to introduce a scheme which would require each of the company's suppliers to make an 'annual voluntary investment' to remain on its books as an approved supplier. He added 'given your many years' experience of dealing with Happy Foods suppliers the board feel that you are ideally placed to inform our current suppliers of the new scheme. The directors would, however, prefer if you could avoid unnecessarily publicising this beyond the discussions with the suppliers themselves.'

Requirement

3.1 Using your knowledge of the *Institute of Business Ethics* three tests (transparency, effect and fairness) evaluate your line manager's suggestion that you should commence the launch of the 'annual voluntary investment'.

See **Answer** at the end of this chapter.

1.7.1 Philosophical model of ethical decision-making

The philosophical model of ethical decision-making offers an alternative approach to evaluating ethical issues, in particular by focusing on whether a suggested decision or course of action in the face of an ethical issue is the right one. It shares some obvious similarities with the *Institute of Business Ethics'* three tests, having a strong focus on stakeholders. By considering each of the four questions the user can determine whether the suggested course of action is appropriate.

1. Do the benefits outweigh the harm to oneself?
2. Do the benefits outweigh the harm to others?
3. Are the rights of individual stakeholders considered and respected?
4. Are the benefits and burdens justly distributed?

Considering a wider range of ethical issues should help to ensure that better business decisions are reached.

1.8 Impact of ethics on strategy

In Chapter 2 we considered the points in the strategy process where ethics may have an impact:

- In the formulation of strategic objectives, some firms will not consider lines of business for ethical reasons.

- External appraisal will need to consider the ethical climate in which the firm operates. This will raise expectations of its behaviour.

- Internal appraisal: Management should consider whether present operations are 'sustainable', ie, consistent with present and future ethical expectations.

- Strategy selection: Management should consider the ethical implication of proposed strategies before selecting and implementing them.

1.8.1 Conflict between ethics and business

Potential areas for conflict between ethics and business strategy include:

- **Cultivating and benefiting from relationships with legislators and governments**: such relationships may lead politicians to ignore the national interest (eg, of the people who elected them) to further their own personal interests.

- **Fairness of labour contracts**: firms can use their power to exploit workers, including child labour, and subject them to unethical treatment in areas where jobs are scarce.

- **Privacy of customers and employees**: modern databases enable tracking of spending for marketing purposes or to discriminate between customers on basis of their value. Staff can be subject to background checks and monitored through their use of email and the location of their mobile phones. This could be particularly pertinent given the rise in the number of staff now using wearable technology while at work.

- **Terms of trade with suppliers**: large firms may pay poor prices or demand long credit periods and other payments from weak suppliers. This has been a particular criticism of large retail food stores in North America and Europe who are blamed for the impoverishment of farmers at home and in developing countries.

- **Prices to customers**: powerful suppliers of scarce products such as energy, life saving drugs or petrol, are able to charge high prices that exclude poorer individuals or nations. Examples here include anti-aids drugs to Africa or purified water to developing countries.

- **Managing cross cultural businesses**: different countries of operation or different ethnic groups within the domestic environment can present ethical issues affecting what products are made, how staff are treated, dress conventions, observance of religion and promotional methods.

2 Marketing and ethics

Section overview

- Ethical issues begin with questioning whether marketing exists to sell people things they don't need and so wastes resources and cause envy and dissatisfaction.

- The nature of products, the means by which they are promoted, the level of prices and the selective way they are made available are also ethical issues.

- Marketers may defend themselves to some extent by noting that ethics are culturally relative and therefore, given that marketing seeks to identify and satisfy needs, it will follow and not lead ethical consciousness.

2.1 Ethical issues in the marketing concept

The most fundamental ethical issue facing marketing is the potential accusation that marketing wastes the world's resources by making things that people don't really need and then using promotion to convince people that they are not satisfied without them.

It is hard to accept this argument in the areas of essential products, but the destruction of clothes, electrical appliances etc, on the basis that they are outmoded or have obsolete technologies, and the huge amount of paper and electricity used to advertise products and to run pop-up and social media advertisements does lend weight to the argument.

The envy created by development and presentation of products that only some can have, such as personal digital players, mobile phones, expensive trainers etc, also contributes to street crime. Sports shoe manufacturer Nike was caught-up in accusations that its slogan 'just do it' was encouraging street thefts of its shoes.

To tilt the argument back in favour of marketing the following points can be made:

- **Value judgements**: phrases like 'things that people don't really need' are not helpful because if people will spend money and effort to get them, who is to say they don't need them?

- **Employment effects**: the production of goods and services creates jobs. This is an ethical good to come from marketing.

- **Proper target marketing may reduce waste**. marketing tries to ensure that unwanted products and marketing effort is reduced. This saves resources.

- **Ethical marketing**: marketing has been used to promote alternative and more ecologically responsible products and ways of life (eg, to quit smoking). This suggests that it is not the practice of marketing that is unethical but rather some of the ends to which it has been put.

2.2 Ethical issues and the marketing mix

The way that marketing is carried out may raise ethical concerns:

Product issues

Some products are dangerous but are sold without this being considered in some parts of the world. Cigarettes and alcohol are obvious examples but increasingly processed foods are being criticised as leading to illness due to high fat, sugar and salt content.

Some products are wasteful of resources or lead to environmental pollution. The sports utility vehicle (SUV) has been a criticised example of this.

Decisions to cease provision of products, or never to offer them at all, can reduce the welfare of society and possibly inflict hardship. Pharmaceutical firms have been accused of suppressing drugs that could cure a condition in favour of continued sales of palliatives.

Price issues

Pricing products to maximise returns may mean pricing them out of the reach of many who want them. Where products are essential, such as life savings drugs or affordable homes, this has clear ethical implications.

Price discrimination remains discrimination. To charge higher prices to people in rural areas compared to towns because competition is less, or to charge people differently because of their gender or age seems unfair.

Pricing low to encourage usage may have the effect of increasing consumption to unhealthy levels. Two-for-one offers on alcohol, or multi-buy offers on confectionary are examples of this.

Promotion issues

The public has expressed concern that they are being 'brainwashed' by clever advertising techniques such as hidden messages in subliminal advertising (flashes of images too brief to be registered and filtered by the conscious mind). It is unlikely that these techniques work as feared but the broader principle that promotion manipulates behaviour remains an ethical issue.

Some images used in advertising and promotion may be offensive to some in society. Promotion has been blamed for causing anti-social behaviour. A soft drink advertisement was withdrawn following protests from schools that children were emulating a character in the advertisement by ambushing and slapping schoolmates so they could experience the 'burst of taste'.

Some advertising is upsetting to casual observers. Road safety advertisements showing slow motion footage of children being propelled over the top of speeding cars have shock value but are potentially very effective.

Place issues

The principal ethical issues here revolve around encouraging or denying access.

Stores have been accused of encouraging consumption of confectionery by mounting displays at children's eye levels at the check-out leading to parents being pestered.

The use of premium rate telephone lines for enquiries and service calls, often with substantial waiting times, has been criticised as a hidden charge. These are also common on children's phone-in quizzes and television shows.

Closures of branches to save cost leaves some customers with a lack of service and poorer quality of life. This has been a common criticism of banks.

Migration of customer service from the High Street to call centres and websites excludes those without IT access, credit cards or those put off by the impersonal contact.

2.3 Ethical marketing

Marketers defend their profession against the issues above in a number of ways.

- **Personal choice**: providing the information given is clear about the content and effects of products it is for the buyer to decide for themselves their ethical priorities, rather than for the firm to decide it for them.

- **Codes of practice**: most marketers abide by voluntary codes of practice in how they promote products and deal with customers. These are developed after taking a balanced view of the issues rather than accepting the assurances of the industry or the accounts of their critics.

- **Societal marketing concept**: marketing is about meeting people's needs and expectations and not about leading them. If issues such as junk food are bothering society, then effective marketing should reduce reliance on the product and as demand falls refinements or new products can be found. Ethical investment funds, cosmetics and energy are all examples of marketing following a genuinely widespread ethical issue and responding appropriately with new market offerings to meet the need.

Interactive question 4: Socially responsible marketing

Your senior partner has requested a memo for developing into a report to a global food manufacturer regarded as being a leading exponent of modern marketing practice.

Requirements

4.1 Explain what you understand to be the advantages of a marketing orientation to food consumers and food manufacturers.

4.2 Identify some of the ethical and social responsibility issues that face marketers in the food manufacturing industry.

See **Answer** at the end of this chapter.

3 Ethical issues in manufacture and procurement

Section overview

- Organisations have a duty to ensure that production processes and products do not cause harm to workers, customers, the environment and wider society.

- Many firms seek to fulfil their own CR commitments by demanding similar commitments from their suppliers.

3.1 Ethical issues in manufacture

The ethical issues in manufacture cover the duties of an organisation to ensure that products and production processes do not cause harm.

The issues raised include the following:

- Ethical relations between the organisation and the environment in terms of pollution, carbon emissions trading and environmental ethics.

- The manufacture, marketing and distribution of defective, addictive and inherently dangerous products and services (eg, tobacco, alcohol, weapons, motor vehicles and some chemicals) that companies knew were harmful to the buyers of those products.

- The use of child labour often in hazardous jobs such as the manufacture of matches, fireworks and carpets.

- Ethical problems arising out of new technologies such as genetically modified food, mobile phone radiation and health.

- Product testing ethics concerning animal rights and animal testing and the use of economically disadvantaged groups (such as students) as test objects.

- The environmental impact of end-of-life cycle products such as discarded electric equipment including computers and smart phones or scrapped cars.

Consumers have moved towards products that are considered more environmentally and ecologically friendly and where people have not been exploited in their manufacture. Hence we now see a greater range of products labelled, for example:

- organically grown
- not tested on animals
- the manufacturer is a carbon neutral firm
- this paper is from recycled sources
- this wood is from sustainable forests
- the chemicals contained in this product are biodegradable

This may be used by a firm as a means of differentiation, to increase competitive advantage.

3.2 Ethical aspects of purchasing and procurement

Many firms seek to fulfil their own CR commitments by demanding similar commitments from their suppliers. This gives rise to **ethical procurement**.

Ethical procurement impacts in several areas:

1 The human rights of workers within supplier firms.

 Many UK firms require that suppliers sign up to the Code of Practice of the *Ethical Trading Initiative*, a charity with representation from industry, government, non-governmental and voluntary organisations. This requires firms to ensure:

- employment is freely chosen (ie, no forced, slave or prison labour)
- freedom of workforce association and collective bargaining are respected
- working conditions are safe and hygienic
- no child labour used
- living wages are paid
- working hours are not excessive
- no discrimination is practised
- regular employment is provided
- no harsh or inhumane treatment is allowed

2 Proper health and safety standards are maintained in operations as they may affect employees and the general public.

3 Environmental protection.

4 Having fair contracting terms and conditions with suppliers.

 This involves fair prices, adherence to reasonable payment terms and having a procedure to deal with suppliers grievances.

 Note: This is an undertaking by the procuring company to its suppliers and is an element of partnership in ethical procurement.

5   Transparency in negotiations with suppliers.

This includes making timescales for contract re-tendering clear and making awards and non-renewal of contracts in good time.

6   Fraud and corruption.

7   There will be zero tolerance of the offering of gifts and inducements by suppliers and also of conflicts of interest.

4   Ethical issues in the use of data

In Chapters 6,13 and 14 we explored some of the ethical considerations concerning the increased use of data in business. As organisations strive to collect greater quantities of data about customers, this has raised concerns that such information will be used to target customers with increasingly personalised marketing messages, to facilitate sales which may not otherwise have been made. Concerns have also been raised about the ethical and legal issues in holding vast quantities of customer data in corporate databases, solely for commercial gain. This issue is further compounded, as it is unclear as to who actually owns the customer data held by organisations and whether or not commercial entities have the right to sell on customer data to third parties.

In Chapter 14 consideration was given to the growing need for organisations to have in place robust security measures over personal data, held in commercial databases, to prevent hackers from gaining access.

5   The concepts of sustainability and corporate responsibility

Section overview

- Sustainability is about maintaining the world's resources rather than depleting or destroying them. This will ensure they support human activity now and in the future. Sustainability is closely linked to the concept of natural capital which was introduced in Chapter 4.

- Corporate responsibility: the actions, activities and obligations of business in achieving sustainability.

- A commonly employed and useful way of thinking about sustainability issues is under three key headings: social, environmental and economic.

In Chapter 3 we discussed the fact that although the primary stakeholders of a company are its shareholders, increasingly there is a need for an organisation to consider other stakeholders and wider areas of social responsibility.

This is enshrined in the concept of corporate governance, covered in Chapter 9.

5.1   What is sustainability and corporate responsibility?

Definitions

Sustainability: The ability to 'meet the needs of the present without compromising the ability of future generations to meet their own needs' (*Brundtland Report*).

Sustainable development is the process by which we achieve sustainability.

Sustainable enterprise: A company, institution or entity that generates continuously increasing stakeholder value through the application of sustainable practices through the entire base activity – products and services, workforce, workplace, functions/processes, and management/governance. (Deloitte *Creating the Wholly Sustainable Enterprise*)

Corporate responsibility: The actions, activities and obligations of business in achieving sustainability.

Sustainability is about maintaining the world's resources rather than depleting or destroying them. This will ensure they support human activity now and in the future. In Chapter 4 we introduced **natural capital**, which is a key part of the concept of sustainability.

Sustainability is not limited to the environment. Interpretations of the scope of sustainable development have developed from a narrow interpretation which focuses on 'green issues' to broader interpretations which include concerns such as:

- Increasing extremes of poverty and wealth
- Population growth
- Biodiversity loss
- Deteriorating air and water quality
- Climate change
- Human rights

A commonly employed and useful way of thinking about these issues is under three key headings: **social, environmental** and **economic** (or **financial).**

Issues	Examples
Social	Health and safety, workers' rights (in the business itself and its supply chain), pay and benefits, diversity and equal opportunities, impacts of product use, responsible marketing, data protection and privacy, community investment, and bribery/corruption.
Environmental	Climate change, pollution, emissions levels, waste, use of natural resources, impacts of product use, compliance with environmental legislation, air quality.
Economic	Economic stability and growth, job provision, local economic development, healthy competition, compliance with governance structures , transparency, long-term viability of businesses, investment in innovation/NPD.

To achieve sustainable success, these three issues must be addressed and balanced; not just the concrete issues such as raw materials or energy use, but also less tangible ones such as relationships with wider stakeholders and employees, whose goodwill is necessary to the long-term success of the business.

Natural capital

During our discussion of natural capital in Chapter 4 we highlighted that a growing number of large organisations are now starting to attach monetary values to the natural capital assets that they use when undertaking their business activities. By attaching monetary values in this way it is believed that the senior management of participating organisations will be better placed to understand the implications that the organisation's activities are having on the planet, which should in turn enable better-informed business decisions to be made.

Worked example: National Grid

In *ICAEW's Natural capital in practice* report, Dunscombe and Glover (2016) highlight the example of National Grid plc, which owns the electricity and gas transmission system in England and Wales. In recent years, National Grid has actively attempted to make a positive contribution to its natural capital. As part of National Grid's Environmental Sustainability Strategy, the company set itself the target of 'delivering sustainability action plans at 50 of its sites' with the aim of enhancing the eco-systems which exist (Dunscombe and Glover, 2016: p.2).

The key challenge for National Grid was how to make the business case for investing in natural capital when its benefits are often 'economically invisible' (Dunscombe and Glover, 2016, p.2).

As part of its sustainability programme, National Grid undertook a project to place financial values on the natural assets on its sites to better understand how the company could make more informed 'investment decisions to secure improved social, environmental and economic returns [...]To date, this analysis has transitioned into action at several sites, where monetising value has helped decision-makers to identify land management options that optimise natural capital value.' (Dunscombe and Glover, 2016, p.3).

Sustainable development recognises the interdependence between business, society and the environment, since without the environment neither business nor society could exist. Thus for businesses to deliver value to their shareholders, they must respond to the needs and priorities of their stakeholders and not exhaust the world's capital.

Corporate responsibility is a strategic business issue, since by addressing their social and environmental impacts, organisations can have a positive effect on their economic performance.

An organisation can adopt different **strategic approaches** to corporate responsibility:

Proactive strategy	A business is prepared to take full responsibility for its actions. Eg, a company which discovers a fault in a product and recalls the product without being forced to, before any injury or damage is caused, acts in a proactive way.
Reactive strategy	This involves allowing a situation to continue unresolved until the public, government or consumer groups find out about it.
Defence strategy	This involves minimising or attempting to avoid additional obligations arising from a particular problem.
Accommodation strategy	This approach involves taking responsibility for actions, probably when one of the following happens: • Encouragement from special interest groups. • Perception that a failure to act will result in government intervention.

6 Sustainable development

Section overview

- This section reviews the mechanisms by which governments, businesses and other global organisations support and promote sustainable development.

The term 'sustainable development' originally appeared in literature on development economics, often as a contrast to the 'unsustainable development' of some countries that were receiving large inward investment from multinational corporations. This was believed to be destroying the social and ecological infrastructure and hence hampering the future development of the countries.

Following the Rio 'Earth Summit' of 1992 and ensuing global political support the need for 'sustainable development' has, amongst political initiatives, led to a focus on firms developing appropriate strategies and thereby becoming **'sustainable enterprises'**. The focus has moved from just developing countries to include impacts on mature home economies too.

6.1 Global initiatives to promote sustainable development

There are a wide variety of UK, European and global initiatives to foster sustainable development, including steps taken by governments, business and other organisations. Such actions are shown to take the form of eight different mechanisms:

- **Corporate policies** whereby the perceived expectations of society convince organisations of the merits of adopting policies on sustainability and publishing information about the policies and their impact.

- **Supply chain pressure** by which the expectations of society drive purchasers to promote a desired standard of sustainable performance and reporting amongst suppliers and others in the supply chain.

- **Stakeholder engagement** enabling those with a particular interest to influence the decisions and behaviour of an organisation, to engage an organisation in ongoing dialogue and a process of feedback to and from stakeholders, supported by information flows about sustainable performance.

- **Voluntary codes** through which society encourages organisations to improve particular aspects of their sustainability performance, often requiring a statement for stakeholders regarding compliance or an explanation of non-compliance.

- **Rating and benchmarking** by which investors and others, or agencies working on their behalf, grade organisations through the use of benchmarks or ratings on the basis of information on sustainability policies and performance and thus influence the behaviour of organisations and stakeholders.

- **Taxes and subsidies** to incentivise organisations to operate in ways that contribute to sustainability, requiring information in the form of tax returns and grant claims.

- **Tradable permits** whereby governments ration allocations of scarce resources or undesirable impacts so as to improve sustainability, requiring information about quota utilisation and prices to support the operation of fair markets.

6.2 Perspectives on sustainability

- An **essential consideration** for which corporations must shoulder responsibility if the Earth is to avoid global tragedy.

- A **fad** pushed by elite political groups and which is now being alighted on by consultants and academics to generate research and consultancy incomes. In June 2017 US President, Donald Trump, announced his country's withdrawal from the 2015 Paris Climate Agreement, on the grounds that it harmed job creation in the US.

- **'Greenwash'** that large corporations can use as rhetoric whilst underneath they continue to conduct their usual disruptive activities.

7 Corporate responsibility

Section overview

- Corporate responsibility can be a source of both risk and opportunity.

- This section considers the reasons why organisations might choose to demonstrate CR, and the extent to which pursuing a CR strategy is congruent with delivering value to shareholders.

- The scope of CR varies with the nature of the organisation.

- Embedding sustainability and CR within an organisation requires the formulation, implementation and control of a strategic plan and the involvement of senior management.

7.1 Why consider corporate responsibility?

Corporate responsibility is no longer just a public relations exercise but is a strategically fundamental driver for business.

CR is both a source of **risk** – the reputational damage that can be done by 'bad' behaviour – and of **opportunity** – companies that are more efficient in their use of energy, for example, will make fewer emissions but will also have lower cost bases.

Attention to **social, environmental** and **economic** aspects of business activity and performance is increasing from customers, suppliers, investors, pressure groups and the community. In a sense each group's support gives a company a licence to operate. Without the support of these stakeholders a business will find its ability to operate effectively is impaired, thus damaging its performance over the long-term.

Firms that misbehave will find fewer and fewer trading partners, consumers will stop buying their products, host nations will withdraw licences or impose fines, local communities will withdraw their support and possibly become hostile and workers will become de-motivated and unproductive. In addition, investors will stop buying their stock, and existing shareholders will sell, banks will increase their lending rates and the cost of capital will increase.

Justifications offered for management seeking to demonstrate corporate responsibility outside a business's normal operations are:

- Self-regulation by the firm or industry now is likely to be more flexible and less costly than ignoring CR and facing statutory regulation later.

- It improves relations with key external stakeholders such as regulators, government and legislators.

- Donations, sponsorship and community involvement are a useful medium of public relations and can reflect well on the business and its brands.

- Involving managers and staff in community activities develops them more fully.

- It helps create a value culture in the organisation and a sense of mission, which is good for motivation.

- In the long-term, upholding the community's values, responding constructively to criticism and contributing towards community well-being might be good for business, as it promotes the wider environment in which businesses flourish.

Tangible benefits of adopting CR include:

- Firms may achieve a lower cost base through the efficient use of resources, which would help improve competitive advantage.

- CR may provide opportunities to enter new markets or attract new ethical customers eg, Innocent drinks.

- Providing new solutions to existing business problems eg, food waste from certain supermarkets which historically went to landfill sites is now delivered to Anaerobic Digestion plants, where it is transformed into electricity that can be used on the national grid.

- A CR policy may help protect the company's licence to operate and its reputation eg, Anglo American, the global mining company is committed to minimising any negative impacts of its operations on the environment and working with local communities to ensure that they benefit from its activities. The focus on safe and responsible extraction enhances its image and helps it retain a social licence to operate.

- CR offers an opportunity to build new core competences, eg, Toyota's 'Prius' was the first mass-produced electric and petrol hybrid car.

- CR may enhance a firms reputation and hence attract more finance from ethical investors eg, by gaining a listing on the FTSE4Good index of companies that meet globally recognised corporate responsibility standards.

Interactive question 5: Being socially responsible

5.1 What are the implications in the

    (a) short term

    (b) long term

of a company acting in a socially responsible manner?

See **Answer** at the end of this chapter.

7.2 Scope of corporate responsibility

The scope of CR varies from business to business. Factors frequently included are:

- **Health and safety**: this includes workplace injury, customer and supplier injury and harm to third parties.

- **Environmental protection**: energy use, emissions (notably carbon dioxide), water use and pollution, impact of product on environment, recycling of materials and heat.

- **Staff welfare**: issues such as stress at work, personal development, achieving work/life balances through flexibility, equal opportunities for disadvantaged or minority groups.

- **Customer welfare**: through content and description of products, non-exclusion of customer groups, fair dealing and treatment.

- **Supply-chain management**: insisting that providers of bought-in supplies also have appropriate CR policies, ethical trading, elimination of pollution and un-recycled packaging, eliminating exploitative labour practices amongst contractors.

- **Ethical conduct:** staff codes for interpersonal behaviour, prohibitions on uses of data and IT, management forbidden from offering bribes to win contracts, ensuring non-exploitation of staff.

- **Engagement with social causes:** this includes secondment of management and staff, charitable donations, provision of free products to the needy, involvement in the local community, support for outreach projects such as cultural improvement or education.

Successful CR programmes focus on issues of most strategic **relevance** to an organisation which offer an opportunity to meet both shareholder and wider stakeholder expectations. Examples include:

- A service organisation might focus on a staff welfare programme to encourage retention.

- A supermarket could stock ethically sourced food, and attract new customers as a result.

- A software company might introduce a new programme designed for the elderly to tackle digital exclusion and create an additional revenue stream in the process.

- A bank may allocate funds to invest in technology to combat climate change.

Interactive question 6: Skin Care Company

You have recently accepted a position as a Chartered Accountant working for the Skin Care Company.

The Skin Care Company (SCC) specialises in making beauty products, predominantly for women. All products are made at the company's UK factory and are sold around the world. The company's founder was keen to introduce a range of ethically produced beauty products made from sustainable ingredients. The founder's vision was to source ingredients from farmers and growers in some of the world's most impoverished regions through establishing long term relationships with suppliers. As a result, SCC pays its growers higher prices for ingredients than competing beauty care companies. SCC's ethical stance helps the company command premium prices for its products and it remains well known among 'ethically minded' customers.

In the years since the founder's retirement, demand for SCC's products has continued to increase and the company has recently finalised plans to list on the London Stock Exchange. One week before the official listing you are accidentally copied in on an email from the company's MD to the Head of Production.

The email reveals that one of the ingredients used in one of SCC's most popular skin care products has been found to contain a toxin which can cause nasty rashes on certain skin types. Although not illegal to use the ingredient in such products, several neighbouring countries have recently commenced an investigation into its safety. The UK government has yet to announce plans to conduct its own investigation.

The MD suggests in the email that because only he and the Head of Production are aware of the exact recipe for the product, they should not reveal this potential problem to the rest of the directors for fear of lowering the company's share price when it floats on the exchange the following week.

Requirement

6.1 Describe the ethical and CR related issues that should be considered upon discovery of the contents of this email and suggest any appropriate actions that should be taken.

See **Answer** at the end of this chapter.

7.2.1 Achieving corporate responsibility

The management of the business must put CR at the centre of its activities by:

1 Identifying the sustainability corporate responsibility issues that are relevant to the organisation.

2 Developing an organisational strategy to embed corporate responsibility into the organisation's corporate policies.

As with all strategic management this involves the formulation, implementation and control of a strategic plan and the involvement of senior management.

There are a number of key factors required for an organisation to **embed sustainability in its day-to-day operations**:

1 Board and senior management commitment.

2 Understanding and analysing the key sustainability drivers for the organisation.

3 Integrating the key sustainability drivers into the organisation's strategy.

4 Ensuring that sustainability is the responsibility of everyone in the organisation.

5 Breaking-down sustainability targets and objectives for the organisation as a whole into targets and objectives which are meaningful for individual subsidiaries, divisions and departments.

6 Processes that enable sustainability issues to be taken into account clearly and consistently in day-to-day decision-making.

7 Extensive and effective sustainability training.

8 Including sustainability targets and objectives in performance appraisal.

9 Champions to promote sustainability and celebrate success.

10 Monitoring and reporting sustainability performance.

Later in the chapter we look at how to ensure that organisations and their stakeholders have the information available to support the mechanisms that will enhance sustainability.

8 Monitoring and measuring sustainability

Section overview

- A sustainable development strategy needs to be implemented and regularly monitored.

- Monitoring involves measuring progress in terms of both processes and outcomes.

- The GRI reporting standards are a global, voluntary code for corporate responsibility and sustainability reporting. It provides a series of standards that organisations can use to measure and report their economic, environmental, and social performance.

8.1 Monitoring process

It is not enough for an organisation to develop a sustainable development strategy. Delivery of the strategy needs to be implemented and regularly monitored:

As with any strategy the implementation and monitoring process involves:

- Identifying the key sustainability issues for the business and the factors that drive them – the social, environmental and economic framework discussed earlier can be used.

- Sustainability issues are not static. Changes to the activities and operations of the organisation may give rise to new issues, so one aspect of monitoring involves giving consideration to any new developments.

- Set targets and standards for sustainability objectives. The standards might originate from government guidance and policy, legislation, public commitments or commonly accepted industry or sector standards.

- Monitor progress towards sustainability objectives in terms of both processes and outcomes.

  Process – is the organisation doing the things that it said that it would to implement sustainability initiatives?

  Outcome – having implemented initiatives is the organisation achieving the outcomes towards which it is striving?

- Report progress and evaluate the implications for future decision making and performance (feedback).

An organisation will need to develop its management information and data analytics systems to meet the requirements of sustainable development monitoring, reporting and evaluation. This may involve making better use of existing financial and non-financial information and data.

Worked example: Big data and sustainability

The amount of data available, coupled to increasingly advanced data analytics systems is now helping UK supermarket chain Sainsbury's monitor the activities of its suppliers, as it strives to meet its sustainability commitments. An article on the *Accounting for Sustainability* website included a blog written by Sainsbury's Brand Director, Judith Batchelar, in which she explains how big data technologies are helping the retailer to achieve its aim of sourcing sustainable wild fish.

'Farmed fish is easier for us to manage, as we know where the farms are and we know how the fish are being managed, including the impact we are having on the local environment. Wild fish is not so easy. Much of it is caught thousands of miles away, in the middle of large oceans, where it is difficult to see what's really going on, let alone manage it. We have to rely on the certification process for the fish, but the paper based system only starts when the fish is landed. We want to know what is happening at sea.' (Batchelar, 2017).

The challenge is made even more difficult as it is estimated that about 25% of the fish caught around the world is caught illegally. In conjunction with technology firm, Satellite Catapult, Sainsbury's is able to actually view, in real time the vessels which are fishing on its behalf. Batchelar (2017) notes that 'earth observation satellites photograph fishing vessels around the world using that vessel's automatic location communicator (they can even see when vessels have switched this signal off). The satellites then collate this data with other data sets which can tell them the vessel's home port, its licence and quota, and the method of fishing it is meant to use. They take this information and, by using complex algorithms, can tell whether the vessel is behaving as would be expected, given everything we know about that vessel…so now we really can "measure what matters" when it comes to illegal, unreported and unregulated fishing. Protecting "Life below water" becomes a real possibility.'

Source:

Batchelar, J. (2017) *Big data: A smart catch for consumers at Sainsbury's.* [Online]. Available from: www.accountingforsustainability.org [Accessed 5 May 2017].

8.2 Reporting requirements

Effective reporting involves ensuring that the organisation is transparent in communicating with internal and external stakeholders.

In the public sector there are a number of organisations that have a role in evaluating the outcomes of sustainability initiatives. These include independent advisory bodies, such as the National Audit Office. In the private sector, reporting of social and environmental impacts is not mandatory. In the case of quoted companies, directors are required to report on environmental matters, the company's employees and social/community issues. An increasing number of organisations now produce Sustainability, Natural Capital or Corporate Responsibility reports, recognising a need to engage key stakeholders on particular issues of public interest.

8.3 Performance measurement

8.3.1 Global Reporting Initiative

The Global Reporting Initiative (GRI) is the world standard setter in sustainability reporting, agreed through a multi-stakeholder approach. In October 2016 the GRI launched the first global standards for sustainability reporting. The GRI standards replaced the G4 guidelines. The standards help organisations to report on the economic, environmental and social impacts that their activities have on the world:

Economic: concerns the organisation's impacts on the economic conditions of its stakeholders and on economic systems at local, national, and global levels.

Environmental: concerns an organisation's impacts on living and non-living natural systems, including ecosystems, land, air, and water.

Social: concerns the impacts an organisation has on the social systems within which it operates.

Performance indicators which could be used to measure the three impacts mentioned above might include:

Economic	Environmental	Social
Revenues and costs	Materials used	Employee turnover and absenteeism
Wages, pensions, other employee benefits	Energy consumption	Diversity of workforce, incidents of discrimination
Retained earnings and payments to providers of capital	Water use	Employee health and safety
Taxes paid, subsidies and grants received	Greenhouse gas emissions	Child labour
Geographic analysis of key markets	Effluents and waste produced	Training undertaken
Return on capital employed	Significant spillages	Bribery and corruption
	Fines and penalties	Community relations
	Impact of activities on biodiversity	Complaints re breaches of customer privacy
		Standard of Product labelling

(Source: GRI 2013)

The GRI standards are intended to show how organisations contribute to sustainable development.

The reporting standards issued by the GRI are the best known example of a global, voluntary approach for corporate responsibility and sustainability reporting. The introduction of the GRI standards is intended to make sustainability reporting relevant and more responsive to new developments.

Organisations adopting the GRI approach are required to follow three standards:

GRI 101: The foundation standard details how organisations should use the standards to produce a sustainability report. It requires organisations to consider how those activities deemed to represent 'material' activities impact on stakeholders.

GRI 102: The general disclosure standard details how organisations should report contextual information relevant to the organisation. It also outlines the reporting process.

GRI 103: The management approach details how organisations manage material activities. GRI 103 is used in conjunction with specific standards.

The specific standards each detail the reporting requirements in respect of the three key areas outlined above: economic, environmental, and social. Organisations select the relevant standards which cover issues relating to the activities they undertake. For example, an organisation involved in burning fossil fuels would use GRI 305: Emissions, to report on these matters.

Each specific standard outlines the reporting requirements, reporting recommendations and provides guidance to the user organisation.

8.3.2 Accounting for Sustainability

The **Accounting for Sustainability (A4S)** project was established by the Prince of Wales to provide organisations with methodologies and tools to enable them to embed sustainability into day-to-day processes and to report more effectively on their sustainability performance.

Worked example: A4S

The aim of the A4S project is to 'inspire action by finance leaders to drive a fundamental shift towards resilient business models and a sustainable economy. To do this A4S has three core aims:

- Inspire finance leaders to adopt sustainable and resilient business models

- Transform financial decision-making to enable an integrated approach, reflective of the opportunities and risks posed by environmental and social issues

- Scale up action across the global finance and accounting community'

The A4S website sets out the importance of making sustainability an embedded issue in the strategy, operations and reporting of all types of organisations.

The work of A4S highlights the roles that Chief Financial Officers and the accounting profession play in ensuring that organisations 'create long term sustainable value by integrating economic, environmental and social matters into their decision-making. The A4S website suggests that the accounting profession can help by:

Influencing and informing
Promoting accounting for sustainability and the benefits of "integrated thinking"

Leading by example
Embedding accounting for sustainability within accounting bodies' strategies and operations

Drive thought leadership
Increasing the understanding of good sustainability practices, by commissioning and participating in work related to accounting and sustainability

Collaboration
Sharing learning and experience with others and to work together to advance better accounting

Training and professional education
Incorporating sustainability into training programmes for employees, suppliers, students, members and others, in professional and academic qualifications and in professional development requirements

Source:

Accounting for sustainability (2017) A4S Aims. [Online]. Available from: https://www.accountingforsustainability.org [Accessed 2 May 2017].

Worked example: Marks and Spencer

Retailer Marks and Spencer takes a proactive approach to sustainability having launched its 'Plan A' sustainability scheme in 2007. The original 'Plan A' set out 100 commitments on the most important social, environmental and ethical challenges facing Marks and Spencer's business. Since this time Marks and Spencer has continually updated its 'Plan A' scheme to include a broader range of commitments. In 2018 a report published on the company's website titled 'Plan A 2025 Commitments' outlined 100 new sustainability commitments up to the year 2025.

Marks and Spencer (2018) highlight that its 'Plan A 2025' is built around three core pillars:

- 'Nourishing wellbeing […] – our goal is to help 10 million people live happier, healthier lives.

- Transforming lives and communities […] – our goal is transform 1,000 communities

- Caring for the planet we all share […] – our goal is to become a zero waste business'. (Marks and Spencer, 2018).

The report highlights comments made by Marks and Spencer's CEO, Steve Rowe, who notes that since establishing 'Plan A' Marks and Spencer has 'substantially improved [its] social and environmental performance, whilst also saving more than £750 million in costs and winning more than 240 awards'. (Marks and Spencer, 2018, p.1).

Source:

Marks and Spencer. (2018) *Plan A 2025 Commitments*. Marks and Spencer.

Interactive question 7: Ashdene Homes

Ashdene Homes is a regional house builder, having considerable knowledge and experience in the South of England where the current UK housing shortage is centred. The company caters for the mid to lower end of the market, with prices normally below £500,000, on relatively small and individual sites which tend to be too large for the resources of local builders but too small for the high volume national house builders. Any mass release of land for development in the South East due to government initiatives is likely to be centred in one area. The development of any such land would take many years given delays within the planning process.

The company, worth £67 million has looked like a takeover target for a while but unfortunately, the company's reputation for internal control has been damaged somewhat by a qualified audit statement last year (over issues of compliance with financial standards) and an unfortunate internal incident which concerned an employee expressing concern about the compliance of one of the company's products with an international standard on fire safety. She raised the issue with her immediate manager but when she failed to obtain a response, she decided to report the lack of compliance to the press. This significantly embarrassed the company and led to a substantial deterioration in their reputation, especially as there have been more press releases about the company's failure to adhere to the high welfare, health and safety, financial, marketing and ethical standards that the founder practised when he started Ashdene Homes.

Requirements

7.1 Outline the implications of poor ethical standards and damaged reputation on the relationship between the affected stakeholder groups and Ashdene Homes.

7.2 What are the main issues concerned with corporate responsibility and why might Ashdene Homes choose to act, or at least claim to act, in a socially responsive way?

7.3 Explain, with reference to Ashdene Homes as appropriate, the ethical responsibilities of an accountant both as an employee and as a professional.

See **Answer** at the end of this chapter.

9 Developing an approach to ethics requirements in the exam

Section overview

- The intention of this section is to demonstrate the thought processes to be adopted when tackling a question involving ethics and the attributes of an answer that will score well in the exam.

- You will find further examples of requirements covering ethical issues in the Business Strategy and Technology Question Bank.

9.1 What will the ethics requirement involve?

Between 7 and 10 marks in the Business Strategy and Technology exam will be allocated to the appropriate discussion of ethical issues, possibly in the context of the ethics of an organisation or an individual working in business who may be a professional accountant.

Scenarios might include topics such as:

- The impact of ethics on strategies and strategic choice.

- Conflicts of interest among stakeholders.

- Attempts to intentionally mislead key stakeholders (by disclosure or non-disclosure of information.)

- Doubtful accounting or commercial business practice.

- Facilitation of unethical strategies.

- Inappropriate pressure to achieve a result.

- Conflict between the accountant's professional obligations and responsibilities to the organisation.

- Lack of professional independence eg, personal financial interest in business proposals.

- Actions contrary to law, regulation and/or technical and professional standards.

Such issues are often not clear-cut and it is important that you can develop a balanced argument, use appropriate ethical language and have regard to any relevant professional principles.

9.2 Recommended approach

The following is a suggestion for the approach to adopt when tackling questions involving ethical issues:

1 Do I have all the facts and/or information? For instance, if the information is from a newspaper report, is it credible?

2 Is there a legal or regulatory issue (criminal or civil law)? For instance, are the persons in question directors who owe statutory duties to their companies? When attempting exam questions in some cases it may be unclear whether or not there is a legal issue, if you are unsure you are encouraged to consider whether legal advice should be sought.

3 Do any other codes or professional principles apply? For instance, is the individual with the ethical dilemma a professional accountant, or is the organisation with an ethical issue subject to its industry's particular code of conduct?

4 Which stakeholders does the decision/action impact?

5   Which ethical concepts/principles/threats are relevant? Eg honesty, confidentiality, conflict of interest and intimidation.

6   If appropriate, consider implications in terms of :

- Transparency?
- Effect?
- Fairness?

7   Ask the key questions of a suggested course of action:

- Do the benefits outweigh the harm to oneself?
- Do the benefits outweigh the harm to others?
- Are the rights of individual stakeholders considered and respected?
- Are the benefits and burdens justly distributed?

8   If this action/decision is NOT taken, what are the issues?

9   Are there any sustainability, corporate governance or corporate responsibility issues?

10   What actions should be taken next?

These steps will be illustrated using the worked example that follows.

Key weaknesses in answering ethical questions have been:

1   Failure to identify the ethical issue (eg, dishonesty, illegality, lack of transparency or unfairness)

2   Failure to use ethical language

3   Answering simply by asserting an opinion rather than applying balanced reasoning using ethical principles

4   Failure to identify appropriate safeguards

5   Application of professional accountants' ethical codes to individuals in the scenario who are not accountants

6   Failure to distinguish between the ethical responsibilities of the individual and those of the organisation

7   Confusing commercial an ethical implications or solely focusing on commercial considerations and ignoring ethical factors.

It is important to note that not all ethical questions will necessarily draw upon transparency, effect and fairness. To produce a good answer when attempting an ethical question it is critical that you adopt a structured approach. In some cases, instead of considering transparency, effect and fairness, it may be worth considering ethics at a personal, business and corporate responsibility level.

Worked example: Pharmaceutical dilemma

Pharma Co is a highly successful global pharmaceutical company. Pharma's board has recently received advance warning of the likely results of a recent study which is not due to be completed for another 12 months. The study is being conducted by Pharma as part of on-going product testing for its drugs that are already available in the market place. Although the study is only 30% complete, the initial indications are that one of Pharma's leading drugs, which significantly improves the quality of life for sufferers of a long-term chronic illness, may cause harmful side-effects if taken at the same time as a newly available over-the-counter medicine that can be self-prescribed for pain relief. The board, mindful of the company's social responsibilities and the potential for bad publicity, is currently discussing what action to take in response to this discovery but is concerned about the harmful impact of any premature announcement on its share price.

Requirement

Discuss the ethical implications of this situation for Pharma and any potential for stakeholder conflict that arises as a result.

Solution

The following solution uses the questions in the recommended approach as a prompt to generate a balanced answer:

Ethical implications

1   **Do we have all the facts and/or information?**

    The study is only 30% complete, so the possibility that in the end the situation may be better than it appears currently should be considered. It is also sensible to double check that correct information gathering procedures are being implemented in the study, and that the preliminary conclusion has been soundly arrived at.

2   **Is there a legal issue (criminal or civil law)?**

    There is likely to be considerable UK and international legislation governing the pharmaceutical industry and the safety of drugs and medicines. This may dictate the responsibilities of Pharma's directors in relation to transparency and communication of any possible safety issues and the timing of any announcements.

3   **Do any other codes or professional principles apply?**

    The pharmaceutical industry will almost certainly have its own code of conduct and guidelines to ensure members behave in an ethical and professional manner. As a highly successful player, Pharma is likely to have a high profile in the industry and will be expected to set high standards of responsible behaviour. Most drugs on the market carry warnings of possible side-effects. A key issue here is the timing of any announcement and the point at which the legislation and/or any professional code of conduct specifies that an announcement and warning of possible side-effects is necessary.

4   **Which stakeholders does the decision/action impact?**

    Pharmaceutical companies are commercial organisations and it is reasonable to assume Pharma's long term objective is to maximise shareholder wealth. If the board announces the research findings and they subsequently prove to be unfounded, then Pharma's share price and shareholders are likely to have suffered unnecessarily. Also sufferers of the chronic illness who stop taking the drug immediately may have a lower quality of life as a result. However were the board not to announce preliminary findings and the tests went on to be conclusive, patients taking the drug may experience adverse side-effects in the meantime.

5   **Which ethical concepts/principles are relevant?**

    Relevant concepts and principles here include issues of integrity and honesty. By announcing the information from the study at this stage, it could be argued that the directors at Pharma would be acting with integrity and honesty, as this would allow users of the drug to make better informed decisions about the combination of medications that they take. This approach would however, create a conflict of interest between the directors' duties to shareholders and Pharma's responsibility to potential users.

    The current situation can be analysed further by giving consideration to the three tests of transparency, effect and fairness.

6   Here it is appropriate to consider **the implications in terms of transparency, effect and fairness**

Transparency – would Pharma mind if it subsequently came to light that the company was aware of the potential safety issues but had chosen not to disclose their concerns until the results were conclusive?

The issue here would be whether a reasonable person would have expected disclosure of the results. Pharma may have grounds for believing that the initial results will not prove representative, given that the study is only 30% complete. If however it is likely that the final results will confirm the initial findings then Pharma would probably not want the fact that it was aware of the problem earlier but took no action ever to come to light.

Effect – whom does the decision affect/hurt?

The possible side-effects may affect a significant number of people if the new over-the-counter remedy is widely used. Any side-effects would also have financial consequences for Pharma in terms of compensation payments and legal costs, as well as reputational consequences – lost customers, knock on effect on image and possible withdrawal of any licence to produce the drug.

Fairness – would the decision be considered fair by those affected?

This partly depends on whether any action taken by the board is seen as a justifiable business decision, which might take into account cost/benefit analysis, risk assessment and normal practice within the industry. Potential drug users may feel it is fairer to be given the information and then be allowed to decide on an individual basis whether they are prepared to risk taking the drug in view of the benefits it confers.

7   **If this action/decision is NOT taken, what are the issues?**

Presumably the worst case scenario is that the warning will be proved correct and Pharma will be forced to make an announcement in 12 months' time regarding possible side-effects (or possibly even to withdraw the drug completely). Alternatively concerns may prove to be completely unfounded or the outcome may lie somewhere in between these two extremes, suggesting there is some cause for concern but perhaps one that can be dealt with regarding a side-effects warning rather than withdrawal of the product.

8   **Are there any sustainability, corporate governance or corporate responsibility issues?**

The sustainability of Pharma's reputation and its long term profitability could be significantly affected if it comes to light that the drug is harmful and that Pharma's board were aware of this in advance but delayed giving warnings.

Stakeholder conflict

Stakeholders are groups of people who are interested in what Pharma does. In the case of Pharma's approach to the safety of its products this would include internal stakeholders (employees, management), connected stakeholders (shareholders, customers) and external stakeholders (government/regulatory bodies).

Here the issue highlights the potential for conflict within and between various stakeholder groups.

Shareholders want profitability so some may prefer Pharma to limit the damage and keep the information confidential until it is forced by legislation and/or regulation to announce it. Users of the drug and regulatory bodies may value safety more highly however and prefer to be in possession of the relevant information to make an informed choice.

Conclusion

Which stakeholders' interests determine Pharma's actions will depend to an extent on their relative power. Clearly Pharma's primary focus is to maximise shareholder wealth. However the users of the drugs are very important to success and may choose to stop buying the product or look to other companies if they think their safety is being compromised. Also shareholders may acknowledge that going beyond the basic requirements and demonstrating a responsibility to wider society will enhance Pharma's reputation and ensure government and public support, giving it a competitive advantage and higher profits in the long term.

Summary and Self-test

Summary

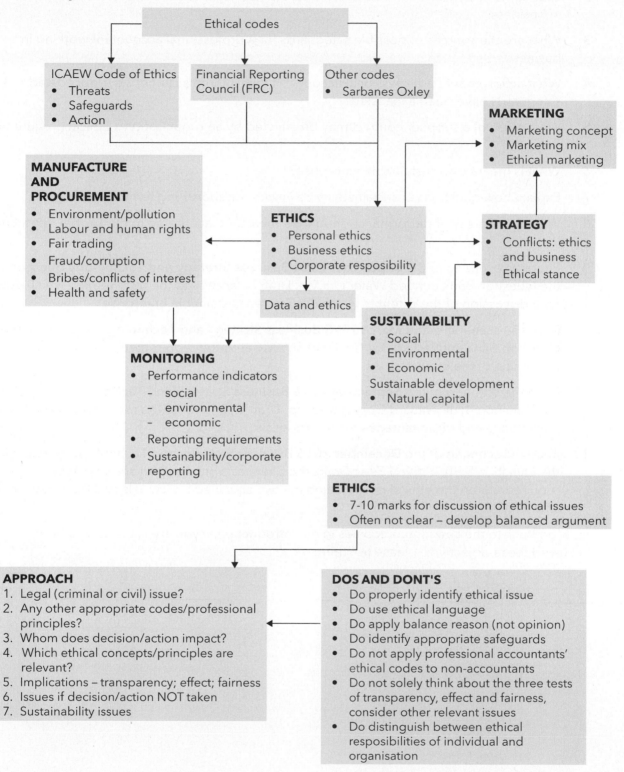

Ethical codes

ICAEW Code of Ethics
- Threats
- Safeguards
- Action

Financial Reporting Council (FRC)

Other codes
- Sarbanes Oxley

MANUFACTURE AND PROCUREMENT
- Environment/pollution
- Labour and human rights
- Fair trading
- Fraud/corruption
- Bribes/conflicts of interest
- Health and safety

ETHICS
- Personal ethics
- Business ethics
- Corporate resposibility

Data and ethics

MARKETING
- Marketing concept
- Marketing mix
- Ethical marketing

STRATEGY
- Conflicts: ethics and business
- Ethical stance

SUSTAINABILITY
- Social
- Environmental
- Economic
Sustainable development
- Natural capital

MONITORING
- Performance indicators
  - social
  - environmental
  - economic
- Reporting requirements
- Sustainability/corporate reporting

ETHICS
- 7-10 marks for discussion of ethical issues
- Often not clear – develop balanced argument

APPROACH
1. Legal (criminal or civil) issue?
2. Any other appropriate codes/professional principles?
3. Whom does decision/action impact?
4. Which ethical concepts/principles are relevant?
5. Implications – transparency; effect; fairness
6. Issues if decision/action NOT taken
7. Sustainability issues

DOS AND DONT'S
- Do properly identify ethical issue
- Do use ethical language
- Do apply balance reason (not opinion)
- Do identify appropriate safeguards
- Do not apply professional accountants' ethical codes to non-accountants
- Do not solely think about the three tests of transparency, effect and fairness, consider other relevant issues
- Do distinguish between ethical resposibilities of individual and organisation

Self-test

Answer the following questions.

1   Explain the three levels at which ethics can exist.

2   Give some examples of threats to self-interest that might arise for a professional accountant in business.

3   What are the sources of possible safeguards for a professional accountant working in business?

4   What action should a professional accountant take if threats cannot be reduced and safeguards have been exhausted?

5   What areas of a supplier contract may be affected by an organisation's ethical procurement policy?

6   What is meant by a sustainable enterprise?

7   Explain how questions of sustainability tie in with the short/long term debate?

8   What three areas of performance should be measured according to the Global Reporting Initiative?

9   Read the scenario of the **September 2014 Business Strategy and Technology** question in the Question Bank entitled *Water On Tap*. Draft an answer to the requirement which asks for a discussion of the extent to which On Tap is a sustainable enterprise.

10 Read the scenario of the **March 2015 Business Strategy and Technology** question in the Question Bank entitled *Rocket Co*. Draft an answer to the requirement which asks for a discussion of the ethical issues.

11 Read the scenario of the **September 2016 Business Strategy and Technology** question in the Question Bank entitled *Guayaporto Ltd*. Draft an answer to the requirement on advantages and disadvantages of the proposals.

12 Read the scenario of the **December 2016 Business Strategy and Technology** question in the Question Bank entitled *Zeter Domestic Chemicals plc*. Draft an answer to the requirement on the ethical issues facing the two specified individuals and the actions each should take.

Now go back to the Learning outcomes in the Introduction. If you are satisfied you have achieved these objectives, please tick them off.

Answers to Interactive questions

Answer to Interactive question 1

1.1 The ICAEW website explains the need for ethical standards as follows.

The work of the accountancy profession is crucial to the effective working of the capital markets (that is the mechanism for the provision of finance to business and the protection of those who supply it). Put very simply, investors may lose financially if their investment decisions are based on inadequate information and this would deter further investment. A loss of confidence in financial reporting could therefore undermine the economy.

Working to the highest standards of ethics and professionalism allows the public, investors and regulators to have confidence in the profession. Your ethical behaviour can protect not only your own reputation but that of the profession as a whole. We have a collective responsibility to apply principles, such as integrity and objectivity, that will enable high quality financial reporting, and effective financial management and business practices; to protect investors, businesses and the wider public interest.

Answer to Interactive question 2

2.1

Threat	Safeguards
Russell Ltd This involves a **self-interest threat** as the consultants' acceptance of the invitation to enjoy the lavish hospitality on offer increases the danger that the consulting team may be reluctant to raise any contentious matters as part of the cost cutting review.	Gifts and hospitality should not be accepted unless the value is trivial and inconsequential.
There is also a **familiarity threat** because involvement in social events with the client is likely to increase the consulting team's familiarity with client staff which may impair their ability to give impartial advice.	In this case it would be appropriate to decline the weekend away, so as not to impair the consulting firm's independence.
Ravencroft White plc This involves a **familiarity threat** because Mr Bootle has been the engagement partner for 11 years and his long association with the client could mean that he does not question judgements made by the client and does not exercise sufficient professional scepticism.	Mr Bootle should be rotated off the audit and another partner assigned to the client. Given that Ravencroft White is a public listed entity, the engagement partner should serve ideally for no more than five years before being rotated off. The five year term for a listed client engagement partner may be extended for an additional period of up to two years if the client's audit committee considers that this extension is necessary to safeguard the quality of the audit.

Threat	Safeguards
Sole Records Ltd Given that the consultant's son works for Sole Records largest competitor there is a danger that a **confidentiality threat** could arise. Mr Minus may be tempted to pass on confidential information about Sole Records' operations to his son.	Mr Minus should be removed from the consulting team and replaced by an independent consultant.
An **intimidation threat** could also exist if the son tries to pressure his father into providing Sole Records with poor consulting advice to give his own employer a competitive advantage. It should however be noted that Mr. Minus's son has only taken up a very junior position with the competitor so in reality his degree of influence over his father's work is likely to be insignificant.	If it is felt that David does not have any influence over his father's work at Sole Records then it may be appropriate for Mr Minus to remain as the principal consultant. This illustrates the need for discretion and tact when assessing ethical issues as a perceived threat may not actually represent a threat at all. Mr Minus may wish to disclose his connection with the competitor to avoid any perceived conflict of interest in his dealings with Sole Records Ltd.

Answer to Interactive question 3

3.1 The board's decision to request an 'annual voluntary investment' from the company's suppliers seems ethically dubious at best. It could be argued that the scheme represents a form of 'blackmail' as failure to comply will result in a supplier's removal as an approved supplier for reasons that are divorced from the quality of the supplies they make.

Applying the Institute of Business Ethics' three tests we can draw the following conclusions:

Transparency

As the board of directors have requested that you avoid 'unnecessarily publicising' the scheme this clearly indicates that they as a collective do not wish to be open about their suggestion and see it publicised at all. Consumer groups, industry bodies and government watchdogs would most likely perceive this move as dishonest, lacking in integrity and going against general wisdom on how business should be conducted. Furthermore, calling the scheme an 'annual voluntary investment' could be regarded as being misleading, as the suppliers are not able to opt out from making the payment without losing a major customer.

Effect

If you were to proceed and introduce the scheme then it is likely that a number of groups could be affected by your decision. Most obviously, the decision to charge suppliers a fee to continue supplying Happy Foods may put them under financial pressures, especially smaller suppliers. The degree of financial distress this may cause is difficult to measure as no details are given as to the size of payments the board at Happy Foods expect the suppliers to make. Clearly for some suppliers the ability to make such payments every 12 months may prove to be unsustainable, thereby forcing them out of business altogether.

Given that Happy Foods has experienced tough trading conditions it seems highly plausible that suppliers will have also been encountering similar financial problems which will only be made worse by the introduction of the scheme. This increases the danger that certain suppliers may need to rationalise their own operations to make the annual payments and maintain supply to Happy Foods. Such moves are likely to impact on the suppliers' own employees (through pay cuts and redundancies).

Consumers are also likely to be affected this decision, as suppliers of ingredients may increase the prices that they charge other food producers that they supply, who in turn increase the prices of the food products they sell. As a stakeholder in this situation you too are clearly going to be affected. Careful consideration needs to be given to the motives of the board in asking you alone to contact the suppliers about the charge. Could this represent an attempt by the board of directors to distance themselves from your actions? In the event that the scheme became publicised in the press it seems plausible that the board could attempt to place the accountability for the scheme at your feet, by downplaying your actions as that of an individual 'rogue' employee acting on their own initiative. Such an occurrence would leave your own career in a potentially precarious position.

Fairness

Although unknown at this point, it seems reasonable to suggest that the affected groups outlined above would most likely consider the introduction of the scheme and your support in facilitating it to be unfair. On the face of it the scheme seems to prop up Happy Foods' own operations at the expense of suppliers who up until now had received fair payment for the goods supplied. This point is exacerbated as the affected groups do not stand to gain anything from the payment beyond what they already had in the first place ie, a deal to supply ingredients to Happy Foods. However, it is worth noting that the notion of what is fair is likely to vary from stakeholder group to stakeholder group.

The perception that your own actions (and those of Happy Foods) could be regarded as being fair is further undermined by the board's attitude to the company's stakeholders, as no consideration appears to have been given to the impact of this decision on them.

It seems safe to say that in this case if you were to follow the board's wishes then you would have failed the Institute of Business Ethics three tests.

Answer to Interactive question 4

Memorandum
To   Senior Partner
From   Accountant
Date   Today
Subject Marketing and responsibility issues

I shall outline the broader perspectives of marketing to food consumers and food manufacturers and consider the implications of these issues.

4.1 Benefits to business organisations, consumers and society

Marketing touches everyone's life. It is the means by which a standard of living is developed and delivered to people and is a human activity directed at satisfying needs and wants through exchange processes. Marketing oriented companies combine many activities – marketing research, product development, distribution, pricing, advertising, personal selling and others – designed to sense, serve and satisfy consumer needs whilst meeting the organisation's goals. The core concepts of marketing are needs, wants, demands, products, exchange, transactions and markets that will benefit the individual, consumers and society at large, organisations and national and international governments. Marketers must be able to manage the level, timing and composition of demand from these different beneficiaries to satisfy their needs and wants. For instance, McDonald's have adopted the broader marketing concept on a global scale through understanding and responding to the changing needs of their customers.

Modern marketing is guided by a number of converging philosophies. The production concept holds that the consumer favours products which are available at low cost and that marketing's task is to improve production efficiency and bring down prices. The marketing concept holds that a company should research the needs and wants of a well defined target market and deliver the desired satisfactions, which is accompanied by long-run societal well being. In marketing-led organisations the entire workforce share the belief that the customer is all important and that building lasting relationships is key to customer retention. A company's sales are derived from satisfying existing customers and attracting new customers. This approach benefits the livelihoods of the employees and suppliers and their staff. Successfully adopting a marketing approach improves customer retention and minimises additional costs. A satisfied customer buys more, stays loyal longer, talks favourably to others, pays less attention to competing brands and is less price sensitive. These benefits are transferred into gains for consumers and ultimately society at large as success breeds success. McDonald's divert much of their energies to ensuring that customers repeatedly return to them satisfied and content with their offering.

4.2 Responsibilities of the modern marketer

Marketing is seen as a social force which not only conveys a standard of living but also serves as a force that reflects and influences cultural values and norms. The boundaries of marketing extend beyond economic considerations. Marketing concepts and techniques are used to promote the welfare of society as a whole instead of the traditional approach of providing products that satisfy consumers' needs efficiently and profitably. They could encompass reduction in poverty, improved education and improved healthcare. For instance, marketing tools are used in promoting healthier lifestyles through better diets, encouraging leisure activities and pursuits and social behaviour. Social marketing suggests that a more ethical and moral orientation be incorporated into companies' marketing strategies: marketers should consider and incorporate the wider social implications of their products and services, such as natural conservation or labour exploitation in emerging countries.

Social marketing does not imply a replacement of the traditional marketing concept but it is an extension so as to recognise and encompass the wider needs of society at large. The criticisms of marketing generally focus on ethical issues and the extent to which marketing is responsible for a variety of social and environmental problems. Whatever the reasons, voluntarily or otherwise, marketers have to consider ecological, environmental and consumer welfare issues together with their wider social role more frequently in their marketing plans and activities. Effective and aware marketers have responded to these developments in a number of ways, for instance, by producing recyclable products and packaging, reducing pollution generated by toxic products or from contamination and protecting consumers against harmful or hazardous products by modifying them or withdrawing them from sale.

Answer to Interactive question 5

5.1 (a) **Short term**

- Additional costs – using greener fuels, buying fairly traded products, rebuilding green areas, paying higher salaries
- Reduced income – no sales to unethical purchasers
- Distribution of wealth to non-shareholders – giving to charity
- Distorts focus – one more target for managers

(b) **Long term**

- Avoids legislative imperative – will otherwise fall to Government to enforce and measures may be more Draconian
- May avoid financial penalties where behaviour is covered by legislation
- Improves PR
- Attracts ethical investors
- Attracts ethical consumers
- Improves staff morale

Answer to Interactive question 6

6.1 **Ethical issues**

Personal ethical issues

As an ICAEW chartered accountant you have a responsibility to follow the ethical code of ICAEW.

Just because a product contains an ingredient which is not illegal for use at the current time does not mean that it is ethical for consumers to use it if concerns over the products safety come to light. The fact that you became aware of the issue with the ingredient via an email which discusses non-disclosure to the other directors supports the need to act.

The first thing you should do is discuss the matter with your manager in the Finance Department, and then contact the ICAEW ethical department for advice.

Directors' ethical responsibilities

The fact that both the MD and Head of Production are aware of the potential problem is a governance issue, and the fact that they are keeping it secret from the remainder of the board is a breach of their duties to the company as a whole and potential shareholders who may invest in SSC when the company floats.

The MD and Head of Production have not however, done anything that appears to be illegal. There is a difference between breaches of legislation and activities that appear to be unethical.

Corporate ethical responsibilities:

The Skin Care Company has a responsibility towards its customers and their wellbeing. Many corporate entities do have a code of ethics which covers all stakeholders, given SSC's historic approach to business it is highly likely that the company does have a code of ethics. Although the other directors are unaware of the issues relating to the ingredients in the product, it could be argued that this is due to poor internal controls, which should identify issues of this nature. The responsibility for maintaining a system of internal controls lies with the board as a whole, and so they could be collectively responsible for the failings to identify any health related concerns.

Answer to Interactive question 7

7.1 When more than one stakeholder group has reason to question the otherwise good reputation of an organisation, the effect can be a downward spiral leading to a general lack of confidence which, in turn, can have unfortunate financial effects. In particular, however, poor ethical standards are likely to affect one or more of the organisation's interactions with:

- **Customers** – Customers will expect certain standards of health and safety and ethical behaviour from Ashdene Homes, especially regarding its treatment of employees. The recent damage to their reputation may reduce confidence among customers leading to reduced sales – with a subsequent impact on corporate profits.

- **Shareholders** – Investor confidence is important in public companies and any reputation risk is likely to be reflected in market value. Shareholders may invest in buying shares, or their wealth, tied up in pension funds, may be invested for them by investment firms. The growth in ethical funds management where investment firms guarantee their customers not to invest in ethically-unsound organisations has led to company directors addressing the issue in earnest rather than giving it cursory attention.

- **Senior management** – Poor ethical behaviour from them creates a poor perception of the organisation in the market. However, poor ethical behaviour from those below can also have a negative impact on such executives and make them wish to disassociate themselves from a failing enterprise; the loss of key talent may be sorely felt by those who remain.

- **Employees** – Although not directly affected, poor ethical standards may leave the employee feeling that they no longer have a worthy association with the firm, which may cause them to leave or be de-motivated as a result. Also, if the organisation exhibits poor ethical standards, employees may feel that they either can or even should follow suit, and a general decline in standards will follow.

- **Suppliers** – Also not greatly affected, but it may be the case that suppliers decide not to deal with Ashdene Homes because they feel that the poor ethical standards will in some way implicate themselves.

7.2 Corporate responsibility (CR) is concerned with companies acting in a socially responsible and sustainable manner. It generally refers to business decision-making linked to ethical values, compliance with legal requirements, and respect for people, communities and the environment.

There is a growing view that the best-managed companies are those that are aware of their wider responsibilities to the social community and to the environment. To ensure that a company honours those responsibilities and protects its reputation, it is necessary to embed these core values into the policies, practices and programmes of the company's systems and decision-making processes.

The CR issues that affect companies vary according to the nature of the company but there are five broad areas where CR might be relevant:

- To treat employees fairly and with respect
- To operate in an ethical way and with integrity
- To respect human rights
- To sustain the environment for future generations
- To be a responsible neighbour in the community

There are several reasons why Ashdene Homes might choose to act in a socially responsible way:

- They might want to act voluntarily to avoid legislation. For example, to avoid excessive pollution of the environment in their methods of working and by buying materials locally to reduce transport use and avoid allegations of their suppliers adding to deforestation.

- They might want to act in an ethical and socially responsible way by making the houses eco-friendly, reducing carbon emissions, having rigorous health and safety checks on their building sites and incorporating recycled materials where possible into the buildings.

- They might want to respond to pressure from shareholders. Some institutional shareholders have a policy of investing only in socially responsible and ethical companies.

- To protect their reputation.

The risk to the company's reputation from adverse publicity about social and environmental factors is always difficult to assess. Ashdene Homes will be aware that adverse publicity can have a damaging effect on customer goodwill – and sales and profits. Management might need to consider CR as a strategic issue when evaluating their strategic options.

7.3 **Ethical responsibilities of a professional accountant**

A professional accountant has two 'directions' of responsibility: one to his or her employer and another to the highest standards of professionalism.

Companies provide a Code of Ethics that all employees are expected to follow to maintain a culture of corporate ethics. Issues to be included in such a Code of Ethics are:

- Avoiding conflicts of interest

- Compliance with laws and regulations

- Rules about disclosure or avoidance of opportunities for personal gain through use of company property or their position in the company

- Confidentiality – extending to absolute discretion of all sensitive matters both during and after the period of employment

- Fair dealing with customers, suppliers, employees and competitors

- Encouragement to report illegal and unethical behaviour

The responsibilities also include the expectation that the accountant will act in shareholders' interests as far as possible and that he or she will show loyalty within the bounds of legal and ethical good practice.

In addition to an accountant's responsibilities to his or her employer, there is a further set of expectations arising from his or her membership of the accounting profession. In the first instance, professional accountants are expected to observe the letter and spirit of the law in detail and of professional ethical codes where applicable (depending on country of residence, qualifying body, etc).

In any professional or ethical situation where codes do not clearly apply, a professional accountant should apply 'principles-based' ethical standards (such as integrity and probity) such that they would be happy to account for their behaviour if so required. Finally, and in common with members of other professions, accountants are required to act in the public interest that may involve reporting an errant employer to the relevant authorities. This may be the situation that an accountant may find him or herself in at Ashdene Homes. It would clearly be unacceptable to be involved in any form of deceit and it would be the accountant's duty to help to correct such malpractice if at all possible.

Answers to Self-test

1   **Personal ethical behaviour**

    This relates to the way you as an individual conduct yourself.

    Business ethics

    This is the way a firm as a whole behaves.

    Corporate responsibility

    This is the belief that a firm owes a responsibility to society and its wider stakeholders, as well as to shareholders.

2   Threats to self interest include: Financial interests, loans or guarantees; Incentive compensation arrangements; Inappropriate personal use of corporate assets; Concern over employment security; Commercial pressure from outside the employing organisation.

3   Safeguards might be generic, created by the profession or regulation or developed in the working environment by the individual or their organisation.

4   In circumstances where a professional accountant in business believes that unethical behaviour or actions by others will continue to occur within the employing organisation, they should consider seeking **legal advice**.

    In extreme situations where all available safeguards have been exhausted and it is not possible to reduce the threat to an acceptable level, a professional accountant in business may conclude that it is appropriate to **disassociate** from the task and/or **resign** from the employing organisation.

5   Contract terms might cover:

    - The use of child labour
    - Human rights
    - Health and safety standards
    - Working conditions
    - Minimum wages
    - Environmental protection
    - Terms for contract negotiation and renewal
    - Basis of contract price

6   Sustainable enterprise: A company, institution or entity that generates continuously increasing stakeholder value through the application of sustainable practices through the entire base activity – products and services, workforce, workplace, functions/processes, and management/governance. (Deloitte: *Creating the Wholly Sustainable Enterprise*)

7   The short term/long term debate refers to the trade off management must make between decisions with short-term impacts on the business and those with impacts on its longer term success. Here the assumption is that sustainability will have an adverse short-term impact on the business, for example due to the enhanced costs of compliance, but that it is essential to its long-term success in the face of mounting social and legal pressure to improve ecological performance.

    Some writers suggest that there may be short-term benefits from sustainability, such as reduced costs from using less energy and other resources or attracting customers who will place contracts or buy the offerings of firms with better sustainability postures (eg, 'carbon neutral').

8   **Economic**: the organisation's impacts on the economic conditions of its stakeholders.

     Environmental: an organisation's impacts on living and non-living natural systems, including ecosystems, land, air, and water.

     Social: the impacts an organisation has on the social systems within which it operates.

9   Refer to the answer to Water On Tap in the Question Bank.

10   Refer to the answer to Rocket Co in the Question Bank.

11   Refer to the answer to Guayaporto Ltd in the Question Bank.

12   Refer to the answer to Zeter Domestic Chemicals plc in the Question Bank.

Glossary of terms

Acceptability	The acceptability of a strategy relates to people's expectations of it and its expected performance outcomes. This often includes consideration of risk and returns.
Acquisition	Concerns the purchase of a controlling interest in another company.
Alliance	An agreement between firms to share a commercial opportunity characterised by each member of the alliance retaining autonomy and pursuing its own commercial interests.
Ansoff's growth vector matrix	Is a model which describes how the combinations of a firm's activities in current and new markets, with existing and new products, can lead to growth.
Asset specificity	Where investments are made to support the relationship which have the effect of locking parties into a relationship to some degree.
Automation	'The creation and application of technology to monitor and control the production and delivery of products and services'. (*The International Society of Automation*, 2018).
Balanced scorecard	An integrated set of performance measures linked to the achievement of strategic objectives. The balanced scorecard consists of four perspectives: customer, internal business, innovation and learning, financial.
BCG Matrix	A tool which examines market growth rates and an organisation's relative market strength in its markets to assess the attractiveness and balance of a business portfolio.
Benchmarking	The establishment, through data gathering, of targets and comparators, through whose use relative levels of performance (and particularly areas of underperformance) can be identified. By the adoption of identified best practices it is hoped that performance will improve.
Big data	Datasets whose size is beyond the ability of typical database software to capture, store, manage and analyse. *(McKinsey)*
	An alternative definition is provided by Gartner:
	Big data concerns 'high-volume, high velocity and high variety information assets that demand cost-effective, innovative forms of information processes for enhanced insight and decision making'. *(Gartner)*
Blockchain	A technology that allows people who do not know each other to trust a shared record of events. *(Bank of England)*

Boundary-less organisations	Boundary-less organisations are entities which are structured in such a way as to make it easier to collaborate with external parties. Such organisations remove the internal barriers that often exist between different functions and departments.
Bowman's strategic clock	Is a model which helps assess the competitive strategy being pursued by an organisation. It contrasts different combinations of price and perceived added value.
Brand equity	An intangible asset that adds value to a business through positive associations made by the consumer between the brand and benefits to themselves.
Business continuity planning	A process through which a business details how and when it will recover and restore any operations interrupted by the occurrence of a rare, but massive, risk event.
Business plan	A business plan is a document which is usually prepared as part of the process of applying for funding. It is a critical document for the potential investor. The contents of a business plan may include; a statement of purpose, a description of the business, financial data and supporting documents.
Business risk	Is the variability of returns due to how a business trades or operates, and its exposure to markets and competitors.
Centralisation	Ensuring decision-making authority is concentrated in one place in an organisation, that is in the centre or strategic apex.
Change agent	Is an individual (sometimes called a Champion of Change), a group or external consultancy with the responsibility for driving and 'selling' change.
Cloud computing	Cloud computing is a model for enabling ubiquitous, convenient, on-demand network access to a shared pool of configurable computing resources (eg, networks, servers, storage, applications, and services) that can be rapidly provisioned and released with minimal management effort or service provider interaction.
Code of ethics	A codification of standards to help prevent wrong-doing and to avoid conflicts of interest and to promote honest and ethical conduct among staff in an organisation.
Competitive strategy	The way that a firm will seek to win customers and secure profitability against its rivals.
Compliance risk	Is the risk arising from non-compliance with laws or regulations.

Confidentiality	The requirement not to disclose information acquired through professional or business engagements to third parties (without specific authority to do so) or to use that information for personal advantage.
Controllable risks	Are those risks which are within the ability of management to control to some extent.
Consortia	Organisations that co-operate on specific business prospects.
Core competences	Are the critical activities and processes which enable an organisation to achieve its critical success factors (CSFs) and therefore achieve a sustainable competitive advantage.
Corporate appraisal	A critical assessment of an entity's internal strengths and weaknesses, and the opportunities and threats it faces in the external environment, to establish its condition prior to preparation of its long-term plan.
Corporate governance	The set of rules which governs the structure and determines the objectives of an organisation and regulates the relationship between the organisation's management, its board of directors and its shareholders.
Corporate responsibility	The actions, activities and obligations of business in achieving sustainability.
Corporate strategy	Is concerned with an organisation's basic direction for the future, its purpose, its ambitions, its resources and how it interacts with the world in which it operates. (*Lynch*).
Cost focus strategy	Providing goods and/or services at the lowest cost in an industry segment.
Cost leadership strategy	Producing at the lowest cost in the industry as a whole.
Critical success factors (CSFs)	Are a small number of key goals vital to the success of an organisation ie, 'things that must go right'. An alternative definition is provided by Johnson, Scholes and Whittington. Critical success factors are those product features that are particularly valued by a group of customers, and, therefore, where the organisation must excel to outperform the competition. (*Johnson, Scholes and Whittington*)
Crowdfunding	Is a way of raising finance by asking a large number of people for a small amount of money. (*The UK Crowdfunding Association*)
Crowdsourcing	The process of getting work or funding, usually online, from a network of people. (*Oxford Dictionary*).

Cryptocurrency	A form of decentralised, digital currency, designed to facilitate the virtual exchange of transactions. Cryptocurrency is encrypted through the use of cryptography.
Cyber security	The protection of systems, networks and data in cyberspace. (*ICAEW Strategic Business Management, Study Manual*).
Cyber risk	Any risk of financial loss, disruption or damage to the reputation of an organisation from some sort of failure of its information technology systems.
Database	A structured collection of records or data that is stored in a computer system along with rules as to the information that will be sought from it, so that queries may be answered by interrogating the database.
Data analytics	The process of collecting, organising and analysing large sets of data to discover patterns and other useful information which an organisation can use for its future business decisions.
Data mining	The process of sorting through data to identify patterns and relationships between different items. Data mining software, using statistical algorithms to discover correlations and patterns, is frequently used on large databases. In essence, it is the process of turning raw data into useful information.
Deliberate strategies	Is the term used to describe those intended strategies which are implemented.
Desk research	Is the gathering and analysis of existing or secondary data. This may use existing company reports and other information from both internal and external sources.
Development strategy	Concerns the decisions about how to gain access to chosen products and markets.
Differentiation focus strategy	Providing a differentiated product or service to an industry segment.
Differentiation strategy	Providing a product or service which the industry as a whole believes to be unique.
Digital asset	Assets which are held in digital form, that is to say assets which are not available in physical form. Common examples of digital assets include: PDF files, images, audio and video files.
Divisionalisation	Division of a business into autonomous regions (geographic divisionalisation) or product businesses (product/brand divisionalisation), each with its own revenues, expenditures, capital asset purchase programmes and profit responsibility
Downside risk (pure risk)	The possibility that the outcome will be worse than expected ie, something will go wrong (the worst case scenario).

Economy	In the context of the value for money (3E's), economy is a measure of actual resources used (inputs) eg, cost of labour per employee or the rent per square metre. The focus is on achieving an output of an acceptable standard at the lowest cost possible.
Economies of scale	Economies arising within the business from the organisation of production (internal economies), or attainable by the business because of the growth of the industry as a whole (external economies).
Effectiveness	In the context of the value for money (3E's), effectiveness is a measure of the impact achieved and considers outputs in relation to objectives.
Efficiency	In the context of the value for money (3E's), efficiency is a measure of productivity. It considers the relationship between the goods or services produced (outputs) and the resources used to produce them (inputs).
Emergent change	Is a type of change which involves a series of continuous open-ended adjustments to the environment.
Emergent strategies	Are those behaviours which are adopted and which have a strategic impact. Emergent strategies adapt to human needs and evolve continuously.
Entity risks	Are all of the risks that affect an entity, including: how it trades, the markets and countries it operates in, the decisions that management make. Entity risk is an umbrella term which encompasses all other types of risk.
Ethics	A system of behaviour which is deemed acceptable in the society or context under consideration.
Explicit knowledge	Concerns the knowledge that the company knows that it has. This includes facts, transactions and events that can be clearly stated and stored in management information systems.
Feasibility	When assessing the feasibility of a strategy this requires management to consider whether the strategy can actually be implemented.
Field research	Involves the collection of new (primary) information direct from respondents. As such it is usually more expensive than desk research and so is only performed if desk research fails to answer all questions asked.
Financial risk	Is concerned with the financial threats which may impact an organisation. Financial risk consists of both controllable and uncontrollable factors. The controllable element of financial risk is concerned with how the business chooses to finance itself. The uncontrollable element of financial risk is likely to relate to factors beyond the entity's control such as interest and exchange rates.

Franchising	Is a method of expanding an organisation which uses less capital than would otherwise be possible. Well known franchisers include IKEA, McDonald's and Starbucks.
Globalisation	The production and distribution of products and services of a homogenous type and quality on a worldwide basis.
Gap analysis	The comparison between an entity's ultimate objective and the expected performance from projects both planned and under way, identifying means by which any identified difference, or gap, might be filled.
General environment	All the political, legal, economic, social/cultural, ecological and technological (PESTEL) influences in the countries a business operates in
Hazard risk	Concerns those risks that the organisation is exposed to as a result of natural events and those factors which would normally be within the control of the organisation, such as employee behaviour and the consequences of accidents.
Human capital	Concerns the collective attributes of an organisation's human resources. It includes the capabilities, creativity, skills and knowledge of an organisation's staff which combine to enable the organisation to create economic value.
Human resource management	Involves 'a strategic and coherent approach to the management of an organisation's most valued assets: the people working there who individually and collectively contribute to the achievement of its objectives for sustainable competitive advantage'. *(Armstrong)*. An alternative definition, is the process of evaluating an organisation's human resource needs, finding people to fill those needs, and getting the best work from each employee by providing the right incentives and job environment – with the overall aim of helping achieve organisational goals.
Incremental change	Concerns a type of change which is characterised by a series of small steps. It is a gradual process.
Industry	A group of organisations supplying a market offering similar products using similar technologies to provide customer benefits.
Industry life cycle	The industry life cycle describes the phases of development that an industry goes through. The key stages of the industry life cycle are: introduction; growth; shakeout; maturity; decline.

Information systems (IS)	All systems and procedures involved in the collection, storage, production and distribution of information.
Information systems strategy	Strategy specifying how hardware, software, and telecommunications can achieve delivery of the information systems strategy.
Information management strategy	Strategy specifying who controls and uses the technology provided.
Information technology strategy	Strategy specifying the systems that will best enable the use of information to support the business strategy.
Innovation	Is concerned with the generation of new ideas of how to do business. It is primarily a creative activity.
Integrity	Involves acting in a straightforward and honest manner in business and professional relationships.
Intended strategies	Are those which are conscious plans imposed by management. If they are implemented, they are referred to as deliberate strategies.
Internet of things	A system of interrelated computing devices, mechanical and digital machines, or objects that are provided with unique identifiers and the ability to transfer data over a network without requiring human-to-human or human-to-computer interaction.
Intelligent system	'[A] computer-based system that can represent, reason about, and interpret data. In doing so it can learn about the structure of the data, analyse the data to extract patterns and meaning, derive new information, and identify strategies and behaviours to act on the results of its analysis'. (University College London, 2018).
	An alternative definition is:
	'Intelligent systems are technologically advanced machines that perceive and respond to the world around them.' (University of Nevada, 2018).
Joint venture	Concerns a contractual arrangement whereby two or more parties undertake an economic activity which is subject to joint control.
Just-in-time manufacturing	An approach to planning and control based on the idea that goods or services should be produced only when they are ordered or needed. Also called lean manufacturing.
Key performance indicator (KPI)	A measure of the level of performance in an area where a target level must be achieved for the business to outperform rivals and achieve competitive advantage.
Knowledge	Is the potential for action based on data, information, intuition and experience.

Knowledge management	Describes a range of strategies and tools that capture all the knowledge that is valuable to an organisation, and deliver it to the people in such a way that it can be acted on quickly, to the competitive advantage of the business.
Licensing agreement	Permission from one party to another to manufacture or sell a product, or to use a brand name.
Limiting factor	A factor which at any time, or over a period, may limit the activity of an entity, often occurring where there is shortage or difficulty of availability.
Marketing	The management process which identifies, anticipates and supplies customer requirements efficiently and profitably. *(Chartered Institute of Marketing).*
Marketing mix	The set of controllable marketing variables that a firm blends to produce the response it wants in the target market.
Marketing research	Is the systematic gathering, recording and analysing of information about problems relating to the marketing of goods and services.
Market segmentation	The division of the market into homogeneous groups of potential customers who may be treated similarly for marketing purposes.
Market structure	A description of the number of buyers and sellers in a market for a particular good, and their relative bargaining power.
Merger	Concerns the joining of two separate companies to form a single company. By contrast an acquisition involves the takeover of one entity by another by purchasing a controlling interest.
Mission statement	A formal document that states the business's basic purpose in society expressed in terms of how it satisfies its stakeholders.
Natural capital	The natural assets (eg, air, water, land, habitats) that provide everyday resources including timber, agricultural land, fisheries and clean water as well as services such as air and water filtration, flood protection and pollination for crops (otherwise known as 'ecosystem services') (Dunscombe and Glover, 2016:p.2)
Network architecture	Concerns the network of relational contracts, within or around, the firm.
Not-for-profit organisation	The primary goals of such organisations are non-financial and can vary enormously. Goals often include meeting members' needs, contributing to social well-being and pressing for political and social change.

Objectivity	Involves not allowing bias, conflicts of interest or influence of others to override professional or business judgement.
Operations management	Concerns the design, implementation and control of the processes in an organisation that transform inputs (materials, labour, other resources, information and customers) into output products and services.
Operational risk	Concerns those risks resulting from the variability in the effectiveness of how the business is managed and controlled on a day to day basis.
Opportunity cost	The cash flow foregone if a unit of the resource is used on the contract/project instead of in the best alternative way.
Organic growth	Involves the expansion of a firm's size, profits, and activities through the use of its own resources and capabilities without taking over other firms.
Organisational structure	How the various functions of an organisation (operations, marketing, HR, finance etc,) are formally arranged into departments or sections, and how responsibility and authority are allocated.
Outsourcing	The strategic use of outside resources to perform activities traditionally handled by internal staff and resources (*thebalance.com*).
Partnership	Involves a joint participation between two or more organisations in the serving of a market or project, characterised by the close interrelationship of operations, exchange of staff and mutual trust and commitment to working with the other(s).
Planned change	Involves following a series of pre-planned steps.
Porter's Diamond	Is a model devised by Michael Porter. The Diamond model helps organisations to understand the determinants of national competitive advantage. The model identifies the following as key determinants: Firm, strategy, structure, rivalry; demand conditions; related and supporting industries; factor conditions.
Porter's Five Forces	Is a model devised by Michael Porter. According to Porter, five competitive forces influence the state of competition in an industry: threat of new entrants; bargaining power of customers; threat of substitute products or services; bargaining power of suppliers; rivalry among existing firms.
Porter's Value chain	Is the sequence of business activities by which value is added to the products or services produced by an entity.

Positioning	Concerns the overall location of a product or service in the buyer's mind in relation to other competing products, services/brands.
Price discrimination	Sometimes also referred to as differential pricing, involves setting different prices for a similar product in different parts of the market.
Price elasticity of demand	Measures how far demand for a good will change in response to a change in its price
Professional behaviour	Involves complying with laws and regulations and not discrediting the profession to which an individual may be a member.
Professional competence and due care	Involves being aware of all prevailing knowledge necessary to provide a professional service
Profit seeking organisations	The primary goal for such organisations is the delivery of economic value to the owners, ie, to increase shareholder wealth.
Product/market strategy	Concerns the decision on what products to offer and the markets to be served. This is closely linked to Ansoff's growth vector matrix.
Qualitative data	Is fundamentally concerned with trends in opinions, thoughts and motivations, as a result it tends to be subjective. Qualitative data cannot be calculated or computed.
Quality assurance	Requires organisations to focus on the way a product or service is produced. Procedures and standards are devised with the aim of ensuring defects are eliminated (or at least minimised) during the development and production process.
Quality control	Involves checking and reviewing work that has been done. Quality control is focused on detecting defects in the output produced, as a result it has a narrower focus than quality assurance.
Quantitative data	Is focused on numerical data which can be calculated and computed.
Rational planning model	A prescriptive approach to strategy formulation. There are three main stages to the model: strategic analysis, strategic choice and strategy implementation.
Relationship marketing	A management process that seeks to attract, maintain and enhance customer relationships by focusing on the whole satisfaction experienced by the customer when dealing with the firm.
Relevant cash flows	Future, incremental, cash flows arising from the decision being made.
Re-positioning	Changing the identity of a product or service, relative to the identity of competing products or services, in the collective minds of the target market.

Resource audit	Involves cataloguing the assets of an organisation by considering physical resources, intangibles, human resources, technological resources and financial resources.
Risk	The possible variation in outcome from what is expected to happen.
Risk appetite	Concerns the extent to which a company is prepared to take on risks to achieve its objectives.
Risk assessment	Involves establishing the financial consequences of each risk event (severity) and its likelihood of occurrence (frequency).
Risk evaluation	The process by which an organisation determines the significance of any risk and whether those risks need to be addressed.
Risk management	The process of identifying and assessing (analysing and evaluating) risks and the development, implementation and monitoring of a strategy to respond to those risks.
Risk register	Lists and prioritises the main risks the organisation faces. It is used as the basis for decision-making on how to deal with risks.
Residual income (RI)	Is a divisional performance measure. It is calculated as:

Divisional profit – (Net assets of division × required rate) |
| **Return on Capital Employed (ROCE)** | Is a divisional performance measure, it sometimes called Return on Investment (ROI)

it is calculated as:

$$\frac{\text{Profit for the period} \times 100\%}{\text{Average capital employed during the period}}$$ |
Scenario planning	Concerns the development of pictures of potential futures for the purposes of managerial learning and the development of strategic responses.
Shared service centre	A number of internal transaction processing activities which had previously been conducted in a number of different departments, or business units, are brought together into one site within an organisation.
Span of control	The number of subordinates reporting to one person.
Stakeholders	Are those groups or persons with an interest in what an organisation does.
Step change	Describes an unexpected jump (upwards) or drop (downwards) in the pace of change. The step is caused by an unexpected event (eg, environmental disaster, unexpected change in government etc).

Strategy	Is concerned with the direction and scope of an organisation over the long term, which achieves advantage for the organisation through its configuration of resources within a changing environment, to meet the needs of markets and to fulfil stakeholder expectations. *(Johnson, Scholes and Whittington).*
Strategic business unit (SBU)	A section, within a larger business, which is responsible for planning, developing, producing and marketing its own products or services for a distinct external market.
Strategic risk	Are those risks associated with long-term strategic objectives.
Suitability	Relates to the strategic logic and strategic fit of a proposed strategy. To be effective, a strategy must fit the company's operational circumstances and strategic position.
Supply chain management (SCM)	The management of all supply activities from the suppliers to a business through to delivery to customers.
Sustainability	The ability to 'meet the needs of the present without compromising the ability of future generations to meet their own needs' (*Brundtland Report*).
Sustainable enterprise	A company, institution or entity that generates continuously increasing stakeholder value through the application of sustainable practices through the entire base activity – products and services, workforce, workplace, functions/processes, and management/governance. (*Deloitte*)
Synergy	Concerns the benefits gained from two or more businesses combining that would not have been available to each independently. Sometimes expressed as the 2 + 2 = 5 effect. Synergy arises because of complementary resources which are compatible with the products or markets being developed and is often realised by transferring skills or sharing activities.
Tacit knowledge	Is the personal knowledge and expertise held by people within the organisation that has not been formally documented.
Targeting	Involves selecting the most attractive market segments.
Threshold competences	The activities and processes involved in using and linking the firm's resources necessary to stay in business.
Threshold resources	Are those basic resources needed by all firms in the market.

Transformational change	Is a type of change characterised by major, significant change being introduced relatively quickly.
Transactions marketing	A management approach that focuses on the product, and develops marketing mixes for a product according to the needs customers satisfy when they buy it.
Transfer price	The price at which one division in a group sells its products or services to another division in the same group.
Unique resources	Are those resources which give the firm a sustainable competitive advantage over its competitors , enabling it to meet its CSFs.
Uncertainty	The inability to predict the outcome from an activity due to a lack of information.
Uncontrollable risks	Are those risks which are outside of the organisation's control. They tend to be driven by external changes.
Upside risk	The possibility that something could go better than expected (best case scenario).

Index

SWOT analysis, 179, 504
Synergy, 380

T

Tacit knowledge, 535
Takeover, 405
Targeting, 220
Technology, 74
Total quality management (TQM), 492
Trading blocs, 85
Transactions marketing, 245
Transfer price, 283
Transformational change, 569
Triads, 85

U

Unavoidable costs, 342
Uncertainty, 318
Uncontrollable risks, 325

Upside risk (speculative risk or opportunity), 318

V

Value chain, 140, 247
Value chain activities, 141
Value drivers, 143
Value system, 144, 247, 495
Values, 44
Vertical Integration, 192
Virtual firm, 155
Vs of Big Data, 128

W

Weihrich's TOWS matrix, 180
Withdrawal, 197
Workforce flexibility, 124

REVIEW FORM – BUSINESS STRATEGY AND TECHNOLOGY STUDY MANUAL

Your ratings, comments and suggestions would be appreciated on the following areas of this Study Manual.

	Very useful	Useful	Not useful
Chapter Introductions	☐	☐	☐
Examination context	☐	☐	☐
Worked examples	☐	☐	☐
Interactive questions	☐	☐	☐
Quality of explanations	☐	☐	☐
Technical references (where relevant)	☐	☐	☐
Self-test questions	☐	☐	☐
Self-test answers	☐	☐	☐
Index	☐	☐	☐

	Excellent	Good	Adequate	Poor
Overall opinion of this Study Manual	☐	☐	☐	☐

Please add further comments below:

Please return completed form to:
The Learning Team
Learning and Professional Department
ICAEW
Metropolitan House
321 Avebury Boulevard
Milton Keynes
MK9 2FZ
E learning@icaew.com